Marketing Communications Management: concepts and theories, cases and practices

Paul Copley

ELSEVIER
BUTTERWORTH
HEINEMANN

AMSTERDAM • BOSTON • HEIDELBERG • LONDON • NEW YORK • OXFORD
• PARIS • SAN DIEGO • SAN FRANCISCO • SINGAPORE • SYDNEY • TOKYO

Elsevier Butterworth-Heinemann
Linacre House, Jordan Hill, Oxford OX2 8DP
30 Corporate Drive, Burlington, MA 01803

First published in 2004

British Library Cataloguing in Publication Data
A catalogue record for this book is available from the British Library

Library of Congress Cataloguing in Publication Data
A catalogue record for this book is available from the Library of Congress

ISBN 0 7506 5294 2

For information on all Elsevier Butterworth-Heinemann
publications visit our website at http://www.books.elsevier.com

Typeset by Newgen Imaging Systems (P) Ltd, Chennai, India
Printed and bound in The Netherlands

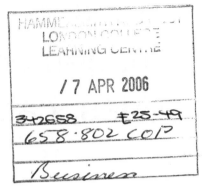

Contents

Figures

Tables

Paul Copley (MA, MPhil, BSc, PGDip Marketing, MMRS, Dip MRS) is Senior Lecturer in Marketing and Marketing Communications at Newcastle Business School, Northumbria University, and is the full-time mode MA Marketing Programme Leader. For the last twenty-five years he has been involved with marketing consultancy, training and development, and research. Post-MA Marketing (Lancaster) experience began with large companies and led on to being involved in consultancy with large business clients as well as working with small business and enterprise support agencies to devise, develop and deliver various programmes for both small and medium enterprises (SMEs) and students in the North of England. Part of this time has been devoted to empirical research into the education and training needs of small-firm owner-managers in the North East of England, leading to the award of MPhil (Newcastle). Prior to this Paul was involved with relatively large companies in marketing services, publicity and international product management, and has a good deal of experience in new product development.

Paul has been an external examiner at undergraduate and postgraduate levels for Dundee Business School and for institutions in Greece and Malaysia, and at postgraduate level for Napier University.

Current academic activities are focused on marketing communications management, interactive marketing, and international advertising and communications, and Paul has taught in this area of study for the past sixteen years. Conference papers, for example to the UK Academy of Marketing and the International Small Business Association, are a constant consideration and have been presented in the areas of marketing communication, semiotics, small business marketing and arts marketing. Paul remains, however, interested in the broad spectrum of marketing strands and is still a committed member of both the Market Research Society and the Academy of Marketing, and is a past Academy track prize-winner.

If the common watchword in successful marketing practice is exchange, then somehow mutual understanding between buyer and seller has to be achieved. This cannot be realized without effective marketing (and corporate) communications, but to be effective communications must be well managed. The increased sophistication of communication elements such as advertising, public relations and sponsorship has been responsible for increased commercial activity and the cluttered environment in which communications have to operate. Good marketing has always been conducted in an integrated fashion, but it is the quest for truly integrated communication campaigns that started in the late 1980s and came to the fore in the mid-1990s that brought about the interest in integrated marketing communications, or IMC as it is known. Recent developments on what has become known as the electronic frontier both challenges and offers opportunities to organizations, and the interactivity that has and is developing because of the technology that has given us the CD-ROM, mobile phones and the Internet is key to successful integration of communication activities.

Most organizations need some form of marketing or corporate communications. This text is designed to service both practitioners and students undertaking formal study. It is particularly geared to the needs of those who are on a course that has basic marketing as a prerequisite. The book has, therefore, been written with the final year undergraduate student, for example BA Marketing or BA Business Studies, and the postgraduate student, for example the Postgraduate Diploma/MA in Marketing, in mind. However, the growth of non-business studies students studying marketing and marketing communications is obviously important, as is the number of overseas students studying such subjects in English. There should also be some interest from professional marketing and non-marketing courses (where marketing is taught) and from marketing and non-marketing professionals in the public and the private sector.

The aim of producing this book is to meet the needs of the above students and practitioners by providing a product that addresses strategic and critical issues, and which dovetails with the current interest in marketing communications (especially advertising and sponsorship) as reflected in the media. More specifically the aims are to:

- provide a book that balances the theory and practice of marketing communications

- provide a managerial approach to marketing communications by first breaking down the various components and rebuilding them into a managerial whole

- provide a usable, accessible book that extends the reader beyond many of the conventional views of the subject; some less conventional but potentially very useful and more critical ideas are introduced

- present marketing communications in the widest possible context by using examples from a diverse range of organizations.

The book therefore draws on as wide a range of materials as possible from small and large firms, consumer and industrial companies, profit and non-profit organizations, public and private sector situations, and uses case study vignettes throughout to add flavour and a more in-depth case at the end of each part to facilitate application. International aspects run throughout the book and an overall international perspective appears as the last of twenty chapters. Importantly, the book makes critical reflections on the prime issues in marketing communications. The book is divided into six parts, each of which contains a number of chapters. Within each chapter there are 'stop points', following the vignettes, many of which are examples of actual occurrences. These 'stop points' are designed to encourage the reader to 'stop and think' about key issues. Typical examination questions, assignment briefing, and a summary of key points conclude each chapter. The main body of the text is followed by a comprehensive index.

A/S	advertising/spend
AA	Automobile Association
ABC	activity-based costing
AIDA	attention, interest, desire, action
AIO	activities, interests and opinions
APEC	Asia-Pacific Economic Co-operation Conference
APIC	analysis, planning, implementation and control
APR	annual percentage rate
ASA	Advertising Standards Authority
ASEAN	Association of South East Asian Nations
ATR	awareness, trial and reinforcement
BA	British Airways
BARB	British Audience Research Bureau
BAT	British American Tobacco
BBC	British Broadcasting Corporation
BBH	Bartle, Bogle and Hegarty
BCG	Boston Consulting Group
BHS	British Home Stores
BLC	brand life cycle
BMRB	British Market Research Bureau
BtoB	business to business
CAMRA	Campaign for Real Ale
CAP	Code of Advertising Practice
CBI	Confederation of British Industry
CEO	chief executive officer
CFC	chlorofluorocarbon
CIPP	Corporate Image Policy Programme
CPR	corporate public relations
CPT	cost per thousand
CRI	Context Research International
CRM	customer relationship management
DAGMAR	designing advertising goals for measured advertising results
DAR	day-after recall
DIY	do it yourself
DM	direct marketing
DMA	direct marketing association
DMU	decision-making unit
DRTV	direct response television
DSM	decision sequence model
EC	European Community
ECVM	European Council of Vinyl Manufacturers
EFTPOS	electronic funds transfer at point of sale
ELM	elaboration likelihood model
EMB	Empire Marketing Board
EPOS	electronic point of sale

ESOMAR	European Society for Opinion Surveys and Market Research
EU	European Union
EVA	economic value assessment
fmcg	fast-moving consumer goods
FTC	Federal Trade Commission
GDP	gross domestic product
GIM	general interest magazine
GM	General Motors
GM	genetically modified
GMO	genetically modified organism
GPO	General Post Office
GRP	gross rating point
GUS	Great Universal Stores
HEM	hedonic experiential model
HTML	hypertext mark-up language
ICC	International Chamber of Commerce
ICMC	integrated corporate and marketing communications
Id	identity
IDM	Institute of Direct Marketing
IGMC	integrated global marketing communication
IMC	integrated marketing communications
IMF	International Monetary Fund
IPA	Institute of Practitioners in Advertising
ISP	Internet service provider
ITC	Independent Television Commission
IVR	interactive voice response
J&J	Johnson and Johnson
JSB	John Smith's Bitter
K&K	knickers and knitwear
M&S	Marks and Spencer
MAE	macro environment
MAN	money, authority and need
MBO	management by objectives
ME	marketing environment
MEAL	Media Expenditure Analysis Limited
MIE	micro environment
MNC	multinational company
MOD	Ministry of Defence
MP	Member of Parliament
MPR	marketing public relations
NEC	National Exhibition Centre
NIC	newly industrialized country
NOP	National Opinion Poll
NRS	National Readership Survey
OFT	Office of Fair Trading
OTC	opportunity to convince
OTS	opportunity to see
P&G	Procter and Gamble
PACT	Positioning Advertising Copy Testing
PC	personal computer
PEST	political, economic, social, technological

PIE	persuasive impact equation
plc	public limited company
PLC	product life cycle
POP	point-of-purchase
POS	point-of-sale
PRO	public relations officer
PRSA	Public Relations Society of America
PWi	Pegram Walters International
QVC	quality, value and convenience
R&D	research and development
ROC	Richness in Occasions to Convince
ROCI	return on communications investment
ROI	return on investment
RoSPA	Royal Society for the Prevention of Accidents
RSL	Research Services Limited
RSPCA	Royal Society for the Prevention of Cruelty to Animals
S-R	stimulus–response
S&N	Scottish and Newcastle
SBU	strategic business unit
SEO	search engine optimization
SIA	Securities Industry Association
SIM	special interest magazine
SKB	SmithKlineBeecham
SMART	specific, measurable, achievable, relevant and timed
SMEs	small and medium enterprises
SOM	share of market
SOV	share of voice
SP	sales promotion
STAS	Short Term Ad Strength
STEP	social, technological, economic, political
SWOT	strengths, weaknesses, opportunities and threats
TEASE	trickster, excessive, adolescent, spirited and entertaining
TGI	Target Group Index
TVR	television rating
UDV	United Distillers and Vintners
UMIST	University of Manchester Institute of Science and Technology
UN	United Nations
USP	unique selling proposition
VALS	Values and Life Styles
VW	Volkswagen
WAP	wireless application protocol
WHO	World Health Organization
Y&R	Young and Rubicam

PART ONE

Marketing Communications in Context

Marketing communications, the most visible of marketing functions, interacts subtlety with corporate communications to form what can be a formidable force for business and other organizations, and one that impacts strongly on society generally. We are apparently exposed to thousands of stimuli each day and many of these are from the marketing and corporate communications' arsenal belonging to myriad companies and other organizations, whether domestic, international or global. This includes the effects of branding, advertising, sales promotions, publicity and sponsorships, personal communications, packaging and so on. Marketers are faced with the challenge of integrating these activities in such a way as to maximize effective and efficient management.

This first part of the book consists of four chapters that take the reader from an introduction to the subject through to a strategic management approach to it. In Chapter 1, the integrated marketing communications mix and its environment is explored. Chapter 2 examines marketing communications theory and what it means for practice. In Chapter 3, behaviour and relationships with the other elements of the marketing effort are examined. Chapter 4 proposes a strategic framework for effective marketing and corporate communications management.

CHAPTER

1

The integrated marketing communications mix and its environment

Chapter overview

Introduction to this chapter

The nature of marketing communication is explored and relationships developed with strategic marketing. Marketing communications, a mix within itself, is seen firmly as part of the marketing mix but in a strategic manner. Marketing communications as an entity is placed within an integrated marketing context surrounded by an ever-present and somewhat turbulent environment.

Aims of this chapter

This chapter seeks to explore the nature and role of integrated marketing communications in relation to the rest of the marketing mix. More specifically it aims to:

- discuss marketing in the twenty-first century in terms of exchange and change

- situate marketing communication within strategic marketing

- explore the future of marketing and marketing communications in integrative terms

- outline the major environmental forces that impinge upon the marketing communications management function.

Marketing, exchange and change

Marketing is said by many to be in a state of transition. Some might say marketing is no longer strategy but a requirement, a necessity. Some of the key issues of debate today are being expressed in terms of marketing, exchange and change, and marketing has for a long time been defined in terms of both exchange and change. Marketing in this sense can be defined as 'A social and managerial process by which individuals and groups obtain what they need and want through creating and exchanging products and value with others' (Kotler et al., 2001).[1]

Exchange

There are differing types of exchange. Fill (1999) lists four:

1   Market – short term; self-interest driven; and independent.

2   Relational – long term, supportive relationships built up between parties.

3   Redistributive – where resources are shared with other parties who work as a collective unit.

4   Reciprocal – that is to do with gift-giving and mutuality as opposed to self-interest of the market exchange.

This has a good deal of meaning in the context of marketing communications since the way in which marketing is seen and practised will have a large impact upon marketing communications and their management. Exchange is becoming much more of the last three, i.e. more relational, redistributive and reciprocal, as the following vignette illustrates.

VIGNETTE

Unilever, Wal-Mart and customer relations

In the past manufacturers have hooked into channels. In the USA for example, the likes of Procter and Gamble (P&G) have become very much associated with Wal-Mart. Procter and Gamble's success or failure in, say, Brazil could therefore be linked to that of Wal-Mart's there (Schultz, 1996). Thus the likes of P&G can be seen as prisoners of their own actions. One of P&G's great rivals, Unilever, does not quite see it this way. As a manufacturer, Unilever wishes to develop closer customer relations in order to sustain growth in the long term. In order to do this it is training its managers in the business of discovering and meeting the needs of customers, but especially those of Wal-Mart, Unilever's biggest global customer. Unilever's 'Wal-Mart Readiness Training Programme' has taken on board the Wal-Mart philosophy of 'eat what you cook'. Just as a chef would sample his or her own dishes, so Unilever's international managers become well acquainted with the retailer by being on the superstore floor stocking shelves, answering customer queries and even helping get the goods from the stockroom to the store. This allows the manager to better meet needs by getting well acquainted with the retailer in terms of its culture, business tools and objectives. This gives Unilever competitive advantage in terms of knowing what a major customer will require in advance, such as when Wal-Mart moved into the UK by acquiring ASDA in 1999.

The training programme includes the philosophy of managers from both organizations working together on live projects, but also that of shared resources. Unilever managers can tap into Wal-Mart's vast database 'Retail Link' that processes on a daily basis point of sale information from every store, thereby providing detailed sales, logistics and accounting data on every item sold – globally. However, knowledge transfer remains the key to the initiative that is seen as a 'two-way street' where, in particular, invaluable insights into how things are run in different countries are gained. Also, of course, managers from other countries can gain a unique insight into the situation in the USA. This includes Wal-Mart's philosophy of low prices maintained by stripping cost out of the supply chain, a plain headquarters complete with plastic chairs and the no-gratuity policy (including paying for one's own sandwiches during a working lunch with Unilever managers). For Unilever, it is all about making sales to the consumer via the customer, so that none of the above is alien. The fourth (of ten) of Sam Walton's (Wal-Mart's founder) laws reads: 'Communicate everything you possibly can to your partners. The more they know, the more they'll understand. The more they understand, the more they'll care. Once they care, there's no stopping them. Information is power and the gain you get from empowering your associates more than offsets the risk of informing your competitors.'

To sum up, two main initiatives underline this kind of partnership approach. First, the dissemination of priceless information via Retail Link; second, the appointment of individual suppliers to be 'category captains', where the supplier acts as an expert consultant to the category buyer and gives objective, impartial opinions and advice such as new consumer trends or a course of action against competitor activity such as the introduction of new product variants. At the end of the day it's about fostering growth in categories. The philosophy is one of doing this in the broad category and inevitably growth will be fostered for Unilever.

Sources: Adapted from Dowman (2000) and Schultz (1996).

STOP POINT

There appear to be two opposing viewpoints. On the one hand, there is the now traditional view of power, conflict and co-operation in channels whereby reward and punishment are the norm, i.e. there are rewards for co-operation and penalties are imposed on nonco-operation (Bradley, 1995). On the other hand lies an apparently opposing view, as described above, that is one of relationships and partnerships and mutual benefits. Are there any real differences between the two? Do they represent two different marketing paradigms or are they part of the same marketing paradigm?

Change

There are differing objectives behind certain communication. Most writers agree on at least four, i.e. inform, persuade, remind and differentiate. The predilection towards the mnemonic and/or the acronym leads writers like Fill (1995; 1999) to rearrange the words to form DRIP, i.e. differentiate, remind, inform and persuade. Change has occurred in the way in which this has evolved. Information then persuasion can be seen quite clearly in the early forms of advertising, followed by the use of reminders and the notion of differentiation of very similar products often being achieved through the communication employed. These days, however, the idea of entertainment is viewed as an essential way to explain the objectives behind certain forms of marketing communication but, in particular, television and cinema advertising. Change of all sorts is important: changing markets, for example the size of Europe as one market or the challenge from Asia. The ability/inability of multinational companies (MNCs) in the past to communicate internationally or even engage in, say, pan-European advertising has been grappled with since the 1960s[2] in terms of communicating with members of the 'global village'. In other words the adaptation/standardization debate as it applies to communication is still alive and kicking with a key question being 'should companies think global, act local?' We have moved into the era of the globalization of markets with very different types of companies emerging, underlining a fundamental change to the business ecosystem. Questions surrounding the new world order and the relationship between MNCs and the development of world regions impinge on many things, not least the communication process.

In particular, the 'information explosion' is upon us. The worldwide dominance of the USA is waning. We have moved chronologically from American manufacturing and distribution dominance in the 1950s and 1960s, through cost-cutting and re-engineering in the 1990s, to the dominance of the media and consumers through ownership of technology and communications in the twenty-first century (Figure 1.1).

The late 1990s have seen technological influence in terms of, for example, digital technology. Corporations such as Eastman/Kodak have digital photography. If this technology were introduced too fast then this would kill off the paper and chemicals business. If too slow then they miss out to the competition. Ultimately the consumer will control this, not corporations. Levi is on the Internet. The consumer who has the technology can order direct. United Airlines offers tickets, hotel reservations and car hire – all on personal computer (PC) software. This is not good news for travel agents. As Schultz (1996) put it, the key to this transition is the transfer of information technology first into channels then to the consumer. Visually this looks something like Figure 1.2.

The future appears to be in the realms of interactivity. Fragmentation has begun and the myth of company/corporate image is dissolving before us. Coca-Cola has a thousand – maybe a billion – images worldwide. The consumer is

Figure 1.1
From manufacturer to technology/communications dominance.

Source: Adapted by the author from Schultz (1996).

1950s/60s – saw America's manufacturing base largely undisturbed with distribution systems developed to get produce out into the marketplace. Communications played a very minor role.
1970s – Japanese introduce quality as a basis for competition.
1980s – saw increased competition based around price in order to clear the market-place.
1990s – saw cost-cutting and re-engineering.
2000+ – will see the dominance of technology and communications.

Figure 1.2
Source of power in the transition from marketer to media and consumer dominance.

Source: Adapted by the author from Schultz (1996).

HISTORICAL	CURRENT	TWENTY-FIRST CENTURY
MARKETER	MARKETER	MARKETER
CHANNEL	*CHANNEL*	CHANNEL
MEDIA	MEDIA	*MEDIA*
CONSUMER	CONSUMER	*CONSUMER*

still small but is growing fast in terms of control. The notions of change and globalization are illustrated in the vignette below.

VIGNETTE

Developments in world regions: Taiwan, South East Asia and global economic tremors

The question is, do we live in one world and if not what kind of world do we live in? On the one hand, there appears to be rapidly converging activity, interest, preference and demographic characteristics leading to readily accessible, homogeneous market groupings. On the other hand, this may very well be stereotyping across cultures that might not be possible, desirable or even necessary. The economy of Taiwan and business developments in that country, and in South East Asia generally, in the past fifty years are interesting. There was rapid growth in the 1990s until the 1997 crisis. Taiwan is part of Asia-Pacific Economic Co-operation Conference (APEC), which includes the Association of South East Asian Nations (ASEAN) countries as well as Australia and a growing number of others. Taiwan has moved to a high-tech, high-wage economy that is more to do with niche exploitation than copycat activity and has used existing technologies in innovative ways. This strategy avoided head-to-head contests for technological supremacy. Taiwanese companies target niches with world-class products specializing in, for example, computer peripherals, microcomputers and the application of specific chips. This has not been a one-way street though. Motorola, Intel, Glaxo, Apple, Boeing, Lockheed have weighed up the 'tigers' and recognized their high potential, and have teamed up with local companies for manufacturing, applied research and applied design. Asia's markets post-1997 have been rather bumpy. Towards the end of 2000, the economic prospects for the region were rather gloomy because of higher oil prices outside the region and a slowdown in US demand for electronics products. Internally concern has been expressed over corporate restructuring and financial sector reforms. However, the global outlook remained positive with projected growth of 4 per cent in 2001 and the International Monetary Fund (IMF) claimed that a slower expansion is not the same as an economic downturn. Current account surpluses, foreign exchange reserves replenishment and manageable short-term debt are cited as positive indicators of stability. They add to this Japan's road to recovery and China's 8 per cent growth for the year 2000. Moreover, various countries are putting new laws and regulations in place to improve the way corporations and banks are run. This costs money and the IMF provides the figures of between 15 and 45 per cent of gross domestic product (GDP) in terms of public sector costs, spread over several years, of bank restructuring in Indonesia, Korea, Thailand and Malaysia. The expectation is one of continuing commitment to reform on the part of governments, debtors and financial sectors in many ways. For example, in Thailand banks are advised to reduce non-performing loans; in Korea the debt of corporations should be reduced by asset sales; and in Indonesia, similarly, with the sale of corporate assets taken by the government. The way the IMF and the World Bank see it, tangible progress has been made in promoting openness and accountability and the development of international standards. The IMF sees itself at the centre of this 'crisis prevention'.

This does not mean that things go back to the way they were. Previous generations of Japanese consumers had to make do with the department store. Japan's twenty to thirtysomethings have much more. The 1000-yen shop, for example, should do well whether the economy is good or bad. Typical of these is Uniglo that sells cheap and cheerful clothes via television advertising to the tune of $2 billion in sales. The driver for this change is the economic crisis, so that the Japanese consumer has stores like Uniglo but also a plethora of shopping magazines and television shows. The Internet and overseas travel have helped educate a new generation of consumers in what they like and how much they should pay. Having said all this, higher priced consumer goods still sell – Louis Vuitton's sales rose by 14 per cent in 1999 making the $800 million mark – but this is a very fluid environment where today's successes can easily become tomorrow's failures.

Source: Adapted from BBC (1994a); Mutsuko and Rutledge (2000); Shigemitsu (2000).

 **STOP POINT**

Late 1997/January 1998 saw the beginning of the economic crisis for the 'tiger' economies. Compare the optimism of 1994 with the pessimism regarding the Pacific Rim then. In addition, the current situation at the time of writing allows us to make a further comparison. The Asian crisis was primarily an economic crisis just as the 'tigers' had been economic miracles. The crisis provided some hard lessons about sound banking and corporate systems, and about the ability to withstand short-term economic fluctuations that can unnerve investors. It also tells us quite a lot about knock-on effects for the marketer. Put yourself in the shoes of a European company wishing to do business with one of these countries and also a domestic company wishing to trade and survive. What contrasting parameters might emerge?

Marketing communications' place within strategic marketing

The basic marketing concept and mix[3] and their meaning to the organization should by now be well understood and will not be discussed here except in terms of the ways in which aspects of the other elements impact upon communication. Marketing communications can be described as being every form of communication relevant to marketing. This invites marketing communications managers to question the efficiency of every item of communication as it relates to and affects the whole strategy. The basic promotional mix elements and their derivatives as the requirements for effective communications and customer understanding have been recognized for some time as being 'above-the-line' advertising and 'below-the-line' everything else, i.e. sales promotion, public relations and selling. The line is an artificial construct devised for accounting purposes within the commission system where 15 per cent of billing was the fee in advertising terms for placing the message in the appropriate space, the rest of the transaction being fee based. It is not unusual, however, to see the term 'through-the-line' being used to indicate changes that have taken place in recent times (see the 'Integrated marketing communications' section later in this chapter). Figure 1.3 shows the relationships between corporate, marketing and communication functions.

The difference between mass and personal communications is obvious. With audiences tending to become more fragmented, mass communication is rapidly becoming a relic of a former era. It is now recognized in many markets that there

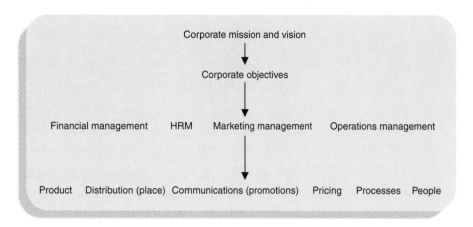

Figure 1.3
Corporate to marketing communications relationships.

is a need for media and media vehicles that match this fragmentation. Mass communication was, traditionally, relatively fast and low cost but with the disadvantages of involving selective perception, poor comprehension of the message, the possibility of only a monologue taking place with poor feedback and the difficulty of measuring effectiveness. Personal communication, on the other hand, has been seen as just about the opposite of this, with high cost per contact at a slower speed but with the opportunity to better get the message across. There is therefore much higher comprehension of the message and the possibility of a dialogue with fast and accurate feedback and, consequently, a move towards 'narrowcasting' rather than 'broadcasting' in all media forms. Traditionally, the view has been that there is a requirement for an explanation of the product/service/organization in order that comprehension is achieved. Promotion (or to put it more accurately, marketing communications) therefore involves many things. For example, legible phone numbers on letterheads, brand name for display on packs etc., product/brand image, price/imputed quality, shape/design of container for recognition on television and shelves, colour of product/pack and even easy-to-follow instructions. The use of a combination of such devices leads, it is argued, to customer/consumer understanding and better positioning of the company/brand. The basic marketing mix then usually includes communication as a fundamental element but the communication itself is a mix of elements. The old promotions mix was usually seen as consisting of *advertising, sales promotion, marketing public relations* and *personal selling*. This is forever developing and mutating. Corporate PR is probably at this point in time seen as being of greater import than product/marketing PR. The optimal mix is determined by factors such as degree of control, cost, credibility, size and geographic spread of target audiences. Fill (1995; 1999; 2002) adds the two new categories of *corporate PR* (as opposed to marketing PR) and *direct response media* (often simply called direct marketing). It will be argued later, in Chapter 14, that *sponsorship* should be taken out of the PR box and stand out as a strategic communication element in its own right. This is shown in Figure 1.4.

This is still the approach of 'putting things in boxes' to provide the practitioner with a kind of shorthand, in the same way as the 4 P mnemonic does for the practitioner considering the overall marketing effort. The aforementioned derivatives of the main communication elements are developing all the time. For example, recent new additions have been in the areas of product placement (a form of the usually mass or impersonal type of communication that includes

Corporate public relations

| Advertising | Sales promotion | Public relations (market/product/brand) |
| Personal communications | Direct marketing | Sponsorship |

Corporate sponsorship

Figure 1.4
The communications mix.

brands appearing within films or television programmes). A useful comparison of the two basic forms is reported by De Pelsmaker, Geuens and Van den Bergh (2001) who use the examples of personal computers and software that have been given away free but come with compulsory consumption of various advertising messages. There are people known as 'troupers' who organize, say, a trip to the theatre for groups of people and who are given incentives to do so (probably a free trip for themselves). This illustrates non-mass or personal communication. Both these ideas would be placed in the sales promotion box, at least in the first instance. Less mainstream ideas, for example language and meaning, including the usefulness of semiology/semiotics referred to in Chapter 6 have, for the past three decades, become increasingly more commonplace. The Marlboro vignette below illustrates the Philip Morris reaction, in the communications arena, to enforced change.

VIGNETTE

Marlboro:
'America's most
wanted' promotion

The tobacco companies, some might say, have had to be inventive, whether this be in developing new products for markets that do not yet exist or, especially, in communications terms. The anti-smoking lobby and other pressures have made this inventiveness a necessity for companies like Philip Morris with brands such as Marlboro if they are to survive.

The Marlboro 'America's most wanted' or, if you prefer, 'If you want it, come and get it', the Grand Larceny case 01/773/5668, is a case in point. This is a promotion that closed after a typical period in which it was sent out through the mail, in a pack that looked like a packet of Marlboro cigarettes, hopefully to known smokers on a database. This forms a classic piece of direct marketing using an unusual approach to sales promotion. Thus there is the pack itself (a videotape box) with a number of objects inside. These include a personally addressed letter, a small leaflet illustrating gifts available in exchange for pull foils, a videotape with a professionally made certificate-18 film on it and a map of Marlboro Country (this also has the application form for entry into a competition, rules, instructions and so on).

The front of the pack uses the Marlboro brand's distinctive colours of red and white, a photograph of Marlboro Country as depicted in poster and magazine advertising, the Marlboro logo accompanied by 'America's most wanted' and 'If you want it come and get it'. The spine of the pack contains the Marlboro logo, 'America's most wanted' and 'Certificate 18'. The back of the pack repeats the 'Certificate 18' warning. The usual Chief Medical Officer's warning on the bottom is included, as are pictures of the three Marlboro brand packs in question. There is some information on the dates of the promotion and eligibility to take part in the offer, and some text that describes the plot. The latter involves felons in Marlboro Country having stashed counterfeiting plates away where the police cannot find them. It is up to you, the recipient, to track the plates down and if you do you will receive the reward of $150 000. To do this you have to watch the video and unravel the clues in it, but also study the map to locate the plates.

The letter has the logo and strap line and is printed on top of a faint map. It gives more detail. You would be one of fifty 'investigators' to have a crack at doing what the 'local law enforcement agencies' could not. You need hard evidence from the map and videotape to follow the trail of events that ultimately would lead you to the reward. There is a tiebreaker of course but, if you get into the last fifty, then you and your partner will be invited on an all expenses paid trip to Marlboro Country to look for the plates and win the $150 000. In the mean time you are invited to consider the pull foil offer on a Zippo lighter, a polished metal ashtray and a white cotton v-neck T-shirt – these are illustrated and the offer is explained in the leaflet.

The leaflet has the same photograph of Marlboro Country as the videotape box and 'America's most wanted gear' above it. It also has 'If you want it come and get it' and the Marlboro logo on it. It has colour photographs of the gifts and information about the pull foils. On the back are the three Marlboro brand packs pictured with 'America's most wanted' above. It has the rules and conditions of entering into the promotion and the usual health warning at the bottom.

The map has the same imagery as the leaflet and videotape box, only it reads 'America's most wanted map'. The back is the same as the leaflet. The instructions, the entry form and rules and conditions are all on the inside next to the full colour map. Albuquerque is probably the most famous place on it, or maybe Amarillo, El Paso or Santa Fe. Maybe the Pecos River and Plains or the Rio Grande are the things you recognize but, whatever strikes you, after a while you know what is meant by Marlboro Country.

You watch the video and you think of Tarantino or Travolta, or someone like that. Maybe it is a Ry Cooder soundtrack because of the bottleneck guitar. If you are watching it as a recipient of the mailing then you are probably doing so to look for clues. You may not know it but the Marlboro product is placed firmly within the film either literally on the hotel desk clerk's counter or simply the Marlboro brand's distinctive red and white, which may be subliminal. Whatever all of this is about, it's certainly about Marlboro.

Source: Adapted from Marlboro materials (December 2000).

STOP POINT

Whether Philip Morris was forced to do this kind of promotion or not is in a sense irrelevant. Restrictions of one sort or another are part of the marketer's environment (see 'The marketing communications environment' section later in this chapter). The challenge is to meet such obstacles and create opportunities, in this case if you are Philip Morris. Consider other challenges that the likes of Philip Morris will have to face. Make a short list of challenges (for example, look at the situation regarding recent advertising bans in the UK and the sponsorship of motor racing by tobacco companies and the pressure to stop this) and consider the kind of communications mix you would devise in order to help meet such challenges.

Integrated marketing communications

Background

Integrated marketing and integrated marketing communications are nothing new, since integration has been around for years with good practitioners. A simplistic view of how IMC works is to concentrate solely on communications elements working together with a 'unified message', where below-the-line activity supports above-the-line activity, and vice versa. This is the drive toward cost-effectiveness and 'careful planning creates marketing communications synergy which reinforces a consistent message or image in a cost effective manner' (Smith, 1993). This is a good start, but what is IMC really? Integrated marketing communications can be described as a process that involves various forms of communications that variously persuade, inform, remind and entertain customers and prospects, affecting and influencing behaviour of target audiences. The IMC process also includes anything and everything that an organization, company or its people and brands do with targets and publics, either deliberately or not. To make good use of all forms of relevant communication makes sense. All in all, the IMC process, like the more general marketing process, starts and ends with the customer or prospect.

What IMC means

Many words are thrown around in this area. Gestalt, seamless, clarity and consistency are but a few examples. As Massey (1994) suggests, the future of marketing communications seems to be integration, just as it was synergy in the 1970s and pan-Europeanism in the 1980s. This is perhaps so, but many would see integration as synergy, and the possibility of pan-European advertising being allowed by a synergistic or integrative approach. Brown (1996) lists eight possible themes to explore the question 'what is IMC?': attitude of mind, one spirit (a single theme to support the brand, the intellectual message where this is the overly simplistic 'one voice, one look' does not account for complexity), one strategy (a single communications strategy that embraces what it needs to achieve objectives), synergy (a unified message where each part reinforces the others, each drawing from each other), equal status among key communication elements where advertising's dominance is challenged, merging disciplines (for example between advertising and public relations or sales promotions), stakeholder emphasis and marketing orientation.

The above can be viewed as a useful addition in understanding IMC. However, the notion that a drive towards IMC and branding without consideration of the customer is short-sighted. At the end of the day, a reiteration of 1950s and 1960s Levitt-style marketing myopia,[4] where the future lies not with outdated constructs that relate to mass communication, but rather with the increasing fragmentation of the mass into one-to-one situations – or something near this. The client–agency difficulties are potentially the biggest area of concern. Until agencies better understand and serve clients' needs in this fragmented rather than mass world, this will not be resolved. There are a number of questions one can ask in this area. The answers to these are attempted below, but some questions remain unresolved here.

What drives IMC?

The overriding factor that drives IMC is the move away from mass communications but at the same time finding ways to get through the clutter in the most efficient way possible. Cost, accountability and a results orientation are now seen as being achieved through the co-ordination of diverse tools targeted at diverse audiences in an increasingly technology-led and global context. Therefore, *financial factors* are important for Schultz, Tannenbaum and Lauterborn (1994), who suggest that the recession, the trend towards pay by results, restructuring of how agencies are paid in terms of billing/income/profit, pressure to reduce media billing and media fragmentation have all contributed towards consideration of IMC. The *sophisticated client*, for many commentators, now is a reality, with such clients being more knowledgeable than in the past. The mystique of advertising is diminished and a power shift has occurred. *Disillusionment with the brand, advertising and agencies* (in a similar vein to the previous point above) appears to be a reality. Own labels are stronger and advertising less revered. Other elements of communications are deemed important. Agencies have had to change, but should see this as a set of opportunities not threats. The *power shift to retailers* generally, and what they need/expect, has meant more scrutiny of the way in which communication is viewed.

What are the benefits of IMC?

The perhaps more practical/practitioner-orientated Linton and Morley (1995) provide a clear list of benefits of IMC to organizations, including creative integrity (theme and style consistent throughout, therefore impact is achieved as opposed to confusion, which can aid campaign build-up and provide materials for other uses), consistency of messages (strap lines and other parts of the message can provide the basis for reinforcement and reminder, leading to the development of the key message, visual standards and consistent use of company colours), unbiased recommendations (usually through one agency and 'through the line' with no worries about earning commission from advertising billing only), better use of all media, greater marketing precision (databases and information processing generally), operational efficiency (needs fewer people, can be a single interface and so creates less conflict, is simple compared to the potentially messy multi-agency situation), cost savings (in administration, rationalization of materials, artwork), high-calibre service (IMC means professionalism for below the line as well as above the line where, overall, service is improved 'through the line'), easier working relationships (one agency means no new learning curves because of knowledge of the client's business, simplified administration, no relearning and ongoing and consistent) and accountability (this has to be true if only one agency is used and value for money should result).

Who benefits from IMC?

Agencies benefit, if they change to meet the needs of clients, i.e. if they apply good marketing practice to themselves. There are lots of opportunities including multimedia. *Clients* benefit where the principal argument is that it was high time clients made their budgets work harder for them. *Consumers* not benefiting means that the full benefit of IMC has not been passed on. There is no real evidence as yet as to whether the consumer is benefiting, but it is certainly looking this way (see Chapter 19 with particular reference to the Internet as an interactive, integrating tool).

What inhibits IMC?

A lack of a clear definition inhibits the development of IMC. There is some debate as to just what IMC really is. Practical difficulties, for example the complexity of different objectives being achieved by different strategy and tactics, do not help. Implementation can be very difficult to achieve. *Cultural factors* inhibit the development of IMC but the main factor is change, or resistance to change. The culture of the organization, for example, may be hung up on flashy advertising on television or it may be that sales promotions have been the norm, linked to bonuses. Any change would be accompanied by conflict. A deeper dimension is provided by Cornelissen (2000), who points to the failure of academia to provide an adequate managerial approach to IMC and suggests that the notion of integration should be rephrased into 'the more operational constructs of interaction and co-ordination between areas'. Useful and memorable constructs should be provided as performance indicators, for example the degree of interaction positively related to the degree of co-ordination between departments.

Where is IMC going?

The organization's *communication function* should be consolidated rather than divided up where 'managers can install co-ordination mechanisms to achieve required levels of interaction between functional areas or departments of communication' (Cornelissen, 2000). In practice, *agencies* are going to have to add value beyond media-buying and creativity, and new structures are emerging. Agencies must seize this opportunity. *Clients* should understand the importance of continuity and that the depth of the relationship will remain, or get even stronger, resulting in a situation akin to relationship marketing that has implications for the role of senior management.

The Haagen-Dazs vignette below provides a good illustration of integration of elements of communication.

VIGNETTE

Haagen-Dazs: 'From food to fashion accessory'

The *situation* for Haagen-Dazs is a case where the media department and the creative department worked closely together to develop a campaign that first created consumer excitement. It then created newsworthy PR, then trade excitement and, consequently, more and more consumer interest, to the point where the whole launch gained an unstoppable momentum. Haagen-Dazs luxury ice cream previously had very little above-the-line activity. The limited amount of local advertising used radio and posters. Local press, cinema and sandwich boards were used to launch the openings of Haagen-Dazs shops. There had been no previous brand launch activity. After being briefed, agency Bartle, Bogle and Hegarty (BBH) immediately started researching. Focus groups were set up among premium ice cream consumers to try to identify the main differences and reasons for purchasing a super premium ice cream over other ice creams. After a lifelong diet of other ice creams, individuals found it difficult to describe the experience of tasting Haagen-Dazs. They kept lapsing into the language of sensual satisfaction. Some elements of this were more tangible than others. The lavishness of the ingredients (fresh cream, egg yolks, skimmed milk and no E numbers at all) invited comparisons with indulgence. The special flavour of the ice cream elevated it to an experience more sensual than just eating. People also seemed to want to enjoy the ice cream quietly and intimately – to savour it without interruptions. They wanted to concentrate on the experience without the distraction. This was not easy to define. Although the ice cream was expensive to market, it was not casually defined as 'up-market, frivolous and young'. Instead, the target market was defined by attitude – they enjoy the best, believe that quality is worth paying for and that they themselves are worth treating (see below how this was translated into media selection). Rather than conducting independent research into the Haagen-Dazs audience, answers were sourced from the extensive qualitative research that was used to guide the creative development of the advertising message itself. Despite the attraction of television advertising for a new brand and the popularity of television with other ice cream suppliers (87.5 per cent of the total ice cream spend went on television), press was preferred since it created a 'feel' with the advertising that could itself be savoured and enjoyed at leisure. In addition, the intimacy of the experience could be better hinted at through the personal one-to-one communication of the press. Television is often a family or social medium that might, in itself, devalue the communication by exposing it to the comment and reaction of third parties. Research showed that women were particularly expressive of these special moments when they are left alone with their favourite magazine. They often save up the magazine for the sheer joy of being alone with a cup of coffee, disconnected from the rest of the world for a few moments of self-indulgence (ideal for Haagen-Dazs).

The principal *objective* was to launch the Haagen-Dazs brand nationally. Then the task was to build brand awareness. Thirdly, the brand had to be positioned as the finest ice cream in the world. The campaign also had to generate strong consumer response since the campaign took place when many of the major multiples were testing the brand. Brand leadership was built *strategically* by creating a new language for ice cream. Other ice creams focus on ingredients or images of happy families. Before advertising came the creation of 'brand ambassadors' – celebrities willing to endorse the brand in press articles. As well as this, the product was given away at all the best places, for example Henley Regatta, and even appeared on the menu at top restaurants. All of this was designed to get the 'chattering classes' chattering. The new advertising talked about end benefits that are sometimes hidden deep below the surface, as opposed to the more traditional style where conscious feelings are expressed about ice cream. Strategically, a series of press advertisements allowed a relationship to be built with the target audience, unlike a one-off advertisement. *Tactically*, although weekend colour supplements and weekend reviews are considered to be highly optional reading, they lack the immediacy of their parent newspapers. The weekend's 'leisurely read' aspect (being read for leisure rather than for information) lent itself to the creation of the values that the brand advertising was trying to develop. The qualitative research highlighted those lazy Saturday or Sunday afternoon moments, languishing in the garden. This is just the moment to whisper Haagen-Dazs, instead of having to shout the message on television. *Implementation* was achieved through Haagen-Dazs using 6 per cent share of voice (SOV) to launch the brand (which is not a large budget for a launch). A small sum was used on PR. *Scheduling* was aided by original research and TGI data was used to blend the shopping and reading habits of the target customer. To ensure that the target market would be exposed to more than one of the four advertisements, the media schedule was compiled with meticulous 'attention to duplication'. The media planners researched and analysed the extent to which readers of each magazine also read the weekend reviews or the weekend magazines. The titles eventually chosen also had to share a commitment to the quality lifestyle that was appropriate to the brand itself. *Evaluation* was seen as a crucial part of the campaign. Although this advertising campaign only had a 6 per cent SOV (share of all the advertising money spent by UK ice cream manufacturers), campaign measurement showed the campaign helped to make Haagen-Dazs the most talked about ice cream brand of the year. It was 'New Product of the Year' for the Marketing Society and it had become brand leader of the take-home premium ice cream sector.

The results confirm the power of good communication. The propensity to purchase (or try it) increased by over 500 per cent. Sales through Haagen-Dazs's own outlets broke all records. Distribution penetration increased through the retail multiples, with Waitrose increasing distribution from their test stores dramatically and Safeway going to national distribution immediately. Prompted awareness almost quadrupled. Haagen-Dazs had a unique positioning as they were 'Dedicated to Pleasure', effectively redefining what premium meant to the consumer.

Sources: Adapted from the BBC (1994b), Haagen-Dazs materials (1996), McCrae (1996) and Smith (1993; 1998).

STOP POINT

Much is written about BBH's advertising campaign on behalf of Haagen-Dazs, but much less on the fact that they created a textbook IMC/integrated marketing campaign. The advertising in fact came almost last and was preceded by a number of communication devices centred on the idea of 'brand seeding' including the use of 'brand ambassadors', getting on posh hotel menus, associations with polo, sailing and the kind of venues where 'debutantes come out and jetsetters mingle' (McCrae, 1996). Consider how important this is if a brand legend is to be created or destroyed by advertising too early and perhaps losing the solid base that can be built through effective word of mouth. Consider also whether or not Haagen-Dazs achieved 'classic brand status' along the lines of Levi or Harley-Davidson.

The marketing communications environment

Environmental factors as an integral part of the planning and managing process are dealt with in Chapter 4 and then throughout the rest of this book. In Chapter 3 such factors are considered in terms of the communication process sender–message–receiver model. The general aim here is to look at the environment in which organizations/marketers and communicators work. The reader should already be familiar with the PEST/STEP/SLEPT-type models of the macro environment and models of the micro environment essential for marketing analysis but which also apply in the communications context. Some writers refer to this as the 'near' and 'far' environment (e.g. Smith, Berry and Pulford, 1997). These are discussed below in three ways: characteristics of the micro and macro environment; strategic environmental issue management; critical components of the micro and macro environment.

Characteristics of the micro and macro environment

Modernist marketing authors like Kotler (e.g. 1984; 1988) appear for many years to have philosophized in terms of the marketing environment. Kotler uses at least two anonymous sayings that mean something in this area. These are 'it is useless to tell a river to stop running; the best thing is to learn how to swim in the direction it is flowing' and 'there are three types of companies. Those who make things happen. Those who watch things happen. Those who wondered what happened' . These allude to the company purpose. This position holds that the purpose should be specific as to the business domain and that products and technologies are transient while basic market needs generally remain. The company should shift its business domain definition from product to market focused. The modernist position sees the marketing environment (ME) as an important concept to the practice of good marketing management. The ME consists of all those factors that affect the organization and its markets, and any factors that affect the relationship between an organization and its markets. Matching takes place in the ME, i.e. the matching of the organization's capabilities to meet customer needs and wants. There is therefore a requirement of management to monitor the ME and adapt product and marketing strategies to meet changing needs. Markets are dynamic and needs fast-changing, so there is, therefore, the need for some form of marketing information system which would necessarily include marketing research and intelligence that should be built into the organization's decision-making process. With many of the aforementioned factors, the organization usually has little or no control over them but can influence them. These factors or components are discussed below.

Strategic environmental issue management

Most managers involved in companies are aware of the importance of environmental analysis. More experienced managers are perhaps also aware of the difficulties of monitoring the environment that is both within and surrounds their organization. In order to implement environmental issue management, four stages of such a process need to be considered. First, *environmental scanning* must take place in order that *key environmental issues* can be identified and an *impact evaluation* allowed before the formulation of a *response strategy* occurs. This applies across the business (including marketing) board but, of course, part of this response is marketing and corporate communications.

Critical components of the micro and macro environment

The micro and macro environment are well-known constructs in general marketing terms and their respective components are depicted in Figure 1.5.

From this general model of the marketing environment the components or elements of each of the micro and macro environments can be seen in relation to what they might mean to marketing communicators.

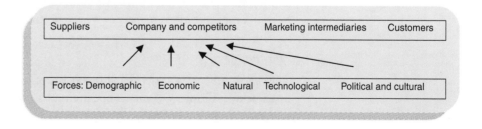

Figure 1.5
Critical components of the
marketing environment.

The micro environment

The *micro environment* (MIE) consists of a number of elements. Taking the elements of the MIE in turn we can begin with the *organization* itself. There obviously exists an *internal* environment within all organizations. Management structures vary vastly but, whatever the structure of the organization, marketing management has the task of making marketing decisions within this context and in the context of corporate mission, objectives, strategies, policies etc. It is especially important to note the notion of conflict within organizations. There are many possible sources of conflict that could occur in organizations, for example how marketing, production and finance interact or how sales and marketing interact (see Chapter 13 for a fuller consideration of internal communications). Every company needs resources of some sort in order to function, for example material and fuel, and there is therefore a need to monitor *suppliers'* prices, shortages, alternatives and perhaps to consider more than one supplier to avoid total cut-off while not getting the benefits of economies of scale. *Marketing intermediaries* include middlemen – agents, manufacturers' representatives, wholesalers and retailers – who have place/time/possession utility. The notion is that such players can act more efficiently and hence more cheaply than a manufacturer. There are also physical distribution firms – warehousing, transportation – who can increase the cost-effectiveness of operations in terms of speed, safety and so on. Marketing services include advertising, PR, marketing research agencies, marketing analysts who can also be classed as marketing intermediaries as can financial services – banks, credit brokers and so on. *Customers* can be consumers or buying for someone else; they might be organizational buyers or resellers; they might be national or local government; they might be at home or abroad. Each type of customer has particular characteristics that call for careful study and, consequently, differing approaches. *Competitors* lie somewhere on a spectrum between co-operation and open warfare. Competition can come in many forms of which there are four from a customer viewpoint:

- desire (where one type is satisfied but not another, for example a new car as opposed to a holiday)

- generic (one problem-solver versus another, for example a car or bike)

- product form (one product rather than another, for example saloon or sports car)

- branding (one brand rather than another, for example own label, Oxo or Bovril stock cubes).

The term *publics* alludes to the organization seeking goodwill, usually via PR activities, on a continual basis. There are a number of established publics: financial (for example the banks), media (press, television and radio) and government (national, pressure groups and local). A related concept, that of the *stakeholder*, has been used relatively recently to describe the actors in such a system as suggested above, which is associated with strengths and weaknesses of organizations and is returned to from a communications management perspective in Chapter 4.

The macro environment

The *macro environment* (MAE) also consists of a number of elements, which are listed below. All micro elements operate under a larger MAE consisting of forces that have been traditionally thought of as uncontrollable (as opposed to the elements of the marketing mix). The forces of the MAE therefore influence opportunities and threats. The organization should be aware of any trends or changes in the MAE. Products developed in the *technological* environment range from 'wonder drugs' to hydrogen bombs to soft-as-floss white bread full of vitamins. It has been argued that new technologies have a creative destruction, especially where real innovation is present and not just gimmicks such as freeze-dried coffee. The accelerating pace of change perhaps underscores the importance of research and development being conducted hand-in-hand with marketing research. Innovation opportunities/threats should be delineated from minor improvements and the need for regulation of, for example, food and drugs recognized. Technology is constantly changing. It can no longer be assumed that current ranges of products will continue to satisfy customer demands. In an early volume of marketing management, Kotler uses the example of non-drip paint as a product that had a profound effect on what had been a stable market. We could extend this now with the recent developments in 'one-coat' paints. Kotler (1984) stated that new technology creates some 'major long-run consequences that are not always foreseeable' and at the time used the example of the contraceptive pill, that 'led to smaller families, more working wives and larger discretionary incomes'. Kotler's argument was that this then resulted in more money being spent on things like holiday travel that in turn would increase airline traffic. Kotler also concluded that the pill had also 'led to a larger average size in brassiere, something the women's lingerie industry has missed entirely' (ibid.).

The *political/legal/ethical* environment involves an increasing and changing amount of legislation. This includes protection of companies from each other; for example antitrust laws (USA) and the Monopoly and Mergers Commission (UK) prevent unfair competition. It also includes protection of consumers from unfair business practices, for example unfair or misleading advertising and packaging, and protection of the larger interests of society against unbridled business behaviour. Acts of Parliament, changing government agencies and changes in their roles (whether this be, for example, leanings toward deregulation or the opposite), the growth of public interest/pressure groups and the notion of consumerism as major social force all have a potential impact. The true nature of the 'sovereign consumer' with many examples of exploitation in many markets such as those for cars, meat, loans, car repairs and insurance (the list is endless) carries on today with consumer magazines like *Which?* and *Watchdog* carrying the flag. The early forms of communication were often trade depicters – an inn sign, a barber's pole and an apothecary's jar of coloured liquid. Now advertising alone is a large (and powerful) industry in its own right. In terms of what can be called the *regulatory* environment there are very many historical/legal/ethical/moral issues. Controls over marketing communications and in particular advertising, i.e. laws (as passed in parliament) or voluntary control (by the industry for the industry to keep up standards) are many and varied. These to some extent can be the same issues regarding consumerism and environmentalism as discussed above. Of the many issues involved suffice to say that all are interesting and some are very important tactically from the communicator's viewpoint. Commentary on controversial communication is abundant in the literature.

The *demographic* environment has many strands to it. An ageing population and therefore new and different markets – for example children, youth, young adults, the early middle aged, the later middle aged, retirees – could form the segments of a market based on age that would change quite radically percentage-wise over the course of time. Increased life expectancy, slowdown of the birth rate, fewer young people, family size/number of children, later marriage, fewer children, higher divorce rate, more women/mothers working, men the target for food manufacturers etc. all contribute to this, as do the rise of non-family households, the single adult and two person co-habiters – all groups with special needs. There are also better education standards, a decrease in indiscriminate television viewing and increases in book and magazine reading and travel to consider. The *geodemographic* perspective sees geographic shifts, rural to urban, urban to rural, city to suburbs, suburbs to city (very important if such shifts mean losing suburban facilities) and regional (say) the North East to the South East.

The *economic* environment is closely linked to demography and markets that require purchasing power that is a function of real income and any changes in disposable and discretionary that are affected by inflation, unemployment and taxation. Such effects may lead to marketing responses such as more cautionary price appeals or time-saving products bought by consumers such as 'yuppies' or 'dinkies'. Savings are clearly pitted against expenditure but this also involves things like credit facilities, lending and mortgages. Changing expenditure patterns, for example when income rises the percentage of income spent on food might very well decrease while that on leisure and recreation increases, need to be recognized.

The *sociocultural* environment involves beliefs, norms and values. Primary concerns are things like 'the institution of marriage', while secondary concerns would follow sentiments such as 'you ought to marry early'. It is said that primary values are more difficult to change than secondary ones – although this is clearly not impossible. Core values are things like 'the American way' and 'Englishness' in terms of culture. Subcultural values belong to groups such as 'teenagers'. Secondary cultural values may involve shifts over time. In one era 'teenagers' may have a particular set of values. These can change quite radically. The sociocultural environment is therefore to do with people's relations with themselves, for example, a 'me society' seeking self-fulfilment, reflected in the use of and expenditure on leisure, recreation and fun. People's relations to others (a 'me' to 'we' shift involving others) are reflected in the use of, for example, 'honesty' in advertising. In terms of ethnicity, Hispanics are seen in the USA as an important subcultural group but this may not be refined enough. In Britain it may make more marketing sense to look at British South Asians as a target group rather than 'the Asian community in Britain', which clearly has a complex make-up. British people's relations to institutions, including shifts in loyalty to marriage or the work ethic, can be readily seen. People's relations to society, again including shifts in loyalty, for example the erosion of patriotism, are also visible, as are people's relations to nature and the universe, again including shifts such as a move from a specific religion to, say, worldliness or some other form of spiritualism.

The *natural/environmental/green* element, with particular reference to the recent rise of environmentalism and 'green' issues, shows clearly the interaction that can occur between the various elements of the MAE and MIE. For example the natural/political/public pressure groups involving 'limits to growth'-type debate and argument.[5] The natural environment therefore involves shortages of raw materials, divided into the following:

- *infinite resources* such as the air we breathe and long-term dangers or shorter-term ones such as the use of chlorofluorocarbons (CFCs)

- *finite, renewable resources* such as forests but with similar long- and short-term dangers

- *finite, non-renewable resources* such as coal, oil and gas.

Increased cost of energy, levels of pollution and government intervention in natural resource management are all items for consideration. All these issues beg the question 'what opportunities are there for the development of new sources and new materials?' Clearly there are opportunities for marketers to communicate benefits or to use particular imagery in this area while at the same time there is the danger of the bandwagon effect, i.e. simply milking an environmental issue by jumping on a current wave of favourable opinion without any real justification for doing so. Environmentalists are perhaps more critical of marketing than consumerists. For example, environmentalists complain more vigorously about (wasteful) packaging whereas consumerists like the idea of convenience packaging. Consumerists worry about deception in advertising whereas environmentalists do not like the idea that advertising leads to greater (than necessary) consumption. The rise of environmentalism has made the marketer's life more complicated, probably much more so than consumerism ever did. The cost of including environmental issues and criteria in marketing decision-making is in many cases not insignificant, but at the same time managers have realized that, at the very least, respecting the environment is in itself worthwhile. This is probably the richest area for marketing opportunities. Kotler (1984), two decades ago, quoting the chairman of Du Pont, makes this point clear. The real environmental challenge is not to be reactive or to try to browbeat but to persuade through real environmentalism what 'I define as an attitude and performance commitment that places corporate environmental stewardship fully in line with public desires and expectations' (ibid.). Again, a communications management perspective on MAE elements will be dealt with in Chapter 4.

VIGNETTE

Corporate and social responsibility

Controls over marketing communications (in particular advertising) come in two forms: the law (as passed in Parliament), and voluntary control by the industry for the industry in order to keep up standards. Some of the laws that have been passed over the years by successive UK governments are the Consumer Credit Act 1974, the Medicines Act 1968, the Sale Of Goods Act 1983 and the Trade Descriptions Act 1968. Some of the UK controlling bodies involved and the codes they expect practitioners to adhere to are the Advertising Standards Authority (ASA), the Independent Television Commission (ITC), the Office of Fair Trading (OFT). In the USA the Federal Trade Commission (FTC) has power and influence but so, too, have other organizations such as the Food and Drug Administration. This is a very large area of study and much that is relevant is naturally beyond the scope of the marketing professional, being the province of corporate lawyers. However, anyone can quite easily get an appreciation of the legal/regulatory environment. The problem is there are so many situations worldwide and the whole issue is compounded by the nature of integrated campaigns, i.e. we are not usually dealing with advertising in isolation but with PR, sponsorship and so on. Added to this are cultural constraints and self-regulatory bodies, making the whole picture quite complex. A further dimension is the development of economic and other groupings like the European Union (EU) and consequently things like European Community (EC) Directives. International marketers should therefore be concerned with laws (international law, misleading claims, government/EC regulations.) and codes (self-regulation by companies, the advertising industry and so on).

Examples of product categories that are of concern are tobacco, alcohol, pharmaceuticals and financial services. Specific target groups that are much written about are children, women and, increasingly, men. Restraint is still very much domestic driven but, for example, EC Directives are becoming increasingly important. A fundamental question is, 'is the business community capable of self-regulation or, left to their own devices, would some firms break the rules?' After all, business exists to make money not moral or ethical judgements. However, intervention is justified for consumer protection. In 1989 within the EC the Consumer Consultative Council (consisting of thirty-nine consumer bodies) existed to express consumer protection opinion. In Germany comparative advertising had been banned since 1909 but the EU appears to like comparative advertising since it apparently assists consumers, and Germany has now followed this lead. Further afield than the EU and EC Directives etc. the world picture is rather diffused. In the Arab world Islam plays a huge part, it being a fusion of culture/religion and law. Of not least importance here is the role and representation of women. Children should not be used in advertising. In many countries, there is concern for dishonesty in advertising, but a strongly held view from the business community is that every merchandise item produced legally should have the right to be advertised.

In many instances it is not the products themselves but blatantly offensive advertising which causes the problem – whether this be real or imagined. For example, a poster campaign in the UK has caused division in the advertising industry itself. The adverts for Club 18–30 (a package holiday company) had sexual innuendo-laden headlines such as 'Beaver Espana' and 'The Summer of 69' that the ASA asked to be withdrawn after 314 complaints. The company said they were inundated with requests for marketing materials from the target audience. More importantly the 'any publicity is good publicity' rule appears to apply for Club 18–30. Pretty Polly's use, on a poster hoarding, of a live model whose cocktail dress is removed to have her posing in high heels, a burgundy bra and a pair of black tights for the press pack is a Trevor Beattie creation. This is the man who allegedly gave us 'Hello Boys' for the Wonderbra (there is some dispute here) but certainly gave us 'f.c.u.k.' after first providing fcuk for the newly positioned and rebranded French Connection fashion house. fcuk saw a plethora of complaints to the ASA. And, of course, there is always Benetton. After the worldwide hullabaloo about shocking images from newborn babies to a nun kissing a priest, from a Mafia killing to a black devil and white angel and so on, came a period of Fabrica (the Benetton art school) and a return to more traditional marketing. This rather more quiet time did not last very long and soon we were seeing more shocking, controversial ideas involving, for example, prisoners on death row, signifying the start of 'a publicity at any cost' campaign followed in 2003 by images of Afghani women, just before the start of the Iraq war.

On a slightly different note, we in the UK have just seen the outlawing of advertising of tobacco products, yet the world's second largest tobacco company, British American Tobacco (BAT), have announced at least two non-commercial sponsorship deals. The University of Manchester Institute of Science and Technology (UMIST) has accepted £50 000 to support a new masters degree in strategic communications that follows Nottingham University's £3.8m deal to fund a school of business ethics. This has led to a number of things, not least a Nottingham University student prize winner appearing on many a news programme to tell his side of the tale – that he has requested that his prize money goes to a cancer charity. Naturally, anti-smoking campaigners accused BAT of attempting to buy 'respectability' on the cheap. Roger Haywood, PR author and chairman of the PR standards council was quoted as calling for other sponsors of the UMIST degree (Tesco, Burson-Marsteller, Allied Zurich, Reuters and the BG Group) to boycott it. British American Tobacco has denied allegations that they exploit smuggling and that they were trying to get round any advertising bans. They were, said the director of corporate affairs, trying to help make the discipline of corporate communications a professional one.

Sources: Adapted from Beckett (1997); Club 18–30 mini disk and poster materials (1995–2000); Hill (1997); Maguire (2000).

STOP POINT Consider which side of this particular fence you come down on. Where do you stand with images and slogans of a sexually explicit nature to sell packaged holidays to relatively young people? How do you view clever approaches like fcuk? Has Benetton the right to use what they call photojournalism or photo realism to sell jumpers and sweatshirts? And are BAT serious when they say they merely wish to support the development of a discipline or profession? Is any publicity good publicity or is there a price to pay that is too high at the end of the day?

Assignment

It has been said that the organization has little or no control over the forces of the MAE but can influence them. Select one of the following organizations and make a list of environmental factors that such an organization might take into account when analysing its markets. Consider the possible marketing opportunities which may exist now or arise in the future in the environmental/'green' part of the marketing environment for such organizations. Follow this through with basic ideas on marketing communications strategy and tactics, especially with regard to message strategy.

- A soap powder/liquid manufacturer.

- A soft drinks manufacturer.

- A car manufacturer.

- A toothpaste manufacturer.

- A packaged holiday company.

- A surface coatings (e.g. paint, varnish) manufacturer.

Summary of Key Points

- Marketing and corporate communications has to operate in a climate of exchange and change. The type of exchange is important but so, too, is the nature of change. We appear to be moving towards an era of media and customer dominance, with a greater relational emphasis on marketing communications practice and one that is increasingly global.

- Marketing and corporate communications' role is mutating continually. The old mix within the marketing mix mnemonic has changed to reveal new strategic tools such as sponsorship.

- The notion of IMC is not acceptable when expressed in very simple terms such as synergy. This needs to be contextualized both within and outside the organization, and will have to become a more functionally endemic part of what an organization is and does.

- The marketing environment is constantly changing. The biggest challenge for marketing and corporate communications management in meeting this change is not so much a result of shifting sands but more to do with dealing with an anthropomorphic, living, growing and mutating entity.

Examination Questions

1 Outline the different kinds of exchange that might exist in marketing. In particular, explain relational exchange, using examples to illustrate.

2 Discuss the notion of power shift from manufacturer to consumer. Use relevant examples to illustrate your discussion.

3 The communications mix is potentially made up of many things and is constantly mutating. Choose two contrasting product categories and highlight the likely communications mix differences when launching a product within each category.

4 'The absence of IMC now is the equivalent of having marketing myopia in the 1960s.' Explain why you either agree or disagree with this sentiment.

5 The marketing communications company has a vital role to play in the achievement of IMC on behalf of clients. Explain this role using examples of your choice.

6 Explain why distributors are of interest to the marketing communicator. Illustrate your response with examples from consumer and organizational markets.

7   Explain the relationship between the micro and macro environments. Discuss the effect of this on marketing communications outputs.

8   The demographic environment clearly interfaces with the economic environment. Explain this interface and illuminate your response with examples.

9   'The natural or green environment is the most important element in any environmental scanning exercise for any company these days.' Explain why you agree or disagree with this statement.

10 Choose any element of the macro environment and put it in the context of a brand of your choice. Discuss the likely communications issues that would have to be dealt with by a brand or category manager.

Notes

1   Some writers do not see marketing this way. Most notably in Europe, Brown (1995), commenting on the marketing concept that he believes is not unassailable, explains that the work of Shigemitsu (2000) 'with its tripartite emphasis on customer orientation, overall integration and profit maximisation [the marketing concept] has been the subject of extensive debate and periodic modification'.

2   See Elinder (1961) for one of the first articles in the literature directly to deal with this subject.

3   The useful shorthand that is the 'marketing mix' has been, and still is, the subject of some debate in academic marketing circles. Building on the problem with mnemonics, for example, Kent (1986) underscores the 'seductive sense of simplicity', the point being that to create something that is a memory aid that then becomes an 'article of faith' is dangerous. It is with this kind of understandable argument in mind that the useful shorthand is used here with caution.

4   Short-sightedness, the inability to see in a truly marketing orientated way. Levitt's original myopia is seen as a classic piece of thought. It is not surprising that Levitt's (1983) article has been reprinted so many times in so many places. See, for example, Enis and Cox (1985), where it is the first of the selected classics chosen to start the book off.

5   The limits to growth debate of the 1970s, centring on the environment, finite oil resources and so on.

References

BBC (1994a). *A Force to be Reckoned With.* (The Business video series). BBC.

BBC (1994b). *The Business – From Food to Fashion Accessory.* (Video and notes.) BBC Publications.

Beckett, A. (1997). Benetton's new babies. *MediaGuardian*, 28 July, 4–5.

Bradley, F. (1995). *Marketing Management.* Prentice Hall.

Brown, J. (1996). IMC – impossible dream or inevitable revolution. *Proceedings of the Marketing Education Group (MEG) Conference*, University of Strathclyde.

Brown, S. (1995). *Postmodern Marketing.* Routledge.

Cornelissen, J. (2000). 'Integration' in communication management: conceptual and methodological considerations. *Journal of Marketing Management*, **16**, 597–606.

De Pelsmaker, P., Geuens, P. and Van Den Bergh, J. (2001). *Marketing Communications.* Financial Times Prentice Hall.

De Mooij, M. (1994). *Advertising Worldwide.* 2nd edition. Prentice Hall.

Dowman, R. (2000). Talking shop. *Unilever Magazine*, **3** (117), 8–12.

Elinder, E. (1961). How international can advertising be? *International Advertiser*, December, 12–16.

Enis, B. M. and Cox, K. K. (1985). *Marketing Classics – A Selection of Influential Articles*. 5th edition. Allyn and Bacon.

Fill, C. (1995). *Marketing Communications: Frameworks, Theories, and Applications*. Prentice Hall.

Fill, C. (1999). *Marketing Communications: Contexts, Contents and Strategies*. 2nd edition. Prentice Hall Europe.

Fill, C. (2002). *Marketing Communications: Contexts, Strategies and Applications*. 3rd edition. Financial Times Prentice Hall.

Hill, D. (1997). Actually, you're supposed to be looking at her tights. *Observer Review*, 21 September, 6–7.

Kent, R. A. (1986). Faith in four Ps: an alternative. *Journal of Marketing Management*, **2** (2), 115–153.

Kotler, P. (1984). *Marketing Management – Analysis, Planning, Implementation and Control*. 5th edition. Prentice Hall.

Kotler, P. (1988*). Marketing Management – Analysis, Planning, Implementation and Control*. 6th edition. Prentice Hall.

Kotler, P., Armstrong, G., Saunders, J. and Wong, V. (2001). *Principles of Marketing*. 3rd European edition. Pearson.

Levitt, T. (1983). The globalisation of markets. *Harvard Business Review*. May–June, 92–102.

Linton, I. and Morley, K. (1995). *Integrated Marketing Communications*. Butterworth-Heinemann.

Maguire, K. (2000). Tobacco firm's new university link-up. At http://www.guardianunlimited. co.uk/Archive.

Massey (1994). An anatomy of integration. *Marketing*, 25 August, 21–24.

McCrae, C. (1996). *The Brand Chartering Handbook*. EIU/Addison Wesley Longman.

Mutsuko, M. and Rutledge, B. (2000). Stoking the yen to spend. *Asiaweek*, **26** (49), 15 December.

Schultz, D. (1996). New trends in communication and advertising. Lecture to the University of Strathclyde Business School, 16 October.

Schultz, D. E., Tannenbaum, S. I. and Lauterborn, R. F. (1994). *Integrated Marketing Communications*. NTC Business Books.

Shigemitsu, S. (2000). Keep learning, Asia. *Asiaweek*, **26** (49), 15 December.

Smith, P., Berry, C. and Pulford, A. (1997). *Strategic Marketing Communications*. Kogan Page.

Smith, P. R. (1993). *Marketing Communications*. Kogan Page.

Smith, P. R. (1998). *Marketing Communications*. 2nd edition. Kogan Page.

Townsend, P. (1991). What big teeth: regulation, Europe and freedom. *Admap*. June.

Wilcox, G. B. et al. (1994). Cigarette advertising and consumption in South Korea. *International Journal of Advertising*, 13.4.

2

Theoretical underpinnings of marketing communication

Chapter overview

Introduction to this chapter

The nature of communication theory is explored in terms of meaning for both marketing and corporate contexts. Many of the theoretical models available were established during the 1960s but some of the key ideas have been around for much longer. Other, more recent, developments have tried to bring buyer behaviour theory closer to that of communications, and this is looked at in Chapter 3. In particular, the traditional view of the communications process has been fused with the 'hierarchy of effects' model to offer further insight into the workings of marketers' communications and the likely effects of such communications on recipients. This chapter concentrates on the ways in which senders of a message can get meaning across to a recipient. These are many and varied but not at all 100 per cent accurate. However, it is recognized that the context in which communications takes place is important and that interactive and relational approaches in such contexts offer an alternative view of communications working in practice. The role of personal influence, the power of word of mouth and the usefulness of adoption/diffusion models are explored.

Aims of this chapter

The chapter seeks to explore and explain the theoretical underpinnings of communication and to underscore the usefulness and limitations of theory to practice. More specifically the reader, on completion of the chapter, should be able to:

- discuss communications in terms of the needs of practitioners
- explain the basic model of communication within an historical context
- explore other communications models and theories that can help inform practitioner decision-making
- assess the impact personal influence has on the communications process
- assess the usefulness of the adoption and diffusion process as an aid to the marketing communicator.

Communications and practitioners

There is concern for the fundamental use of the very basic model of the (marketing) communication process used by many writers of textbooks to suggest the availability of, at the very least, a framework for marketers to help manage their various forms of communication – whether mediated or interpersonal. Buttle (1995) provides a useful history/ancestry of communication (and marketing communication) theory and points to the lack of explicitness regarding theory. The simple argument is that theory should inform practice otherwise it is pointless, but practice needs some theoretical underpinnings to provide stability.

This argument is central here since we are concerned with practitioners and what they can gain from the theoretical stances taken by writers – whether practitioners themselves or academicians – in order to provide a framework or even simply a basis from which to build the desired model. The vignette below illustrates the need for vigilance and a problem-solving outlook.

VIGNETTE

Sainsbury: why do a Basil Fawlty without Manuel?

By August 1999 Sainsbury, the supermarket chain, had become the centre of a row with competitors over a new advertising campaign that was said to be misleading. The 'no genetically modified food where you see this label' line over the Sainsbury logo followed by a claim that Sainsbury 'are the first major supermarket to start making all own-label food without genetically modified ingredients', all in the name of customer care, had infuriated the likes of Iceland, Marks and Spencer (M&S) and Waitrose. These companies claimed themselves to be the first, and Russell Ford (Iceland's managing director) went as far as to accuse Sainsbury of telling 'a blatant lie'. Further, the accusation that the advertising gave the impression that all of what Sainsbury do is genetically modified (GM)-free, when clearly a lot of branded (as opposed to own label) goods are not, has been made.

Sainsbury vigorously denied any attempt to mislead but this controversy follows on from a previous Christmas campaign that starred John Cleese, the well-known comedy actor (among many other things) who is as least as famous for his Basil Fawlty character in the 1970s BBC comedy *Fawlty Towers* as he is for the earlier *Monty Python's Flying Circus* television programme or the later hit film *A Fish Called Wanda* with Jamie Lee Curtis. The 'Value to Shout About' promotion had backfired badly. It was voted the worst campaign of the year by the industry. Store staff complained it made them appear stupid but, more fundamentally, traditional mid-range shoppers stayed away from what seemed a store that was going in a downward direction while attracting price-conscious shoppers who were simply after bargains, hitting sales and, presumably, profits. Some estimates put a value on price per share loss of 34p (£600 million in value). Sainsbury were a poor fourth to the other big three supermarkets and the overall effect on image was one of portrayal of a value store.

Job losses, the sacking of agency Abbott Mead Vickers and some restructuring followed, along with rumours of takeovers and mergers. Tesco had emerged as the champion with Sainsbury playing catch-up with ideas previously rejected but used to good effect by arch-rival Tesco. Allegedly the Queen buys Tesco Christmas puddings, and globalization is at work on the high street. For Sainsbury, like many others, this meant reinvention and renewal. This requires vision of the sort shown by Time Warner and AOL whose merger saw the potential for the smooth and integrated flow of information. Sainsbury appear to have recovered from the 'Value' debacle that for some, almost inadvertently, repositioned the brand from middle market, middle England to that of a value store. Sainsbury clearly now feel that they are on a winner with their current celebrity endorser, television's 'Naked Chef', Jamie Oliver, one of British television's most popular chefs.

Source: Adapted from BBC (1999a; 1999b); Finch (1999); Harbridge (1999).

STOP POINT

It is easy, with hindsight perhaps, to see what went wrong with the Sainsbury campaign. The use of Cleese in this way was an error of judgement, especially given the wonderful opportunity to exploit one of the best known and funniest comedy actors in the business. What else could Sainsbury have done with such a character in your view?

A model of mass communications

Numerous models have been developed in this area that help further develop this general framework for understanding. The commonest form in the textbooks deals with the problems of one-way mass communication, although it does have a feedback loop that indicates that the source is likely to search for, or expect some form of, recipient feedback. The source is usually the marketing organization and the receiver the consumer, though not always. To complete this process accurately is a very difficult task to achieve. The process looks simple but in practice is far from simplicity. The basic model is shown in Figure 2.1.

For this to be of any practical use in the real world, it has, of course, to aid the marketer in terms of effective and efficient communications. Fundamentally, the idea is for the communicator to be in a position to understand the (target) recipient well enough to be able to encode desired messages with a high degree of certainty that there will be no 'noise' in the system. The task is to understand how decoding will occur and allow for the subsequent transfer of pure, unadulterated meaning.

The most frequently adopted model of the communications process in marketing terms is that of Schramm (1971a), revised from Schramm's 1954 model which itself was derived from Lasswell's (1948) semantic description, and Shannon and Weaver's (1962) 'model' of the communication process. Many authors, such as Fill (1995; 1999; 2002) and Belch and Belch (1995), use this as a fundamental building block. The elements of the process for our purposes

Figure 2.1
A basic model of the communications process.

Noise				Noise
Source (Communicator)	Encodes	Signal (Message)	Decodes	Destination (Receiver)
		FEEDBACK		
			Noise	

here need to be explained and broken down into their own constituents in order that the model can be better understood. Taking these in turn:

1   *Sender/source.* A person, group of people, company or some other organization may wish to transmit/relay an idea, set of ideas or a proposition in order to share something with another party. This out of necessity includes the encoding of a message in some shape or form with the intention of achieving one or more of the communications objectives, and necessarily involves the sender/source itself as part of that message. The source characteristics outlined in the Kellman model below apply here so that salespeople, advertising and so on should have elements of trust, likeability, attractiveness, power or other characteristics in order to influence and persuade.

2   *Encoding.* If the problem is perceived incorrectly by the source then the wrong concept might be developed and encoded, making the communication faulty. Some form of situation analysis is useful here. We are concerned about actuality and perception, where any mismatch is the perception itself in the mind of the transmitter. This makes a lot of sense in the real world of everyday experience where thought/ideas have been translated into symbolic form. The problem lies in the task of getting the right sentences, words, symbols and so on, that will communicate effectively, from a vast array of verbal and non-verbal elements.

3   *The message.* The message is the symbolic representation of the sender/source's thoughts/ideas. If the source does not say what he or she means, even if the problem is understood, then the message strategy will be faulty. Objectives should be met by using the best combination of marketing communications tools – advertising, packaging and so on – with the right kind of message at the right time. The message itself has no meaning. Meanings are part of the message user, i.e. sender/source or recipient/receiver. Many options are available to the communicator including one- or two-sided arguments, open/closed conclusions and rational/emotional appeals. All this adds up to creative strategy.

4   *The medium.* As the conduit/channel for the message, the medium (or particular vehicle) and its nature and characteristics are of crucial importance to marketing communicators whether this be via a newspaper, a trade show or a salesperson. Messages are often viewed as mediated (if, for example, a salesperson is involved) or unmediated (if, say, an advertisement is used). The medium or media vehicle might be an upmarket, glossy magazine. The advertisement might well use references to, say, the works of Cezanne to sell crystal glass products. This would require a certain knowledge of art and especially painting (even if only gained through simplistic magazine articles!) on the part of the reader in order for the advertisement to work on that reader. In other words, as McCluhan[1] said a long time ago, 'the medium is the message' or at least it is part of it.

5   *Decoding.* This involves the deriving of meaning from the received message that is a composite of the actual message sent and any influences the medium may have had upon it. If the receiver does not understand the message or does not interpret it in the way it was meant then communication is faulty. Many feel that in marketing communications terms there is a need for clarity and simplicity where, for example, key selling points are understood. Others advocate much more complex approaches involving devices such as metaphors or metonyms.

6   *Recipient/receiver.* The receiver is normally the person, people or organization (hence the reason why some writers prefer to use the catchall 'decision-making unit' – DMU) with whom the sender wishes to share thoughts, ideas and so on. This, of course, will not always be the case since, clearly, others will receive the message that is not intended for them. The receiver might understand the message but might ignore or forget it. In marketing communications circumstances some believe that repetition can 'educate' the customer/consumer over a period of time.

7   *Feedback.* This loop of the process provides the sender/source with a channel of evaluation of the message encoded and sent. This can be viewed in two ways: first, in terms of how accurately the message has hit the target; second, in terms of the degree of correctness of interpretation on the part of the recipient/receiver from that which was intended. This then allows the sender/source to correct any ineffectual or misdirected messages. Typically viewed in marketing terms as a marketing research opportunity, this involves straightforward activities like coupon redemption in sales promotions but also things such as awareness scores, image studies and tracking studies. Some of this may be continuous rather than ad hoc.

8   *Noise.* The notion of noise can be misconstrued. It is not a question of making enough noise in order to be heard, like a shelf screamer in a supermarket that is designed to attract attention. Rather, the term 'noise' was used originally to denote interference or impedance, for example of a radio signal. These are terms often used interchangeably to describe the blocking or distortion of the message at any stage in the marketing communications process. This can take many forms, from the poor signal on radio or television resulting in poor sound and/or vision to the lack of knowledge or information that causes a consumer to be unable to fully understand the message. Noise can therefore be physical or cognitive and can be anything from interruption by a secretary to the amount of clutter in a newspaper or magazine.

Critique of the original process

It is, of course, recognized that the marketer is not the only player in this game. The target is another player, but other influences are also part of the process – the bullet theory (Schramm, 1971b) or hypodermic effect (Klapper, 1960) having been rejected for some time with an emerging preference for interactive and integrative rather than linear thought. Buttle (1995) provides a clear analysis of commonalties within the various representations of the communication process, identifying four such commonalties and concluding that marketing communications theory fails to draw on the very disciplines it should. Four common themes emerge in what Buttle calls 'normal marketing communications'. These are:

1   Focus on the individual, where family/household, institutional and cultural levels are left out. For example, the age-old 'what we do during the commercial break' question or the social context of advertising reception would apply to family or household contexts. Institutional effects involve the message production and delivery systems of companies, agencies and so on that are an interlocking network of institutions are things like voluntary codes and lobby groups. Cultural effects are both cognitive and critical. Cognitive effects involve, for example, cultural values and mores, whereas critical effects

involve Marxist and feminist views, dealing with institutional structures and the way society is organized.

2   Focus on individual messages, clearly a problem if estimates such as the one that suggests that 3000 marketing-controlled messages bombard individuals each day are true. Cumulative impact should be taken into account. Added to the effect of marketing communication stimuli, other stimuli existing outside the marketing communications area have impact.

3   Focus on source's intent where cumulative impact, shared meaning, derived symbolic meaning and not least meaning derived from non-promotional marketing and other variables are bound to have some sort of effect. Belief in the notion of the passive audience is long gone. The view that 'people do something to the content' has superseded the view that the communications content 'does something to people', at least in the minds of those who favour the interactive approach. The notion of source intent is clearly not without problems. The relationship (between content and audience) to message content whereby the 'exposure tradition' holds that power is in the content, whereas the 'gratification tradition' holds that power is in the hands of the audience. The 'interactive tradition' has power with both.

4   Focus on co-orientation, whereby to avoid problems with fidelity the communicator can opt for a closed text to avoid misreading, misunderstanding and so on. This, of course, ignores social and other contexts people necessarily operate in and that might produce multiple meanings because messages get 'contextualized'.

Buttle therefore condemns the usual marketing communications theory as ill informed and narrowly focused. The danger in educational/learning terms is that lecturers think that this is what students need in order to be practitioners. Much of this is steeped in 1940s and 1950s thought, with many important parameters unaccounted for and ignored. In a sense one can argue that such parameters are accounted for within the notion of 'realm of understanding/field of experience' as depicted in Figure 2.2.

Realm of understanding/field of experience

This is often included in representations of the marketing communications process to indicate the possibilities of overlap between sender and receiver so that 100 per cent commonness of field of experience – what Shimp (1997), calls 'perceptual field' – is a possibility. It is in this light that one cannot escape the feeling of opportunities being lost through not pursuing greater understanding of such effects. The marketing communicator, it could be argued, has a lot to gain from the participation of a broader spectrum of professionals such as sociologists, anthropologists, semioticians, cognitive scientists and, even, psychoanalysts. This is a qualitative shift that suggests 'a new phase in the attempts to penetrate the secrets of the black box' (Mattelart and Chanan, 1991).

Dealing with both the theoretical and applied side of semiotics, Hetzel and Marion (1995a; 1995b) are concerned for its use in consumer marketing research. They use Fouquier's 1984 work to depict the communication process in terms of the 'field of semiotic description' (Hetzel and Marion, 1995a). The way in which the semiotician tackles the real world is by seeking to describe not what is real but that which is constructed in and by a particular discourse. Self-images of senders

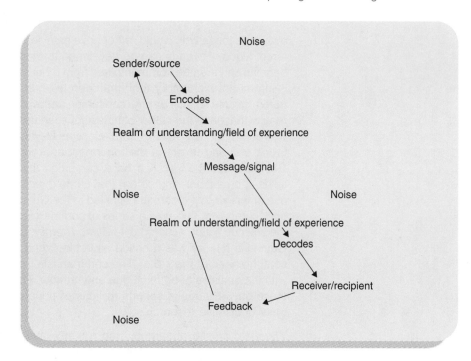

Figure 2.2
The marketing
communications process.

Source: Adapted from Fill (1999);
Shimp (2000).

and receivers and the constructed world must be taken into account. The act of communication therefore moves to a constructivist position from an ontologist position. Semiotic reality is the reality of language (used in the widest sense of the word) and its goal is to build models that are constructed with a certain meaning. This might be in a piece of film or architecture or, indeed, an advertising image or corporate identity. Constructed cultural objects allow for communication, with varying degrees of success, in this research paradigm where language is used as a model for all forms of cultural discourse, and therefore semiologists borrow from the structural linguists (principally de Saussure) of the first half of the twentieth century. Language is seen as a whole system of rules governing the selection and combination of different signs out of which meaning is produced. Since the transfer of meaning is fundamental to marketing communications, there is much to be gained for the marketing communicator from its study and use (see Chapter 6).

VIGNETTE

Is Dairy Box your granny? Is Waterford Crystal glass not just for grandmothers anymore? The semiotic and projective technique's contribution to brand communication and development

The range of research techniques available to researchers is vast but possibly the most common form is the focus group. Projective techniques, often seen as the pariah of marketing research because of their lineage with largely discredited motivation research techniques from marketing's early days, have gained some credibility through their use in focus groups by large companies like Guinness. The use of such techniques form Peter Cooper's viewpoint to fit the product to the message and the message to the product. Peter Cooper is a psychologist with vast experience of consumer research of this sort. Cooper gets participants to cut up pieces of magazine images in order to explore the personalities of brands of chocolates such as All Gold and Dairy Box. Research like this, it is argued, allows the researcher to explore how a brand expresses itself. Cooper uses role-play as a means of exploring ways of segmenting markets and developing brand personalities. This is illustrated by its application to the market for painkillers, where the market can be broken into those consumers who would prefer pain to be attacked and driven away and those who would rather have pain soothed away. From this basis different kinds of brands can be developed to meet different kinds of need. The benefits can then be communicated from a better understood base. Clay modelling as an exploratory tool has been used in many contexts. Cooper illustrates its use in discerning consumer perceptions of political parties, with results that have the clarity of hindsight even though this work was conducted well before the UK 1997 general election. Psychodrawings have been used in terms of trying to get at the innermost and outermost properties of brands. Guinness spent £5 million on a campaign involving Celtic imagery (wheat fields, the seasons and so on) that came directly out of psychodrawings. The use of this kind of technique also led to the Guinness 'Its not easy being a dolphin' campaign. This was a series of commercials starring Rutger Hauer, from the science fiction action movie *Blade Runner*, as the embodiment of a pint of Guinness (Hauer was dressed all in black and his blond hair used to represent the head of the stout). The commercials themselves were cryptic pieces with the qualities of both intrigue and humour. These ran for several years and these days Guinness spends millions of pounds each year on semiotic and other qualitative research.

Waterford crystal apparently had a stuffy image. Despite this and over 200 years of history, the hand-cut goblets and bowls that were the epitome of old-fashioned and stuffy elegance have been replaced by a new generation of Waterford glassware. In 1991 Waterford introduced Marquis, the first new brand that has innovative crystal patterns with designs ranging from contemporary to traditional. Waterford Holiday Heirlooms have a history too, dating back as they do to Victorian times and are 'designed to bring us back to a time when a gift was truly an offering of love'. The brand has also been extended to include table linens, bone china and, even, pens. Waterford is now Waterford Wedgewood plc and this group also comprises others such as metalcraft and ceramic companies. Dinnerware patterns take their inspiration from established Waterford Crystal designs and from Irish tradition and heritage. Sales to the elderly have been replaced by a designer-driven (for example, John Rocha) contemporary approach. Other designers followed, including links with Jasper Conran and Versace. Success in the USA is key to Waterford's success. A symbol of its status in the USA is the Waterford designed and built Times Square Millennium Ball used to herald in the New Year in 1999/2000. Yet it is only in recent times that Waterford has begun to use its Irishness. 'Ireland would not have been the best kind of association if you wanted to market something as being a luxury product . . . it had a reputation of "pigs in the parlour" and backwardness'. So says Michael Dennehy, the company spokesman. The last ten years, however, have seen an Irish economy transformed. The Waterford factory is the country's fourth most visited tourist attraction and the vision is for even more expansion into the tabletop luxury goods business with the aim of being on a par with Gucci, Louis Vuitton or Burburry. President of Waterford Wedgewood, Redmond O'Donoghue, says that it is no secret that there is a hunger, or at least an appetite for acquisitions, especially in leather luggage, watches and jewellery. Chairman Tony O'Reilly has said that it is the brand and its image that matters and not where the actual product is made. Waterford crystal could be made anywhere in the world but still uses its Irish heritage to very positive effect.

Sources: Adapted from BBC (1997); QED (1995); Stanley (2001); www.waterford.com/wfdinner.html accessed in 2001; www.waterford.com/holiday.html accessed in 2001.

STOP POINT

Think about the credibility of getting participants to cut up pieces of magazine images in order to get at the personalities of brands such as All Gold and Dairy Box. How does research like this allow the researcher to explore how a brand expresses itself? Has role-play as a means to exploring ways of segmenting markets and developing brand personalities any credibility? Has clay modelling as an exploratory tool any credibility either? These techniques and the use of psychodrawings in terms of innermost properties of the brand and outer properties and the ideal Guinness drinker are at least interesting, but what are the kinds of problems that will arise when it comes to the analysis of findings? Culture, branding and communication can combine to create potent meaning. Waterford's use of Irishness, now that the image of the Irish is positive not negative, is instinctive. Think of Waterford crystal in simple semiotic terms. What is the difference between a literal meaning and a constructed meaning for the Waterford brand? What kind of constructed image is being sent by a (newly) constructed sender to a newly constructed receiver, in a newly constructed world in Waterford's case? Think about the added dimension of a new age Irishness (itself constructed from tradition, heritage and modernity) in terms of meaning for the Waterford brand.

Kellman's source characteristics model

A trend (started in America) in recent years in advertising has been to use chief executive officers (CEOs) like Bernard Matthews (UK, turkey food products) or Victor Kiam (USA and globally, Remington shavers) to get across enthusiasm, likeability and so on. Similarly, endorsers such as Sir Robert Mark, a former top police chief, are thought to be very credible with issues such as road safety and, hence, are good, credible endorsers of, say, quality car tyres that will stop well in difficult conditions. Another current example would be the aforementioned television 'Naked Chef', Jamie Oliver. Likeable yet credible (he is streetwise and plays the drums on chat shows), Oliver is the endorser of the retailer Sainsbury (especially Sainsbury's food). That is not to say that all sources have to be celebrities. Sales staff can have credibility through the way they dress or they can acquire credibility through gaining knowledge. Fill (1999) uses the Kellman source characteristics model to show how the ways in which sources obtain and retain their characteristics can then be used in message strategy. Kellman's source characteristics model again dates back some time (to the 1960s). Credibility (trustworthiness), attractiveness (identification, likeability) and power (compliance, reward and punishment) all potentially go towards building source characteristics.

High *credibility* is not necessarily the most effective characteristic in certain situations, as might be expected. Fill (1999) uses Eagly and Chaiken's (1975) work to illustrate how high/low credibility sources can be equally effective. The use of a high credibility source is of less importance when receivers have a neutral position. This is clearly plausible with regard to low and high involvement and where risk is involved. It is also dependent upon product type. Everyday products like insurance can be promoted in this way. Credibility can also come with association. Fill (1999) uses the example of Dennis Fire Engines to illustrate the reliablity of its equipment chosen, i.e. Dennis is associated with the bravery of the fire crews as often seen on news bulletins and other media coverage.

Research by Newell and Shemwell (1995) supports the importance of credibility for CEO endorsers where source credibility has a strong direct impact on purchase intentions. This research underlines the importance of testing with the target market the believability of the executive concerned. These researchers suggest that, for example, for radio and television, warmth meter tests might be appropriate in establishing a sounder theoretical base in the area and, in particular, for measuring believability. Also, the findings from this research support a model in which beliefs about product/brand attributes mediate the effect of source credibility on behavioural intentions, leading to the assertion that CEO endorsers may be better suited to informational advertising rather than advertising that emphasizes affective associations and brand recognition. If a product needs supporting at the introductory or growth stage of the product life cycle the CEO endorser might be used to communicate significant product improvements (Newell and Shemwell, 1995).[2]

Empathy or correlation between source and recipient means that the receiver will find the source *attractive* and a relationship can then develop where the latter sees him or herself in the situation depicted, say, through slice-of-life advertising, i.e. relates to it and identifies with it and the problems it solves.

Power and therefore compliance are important in some situations. The receiver complies in order to obtain a reward or avoid punishment. Power is more easily seen in personal communications situations where both the 'stick' and the 'carrot' are in evidence. Expense accounts, type of car allowance, bonus rewards and penalties, and so on are commonplace. Salespeople may have power to give discounts and sales managers to give incentives, for example.

VIGNETTE

Blimey, the Oxo family has been usurped by lager, sex and football

There are many examples of source characteristics used in communications. In the UK the (now defunct) Oxo family would be typical of the composite source of an affable message involving traditional family life. This quintessential middle-class family with a liking for gravy has a history stretching back to black and white commercials and 'Katie in the kitchen' but is no more. The latter-day Oxo family of Lynda, Michael and two children had carried on the tradition of slice-of-life, soap opera advertising with its dining table and other artefacts featuring in the sketches that spanned sixteen years. A move towards 'real-life' domestic scenes, including a group of young lads exhibiting laddish behaviour, seemed inevitable so that demographic and other changes could be met. 'The Oxo family was a great British institution but times have changed and the new campaign holds up a mirror to life in Britain today' says an Oxo spokesperson.

The radical departure involved a new family and a three-bedroomed council house in Dagenham, Essex. Louise and Paul and children, Fred and Becky, were seen tucking into a spaghetti bolognese. The idea of four lads, one of whom cooks for the others (using Oxo of course) during a television football match and lager-drinking session, has to be classed as a radical departure. A couple enjoying a romantic meal while the viewer is made to feel that they are playing 'gooseberry' provides a sexy, free-and-easy image. Another demonstrates what happens when the power of love overtakes hunger.

The campaign of one-off ads 'focuses on family life as it is lived today with interchangeable characters who will strike a chord with every viewer'. The rather ironic logic is that families are not sitting down together to have dinner because they are too busy watching advertisements on the television. This is at least partly true and is part of the fragmentation that is happening all around, including pre-cooked meals that include the gravy. This has been called the television dinner – invented circa 1953. By 1997 two-thirds of British families had given up the dinner table for the television. By 2001 one in twenty families only eat together on special occasions such as Christmas Day.

Source: Adapted from Gregoriadi (1999); BBC News Online (1999a; 1999b).

STOP POINT

The Oxo family as a credible and likeable message source was clearly of value to marketers for a good number of years. For obvious reasons, this would no longer be the case and to carry on using the nuclear family in its traditional form would not have been wise. Think about the next stage of development for the Oxo brand. Laddism, for example, is said to be coming to an end and, while the target might still be young, single consumers, who or what might the source of the message be if credibility, attractiveness and/or power are to be harnessed?

Step flow or personal influence models

These models are very simplistic and usually involve one-, two- or multi-step flows, opinion leaders/formers/followers[3] and, necessarily, innovator theory and the strength of word of mouth (also dealt with in Chapter 3 from a behaviour point of view). Numerous models have been developed in this area that are said to provide general frameworks for understanding. Step flow or personal influence 'models' were established by the 1960s. Here the message is encoded, transmitted and decoded by the receiver, but this then includes the role of the opinion leader and word of mouth with others to move from one- to two- to multi-step flows of the message, which necessarily mutates and where the meaning intended by the sender can be either enriched or changed in some other way. This is illustrated in Figure 2.3.

Bullet theory would have us believe that a message can be shot like a bullet at a target. However, the simplest of situations becomes very complex. Each target can

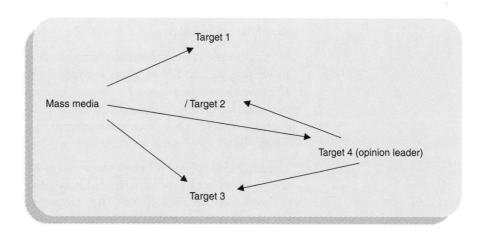

Figure 2.3
Step flow or personal
influence models.

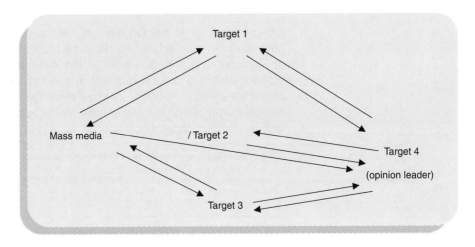

Figure 2.4
Multi-step flow and personal
influence model.

either be passive or reactive, depending on the effect of the message. Figure 2.3 illustrates the situation where target 1 is passive (illustrating one-step flow) whilst target 2 is blocked from the message by some sort of noise. Target 2 is informed of the message by target 4, who is also an opinion leader. Target 3 receives the message directly but is also informed by the opinion leader, target 4, who in this case has received the message but in other cases may not have done but might still have influenced other targets. In other words, the mass media is not the only influence and may not be an influence at all. Some form of multi-step flow of information is much more likely in reality. This is illustrated in Figure 2.4.

Opinion leaders, formers and followers are important links in the communications chain. From the above it can be seen clearly that interaction takes place. Closely related to this is the power of *word of mouth*, whereby personal recommendations can enrich the communication process. Fill (2002) provides a clear description of the potency of word of mouth that can give a depth of credibility other forms of communication cannot. Fill's interpretation of Dichter's (1966) ideas are: *product involvement* (people have a high propensity to discuss matters that are distinctly pleasurable or unpleasurable), *self-involvement* (people might wish to show ownership for prestige reasons or may wish to seek reassurance to reduce dissonance), *other involvement* (expressions of love, friendship and caring are aspects of the motivation to help others whereby product benefits can be passed on or shared) and *message involvement* (motivation to discuss products comes from the marketing stimuli that surround them, in particular advertising, provoking conversation and to stimulate word-of-mouth recommendation).

Getting people talking about the brand is clearly important but so, too, is the advertising or actually wearing branded clothes. Whichever, the marketer's objective should be advocacy. Getting the brand and advertising talked about in a positive manner is often the objective. Many companies have been successful at this for their brands, for example Guinness, Boddingtons and John Smith's Bitter.

Targeting those who will carry the message on is therefore clearly important. *Opinion leaders* can therefore be ordinary people but they will be predisposed to having an effect on others.[4] They are normally of the same social class but have a higher status within a particular context. For example, an opinion leader may be a colleague who just happens to have the biggest influence when it comes to a particular activity. Within this context opinion leaders may have the highest level of confidence because of their knowledge base (of products and brands, the activity itself, the media, for example specialist magazines), be more outgoing and so on. Opinion leaders can be used in advertising of any sort. They are used to promote washing powders, for example, on the consumer side.

Closely allied to the opinion leader is the *opinion former,* who is normally some form of professional rather than an ordinary person who for whatever reason has some form of authority or status. Celebrity endorsers can be seen as opinion formers, especially on the consumer side where many examples exist from breakfast cereal to packets of crisps. On the organizational side, an example might be a civil engineering project manager who could be used to sway an entire industry's buyers into at least considering a particular brand of, say, rough terrain dump truck.[5] It need not be actual people who form opinions. It may be that UK wine experts in the UK like Oz Clarke, Jancis Robinson or Malcolm Gluck form opinions, especially through their columns in national newspapers, but it can be entire television shows and other media items that become formers of others' opinions on anything from forklift trucks to cars, wine and restaurants. It is not always the case that an opinion former is a deliberate ploy to shape things, as the Jack Daniel's vignette below illustrates.

VIGNETTE

Step flow personal influence models: Jack Daniel's gets lost in space

'Drinks' is an area where controversy has reigned. Asda, now part of Wal-Mart, was steeped in controversy over cries of 'copycat' from, among others, Grand Metropolitan (now Diagio). Why copy? Presumably because it's worth it to the likes of Asda to piggyback on classic designs. Jack Daniel's is a case in point. The way this brand has won its way globally into the consciousness of millions of people is impressive. It is a necessary rock and roll accessory and even an icon of the art world. The images in fashion photographer Carl Moore's photographs are said to be trivial, over-styled and emotionally hollow, and he is apparently happy to have it this way. African-American models wearing western apparel are set against red and blue backdrops. Props include bales of hay and bottles of Jack Daniel's. Moore shows the observer roles and codes that are familiar and not something that imprisons. Thus, it can be said with a fair degree of certainty, that Jack Daniel's is many things including the Jack Daniel's Country Cocktail, an art object (or at least part of an artistic photographic image) and an essential part of a poem:

no one notices the man wiggling like jelly at the front door

no one suggests we put a screen in between

no one notices the pale negro drinking Jack Daniel's in the basement is a world class chef you can't light a match to

no one notices his cousin-in-law with the verdant Frederick Douglass hair never been dyed will distract my guests from soggy green beans with almonds (Janice Lowe – see Extended family, 1998).

It is also the sponsor for *The Buzz* magazine's Jack Daniel's Interview that features interviews with film stars such as Matt Leblanc and Gary Oldman (around *Lost in Space,* the remake of the cult 1960s television show).

The official line is that Jack Daniel's Old No. 7 is a simple reminder that some things just never change. It is old time Tennessee sour mash whiskey, not bourbon. It is 'charcoal mellowed smooth, drop by drop though ten feet of charcoal made from sugar maple' (see note 3). The reality is much more complex.

Sources: Adapted from Brett (1998); Extended family (1998); The Grocer (1997); Mitchell (1997); Woods (1998); www.jackdaniels.co.uk/oldno7/tourfive.asp;[6] www.jackdaniels.co.uk/oldno7/distill.asp.

STOP POINT

Consider word of mouth and personal influence in the world of the Jack Daniel's brand. Why is it that actors, poets, artists and rock stars appear to want to be unofficial yet potent spokespeople for this brand? Make a list of communication tools and devices that would make up an optimal communications mix for this brand.

Innovation theory and relational exchange

The innovation curve (Rogers, 1962) is well covered in basic marketing theory and texts, and should already be known to the reader. This links to the previous section in that innovators and early adopters of products/brands and ideas generally have opinion-leading and opinion-forming characteristics. This deals with prior conditions of previous practice, felt needs/problems, innovativeness and norms of the social systems that feed into communications channels thus:

Knowledge → Persuasion → Decision → Implementation → Confirmation

This is influenced by the characteristics of the decision-making unit (sociometric, personality, behaviour) and the perceived characteristics of innovation (relative advantage, compatibility, complexity, trialability and observability) leading to either continued or later adoption or rejection by discontinuance or continued rejection.

As with all stage models each stage is sequential, hierarchical and in this sense is open to the usual criticism of stages being left out, being out of sequence etc. This model is, however, useful from the marketing communications perspective with regard to objectives and strategy (for example providing persuasive information through a particular media vehicle). Rogers' five stages are:

1 *Knowledge* – the DMU becomes aware of the innovation but has nothing to go on. The opportunity is there to provide (persuasive) information through channels such as the media.

2 *Persuasion* – the perceived characteristics of the innovation become important, as do the messages from the media, opinion leaders and so on.

3 *Decision* – attitudes are formed and a decision to adopt or reject the innovation made. Communication is clearly important in this.

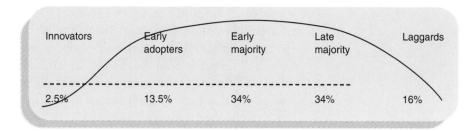

Figure 2.5
The diffusion process.

4   *Implementation* – the DMU needs to know how to access the innovation for trial, if it is not rejected, and communication has its role to play in this.

5   *Confirmation* – post-trial the innovation will either continue or be delayed or be rejected. It may well be readopted or rejected continuously. The DMU can be assisted in this process by persuasive communication, helping to dispel worries or negativity and reaffirming the original decision with post-behavioural consolidation.

The process of adoption and diffusion of innovations is theoretical and the curve need not be normal as depicted, but can be skewed depending upon the make-up of the population or sample. It can also have a shorter time span to indicate the rate of diffusion. The importance of innovators and early adopters in terms of word-of-mouth communications should not be underestimated. The normal diffusion process can be visualized as in Figure 2.5.

Taking each of these types in turn, *innovators* have high disposable income and are risk-takers, including with unknown products or brands. They have opinion leadership characteristics. *Early adopters* also are opinion leaders and they are the biggest influence on the speed of adoption and diffusion. They tend to be young(er) and have an above the norm education. The *early* and *late majorities* are the 'admass' of opinion followers who watch more television and read and take publications less than the previous two groups. Respectively they will be slightly above and slightly below the norm on characteristics such as income, education and so on. *Laggards*, as the tag suggests, are very slow to take up innovations and generally would be attracted by sales promotions on the pricing of products, which might be 'last year's model'. Generally they are low on characteristics such as income, education, reading specialist publications and status.

Clearly there are other ramifications for communicators in this scenario. Targeting parameters such as age, income and education clearly needs to be addressed as does the communications mix in relation to the speed of diffusion and other factors that might cause a skewed distribution curve such as nature of the product and the market in question for example, a company dealing in specialist products might have a highly specialized market to cater to, which is populated by very innovative people. Similarly the other extreme may be the case with little or no innovation taking place.

Organizational exchange

Rather than the linear approaches discussed above, it is much more likely that communication occurs in a particular context within which there are many variables. Fill (2002) uses Littlejohn's (1992) four main contextual levels to illustrate how communication events can be linked together. This hierarchical structure consists of interpersonal, group, organizational and mass communication. Fill (2002) uses McEwan's (1992) work (after Goffman, 1969), to underline the importance of mutual understanding of each of the other players' behaviour that permits both formal and informal communication procedures to be established leading to increased levels of *trust*. As this grows there is likely to be transference from formal to more informal roles. This is therefore a (social) behaviour approach. Fill also uses Taylor and Altman's (1987) work on social penetration to further discuss relational communication theory. Disclosure of increasing amounts of personal and organizational information develops levels of intimacy that serve to build interpersonal, inter-organizational relationships. This begins with orientation (disclosure of public information only). This can then lead to exploratory affective exchange (expansion and development of public information), then affective exchange (disclosure based upon anticipated relationship rewards, of deeper feelings, values and beliefs) and, finally, stable exchange (a high level of intimacy where partners are able to predict each other's reactions with a good level of accuracy).

A wider array of participants might be inevitable where a communications network can be seen. Organizational boundaries in this scenario would be transcended to form an intra-organizational network. This again may be formal or may have developed towards the informal.

Brand image and trust

The components of brand image are seen as being potentially both rational and emotional, and this is fundamental to the notion of what a brand really is in any given situation. The Research Business has developed, for example, their Brand Works brand facet model which when applied to a particular brand would yield a mix of facets. Taking Toshiba as an example, this brand apparently has saliency (emotional closeness/distance of consumer to brand) and brand personality (personification of the brand that demonstrates how the brand's core emotional character has been projected to the consumer). Whatever facets there are to a particular brand, it seems likely that trust plays a vital part in the process that leads from consumers' perceptions and experiences of a brand to brand loyalty. Trust, pragmatically, is seen as a powerful marketing weapon in the armoury and is something that can be lost and won (Bainbridge, 1997). Trust in this light becomes an important brand attribute making major fast-moving consumer goods (fmcg) brands more powerful than the Church (according to the Henley Centre's 'Planning for social change 1998' report). Marks and Spencer have trust and this enables them and others, such as Virgin, to extend into hitherto unknown (to them) areas but where consumers welcome brand extension under certain conditions. Marks & Spencer and Tesco in this sense have become choice editors, manufacturers in their own right (own label) and service providers. These organizations know that trust can be just as easily lost as won and is best kept by a philosophy that runs across the whole organization, not just within the marketing department. This raises questions of who should be the guardian of the brand image and just how far is it credible and fair to stretch brands and still maintain a long-term mutually beneficial consumer–brand relationship.

Trust, commitment and loyalty in the brand–consumer relationship

There is interest in relationship quality that stems from trust and the high degree of certainty of predictable and obligatory behaviour that leads to sales, giving the seller integrity and the process a high degree of certainty (Crosby, Evans and Cowles, 1990). The process proposed by Morgan and Hunt (1994) is central here, i.e. that trust leads to commitment which leads to loyalty and that this is essential for successful relationship marketing. What is proposed is that this process is transposed to the consumer–brand relationship, thus the brand inspires the same degree of relationship quality that is usual in human relationships. This trust in brands requires investment that carries with it some degree of risk that consumers will cease to co-operate and cease resisting attractive alternatives. Trust within the consumer–brand context has not been adequately explored and lacks suitable definitions and measurement. The analogy of marriage – mutual social trust leading to commitment and the establishment and maintenance of exchange relationships – is helpful in conceptualizing how consumers might choose brands, as are the ways in which people choose friends based on personality. The resultant loyalty to brands is rather more than the simplistic notion of repeat purchase over time.

VIGNETTE

John Smith's Bitter: a widget, plain, honest Jack Dee and some penguins

Comedian Jack Dee was signed up to combat Guinness and Boddingtons in the battle for the UK canned bitter market in the early 1990s. His fee was rumoured to be £750 000 and Dee was not that famous. Little did anyone know that he would eventually, nearly ten years later, take part in and win a game show on Channel 4 called *Celebrity Big Brother* that was created in aid of the charity Comic Relief, with great aplomb and with his personality intact. The publicity surrounding this show was masterly, with the sullen Dee allegedly escaping from the Big Brother house. The idea behind the show was that a group of people are thrown together for a period of time until they are nominated to be evicted, with the public then voting them out. The last to remain is the winner. During the six-week-long show Dee was involved in many things, all of which were on videotape. For example he was seen escaping from a back door then 'caught' in the compound and brought back. This is reminiscent of a prison escape and Dee played his part superbly well. The first round of voting alone raised £115 000 for Comic Relief. Over 3 million viewers had voted and 12.3 million tuned in to watch live as Dee's wife Jane met him at the door of the house where he said 'It feels great to be out' as if being let out of prison. The show eventually gave Comic Relief over £500 000 and had gripped the country for six weeks.

Dee was seen in both instances as a 'no nonsense' character who would not 'suffer fools gladly' and this matched the John Smith's Bitter brand proposition. According to the Institute of Practitioners in Advertising (IPA) this case gives hope to brands that face stiff, new competition. After thirteen years as market leader the brand suddenly faced a new challenge – a new in-can device that created the 'draught in a can' at the quality end of the market. Within two years these brands had taken 15 per cent (volume) and 24 per cent (value) of the off-trade market. John Smith's Bitter already had Jack Dee and they added a 'widget' (a word similar to 'gadget' meaning a small mechanism or device), which meant that the product did not need advertising gimmicks to support it (a gimmick in itself, but who was to know?). The advertising included commercials involving dancers and penguins. The penguins, for example, perform for Dee but are rejected because no gimmicks are required. The 'widget' enhanced the original 'no nonsense' Jack Dee theme, causing can and pub sales to be successfully stimulated. This was despite criticism of the product itself. It is, after all, no longer a real ale but rather a smooth-flow nitro-keg beer that trades on the name of its cask original. According to the Campaign for Real Ale (CAMRA) 'They confuse many customers, especially when bar founts are topped by dummy hand pumps'. The Campaign for Real Ale cites the amount spent by the big brewers on promotion rather than devoting money to real ale as the biggest problem, with three times the amount being spent on John Smith's Bitter than on cask alternatives such as Directors Bitter or Courage Best Bitter.

The John Smith's Bitter 'no nonsense man' is a cardboard cut-out that followed Dee as the star, appearing on television, posters and in-outlet advertising and was a favourite prize to take home in student-flat land. For this kind of product, especially in canned form, the invention of 'draught in a can' via the widget had been innovatory. The combination of the new technology, Dee and a lot of off-the-wall creative thinking led to the John Smith's Bitter brand remaining the bitter market leader.

Sources: Adapted from Ananova (2001a; 2001b); BBC (2000; 2001a; 2001b); CAMRA (1999); Freeserve (2001); IPA (1995); Scottish and Newcastle (2001).

 **STOP POINT**

The plain, no nonsense personality of Jack Dee was for a while a perfect match for that of the John Smith's Bitter brand. Consider how important this matching is when considering employing the celebrity endorser. Consider also how important, in the face of stiff competition, it is to marry ideas together in order to win over the majority rather than just those willing to try new things.

Assignment

Write a paper of approximately 2000 words that illustrates how management might benefit from the consideration of communications theory. Include in your response ideas around:

- relationships and trust
- interaction and networking
- informal as opposed to formal communications.

Summary of Key Points

- The communications process can be modelled with source of message as the encoder and the recipient the decoder. The message may be distorted by 'noise' in the system.

- The original process has been criticized for its overly simplistic view of communication and much more has to be considered in the process to make sense of reality. Considering the realm of understanding and field of experience of both sender and receiver caters for some of this.

- Source characteristics can be broken down into credibility, attractiveness and power to include trustworthiness, identification, likeability, compliance, and reward and punishment.

- Step flow and personal influence models can be useful in the understanding of flows of information and the role of the opinion leader and former. The strength of word of mouth is clearly important here and within innovation theory.

- Relational exchange and communications theory shed more light on the communicator's task in terms of organizational and consumer markets. Networking is increasingly important with the former, and with the latter trust, commitment and loyalty need to be understood in a more holistic manner.

 ## Examination Questions

1 Explain the basic model of communication. Illustrate how this can help marketers in their communications' decision-making.

2 Discuss the kinds of problems the marketer has when attempting to encode particular ideas. Give examples of the kinds of tools and choices at the marketer's disposal.

3 Explain what a message is in terms of its social context and its elements. Illustrate the kinds of signals that can be transmitted to different targets by the same marketer.

4 Elaborate, using examples, on the use of semiotics in the communication process generally, and in terms of encoding and decoding in particular.

5 Explain the role of feedback in the communication process. Illustrate why the situation is more complex than the simple feedback loop looks on communications diagrams.

6 Discuss 'noise' as an integral part of the communications process. Use a key source of 'noise' to illustrate your discussion.

7 Explain and expand upon the 'source characteristics' model using examples from both consumer and industrial/business-to-business fields.

8 List the key management benefits to using communications theory, illustrating the kinds of theory that could be useful at different stages of the management process.

9 Explain the basic idea behind 'step flow' models. Illustrate the importance of word of mouth and opinion leadership.

10 Critically examine the usefulness or not to marketers of the theory of adoption and diffusion of innovations.

Notes

1 Marshall McCluhan famously remarked that the 'world is a global village' (see Chapter 20) and 'the medium is the message'. With the latter, the medium is seen as all important and in this sense it is not what you say or even how you say it but the means by which it is said that carries

the day – the day being the 1960s when television was at its zenith. Some make comparisons, at the beginning of the twenty-first century, between television then and the Internet now.

2 These writers note that the research finding should be viewed as being context specific and that much more work would be needed before any generalizations could be made.

3 Opinion leaders and formers are described and illustrated later in this chapter. Opinion followers are those people in a particular context who simply follow the leader/former.

4 Not just in brand/marketing terms but in many other walks of life that may or may not interface with marketing activities.

5 The term 'brand ambassador' has also been used by the likes of Haagen-Dazs to describe someone in the media spotlight who is prepared to become an advocate of the brand in a PR manner, as opposed to celebrity endorsers who are allied to advertising.

6 Take the tours that the Jack Daniel's website offers. Substitute 'one', 'two', etc. for the 'five' given here.

References

Ananova (2001a). Jack Dee is people's choice for Big Brother. At www.ananova.com/entertainment/story/sm_239721.html, accessed March.

Ananova (2001b). Jack Dee pleads to be evicted. At www.ananova.com/entertainment/story/sm_240577.html, accessed March.

Bainbridge, J. (1997). Who wins the national trust? *Marketing*, 23 October, 22–23.

BBC (1997). *No. 2 Heinz*. Television series Branded.

BBC (1999a). Sainsbury loses out in store wars. At www.news.bbc.co.uk/hi/english/the_company_file/newsid_273000/.

BBC (1999b). What's gone wrong with the great British brands? At www.felixent.f9.co.uk/hnh/br901.htm.

BBC (2000). Stars on the sell. At http://news.bbc.co.uk/low/english/uk/newsid_894000/894865.stm, accessed August.

BBC (2001a). Dee big winner of Big Brother. At http://news.bbc.co.uk/hi/english/entertainment/newsid_1225000/1225722.stm, accessed March.

BBC (2001b). Jack Dee tries to escape from Big Brother. At http://news.bbc.co.uk/hi/english/entertainment/newsid_1214000/1214552.stm, accessed March.

BBC News Online (1999a). Has dinner had its chips. At http://news.bbc.co.uk/hi/english/entertainment/newsid_434000/434461.stm.

BBC News Online (1999b). Oxo puts sex on the menu. At http://news.bbc.co.uk/hi/english/entertainment/newsid_572000/572108.stm.

Belch, G. E. and Belch, M. A. (1995). *Introduction to Advertising and Promotion*. 4th edition. Irwin.

Brett, A. (1998). www.thebuzz.nireland.com/Jack08.html, accessed August.

Buttle, F. A. (1995). Marketing communications theory: what do the texts teach our students. *International Journal of Advertising*, **14**, 297–313.

Campaign for Real Ale (CAMRA) (1999). Beer giants are slated as 'Gravediggers of Real Ale'. www.camra.org.uk/news/julysept99/nitro.htm.

Crosby, L., Evans, K. and Cowles, D. (1990). Relationship quality in services selling: an interpersonal influence perspective. *Journal of Marketing*, **54**, 68–80.

Extended family (1998). *The American Poetry Review*, **27** (2), 42. At http://web3.infotrac.galegroup.com/itw/ifomark/156/691/4312273w3/.

Fill, C. (1995). *Marketing Communications: Frameworks, Theories, and Applications*. Prentice Hall.

Fill, C. (1999). *Marketing Communications: Contexts, Contents and Strategies*. 2nd edition. Prentice Hall Europe.

Fill, C. (2002). *Marketing Communications: Contexts, Strategies and Applications*. 3rd edition. Financial Times Prentice Hall.

Finch, J. (1999). Rivals maul Sainsbury GM ad. *Guardian*, 19 August. At www.guardian.co.uk/gmdebate/Story.

Freeserve (2001). Jack Dee's full Mountie. At www.thenuttyboy.freeserve.co.uk/jack_dee.htm.

Gregoriadi, L. (1999). Oxo serves up new recipe. At www.guardian.co.uk/Print/0,38583943606,00.html.

Harbridge, J. (1999). Profits a store point for Sainsbury. 2 June. At www.news.bbc.co.uk/hi/english/the_company_file/newsid_355000/.

Hetzel, P. and Marion, G. (1995a). Contributions of French semiotics to marketing research knowledge. *Marketing and Research Today*, February, 35–40.

Hetzel, P. and Marion, G. (1995b). Contributions of French semiotics to marketing research knowledge. *Marketing and Research Today*, May, 75–85.

Institute of Practitioners in Advertising (IPA) (1995). *The Advertising Effectiveness Awards*. Notes and video. IPA.

Klapper, J. T. (1960). *The Effects of Mass Communication*. New York Press.

Mattelart, A. and Chanan, M. (1991). *Advertising International*. Routledge.

Mitchell, C. D. (1997). New narratives. *Art in America*, **85** (11). At http://web3.infotrac.galegroup.com/itw/ifomark/156/691/4312273w3/.

Morgan, R. and Hunt, S. (1994). The commitment-trust theory of relationship marketing. *Journal of Marketing*, **58**, July, 20–38.

Newell, S. J. and Shemwell, D. J. (1995). The CEO endorser and message source credibility: and empirical investigation of antecedants and consequences. *Journal of Marketing Communications*, **1**, 13–23.

QED (1995). *It's Not Easy Being a Dolphin*. Channel 4 television series.

Rogers, E. M. (1962). *The Diffusion of Innovations*. Free Press.

Schramm, W. (1971a). How communication works. In *The Process and Effects of Mass Communication* (W. Schramm and D. Roberts, eds), University of Illinois Press.

Schramm, W. (1971b). The nature of communication between humans. In *The Process and Effects of Mass Communication* (W. Schramm and D. Roberts, eds), University of Illinois Press.

Scottish and Newcastle (2001). Ales/stouts. At www.scottish-newcastle.com/beer/ales.html.

Shannon, C. E. and Weaver, W. (1962). *The Mathematical Theory of Communication*. University of Illinois Press.

Shimp, T. A. (1997). *Advertising, Promotion and Supplemental Aspects of Incremental Marketing Communications*. 4th edition. Dryden Press.

Shimp, T. A. (2000). *Advertising, Promotion and Supplemental Aspects of Incremental Marketing Communications*. 5th edition. Dryden Press.

Stanley, B. (2001). Waterford crystal shatters its stuffy image in a bid to boost sales. At www.naplesnews.com/01/02business/d576942a.htm.

The Grocer (1997). Where customers vote with their feet. *The Grocer*. At http://web3.infotrac.galegroup.com/itw/infomark/156/691/43122731w3/.

Woods, B. (1998). The flavour meister. *Food and Beverage Marketing*, **17** (1), 8–9. At http://web3.infotrac.galegroup.com/itw/ifomark/156/691/43122731w3/.

CHAPTER

Behaviour and relationships

Chapter overview

Introduction to this chapter

The nature of behavioural theory in relation to marketing communications is explored and relationships examined and developed with the context of the marketing communications mix. Target market behaviour has to be understood. The theoretical focus of this understanding has become, over the last four decades, the cognitive, affective and behaviour stage models that are the hierarchy of effects or response type. On the other hand, the buying process has also been modelled. The marketer needs to know the who/why/what/how/when and where[1] about buying. It is the 'why' that is the most mystifying and problematic but it is clear that what is bought is an important consideration, especially in relation to the amount and kind of information sought.

Aims of this chapter

The main aim of this chapter is to consider behaviour theory in relation to the communication process. In particular the chapter seeks to:

- place communication within a cultural context and discuss other environmental trends and influences on buyer behaviour

- outline the major inputs of buyer learning theory and show the complexity of buyer behaviour

- facilitate understanding and use of the buyer decision-making process.

Communication, culture and other environmental influences on buyer behaviour

Communication and culture is looked at more closely in the international context in Chapter 20. However, it is so crucial to the workings of marketing communications that it is felt that there is a need to deal with the usual cultural issues and those of buyer behaviour and to attempt a synthesis of the two approaches at this early stage in this book. Culture has many definitions. International study relies heavily on the work of Hofstede[2], who refers to culture as the collective mental programming of the people in an environment, where culture is not a characteristic of individuals. Culture therefore encompasses a number of people who were conditioned by the same education and life experience. Marketers should therefore be concerned with the size of markets and, of course, demographics and other factors that give rise to trends within markets or segments. For example, time pressures have given rise to convenience foods. The home environment has become somewhat of a cocoon leading to many changes in home entertainment, 'do it yourself' (DIY) products and so on. Indulgences such as weekend breaks and excitement, fantasy, health and many leisure pursuits are other examples. The ability to measure the size of such markets is of little use if the product and communications do not fit in with the culture. People worldwide share certain needs, but needs may be met differently in different cultures. Language as a cultural variable is important but, more than this, other cultural elements include things such as customs and religion.

Culture is important in communication because it differs between societies. What may be very acceptable in one country might not be acceptable in another. This is because culture is learnt. Culture may be seen as the sum total of learned beliefs, values and customs. These then shape and influence the buyer behaviour of people in a particular societal context.

Subculture, social class and reference groups

When considering the importance of buyer behaviour in the development of effective marketing communications strategy, the marketer must also take notice of the fact that very few consumers live, work, or make decisions in social isolation. Individuals are influenced by culture – traditions, lifestyles and so on associated with a particular country. A culture can affect the ways that consumers seek to satisfy needs, the weighting given to choice criteria, the preferred brands and so on. The study of culture is also useful in understanding and use of cultural stereotypes in advertising. For example, to make a product look chic it might be placed in a French, or more specifically Parisian, setting. In other words the context in which the consumer receives the communication plays a very important part in the process, so that if a consumer listens to a radio advertisement in the workplace, he or she may well do so surrounded by work friends and colleagues. More broadly, most people live as part of a community and as such are subject to the norms, values and influences of those around them.

Groups are very influential on individual consumers. *Subcultures* are smaller groups where beliefs, values and so forth are different to those of the mainstream. Like any segment, subcultures are based upon some parameters such as age, religion, ethnicity and so on. Subcultures will only be important to marketers if they conform to the rationale behind segmentation, i.e. whether they are substantive or accessible. Also, there may well be sub-subcultures that exist. A subgroup of the British Asian might be the British South Asian. It may be that the *social class* a person is in, or aspires to be in, is a key factor for the marketer. Most societies are stratified into some form of class system where relatively homogeneous groupings exist based largely in the past on, for example, income, educational platform and occupation. This notion does differ from country to country but in many countries the stratification is very similar, based as it is on a grading system originally designed by sociologists. In the UK the social grades of A, B, C1, C2, D and E were used for some time as a way of describing socioeconomic types in the population. However, the influence of others in the various groups to which an individual might belong, such as family, was recognized. *Family and home life* are a constantly changing part of the environment. Learned behaviours are not uncommon. Not spending enough time with children has resulted in behaviours on the part of working parents that are far removed from previous generations. *Family lifecycles* have also changed. The traditional move from being single to being a newlywed, to having young children then growing children (full nest) to empty nest (children move out) and being on one's own (remaining partner, spouse having died) is no longer a certainty (not that it ever was for some people). Changes such as both parents working have meant, for example, dual incomes. Communicators have consequently had to use different media and media spots to be able to cater for these changes. Returning to work has meant that for many mothers, work colleagues are as important as daytime television or radio spots. Of course, a reality these days are things like divorce and remarriage. This has given rise to the so-called 'second chancer', a segment that has different characteristics again to those aforementioned. For example, they tend to be older than 'normal' married people and have a higher household income, are more content with life and spend time seeking to enrich their lives rather than to please others. *Reference groups* are those groups with members whose presumed perspectives or values are used by an individual as the basis for his or her judgements, opinions or actions. Marketing communications often seeks to replicate the communication and interaction between individuals within groups where one member offers a solution to other members' problems. Sales promotional strategies will often encourage the group interaction. For example, a wine club may offer a discount or some other incentive for a member to introduce a friend (Belch and Belch, 2001). Marketers have long used reference groups for aspirational advertising and have long been aware of disassociate groups, i.e. groups to which consumers do not belong (or do not wish to belong) but which can be used in advertising.

Culture and consumer behaviour

Hofstede's 'five dimensions of culture' model is used extensively by de Mooij (1998). These dimensions are power distance, individual (versus collective), masculine (versus feminine), uncertainty avoidance and long-term orientation. These dimensions are discussed more fully in Chapter 20 but suffice to say here that this model represents yet another typological system of classifying people by cultural parameters. This kind of approach might be acceptable to some, as might Mueller's context work (Mueller, 1996). To others, however, generalizations of culture can often be more harmful than useful. While it might be the case that segmentation studies are useless unless a segment is substantial and accessible, fallacies should be avoided. For example, a need such as self-actualization (see Maslow's hierarchy of needs later in this chapter under 'Motivation'), if seen as an individualistic concept, might give the impression that self-actualizers will only exist in low-context cultures. This would be a very superficial approach that underscores the need for a deeper understanding of cultural models. A cornerstone of the systems that have been developed to look at cross-cultural classification is the original Values and Life Styles (VALS) system devised by Maslow and Rockeach in 1975. This and VALS 2 (in 1989) are probably the best known lifestyle and values approaches that characterize culture and aspects of buyer behaviour but others have followed. A VALS-type system is illustrated in Chapter 4 and returned to in various parts of this book.

Buyer behaviour can be defined as the things buyers do while satisfying wants, needs and desires. This is done through searching for and selecting purchases, using these products and services, and then re-evaluating their usefulness and either going on to repurchase the same products and services or rejecting them. This process may be almost involuntary or impulsive but at other times more detailed and exhaustive.

VIGNETTE

IKEA: extending the brand into the 'second chancer' segment

Putting it into practice, or implementation if you prefer, can be the most difficult part of any business activity. Doing this on a global stage is even more daunting but IKEA have achieved this with apparent aplomb. The IKEA business idea is to offer a very wide range of home furnishings with good design and availability but at low prices, making their products functional and affordable. IKEA therefore claim to 'side with the many' rather than the few who can normally afford good design. IKEA claim to appeal to the needs, tastes, dreams, aspirations and wallets of almost everyone. Their claim is that they have a partnership with the customer. They do their part by having good design ideas that allow products to be manufactured using pre-existing processes. They buy in bulk from all around the world so as to get the best deals. This allows IKEA to offer the low prices for which they are famous. IKEA admit, however, that the partnership with the customer contributes towards this by the very nature of the flat-packed products that are for the most part self-assembly. 'This means we don't charge you for things you can easily do on your own. So together we save money . . . for a better everyday life.' This is a good proposition. The self-serve warehouse is promoted as an experience in itself, a day out. You can even dine there and then take your furnishings home with you.

This has not always been the IKEA market position. Since its humble beginnings in founder Ingvar Kamprad's childhood somewhere in the 1930s and the official 1943 founding of IKEA – Ingvar Kamprad Elmtaryd (the farm he grew up on) Agunnaryd (the village near the farm) – to the present day, IKEA has travelled from nothing to a presence in twenty-nine countries around the world. IKEA has therefore literally moved from matchsticks through a vast range of furnishings in six decades. The first showroom was opened in 1953. By 1956 flat packs had begun. Designers joined the growing number of employees. Particle board arrived by 1969 and by the early 1970s so had modern plastics. IKEA moved outside Scandinavia in 1973, opening up first in Switzerland, then Austria, the Netherlands and Belgium – reaching the USA by 1985, with by then thousands of employees. The company says that

'At first, we weren't sure the USA needed IKEA. After all, what could we bring to the country that has everything?' They soon realized that the need for useful, attractive home furnishings at 'prices for every wallet' is everywhere. So by 1998 they had opened in China and by 2000 in Russia. IKEA offers products for virtually every home furnishing eventuality, from the bedroom to the kitchen, from adults to children, from simple everyday objects to products with a great deal of design input.

From the start marketing and customer satisfaction has appeared a natural part of IKEA's *raison d'être*. Even its first showroom, opened in 1953, was created for competitive advantage through three-dimensional presentation. Design is and has been for most of IKEA's history a key component and the source of many prizes. It is the past decade that has seen IKEA's appeal spread to a broader group, not just lower-income groups such as students or families with young children. By the late 1990s, the UK consumer was being invited via IKEA's television advertising to 'chuck out the chintz', and come on down to IKEA to replace this dreary old stuff with shiny new IKEA products. IKEA had already been successful elsewhere. For example in Belgium, from the early to mid-1990s, IKEA nearly doubled the number of customer store visits and its turnover, and brand awareness soared after a successful integrated marketing communications campaign involving television, radio, newspapers, magazines and employees themselves.

Recognizing that the environment out there is in a constant state of flux, IKEA have not been slow in targeting newly divorced people. A campaign in America featured a divorced woman and her daughter shopping for furniture after the ex-husband had kept the household goods in the divorce settlement. This group of 'second chancers', as a whole, has potentially a great deal of disposable income and the kind of needs that organizations like IKEA can satisfy – in many markets throughout the world. Similarly, IKEA has not been shy to approach the gay community. In 1994 IKEA were running an advertisement in the USA that depicted two gay men shopping for a dining-room table together. This was some time before competitors understood the attraction of this lucrative market.

Sources: Adapted from Baack and Clow (2002); www.ikea-usa.com/about_ikea/our_vision/better.asp; www.ikea-usa.com/about_ikea/timeline/slash.asp; www.ikea-usa.com/about_ikea/timeline/fullstory.asp; www.ikea-usa.com/about_ikea/timeline/years_1940.aspp; www.ikea-usa.com/about_ikea/timeline/years_1950.asp; www.ikea-usa.com/about_ikea/timeline/years_1960.asp; www.ikea-usa.com/about_ikea/timeline/years_1970.asp; www.ikea-usa.com/about_ikea/timeline/years_1980.asp; www.ikea-usa.com/about_ikea/timeline/years_1990.asp (all 2002). De Pelsmaker, Geuens and Van Den Bergh (2001).

STOP POINT

What makes a global brand if cultures and subcultures are so very different around the globe? Should marketers focus on differences or look towards similarities? How have IKEA managed to satisfy the needs and wants of so many diverse peoples? Perhaps the only way is through a marketing approach that is flexible rather than rigid, open rather than closed, forward thinking rather than backward looking. Map out the importance of design, of store layout and other aspects of IKEA's operation that you feel contribute to the overall image of the company and brand.

The complexity of behaviour and buyer learning theory

The basic buying impulses of incentive, purchasing power and availability are fairly simplistic. Satisfying needs, whether physical, social, emotional and so on, can be seen to be easily achieved through situational factors such as living in a particular environment that predetermines, for example, what one eats. The weather, utilities, services available and so on may be determining factors in buying behaviour. Motorway services might not be the preferred place to refuel one's car and body but may in some circumstances be the only option. Getting cash from a machine in a wall might be the only means of obtaining spending money on a holiday island using a particular credit card and PIN number. More complex theories of consumer and organizational buyer behaviour and of consumer and organizational buyer decision-making abound in the literature, as do models of buyer behaviour. There is also a need to reflect on the practical analysis of buyer behaviour in relation to marketing communications. The intimate relationship between the two processes of buyer behaviour and marketing communications is well recognized in the traditional marketing literature. The notion of *involvement* is fundamental to this since this represents the degree to which a stimulus of some sort, marketing or corporate communications originated included, is relevant to an individual's need or want. The greater the relevancy, the more extensive the search is likely to be. The degree of involvement can depend upon many things including low or high cost of the item and whether the purchase situation is an ongoing one or a one-off or even impulse. It is not simply the case that because an item is low in cost that it is low in involvement.

Motivation

Motives, or why we feel compelled to take particular actions, can be viewed from a number of different standpoints. The commonest approach over decades has been to look at Maslow's '*Hierarchy of needs*'. This model suggests that human needs are built on a pyramid structure, with the most basic (physiological needs – hunger, thirst and so on) at the base of the pyramid, whereby humans need things like food, shelter and sex in order to sustain life. Next up the hierarchy are safety needs involving security and protection from physical harm, followed by social needs where love, affection, belonging and acceptance are desired. Esteem needs are next in the pyramid, where a sense of accomplishment, status and respect from others is sought. At the top of the pyramid is the need for self-fulfilment and the realization of ones own potential, called self-actualization. The simple premise here is that the lower level must be satisfied before other levels, i.e. once basic needs are met the human can move up the pyramid to higher-order needs such as those at the top of self-actualization. The reality is far more complex than this simple concept. Many products are sold on different levels. A product that nourishes might well be sold on parental love (social). A person wishing to achieve the ultimate in self-actualization by climbing a mountain or shooting some rapids might well ignore safety needs from the start. On the other hand, in simpler situations, it is easy to see how needs can be different within a product category. Volvo some time ago was emphasizing safety and love for children in its advertising.

Human motives can be understood further by studying *personality*. The *psycho-analytic theory* of Freud explains much about motivation and personality, and this has been applied to consumer behaviour situations. This is a probe for deeper-seated motives that are the basis for buying behaviour and purchase decisions but that are unclear even to the consumer. Probing the unconscious appeared to provide the answer. Motivational research (pioneered by Ernest Dichter and others), which saw the development of new (for the time) methodologies and tools including projective techniques and association tests, was seen as interesting but problematic. The focus group and to some extent the depth interview did grow and flourish but some of the 'stranger' tools were discredited, although certain tools and techniques are still used today (see Chapter 18). At best it might be said that interesting insights can be had from such research, although some large companies such as Guinness continue to support these kinds of techniques. It is easy to be sceptical of motivational research when the outcomes suggest, for example, that women bake cakes because this is the symbolic act of giving birth, or that men smoke cigars as a substitute for thumb-sucking. The use of small samples is a perennial problem in any research field. This, of course, negates the use of generalizabilities, where the research leads to insights but really might only discover the idiosyncrasies of a few individuals. Interpretation of results is another problematic area. If the researcher is using projective techniques to facilitate an outcome through providing a means of expression such as cutting and pasting magazine images or psychodrawings, there is still the problem of the interpretation as to what the image might mean. Still, these techniques are believed to enrich and enhance qualitative research. The sage advice is that they should be used with caution and in the end it might be worth remembering that sometimes a cigar is just a cigar.

Perception

External information exists in many forms. How we perceive stimuli, whether marketing-controlled or otherwise, depends upon how we receive and select information and organize it for our own devices. Belch and Belch (2001) divide perception into three areas. First is how consumers sense and attend to various information. Here consumers use the senses to create a representation of the stimulus but the marketer can manipulate this situation by using the senses in a particular way. For example, with perfume the marketer can not only use eye-catching visuals in a magazine advertisement but can also allow the consumer to sample the product and take advantage of the sense of smell by using a strip or scratch mechanism to release a small quantity of the perfume. Second is the selection of information where the consumer's personality, needs, motives expectations and experiences are the psychological factors that explain why the consumer focuses on one thing but ignores another. The consumer will attend to a stimulus that is perceived to be a problem solver. Third, the consumer then interprets the stimulus depending upon the internal psychological factors at play but will be selective with regard to exposure, attention, comprehension and retention. The consumer therefore might either choose (or not) to be exposed to stimuli by channel flicking while watching television. Consumers are also very capable of screening out many of the stimuli that they are exposed to every day. In other words they choose to focus on some but not on others. The marketer's job is to get through this clutter and get attention, but even if this is successful the consumer may still selectively comprehend only certain ones depending upon their own attitudes, beliefs and so on. Information may more often than not be interpreted in a way that supports a particular position. The final, retention, stage of this selection process is perhaps the trickiest for the marketer, since the consumer will only see/hear what he or she wants to see/hear and will disregard all the rest of the information. The marketer, however, has quite an armoury at his or her disposal in order to induce in the consumer retention of the message rather than not. Images, rhymes, symbols, associations, jingles, pop songs or memorable tunes and many other devices can be used as emotional triggers[3] to aid memory and help consumers learn about brands and so on.

Cognition

Consideration of cognition in terms of buyers involves intellect and processing of information. This can be viewed as a rational process whereby information is sought, stored, evaluated and used in an intra-personal manner (Pickton and Broderick, 2001). The consumer and buyer decision-making processes, which form the central plank of most models of buying behaviour, are dealt with in a separate section later in this chapter. Marketers should be aware of the major influences on their customers or potential customer and consideration of the more general model can help with this. Other more specific models are discussed below.

Information processing model

A message may fail at any one of the stages prior to its retention. A message might not be understood or remembered or acted upon. The consumer and the type of purchase situation will affect this process. If the consumer is inexperienced, and the purchase situation is high involvement or risky, then the consumer is more likely to pay attention to a message than for routine low-involvement situations. Television advertising with simple messages and involving devices such as jingles, music, celebrities, humour and so on is ideally suited to this type of situation since the consumer is not really interested in what is said. Conversely, printed advertisements or brochures are more suitable for the high-risk purchase situations where the consumer is motivated to gather information in order to make the important decision.

As already discussed in Chapter 2, marketing communicators should be aware that a huge difference can exist between meaning intended by the sender and the meaning as interpreted by the receiver of messages. As in the old adage mentioned above, people see and hear what they want to see and hear, and disregard the rest. The communicator should try to understand what happens in a consumer's mind from the first exposure to a message to the ultimate response, whether this be to ignore, take notice but quickly forget or forget after a period of time, store in memory and act later or act immediately, and so on. The literature suggests a five-stage model that a marketing communications message needs to pass through for it to be effective, i.e. retained in the memory. The stages are exposure, attention, comprehension, acceptance and retention.

1   *Exposure* – information processing begins when a message reaches at least one of the senses among target audience members. There are many estimates as to how many stimuli a person on average is exposed to in a day. Some say 3000 while others see it as less than this at 1800 (Kotler, 2000). Not all of these would be noticed by any means and the ability with, for example, television to zap or zip allows the receiver to terminate the potential exposure before it begins, making it increasingly difficult for marketers to communicate.

2   *Attention* – is the allocation of processing capacity to an incoming message. Since capacity is limited, some messages will receive attention and others will be ignored. An affective (feeling or emotion) reaction might precede a cognitive reaction, which is then followed by a more elaborate affective reaction. In this case there is a primary emotional response to a stimulus that determines whether a consumer is going to pay attention to it, produced by needs, attitudes and so on (see 'Attitudes' below).

3   *Comprehension* – the desired meaning being attributed to a message depends on how a consumer categorizes and elaborates a stimulus through the use of existing knowledge and beliefs. This has been called field of experience (Shimp, 1997) and realm of understanding (Fill, 2002). Categorization occurs when the incoming stimulus is compared with the memory content (something else in the memory bank such as the use of a particular technique in the past) to be classified and assigned meaning. The categorization will therefore involve the consumer associating this new information with something already existing. The consumer therefore engages in *elaboration*, the integration between new information and existing knowledge.

4   *Acceptance* – the consumer's comprehension of a message does not automatically lead to its acceptance. He or she may understand a message but not alter buying intentions or behaviour. In this case acceptance probably means having to change consumer attitudes.

5   *Retention* – is the stage where the stimulus finally is transferred into the memory, i.e. the message is noted and stored for use on a future occasion, the next relevant purchase occasion for example.

Simulated consumer decision-making process models

Two tools have been developed in this area to simulate decision-making processes. The 'rational consumer'-based *elaboration likelihood model* (ELM) advocates that consumers take time to consider messages designed to change attitudes. Information is processed via a central and also a peripheral route. If the key message from a piece of communication is believed then it will come in through the central route, making the message more likely to be firmly held, last longer and be resistant to change. This makes repetition of the message important since the more the consumer sees the communication, the more likely he or she will attend to the core message and take it through the central route. It is the less than key messages that come in through the peripheral route. The result here is a lessening of the grip held, held for less time and less resistant to change. BMW's 'The ultimate driving machine' strap line might come in through the central route while the voiceover tone of voice might come in peripherally. However, two intervening variables have been established here. First, motivation plays a key role. The more motivated a person is to search for information, the more likely he or she is to process information via the central route. Second, the consumer's ability and desire to use cognitive skills will determine whether or not the information will be used via the central or peripheral route. Someone who likes to engage in thought, and can, will be in the former mode.

The less than rational consumer, the person who impulse buys or buys for fun fits in with the *hedonic experiential model* (HEM). The HEM tends not to follow a rational cognitive, systematic and reasoned consumer processing approach.

Shimp (1997) introduces the fun, fantasies and feelings of the hedonic, experiential model after Hirschman and Holbrook (1982), who were two of the first to challenge the traditional view of consumption, particularly from the (marketing) research methodological standpoint.[4] The hedonic experiential model assumes the tendency exists to maximize pleasure and minimize pain. Following such impulses ignores longer-term consequences of action in favour of short-term pleasure. Here the consumer will relate to emotions and feelings. Fun and new or unusual experiences might be being sought in certain situations where more rational considerations such as price do not matter as much as the experience. Things on the outside of the ELM model become central in the HEM model.

Cognitive maps can help explain the links between various ideas and to assess and evaluate information. Baack and Clow (2002) describe these as simulations of the brain's knowledge structures containing assumptions, beliefs, attitudes, interpretations and so on about the world. For new situations these structures help the individual produce an appropriate response. Linkages are made between competing brands in terms of attributes and this helps the consumer make decisions. For example, if the decision is about which fast-food restaurant to visit, the consumer might think of McDonald's and the choice of food (say a vegetarian option), the service (going on past experience it was really fast) and the décor (last time it was nice and clean), and so on. The consumer might think about these factors in relation to Pizza Hut, KFC, Burger King and a few others. Baack and Clow also discuss levels and layers (beyond the actual message to include other things that might matter such as parking availability, ambience and so on) in terms of linkages. They also discuss linkages that already exist and messages that have no linkages at all to demonstrate the complexity of what on the surface is a simple situation. Obviously, different reactions will take place depending upon the levels and layers of linkage that exist and whether or not the message already has linkage with the brand or company. Repetition is important for transference from short- to long-term memory and the message is processed and fitted into previously constructed cognitive maps. Added to this is the idea that the marketer could link the message to a new concept that the consumer may not even have tried. Since, from a marketing perspective, it is easier to strengthen linkages that already exist, it would be worthwhile setting up links, even if tenuous, to build upon later. Marketers should continually look for linkages that will have allure for consumers and help gain trust, commitment and maybe, even, loyalty.

Learning and the consumer learning process

Clearly, the amount of experience and information that a buyer has will affect the type of decision-making process they are likely to go through. The ways in which consumers learn about things has an influence on the marketing communications strategy.

Learning theories

Learning has been described as 'the process by which individuals acquire the purchase and consumption knowledge and experience they apply to future related behaviour' (Belch and Belch, 2001). The two basic approaches of behavioural and cognitive learning are well established in the marketing literature. *Behavioural learning* emphasizes the role of external, environmental stimuli in terms of the Behaviourist stimulus–response (S-R) 'school of thought'. Learning through *classical conditioning* can play an important part in marketing. Pavlov, the Russian physiologist, had sorted the unconditioned stimulus and response out from the conditioned stimulus and response in terms of food, dogs and the ringing of a bell. In other word, the dogs originally salivated (unconditioned response) when they saw the food (unconditioned stimulus), but a conditioned response of salivation to a conditioned stimulus (not food but the ringing of a bell) was to be had. The contiguous presentation of the two stimuli is essential for the association to work, and the more this happens the stronger the association. It was surmised that the consumer could also be conditioned to form favourable impressions and images of various brands through an associative process. Marketers strive to associate their products and services with perceptions, images and emotions known to evoke positive reactions from consumers. This has interesting implications for the use of many tools and techniques such as celebrity endorsements or the use of music in advertising. What is hoped for is a more favourable attitude towards a brand when it is placed in certain situations with emotional triggers, such as likeable music, that are well received. Of course, the opposite might be the case so that rather than the arousal of positive feelings, negative ones ensue.

The principles of *operant or instrumental conditioning* have been used by marketers through the use of the concept of reinforcement, i.e. reward or punishment as a consequence of action or indeed inaction. Behaviourists such as Skinner, using pigeons, have shown that reinforcement of behaviour strengthens the S-R bond. Positive experiences will reinforce while negative ones will have the opposite effect. Marketing communications can emphasize the benefits of purchase of a particular brand. Advertising can instruct the consumer to use a product to solve a problem (say, deodorant). Sales promotions can reward a purchase with an additional benefit such as an offer the next time round. Belch and Belch (2001) point out that *schedules of reinforcement* can have an effect on the speed of learning. Continuous reinforcement can mean loyalty but if the reinforcement stops the consumer is likely to switch brands. Learning might be slower with *intermittent or partial reinforcement* but lasts longer. Therefore, if appropriate, the cost of using the latter rather than the former would suggest there are instances when intermittent reinforcement could be employed.

Shaping is another option whereby the reinforcement of successive acts leads to the concept of the diminishing reward. The marketer might begin with free samples to achieve trial, followed by coupons to induce purchase for a small financial outlay and then a larger one until, finally, the consumer purchases without inducement. The use of such techniques is the foundation of sales promotion strategy for new brands but the overuse of them can have a disastrous effect on brand image.

Cognitive learning theory advocates much of what is discussed below in terms of the buyer decision process. Problem-solving, information-gathering, choices and decision-making, mean that marketers need to respond to this type of learning by providing information in the right sort of detail and format. For example, salespeople and brochures might be enough to do this. On the other hand, detailed infomercials (perhaps using two-sided arguments that replicate the problem-solving process, that is, make it easier for the consumer to weigh up the pros and cons of different brands by presenting them with a carefully edited version) might be required. The avoidance/reduction of cognitive dissonance by not overstating brand strengths in the first place, or follow-up communication post-purchase are other examples of tools that can contribute to this end. Of course, as indicated earlier in this chapter, environmental influences on buyer behaviour are expected and do exist, so that learning would not simply occur cognitively, in a vacuum.

The evoked set[5]

As part of the evaluation of alternatives (see the consumer decision-making process below), the 'evoked set' has become a useful construct. The evoked set is basically a list of those preferences or options that a consumer places in a sort of shortlist. In brand terms, the evoked set is those brands within a product category from which the consumer creates a menu, excluding all other potential menu members in the process. This helps make brand choice manageable and it saves time and energy in making decisions. The marketer's job then is to make sure that his or her brand is in the evoked set or on the menu. Salience or 'top of the mind awareness' is important here to gain entry onto the consumer shortlist and this can be achieved through the use of other marketing communication devices such as in-store sales promotions; such devices can be used to help the consumer make the final choice of a brand from the evoked set. Typically a consumer might have four or five alternatives on the menu, including a particular own label. These brands will have arrived there by some means such as advertising. Belch and Belch (2001) point out that evaluation criteria will be much broader than simply this, since products or services come with 'bundles of attributes'. They use Peters and Olson's distinction between functional and psychological consequences to highlight the difference between more concrete and tangible consequences of a particular brand choice (say taste) and the more abstract and intangible ones such as how a brand makes the consumer feel. However, it is not until the consumer is in the store that the final decision to purchase will be made. The consumer may choose one particular brand from the menu simply because of an attractive sales promotion or an end-of-aisle display.

The Ehrenberg and Goodhart (1979) awareness, trial and reinforcement (ATR) model suggests that it is the big brands that benefit from consumer behaviour regarding brand switching. As long as the brand is the most frequently purchased (but not the only one purchased) then brand management is doing its job. This suggests that consumers shop around to check that consumption patterns bring the best results (Pickton and Broderick, 2001). Baack and Clow (2002) add that the consumer may very well take a multi-attribute approach and actually rate these attributes across brands. Also, consumers may partake in affect referral whereby they will buy a particular brand of a product category that there is no experience of simply because there is trust in the brand already from experience elsewhere. Latterly this has been proven to be the case with rather diverse product categories and not just the obvious ones such as Cadbury chocolate and other confectionery and cakes. Virgin, for example, has been successful in music, soft drinks, airlines, financial services and so on.

Attitudes

Attitudes are learned predispositions towards things that will influence the person's perceptions, feelings and, ultimately perhaps, behaviour towards those things. The thing might be, for example, an object, a person or an idea and the attitude might be trivial or more strongly held. The literature suggests that attitudes have three components:

1   *Cognitive* – mental images, interpretation and understanding of the thing.

2   *Affective* – feelings and emotions towards the thing.

3   *Conative* – intentions, actions and behaviour with regard to the thing.

This sequence might change but in this example, from a marketing standpoint, the consumer has first to get some idea about the thing (say an advertisement for a particular brand) that might involve humour. Then they are in a position to get a feel for both the commercial and its content, including the brand and to feel good about the experience. The consumer is now in a position to act (or not) in one way or another and that action might be to try the brand because of the positive feelings toward it. The consumer may be made to feel first, then take action (try the brand) and then understand it so that the sequence might be different (see hierarchy of affects below). Therefore, in marketing terms it is much more relevant to talk about, for example, attitudes towards brands, advertisements or the celebrity endorser used within the advertisement. Attitudes are important to marketers and marketing because they hold the key to positive or negative leanings consumers may have toward a company or brand. Having a favourable attitude towards a brand may not necessarily lead directly to purchase since some other intervening variable such as price may get in the way, but clearly attitudes and the verbal expression of attitudes and opinions are highly sought after by marketers in their pursuit of creating more effective communications.

Multi-attribute attitude models are particularly useful to marketers as they view an attitude object, such as a brand, as possessing a number of attributes that provide the basis on which consumers *evaluate* and form attitudes (Belch and Belch, 2001). Thus consumers have *values* that become *beliefs* about specific brand attributes and attach different levels of importance to these attributes. By appealing to basic values, the marketer can influence consumers that a particular brand can help them achieve a desirable outcome. For example, toothpaste may have the attributes: cleans teeth, freshens breath, reduces tartar, reduces risk of gum disease, tastes nice, looks nice, pump dispenser or a certain price level. Having clean, white teeth might reflect the basic personal value of self-respect (but not necessarily in all cultures). Marketers, through product positioning, can associate brands with one, some or all of these attributes. The brand which is associated with those attributes that are important to a particular consumer will most likely go into the evoked set, and might be purchased. In fact, many brands may offer the same level of performance, but it is the brand that is associated with those attributes by the consumer that will be preferred. Belch and Belch point out that *salient beliefs*, i.e. beliefs concerning specific attributes or consequences are activated and form the basis of the attitude, and that such beliefs will vary across market segments, over time and across different consumption situations. Attitude change can be brought about through understanding such beliefs in four ways:

1   By increasing or changing the strength or belief rating of a brand on an important attribute. Reinforcing a brand attribute is an example of this where a Toyota is 'the car in front' and a BMW is 'the ultimate driving machine'.

2 Changing consumers' perceptions of the importance or value of an attribute. Tapping into current trends or fashions can help achieve this. The Co-operative Bank in the UK made a big play for the moral high ground on not investing in oppressive regimes, as part of the values of their own heritage and *raison d'être*.

3 Adding a new attribute to the attitude formation process, in a similar vein to 2 above, only with something new added. Belch and Belch (2001) use the example of product improvement by Jeep's introduction of 'Quadra-Drive'.

4 Changing perceptions of belief ratings for a competing brand. More prevalent in the USA than anywhere else, this leads directly to comparative advertising and the use of knocking copy where the marketer compares the brand, in a more favourable light of course, to the competition.

Hierarchy of effects

When a message is sent to an audience it is assumed that the audience responds in some way. There are many possible responses that can be grouped into three distinct categories: cognitive, affective and conative. All messages attempt to influence at least one of these responses. The hierarchy of effects therefore states that a consumer must pass through a series of stages from unawareness to purchase and brand loyalty. A number of 'models' have been developed over the years and a précis is shown in Table 3.1.

Table 3.1
Various hierarchy of effects models

Model	Cognitive	Affective	Conative
AIDA (St Elmo Lewis, 1900)	Attention	Interest, desire	Action
AIDAS (Sheldon, 1911)	Attention	Interest, desire	Action, satisfaction
AIDCA (Kitson, 1921)	Attention	Interest, desire, conviction	Action
AIDA (Strong, 1925)	Attention	Interest, desire	Action
DAGMAR (Colley, 1961)	Awareness, comprehension	Conviction	Action
Lavidge and Steiner (1961)	Awareness, knowledge	Liking, preference, conviction	Purchase
Adoption (Rogers, 1962)	Awareness	Interest, evaluation	Trial, adoption
Howard and Sheth (1969)	Attention, comprehension	Attitude, intention	Purchase
On line info (Hofacker, 2000)	Exposure, attention	Yielding, acceptance, comprehension, perception	Retention

These deal then with the think–feel–do sequence of events regarding the cognitive (awareness, knowledge), the affective (interest/liking, desire/preference/conviction) and the conative or behavioural (action/purchase). They are subjected to the usual criticism that is applied to stage models but also that knowing the level of communication input in order to facilitate change is difficult to measure. Until this is known an optimal communications mix cannot be devised and implemented. The state of mind of the customer and changes to the usual think–feel–do sequence are important in terms of levels of involvement. This was recognized by Vaughn (1980), for Foot, Cone and Belding. This agency was concerned with the importance attached to products. High-involvement products that tend to follow the think–feel–do sequence are those like cars, furniture, loans and appliances (classical hierarchy of effects). Those that follow the feel–think–do sequence tend to be jewellery, perfume and fashion because the consumer wants to be emotionally attracted by the brand image. Low-involvement products that follow a do–think–feel sequence tend to be things like detergents, food and toilet paper, that are bought without too much cognitive effort. Low-involvement items like sweets, soft drinks and ice cream follow a do, feel, think sequence and are thought of as 'life's little pleasures' (De Pelsmaker, Geuens and Van Den Bergh, 2001).

Here then involvement, the importance of the product to people as expressed by the buying decision, is recognized. Risk comes into play with regard to performance and psychological aspects. However, this can be challenged in the sense that some seemingly simple products are no longer low-involvement products. The Ogilvy Centre for Research and Development (1984) distinguish between performance risk such as the product not coming up to scratch or living up to what is expected and psychological risk. This latter type of risk exists where the choice of a particular brand reflects badly on the purchaser in the eyes of others. Within this there are badge categories where the brand name remains prominent while the product is used, such as beer or blue jeans. There are also closet categories where only the purchaser knows the brand name. A particular brand of petrol would be an example of a closet brand. Both of these categories can be linked to the consumer's self-image. This can perhaps be more clearly seen with the badge-type brand whereby use of the brand makes the person feel better about him or herself. Motives for buying a particular brand of an otherwise banal product like toilet paper or cleaner can therefore be complex. Advertisers have understood this for some time, finding very clever ways, for example, to get around the anxieties attached to many aspects of the toilet.

The Ogilvy Centre also distinguish between new and established brands in terms of how communication works. For an established brand salience (top of the mind), reinforcement and repurchase is the expected sequence. For new brands the picture is rather more complex. Four models are suggested:

1   For new brands that are distinctive and high risk, awareness should be followed by comprehension, then attitude formation and purchase.

2   For new brands that are distinctive and low risk, awareness should be followed by purchase then comprehension and attitude formation.

3   For new brands that are similar to competitors' and high risk, awareness should be followed by attitude formation, comprehension and purchase.

4   For new brands that are similar to the competition and low risk, awareness should be followed by purchase then attitude formation and comprehension.

Types of customer

The development of successful marketing communication programmes begins with understanding why consumers – or customers – behave as they do. Consumer behaviour can be defined as the process and activities people engage in when searching for, selecting, purchasing, evaluating and disposing of products and services so as to satisfy their needs and desires. So marketing communicators need to recognize that while much of promotional activity has the goal of influencing consumers' purchase behaviour, the purchase is only a part of what can be a long and detailed process of information search, brand and retailer comparisons and evaluation. Armed with customer knowledge, marketing communicators can begin the task of developing effective message strategy, choosing appropriate media, deciding the promotional mix weighting, setting objectives and so on, i.e. designing, developing, planning and executing a communications campaign.

A customer who learns before anything else and is highly involved in a buying decision, looking at a large range of alternatives, comparing features, prices and so on expresses a high-risk position. The marketer will need to provide technical detail using print media, and sales staff and friends/family might also be consulted so communications should be designed with the multi-step flow of communication in mind. Such a customer will therefore go through a *think–feel–do* sequence to resolve a problem.

A customer who buys quickly with little thought or evaluation, and then evaluates post-purchase usually does so because there is little difference between products on offer and little risk involved. The marketer will need to help the consumer justify their purchase, thus avoiding cognitive dissonance. Such a customer will go through a *do–feel–think* sequence.

Many products purchased in a routine fashion are associated with low risk, where there is little between brands and the consumer has experience of purchasing the product. The marketer needs to remind the consumer that the brand is still there and provide reasons why it should remain as part of the consumer's repertoire and try to avoid switching since this customer will *think–do–feel* in sequence.

The trained, professional buyers will tend to be methodical and follow set practice for risk reduction. Much of this is routinized but on occasion there will be more highly involved purchase. This customer then is either *do–think–feel* (routinized) or *think–feel–do* (new task).

VIGNETTE

Fentiman's invigorating and refreshingly botanically brewed beverages

In terms of product development, Fentiman's is unique in that its products are entitled 'brewed botanical beverages'. These are products that are brewed from herbs and bruised roots. There is a natural fermentation and it sells the products at not more than 0.5ABV so they can be merchandized as Adult Soft Drinks. These products were originally sold in half-gallon stone jars over forty years ago and Fentiman's history goes back to the early 1900s, so Fentiman's markets them as the Original Adult Soft Drinks. There certainly is not another brewed and fermented product in this category. Therefore Fentiman's possess a strong point of difference and a unique process that does deliver a 'real flavour benefit'. The product line includes old-fashioned brewed Ginger Beer and Victorian Lemonade, a brewed lemonade. The company felt it would be useful to include the ingredients, such as burdock extract, elder flower, lime flower, hyssop, cinnamon, red clover and nettle in the product description.

The resurrected company was brought back to life by the great-great grandson of the founder Thomas Fentiman, Eldon Robson. The company, although involved with a form of retro marketing, are not behind the times. Fentiman's have moved to a screw top for ease of opening but this has not affected the traditional image of the bottle since, in addition to the loss of the traditional cap, there is a wrap-around label. The name is a strong communicator and as such is crucial to positioning. 'Brewed Botanical' can be defined as natural and healthy. Perhaps the company should be pushing the ideas of natural, healthy, nutritional – and even provide nutritional value, calorific content and so forth on the label. The existing information on the bottle explains what Fentiman's and brewed botanical beverages are all about. This is even better explained on the Fentiman's website.

Fentiman's have been on the shortlist of a competition sponsored by the Ministry for Agriculture, Fisheries and Foods, have appeared on the BBC's *Food and Drink* programme and in the BBC's *Good Food* guide in the 'Tried and tested' section. Much praise can be found in the industry for this five-star rated range of soft drinks. Distribution has been selective, which enhances the Fentiman's image. Fentiman's has been distributed through Boots, Oddbins, Sainsbury, Tesco, Somerfield and other multiples. With the addition of a screw top for ease of opening Fentiman's is likely to get the product into places with a good takeaway trade and with certain pubs and cafés, particularly those with a 'real ale' image, most surely falling for Fentiman's charm.

The locally (to the North East of England) famous Fentiman's dog's head (a Crufts winner called Fearless) was re-created as the company logo. Other signifiers have been used and Fentiman's has become somewhat stylized, like Jack Daniel's but without the alcohol. The stone jar (grey hen) is seen as important to the understanding of the nature of brewed botanical beverages. All in all Fentiman's signifies sophistication, albeit at a price. But you get what you pay for.

Sources: Adapted from www.fentimans.com/pedigree.htm; www.fentimans.com/findus.htm; www.fentimans.com/ourlogo.htm; www.fentimans.com/botanic.htm; www.fentimans.com/sedimentally.htm; www.fentimans.com/index.htm (all 2002); and UK Trade and Investment (2003); Waitrose.com (1999).

STOP POINT

There has been due consideration as to how Fentiman's can get a clear message across to general public end-users about what the product can do, and about its quality and authenticity. The trade has also been carefully considered. Given the nature of the product and its premium price, consider where the Fentiman's range fits in with the models outlined above.

The buying decision-making process

As was seen above from consideration of the types of buyer there are, consumers differ radically most of the time from the organizational, industrial or business-to-business buyer in many ways but especially in terms of their buying behaviour. Both of these decision-making processes are considered below.

The consumer buying decision-making process

The consumer's purchase decision process is generally viewed as consisting of steps through which the consumer passes in purchasing a product or service. Belch and Belch (2001) highlight the relevant internal psychological processes of motivation, perception, attitude formation, integration and learning that have already been discussed above, in relation to the *stages in the consumer decision-making process* that are a staple in many texts, i.e.:

Problem → Information → Alternative → Purchase → Post-purchase
recognition   search   evaluation   decision   evaluation

This consumer decision process is central to models of consumer behaviour such as that of Engel, Blackwell and Miniard, (1997). Thus the decision process is fed into at various stages by the memory but also by environmental influences and individual differences. The decision-making process may not be followed in exactly these stages. Little or no alternative evaluation may be made in certain situations, for example where there is no risk involved with low-value, frequently purchased items. However, as a general model of consumer decision-making, these stages are worth exploring.

Problem recognition

This occurs when a consumer recognizes or perceives a need and is motivated to solve the problem. It is caused by a difference between a consumer's ideal or desired and actual states. This need or want may be caused by being out of stock of a particular item in the pantry or fridge or dissatisfaction with a current product/service. New needs/wants and related product purchases, for example the purchase of, say, a Sony Play Station 2 that leads to the need for games and accessories etc., do emerge. The availability of new products, and other marketer-induced problem recognition through advertising, sales promotions and even the in-store bakery, are part of this stage of the consumer decision-making process.

Problem recognition can be a straightforward process – it is the way that consumers perceive the problem and become motivated to solve it that will influence communication strategy. They may be motivated by, for example, price, status, safety or other such parameters. The *motivation* to take actions to solve such problems can be complex. This can be partly explained by Maslow's hierarchy of needs (as discussed above). If the marketer wishes to understand underlying reasons why consumers behave as they do, then motives should be understood.

Information search

Perceptions are important in marketing. Consumers perceive a need or problem that can be satisfied by a purchase of an item, so that they begin to search for information needed to make this purchase decision. The initial *internal* search usually involves a memory scan to recall past purchases or stored knowledge about companies, brands, advertising images, etc. This is often all that is needed for routine purchases such as favoured brands. An influence here might be dissatisfaction with the last external purchase or strong *word of mouth* from a friend or a new advertisement for a competing product. This kind of influence is external but may not be sought. Depending upon the importance of the purchase decision and the extent of perceived risk associated with the purchase, additional information may be needed (*external search*). This will be acquired from personal sources (friends, relatives, etc.), marketing sources (such as salespeople, advertising, point-of-purchase displays) and public sources (such as reports/features in the media that are not necessarily PR induced). The *evoked set* (as discussed earlier) is important here. This menu is not necessarily permanent and it is the marketer's job to get the brands into the target's evoked set. Baack and Clow (2002) maintain that the individual's ability to search depends on both educational level and predisposition to search. This might involve cognitive reasons or simply that the particular individual has an enthusiasm. The latter point is linked to *opinion leadership* and also the motivation to solve needs. Costs (actual cost of item, time spent, opportunity cost in terms of other activities and so on) of the search and rewards in terms of benefits for so doing are obvious factors. Baack and Clow (2002) summarize external information search in terms of ability, motivation, costs and benefits. They maintain that if the perceived cost of the search is low but the benefit high, then there will be high motivation for the consumer to search but he or she will still need to have the ability to do so and to find the right kind of information.

Clearly knowledge as to how consumers acquire and use information from external sources is important to marketers in formulating communication strategy. How consumers sense information, select and attend to various sources of information and how the information is interpreted and given meaning are important. This is the perceptual process (see 'Perception' above), defined as the process by which an individual receives, selects, organizes and interprets information to create a meaningful picture of the world (Belch and Belch, 2001). Marketers should have an opportunity to facilitate this process, the key being the provision of the right information in a timely fashion that will allow for comparisons to be made (Baack and Clow, 2002).

Alternative evaluation

Advertising and promotions are used to create favourable attitudes towards new products/services or brands, to reinforce existing favourable attitudes and to try to change negative attitudes. Integration strategies are used by consumers to compare brands so that they combine any number of sources of knowledge, meanings and so on in order that they may make a decision. This may be kept very simple in certain situations where it may be that price is the only parameter. More often, after information acquisition, the consumer begins the process of evaluating various products, brands, stores, etc. Some options will be dismissed if they do not match with the consumer's choice criteria. The remaining options are the *evoked set*. The goal of marketers is to ensure that their brand is contained within this evoked set, i.e. that it is at least considered at this evaluation stage. For example, repetitious/reminder advertising is used to keep brands 'top of mind'; new products will have awareness objectives to get the brand into the evoked set etc. The role of the brand is important here since a positive attitude towards a brand should help to make other brands from the same company part of the evoked set. Evaluative criteria are the dimensions or attributes of product or service that are used to compare the different alternatives. They can be objective, for example price, guarantee or delivery, and subjective, for example styling, fashion or status. The importance of the various criteria will vary depending on the consumer, the type of decision, their lifestyle and so on.

Purchase decision

The consumer may make a purchase decision but this is not the same as making a purchase. The decision to buy a particular brand may have been made as a result of the evaluation at the last stage, but the detail of availability, price/terms negotiations, service, delivery and so on may affect this. The actual purchase may take place fairly quickly after the decision to buy has been made, or may involve further information search and decision-making. On the other hand, it may be that the decision turns out to be merely a purchase intention involving other alternatives within the evoked set. The important role of in-store displays and other information, sales promotions and sales staff becomes evident at this stage. Brand and store loyalty are useful for the consumer as they cut down on the evaluation and decision-making stages but this is not easy to achieve, particularly in some product categories where consumers are prone to be fickle. Hence the use of techniques to keep the brand salient. It is perfectly feasible, therefore, that someone or something will come between the consumer and the brand. This might be some form of contextual change such as shortage of money, the influence of a friend or a competitive offering. It may even be an impulse buy or simply a change to try something different.

Post-purchase evaluation

Satisfaction or not with the purchase is key to this stage. If the product/service meets or exceeds expectations then the consumer will continue to evaluate a product/service while using it – comparing their expectations with the actual performance. Feedback from this stage will influence the evaluation and choice of brands/retailers for future purchases. Positive feedback means the brand will remain in the evoked set, and the attitude will be strengthened. Of course, the opposite may be the case where negative feedback and attitudes may lead to the elimination of the brand from the evoked set. *Cognitive dissonance*[6] may come into play at this stage. This has been described as mental or psychological tension. The consumer will attempt to reduce dissonance by seeking the opinions of others, using advertising and so on to seek reassurance. This will serve to remind them of why they made the purchase in the first place. It could also involve reflecting on the inferiority of those brands that are rejected, in order to satisfy themselves that a good decision has indeed been made. The importance of this period of activity has not been lost on major marketers either to support the choice of their own brand or to seize on an opportunity for new business where dissatisfaction prevails. It is therefore not surprising to see refund policies, guarantees, warranties and so on in order to enhance satisfaction and provide reassurance. Marketers should also remember that they should be in the business of retaining customers but also that by keeping customers satisfied and reassured, positive word of mouth will result. Obviously, negative word of mouth (and even brand/company damage) might be the outcome if the customer is not happy with the purchase.

The organizational buying decision-making process

The types of goods and services are, of course, different in the buyer (as opposed to consumer) situation. The buyer buying decision-making process reflects the purchase of industrial equipment (machine tools, computers and so on), operational equipment (such as office furniture), component parts and many other things. There are many examples such as process material, maintenance and replacement parts, operating supplies (such as photocopier toner), raw materials and products that are finished but for resale. Distribution chains can vary enormously in different industries and situations but selling direct, as a result of the Internet, is said to be on the increase. Customers can vary too but are usually manufacturers, resellers such as wholesalers or retailers and, not least, local or national government organizations such as the Ministry of Defence (MOD).

As with the consumer, the marketer in the buyer situation has to know and understand the target customer, whether this is a commercial organization, a school or a hospital or, indeed, a business service such as telephone, legal or insurance. The notion of the *buying centre* as a composite 'MAN' (money, authority, need) or DMU has been an acceptable way of describing the group of individuals involved in the buying decision. Long ago the five buying centre roles were established in the literature: *users* (the people who actually use the product or service); *buyers* (those who actually make the purchase); *influencers* (people who either formally or informally shape the purchase); *deciders* (the people who authorize decisions); and last but not least the *gatekeeper* (the person or function who controls the flow of information such as rules or alternatives within the rest of the buying centre). These roles may overlap and the nature of each will depend upon the size of the organization. The very small company may have one person acting out all five roles. A large corporation could well have elaborate and sophisticated structures. In other words the buying process is unique to each organization.

The marketer must understand these roles and the buying centre as a whole for each of its customers if the salesperson is to be successful. There are a number of factors that may influence the various members of the buying centre. These include internal organizational factors (finances, human resources and so on), the make-up of the individual players (for example attitude towards risk-taking or motivation), cultural factors (managerial style, for example, might be driven by the organization's American or Japanese origins), and social factors (such as the need for social acceptance).

The buying situation as discussed above will also have an influence on the ways in which the buying centre will behave. The *routine*[7] (straight or modified rebuy) purchase may only involve the buyer, especially in the case of the straight rebuy. In the case of modified rebuy the various influencers may come into play. However delivery is crucial and penalties often apply for lateness. It is the *new buy* situation that will see the five roles of the buying centre becoming activated, since needs, specifications and vendors all need to be identified, evaluated, selected and terms negotiated. This becomes the basis of the buyer buying decision-making process that is the equivalent of the consumer buying decision-making process (Baack and Clow, 2002). The elements of this are as follows:

- identification of needs
- establishment of specifications
- identification of alternatives
- identification of vendors
- evaluation of vendors

- selection of vendors

- negotiation of terms.

Rather than physiological needs as with the consumer, here needs are for maintenance, financial services, parts and so on. Once this is established specifications can be written, often by experts such as engineers. Alternatives and suppliers (whether in-house or external) can then be identified and proposals from perhaps a number of organizations evaluated. This evaluation will involve some or all of the buying centre members depending upon the size of the purchase, risk and so on. Selection and negotiation follow but this may not be a straightforward situation based on monetary value since other factors may come into play. The simple fact that one supplier might provide for all of the organization's needs at a very favourable price might swing the decision that way. Marketers should be aware of how the organization is likely to behave throughout this process and what is likely to influence the situation in a posititive manner. Baack and Clow (2002) note that several recent trends have had a big impact on the buying process. First, the notion of a 'buying community' can be a very real and powerful force, especially regarding SMEs. This constitutes an interlocking network of business owner managers, trade associations and social organizations. Second, the impact of the Internet and e-commerce cannot be ignored. Third, reputation and image can be enhanced by the development of global corporate brands. Fourth, database-mining and integration is now a powerful force. Fifth, it is now recognized that new methods of breaking into the buying centre must be developed if the firm is to succeed. This includes effective internal marketing and full use of employees as ambassadors for the company. It is for these reasons that the development of effective IMC, as discussed in Chapter 1, cannot be ignored.

Variations in buyer decision-making and communication implications

The decision-making process described so far will not apply in every type of purchase situation. Consumers may miss some of the five stages, or mix up the order in which they occur. High involvement, i.e. important decisions will usually follow the model as described. However, where the consumer feels confident about a purchase, due to previous experience, or it is not felt to be very important, for example a bar of chocolate purchased on impulse, then stages such as information search and evaluation will be minimized or will disappear.

Marketers of brands which are routinely purchased, for example fmcgs, will seek to keep their brands in the evoked set, and try to maintain high levels of brand awareness through reminder advertising, regular sales promotions and prominent end-of-aisle or shelf positions in-store. Marketers of new brands face a different challenge since they need to disrupt consumers' routine behaviour and get them to consider a new alternative, as in the Ogilvy Research Centre observation discussed earlier. High levels of advertising to build awareness will be needed, together with sampling, price deals, high-value coupons and so on to gain trial. For more complex, high-involvement purchase situations, consumers probably have limited knowledge of brands and need to go through an extensive external information search. Informative advertising, brochures, highly trained salespeople, in-store displays/information will be needed to assist the decision-making process. This is also the case for the buyer unless the rebuy situation prevails.

Communications implications of low-involvement cases are that consumers will have little motivation to learn marketing messages, so they need to be repeated often to enhance learning and inhibit forgetting (classical conditioning). Print is preferable for high involvement where information is sought and a self-controlled pace of learning is desired (although broadcast is useful to 'intrude' to enhance the build-up of awareness). In low-involvement situations broadcast media is preferred so that messages will be received regardless of whether they are sought. Belch and Belch advocate the use of the multi-attribute attitude model to show key issues to discuss, particularly in low-involvement cases, where messages should also be kept simple with continuity across different areas of the campaign. Also, pricing issues generally do not dominate high-involvement decision-making as there are several key attributes to consider, but may be the dominant variable in low-involvement decision-making and should therefore be included in the message (Belch and Belch, 2001).

VIGNETTE

A fistful of lattes or when is a coffee more than a coffee? When it's Starbucks

Sitting at a Starbucks in Kuala Lumpur during a break while on business was an experience, but not that different an experience to the one in my native Newcastle in the North East of England, apart from the weather of course. I had read a brief account of Starbucks in Baack and Clow's (2002) book, and the reasons why Starbucks had been able to convince Americans that they should spend a lot of money on latte and scones. Its phenomenal growth is apparent and quite an amazing opportunity, especially the lack of competitors. For all of America's melting pot mix of peoples, a concept common to many mother countries – the coffee bar – had not really taken off.

Starbucks is very young (founded in 1971 but Howard Schulz bought it in 1985 to start what can be seen today) and yet is one of the most recognized brand names around the world. Starbucks has won many awards, for example *Business Ethics Magazine's* '100 Best Corporate Citizens 2000'. The key to Starbucks in America appears to be the freshness of the coffee, it being never more than an hour old. Other factors come into it such as service, locations and other attractive features such as music and, not least, the quality of its products through careful sourcing of raw materials. This has given Starbucks the edge with consumers and has generated business-to-business interest as well.

This all tied in with the Kuala Lumpur experience. Very good coffee with very good service in a convenient location and, having read Baack and Clow's account, this did not surprise me. On the contrary, I could glimpse the coffee culture scene in the USA from afar. This seems set to continue with the effort that Starbucks are putting in to marketing and marketing and corporate communications: the Starbucks Card, for example, designed for personal use and gift-giving and as a form of currency that not only provides the customer with the incentive of not having to have money but also quickens service. Rather like a pay as you go mobile phone you simply load the card up and proceed to spend.

Starbucks also has a stated position on genetically modified organisms (GMOs), fair trade and organic milk. It has a Green Team that ensures the use of reusable cups, coffee grounds as compost and recycling among many other things. Starbucks does not franchise to individuals. It has six guiding principles to help in decision-making:

1 Provide a great work environment and treat each other with respect and dignity.

2 Embrace diversity as an essential component in the way we do business.

3 Apply the highest standards of excellence to the purchasing, roasting and fresh delivery of our coffee.

4 Develop enthusiastically satisfied customers all of the time.

5 Contribute positively to our communities and our environment.

6 Recognize that profitability is essential to our future success.

The Starbucks environmental mission statement includes:

1 A commitment to understanding environmental issues and sharing information with partners.

2 Developing innovative and flexible solutions to bring about change.

3 Striving to buy, sell and use environmentally friendly products.

4 Recognizing that fiscal responsibility is essential to Starbucks environmental future.

5 Instilling environmental responsibility as a corporate value.

6 Measuring and monitoring progress for each project.

7 Encouraging partners to share the Starbucks mission.

Source: Adapted from Baack and Clow (2002); www.starbucks.com/aboutus/gmo_update. asp; www.starbucks.com/aboutus/pressdesc.asp?id = 218; www.starbucks.com/investor.asp; www.starbucks.com/aboutus/environment.asp; www.starbucks.com/aboutus/timeline.asp; www. starbucks.com/aboutus/recognition.asp; www.starbucks.com/aboutus/greenteam.asp; www. starbucks.com/aboutus/envaffairs.asp; www.starbucks.com/aboutus/origins.asp.

STOP POINT

Starbucks has clearly been a success with consumers. Consider the decision-making process and the communication used by Starbucks. What type of consumer uses Starbucks? What would you speculate would be likely post-purchase behaviours if any? Consider also the buyer buying decision-making process. What are the likely stages that Starbucks will have to go through if they want to be successful in the business-to-business arena? What kinds of business-to-business communication will be needed to ensure success?

Assignment

Review consumer and trade/business and management magazine advertisements and identify and provide an analysis of one exhibit you feel is aimed at each of the types of consumer or buyer, and comment on anything you perceive might be to do with the buying decision process outlined in this chapter.

Summary of Key Points

- The size of markets is important but the ability to measure this is of little use if your product and communications do not fit in with the culture.

- People worldwide share certain needs but needs may be met differently in different cultures.

- Language is a cultural variable but culture is much more than this. It includes things like customs and practices and involves values, symbols, heroes and rituals as expressions of culture.

- There is often discussion of global culture but it is more realistic for marketers to look at models such as high/low context of culture as well as the characteristics of culture and aspects of consumer behaviour. Models of consumer behaviour have cultural elements as have lifestyle and value approaches. Cross-cultural comparison models of advertising, for example, have been made.

- Buyer behaviour theory is quite complex but can be broken down into component parts such as motivation, perception and cognition. The same can be said of buyer learning theory in terms of classical and operant behavioural theory and cognitive learning theory. The evoked set, attitudes and the hierarchy of effects are also key to understanding behaviour.

- The buying decision-making process can be modelled but should be used with caution in either the consumer or organizational buyer context. There are variations to the conventional models and also communication implications of such variations.

Examination Questions

1 Distinguish between beliefs, attitudes, opinions and interests. Explain the elements of culture that are likely to be important in any given situation using examples to illustrate.

2 Using an example of a values and lifestyle model, explain why understanding of cultural elements alone is not enough for effective marketing and marketing communications practice.

3 Illustrate the importance of 'word of mouth' and opinion leadership in terms of buyer behaviour. Explain how peer group pressure might be made to work in magazine advertising.

4 Critically examine the usefulness or not to marketers of Holbrook and Hirschman's hedonic and experiential theory of buyer behaviour. Contrast this with the more traditional ELM.

5 Explain the role that family members might have within the consumer buying decision-making process.

6 Explain selective perception and retention in terms of a communicator's effort to 'get through the clutter'.

7 Differentiate between ordinary and subliminal advertising using examples to illustrate.

8   Compare and contrast the consumer and organizational buyer in terms of the hierarchy of effects sequence.

9   Explain the five stages of the conventional consumer decision-making process. Contrast this with the organizational buyer decision-making process.

10   Discuss the likely variations in consumer and buyer decision-making and illustrate with examples of communications implications.

Notes

1   This can be made memorable by thinking of Rudyard Kipling's 'Six wise serving men' that taught him all he knew, 'Their names are What and Why and When, and How and Where and Who' (Oxford University Press, 1979: 300).

2   Geert Hofstede's large and diverse study of IBM employees around the globe is used by many writers but in marketing and communications' terms particularly by De Mooij (1994; 1998). See also Hofstede (1990).

3   Belch and Belch (2001) note that *subliminal perception* is a possibility whereby consumers perceive a message subconsciously. The possibility of using such triggers or cues is intriguing but problematic in an ethical sense. Also, the use of such 'hidden persuaders' could pave the way for a consumer backlash if the company concerned were 'found out'.

4   In their seminal article, Hirschman and Holbrook (1982) dispel the myth of the traditional view of the consumption of products with their belief that consumers behave in a far more sensorily complex, imaginative and emotion-laden way, which is why they are interested in multiple facets consumption. They are therefore interested in things like the way the scent of a perfume involves the recall of an event that actually occurred (past episode in a romance) and indeed in fantasy imagery whereby the consumer constructs an imaginary sequence rather than an experienced, historic one.

5   Baack and Clow (2002) distinguish between the inept and the inert set. The inept set are brands not considered even though they are in the person's mind because they elicit negative feelings through a bad experience or an influential negative comment. The inert set are brands that again the consumer is aware of but has negative feelings about. Thus neither of these sets becomes part of the final evoked set, unless something happens whereby the linkages become stronger rather than weaker and the consumer feels more positive than negative about a particular brand.

6   A theory of cognitive dissonance as espoused by Leon Festinger proposed that a feeling of psychological tension or distance can occur which causes post-purchase doubt in a consumer after a difficult (but not necessarily costly in money terms) purchase is made. The consumer wishing to reduce the tension may seek to do so with a variety of post-purchase behaviours such as checking prices, seeking further information and so on to satisfy themselves that they have made a good purchase decision.

7   There is an inherent danger that vigilance will be eroded and mistakes made. The attractiveness of computerized automated systems for stock control and just-in-time management is very understandable.

References

Baack, D. and Clow, K. E. (2002). *Integrated Advertising, Promotion and Marketing Communications.* Prentice Hall.

Belch, G. E. and Belch, M. A. (2001). *An Introduction to Advertising and Promotion.* 5th edition. Irwin.

De Mooij, M. (1994). *Advertising Worldwide.* Prentice Hall.

De Mooij, M. (1998). *Global Marketing and Advertising: Understanding Cultural Paradoxes*. Sage.

De Pelsmaker, P., Geuens, M. and Van Den Bergh, J. (2001). *Marketing Communications*. Financial Times Prentice Hall.

Ehrenberg, A. and Goodhart, G. (1979). *Essays on Understanding Buyer Behaviour*. J Walter Thompson.

Engel, J., Blackwell, R. and Miniard, P. (1997). *Consumer Behaviour*. 7th edition. Dryden.

Fill, C. (2002). *Marketing Communications: Contexts, Strategies and Applications*. 3rd edition. Prentice Hall.

Hirschman, E. C. and Holbrook, M. B. (1982). Hedonic: emerging concepts, methods and propositions. *Journal of Marketing*, **46**, Summer, 92–101.

Hofstede, G. (1990). *Marketing and Culture*. University of Limburg.

Kotler, P. (2000). *Marketing Management: Analysis, Planning, Implementation and Control*. 10th (Millennium) edition. Prentice Hall.

Mueller, B. (1996). *International Advertising*. Thomson.

Ogilvy Centre for Research and Development (1984). *How Advertising Works: an Up-to-Date View*. Ogilvy Centre for Research and Development.

Oxford University Press (1979). *Oxford Dictionary of Quotations*. 3rd edition. Oxford: Guild Publications.

Pickton, D. and Broderick, A. (2001). *Integrated Marketing Communications*. Financial Times Prentice Hall.

Shimp, T. E. (1997). *Advertising, Promotion and Supplemental Aspects of Integrated Marketing Communications*. 4th edition. Dryden.

UK Trade and Investment (2003). Food and beverages – invigorating and refreshing botanically brewed beverages. www.uktradeinvestusa.com/dbuk/sector/products_show.asp?

Vaughn, R. (1980). How advertising works: a planning model. *Journal of Advertising Research*, **20** (5), 27–33.

4

Managing the communications mix

Chapter overview

Introduction to this chapter

The concept of marketing communications planning, utilizing the different models/theories of the process, is well developed in the literature. It begins with some form of analysis as a first 'where are we now' stage. This can involve considerable detail. The communications mix needs to be part of a carefully planned strategy in order to maximize effectiveness, to obtain a unified message. The key purpose of this chapter is to provide a decision sequence model (DSM – a framework and template) that can be easily adapted by the manager of communications of one sort or another in different contexts. This, broadly, is the analysis, planning, implementation and control (APIC) system for managing, *à la* Kotler,[1] communications.

It is recommended that practitioners develop a decision sequence model/framework that includes marketing communications theory, the communications environment, and key issues in understanding consumer behaviour such as information processing and decision-making. There is therefore a need to deal with the development of communications strategy and then with implementation and execution of such a strategy. It is from this point that marketers can begin to develop marketing communications.

Aims of this chapter

The main aim of this chapter is to propose a management framework for use across the remainder of the book. More specifically the chapter aims to:

- explain what the DSM is and what it offers to marketing communicators
- explain the elements of the APIC system in broad DSM terms
- provide some critique of the adoption of such an approach
- provide a framework for the management of the marketing communications function.

Decision sequence models

The DSM is a commonly used model that deals with both the 'art' and 'science' aspects of communication. A decision sequence framework holds a logical sequence of decisions that managers make when preparing, implementing and evaluating marketing communications strategies and plans. The decision sequence imposes a managerial framework on a process that is often otherwise conducted by 'the seat of the pants'. In this book a vertical representation is used (which is the commonest form). It is acknowledged that other authors such as Shimp (1997) offers an approach that is horizontal, but deals essentially with the same kinds of issues of marketing structure, environmental monitoring and management, the brand decision process and brand-equity enhancement.

The APIC system

APIC is a memorable piece of shorthand for:

Analysis of the present situation (regarding the company, the product, the market, the target customer – where we are now), followed by

Planning, including objectives and positioning (direction and mapping, where we want to go) and strategy and tactics (mix choice within creative and media boundaries – how we get there), then

Implementation (costing, budgeting, production, scheduling – how we put it into practice) and, finally,

Control (research, monitoring and evaluation – did we get there?).

Analysis – where are we now?

Analysis is necessary to guide the assessment of the problem, the 'current state of the world', the 'where are we now' review. This requires a number of assessments.

An assessment of actual and/or potential targets: the customers or prospective customers

Descriptors of the target market must be derived so that the most appropriate segment of consumers can be reached. This classification process needs to identify customers/consumers on a number of criteria such as demographics, usage levels, knowledge and so on. Perceptions (of product, the competition) are important. In order to communicate with targets, it is advantageous to assess their perceptions of the product, its competition, and the relationships between the consumer and the product class. Processes (decisions on where the brand can be bought and how, e.g. in store or at home) are also important, i.e. to learn how consumers process information and make decisions is very useful. How involved customers/consumers are in decisions and how product/brand decisions are made in the home or in the store are also useful.

Mass marketing is a thing of the past – the 1970s saw segmentation and line extension. Niche marketing followed into the 1980s and the forecast is for atomization – we are all capable of being a target segment since we are all very unique. Databases via research and technology are of increasing importance.

Aggregation – mass marketing – is therefore a very rare occurrence. Not even the classic examples of commodities such as sugar and coffee escape this. Goods are no longer standardized. For this to work, everyone must have the same basic needs and wants, and a marketing mix to match these needs to be designed. This is highly unlikely even though economies of scale – 'you can have any colour you like as long as it's black' – are attractive with lower costs, including those of advertising. Homogeneous groupings – dealing with smaller groups – are perhaps more of a reality. This might not be perfect but the consumer appears willing to compromise with something that is nearly what they want.

Segmentation is at the heart of modern marketing. It deals with market segmentation bases and, therefore, market targeting (ways to cover the market and identifying attractive segments), market positioning and product position in the market. Steps in the market segmentation process include:

1 Determine market boundaries – consider basic needs/wants to be served.

2 Decide which variables/bases to use; this might entail using a hunting expedition, through some sort of marketing research/survey.

3 Collect and analyse data, which requires the usual instrument design and implementation followed, usually, by a more in-depth look at the segment via focus groups.

4 Develop profiles of each segment and relate them to actual buying behaviour.

5 Target the segments to be served, which involves matching company offering to needs/wants.

6 Design the marketing plan, which would of course include marketing communications involving image and so on (Hiam and Schewe, 1992).

Targets should have been arrived at by this stage and certain tools used. These tools are described below.

Customer databases

Parameters such as demographics, psychographics, behaviour/usage and geography can be used to build databases. Philip Kotler has said for a long time that the organization is in danger of drowning in information (for example Kotler, 1994). The organization should make sure the data is relevant to a particular context and, indeed, that measurement of true customer value is possible at all (Schultz and Kitchen, 2000). This again goes back some way in time where writers such as Kotler have always called for segments to be substantive. Only by understanding how customers like to be contacted will the company be able to truly interact with them. Customer care is central to what marketing is, not least because, as anyone who has been in a real marketing job knows, it is better to keep customers than to lose them and have to seek even more new ones. It is not easy keeping customers. The wrong attitude on the part of the receptionist is enough with some. With others who are loyal in the extreme, gradual erosion of such loyalty will inevitably be the outcome should the company's quality control slip or level of service diminish. This being the case, there is a need to ask how it is that so many organizations from retailers to manufacturers to service providers cannot, or will not, show a willingness to care for their customers in order to keep them.

There is also a need to question the link, if any, with the suggested failure of marketing to make a full impact on the management of business, commercial and public sector organizations alike. But this is not a new phenomenon. It was, after all, marketing theory that provided the focus on the importance of change to organizations.

These ideas had matured by the 1970s in most of Europe, and earlier of course in the USA. Today it is assumed that there are many organizations that are finance-led by chief executives who are paid salaries and bonuses based on the efficiency and effectiveness of the organization during their period of tenure. Short- and long-term successes are clearly important here and it is not so much definitions of marketing (of which there have been an incredibly silly number churned out mostly by academics over the years) and its concepts, but how the organization defines marketing. A simple definition that seems apt to use here is 'the creation and development of a customer base'. In short, the company must start with segmentation and identify target groups from the outset, and follow on towards objectives and where the company/product/brand should be positioned.

Product differentiation and branding

Product differentiation should be based on customer perceptions, for example association of the product with something that is valued. For this to work there are three requirements: the customer must be able to distinguish between products, the differences between competing products should not be small/trivial and the customer must care about the product. One way might be to focus more narrowly and accurately than competitors and this might require one-to-one marketing. In practice this is doubtful and some form of homogeneous grouping would be necessary even for a company like, say, Porsche. A number of different kinds of contact would be expected. Here, Schultz and Kitchen (2000) advocate understanding via a brand contact audit. This should tell the company how (and in how many ways) customers are in contact with the brand but also what they might prefer.

Bases for segmentation

Many things qualify as a base for segmenting a whole into constituent parts. Clearly segments must be attractive but several question areas arise:

1   Can the segment be identified? Can it be measured? Are there shared characteristics?

2   Is it large enough to be worthwhile? Is it substantive? Not just in volume but in value?

3   Can you reach it? Or is it too general a mass that segmentation is not possible? Often, where there is a media vehicle, there are the means.

4   Is it responsive? Will targets want the offering?

5   Is it stable? Or is it likely to be volatile? Is it fickle?

Bases are therefore at the centre of targeting. For consumer marketing many bases have been developed but the use of demographics, psychographics and to an extent geodemographics is common. There are others such as benefit segmentation, and rather different approaches for industrial/organizational markets such as location, industry type and size. Most writers would agree that there are basically two types of base for consumers – descriptive and behavioural. In organizational markets, bases such as customer size, location, industry classification, usage rate and nature of operations are commonly used.

1 *Descriptive* variables can be grouped into *geographic*, i.e. regional/country using government statistics to help measure size and so on. Examples involve products such as beer, soft drinks, refreshing drinks (perhaps for climatic reasons) or cider as opposed to wine (in northern France this is important because cider is consumed in the north). Internationally it may be attractive to group countries into, say, the Middle East, but this can cause problems because they are different. *Demographic* variables are age, sex and socioeconomic class and are easy to measure and can prove to be good indicators of needs and wants but rarely stand alone.

2 *Behavioural* variables can give the marketer an insight into the motivation. People may qualify to be a 'member' of a target market but may take no part in it, nor wish to. These include *user status*, i.e. some members of the market may never have been users, and they have to be persuaded otherwise. Some will have been users and lapsed, while others remain users (brand loyal, or loyal to a menu of brands for the same type of product) and so on. Each group needs to be assessed and approached accordingly. *Usage* involves distinguishing non-users from light and heavy users and so on. Here the 'Pareto principle' may be assumed, that is, 20 per cent of the market will account for 80 per cent of sales. This indicates the importance of small groups of consumers. *Benefit* segmentation assumes that the difference in benefits sought is the basic reason for the existence of different market segments. This is very plausible and is at the heart of modernist marketing philosophy – the old dictum that 'people do not buy drill bits, they buy holes' exemplifies this. *Personality* attached to brands deliberately for the purpose of matching product to target can be a segmentation base. Attributes such as dominance, thoughtfulness and impulsiveness are very plausible but rely on an understanding of buying behaviour where there are so many other variables in operation it is difficult to have one personality trait win the day. *Lifestyle* is a 1970s phenomenon that still lives on today and is still based upon A (activities), I (interests) and O (opinions) studies whereby the marketer is not reliant solely upon the old A, B, C1, C2, D and E (in the UK) socioeconomic classification system. Shared need based on what consumers like, not what they earn, is the rationale for employing such studies. Plummer's (1974) 'lifestyle dimensions' list of AIO has been replicated many times and this includes, for example, work and social events (activities), family and community (interests) and social issues and politics (opinions).[2]

The use of survey research of some sort is, of course, a requirement in order to arrive at a typology for a particular market. Leaving aside any marketing research-type problem, you might wish, as marketers, to question this approach in itself. It is very plausible from the advertising viewpoint but putting the VALS-type typology into practice can be infinitely more difficult than devising communication to influence such types.

Other bases such as *social class*, *occasions* and *stage of buyer readiness* (how much they know about a product/brand and how aware they are) may be applicable and can also be used as bases for segmentation, but are often part of a combination of tools.

Geodemographic systems

Geodemographic systems have also been around since the 1970s – since the ability to use IT to process information into a usable form became available. Acorn (a classification of residential neighbourhoods) was the first such system in the UK. This was followed swiftly by another system called, aptly, Mosaic. Such systems are used in direct marketing campaigns and by companies wishing to locate to an appropriate area with particular housing or other characteristics. In short they are mapping systems, geographically, but with a demographic breakdown thrown in. Different countries have different approaches that are based on the same principles as, for example, the American approach to geodemographics.

Industrial, organizational or business-to-business bases

Industrial, organizational or business-to-business bases may take the form of customer size, location and so on. Chisnal (1989) uses the simple example of the car market, which can be broken into 70 per cent company and 30 per cent private new registrations. Chisnal's example of the industrial paint industry highlights *size of firm* and *type of paints related to specific end uses* (for example deck finishes in the marine coatings sector) as potential bases for segmenting the industrial paint industry.

There is therefore a need to understand the organizational DMU, as opposed to the consumer, where purchase motivations need to be understood. Also, perhaps even more so than with consumer systems, within organizational marketing there is a need for very specific, tailored approaches. Another example, this time from the banking business service sector (business-to-business banking), sees the market being segmented into four (defenders, prospectors, analysers and reactors), after Miles and Snow, 1978, by 'business strategy'. Within this typology *defenders* rarely change their banking requirements and compete on price, delivery and quality. They invest in processes, have mechanistic structures and are businesses that are run by accountants and production people. *Prospectors* readily change their banking requirements and are almost the exact opposites of defenders. *Analysers* are those who ponder about all aspects – their requirements and ways of doing business. *Reactors* are inconsistent and faddy with their banking requirements. These types can be said to be mutually exclusive, internally homogeneous and collectively exhaustive, i.e. making up the whole of the business banking sector (James and Hatten, 1995).

An assessment of product class

This requires knowledge of customer/consumer perceptions, attributes and benefits of the product/brand, performance of the product/brand and the uniqueness offered by the product/brand. Part of this assessment comes from the study of consumer perceptions, but the analyst must also evaluate the attributes and benefits of the product, how well each of the brands performs in these areas and what unique features/benefits are offered. Additionally, this analysis should consider past strategies and market shares for the brands in question.

An (internal) assessment of the company/organization

This involves assessing the strengths and weaknesses and the understanding of corporate goals and philosophy, financial and production capabilities, and marketing support (distribution, sales and so on).

An (external) assessment of the micro (for example competitors) and macro (usually found in PEST/STEP form) environment

This involves an assessment of opportunities and threats being made. Analysis, therefore, necessarily includes information on previous marketing strategy, buyer information-processing, buyer decision-making processes, stakeholders, any intra-organizational issues, and any research and evaluation that may have been conducted, usually on aspects of the environment. Most of the marketing communications planning models alluded to above share this common initial stage of analysis.

VIGNETTE

Simply heaven and hotter than hell: Club 18–30 and club culture in the summer of 2002

Complaints arrived and the UK Advertising Standards Authority and the ASA asked for Club 18–30 advertising to be withdrawn after 314 complaints were received. The mid-1990s saw the height of Club 18–30's dominance of the clubbing market. Now metropolitan club land culture has been added to the mentality of the youth holiday market, highlighting how things change and the need for constant monitoring and analysis. Niche marketing of holiday packages is the order of the day. Over 1 million UK teens to twentysomethings take at least one all-inclusive holiday each year. Another development is the increased sophistication with which these holidays are marketed. The stability of the economy and the strong pound has meant that this group have been able to spend a lot on such concepts as 'clubbing', a shift from the earlier 'sun, sand, sea and sex' packages. The market has been seriously shaken. Standalone youth brands from Thomson include Club Freestyle and, from Airtours, Escapades. Cosmos have joined forces with The Ministry of Sound to form the Clubber's Guide. With the latter, the brochure was slick, putting across an image that was 'elite' and 'ultra-cool'. This was an attempt to re-create 1980s Ibiza hedonism. Chris Medd, Cosmos's product manager was quoted as saying, 'We aim at a breakaway crowd willing to pay a little bit more. We are not going to bang on your door at eight in the morning to get you on a donkey'. The Ministry of Sound's popular website, monthly magazine and record label all helped to communicate this brand to the target and, if anything, the Ministry of Sound had the upper hand. Club Freestyle also aimed upmarket at serious clubbers. Thomson preferred the stand-alone brand and individual club promotions. Escapades promoted value for money through local radio and Club 18–30 took a broad approach offering gigs and excursions. A move away from the 'Beaver Espana'-type advertising to brand tie-ups with Diamond White and the *Daily Star* is one way to target the mass market. They also had a bright pink, half-sized brochure that helped with the lack of space in agencies. This was said to be both eye-catching and small enough to fit in a handbag. It also had a pair of breasts on the front cover, something its target did not seem to mind. Splash, owned by First Choice operated only out of one resort, San Antonio. It was promoted via a *Viz* comic type of brochure and managing director, Chris Read, called his target 'Saturday Nighters' rather than clubbers. First Choice also had 2wenties and decided to reintroduce Turkey as a summer 2002 destination. Turkey was seen as good value for money with new excursions introduced.

Some claim the market appears now to be static, although Club 18–30 claimed to be growing at a rate of 5 per cent per annum, with the new entrants expanding the market not taking market share. The target seems passionate about taking holidays and research shows that they will forgo other things in order to do this. Others think the market seems to be expanding at the edges but the challenge is to keep the target interested. This means innovative thinking. So far Clubber's Guide has introduced weekend clubbing breaks to European cities and Airtours have put in a long-haul destination to Mexico. Club 18–30 sell on being exclusive – only like-minded people together, no families or old people – and many bars stay open until 04.00. They have introduced 'The Works' in Majorca and Zante (full English breakfast, fridge full of beer and a weekly barbecue included). Their 2002 brochure informs which properties will be showing World Cup football. As well as being innovative, there is sage advice from the industry:

- Know your clubs – what is happening in particular clubs on particular nights.

- Know your resorts – a UK garage fan will apparently be happy in Ayia Napa but not in Benidorm. Learn about the music in relation to the resorts.

- Sell club passes – inform your customers of entry costs and offer passes where appropriate.

- Cheap is not always best – clubbers do not necessarily want cheap hotels.

- Suggest short breaks – to the resorts but also city breaks such as to Berlin or Reykjavik.

Sources: Adapted from Travel Trade Gazette (2001a; 2001b; 2001c; 2001d).

STOP POINT Consider the importance of analysis for companies with brands like Club 18–30. Knowing the customer is one important thing but others are just as important. Draw up a list of the kinds of issues you would recommend to be included in the analysis step of a decision sequence model for brands such as these. Use the pro forma in Figure 4.2 near the end of this chapter to do this.

Planning: where do we want to go and how shall we get there?

Objectives and positioning: where do we want to go?

Objectives

Objectives are involved with direction. There is a need for a clear statement of the 3 Ts:

Target market.

Time deadline.

Task of message.

Positioning describes how the target should perceive the product relative to the competition. Objectives can be viewed in two ways. The first is hierarchical, from the mission down to the marketing communications level, i.e.:

1 *Business mission* includes overall vision and involves corporate values, leadership and so on.

2 *Business-level objectives* include survival, growth, expansion and so on.

3 *Marketing-level objectives* include market share achievement, sales by volume or value or profit.

4 *Marketing communications objectives* include creation of awareness of and interest in the brand.

The second allied to the 3Ts, is that objectives should also be SMART, i.e. specific, measurable, achievable, relevant and timed. Most if not all writers would agree with this and the fact that the role of objective-setting is to constrain strategy and help eliminate the large number of strategy options. Management by objectives (MBO) is as old as time. Rothschild's (1987) list of reasons why we should use the MBO approach includes the idea that objectives give direction, are a means to performance measurement and are consistent with time management. In marketing communications terms, the DAGMAR model as discussed in Chapter 3 is perhaps the best known of the hierarchy of effects. This stands for designing advertising goals for measured advertising results and looks to measure the result of a specific communication task in terms of the think–feel–do/cognitive–affective–behavioural hierarchy of effects on a defined audience. This attempts to measure the degree of change in a given time period as one moves through the hierarchy. An example might be to make 70 per cent of the target audience aware of the new product and to achieve a 50 per cent understanding of the proposition with 40 per cent convinced, but the expectation that, when it comes to it, 20 per cent will purchase in the first period.

The distinction between marketing and marketing communications objectives should be clear. In the above simple example the marketing objective is to achieve 20 per cent market share in the first trading period, say, a year. The marketing communications objectives to help achieve this could be many and varied, with the first being creation of 70 per cent awareness through, say, advertising but for conviction a combination of advertising and public relations may be used. Towards purchase sales promotion could very well have a role and so on.

Positioning

This means seeing things from the customer's perspective (and sometimes vis-à-vis the competition). It consists of all action taken to make sure that the marketplace's perception is managed. Strategic positioning is a result of communicated perceptions about a product or brand (whereas image is a more global impression). Position is a reference point in relation to the competition, and involves product attributes/features with related perceived or otherwise benefits which can be seen in the statements made about the product/brand in marketing communications, whether this is verbal or non-verbal (or both). BMW thus becomes 'the ultimate driving machine', Volvo is first of all safe, then has longevity and now is well designed. There are many ways to achieve positioning: through actual attributes, through benefits/solutions to problems, through price/quality and so on. In terms of developing a positioning strategy, Hiam and Schewe (1992) offer a seven-point system:

1   Determine relevant product/market – or more than one if applicable.

2   Identify the competition – whether primary (Perrier versus other bottled water) or secondary (Perrier versus other soft drinks).

3   Determine how consumers evaluate options – marketers must understand the standards by which consumers evaluate and reach decisions.

4   Learn how competitors are perceived – based on the same kinds of parameters.

5   Identify gaps in positions held – this helps pinpoint gaps that are attractive and those that are not!

6   Plan and carry out the position strategy – design a programme.

7   Monitor the position – seek to check for adjustments.

An example of perceptual mapping is provided in Figure 4.1.

Rothschild (1987) proposes several strategic issues for positioning/repositioning including consideration of relevant targets, the simple logic being that it is better to dominate a segment than to try to be all things to all people. Another Rothschild issue is consideration of the entire product line and position products/ brands so that the portfolio is optimized. Rothschild also suggests consideration of alternative bases as described above. This is qualified by whether the brand is leader or follower (never attack the leader straight away), the current positioning of competition and the resources available.

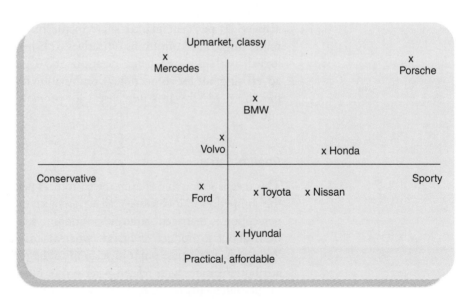

Figure 4.1
A typical perceptual map of the UK car market.

Lifestyle segmentation: Young and Rubicam's 4 Cs (cross-cultural consumer classification) and other such systems

Young and Rubicam's (Y&R's) 4 Cs system has been developed in the UK and has been extended to France and Holland. It is a VALS-type system of classifying people into groups with similar needs. Young and Rubicam are concerned with innermost needs. They maintain it is not a question of how much money we earn but how we want to spend our money, what we buy and the kind of advertising that will work on different people with different needs. The characteristics of the people described and the kind of advertising that might appeal to them are the issue for Y&R. The classification types are the *mainstreamer*, the *aspirer*, the *succeeder* and the *reformer*. The mainstreamer is apparently in need of things like security. The aspirer, as one would expect, wants the good things in life. The succeeder already has these but wants control. For the reformer it is the quality of life that is important. Any communication aimed at these groups should reflect the characteristics of each. For the first, the Legal and General umbrella is symbolic of security. For the second, the Halifax credit card and the relaxed Lionel Richie lyric of 'Easy like Sunday morning' has aspirational meaning. The British Airways 'Red Eye' or 'Boardroom' advertisement shows an executive in control at a business meeting despite flying over the Atlantic. For the fourth, a punk-like character saves an old man from a scaffold collapse (and not attacking him as you are led to believe at first). 'The whole picture' is provided courtesy of the *Guardian* newspaper.

Pegram Walters International (PWi) have developed 'Global Village' 1 and 2, a system not dissimilar to that above. This system gets to know targets such as teenagers. Pegram Walters International found that the language today's 'global youth' understands is communication they recognize, pay attention to and remember. This leads to respect for the communication and the brand. Global Village 1 was a study conducted in 1990. Global Village 2, conducted in 1997, looked at the essential aspects of communication with teenagers in the UK, the USA, Russia, Singapore, Spain and Germany. Both qualitative and quantitative research was used, as expected, to look at how 12–18-year-olds respond to and talk about advertising and other communications. The conclusion from this study was that certain components appear to be key to teenager language, which specialize in the television advertising medium. This leads PWi to conclude that the most effective advertising will combine messages and images that reflect a teenager's personal values with a brand message that imparts some wisdom and a format with a narrative structure – otherwise it will be 'just another advertisement'.

Another international agency, Context Research International (CRI), offers a three-point research programme that should help create advertising messages that cross borders. Rather than assume an image will have the same meaning in Germany as it might in the UK, CRI suggest that research can make the communication offered to the target more effective by, first, evaluating the brand and choosing the advertising theme. Second, use research to identify how the theme can be expressed in each market. Third, CRI advocate testing creative ideas in each market. Some tailoring may be required but a better value campaign is the result, according to CRI.

Similarly, the Harris Research Centre has developed a system called Semiometrie to more reliably understand cultural differences. One such application was a survey in the UK, Germany, France, Italy and Spain. Some 12 000 respondents aged 15 and over were subjected to both quantitative and qualitative treatments with a view to establishing values and emotions. Factor analysis found that four first factors are common to Europe (but different else-where): duty as opposed to pleasure; community as opposed to singularity; materialism as opposed to culture; and idealism as opposed to pragmatism. At the same time further analysis using Semiometrie demonstrated that mentalities are extremely different from one country to another.

Source: Adapted from Flaster (1997); Morrison (1998); Pepp and Bacattelli (1998); QED (1995).

Perhaps the only way to have effective communications is through some form of system to first help establish the target(s) and then help devise branding and communication messages that will fit, especially when crossing borders. Targeting is not the biggest problem. The biggest problem is one of the marketer being able to approach such targets effectively. Think about systems such as those above in differing contexts. What kind of research would be required? What kind of tailoring might be needed for different markets?

Strategy: how do we get there?

Strategy has to be created and co-ordinated even when developed independently. The *communications mix* can be considered in many forms and in an integrated fashion. If *objectives* are to do with direction, then *strategy* involves choosing the best means, in terms of both being creative and the type of media, of achieving them. Strategy involves both '*push*' to the trade, and '*pull*' to persuade end-users to demand. Sometimes these may be combined with a *profile* strategy to build goodwill at the same time (Fill, 1995; 1999). Schultz and Kitchen (2000) suggest that strategy itself is a pluralistic concept and attack, for example, the hierarchy of effects as an outdated concept, the problem being that such concepts are descriptive and not prescriptive. Only when a clear understanding of marketing dynamics is a reality can campaign implementation be successful.

Creative strategy and tactics

Creative strategy is dealt with more fully in Chapter 6. One of the most important elements of an integrated marketing communications programme is the message. Traditionally, advertising has been used to communicate information about a product or a service. Within an IMC framework the message is transmitted through the packaging and promotions, as well as through advertising. Information is still an important component but creative strategy also has to create and support brand images/positioning, demonstrate how a product/service can solve a problem or satisfy consumer needs, and persuade and shape consumer decision-making and brand choice. It also might have to remind consumers why they purchased a brand in the first place, or reassure them (reduce dissonance) that they have made the right decision. In IMC persuasive communication is paramount, advertising and PR are most effective in persuading audiences that information is accurate and attitudes need to change, and sales promotion and personal selling are persuasive in gaining action.

The link between objectives and creative strategy is made with a model of the sequence of persuasive objectives for marketing communication that begins with name or brand awareness (Burnett and Moriarty, 1998). If this is the objective they suggest a move through the provision of meaningful information, changing perceptions or attitudes, creating conviction, providing reasons to change behaviour, and reinforcement and reminder. Together all the communications tools should provide sufficient motivation to the audience to prompt a change in behaviour. The communication objectives should therefore be sequential (as in attention, interest, desire, action – AIDA), using the communications tools as appropriate to the stage in the sequence.

Creative strategy therefore is a key stage in the communications planning process, and should determine what action is required from the audience, what the messages should say or communicate – the 'big idea' as it has been called. Creative tactics are how this is executed and these involve media considerations as well as the actual design of an advertisement or press release. The importance of creativity in marketing communications in an overcommunicated society to develop a position and differentiate products/services should not be underestimated. However, just because promotion is creative or popular does not mean it will achieve the objectives it sets out so to do. Good communication is effective, not necessarily creative. Belch and Belch (1995) define creativity as 'the ability to generate fresh, unique and appropriate ideas that can be used as solutions to communications problems'. They go on to say that to be appropriate and effective a creative idea must be relevant to the target audience.

Media strategy and tactics

The marketer first has to understand the media before being able to plan the media. The media can, therefore, be looked at in two ways: the nature, pros and cons and characteristics of the media should be appreciated, and then media planning can be considered.

Nature, pros and cons and characteristics of the media

The various media at our disposal quite obviously have certain characteristics. Some of the pros and cons are listed in Table 4.1.

The real task[3] is choosing media categories and vehicles. The inclusion of those media at the cutting edge of technology is much the same as for previous

	Advantages	Disadvantages
Magazines	Long life	Long lead times
Newspapers	Short lead time	Short life
Television	Animation	Expensive
Radio	Sound	Spoken message only
Posters	Can be dramatic	Short message only
Transport	Low cost	How effective?
Signs	Low cost	How effective?

Table 4.1
Characteristics of various media

generations who viewed television is essential. Whether the Internet is the ultimate narrowcasting medium or whether a truly in-home multimedia environment will exist are questions not yet answered. The various media are often selected for their geographical reach, the ability to dramatize, frequency of exposure and so on. This being understood, the practitioner could then move on to more important things such as planning, costs and so on.

Media planning

Media strategy is the subject of Chapter 7 where greater consideration is given. The media planner has to decide which media are feasible and pick the main medium and how it should be used. He or she then has to decide on support media based on, for example, creative suitability in terms of the ability to dramatize, and experience of effectiveness, availability and lead time (long/copy deadlines), regional availability, competition, effect on trade and sales force, coverage and cost per thousand. Media planning is therefore about matching the media to the target audience after careful consideration of many things but, especially, audience characteristics. International campaigns are shaped by strategy, i.e. whether the multilocal or global (or something in between) approach is taken. For a number of years international media vehicles such as the *International Herald Tribune*, the *Wall Street Journal*, *Time*, *Fortune*, *Newsweek*, *Reader's Digest*, *Cosmopolitan* – to name but a few – have been available to marketers, even if some have been English-language only. In short the media planner has to understand the media planning process through to evaluation and within this must intertwine creative and media work.

There is concern here, therefore, with things such as changes in media technology, the development of mass markets, the standardization of brands, and changing lifestyles of consumers. This adds up to the central question of *narrowcasting*, i.e. using highly selective media for special target groups. MTV is an advert channel. It has a target audience of 14–34-year-olds and is therefore to some extent an opportunity for global narrowcasting.

Media selection costs can be extremely high. Buyers must be aware of how to reach target audiences via the best and most advantageous media, of negotiations for favourable rates and of size, length and frequency. Traffic and production (artwork, scripts and associated deadlines, timings and so on) have to be controlled. Supporting publications for wider coverage and experience of such media are also important considerations. In short they should be able to choose the channel(s) of communication that can give the message the best chance of being clearly expressed, communicate to as many of the selected audience as possible at the lowest cost and eliminate the problems of judgement via facts/figures to support the message. Buyers therefore must have information, authority, respect and persistence.

Choosing appropriate media is of crucial importance. The notion that the 'medium is the message' is not without foundation but has been challenged to some extent in the new electronic media. There is a link between marketing and media planning, i.e. from marketing plan down a hierarchy to media and creative plan. This implies a consideration of marketing objectives, product, profit, channels, resource constraints, IMC strategy and the target audience as a necessary part of the planning and managing process.

Implementation

Implementation needs to be considered in a test market fashion before full-scale commercialization, but not every company will do this automatically. Budgets need to be realistic and within resources. As strategies are developed, budget constraints need to be considered and objectives perhaps reviewed, since there may be a need to change objectives/strategies because of overly ambitious campaign development.

Spend issues

Funding

Lack of certainty as to what the money actually does has not helped the spend situation (recall the Leverhume words to the effect that 'half the money I spend is a waste, the problem is I don't know which half'). Measurement is the key to understanding this but it is clear that senior management, while recognizing the need for communications, have in the past treated it with a certain amount of derision.

Appropriation

Spend is dealt with in detail in Chapter 7. The tried and tested methods of arriving at how money should be spent are relatively well established in the literature. The conclusion drawn by most if not all writers in this area is that no one method prevails or is best at any given time. It is argued that spending on promotion is an investment and should be viewed as such, and not as a cost or expense as accountants would have it. Personal communication is often but not always associated with fixed costs, and the rest of the mix with variable costs. The former applies to sales management and the latter to brand or product management. If 80 per cent of new products fail then it is necessary to spend to get the 20 per cent to succeed, but also to bring the failure rate down. This is allied to brand-building in the longer term. Generally speaking, personal communication dominates appropriation in organizational markets and advertising in consumer markets.

Budgets

Budgets are to do with timing of spread of financial resources. Media scheduling has to be considered. Appropriation is the total sum allocated, while a budget is specific to the media or a market. These are the two broad tasks the organization faces. The size in the end depends on objectives that, of course, may have to be revised in the light of the amount of money available. It also depends on the stage in the company and the competitive environment. Costs depend on which media slots are bought and how much is spent on production, administration and research. A reserve of some sort should be considered.

Control

Evaluation

Evaluation is necessary in order to find out if objectives are being achieved. This then merges with a new situation analysis. There is a need, however, to consider research at each stage of the model and what research and evaluation means for different kinds of communications mix elements. Evaluation of the marketing communications effort can involve the obvious – sales increases for example – but to be 100 per cent sure is the impossible dream. This kind of evaluation is very tempting, especially in today's climate of pressurized performance. Cause and effect, especially with advertising, is not as concrete as it is with, for example, sales promotion coupon redemptions.

Research

Research has become one of the cornerstones of modern communications management and is vital in giving direction to a campaign. Research should be regularly used to both create and assess the creative effort. Most authors consider communications research in terms of pre-, during and post-testing, i.e. diagnostic testing of messages for the development of effective communication as well as assessment of how well objectives have been achieved in terms of sales or market share indicators, or attitude changes. This might involve campaign tracking and evaluation. Some typical research activity within a communications decision sequence model is outlined below.

Situation analysis and targeting – consumer research, competitive research and product research.

Targets, objectives and positioning – internal and feasibility research.

Strategy development – developmental pre-test of concepts.

Budget – final pre-test and execution of production.

Implementation – test marketing and internal feasibility research.

Evaluation – Post-test against objectives.

New situation analysis research – cycle begins again.

Clearly there are good reasons for wishing to measure the effectiveness of a communications campaign, such as avoiding costly mistakes, discovering other ideas and increasing efficiency, but this comes at a cost, not just in money but in time where delay might mean lost opportunities. *Return on customer investment* (ROCI) is seen as mandatory by Schultz and Kitchen (2000), who also see much of the above as being 'too soft'. Because in communication terms the measurement of return on investment (ROI) was too difficult or impossible, managers switched to trying to measure communication effects via the hierarchy of effects etc. Schultz and Kitchen advocate the importance of measurement time frames, both short and long term, as a basis of communications planning and completing the communication planning matrix. Schultz and Kitchen advocate an outside-in rather than inside-out approach to budgeting, i.e. that money spent on communication should be driven by the amount spent by the customer. This will drive spend down and profits up. Schultz and Kitchen's is a 'closed-loop system' for identifying the value of customers and prospects. A key concept here is that of *incremental returns* in terms of calculating ROCI. However, the simple formula (rather similar to marginal analysis) works at a very superficial level unless, as Schultz and Kitchen point out, 'hurdle rates' for investments are set, i.e. minimum percentage returns are set. Also advocated is the notion of short- and long-term brand aspect measurement. This approach means investment in brands but also measurement of brand equity in terms of price willing to pay, advocacy and so on. Interestingly, Schultz and Kitchen then return to attitude and behavioural measurement, albeit in an explanatory rather than predictive manner. Activity-based costing (ABC), which means attributing costs directly to customers/potential customers, and economic value assessment (EVA), i.e. the economic worth, are very much investments in the communications approach rather than treating communications as a cost.

VIGNETTE

Putting it into practice: limited resources and SMEs

Many small firms are constantly looking for new ideas for niche products. It was suggested to one small firm by a local enterprise promotion agency that there might be an opportunity aimed at gardeners with a product that would help lift off ingrained dirt after working with soil. At the same time the company was working with another support agency regarding the general marketing of products, and mentioned this new idea to the marketing adviser. After some research the adviser felt that there was definitely a niche market for a product of this nature, which should be much better than a simple barrier cream, and suggested the company form a separate marketing company to develop and market it. With his marketing expertise it was felt that he would be a perfect third partner, and he agreed to join as a director and investor.

The new company was formed and the first version of the product was formulated. A professional gardener was persuaded to test it out, and he very quickly came back with the comment that one of his main problems in gardening was infection of small cuts and grazes caused by thorns and sharp stones. He added it was not always desirable to wear gloves, and even then dirt could get trapped inside them. The antiseptics and bactericides were researched until the company found what was felt to be the best on the market, and this was added to the product in the recommended quantities for maximum effect. The professional gardener and other testers were delighted with the results, and by the end of the year all the packaging was designed and the first production batch of product made.

The company then carried out a press release mailing to over 1000 newspapers and magazines, and from the resulting publicity sold over 150 bottles by mail order all over the country. Many of these customers placed repeat orders, which suggested to the company significant proof that the product, now a brand, was doing the job for which it was designed. Mail-order sales quickly totalled over 500 bottles. A leading PR company in the area was engaged to provide press releases and promotional activity, and the company also worked closely with a brokerage that bought media space and advised on advertising. Accordingly, the company produced a commercial that was first shown on regional television in May the following year.

The retail launch was scheduled for just before Easter, through garden centres. The company was well supported by local garden centres that ordered as soon as they saw the bottle. A top horticultural agent began acting for the company in the north and he gradually increased the number of outlets who stocked the product. A stand was booked at a gardening and leisure exhibition in September where the prototypes of two new and complementary products to build the brand into a range were shown. A significant number of serious enquiries, including some from overseas companies, were received. While the major wholesaling chains were not enthusiastic about stocking and selling the brand the company went ahead and appointed a national selling group to take the brand to the independent chemist trade, as the range has many other applications outside the gardening sector. Once again, although they felt the product had good potential, the company had problems persuading the major chemists' wholesalers to stock the line to deal with referred orders. The company realized that the brand could not really start selling until this started to happen. An arrangement was agreed for the brand to sponsor a national not-for-profit gardening competition to the tune of 10p for every bottle sold in the UK in return for the use of their publicity machine and other PR opportunities. To pay for communication the company set a sales target of at least 250 000 bottles in the next year of trading to allow an annual marketing communications spend of 30p per bottle *including* the 10p to the not-for-profit competition.

A preliminary report on the results of a questionnaire (to be administered to the general public) was expected to give the company some ideas about the following:

1 How the public would react to the existing packaging and the kinds of devices/on-pack messages, on-counter displays, leaflets, etc. that would help sell it. Also opinions about the appeal the product might have in terms of age, class, sex and so on in its present form.

2 Both creative and media ideas, an integral part of the marketing effort, needed to be informed by opinion and perceptions relating to design, messages and so on, and the kinds of media and media vehicles that might work most effectively, and these were sought using the questionnaire.

The company decided to conduct more research in order to get a clearer message across to general public end-users about what the product can do. This included more on the above, any PR possibilities, any future developments in packaging such as tubes, any export considerations such as labelling requirements for the EC and any other marketing communications opportunities.

Source: A composite based on the author's experience.

STOP POINT

Consider the prospects and problems for this brand and its owners. Think about the financial limitations that are common to all SMEs, especially when it comes to advertising costs. Other, less costly, tools are available to companies like this one. How effective are these alternatives likely to be? The company should be applauded for its attitudes towards marketing communications and research, but should the company attempt a more integrative approach?

A critique of the APIC DSM

Finally, the old battle has been won. Corporate and marketing communications now leads and does not simply support, and is seen as an investment rather than a cost. Management of the corporate and marketing communications functions has traditionally been under command and control management (Schultz and Kitchen, 2000). There is concern for the day-to-day management of communications and before the process of implementation of communications strategy begins, key issues in the communications environment must be understood. Of the numerous communications (especially marketing communications) planning models that can be considered, most contain very similar stages or processes. In an attempt to move away from this approach Schultz and Kitchen (2000) offer an eight-step, cyclical model that is an integrated global marketing communication (IGMC) planning process. What is clearly different to other models is their approach to return on investment, stage six in the model entitled 'Estimate of return on customer investment (ROCI)' (see Schultz and Kitchen, 2000).

Brown (2001) is perhaps the UK's greatest APIC critic. For Brown, APIC is a modernist marketing ideal. As a postmodernist, Brown prefers to see TEASE as the acronym to entice us in. This stands for marketing as

Trickster

Excessive

Adolescent

Spirited

Entertaining.

The problem for many brought up on the Kotleresque approach to marketing management is that even Brown's 'retro-orientation' can fit into the APIC system. Brown recognizes this and acknowledges that it might appear that it is just another version of the argument that 'marketing is artistic, marketing is creative, marketing is right-brained'. But still Brown insists that TEASE 'comprises the Big Crunch' and is 'a replacement for APIC, not sugar on top of it'.

VIGNETTE

The IPA guide to advertising effectiveness

In order to provide another alternative view of a marketing communications management system, the IPA view is considered. The IPA training video referenced here deals with six companies and their respective agencies involved in the IPA Effectiveness Awards for 1994. It puts forward a six-part framework for effective advertising which is a combination of how advertising works in particular situations and a strategic approach. The elements are:

1 *Joined up thinking* – this links processes and gets above the clutter. Boddingtons (BBH) is the example here with the 'Cream of Manchester' campaign which took the brand out of the Granada/Manchester area to success nationally while not alienating the traditional Boddingtons drinker. Humour is the creative vehicle. John Smith's Bitter (BMP DDb Needham, widget, no-nonsense) and BMW (WCRS, performance, exclusivity, quality, luxury) also show evidence of joined up thinking.

2 *Strategic impact* – this involves a direct link with business mission and to some extent builds on the older notion of unique selling proposition (USP). The Cooperative Bank (BDDH) is the main example here. The ethical side of consumer behaviour is the key with 'The Bank with a Conscience' the overall theme which links in directly with the bank's philosophy and vision.

3 *Creative excellence* – capturing the imagination is key here and to some extent reflects David Bernstein's (1984) 'creative ideas' and David Ogilvy's (1983) 'big idea' approach. Through humour and aggression Pepperami

(S P Lintas) achieved notoriety and cult status with 'It's a Bit of an Animal' campaign. Creativity is said to be useless in isolation but flows out of strategic thinking. This can be seen in British Airways' (BA's) core values campaign that reflect status and prestige to capture the hearts of business people. In 'Manhattan' and 'Redeye' there is no lowest common denominator.

4 *Media ingenuity* – Boddingtons' media strategy was unusual. Their use of press, especially the Sunday colour supplements, had not been done before in the UK for beer. This was certainly not mainstream, and word of mouth was expected to be highly influential, classically relying on opinion leaders etc. for multistep flow. Pepperami spent only £800 000 (10 per cent of the norm) and did not pursue the usual audiences consisting of young people (the target) but did pursue an audience of which they would still be a part.

5 *Campaign leverage* – integration is a key word in all of this – 'going beyond the going beyond', or pushing out the boundaries – which it was felt that BA, Boddingtons and the Cooperative Bank had to do to achieve their various objectives.

6 *Product innovation and consistency* – this advocates 'new news', features, ideas, consistency and as such appears very similar to the joint brand image (Ogilvy)/USP (Rosser Reaves) approach advocated two decades earlier. The John Smith's Bitter widget, combined with the humour of Jack Dee, is consistent throughout. The paradox is one of using innovation with the notion of continuity but a balance of the two is achieved through the use of Dee and the humourous settings. John Smith's Bitter manages to get away with the gimmick of having 'no gimmicks'. With BMW the balance is achieved also between image and change, and with the Cooperative Bank between generic ethics, impeccable credentials and guarantees.

Source: Adapted from IPA (1995), video and notes.

STOP POINT

What are the similarities and the differences between the APIC approach and the IPA system? Map these out and begin to build a framework in your own terms using language that has meaning to you.

A framework for managing communications

Figure 4.2 is a summary of the management framework that has been discussed above and will be used during the rest of this book.

Assignment

Choose an organization – a business, a charity, a local authority function – and apply the management framework to part of its communications activity. For example, problems or opportunities may exist now or arise in the future in the environmental/'green' part of the marketing environment for such organizations.

ANALYSIS

Targets/potential targets (customer/prospect)	TARGET 1	TARGET 2	TARGET 3
Customer database (size, profitability, % share)			
Bases for segmentation and targeting			
Descriptive			
Behavioural			
Opinion leader			
DMU			

Product	TARGET 1	TARGET 2	TARGET 3
Perceptions			
Attributes			
Benefits			
Performance			
(Sales, profits, against previous, average, best)			

Company/organization	STRENGTHS	WEAKNESSES
Corporate goals and philosophy		
(Mission, vision, policies)		
Capabilities and competencies		
(Resources, financial, technological, managerial)		
Marketing mix/strategy		
Trends in buyer information process		
Trends in buyer decision-making process		

Micro environment	OPPORTUNITIES	THREATS
Stakeholders		
Competition		
Suppliers		

Macro environment	OPPORTUNITIES	THREATS
Sociocultural		
Technological/scientific		
Economic		
Political/legal		

PLANNING

Targets	TARGET 1	TARGET 2	TARGET 3
Targets			
Time			
Tasks			

Objectives (SMART)	TARGET 1	TARGET 2	TARGET 3
Business mission			
Business objectives			
Marketing objectives			
(Penetration, development, diversification,			
actual sales/profit)			
Marketing communications objectives			
(Awareness, develop interest)			

Position	TARGET 1	TARGET 2	TARGET 3
Perceptual map parameter 1			
Perceptual map parameter 2			
Perceptual map parameter 3			
Perceptual map parameter 4			

Strategy	TARGET 1	TARGET 2	TARGET 3
Communications mix			
Creative strategy and tactics			
Rational message			
Emotional message			
Media strategy and tactics			
Media type			
Media vehicles			

Figure 4.2
Management framework
summary.

IMPLEMENTATION			
Funding	**TARGET 1**	**TARGET 2**	**TARGET 3**
Appropriation and budgets			
Scheduling			
People			
Media			
Traffic and production			

CONTROL			
Research	**TARGET 1**	**TARGET 2**	**TARGET 3**
Pre			
(Concept testing, product testing, test marketing, etc.)			
During (monitoring)			
(Aided, unaided recall, recognition, objectives being achieved, e.g. sales)			
Post (evaluation)			
(Aided, unaided recall, recognition, objectives achieved, e.g. sales)			

Figure 4.2
(Continued)

ACTIVITY	TIME PERIOD							
	Jan	Feb	Mar	Apr	May	Jun	Jul	Aug
Advertising medium (1)	x	x	x	x	x	x	x	x
Advertising medium (2)	x		x		x			x
Public relations (1)	x							x
Public relations (2)		x	x	x				
Public relations (3)						x	x	x
Sales promotion (1)	x							
Sales promotion (2)								x
Exhibition (1)	x							
Exhibition (2)					x			
Exhibition (3)							x	

Figure 4.3
Example of a Gantt chart.

Follow this through with basic ideas on the rest of the marketing communications framework. In particular create simple Gantt charts to illustrate scheduling of (1) communications tools, (2) advertising media and media vehicles, and (3) production of materials and other traffic issues. A Gantt chart is a simple device that can easily be constructed and is designed to provide a snapshot of activities over time periods; as, for example, in Figure 4.3.

Summary of Key Points

- Most writers would subscribe to some form of decision sequence model when attempting to manage marketing communications. There are, however, challenges to the APIC type of system.

- Analysis deals with assessments of customers, products, the organization and its environment. This is the 'Where are we now?' question.

- Planning deals with targets, objectives and positioning. This is the 'Where do we want to go?' question. This is followed by consideration of creative and media strategy – the 'How do we get there?' question.

- Implementation is a consideration of 'How do we put this into practice?' and involves the allocation of spend to the campaign.

- Control involves evaluation and research and is the 'Did we get there?' question. This is not only a check on whether objectives have been achieved, but also a consideration of the place of research in the entire framework.

Examination Questions

1 Explain why you agree or disagree with the contention that the APIC-type model is useful as a framework for communicators to operate within.

2 Outline what you consider to be the important elements of the analysis stage of a marketing communications' DSM.

3 The planning stage of a DSM involves consideration of 'where do we want to go?' and targets. Discuss the importance of establishing targets early on in campaign planning and managing.

4 Explain the usefulness (or not) of perceptual mapping using illustrations of your choice to aid the explanation.

5 Creative strategy is part of 'how do we get there?' Discuss, broadly, the difference between rational and emotional appeals.

6 Discuss the importance of involvement with particular reference to creative appeals.

7 Media strategy is also part of 'how do we get there?' Explain why you agree or disagree that a firm understanding of media characteristics should be the first step in this part of the framework.

8 There are a number of practical issues when considering how to put a campaign into practice. Discuss at least one such issue for a product of your choice.

9 Discuss the logic behind pre-, concurrent and post-testing within the marketing communications arena, using examples to illustrate.

10 Comment on the idea that the battle to view marketing communication as an investment not a cost has been won. Explain what you understand the terms ROCI and TEASE to mean.

Notes

1 For a nearly thirty years Philip Kotler has used APIC effectively as the subtitle of his *Marketing Management* (for example Kotler, 1994) tome. While this approach is used here, not unlike many other authors in the communications area such as Fill or Belch and Belch, it is acknowledged that other writers are somewhat critical of this paradigm, notably Brown (2001).

2 Following the AIO idea, the original VALS model as devised at the Stanford Research Institute in the 1970s by Maslow and Rockeach blended demography with lifestyle variables. This was replaced in the 1980s by VALS2.

3 The reader is urged to familiarize him or herself with the various characteristics of the media if unfamiliar with them.

References

Belch, G. E. and Belch, M. A. (1995). *An Introduction to Advertising and Promotion*. 3rd edition. Irwin.

Bernstein, D. (1984). *Company Image and Reality*. Cassell.

Brown, S. (2001). *Marketing – the Retro Revolution*. Sage.

Burnett, J. and Moriarty, S. (1998). *An Introduction to Marketing Communications – an Integrated Approach*. Prentice Hall.

Chisnall, P. (1989). *Strategic Industrial Marketing*. Prentice Hall. (Chapter 6.)

Fill, C. (1995). *Marketing Communications: Frameworks, Theories, and Applications*. Prentice Hall.

Fill, C. (1999). *Marketing Communications: Contexts, Contents and Strategies*. 2nd edition. Prentice Hall Europe.

Flaster, C. (1997). First get the language right, then tell them a story. *ResearchPlus*, November, 11–12.

Hiam, A. and Schewe, C. D. (1992). *The Portable MBA in Marketing*. Wiley. (Chapter 8.)

Institute of Practitioners in Advertising (IPA) (1995). *Advertising Effectiveness*. IPA.

James, W. and Hatten, K. (1995). Further evidence on the validity of the self-typing paragraph approach: Miles and Snow's strategic archetypes in banking. *Strategic Management Journal*, **16** (2), pp. 161–168.

Kotler, P. (1994). *Marketing Management – Analysis, Planning, Implementation and Control*. 8th edition. Prentice Hall.

Miles, A. and Snow, C. C. *Organisational Strategy, Structure and Process*. McGraw-Hill.

Morrison, V. (1998). The real values behind national stereotypes. *ResearchPlus*, Autumn, 6–7.

Ogilvy, D. (1983). *Ogilvy on Advertising*. Pan.

Pepp, M. and Bacattelli, I. (1998). Researching the way into adland Europe. *ResearchPlus*, Autumn, 18–19.

Plummer, J. T. (1974). The concept and application of lifestyle segmentation. *Journal of Marketing*, **38**, January, 33–37.

QED (1995). *It's Not Easy Being a Dolphin*. Channel 4 television series.

Rothschild, M. L. (1987). *Marketing Communications*. Heath.

Schultz, D. E. and Kitchen, P. J. (2000). *Communicating Globally*. Macmillan.

Shimp, T. A. (1997). *Advertising, Promotion and Supplemental Aspects of Integrated Marketing Communications*. 4th edition. Dryden.

Shimp, T. A. (2000). *Advertising, Promotion and Supplemental Aspects of Integrated Marketing Communications*. 5th edition. Dryden.

Travel Trade Gazette (2001a). Clubbing operators spin the marketing decks, *Travel Trade Gazette*, 26 March. At http://web5.infotrac.galegroup.com/itw/infomark/191/445/17565313w5/purl=rcl.

Travel Trade Gazette (2001b). 2wenties returns to a safer Turkey, *Travel Trade Gazette*, 11 June. At http://web5.infotrac.galegroup.com/itw/infomark/191/445/17565313w5/purl=rcl.

Travel Trade Gazette (2001c). Viewpoint: keeping abreast of the youth market, *Travel Trade Gazette*, 11 June. At http://web5.infotrac.galegroup.com/itw/infomark/191/445/17565313w5/purl=rcl.

Travel Trade Gazette (2001d). Club 18–30 is in the pink with summer 2002 launch, *Travel Trade Gazette*, 18 June. At http://web5.infotrac.galegroup.com/itw/infomark/191/445/17565313w5/purl=rcl.

Travel Trade Gazette (2001e). How to sell clubbing holidays, *Travel Trade Gazette*, 23 July. At http://web5.infotrac.galegroup.com/itw/infomark/191/445/17565313w5/purl = rcl.

Advertising as Art of Persuasion, Strategic Thinking and Managed Discipline

Effective advertising can only be achieved through understanding the subject as a management process. There are various steps to this kind of process, but before this can be achieved the various functions performed and the creativity involved have to be understood. In this sense advertising can be seen as both 'art' and 'science'.

This second part of the book consists of four chapters. Chapter 5 deals with advertising theory, branding and practice. Chapter 6 deals with creative strategy. Chapter 7 deals with media choices in terms of characteristics and planning and spend issues. Chapter 8, following on from Chapter 4 in Part One of this book, facilitates a strategic framework for effective advertising management for a Scotch whisky brand.

Advertising theory, branding and practice

Chapter overview

Introduction to this chapter

The main concern in Chapter 2 was for the fundamental use of the very basic model of the (marketing) communication process. The critique of communications theory used in Chapter 2 applies equally here in terms of advertising, so that advertising practice without theory (and vice versa) is problematic. In this chapter the theoretical and practical nature of advertising is explored, particularly in relation to branding. Two key practitioners' views that have been influential over the past five decades or so are examined and explained. As with the broader communications argument, in this chapter we are concerned with practitioners and what they can gain from the theoretical stances. The nature of this, of course, will be dependent upon the type of product, whether new or established, a physical product or service, low cost or expensive, consumer or industrial, and will determine the importance of advertising in the communications mix in any given context. It will also depend upon the type of market, whether it is a growth or mature market for example, which will also have an impact on the use of advertising. The product/brand/market life cycle, objectives and policies of the organization, economic outlook, competitive activity, promotional resources and many other parameters will determine the nature and importance of advertising activities.

Aims of this chapter

The overall aim of this chapter is to consider advertising and branding in the context of what theory has to offer practice. More specifically, on completion of this chapter, the reader should be able to:

- discuss the nature of advertising in the twenty-first century in terms of theoretical development

- define advertising in comparison with other elements of the communications mix

- explain the relationship between advertising and branding decisions and how advertising is used to create brand value

- outline the major practitioner influences on current day advertising and to establish a link between past and present.

Advertising theory

Advertising as art of persuasion

Advertising has been seen as both a positive and negative force in society. As indicated above, it is not the intention here to get too deeply involved in the ethical debate that surrounds what has been called the 'second oldest profession'. Since the 1960s the debate has been about whether advertising shapes society (see especially Vance Packard's (1957) 'Hidden Persuaders') or whether it merely reflects societal norms in order to do its job and sell things. Issues include, for example, the controversial advertising of Benetton or the 'pester power' of children who make their parents' lives difficult because of an advertisement they have seen for an £80 pair of trainers or the latest Play Station 2 game at £50 a time.

Advertising can be said to be art – for the most part. The old adage of Lord Leverhulme[1] underscores this notion, or perhaps the corollary of 'not an exact science' should be used. Pure transfer of meaning is difficult, if not impossible, to achieve and this is true of mere information-giving, leaving aside the problems associated with persuasion. As communication strategies are developed, the organization, as we have seen in Chapter 1, has a number of alternatives available in terms of the communications mix. The elements of the mix can be described and grouped in a number of ways. For example, communication can be mass (as with advertising) or personal (as with selling). Alternatively, communication can be paid for (for example advertising or exhibitions) or free (publicity or word of mouth). Communication can also be a mix of these, that is:

- mass and free (publicity)

- mass and paid for (advertising)

- personal and free (word of mouth)

- personal and paid for (selling).

There has always been confusion over the difference between advertising and publicity. Confusion still remains over what is paid-for sponsorship rather than advertising. The sponsorship by Cadbury's (chocolate) of the British television soap opera *Coronation Street* on ITV, however, can be seen to be very different from a Cadbury advertisement through the objectives behind the different forms of communication. As well as this, the comparative advantages and limitations of personal as opposed to mass communication can be expressed in terms of other factors. Mediated communication like advertising has long been recognized as a fast medium that has a low cost per contact. It can attract attention and engage people with a message but has to try hard to do so. Advertising has so far been a one-way flow of message content, and its effects have been difficult to measure. Compare this with personal communication, which is often face to face, provides instant feedback and allows messages to be tailored to individuals. Advertising is a paid-for communication that usually involves mass media such as television. However, as technology changed, advertising became less mass and more personalized, introducing media such as mobile phones using text messages. Compare the strong degree of control that the advertiser who is paying for the communication has, compared with seeking publicity where messages have to be filtered through editors and others.

The advantages of advertising over other forms of communication are well known to be in terms of control – the sender pays for the space and can therefore say what he or she likes, where and when to say it and to whom, providing this is within legal and regulatory frameworks. The low cost per contact and the creative power of advertising means that it can be very cost-effective, especially in consumer markets where there is little between brands other than the ingenuity of the advertising that becomes part of the brand's architecture. On the other hand, the disadvantages of the non-personal nature means there is no opportunity for immediate feedback, and costs of production and media can be very high yet credibility can be low. Most people know that advertising exists to persuade and if they so wish viewers, listeners and readers can 'screen out' messages either psychologically through selective perception or physically by, for example, leaving the room when the commercial break is on. Another disadvantage of advertising as mass communication is that messages were thought to have to be very general in their appeal. These days, however, the fragmentation that has occurred in the various media means that there are smaller groups of recipients of messages, and marketers therefore have the ability to target these more with more specific messages. Also, the idea of narrowcasting within broadcasting whereby a mass medium such as television can be used by using audience research and analysis has been with us for some time.

Advertising is by and large seen as an art – the art of persuasion – and can be defined as 'any paid for communication designed to inform and/or persuade'. It is much more than this though, as alluded to in Chapter 1. It is part of the fabric of everyday life. Television advertising in particular has changed from being exclusive and even exotic to being prosaic and everyday. This underscores the importance of the McCluhanism 'the medium is the message', or at least part of it.

How advertising works: communications models

For advertising to work at all it has first to be seen, read, listened to; then comes belief, being remembered and even acted upon (Crosier, 1999). Thus, as discussed in Chapter 2, various models from fairly early on in the twentieth century were developed to try to understand the processes involved in moving from states of unawareness to awareness through to actual behaviour to try to measure communications' effects. Thus we have Strong's 1925 AIDA through to Colley's 1961 DAGMAR, the think–feel–do sequence and its derivatives. Also as discussed in Chapter 2, there has developed an attempt to show the problems of measuring the actual effect of a particular form of communication, not least advertisements. This is descriptive, and does not tell us why people respond as they do to advertisements, yet is consistently used to help form objectives. AIDA and its ilk are still the implicit conceptual underpinning of much of present-day advertising strategy. Indeed, as Crosier (1999) points out, it has to be conceded that a 'deficient but codified basis for objectives formation is preferable to no common framework at all'. Further, Crosier relies on McDonald (1992) and Fratzen (1994) to provide a critique of the hierarchy of effects. Thus Crosier concludes that the measurement of cognition is possible, of affectation possible but difficult, and of behaviour possible after the fact but to predict accurately is very difficult.

The advertising process that follows the communication process was dealt with generally in Chapter 2. However, this model was originally developed to deal with the problems of one-way mass communication. The sender or source of the message in advertising terms is usually the organization. The message may be handled by some form of communications company. The sender/source itself is usually part of that message. Advertising may have elements of trust, likeability, attractiveness, or power in order to influence and persuade. The celebrity endorser may be used to get across enthusiasm, likeability and so on. Encoding deals with problems where the advertiser's job is to perceive correctly the problems to be solved and to create the right concept and to develop the advertising in terms of the right sentences, words, symbols or whatever else from the vast array of verbal and non-verbal elements. The advertising message is the symbolic representation of the sender/source's thoughts/ideas. Decoding involves the deriving of meaning from the received message that is a composite of the actual message sent and any influences the medium may have had upon it. Feedback is the loop of the process that provides the sender/source with a channel of evaluation of the encoded message. Most feedback activity occurs in the area of advertising research. Noise (interference or impedance) is the blocking or distortion of the message and this has a particular bearing on advertising. It might be a lack of knowledge that causes a consumer to be unable to fully understand. This can therefore be physical or cognitive and can be anything from interruption though channel flicking to the sheer amount of clutter in a newspaper or magazine. Realm of understanding/field of experience is used to indicate the possibilities of overlap between sender and receiver so that 100 per cent commonness of field of experience is achievable. In advertising terms, prior knowledge of a particular brand or the residual effect of a previous campaign would be part of this.

Other communication models

Step flow/personal influence models, innovation theory and hierarchy of effects all have resonance with advertising. It is the latter, hierarchy of effects, to which most attention has been paid and yet it is the most problematic. Clearly, advertising has been the most prolific communications tool used to gain awareness and interest, within the think–feel–do sequence of events regarding the cognitive (awareness, knowledge), the affective (interest/liking, desire/preference/conviction) and the behavioural (action/purchase). This has been subjected to the usual criticism (see Chapter 2) that is applied to stage models but also knowing that the level of communication input in order to facilitate change is difficult to measure. Until this is known an optimal communications mix cannot be devised and implemented.

Another common model applied to advertising is the *Kellman source characteristics model*. The ways in which sources obtain and retain their characteristics that can be used in message strategy were discussed generally in Chapter 2 and the use of a celebrity endorser is discussed in Chapter 6. The model elaborates how credibility (for objectivity, relevancy, expertise, trustworthiness and so on), attractiveness (through identification with the source) and power (when the source can reward and punish and therefore involves compliance) can be used in communications but especially in advertising. High credibility is not necessarily the most effective in certain situations, as might be expected. The use of a high-credibility source is of less importance when receivers have a neutral position. This is clearly plausible with regard to low and high involvement and where risk is involved. Everyday products like insurance can be promoted in this way. Empathy or correlation between source and recipient means that the receiver will find the source attractive and a relationship can then develop. The latter sees him or herself in the situation depicted, say, through slice-of-life advertising, i.e. he or she relates to and identifies with it and the problems it appears to solve. Many advertising examples exist of credibility and attractiveness. In the UK the Oxo family would be typical. However, the use of power characteristics is rarer and is more easily seen in personal communications situation where both the stick and carrot are in evidence – expense accounts, type of car allowance, bonus rewards and penalties, etc.

The context of advertising

The context of advertising determines much of what is eventually practised. The industrial setting is often radically different from that of the consumer but within the notion of 'consumer advertising' there are very different contexts. Fast-moving consumer goods advertising may be very different to that of consumer durables. The business-to-business (BtoB) situation has many contexts and it is erroneous to assume that industrial equates to BtoB, or that all non-consumer advertising can be grouped under the umbrella of 'organizational'. This is the reason why this book does not have a dedicated chapter on BtoB advertising or communications. It is believed that it is far better to look at advertising within specific contexts, perhaps on a market or industry basis. The vignette below is but one of myriad contextual examples, i.e. the luxury car market.

VIGNETTE

The luxury car market: BMW, the ultimate driving machine

BMW have been a huge success, especially in the UK. Advertising has had a major role to play in BMW's success. WCRS, the London-based advertising agency wanted the advertising to enrich BMW's reputation for performance but at the same time communicate the breadth of the range. The core values of performance, quality, service and exclusivity needed to be extended into all models. The advertising itself was adjudged to have added value and to have helped project exclusivity into a context that is not exclusive. The campaign was awarded the IPA's Advertising Effectiveness 'Grand Prix' in 1994 for 'its sustained, demonstrable success, added to the way the case faced up to the particularly difficult challenge presented by the car market, where multiple factors impact strongly on consumer choice'.

Award-winning advertising therefore helped make BMW an 'auto icon', with 'suave authority and cool restraint'. The brand proposition is now established as exclusive with advanced technology (country-of-origin effect, performance) used. The medium used was prime slots on television, creating a 'television poster', rather than the conventional television advertisement. The use of James Bond product placement is the 'ultimate product placement' for a context like this. The BMW reputation has grown over the past twenty-five years and the company has consistently generated a profit in the UK. This success reflects a combination of diligent brand management and the conception and production of world-class products. BMW's market share and profits have been maintained because of customer demand and not heavy discounting.

BMW cars are most succinctly described through their famous advertising strap line 'the ultimate driving machine' that summarizes the corporate philosophy. Many product features and innovations that contribute to the driving experience have been the focus of some of the most famous car advertising ever, including 'Shaken. Not stirred', 'Balance' and 'Twins'. BMWs are driven by and large by older people for whom golf remains the most popular hobby, and they are increasingly loyal. BMW gained the most sales from GM and also Ford, and those BMW customers who choose to leave the brand and go on to buy a competitor's car tend to go to Mercedes-Benz.

BMW do engage with other communications, especially direct communications and other tools such as 'Packington Hall'. This is an invitation-only event to a selected range of customers inviting them to the Motor Show as guests of BMW, including hospitality at a nearby stately home. There is also Brands Hatch, a campaign sent out to attendees of the BMW Nigel Mansell Driver Training school. There is of course the *BMW Magazine*, a complimentary subscription to *BMW Magazine* being sent to all new car customers for a period of three years, the likely ownership period. BMW does not use things like inserts since it is felt inappropriate for a brand like BMW. For the same reason BMW does not endorse the use of anything other than communication that supports the proposition that BMW consists of exclusivity, advanced technology and performance. However, in recent years BMW's advantage over competitors in terms of brand perceptions has been eroded. Many of BMW's rivals have begun to stake a claim on the traditional BMW attributes of performance, most notably Volvo's recent campaigns that have overtly focused on the performance element of their cars to overcome their tired safety-first image.

The advertising of late has begun to widen the gap between BMW and its rivals. This is not simply a perceived gap, it is an actual difference in the very nature of the cars. This advantage which BMW is now attempting to highlight is that of 'driving'. Driving is at the heart of all of BMW's communications. 'Driving' is not simply another word for 'motoring', it is about dynamism and the entire experience of driving a BMW which cannot easily be imitated by any of its rivals. These dynamic driving qualities are prevalent throughout all BMW communications, both in advertising and direct marketing. These different executions of 'dynamic driving' range from the television advertisement 'soundtrack' to the press advertisement '50/50' which highlights BMW's near perfect balance which it tries to achieve with each car's weight distribution.

Product innovations continue to cause a great deal of interest in the motoring press in the latest BMW or BMW concept car which is being considered for production, with two new product launches of late that have generated particular interest, including the Z3 Coupé that builds on the popularity of the Z3 Roadster. BMW will continue to move forward and while they will engage with relationship marketing and customer service elements such as the BMW Card, advertising will continue to have a major, if not leading, role in the BMW communications mix, where brand values will continue to be emphasized.

Source: Adapted from the IPA (1995); IDM (1997); Crosier (1999); BMW (2002).

STOP POINT

Consider what the BMW brand proposition is. What role does BMW advertising have in emphasizing brand values? How does BMW's advertising integrate with other elements of the communications mix?

Branding and advertising

The meaning of 'to brand'

Just as mass marketing is a thing of the past so, too, is the generic product. Even at supermarkets where there are products that are not labelled as individual brands per se, they are often still branded in a particular basic fashion, such as Tesco's own-label 'value' brand. The brand image is a perception on the part of the consumer. It is a perception of what the marketer has created in terms of brand identity. Chapter 13 provides a more detailed discussion on the relationship between identity and image (at the corporate level) but, for now, suffice to say the consumer has a perception that is called the brand image and uses this as a shorthand in order to aid decision-making. The benefits of branding are, according to marketers and those who are pro branding, myriad. These include providing choice, saving time and money, and guaranteeing product quality, while those against point to waste, particularly with packaging, and high prices.

Brands are configured from a basic product but are added to with tangible and intangible attributes. Another way of looking at this is to take the view of David Bernstein (1984), who sees the brand as a product with clothes on that grows and matures in much the same way as a baby comes into the world and grows up. Levi, Lee and Wrangler offer similar denim jeans, but they are very different brands with different personalities. This is because of the symbolism used, the communications (particularly advertising) created and the behaviour of the parent and brand itself. Blind testing is a testament to the power of the brand and when a brand is stripped of its 'clothes' back to the original product this can be very revealing.

Brands therefore consist of the following:

1   Core product[2] – the actual, physical product or service that is generic and easy to copy.

2   Tangible attributes – that is, design, performance, ingredients, parts, size, shape, pricing and harder to copy.

3   Intangible attributes – that is, value, image, distributor's image and much harder to copy.

Brands are therefore built through the use of names and other signs and symbols to create a symbolism that becomes an identity. This makes the brand memorable and may describe the benefit sought by the consumer, as with Slim Fast or Head and Shoulders. It may use association with activities, such as Range Rover, or it may be distinctive such as the Apple Corps distinctive coloured apple logo. Pronunciation and phonetics are important, as recognized many years ago by Kodak, which is acceptable in many markets throughout the world without alteration or adaptation.

Other issues surrounding branding are beyond the scope of this chapter and, indeed, this book but some are returned to in Chapter 13. Brand strategy (in terms of monolithic, family and umbrella branding), brand extensions (in terms of resource saving and IMC) and co-branding (in terms of relationship marketing and collaborating partners such as Visa and bankers such as HSBC and others) are important and should be pursued outside of this text.

Advertising, brand image and objectives

Today, the primary role of advertising is to help build brands. In the old days shopkeepers knew their customers personally. Then, they saw them on a daily basis, but now this relationship has to be simulated. One way of achieving this is to use branding. If the object is to bring product/company and customer together in a relationship of trust, commitment and perhaps even loyalty, this poses real difficulties/dilemmas for the use of certain tools. For example, the use of sales promotion might be seen as some form of bribery but if used more subtly can be a real relationship management tool in order to keep customers, for instance the loyalty bonus card. In order to achieve this, objectives have to be clear.

In essence advertising objectives can be viewed in the same two ways as outlined generally in Chapter 4. First, objectives can be viewed in a hierarchical form, from mission down to marketing communications and then advertising. Second, they should be viewed as being SMART. Remember the role of objective-setting is to constrain strategy and help eliminate the large number of strategic options. The MBO approach includes the idea that objectives give direction, are a means to performance measurement and are consistent with time management. In advertising terms, the DAGMAR model discussed in Chapter 4 looks to measure the results of a specific advertising task in terms of the hierarchical 'think–do–feel' cognitive/affective/behavioural system for a defined audience. There is therefore an attempt to measure the degree of change in a given period of time as one moves through the hierarchy. The example given in Chapter 4 can apply here, i.e. advertising can be used to make 70 per cent of the target audience aware of the new product and to achieve a 50 per cent understanding of the proposition, with 40 per cent convinced, but with the expectation when it comes to it that only 20 per cent will purchase in the first period.

Advertising is therefore used to build brand awareness but also to provide information if necessary. Brand image and identity cannot be built and sustained without some form of advertising. In the previous chapter the management model used placed objectives and direction clearly at the start of the communications' management process. Advertising objectives are no different in this regard, as advocated earlier. Advertising objectives should be debated by all those with influence during a campaign. This requires that the objectives behind the campaign be explicit rather than implicit, since without this kind of precision a vacuum is likely to be filled with ambiguous creative media outcomes. Most writers around his subject would therefore advocate SMART to avoid any vagueness and to provide a framework whereby objectives can be measured. Perceptions, attitudes, predisposition and so on need some form of measurement otherwise they are of little use in terms of communications and in particular advertising effects.

As alluded to in Chapter 4, Schultz and Kitchen (2000) go further and move away from mere communication effects towards ROCI. Key to this concept is that of incremental returns in terms of calculating ROCI. This especially applies in the advertising context where activity-based costing (ABC) and economic value assessment (EVA) view advertising as investment not cost.

Brand image and trust

By creating satisfaction and attempting to gain loyalty the marketer enters into a binding contract in the marketplace. This is achieved through being courteous, accessible and responsive, and so produces an affinity with and liking by the customer of the brand owner. The intensity of the relationship that then follows will affect the degree of loyalty. For Duncan (2002), this is about expectations, and provides a scale from awareness through to identity, being connected, continuity and, finally, advocacy, that a consumer might move up or down. Duncan reminds us we should not forget the negative, i.e. if a consumer is disappointed, then not only is he or she not an advocate for the brand, but also may very well be a vocal disparager of it. Total brand loyalty[3] is, these days, an unrealistic prospect but this does not negate branding. Indeed, this is far from the case with estimates hovering around some form of the Pareto principle of 80/20.[4] In some instances brands can be worth a considerable percentage of the worth of the parent, and Philip Morris is said to have paid six times the value of the company's assets when it acquired Kraft (Duncan, 2002). Brand awareness, association, perceived quality, proprietary assets such as trademarks and, to an extent, loyalty can all be measured in some way, leading to brand equity. While the customer/consumer gets the benefit of less risk, easier decision-making and so on the company benefits from, for example, reduced costs and increased sales and revenue since it costs less to sell to loyal customers who are probably heavier users.

As suggested in Chapter 2 there is interest in relationship quality that stems from trust. There is a high degree of certainty of predictable and obligatory behaviour that leads to sales and gives the seller integrity and the process a high degree of certainty (Crosby, Evans and Cowles, 1990). The Morgan and Hunt (1994) trust/commitment loyalty schema promotes the idea that this is essential for successful relationship marketing. The brand inspires the same degree of relationship quality that is usual in human relationships, but this is investment that carries with it some degree of risk that consumers will cease to co-operate and cease resisting attractive alternatives. The marriage analogy mentioned in Chapter 2 can help in conceptualizing how consumers might choose brands, as are the ways in which people choose friends based on personality. The resultant loyalty to brands is rather more than the simplistic notion of repeat purchase over time. There is a much more complex notion of brand loyalty, involving frequency of usage, share of portfolio and attitudinal loyalty. In other words brand loyalty is commitment. Rather than a formula of trust + commitment = loyalty, there is a holistic process where trust, commitment and loyalty become one and the same. What has been suggested is a modification of an existing model that will then reflect key areas of the consumer–brand relationship.

Trust in reliance is the key variable within the consumer/brand relationship but this is shaped by:

- opportunistic behaviour (a negative influence on the relationship since it is deceit-orientated)

- consumers' predetermined set (recognition that consumers can be influenced by factors not necessarily within their direct control, i.e. parental influence and life stage)

- communications (formal and informal sharing of meaningful and timely information).

Commitment exists when the consumer believes that an ongoing relationship with the brand (from a repertoire) is so important that they wish to maintain it through maximum effort and believe that buying the brand will result in a positive outcome. Commitment can be deemed to be attitudinal and is influenced by:

- shared values (extent to which both the consumer and the brand have common behaviours, personalities, goals, functions, ideals, representations, attitudes and policies)

- relationship benefits (brand should consistently satisfy the consumer both in its functionality and the way in which it represents the consumer to others)

- relationship termination costs (expected loss suffered, both financial and emotional).

It is posited that trust and commitment reinforce one another within this process towards loyalty. If this bond weakens then, naturally, loyalty will weaken. It has also been suggested that where consumers trust in, and are loyal to, a repertoire of substitutable brands this is largely dependent on perceived involvement. Naturally, where involvement in a product category, or the brand itself, is high the costs and benefits are high and the consumer may give more thought to the other variables.

The components of brand or corporate image are seen by many as being both rational and emotional, as explored further in Chapter 6, which is fundamental to the notion of what a brand or organization really is in any given situation. Bhat and Reddy (1998) use the terms functional and symbolic in respect of brand or corporate positioning where a brand can be both, or one or the other. The symbolic offers either (or both) prestige and self-expression. The functional meets immediate practical needs. The Research Business have developed, for example, their Brand Works brand facet model which, when applied to a particular brand, would yield a mix of facets. Taking Toshiba as an example, this corporate brand apparently has saliency (emotional closeness/distance of consumer to brand) and its corporate brand personality (personification of the organization that demonstrates how the corporate brand's core emotional character has been projected to the consumer). Whatever facets there are to a particular brand, it seems likely that trust plays a vital part in the process that leads from consumers' perceptions and experiences of a brand to brand loyalty. Trust, pragmatically, is seen as a powerful marketing weapon in the armoury and is something that can be lost and won (Bainbridge 1997) and something for both parties to win with. There can be a win-win mutual benefit bargaining rather than the win-lose adversarial bargaining where consumers expect information and to be taken seriously otherwise the relationship will be damaged (Fletcher and Peters, 1997). Trust in this light becomes an important brand attribute making major fmcg brands more powerful than the Church (according to the Henley Centre's 'planning for social change 1998' report). Marks and Spencer have trust and this enables them and others, such as Virgin, to extend into hitherto unknown (to them) areas but where consumers welcome brand extension under certain conditions. Marks and Spencer, Tesco, etc. in this sense have become choice editors, manufacturers in their own right (own label) and service providers. They know, however, that trust can be just as easily lost as won and is best kept by a philosophy that runs across the whole organization, not just within the marketing department.

Mission, vision and international brands

The importance of corporate mission and vision which deal respectively with 'what you are doing' and 'where and what you want to be doing' as an organization, at some time in the future, cannot be overlooked. Mission should be viewed as a strategic discipline, part of the intellect of the organization, the cultural glue that binds the organization's often disparate elements – in essence the soul of the organization and the reason for being (see Chapter 13). This plays an important role in brand development and can contribute toward *competitive strategy and comparative advantage*. International and global branding and advertising will be addressed in Chapter 20 but it is worth briefly addressing this issue here. This clearly involves some discussion on the benefits of advertising, including the encouragement of competition, economies of scale, product development, stimulation of economic growth, improved products due to competition among brands, lower prices and greater variety. Conventional wisdom seems to say that no amount of advertising, however good, will enable a poor product to succeed. However, besides being used to communicate the benefits and availability of a product, it can explain how a product may be used to best advantage.

VIGNETTE

After Eight – Et ne dites pas, 'ils sont fous ces Anglais', pas avant d'avoir goute des After Eight

This was the final text in the first commercial which introduced After Eight to the French marketplace in 1971. Prejudices were overcome and new habits introduced. The After Eight concept was seen as sacrilege by the French and as nothing at all by the Germans, who knew nothing of after dinner gatherings/habits of the English, or the Italians, who were not accustomed to mint and chocolate mixed and were not used to buying big boxes of chocolates let alone holding English-style dinner parties.

The name came from inspiration rather than anything else. A Rowntree (brand owners until Nestlé bought the Rowntree MacIntosh brands in the mid-1990s) executive heard of a shirt in America called 'After Six' and thought 'Why not After Eight?'

Packaging was designed to be upmarket to reflect special occasions which would communicate both verbally and pictorially via a trademark, i.e. a Louis XIV ormolu clock (moulded, embossed, gilded bronze) showing the time as a few minutes after eight o'clock against a distinctive green background. The product itself was individually wrapped in brown glassine envelopes also bearing the trademark.

The brand was perceived as uniquely presented to be enjoyed after dinner or on comparable occasions and associated with elegance, sophistication, social status of the hostess and guests, i.e. reflecting good taste of the giver, flattering the receiver but affordable. All of this is meant to evoke the dinner party – the candelabra, the crystal brandy glasses, black ties and cigars, the old English country house, butlers, chauffeurs, Rolls Royces, etc. In other words this is highly aspirational.

With the advertising, the tone of voice, choice of cast and selected scenarios had to reflect the above evocations. Testing began in 1962 in Scotland then 'Dinner Table' was put on air in 1964 on Yorkshire TV – resulting in 64 per cent sales increase compared with 18 per cent in other parts of the country. Thus the brand acquired its one and only personality.

Regarding international marketing, the key and obvious question was 'would the brand's added value apply in other markets. JWT had handled the UK account but Lintas were given the account for Germany, the Netherlands, Italy and France. The UK commercials were not simply dubbed to save money. The decision was made to keep the 'Englishness' of the brand but to create quality advertising in each of the chosen markets to make sure no brand image damage occurred. The English dinner party was a problem so adaptations had to be made:

- *Germany* – a high society soirée was invented where the entire concept was highlighted using a butler but emphasizing they were made in Germany. Launched via glossy magazines in 1966, After Eight was a major brand by 1969.

- *The Netherlands/Italy* – launched in 1969 basically as in Germany with minor adaptations.

- *France* – in France confectionery products were not associated with social activity, English food was not taken seriously and peppermint in chocolate was unheard of. Through qualitative research the company made the decision to keep the concept, including the Englishness, which was dealt with purely through advertising: (voice over) 'The English have always had a certain way of life – a sense of refinement if you like . . . Here is a new fashion from London for after dinner – After Eight. Fine leaves of chocolate filled with melting mint. Yes, you heard – mint and chocolate. And don't say, 'they are mad, these English', before having tasted After Eight.'

Sources: Adapted from After Sex Mints (2002); After Eights – Jungle Dinner Party (2002); Parker (2000); Rijkens (1992); http://www.dooyoo.co.uk/tv/misc_tv/after accessed December 2002; http://www.nestle.com.search/search_home.asp, accessed October 2002; http://www.greenpeace.org./pressrelease/geneng/1999nov3.html, accessed April 2002; http://www.nestle.com.in_your_life/iyl-home.html, accessed October 2002; http://www.oneworld.org./ni/issue275/boycott.html, accessed April 2002.

STOP POINT

There is some speculation as to what, these days, constitutes a special occasion and some suspicion of 'crusty lords and bejewelled hostesses'. Does the modern woman have a different set of values in a different lifestyle? Does the After Eight concept need revamping without repositioning? Whatever happens, the company, even though part of Nestlé, will stick to the Rowntree MacIntosh principles and guidelines as laid down in 1985 in terms of product, position and advertising. Or will it? The answer, up until the time of writing, seemingly is yes, but while the dinner party concept has been retained, new advertising injects humour into the situation to target a slightly younger audience. The packaging has changed, away from its dark green and gold box, so it appears to be a makeover rather than a change in direction. In terms of international brand configuration, consider the positive and negative effects on Nestlé brands from the marketing environments and its own behaviour. Outline what you see as plus points in Nestlé brand stewardship. Nestlé clearly wish to protect the brand against ambush, as can be seen by their unsuccessful bid to stop the brand 'After Sex Mints' being registered in the UK. It was found that the word 'sex' would be unlikely to be heard as 'eight'. And, after all, the brand name After Eight was derived, allegedly, from a brand called After Six, albeit for a shirt!

Advertising practice

Practitioners' views on advertising

Historically, at least three strains of thought have established themselves as cornerstones of what advertising is or should be. Central to this, apparently, is the search for the 'big idea', for example a strap line with endurance and longevity such as Nike's 'Just do it'.

First the *USP* was a concept developed by Rosser Reeves (1961) of the Ted Bates agency. He suggested there are three characteristics of a USP:

1 Each advertisement must make a unique proposition to the consumer rather than simply words or product puffery or window dressing. Each advertisement must provide a tangible benefit to the consumer so that they can say 'If I buy this product I will get this benefit'.

2 The proposition must be one that the competition either cannot or does not offer. It must be unique either in the brand or in the claim.

3 The proposition must be strong enough to move people. That is, pull over new customers to your brand, either through taking market share from competitors or expanding the size of the market or both.

Reeves felt the attribute, claim or benefit that forms the basis of the USP should dominate the advertisement and other communications and be emphasized through repetition. For example Volvo, originally at least, meant safety. However, for this approach to work there must be a truly unique attribute or benefit. The position must give them a sustainable competitive advantage, i.e. one that cannot be copied easily. This, of course, is based on the premise that the consumer thinks rationally and the advertising must also operate in a rational way. Something as mundane as a soap powder or surface cleaner can be given a USP, for example speed, which has concrete benefits to the consumer (time saving, not hard, boring work, etc.). The advertising's task is then to get this benefit across and it may simply use a colour change to demonstrate the speed of the brand's action. However, a USP may be achieved by other means. A change in product form (from powder to liquid) or packaging (a new way to get the product out of the container) can be the basis of the USP. It is also the case that the USP will not work on certain products where emotion is involved. This can occur in the seemingly rational world of industrial marketing where prestige of supply is involved. One thing that can be said, for a while at least, is that the USP worked for Ted Bates as an agency, where the USP for the agency's services was the USP.

The *brand image* is almost the opposite of the USP and appears to work in many product/service categories where competing brands are very similar and the USP may be difficult to implement or there may not be a USP. Brand image was championed by David Ogilvy, founder of Ogilvy, Benson and Mather and often referred to as 'the Pope of the profession'. Ogilvy advocated that advertising's task was to develop a strong, memorable identity for a brand through 'image advertising' where an image is developed that will appeal to product users. Thus Ogilvy, contra Reeves, comes down largely on the side of emotion rather than reason, but not exclusively so. Ogilvy was interested in brands and personality, seeing the job of advertisers being to match a brand's personality to that of the target. There was a need to give the brand a 'first class ticket through life' and the consumer a 'first class ticket to product quality'. To achieve this, the brand must first be given a personality. If a brand is a product with clothes on, then personality is what it wears. This is a set of associations, favourable connotations or positive psychological overtones, or what Ogilvy (1983) called chemistry rather than the literal product. Put the same whisky in two milk bottles and blind test them. The drinker will think the drinks are quite different if they are told they are, even though it is the same whisky. They are in fact 'tasting images'.

Practitioners' attitude toward their creative task

In practice, the rational and emotional approaches are often used in conjunction to form creative strategy (see Chapter 6) and as Ogilvy rightly said, there is not necessarily a conflict between image and fact. This was not lost on John Hegerty, of Bogle, Bartle and Hegerty when creating the magazine advertising for the super premium ice cream brand, Haagen Dazs. Here double-page spreads were used with imagery on the right-hand page (emotional, sexual and sensual) and factual information on the left (rational, quality of ingredients, etc.). The *positioning* attitude towards advertising favoured by many, including Reis and Trout who championed this in the 1970s, has become a popular basis of creative development. The basic idea is that communications activity is used to 'position' the product or service in a particular place in the consumers' minds. Positioning can be on the basis of the brand in relation to the competition, product attributes, price, quality and so on. A brand can be positioned on rational or emotional bases, or both.

Most advertising practitioners have some form of system as to how advertising should work. This helps to resolve the potential conflict between communication planning, effectiveness and creativity. The idea that creativity can be planned or harnessed in some way may not sit quite right with some people, but this is what advertising practitioners have to try to achieve. They, along with brand and marketing managers, are responsible for the message (what is said), the media (how the message will be carried) and the timing (or manner in which the message will be carried), among other things. This might be called creative planning, since it deals with strategy, execution and production.

According to the agency D'Arcy, Masius Benton and Bowles, the position must first be clear and the target must be able to see what the product is for and why they should be interested in it. Benefit(s) should also be clear and compelling. Uniqueness on it own is not enough. This means the offering should be 'describable in a simple word, phrase, or sentence without reference to any final execution', and 'be likely to attract the prospect's attention'. There should be a clinching benefit and the advertising should allow branding through which the prospect can vividly experience the product or service. In this agency's opinion, brand personality gives the product an extra edge where 'all brands do something, but the great brands also are something'. D'Arcy also proclaim that agencies 'must dare to be different' where the agency itself must 'stand out' and 'not emulate but annihilate' the competition. The big idea, an Ogilvyism, is also advocated by this agency, where the advertising must be single-minded, and 'should be all about that one big thing'. This may be emotion rather than reason. A 'tear, a smile, a laugh . . . an emotional stimulus' that the viewer will want to see 'again and again'. However, the advertising should also be 'visually arresting . . . compelling, riveting, a nourishing feast for the eyes'. Finally D'Arcy advocate 'painstaking craftsmanship . . . go for the absolute best in concept, design and execution'.

VIGNETTE

Gordon's Gin . . . of all the gin joints, in all the towns, in all the world

Gin has a long history stretching back over centuries. Essentially it can be traced back to Holland around 1600. Gin is the juniper-flavoured grain spirit known as 'jenever' and sometimes 'genever' and in Britain 'Hollands' and 'Sciedam', after the town in which many distillers were based (it was first distilled in the town of Leyden). Apart from its role in the film *Casablanca*, gin has quite a reputation and is the likely source of the term 'Dutch courage'. The notorious drinker-comedy actor W. C. Fields apparently once said, 'I never drink anything stronger than gin before breakfast'. It is probably gin's reputation first as a medicinal cure for kidney woes and then as a means of abortion, followed by the gin palaces of Victorian London that pose downside problems generically if not at the brand level.

Gordon's (a London 'dry gin') is sold worldwide by United Distillers. It is a primary gin brand within the growing white spirits market, but gin as a category has been in decline and this has affected Gordon's – although still the world leader selling primarily in the UK, USA, Spain and South Africa where it is produced in each and collectively these represent 90 per cent of world volume. In the USA it is third to Seagram's and Tanqueray and in Spain it faces stiff competition from Larios (a Gordon's 'me too' originally). In South Africa it is strong but does have a rival in Mainstay. In Germany, France and Italy it is brand leader but these are small markets. Duty free sales are increasing with UK, Germany and USA sales accounting for almost half.

Gordon's has a global reputation. It has heritage and credibility with consumers and the trade but its market position varies from culture to culture and the stage in the life cycle and, of course, competition. In the USA and Spain Gordon's has a lower image linked with a lower price and, therefore, is price sensitive in these markets. In contrast, Gordon's is viewed as rather upmarket in the UK, a mature market where the brand has a premium price.

Gordon's is now up against brands such as Absolut vodka which are highly prestigious. Young adults seek prestige brands and there is a trend towards 'easy to take' spirits, greater health consciousness, greater fashionability of vodka, tequila and white rum, greater use of wine/champagne and a slow decline of formerly high-flying brands such as Martini. Martini is still perceived as having quality, strength and mellowness. These seem important variables for brand acceptance. Gordon's is seen as adequate, acceptable and everyday in some markets and up against Beefeaters, Tanqueray and Bombay directly. In others gin has high status, is fashionable, youthful and fun when used as a mixer but is seen as masculine, older, quiet, contemplative and relaxed when drunk neat. Gordon's as an English brand is associated with high status. For many, then, the image is high quality, a premium brand that is aspirational, luxury, stylish and modern, associated with the British elite, masculine, independently minded people as well as being fun, sociable, friendly, sexy and frivolous. Other factors are the clarity of the liquid, freshness, coolness and bubbly (with tonic) and associated with tonic, i.e. G&T. Generally, research has shown that gin appears to be associated with things like maturity, responsibility, success, sophistication. In other words some form of differentiation for Gordon's from, for example vodka, could therefore be achieved.

Sources: Adapted from Hankinson and Cowking (1993); http://www.behind-bars.net/gin.html, accessed April 2002; http://www.beveragebusiness.com/art-arch/07lewis.html, accessed April 2002; http://www.cigaraficionado.com/Cigar/Aficioado/drinks/spirits/MW0796a.html, accessed April 2002.

STOP POINT

If Gordon's were looking for distinct target groups out of this, what would you advise? Think about what would appeal to the young, mid-twenties, male and female, slightly upmarket target, seeking sophistication and fun. What of the older, value for money seekers who are not particularly brand loyal, who are male or female middle income conservatives who reject the 'yuppie' image but like G&Ts? Then there are the Gordon's loyalists of any age who value the brand and derive status and prestige from it and who conform to the rituals of their lifestyles, looking for sophistication, tradition and heritage.

Assignment

Choose a city – Milan, Glasgow, Kuala Lumpur, London, Newcastle, Athens – and apply the branding framework that would help reshape its image. Make a list of the things that would allow you to effectively brand the city. For example, is the city environmental/'green', or is there some other part of the marketing environment that allows you to use the city's attributes. Follow this through with basic ideas on the role of advertising in the promotion of the city. Devise some form of symbolism and slogan that would be appropriate to the new brand.

Summary of Key Points

- Advertising can be seen as a positive or negative force in society. On balance it is probably seen by most as positive.

- Advertising is seen by many as art not science, where the transfer of pure meaning is difficult if not impossible.

- Different objectives drive different communications and the difference between elements of the communication mix is reflected in the objectives, which should always be SMART. A fundamental difference between advertising and publicity is degree of control.

- Measurement of communications (especially advertising) effects has been replaced by ROCI, but it is still fruitful to apply the basic communications process to advertising.

- The context of advertising is important. Advertising has different roles in different contexts and is more important in some rather than others.

- Advertising can emphasize brand values and explain what the brand proposition is.

- Branding appears to be here to stay. Core, tangible and intangible attributes make the brand and create brand equity.

- Brand loyalty is something of a myth but trust and commitment and perhaps loyalty are worth striving for.

- There is a link between mission, vision and branding. There is an intimate link between branding and culture.

- Practitioner views as to how advertising and branding work are important and influential. The USP and brand image stances have produced a rational versus emotional myth. Positioning has been prevalent for over three decades.

Examination Questions

1 Discuss the notion that advertising can be said to shape society or merely reflect societal mores.

2 'Advertising is not and could never be a science. At best it is managed art.' Discuss this statement using examples to illustrate why you agree or disagree.

3 Explain the characteristics that distinguish advertising from other elements of the marketing communications mix. In particular highlight the differences between advertising and publicity.

4 Distinguish between business, marketing and advertising objectives by using examples of your choice. Discuss the requirement to be SMART with advertising objectives.

5 'Return on customer investment is more important a measure than the effects of communication on behaviour'. Explain what this means.

6 Explain, using examples to illustrate, why the context of advertising makes advertising more or less important in the communications and marketing mix.

7   Brand values and proposition are fundamental to advertising. Explain the role, if any, advertising might have in this area.

8   Explain what is meant by core, tangible and intangible attributes in relation to brand equity. Explore the relationship between loyalty, trust and commitment for a consumer brand of your choice.

9   Explain the link between mission, vision and branding in the context of a major consumer brand such as Levi.

10 Explain what USP and brand image mean. Provide examples from each and also an example of a brand position.

Notes

1   Lord Leverhulme, founder of Unilever, once famously said something like, 'Half the money I spend on advertising is a waste. The problem is I don't know which half'.

2   It is interesting to note that there may well be exceptions to the tried and tested model of branding. Where fashion comes into it, it may well be that designers such as Jean Paul Gautier or Donna Koran may be at the core, and the physical product does not matter. Some believe that designers of this stature could put their name on almost anything, and it would be the name that counted.

3   This may only exist with the less fickle Bon Jovi or Rolling Stones rock band follower or Newcastle United or AC Milan football fan.

4   That is, 80 per cent of something provides 20 per cent of something else. In this case 80 per cent of turnover might be produced by a brand that represents just 20 per cent of a company's products while the remaining 80 per cent of products only produce 20 per cent of turnover.

References

After Eights – Jungle Dinner Party (2002). At http://www.dooyoo.co.uk/tv/misc_tv/after, accessed December.

After Sex Mints (2002). (Trade mark case.) At http://www.patent.gov.uk/tm/legal/smarries/2002.

Bainbridge, J. (1997). Who wins the national trust? *Marketing*, 23 October, 22–23.

Bernstein, D. (1984). *Company Image and Reality*. Cassell.

Bhat, S. and Reddy, S. K. (1998). Symbolic and functional positioning of brands. *Journal of Consumer Marketing*, **15** (1), 32–43.

BMW (2002). How are BMWs advertised and promoted in the UK. At http://www.bized.ac.uk/Admin/info/old2bmw/bmw13.htm.

Crosby, L., Evans, K. and Cowles, D. (1990). Relationship quality in services selling: an interpersonal influence perspective. *Journal of Marketing*, **54**, 68–80.

Crosier, K. (1999). Advertising. In *Marketing Communications* (P. J. Kitchen, ed.), pp. 264–288, Thomson International.

Duncan, T. (2002). *Integrated Marketing Communications*. McGraw Hill.

Fletcher, K. P. and Peters, L. D. (1997). Trust and direct marketing environments: a consumer perspective. *Journal of Marketing Management*, **13**, 523–539.

Fratzen, G. (1994). *Advertising Effectiveness: Findings from Empirical Research*. NTC Publications.

Hankinson, G. and Cowking, P. (1993). *Branding in Action*. McGraw Hill.

IDM (1997). *The Launch of the Latest BMW . . . and It's Not a Car (1997/8)*. IDM.

Institute of Practitioners in Advertising (IPA) (1995). *The Advertising Effectiveness Awards*. Notes and video. IPA.

McDonald, C. (1992). *How Advertising Works: A Review of Current Thinking*. NTC Publications.

Morgan, R. and Hunt, S. (1994). The commitment-trust theory of relationship marketing. *Journal of Marketing*, **58**. July, 20–38.

Ogilvy, D. (1983). *Ogilvy on Advertising*. Pan.

Packard, V. (1957). *The Hidden Persuaders*. David McKay Co.

Parker, P. (2000). After Eight. At http://www.tuesdayonline.freeserve.co.uk/food/after8.html.

Reeves, R. (1961). *Reality in Advertising*. Alfred Knopf.

Rijkens, R. (1992). *European Advertising Strategies*. Cassell.

Rothschild, M. L. (1987). *Marketing Communications*. Heath.

Schultz, D. E. and Kitchen, P. J. (2000). *Communicating Globally*. Macmillan.

6

Creative strategy and the role of semiotics

Chapter overview

Introduction to this chapter

Creative strategy is a key stage in the communications planning process, and should determine what action is required from the audience, what the messages should say or communicate and what the 'big idea', alluded to in the previous chapter, is if it exists at all. Creative tactics need to be executed and this usually involves media considerations as well as the actual design of an advertisement, a piece of packaging or a press release and so on. The use of semiotics by marketers is on the increase, and this is particularly relevant to the creative side of things. Semiotic analysis looks in from the outside (outside in), as opposed to the more traditional approaches that try to get inside the person and get at their perceptions and so on (inside out). As such, semiotics as an analytical marketing tool has huge potential.

Aims of this chapter

This chapter seeks to explore the nature of creativity in relation to communication. More specifically it aims to:

- discuss creative strategy and explain the nature and role of the creative brief

- highlight the commonest creative appeals available to marketers

- discuss the execution and evaluation of creative ideas

- explain the basic nature of semiotics and how marketers can use this as an aid to creative strategy development.

The importance of creativity in marketing communications

The nature of creativity

Creativity is an important factor in our overcommunicated society, especially when developing a position to differentiate products/services. Just because a promotion or an advertisement is creative or popular does not mean it will achieve the objectives set. Communication should be effective and not necessarily creative in this sense. Creativity is about finding new and appropriate ideas or directions in order that communications problems can be solved. There may be tension between effectiveness and creativity. Schultz and Kitchen (2000) provide the idea of 'creative templates', where there are four drivers of creativity in communication. These are the consumer, the competition, the environment and the product/brand. Generating ideas through some form of research in these areas has been commonplace for many years. Everything is capable of receiving creative treatment. There may be a 'way of doing things' in certain contexts where the same creative ideas cannot be done in other contexts. This is usually for cultural reasons of one sort or another. It may be culture in the sense of religion or language so that certain words or representations (for example through the use of nudity or sexual images) prohibit the transference of a creative idea from one context to another. For example, it may be difficult, if not impossible, to transfer an idea generated in a consumer context and transfer this to an industrial one, i.e. humour, sex, fantasy and so on might never be used in the context of communicating the benefits of certain medical products like urological catheters. Similarly it is unlikely that facts, figures and logic would be used in the context of tobacco products. Some might say that in many instances it is the personality of the brand and not logic that is important.

In short, despite a certain creative approach being successful, it cannot always be reused. However, Schultz and Kitchen (2000) emphasize the notion of patterns or templates that can help screen out unproductive ideas and help establish productive creative ideas. Six 'creativity templates' were derived from research involving a sample of 200 advertisements. Rather than deriving a creative approach from more research, the use of these templates can help the creative function to replace, for example, the cultural driver in one marketplace with another for a different context. In this way symbols can be changed and extended to existing and new products.

Creative planning

The message is what is to be said through media of one sort or another in a particular manner at particular times. It may appear a contradiction in terms to talk about 'creative planning' since one might assume that to be creative one must be free to do as one pleases. This is not the case at all. Creativity has to be harnessed and managed. The communication has to position the product, company or brand for the target audience so that they know what it stands for, what it is for, whom it is for and why they should be interested in it. Then creative work can begin to show, for example, benefits or the 'big idea'. There should be a development of a dynamic, creative communications concept that uses all tools and techniques including brand personality (as discussed in Chapter 5), doing something different and even outstanding. Perhaps this means providing something that is visually or aurally arresting that becomes compelling viewing or listening.

Creative strategy development

Creative strategy is based on several factors. First, the identification of the target market must be made. Second, the basic problem, issue or opportunity the communication must address has to be identified. Third, the major selling idea or key benefit needs to be communicated. Finally, any supportive information that is required should be included. Once these factors are determined a creative strategy statement should describe the message appeal and execution style. This will necessarily include *copy platform* or *creative brief*, i.e. the platform for creative strategy in the form of a document that underpins the rationale behind the message, the creative concept and execution. This written document thus specifies the basic elements of the creative strategy including the basic problem or issue, communications objectives, target audience(s), major selling idea or key benefits, a creative strategy statement and supporting details, encapsulating all important points. The '*big idea*' will either be rational (a USP) or emotional (brand image) or a mixture of both. Creative ideas can be arrived at by a variety of means from the use of free association and juxtaposition of ideas to form new ideas to convergent, divergent and lateral thinking in the search for new ideas. Brainstorming sessions, usually run in a focus group way by a trained interviewer or psychologist, are another form of free association that can be used as a vehicle for arriving at new, creative approaches. These kinds of techniques allow marketing people to produce 'rough roughs', crude but effective drawings or computer-generated visuals but also scripts and/or storyboards and so on that help improve the communication process between company/organization and agency/communications company. In many instances it is the creatives who develop such techniques. For example, Catling and Davies (2002) report on the briefing given by Cadbury Schweppes to consider new toppings for ice cream. They proceeded by inviting lots of the eventual target (children) to try the products out and listened to their views on what was 'ugh and what was yum' in order to get a new perspective on the product. In this way ideas can emerge from a process of generation to selection/discarding and verification of final idea(s). The 'big idea' is discussed below in terms of appeals. The creative sequence becomes:

Strategy → Briefing → Output

The contents of the brief should be just that – brief. This document should be a short account of why the campaign is necessary, its objectives, the target(s), the main idea, the tone of voice, expected reactions of the target(s) and any production, traffic or media requirements. This latter point might include ideas on 'triggers' (words or other useful devices), facts and so on. The brief should not be too prescriptive as this would constrain too much the people who have to work on it.

Communication appeals and execution

Having developed a creative strategy that clarifies *what* the communications should say, marketers and their agents need to decide how this message can be executed. An appeal refers to the approach used to attract the attention of consumers and/or to influence their feelings towards a product, service or cause. The creative execution style refers to the way a particular appeal is turned into a message that can be presented to the consumer.

Creative strategy should strive to achieve successful communication. A number of approaches can be taken either individually or in conjunction with others: *using the product/brand* to explain and compare vis-à-vis the nature of the proposition, the competition and so on. Thus, for example, a visual technique or some form of demonstration may be used to make clear and simple what otherwise would be a complicated proposition. The use of visuals to show liquid flowing into an engine (oil), a body (a heartburn remedy) or a washing machine (a liquid detergent) are commonplace illustrations. Direct comparisons with other, competitive brands are commonplace in the USA but less so in Europe. However, even in Europe, increasingly 'knocking copy' is being used to show a brand in comparison with a competitor. Comparison comes in other forms such as a 'challenge' or direct price comparisons, for example Tesco versus Sainsbury rather than Tesco simply declaring low or lower prices. A before/after demonstration such as that for Head and Shoulders anti-dandruff shampoo or 'torture tests' using extreme examples to prove a product feature, such as strength, are common. Very strong glue shown to be able to hold the weight of a man or machine is one example. Also the brand or product may be portrayed as a hero, where it is the star and is given an identity and personality as with, for example, Mr Muscle. *Using people* is common in communication. This can be either direct or indirect in its approach. The former uses a medium on a one-to-one basis, with someone talking directly to the audience. The presenter may be a celebrity, an unknown, an animated character or a puppet. An example of the use of this is a selling situation or in advertising that uses a presenter where a testimonial is employed, usually underscoring a feature such as safety. The indirect approach involves things like enacting a story as with the many slice-of-life soap operas such as the Oxo family or the Nescafé couple. The use of *brand properties* should result in identification with the brand, the difficulty being having the brand remembered and not merely the creative treatment such as a humorous sketch or the actor/comedian him/herself.

Types of appeal

There are many types of appeal that can be ued by the marketer, but not every appeal is suitable for every occasion. Animation can make a brand come to life and a cartoon character can symbolize a brand or organization. Kelloggs Frosties' 'Tony the Tiger' is typical of this treatment and there are many others such as the Jolly Green Giant (canned sweet corn). Others include humour, shock and other devices that play on the emotions. At the broadest level, appeals are broken down into two categories – rational/informational and emotional. Involvement plays a vital role here where generally speaking the higher the involvement the more likely the appeal will be rational, using product characteristics and subsequent benefits and information. Where low involvement is prevalent, emotional and image-based appeals are likely to work especially where there is hedonic consumer behaviour on display.

Emotional appeals are often referred to as 'soft sell' and include many techniques such as fear, humour, sex, music, fantasy and surrealism. These can be used to play on personal states such as safety and love or on social states such as status or rejection. Marketers use emotional appeals to produce positive feelings that evoke a favourable evaluation of the brand in the mind of the audience. The negative consequences of an action or inaction can be presented in a *'fear appeal'*. For example, a person may be perceived as being someone stranded in a flood-affected house but who has not taken out insurance. Fear can also be used with the threat of social rejection if the product is not used. For example, a deodorant or sanitary protection product can be depicted as a heroic problem-solver – but the communication tells the viewer that if they do not use the brand the implication is that they could be in trouble. Fear appeals need to be used with caution since the recipient of the message will selectively screen out a message that is too strong and that causes cognitive dissonance as with, for example, anti-smoking or drink-driving campaigns. *Humour* is well known for its ability to attract attention and interest. It also creates a favourable and positive mood. However, ironically, the success of humour in doing this can detract from the message/brand, i.e. the humour works but not to the benefit of the brand. The comedian/celebrity used may be remembered and liked but the brand/brand name may be lost and not recalled or recognized. The trick then is to have successful humour that is associated with the brand. *Sex* is good at getting interest, and can be used more subtly or openly if in the guise of sensuality. *Music* of various types can be a psychological cue for gaining attention, enhancing visual images and generally reminding the target that the brand is still out there. *Fantasy and surrealism* is used by, for example, Guinness to stimulate and interest the audience. This is particularly useful where the brand proposition is such an experience. For example, the suggestion is one of a magical experience with Disney.

Rational appeals focus on the consumer's practical, functional or utilitarian need for the product/service. They often emphasize features and benefits and facts. In an informative way the message tries to persuade consumers to buy the brand because it is the best available at meeting their needs. Common rational appeals include comfort, convenience, economy, health, touch, taste, smell, quality, dependability, durability, efficiency, efficacy and performance. Information appeals tend to be very factual where higher levels of involvement mean that information will be processed.

Combining rational and emotional appeals

Of course, many messages will contain both rational and emotional elements. Haagen-Dazs (see Chapter 1) is a classic example where, after specific public relations and sales promotion tools were used, the advertising campaign was launched in the UK using magazines as the main medium. On one side of a double-page spread was a sensual image of near naked couples embracing in erotic clinches but always with the brand in full view. On the other there were facts about the quality of the ingredients use to produce the super premium brand, thus showing that emotion and reason could work well together. This echoed the words of David Ogilvy, who famously said that there should be no conflict between images and facts.

Communication execution

Rational appeals can therefore be presented in a number of ways. They could also be presented as a slice of life where a problem is presented in a factual way together with the solution, usually the brand. Demonstration is another means to this end as is comparison with other products or brands. Where appropriate, technical features can be turned into benefits and favourable price can be used as leverage. Other ideas include the announcement of new products, service or extensions in the range, and this can give the audience reassurance of caring, inventiveness, quality, value, reliability and so on. It may be that a simple straight or factual message or a straightforward presentation of information concerning the product/service is appropriate.

Emotional appeals are more likely to be executed through the use of animation, especially with children but increasingly more with adult since the advent of the 'adult cartoon' in television programming and other media forms. Also used are characters or personality symbols that might be represented by actors (Cap'n Bird's Eye) or cartoon characters (Tony the Tiger) and even people in costume (the Honey Monster) and line drawings (Pru from the Prudential). On an emotional level these can create interest, mostly for low-involvement products. Fantasy and surrealism are used in the execution, as with the now famous magazine and poster campaigns for Benson and Hedges cigarettes. Similarly drama, slice of life and demonstration can be used to deliver emotional appeals as well as rational ones.

VIGNETTE

Sex and bopping: Kylie, the girl with the golden bum

Sex sells

Sex sells, as everybody knows. Some argue that it is pressures from the MTV generation that cause the marketing communications industry to liberally use sex as the key appeal, especially in advertising. New and interesting ways of 'talking' to audiences, getting through the clutter, making something stand out from the crowd is the name of the game. One way of doing this is through the use of sex appeal. Certain industries are, more than other industries, affected by this kind of appeal. It is generally considered to be a mistake to use sexual imagery when there is no relationship with the product or brand attributes. This might very well grab attention and so on but would be seen as a poor creative decision since the images would simply overpower the message in the brand offering. The use of sexual imagery, especially the kind that objectifies women, can draw the fury of society upon the marketer. Sometimes, of course, this can work in the sense that a great deal of publicity can be had from entering into this game. The 2002 UK Motor Show held at the National Exhibition Centre (NEC), Birmingham, England, appeared to court this kind of publicity through the use of an image of a women in bra and panties pointing the way to the exhibition venue. A few days after the first poster went up the whole county knew not only that it was Motor Show week, but also where it was being held. This was achieved through the massive coverage the posters received on British television and in newspapers. The debate centred around this question: How can an industry where more than half of its customers and potential customers still carry on, as it has so notoriously in the past with 'lovelies on car bonnets', objectifying women? This was either a case of extreme serendipity or an informed, calculated risk on the part of the motor industry – a campaign carried out to perfection with great timing and aplomb.

Fashion, popular music, television programming and other such arenas

The fashion industry in particular is susceptible to this because of its very nature but so are others that are part of popular culture, with much intertwining of clothes, music, perfume, film and television. According to some marketers and advertisers, there is a necessary new vulgarity that is the key to success, especially in these kinds of industry where graphic sex is commonplace. While worries about AIDS and other sex-related concerns have spawned new pressure groups that contest the use of such imagery in advertising, film, television programmes and so on, these are perhaps not the greatest threat to the successful use of sex to sell. This threat probably comes from the very same source – people and their attitudes toward sexual (and other taboo) imagery. As society changes, so do its mores, norms and values, which differ from society to society anyway, thus providing marketers with problems and dilemmas when crossing borders.

And then there is Kylie

'Pop Princess' Kylie Minogue had a very good year in 2002. The statistics are there for all to see, and even the tough American market apparently succumbed to Kylie's charms. In March 2002 the *Sunday People* was reporting that 'Kylie is the hottest property we've seen in a long time'. Apparently the single 'Can't get you out of my head' topped the dance chart in the USA and the album 'Fever' went straight in at number 3 on the Billboard chart. However, it is her pert bottom, aided and abetted by a pair of golden hot-pants worn in the video for the single 'Spinning around' that did the trick. This was pure, raw sex that helping to sell singles and albums. However, Kylie now has some degree of music credibility. She has been around as a singer (as opposed to her other life as an actor, not least as Charlene in the Australian soap opera *Neighbours*) for fourteen years. She has sold more than 30 million records, has had number one hits across Europe and has so far done very well in America in what for her is a 'second bite of the cherry' having not succeeded in breaking into the American market at the first attempt. Her associations with singers such as Michael Hutchence and Nick Cave have added credibility (although the same might not be said of her association with the Manic Street Preachers). More credibility has come from her performance at the 2000 Sydney Olympics Ceremony and her association with the Nicole Kidman/Ewan McGregor film *Moulin Rouge*. She has also won 'Brit', NME and other awards. The usual mix of promotional devices for a pop artist such as Kylie will no doubt be used in the future. The usual touring, store appearances and, of course, television and video and now web-based activity will occur.

However, while Kylie started off with a squeaky clean girl-next-door image, she finally declared that she wanted to start singing about sex and with this came a new image – so much so that despite being in her thirties, Kylie is successfully taking on much younger competition. As 2002 saw her elevation into Madame Tussauds, Kylie Minogue was seen as being irresistibly cute, sexy, flirtatious, playful, cheeky, loveable . . . but also an artist, showgirl, a songwriter and a powerful performer. Kylie's new range of knickers (actually lingerie, but the tabloids focused on the knickers) was launched in 2003 with the name 'Love Kylie'. However, for some at least, it was undoubtedly the gold lamé hot-pants in the video 'Spinning Around', a device that landed the tabloid and music press label 'SexKylie', that did the trick.

Sources: Adapted from Bletchly (2002); www.freecfm.com/k/kylie/data/mainpage/index.htm, accessed 4 October 2002; www.askmen.com/women/singer_60/63b_kylie_minogue.html, accessed 10 April 2002; www.askmen.com/women/singer_60/63c_kylie_minogue.html, accessed 10 April 2002; www.fmrecords.com.au/news.cfm?NewsId=167, accessed 2000; www.totallykylie.com/TK/Main/main.htm, accessed 31 March 2002; www.hellomagazine.com/profiles/kylieminogue/, accessed 4 April 2002; www.rollingstone.com/artists/bio.asp?oid=3133&cf=3133, accessed 2002.

STOP POINT

Consider the use of sex, nudity, eroticism and other such devices by marketers and others. When considering advertising in particular the argument goes back to the fundamental question asked in Chapter 1, i.e. does advertising shape society's values or merely reflect them?

Is there a difference between marketing communications content and images and that of television programmes, since with the former an attempt is being made to change (purchase behaviour) while with the latter the goal is merely entertainment?

And is the 'writing on the wall' for the use of such techniques as society changes and they are no longer the devices they were to grab and hold attention and get through the clutter of thousands of similar stimuli each day?

Message strategy design considerations

The message style

Linked to appeals is the design of the message. A consideration of the need to provide information or the use of pleasure and enjoyment in consuming the message should be made; thus the emphasis on rational or emotional (as discussed above). The amount and quality of the information that is communicated, and the overall judgement each individual makes about the way a message is communicated has to be considered. Messages might be product orientated and rational, or customer orientated and based on feelings and emotions, or indeed both. As a 'rule of thumb', high-involvement decisions are likely to require an information emphasis – key product attributes and benefits – and low-involvement decision-making requires the message to create images in the mind of the consumer and an emotional response. However, high-involvement decisions, though requiring an information search and so on, might well have an emotional side and there may well be room for an emotional element within the message. Whichever, the more a receiver likes a message the more likely there is to be a positive response to it. *Likeability* then is linked to a favourable attitude or predisposition towards the brand or the organization, which is a desirable state. To achieve this the marketer is likely to choose some form of entertainment, for example humour, in order that the target likes the communication and, hopefully, the brand or organization.

Message pattern

Messages can be designed so as not to cause problems with the audience. *Conclusion-drawing* (as opposed to the audience interpreting what they want) can be considered. This is explicit rather than something implicit and will only work if the issue is complex enough to warrant it, or if the audience education level is relatively low so that they will accept a conclusion. Better educated audiences prefer to draw their own conclusions and less well educated audiences may have to be told what to do, i.e. conclusions need to be drawn for them. The urgency of the situation may make it sensible to draw conclusions but the level of involvement probably overrides most considerations since, if a lot of information-gathering is going on, this negates the idea of conclusion drawing. *One- and two-sided messages* can offer argument for and against a particular benefit or issue. A one-sided message, for example 'Guinness is good for you', 'Foster's, he who thinks Australian drinks Australian' or 'Philips, simply years ahead', will work to reinforce the brand for those who already believe in it, especially in situations where the targets are less well educated. These are messages that present just one argument, in favour of the product or issue. The two-sided message can be used when trying to explain and persuade. The target is likely to be better educated and willing to consider the argument, where the good and bad points of an issue are presented and are more effective when the receiver's initial opinion is opposite to that presented in the message or when scepticism exists. With sound argument, credibility is improved and a more positive perception of the source can occur.

The presentation order

The presentation order of points, issues or benefits is important. The 'primacy effect' uses messages that make the strongest claim first and therefore uses anticlimax. This is the direct opposite of the 'recency effect' where the strongest claim is made last, which uses climax. Generally speaking (although the approach usually depends on degree of involvement), personal communication techniques use the recency effect. This means that a persuasive build-up via argument allows the key selling point to be made at the end. Where fast attention-grabbing is the goal, the use of key points at the start is more appropriate. The decision to place main points at the start or end of the message depends on the audience involvement. A low level of involvement will require an attention-getting message component at the beginning. For high involvement the audience will be interested enough in the information to stay with the message until the end, so building up to the key selling points can be very effective. Television advertising is more likely to involve the primacy effect: personal selling of the recency effect. *Repetition* either within the message or the message as a whole has been proven to work but can be expensive and the danger is one of brand damage if the frequency of the message is too high. Music and jingles in particular have been used successfully within advertising and elsewhere (for example in-store as with B&Q and the song 'Nobody does it better'). Slogans and tag lines/strap lines similarly are used with frequency to work on the memory, often employing mnemonic devices such as rhymes and rhythms.

Source of the message

The importance of source credibility, attractiveness and power was discussed in Chapter 2 and is part of the message strategy. The decision needs to be made about who will be the presenter of the message. For example it might be the organization itself, a spokesperson, the CEO, a celebrity and so on. The key to source credibility is trust, and the audience must believe the source and their motives. The key components to developing credibility/trust are expertise, knowledge, motives, likeability and similarity to consumer. Often corporate or brand names carry a good reputation so these are included as part of the source.

Message integration

Message integration is similar to the integration discussed earlier in Chapter 1 in terms of 'the single voice' or the 'Gestalt', the whole being 'greater than the sum of the parts'. A marketing communications message can be made up of many components: the headline, copy, layout, illustrations or photographs, strap line/tag line, brand/organization logo and so on. Obviously the better these components work together, the more likely it is that effective communication occurs.

Thus the components of any message have to work together. In print headlines (the words in the leading position that are read first and positioned to get attention) have to work with body copy (the detailed text with the key message). Visuals are often used to attract attention or support the headline and copy. They also make the message more interesting to the target. Layout refers to the physical arrangement of the elements. With broadcast media there is usually an audio element. This may be in the form of a voice-over, or a presenter talking to the audience directly or an indirect message carried through, for example, a slice-of-life-type advertisement. Music can work to create positive emotions and mood. This can be associated with a brand and can be used as a background element in store or within an advertisement. Jingles are a variation from more subtle background, mood-creating music and are often used for low involvement type products or services. Jingles can become very much a part of the brand.

Advertorals and infomercials

Another device invented in order to escape message clutter is the *advertoral*, i.e. an advertisement plus an element of editorial. Obviously this would be a longer slot, say, for two minutes on television that would not only advertise the brand but also combine it with a story. For example the viewer may be taken into the world of classical music with facts about the life and works of classical composers. Later in the piece the actual product on offer – a classical music compilation CD set – can be introduced, as can an extra CD at a special price. In this way the viewer is drawn into the message. This technique does bring into question the ethics of the use of such communication. In a similar fashion the *infomercial*, i.e. information plus commercial, has been criticized as a potentially unethical way of doing business. Informercials are usually much longer pieces whereby the viewer is urged to 'pick up the phone' having been introduced to the product by way of demonstration and then urged to buy it, thus moving the viewer from zero information to purchase in a relatively short space of time. Such techniques are linked closely to 'cooling off periods' where refunds, by law, have to be made within a given space of time.

VIGNETTE

Wild Turkey and Jim Beam Bourbon meet the Scottish Islay malts in message strategy design

Bourbon

American Bourbon and Scottish malt whisky have a lot in common, perhaps not in the taste but certainly in the design of brand communication. History and tradition have a lot to do with this. Colonial America and the county's 'only true native bird', the wild turkey, provide a rich tapestry of life to tap into. As part of a web-based promotion the producer of the Bourbon brand *Wild Turkey*, Austin Nichols and Co., uses a collection of regional recipes for preparing wild game, claiming that from the start Wild Turkey has been a traditional accompaniment to wild game. Like many others, Wild Turkey is proclaimed as America's premier bourbon, which is matured slowly in oak barrels and truly 'an American original'. *Jim Beam Bourbon*, which dates back to the late 1700s, has been called 'Kentucky tea' by its own master distiller, Booker Noe. Jacob Beam, a farmer and mill operator aged some corn whiskey in oak barrels that had been charred by fire to produce the distinctive amber coloured liquid. Through the generations Jim Beam has become known as the classic Kentucky bourbon.

Islay malts

Ardbeg is produced in a distillery that can be traced back to 1794. Ardbeg is renowned for its heavy peatiness. It is 'earthy, very peaty, smoky, salty, robust. A bedtime malt'. The *Bunnahabhain* (meaning 'mouth of the river') Distillery was founded in 1827 on Islay. In the early 1920s the distillery was acquired by a large international drinks organization, but since a successful management buyout in 1988 a small but committed team has run it. The Bunnahabhain is a medium, smooth, soft, mellow, light, gold-coloured drink with a hint of peat, as with Islay malts generally. There are five others on Islay – *Black Bottle Whisky* is the Islay blend that reflects the essence of Islay malts

So what have Islay malts and bourbons got in common?

In the whisky/whiskey and bourbon markets, packaging is at least as important as advertising – and some would say is as important as the product itself. Image is a highly relevant factor in customer decision-making. Brand packaging, and message content of television, magazine and other advertising needs to be viewed in the light of this. The tendency toward tartan and heather and other similar pieces of symbolism is tempting but very dangerous when considering brand identity. Developing 'Scottishness' or 'The deep southern roots' of the brand is one thing, but it is how the message is constructed that matters. *Jack Daniel's* has very successfully exploited 'Southern roots' when marketing their product to the UK and other markets. There are many devices involving tradition and other representations of Scotland (if indeed this 'origin effect' is desirable). For example, Scottish kings used the Stone of Scone to swear in their nobles but was forcibly taken by the English in the thirteenth century and placed in Westminster Abbey. The stone was returned to Edinburgh Castle in November 1996 – but legend has it that this stone is merely a replica. The real Stone of Scone, it is said in legend, was hidden on Tara in Ireland in 1292 before the English could get their hands on it. Some might argue on the Isle of Islay that it has associations with sword Excalibur and the stone is the Stone of Destiny that Excalibur was pulled from. Of course, it has not been found on Islay, but the story could be part of Scottish folklore.

Sources: Adapted from www.obfuscate.com/obfuscate/wt/page2.html, accessed 13 January 2003; www.wildturkeybourbon.com, accessed 2003; www.weeklystandard.com/Utilities/printer_preview. asp?idArt... (Matt Labash, accessed 6 May 2002); www.jimbeam.com/jb_web/content/ Heritage/default.asp, accessed 2003; www.blackbottle.com/bb_content.html, accessed 2003; www. blackbottle.com/whiskies/bunnahabhain/bb_content.html, accessed 2003; www. blackbottle.com/ whiskies/ardbeg/bb_content.html, accessed 2003; www.tartans.com/articles/stoneofscone.html, accessed 31 January 2003; www.durham.net/~neilmac/stone.htm, accessed 31 January 2003.

STOP POINT

What role do you think that the 'source' will have in whisky/whiskey or bourbon marketing communications message strategy decisions? Consider the viability of the proposed position using 'Scottishness' or 'Southern roots' as part of the brand. What role, if any, would there be for other elements of the mix such as PR, sales promotions or packaging?

Evaluation of creative strategy/work

Ultimately the responsibility for the creative strategy and implementation/ execution is that of the 'client', i.e. the marketer. Communications companies/ agencies may be used to bring their creative and production expertise, but the management of a brand image position firmly rests with the commissioning organization. Most communications campaigns will involve a certain amount of pre- and post-testing to ensure that a particular type of execution is delivering the objectives of the communication. Only where the creative function is confident that transference of ideas can take place will this be minimized. The creation of an effective message depends on the following: the style, the pattern, the perceived source and the presentation of the message to the target audience. There are also techniques which advertisers can use to try to ensure that their message is perceived and understood.

Projective techniques and their use in brand and communications research

Conventional research can be used in conjunction with other, less common techniques. Once initial ideas have been generated and background research carried out, the researcher can discover the cultural landscape. Projective techniques can be added to the research toolbox to help facilitation and achieve greater depth. The range of research techniques available to researchers is vast but possibly the most common form is the focus group. Projective techniques have gained some credibility through their use by large companies like Guinness. The idea is to fit the product to the message and the message to the product. For example, there is difficulty in terms of the credibility of getting participants to cut up pieces of magazine images in order to get at the personalities of brands such as All Gold and Dairy Box. Similarly, role-playing is a means of exploring ways of segmenting markets and developing brand personalities or the use of clay modelling as an exploratory tool and psychodrawings in terms of innermost properties of a brand.

Projective techniques as research were born out of psychoanalysis and these vary enormously in form but are generally attempts to use the chain of ideas mechanism. They use a projection of the corporate/brand image into something else, for example what a third person might say, think or feel about an idea, object, brand or company. The researcher might ask the respondent to think about, say, Tesco (the multiple) as an object or an animal in order to get at the innermost self and cultural meaning – which is not accessible to the conscious mind. The argument is that if you are a food company then your image can only be interpreted within the parameters of cultural meaning and in this case within the context of the rituals of eating, socializing, etc. Advertising in many cases is in the business of constituting peoples' emotions and can either be dreamt up by practitioners (adman/woman or brand manager) or can be devised after some form of research. This might be a conventional focus group or a projective technique and where those who take part in studies may/may not be representative of a particular target group.

Semiology and semiotics

The outside-in (rather than inside-out) approach that is semiotics, sees the context or culture as the object of study not the consumer (Lawes, 2002). Mostly recognized as the domain of intellectuals and philosophers, semiology in the European tradition and its more precise derivative, semiotic analysis, have been used by academics and to some extent practitioners – sociologists, sociolinguists and the like – have also shown interest. Latterly interest has been shown by marketing academics and to some extent practitioners. Since then various attempts to apply semiotic analysis to marketing communications problems, especially in the area of corporate communications (image and identity), have been made. The obligatory jargon of the semiologist and the consequent irony of the difficulties faced when attempting to apply semiotics to situations involving communication has not helped. Some have, unconvincingly, claimed to construct images through semiotic research. Others use semiotics to deconstruct images in an attempt to show how semiotics works in marketing situations, an approach which is not necessarily helpful in constructing images that meet the needs of the marketing communicator. Lawes (2002) is rather more convincing with a two-stage approach. Stage 1 involves brainstorming and free association coupled with other data – 'cultural evidence' that can be many and varied things from previous advertising, newspaper reports, television or Internet information. An accurate impression of the cultural context in which materials exist can in this way be had. Stage 2 is the analysis stage for which one needs some tools that help thought to be organized in a particular way and can help similarities and differences to be noticed within sectors or categories (see later in the semiotic analysis section).

Semiotic usage is an attempt to get at 'the truth' in a culturally driven and specific context and can help the marketer recognize what the organization is really saying about itself or what it is not saying, or what the competition is saying about itself. It is capable of providing, first, codes of the organization's own and those of others. It can also highlight subtle differences in behaviour that can aid more effective communication. Through semiotics, consumer culture can be monitored and changes detected as with emergent and discontinued codes, personal expression through taste or how consumption interacts with lifestyle.

Opposite to the position of the determinist theories as to how advertising works lies the relativist position where the receiver is no longer a passive receiver of messages but brings in his or her own experiences and culture, even if this response is a silent one. For Brown (1995) semiotics appears to be a relativist philosophical heresy. For some it is perhaps not so black and white. As mentioned in Chapter 2, the advertising industry increasingly uses the work of sociologists, anthropologists, semioticians and other professionals who are expert in particular aspects of qualitative research (Mattelart and Chanan, 1991). Language is used as a model for all forms of cultural discourse and therefore semiologists borrow from the structural linguists (principally de Saussure) of the first half of this century. Language is seen as a whole system of rules governing the selection and combination of different signs out of which meaning is produced. A useful distinction between semiology and semiotics is provided by Beaumont and Crosier (1995), i.e. semiotics has replaced (or provides an alternative to) structuralism as the analytical tool for practical application. Semiology is the real science, the study of the system of signs where a sign is something that has significance within a system of meaning. In the de Saussure mould, the key elements of semiotic analysis are:

- the signifier – the material vehicle, i.e. sounds/images, words/pictures

- the signified – the idea, the mental construct.

Thus the colours gold and purple have particular meaning or connotations. The meanings of signs are not static and do change over time. Marketers need to know this and should be the masters of the language of signs. Cadbury use the colour purple in a Romanesque kind of way to suggest luxury, purple being a royal colour, but this has to have the same meaning over time in order to work. As Lawes (2002) points out, social mores at any given time might dictate what certain things mean. For example, expensive wrapping using the colour gold, etc. might be thought of as constituting luxury. Upmarket, 'luxury' biscuits wrapped in corrugated cardboard might be a way of saying 'I am environmentally friendly'. This has everything to do with lapsed or residual, dominant or emergent codes that are unspoken rules that link signs to meanings. Also, cross-culturally, that which is signified may not be the same in different cultures. Try asking people from different cultures whether they understand the concept of a butler. This can be very difficult if they have not experienced this phenomenon. This kind of dilemma arose for Nestlé with the Rowntree chocolate brand Kit Kat. The brand's strap line had been 'Have a break, have a Kit Kat', based on the British (or even English) notion of a tea break. Nestlé decided to keep the concept of a break (we all need a break from work from time to time) but without the tea break association that does not exists in the many cultural settings to which they wanted to take the brand.

Constructs derive their meaning from their differences from other, related, phenomena rather than their intrinsic characteristics (Brown, 1995). Semiology is therefore understood here in a post-structuralist way – open exploration rather than the positivist, structuralist 'self-delusion' (Beaumont and Crosier, 1995). There is a structured relationship between the signified and signifiers where signs are arbitrary and do not simply correspond to their referents. What they stand for is the real world and we perceive the world through classificatory and combinatory systems which language provides. Reality is therefore relative to how it is constructed or signified by language.[1] Ideology can enter into the process of signification to provide its own imaginary view of reality. This fits Brown's (1995) number 4 cell description of postmodern marketing research rather than number 2, i.e. that of traditional qualitative research. In terms of ontology (nature of being) and epistemology (knowledge) Brown has four cells: traditional marketing research (realist/realist); traditional qualitative research (realist/relativist); interpretivist marketing research (relativist/realist); and postmodern marketing research (relativist/relativist).

The composition of advertisements and the configuration of the corporate/brand identity used in those advertisements and elsewhere are seen as crucial to successful communication. The observer of the image has to bring with him or her knowledge of denoted codes and connoted associations for interpretation of meaning. There is an assumption that the individual psyche, like the image, is structured like a language. Meaning arises from the relation between culture and nature. Advertising and corporate/brand images therefore mean nothing to those people who:

- cannot distinguish between the literal denoted meaning and the associated connoted meaning

- cannot distinguish between loose individual signifying elements of the paradigm and their joining together by the rhetorical rules of the syntagm

- cannot be directed or positioned by arrangement to make ideological meaning from it since such meaning is produced out of the formal arrangement of chaining signifiers which by themselves are polysemic or ambiguous.

For example, an arty advertisement in an upmarket, glossy magazine that uses references to the works of Cezanne to sell crystal glass products would require a certain knowledge of painting. This knowledge may have been gained through simplistic magazine articles, but the reader might be in a position that allows the advertisement to work on that reader. Brand names like Coke and Virgin may bring to mind the idea of soft drinks but also they bring other things to mind, depending not least on whose mind it is. The signifier 'Coke' has many meanings – as in coal, soft drink and cocaine (Brown, 1995). As a student once remarked on the launch of Virgin Cola: 'Oh good,' she said 'That means I'll be able to go into the bar and order a Virgin on ice.' As Brown (1995) succinctly puts it, 'meaning, in short, turns out to be very difficult to tie down'. So for Brown, contra de Saussure, the signified and signifier are not at all like two sides of a coin, but are more like two shifting layers.

Differences in cultural knowledge are crucial and crucial to this knowledge is the acquisition through language of what Sinclair (1987) calls 'gendered subjectivity', that is to say, the observers' identity within the sexual order of society and the illusion of their wholeness as individuals where subjectivity is the function of language not a pre-given, fixed human characteristic. Rather, the human subject is inserted into a pre-existent linguistic order that forms its relation to meaning. The observers of the image cannot therefore take their own meanings in accordance with how the text filtered their cultural experience because the very notion of a coherent consciousness based on individual experience is imagery – an illusion produced by language in all texts and the basis of all ideology. Brown (1995) points to the Japanese term for blue, *aoi*, but which also applies to objects which are green, i.e. there is often no equivalence but which is something often assumed to be inevitable, i.e. we are the product of language. Brown concludes that 'Language proceeds and exceeds us'.[2]

Semiotics and branding

Using Kapferer's (1991) and Semprini's (1992) work on brand identity elements, Hetzel and Marion (1995b) see the real challenge for companies as understanding the relative importance of each element of brand identity and the nature of relations between the various elements. Semprini's hierarchy of mutual relationships, based on semiotic theory, is based on the notion of the brand offering a discourse and meaning being produced by generation and narration, coming about 'through gradual enrichment around an elementary core in which only the constitutive values of society exist'. Such values only acquire reality by 'rising back upwards towards the discursive surface' where they are 'implemented by narrative structures' and are subsequently 'enriched by the figures and objects of the world as we know them around us'. So a journey by meaning is travelled from simple to complex, i.e. the sign is transformed into signification through a generative journey in three stages: axiological, narrative and discursive.[3]

Conventional versus semiotic research

The problems and controversy that surround methodological approaches that necessarily use, for example, focus groups and potentially projective techniques, or 'confessional interviews' have not gone unnoticed. The use of qualitative (usually as opposed to quantitative) research methodology has been a debate for some time, and still is in marketing circles. For example, the call for a 'humanistic approach' (not just positivistic inquiry) where rich insights can be gained (Donnellan 1995) is not unusual.

Conventional research looks at what (say) advertising, brand or corporate images mean to respondents willing to participate in the research study. It also looks at signs and symbols through the use of conventional procedures, e.g. free response, multichoice, etc. and may go as far as using a third party usage with rating scales (Foster, 1995). With less conventional research, there is a desire to gain an objective (rather than subjective) set of stimuli that produce consistent response across individuals yet also a need to get into the unconscious (Hussey and Dunscombe, 1998). Patterson (1998) distinguishes between brand image and brand personality by using Aaker's brand work to illustrate the dimensions of the latter – excitement through daring, and spirited or sophisticated through glamour, charm and so on – which allows consumer to choice between similar things through a matching of brand personality with their own. As brands become similar, consumer choice based on brand personality is an implicit, internal experience by the primal, subconscious brain. Hussey and Dunscombe point to brand identity as being the explicit, external features of the brand's image observed by the rational/conscious brain. It is these that are easily articulated by consumers in research but this does not help in the matching of brand personalities with those of consumers. Hence the use of Heyden et al.'s (1995) 'implicit model of consumer behaviour' which considers the relationship between brand image (brand identity and personality) and consumer needs (rational and emotive). The outcome for Hussey and Dunscombe is consideration of three 'sets': ascription, gratification and animation. The first two deal with, respectively, motives and what respondents feel they 'get out of it', and are used to define the vectors of implicit space. The third deals with personification and the characteristics that project personality. The Hussey and Dunscombe study involved respondents being shown photographs of brands and the matching of these to cars and animals so that, for example, in instant coffee terms, the results suggest that Nescafé Gold Blend is a Porsche (high status, expensive), Bird's Mellow a (Rover) not the new BMW Mini (standard, cheap, etc.).

In much of the literature, *semiotic approaches* deal in deconstruction rather than construction. In deconstructive terms this is the underlying message and how words and pictures work together to reinforce the message and how alphapictorial components use gesture, art, myth and symbol to give emotional impact (Zakia and Nadin, 1987). Semiotics is concerned with how meaning is created. It is therefore interested in signs in society where communication takes place at a distance, often on a 'mass-market mind'. *Semiotic research* does not, therefore, result in the kind of reporting conventional research usually provides. Conventional research looks at, say, how the company is perceived often at the most superficial of levels and is accompanied with the problems such an approach brings. Semiotic research attempts to look at deeper levels of meaning using appropriate analytical tools and techniques. This leaves behind many of the problems associated with the superficial approach but, by definition, brings with it problems in design, implementation and interpretation of results.

Zakia and Nadin (1987) create what they call an *interpretant* matrix through deconstructing an advertisement by choosing three characteristics, which are:

- iconic (signs resembling that which they stand for – a painting of an object looks like the object)

- indexic (signs that are indicators of a fact or condition – smoke usually indicates fire)

- symbolic (signs that bear an arbitrary relationship to that which they stand for – an object stands for that object we identify with the word).

Zakia and Nadin apply these in a vertical column of the matrix along with (seemingly arbitrarily chosen) meanings – exotic, sensual, sophisticated, androgynous. Isolating the alphapictorial elements that they (the interpreters) feel support the meanings assigned does this. A brand of perfume, for example, can be seen as exotic in terms of the use of: a foreign flower (iconic); Paris, France and a snake around a woman's neck smelling the perfume (indexic); and the text in French, the native woman, the serpent/Garden of Eden, the 'phallic' neck of the flower (symbolic). Of course, other referents are used for other aspects of the brand so that 'sensual' is shown by partially opened lips (iconic), feminine finger-pointing (indexic) and warm colours, coiling serpent, interlocking fingers (symbolic). Such approaches can be easily criticized and perhaps especially, for example, Zakia and Nadin's claim for managerial implications at the end of their article. However, the semiotic approach does provide researchers with the means to both find new hypotheses and to analyse collected data in what is in effect a relativist position on communications and brand image research.

Kaushik and Sen (1990) have attempted to decode advertisements, but also to decipher the differences that exist between brands and their personalities, by asking respondents to associate two distinct brands of washing powder with any gods and goddesses of the Hindu Pantheon. This attempts to explore all levels of signification without subjective interpretation of qualitative data. This is done through using three levels – exegetical, contextual and cultural context. Words to describe the first in this context are powerful, angry, life preserver. For the second, the contextual level, an example would be 'to fight evil'. For the third, the cultural context, the goddess might be seen as having an accessible image. The interpretation of this regarding the brands might be, for example, that one is seen as powerful but harsh and the other powerful but gentle.

The Fouquier 'field' model has been adapted from the well-used Schramm model of the communication process as discussed in Chapter 2. This has obvious linkages with the semiotic approach to meaning. Thus the Schramm model is easily modified to incorporate the essence of the semiotic approach (Hetzel and Marion, 1995a). Hetzel and Marion go on to discuss five models of influence of messages – transmission, construction, impression, stimulation and insemination – and are concerned with two types of contributions of semiotics to consumer behaviour (research), i.e. co-interpretation and enunciation. Thus the semiotic approach provides researchers with the means to both find new hypotheses and to analyse collected data.

The difference between conventional marketing research and Brown's postmodern approach illustrates this dichotomy. To many involved in marketing and marketing research this is acceptable as long as the 'model' remains hierarchical and fits in with cell 1 of Brown's grid. The other cells, however, may pose some problems for those who either take the positivist stance by inclination or for those under pressure to justify, in a cause and effect-like way, decisions to conduct research. This costs good money but which appears, on the surface at least, to be if not spurious or eccentric then perhaps strange. The traditional qualitative research of Brown's cell 2 has its critics, i.e. critics of depth interviews and focus groups/group discussions, as does the interpretative research of cell 3 – mostly in terms of generalizability and interpretation of findings. The stuff of cell 4 is, of course, even more problematic in terms of methodological approaches in research design. Postmodernism contends that individuals do not have unmediated access to external reality and questions the existence of the free-thinking 'subject', i.e. the human condition is not constitutive but constituted where knowledge people imagine they possess is 'unreliable, dispersed, fragmented, pre-existing and an epiphenomenon of language' (Brown, 1995).

Semiotic analysis

It is interesting to note that Tesco have recently run a graduate recruitment campaign which uses the line 'If Tesco is just a shop, here's a village in the south of England' accompanied by a photo of London Bridge, Big Ben, etc., i.e. London. If semiotic analysis is applied in such situations, the hope is that structured recall of advertisements designed on this basis will result in the creation of pleasurable/positive emotions that will be triggered when brand/company is viewed. Jhally (1987) uses Williamson's work to illustrate the importance of transference of meaning from one sign to another where the transference is accomplished by the juxtaposition within the formal internal structure of the advertisement but requires the active participation of the viewer.

Once information is in place, analysis follows. Some of the tools that can be used are listed by Lawes (2002) as being:

- visual signs
- linguistic signs
- aural signs
- the implied communication situation
- textual structure
- information structure
- visual emphasis
- genre

- binary oppositions and contrast pairs

- communication codes.

This, for Lawes, is the semiotic tool kit. These tools can be used in studies that precede other research whereby hypotheses for testing can be developed and qualitative research objectives can be sharpened. With conventional qualitative analysis, a research report would comment on how an informant responded to a particular question or stimulus. Semiotic analysis, however, can do a number of other things. Cross-culturally semiotic analysis can provide usable information without the cost and other problems of setting up interviews, focus groups and so on. Materials from popular culture can provide an insightful project. Semiotics is a streamlined, efficient methodology that allows competitors' communication to be analysed and used to advantage, and it can be very cost-effective, allowing a maximum quantity of information out of a data set.

VIGNETTE

The semiotic sandwich and other food for thought

Advertising campaigns and corporate/brand images can be coded in the language of signs that can be understood by a shared consciousness principally using the symbolic workings of colour and form. For example, red is urgent, forward, leaping, and the symbolic use of this would be things like red for danger or leaping flames. In contrast, blue is cool, distant and the colour of an apparent recession into the distance as seen in a cool pool, an infinite sky or a faraway horizon. The basic premise is that social attitudes and values are embodied in signs and symbols. These can be found everywhere but in particular in logos, advertising, retail design, media exposure, etc., which build up brand and corporate images in the minds of consumers. Just how signifiers set off chains of ideas in the mind of consumers so that the image feels like the true and natural representation of the company/brand and how it thinks and feels is of prime importance here. Consider two brands, Panzani (in terms of deconstruction) and Peperami (in terms of construction), of brand identity and hence image.

Panzani (pasta, pasta sauces)

Cultural discourse is about coded meaning in any given culture. The much quoted Barthes (1973) looked at French popular culture and consumption and the mythological discourses of the bourgeois class, especially where nationalism or fetishism was involved, for example with wine. Panzani advertising deconstructed semiotically by Barthes is presented independently by John Sinclair and by Daniel Chandler as a good example of deconstruction using semiotic tools. The piece of advertising analysed is principally a still-life composition (typical of coffee-table magazine advertising, where the knowledge on which the signs depends is highly cultural) which uses form, colour and tones: packets of the (dried) pasta, a tin and sachet of sauce, some tomatoes, onions, peppers and a mushroom all spilling from a half-open string bag. In semiotic analysis, a bag and the vegetables signifies the pleasures of shopping for, and the preparation of, fresh food and, second, the juxtaposition of the packaged foods. The composition and colours call upon French cultural knowledge of food and 'Italianicity' (not for an Italian viewer for whom the name would not have the same connotative meaning, but for a French audience) for signification. The advertisement therefore *denotes* a literal image – just a bag and so on and *connotes* an ideological meaning, i.e. that the packaged brand of food is exotic, aesthetic and just like natural food. We are invited to take the ideological meaning where the arrangement of the objects and anchorage of the sales message take out other meanings. The connoting signifiers are scattered or discontinuous in themselves, being drawn from different paradigms but they acquire meaning by being joined together by rhetoric of apparently natural relationships in a syntagm (order) within the advertisement. That signified from this 'return from the market' or 'shopping for oneself' is the freshness of the products and the domestic preparation implied. A second, less apparent sign is that of the Italian tricolour of yellow, green and red. Overall the image transmits the idea of 'a total culinary service' through the brand.

Peperami (Van Den Bergh's)

The award-winning campaign 'It's a bit of an animal' was devised after National Opinion Poll (NOP) research on the UK market in 1993 showed that only 25 per cent of the population had ever tried Peperami after eleven years on the market. By mid-1994 the figure was 35 per cent. July to September 1993 saw sales leap by 42 per cent. After the advertising had ended, sales were up 23 per cent on the previous year's level. The brand personality consumers embraced came out of more than fifty rough advertising concepts (from eccentricity to aggression) tested using 'confessional interviews' and semiotic analysis. This enabled the agency S P Lintas to gain an insight into how consumers relate to Peperami, i.e. the end-user – young males – rather than the purchaser – housewives. Since then Peperami has developed, especially on the Internet. There is a web-based 'Animal' game that uses Ade Edmondson's voice as the voice of Pep, the Peperami 'animal'. And there is Snackopolis, home of Peperami, Pep and the mad midget scientist Pepereinstein . . . enough said?

As Chandler observes, 'meaning includes both denotation and connotation'. The challenge to the marketer is to learn from deconstruction of images but at the same time to better use semiotic analysis in the construction of effective communication.

Source: Adapted from Chandler, D. (2003); IPA (1995); Sinclair (1987); www.microtime.co.uk/animal/story.htm/, accessed 5 February 2003.

STOP POINT

And the sandwich? Well the next time you attend a meeting and someone brings a sandwich with them and your natural tendency would be to think that it just their lunch, then think again. What is that sandwich really saying. Is it not a signifier that signifies that this person is so busy they have not had time for lunch? Or in fact they are so busy they have not had time to open the sandwich? What else is being said through that sandwich?

Assignment

Watch a series of current television advertisements. While watching them, attempt to analyse what you see with reference to objectives, source, style – informational versus emotional. Watch out for pattern, i.e. conclusion drawn, one- or two-sided order of presentation, primacy or recency effects. Look also for appeals being used, i.e. the use of slice of life, fear, animation, humour, music, sex, fantasy and so on. Now do the same with newspaper advertising, magazines and with packaging. Think about the research opportunities within this. What use would conventional research be put to? Is there any scope for semiotic analysis?

Summary of Key Points

- Creativity is an essential factor in overcrowded marketplaces but tension can exist between creativity and effectiveness.

- It may be difficult or impossible to transfer creative ideas between contexts but unproductive creative ideas can be screened out. Creative ideas must be planned and managed. A good creative brief will assist in this.

- Creative appeals are used to attract attention and/or influence feelings or indeed move the customer towards a particular behaviour.

- The product or brand and people can be used in the creative process so that brand characteristics, celebrities, reference group images and so on become an integral part of the process.

- Appeals are broadly either emotional or rational but a combination of the rational and emotional is not only possible but in many cases desirable.

- There are many creative executions to choose from, for example the use of the surreal in an animated form. There are also design considerations such as conclusion drawing and one- or two-sided messages. The presentation order involves decisions on primacy/recency effects. Repetition, music, slogans and strap lines are other considerations.

- The source of the message clearly has characteristics that can be invaluable.

- Message integration, as with IMC generally, requires a Gestalt-type approach with elements of the message working together.

- Advertorals and infomercials are alternative choices to get consumers to take action 'on the spot' but there is clearly an ethical and legal dimension to this approach.

- Evaluation of creative work can be conducted through conventional or less than conventional means. With the former, questionnaire and focus groups are commonplace examples. With the latter, semiotics is one of a number of alternative approaches to understanding perceptions and so on. Tools and techniques used might be projective in nature and these can help with the coding and decoding of signs that can be understood by a shared consciousness.

Examination Questions

1 Explain what you understand creativity to be. Discuss the idea that creativity can be planned and managed, using examples to illustrate.

2 Outline what you consider to be the important elements of a creative brief. Say why, using examples, it might or might not be possible to transfer creative ideas from one context to another.

3 Discuss the kinds of creative appeals that are available to communicators. Consider the usefulness of combining emotional and rational appeals in some instances. Illustrate your response with an example of one such combination.

4 Explain the range of creative executions available to marketers. Choose one such execution in particular and discuss its pros and cons in relation to a particular brand.

5 Creative decisions may include use of the source as part of the creative effort. Explain why this might be so and provide examples to illustrate.

6 Discuss the importance of integration of elements of a message with particular reference to creative appeals and brand recall. Illustrate with examples.

7 Distinguish between the advertoral and infomercial. Using examples to illustrate, explain the advantages and disadvantages of their use.

8 Explain in principle what projective techniques are. Discuss how such techniques can help develop creative strategy using examples of brands to illustrate.

9 Explain what is meant by the term 'semiotics'. Compare and contrast more traditional approaches to evaluating creativity with semiotic analysis.

10 Discuss the possibility of combining projective techniques with semiotic research. Use an example to explain and illustrate the use of projective techniques within the semiotic arena.

Notes

1 It can be argued that reality might not change when language changes and that we can have reality without language, i.e. through other constructs.

2 Interestingly here Brown's word has to be taken on this since it is outside my field of experience just as Eskimos having many words for snow is!

3 This is a good example of the semiotician using rather opaque language to describe what really are simple concepts.

References

Barthes, R. (1973). *Mythologies*. Paladin.

Beaumont, L. and Crosier, K. (1995). Semiotics in the service of marketing communications decision makers. *Proceedings of the 1995 Marketing Education Group Annual Conference*, University of Bradford, July, 20–30.

Bletchly, R. (2002). The girl with the golden bum. *Sunday People*, 24 March, p. 13.

Brown, S. (1995). *Postmodern Marketing*. Routledge.

Catling, T. and Davies, M. (2002). *Think!* Capstone.

Chandler, D. (2003). Available at www.aber.ac.uk/media.Documents/S4B/sem06.html, accessed 5 February.

Donaldson, E. (1995). Changing perspectives on research methodology in marketing. *Irish Review of Marketing*, **8**, pp. 81–90.

Foster, J. (1995). It's very nice, dear, but what does it mean? *Research*, May, 20–21.

Hetzel, P. and Marion, G. (1995a). Contributions of French semiotics to marketing research knowledge. *Marketing and Research Today*, February, 35–40.

Hetzel, P. and Marion, G. (1995b). Contributions of French semiotics to marketing research knowledge. *Marketing and Research Today*, May, 75–85.

Institute of Practitioners in Advertising (IPA) (1995). *The Advertising Effectiveness Awards*. Notes and video. IPA.

Jhally, S. (1987). *The Codes of Advertising*. Routledge.

Kaushik, M. and Sen, A. (1990). Semiotics and qualitative research. *Journal of the Market Research Society*, **32** (2), 227–242.

Lawes, R. (2002). Demystifying semiotics: some key questions answered. *International Journal of Market Research*, **44** (3), 251–264.

Patterson, M. (1998). Split personalities: the semantics of brand image. pp. 430–434.

Schultz, D. E. and Kitchen, P. J. (2000). *Communicating Globally*. Macmillan.

Sinclair, J. (1987). *Images Incorporated*. Croom Helm.

Zakia, R. D. and Nadin, M. (1987). Semiotics, advertising and marketing. *Journal of Consumer Marketing*, **4** (2), 5–12.

Media characteristics, planning and spend issues

Chapter overview

Introduction to this chapter

In this chapter, the three broad areas concerning media characteristics, media planning and spend issues are addressed. The changes that have taken place in the media in recent times are immense. The Internet (see Chapter 19) of course is remarkable but not the only consideration as targeting and fragmentation has evolved, putting the characteristics of the new media in sharp relief against the more traditional media types. The changing characteristics of target audiences have created even more challenges when matching media to targets. Planning media in a strategic fashion is addressed to the point that prepares the reader to be able to carry on with the more detailed aspects of media planning. Allocation and budgets are addressed in a theoretical as well as a practical manner.

Aims of this chapter

The overall aim of this chapter is to explore the nature of media characteristics and how media can be planned in relation to the amount of money available. More specifically, on completion of this chapter, the reader should be able to:

- appreciate the nature and role of media within marketing and marketing communications
- explain the emergence of the 'new media' in relation to the 'old'
- explain the role of media planners and buyers
- outline the media planning process and explain this in relation to other marketing communications elements
- explain reach, frequency and weight of media and discuss the relationship between these
- discuss scheduling in relation to cost and cost per thousand (CPT)
- explain the theoretical and practical approaches to allocation and budget-setting.

The characteristics of the media

The 'medium is the message', according to Marshall McCluhan in the 1960s, suggested that different media can have differing effects on recipients. Over time the effects of the media have changed as the move from the more passive to the more active or interactive recipient of messages has occurred. Television in the past may very well have washed over audiences fascinated by the new medium and its stars of varying sorts, depending upon the type of programming. Advertising on television was particularly attractive and could lull consumers into consuming, or at least buying. Now, while general interest magazines, newspapers and programming still have a place, special interest magazines, newspapers, websites and television and radio programmes have evolved to meet needs of specialist groupings that were perhaps once part of a mass audience. This gives rise to issues of duplication and repetition. The criteria for choice lies within the characteristics or qualities of different media and media vehicle types. However, quantitative measures of how much of the target is reached are important. This said more qualitative measures as to how the media are consumed and the technical characteristics of the various media such as colour reproduction, quality of print and so on also have to be considered. The various media at the communicator's disposal quite obviously have certain characteristics, which were discussed briefly in Chapter 4.

Wading through all the various good and not so good points can be pedantic but knowing the media is essential grounding in order to complete the real task of choosing the right media categories and vehicles. This necessarily includes the Internet and other electronic-based means of delivering messages such as the CD-ROM. Those media at the cutting edge of technology can now be viewed in much the same way as previous generations viewed television, radio and print. A key question might be whether or not the idea of 'narrowcasting' (in essence effective targeting) is more achievable with these new tools. Another question is how much longer will it be before we have available to us a truly in-home multimedia environment? The various media are often selected for their geographical reach, the ability to dramatize, frequency of exposure and so on.

The overall goal within this area is to devise an optimum situation for the delivery of promotional messages to particular target audiences. The structure of the media industry itself has changed, while there are obvious media specialists now it is noted that there have been media independents since the 1970s. As advertising agencies mutated into the communication companies of today, one of the first changes was the creation of media companies and brokerages, the owners of which were often employees the old media departments of the larger agencies who decided to shed this function and to use such independents. As multimedia schedules became the norm, so too did computer software that could handle such complexities, but this has not seen the demise of the media buyer as a function as some had predicted. Organizations strive to be more effective and efficient in many other areas and this includes the media context.

The electronic media

Traditionally, the two main forms of electronic broadcast media have been *television* and *radio*. They are mass media that can reach large audiences at a relatively low cost per target. There has been a large growth recently in the number of electronic vehicles due to the developments of cable and satellite television, and also the introduction of many more commercial radio stations including Internet radio.

Developments of satellite, cable and digital transmission are here and still happening. As advertising media there are problems but also opportunities. On the downside *television's* absolute (i.e. for the actual, say, 30-second spot) costs are high but relative (i.e. per contact) costs are low. Audiences have been encouraged in a way by the advent of the handset. There is a high level of repetition and the message has a relatively short life. There is a lot of 'clutter' and fragmentation as the medium has gone through rapid change. On the plus side the medium is flexible, still has prestige (although some might say it is too prosaic now for this to be a characteristic), can allow dramatic effects and is highly creative. There is scope still to reach relatively mass audiences, with major soap operas reaching many millions, to more specialized programming with perhaps only a few thousand. Commercial *radio* was strongly regional in countries like the UK. National coverage such as Virgin and Classic FM is now firmly secured. One of the downside issues in the past was the perception that radio would not capture attention or would have a very big span of attention. It was thought that because it was not a visual medium it would be 'aural wallpaper'. Couple this with the low prestige of especially local radio and it is not surprising that radio was a much underused medium, especially when no real national possibilities existed. However, on the upside, costs have been much less than television, and radio offers national and regional coverage. It also provides the ability to target via programming such as 'drive time' and sports coverage slots and so on. The realization that radio's key characteristic is the use of imagination has made radio a popular choice for particular campaigns. Used cleverly it can become a visual (pictures in the mind) and not just background noise. It is a portable medium that can be listened to in a variety of locations and is therefore both flexible and capable of involving the audience.

With other electronic media, interactivity is considerably higher and in many instances there are immediate responses. Targeting is possible and there are relative low costs and a good degree of flexibility. On the downside, there are often high set-up costs, poor security and slow developments (despite the pace of technological change) and targeting might be segment specific in some instances. Therefore *mobile phones*, now with text and picture messaging, *teletext* and, even, *facsimile (fax) machines* are available to marketers who can either keep in touch in a regular way with customers or use random messaging (but this is in danger of being perceived as 'junk mail'). The ubiquitous *CD-ROM* has an uncertain future as does *video* but these are currently still considerations when reviewing the various media and their qualities. *The Internet and e-commerce* is now here with the World Wide Web (the Web) as the main commercial arm of the Internet. The number of users will be into billions in the next few years and its use in the business-to-business marketing context has until now outpaced that of the consumer. However, consumer e-commerce is catching up. The aforementioned problems of security and also of cost of access will not exist forever. Thus through websites both the organizational customer and consumer can 'shop' for twenty-four hours a day, 365 days a year anywhere in the world, or at least the cyberworld. Direct sales, public relations and so on are conducted through this medium (see Chapter 19).

VIGNETTE

What have *The Simpsons*, television movies, *Star Trek, Indiana Jones* and bi-directional infrastructure got in common? The Barry Diller factor, that's what

By 1993 there was much discussion around fibre optics and the bi-directional infrastructure of television in terms of education, movies, games, information sources, sport and so on. This, it is said, is the future of television. By the early 1990s 64 per cent of Americans had access to cable television and now this figure is even higher, but many less well off people do not have access to cable. There is an opportunity for 'programmability', i.e. the ability to interact with consumers' preferences and target toward those preferences. Advertisements, it is predicted, will come in different versions and the consumer will have the ability to choose a Coke advertisement in Italian if that is what is required. If the consumer decides that he or she is in the market for a car then a message will be provided to match the consumer's profile. Within this there is some speculation that the 'medium is the message' adage is over. The message, or rather a bit of it, is deliberately created for the medium. All this means that certain types of people will be able to participate in society, the fear being that some will not.

Aspirational programmes means aspirational advertising and this can be seen as a positive thing as well as a negative one. Some people argue that there will be a community that will replace the state/centralized authority by putting the power in the hands of the people – a 'Jeffersonian vision'. Companies such as United Artists and Microsoft are very active in this area, being very interested in the future of interactive television. Barry Diller is a major player with an impressive curriculum vitae. He was made Chairman of Paramount Pictures by the age of just thirty-two, having carved out a career that began at ABC but led to the development of made-for-television movies that explored 'social problems' rather than the conventional movie fare. Made-for-television movies were firmly established by 1972 as part of network programming. By this time Diller was just thirty and at forty-two he quit Paramount (with *Taxi* and *Cheers* among others under his belt) to join Fox Broadcasting to organize a fourth network to compete with ABC, CBS and NBC. This was up and running by 1987 and was on five nights a week by 1990 with reality programming and, not least, *The Simpsons*. Diller moved on again with a spell at QVC (and a $25 million share in it) and by 1995 had quit and bought into cable networks.

Barry Diller may have failed in his takeover attempt of Paramount but he is probably *the* Hollywood producer who became concerned with the interactive nature of television. The industry sees him as innovative, a revolutionary, a pioneer, a media evangelist and, seemingly, a hero of sorts. Diller sees himself as being in the 'everything business'. If the old convergence was 'televisions, computers and telephones', the new convergence is 'information, entertainment and electronic commerce'. Diller seems to be able to move easily between high and low concepts but also believes in computers, and that nothing completely displaces anything else (we still have radio, television and video rental). The future will include things that are not about computers or interactivity, such as leisure pursuits, but there will be e-commerce, digital technology and mobile phones. In the USA and Europe we have seen the success of the DVD, and this is set to happen in the Asia-Pacific region in the next few years despite the success of its rival, the VCD. Electronic or digital cinema has arrived, another shake-up, reputably as big as the one when 'talkies' arrived, but with digital rather than film or celluloid delivery.

Sources: Adapted from DVD player base to increase fivefold in Asia-Pacific over next four years, available at www.screendigest.com/rep_ecinema.htm, accessed 5 February 2003; Electronic cinema: the big screen goes digital, available at www.screendigest.com/rep_ecinema.htm, accessed 2000; Los Angeles Magazine (1999); Milmo (2001).

STOP POINT

The advent of differing formats is nothing new. The expectation is that science and technology will on a continual basis provide new and exciting ways to communicate and so on. What is new is the convergence of information, entertainment and e-commerce. Explore what you think Diller means by this as opposed to the old convergence of televisions, computers and telephones. Explore where interactivity might fit into this.

Other media

Direct marketing

Direct marketing of one form or another has been around for many years but in recent times, largely due to information technology and data handling, this kind of activity has grown considerably. Direct marketing (considered more closely in Chapter 10) includes *direct mail, telemarketing* and *direct response* to press or broadcast media advertising and the *Internet*. Where appropriate, more sophisticated interactivity will take place such as with satellite television advertising. Direct marketing is often used to make an offer there and then but is also to provide more detailed information. This might be in the form of a reader/viewer offer with the media vehicle and marketer sharing profits. In this case no charge for space taken would be made but the marketer would, of course, supply the product. It has been successfully used in many integrated campaigns but on the downside it has been associated with 'junk mail', i.e. unsolicited and often unwanted mailings viewed as rubbish to be 'binned' (often unopened) by recipients. If used properly through good database management, it can be a very cost-effective way of maintaining contact with customers. The same logic applies to *telemarketing* where prospecting calls can be viewed as 'junk calls' if they are not relevant to the recipient or indeed interrupt them at inconvenient times. This is different from calls from prospective customers who respond to the marketer's stimuli via the telephone when it is convenient for them in order to place an order or gather information. Again, the same logic applies to *e-mail*.

Print media

Despite the impact of the Internet, newspapers and magazines are still popular. Branding is strong and behaviour often habitual. Here the classic activities, interests and opinions can be clearly seen. Magazines, in particular, reflect interests and lifestyles so that targeting can be very accurate, allowing marketers to understand the characteristics of the target and work on this through advertising, editorials (where effective PR and press relations are at work), offers and other sales promotions such as competitions. Generally, the printed word allows for detailed explanations, and the supply of facts and figures if appropriate, which can be particularly useful where there is high involvement. From a PR perspective, an editorial in print has high credibility among readers of newspapers and magazines, the logic being that if a reader buys and trusts a particular periodical, then he or she will trust any PR-based write-ups, feature articles and so on. *Newspapers* have a wide reach, high coverage and are of course national and regional vehicles and, while many are published daily, some are weekly or Sunday newspapers. The reader controls the speed of consumption and chooses what he or she wants to read and ignores other parts of the paper in the time frame that he or she dictates. Detailed information can be provided and coupons used at a later time. Newspapers have short lead times, usually a day or two and now most offer colour, different sized advertisements and varying placements, for example on the back page. On the downside, they are disposable, often only skim-read and have a very short life span, therefore exposure can be at best a fleeting glimpse. There is much clutter and advertisements can often end up with poor reproduction and this can lessen their impact or even damage the brand. *Magazines*, especially hobby, lifestyle or special interest magazines (SIMs) usually have targets with high attention to what is on offer. There are titles targeted at male and female readers, and other targets such as the lesbian and gay community. As well as SIMs there are general interest magazines, or GIMs, that appeal to a wider spectrum of reader. Visually, the quality of magazines is usually very high. Certainly with the 'glossies' this is deliberately so, to offer the quality required by advertisers such as Chanel or Boss. This might be less appropriate in other contexts but generally good-quality paper and colour print are the norm. Magazines have longevity, i.e. a much longer shelf life than newspapers and readership is usually higher than circulation, i.e. there is more than one reader per copy. On the downside, lead times are long – weeks or months as opposed to days. Special editions are common. With business-to-business magazines there is often an edition tied to a particular event such as a trade show at a particular time, and space has to be booked well in advance. Using inserts may help this situation but while most magazines offer little wastage in terms of hitting the target, absolute costs can be very high, especially with consumer magazines. It would be wrong to assume that magazines are a visual-only medium since sampling has been successfully done, especially for perfumery but other products too, for a number of years now so that the tactile nature and other qualities of the product or brand can be conveyed.

Out-of-home media

This category is now very wide with many media and vehicles including cinema, billboards or poster hoardings, transport (outside as well as in), in-store promotions, shopping trolleys, parking meters, window displays, sports arena and sports apparel, banners from planes and projections onto buildings. Apart from cinema these media are mostly used as support media to other lead media such as television. Out-of-home media can provide triggers that jog the memory by using short, simple messages. The characteristics of *cinema* can be very similar to those of television but it is an out-of-home medium. Therefore, recipients of any marketing communications (in particular advertising of course) will have selected a particular cinema and a particular film, possibly in a social setting but certainly a context that has different atmosphere, mood and other qualities. The creative impact of cinema advertising can be extreme in comparison to the 'box' (a nickname for television) – darkened auditoriums, large screen, wide screen and stereo or even surround sound. The advent of some of these cinematic qualities as part of home viewing is also here with, for example, wide screen televisions, surround sound and in effect mini-cinemas available. *Outdoor* media such as posters and so on are limited in scope but have high reach and frequency, low cost, good coverage nationally and regionally, and provide targeting opportunities. They have a 'poor relation' kind of image in comparison with other media, long production times, and impact is difficult to measure.

Transport media have high length of exposure and low costs but biased recipients of messages since many are travellers of one sort or another. There is also a lot of clutter around such media. *In-store* opportunities are numerous including shelf screamers and those at point of purchase. These are inexpensive and flexible and can be persuasive and attention grabbing. However, if not done well they can cause damage to the retailer and to the manufacturers' brands, especially if they appear tatty and cluttered. They are also biased towards shoppers, as might be expected in the context in which they are used.

VIGNETTE

QVC home shopping: is Jon bon Jovi part of the bi-directional infrastructure of companies like this?

The answer is of course yes. The early to mid-1990s saw discussion emerge in the media around home shopping and the notion of quality, value and convenience (QVC). QVC is the home shopping channel set up by Joseph Segel in 1986. QVC is a very powerful force in this sector of retailing. Covering first the USA then Latin America, the UK and then the rest of Europe, this expansion is set to continue. QVC is currently in 84 million homes in the USA, 9 million via BskyB in the UK, 27 million in Germany and 5 million in Japan. QVC operates out of Pennsylvania but has communication centres across the USA and 14 000 employees worldwide. This means that QVC is the leader in electronic retailing with 96 per cent of all cable homes and 16.5 per cent of all satellite homes in the USA. In 2001 sales exceeded $3.9 billion with worldwide telephone calls in the region of 133 million and 92 million units shipped. QVC introduces 300 new products and adds 40 000 new customers every week. Programming varies but, typically, in England this will consist of seventeen hours plus seven 'night time' hours consisting of the best of the previous seventeen. This varies from country to country. QVC is one of the largest purveyors of 14-carat gold jewellery for which QVC has created its own special packaging to ensure safe transit. All jewellery lines account for 31 per cent of QVC programming. QVC now has an on-line interactive shopping division with QVC UK and QVC Germany having their own websites.

So what has Bon Jovi got to do with television and on-line shopping? Everything it seems. QVC do a lot of things, including becoming involved, in April 2003, with the American Legacy Foundation and the 'Circle of Friends' Sunburst Pin. This pin is a symbol of 'hope and inspiration' for women and their families. Circle of Friends is a grassroots movement supporting women who want to stop smoking and QVC have become involved with selling the pin to raise money to be able to offer grant support. Rock band Bon Jovi's involvement with QVC is quite another matter. At about the same time, on 12 April 2003, Bon Jovi made an unprecedented live appearance on QVC from its sold-out 'Bounce Tour' concert in San José. In addition, exclusively to QVC shoppers, was a Bon Jovi Limited Tour Edition Bounce CD and DVD/VHS package. QVC also ran segments of the band's live performance during late evening slots. The eight o'clock live slot allowed viewers a backstage glimpse of the sound check and to talk on air to band members. Both Jon Bon Jovi and John Kelly, QVC's vice-president of merchandising, have praised the Bon Jovi–QVC alliance. Jon Bon Jovi is quoted as being 'really excited about working with QVC' which 'allows us to reach out to our fans across the country' and to offer 'another way to experience a Bon Jovi live show'. Kelly sees QVC–Bon Jovi as 'a perfect fit'.

Another feature of Bon Jovi marketing is the 'AmericanXS' programme that provides CD owners with a pin code that allows for website registration where they will find exclusive downloads, contests, video footage and offers on concert tickets. The Limited Tour Edition copies of Bounce also have the code. Apart from the band's obvious chart success, Bon Jovi have headlined the NFL Kickoff in Times Square, performing live in front of half a million people before helicoptering to the Giants' stadium to perform during halftime of the opening game of the season, which is a first. In addition the NFL have adopted Bon Jovi's 'It's My Life' as its designated signature song. This will be played in conjunction with all future Super Bowl Championship celebrations.

Sources: Adapted from www.qvc.com/corporatefacts/corporate, www.qvc.com/mainhqwel.html?, www.qvc.com/cp/cp_press_bonjovi_0402.html and www.qvc.com/cp/cp_press_american_0409.html, all accessed 2003.

STOP POINT The advent of QVC came as part of the changing characteristics of the media, especially television and the way we consume its output. Is the QVC–Bon Jovi alliance the epitome of interactivity? What elements of traditional marketing activity are present with Bon Jovi marketing?

Media planning

Donnelly (1996) maintains that up to 90 per cent of appropriation is spent on buying actual space or slots. Choosing appropriate media is of crucial importance. The notion that the 'medium is the message' is not without foundation but has been challenged to some extent in the new electronic media, as suggested in the vignette above. Burnett and Moriarty (1998) provide the link between marketing and media planning, i.e. from the marketing plan down a hierarchy to the media and creative plan. They also qualify this in a seven-point framework of a media plan that should consider marketing objectives, product, profit, channels, resource constraints, IMC strategy and the target audience.

Role of the media planner

Armed with the information above, as suggested in Chapter 4 the planner has to decide which media are feasible, and pick the main medium and how it should be used. The matching of the media to the target audience after careful consideration of many things but especially audience characteristics is the next step. The media planning process, including evaluation, must intertwine creative work.

Whether you go along with either of these you might still consider 'zapping' (the 'do they watch or make a cup of tea' debate) to be the major problem but that a striking, strong advertisement is still the order of the day to break through the clutter. The number of sets per household, time shift viewing and zipping through videotape are still problems so it is up to the creatives to solve them if they can. We are concerned here, therefore, with things such as changes in media technology, the development of mass markets, the standardization of brands and the changing lifestyles of consumers. This adds up to the central question of *narrowcasting*, i.e. using highly selective media for special target groups. The Chapter 4 example of MTV as a commercial channel that carries advertising is useful here. It has a target audience of 14–34-year-olds and is therefore to some extent an opportunity for global narrowcasting.

Reach, frequency, gross rating points (GRPs), placement and cost of that placement are all important, and most writers deal with these and admit to their relative simplicity. But it is not necessarily a case of simplicity being a virtue. Many practitioners now believe that this is not enough and are using focus groups to help understand targets more fully. The simple notions of reach (how many) and frequency (how many times) and GRPs/television ratings (TVRs) (reach $\times$ frequency and cost per thousand – the cost of reaching that many of the target audience) are of little use on their own. Typically, for example, creative content has an effect on advertising effectiveness and would have to be weighted in some way to be entered into any calculation. This is clearly problematic. Audience duplication is another problem that needs to be addressed.

Role of the media buyer

Some argue that the role of the media planner, which is basically a matching one, has been diminished by the introduction of basic software. Others suggest that the role has merely changed and is just as important as ever, if not more so. Media costs can be extremely high as suggested in Chapter 4. Buyers must be aware of how to reach target audiences via the best and most advantageous media, negotiations for favourable rates, size, length and frequency also of traffic and production, artwork, scripts and associated deadlines and so on.

Situation analysis for media decisions

Media planning is a central part of communications (and particularly advertising) management and is influenced by a number of factors (Figure 7.1):

- *Company sources* – understand the company in terms of targets/prospect profiles, purchase cycles, distribution patterns and so on. Clearly it is important/necessary to know early on the target audience in order that matching with readership/viewing/listening profiles can take place.

- *Marketplace sources* – understand the marketplace, monthly sales (past and projected), sales areas, rival advertising and so on.

- *Message sources* – know what to say and how through knowledge of themes, copy platform, levels of awareness (from research) and so on.

- *Media sources* – know the media. This is an industry in its own right led by Nielsen globally and in the UK by, for example, the British Audience Research Bureau (BARB) which operate a 4500-strong sample with 'Peoplemeter'. The British Market Research Bureau has a 24 000-strong sample with TGI (Target Group Index). Media Expenditure Analysis Limited (MEAL) and many others attempt to understand audience characteristics and behaviour. This of course is not just concerned with broadcast media, and older instruments are still used, for example door-to-door and telephone surveys and also diaries. With print media in particular, the Audit Bureau of Circulation service is highly valued – in order to find the best place and time when the audience is likely to use the message (often called aperture or window of opportunity). The net result is that good use of media sources puts

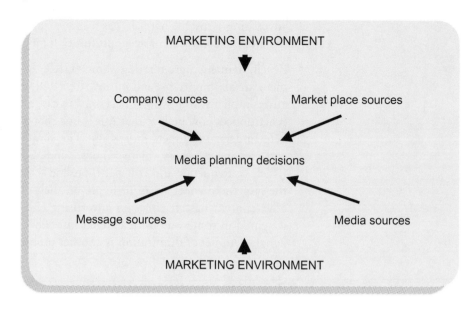

Figure 7.1
Factors influencing media planning decisions.

the marketer in the position to be able to say what their audience profile is. It may be that 70 per cent of ABC1 men watch a particular programme but only 3 per cent of C2DE men watch the same programme. This kind of analysis is only possible with good media source information.

Objectives

Reach

Reach involves the opportunity to see (OTS) and this helps advertisers to measure how many people have an OTS the advertisement but does not indicate how they react to it. This is usually measured in a four-week time period. There are complications regarding multimedia (most examples given in textbooks are of the single-media vehicle variety for simplicity as illustrated in Figure 7.2) and duplication. Also, placement is very important, whether this is different times of day for a television channel or within a magazine or newspaper. When the goal is cognitive (attention/awareness), then the reach objective will be high and therefore an attempt to minimize duplication will be made. When the goal is affective it may not be possible to achieve the same level of cover because of costs. A simple example of reach is that if 70 per cent of the audience of 10 million viewers that watch a particular news programme are ABC 1 men and if 9 million ABC1 men exist in a particular market, then 78 per cent of the target can be reached, i.e.

$$\frac{\text{No. of target viewers} = 7}{\text{Size of target market} = 9} \times 100\% \qquad [7.1]$$

Put another way, 78 per cent of the ABC1 men market can be covered using advertising around such programming. Reach will always be lower than coverage unless the universe is reached, i.e. 100 per cent of the target. The marketer can build towards achieving this but often through repetition and duplication where a complex media and media vehicle mix may exist. It may be possible to reach 100 per cent of the target but the marketer has to ask the question, 'at what cost?' *Effective reach* in the end must be measured not just in OTS or

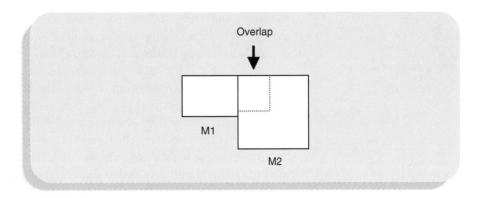

Figure 7.2
Simple example of effective reach.

exposures but at the very least awareness of the message. A way to tackle this issue is to think in terms of gross versus net reach. With the former a person will be counted twice and with the latter only once. As a simple illustration let us suppose we have two media types that overlap as illustrated in Figure 7.2.

The first medium, M1, and the second, M2, have a common overlap area, O. Gross reach and net reach can be expressed as:

Gross reach, $GR = (M1 + O) + (M2 + O)$ [7.2]

where a person in the overlap area would be counted twice.

Net reach, $NR = M1 + M2 + O$ [7.3]

where a person in the overlap area would be counted only once.

Effective reach is generally accepted to be achieved between three and ten exposures during this four-week period (Shimp, 1997). As usual cost considerations dominate and the use of television may well deny this number of exposures in a schedule. However consideration of reach in this way coupled with effective targeting can improve the efficiency and effectiveness of reach. A large reach can be had using television but in terms of the target specialist magazines may be more effective.[1]

Frequency

Frequency involves the ideas of 'wear-in', i.e. starting with one exposure and building more, and 'wear-out', whereby the optimal number of exposure has been achieved and wastage is occurring. Frequency therefore deals with how often or the number of times the target audience is exposed on average in that period. There is no real consensus in this area as to what is best. Overexposure is seen both as a waste and potentially brand-damaging. The target might read the cost of frequent exposures as being paid for by them, in the price of the brand. Underexposure is seen as ineffective in achieving objectives and moving people. Repetition can be beneficial but only in a balanced way. The deliberate repetition of some advertising is so that the audience sees the message more than once. *Effective frequency* is a measure of the number of times the target needs to be exposed in order to achieve the objective, and several writers have estimated this. A key question therefore is 'how many exposures do we need to achieve our objectives', the answer to which will depend on the nature of the objectives. For example Krugman (1972) estimates three opportunities to see is the optimum: the first provides understanding as to what is being advertised, the second relates to recognition and what the communication means, and the third stimulates some form of action. Krugman's upper limit is apparently ten exposures, anything beyond which being wasteful. Krugman's 'rule of thumb' of three exposures is one to get over 'what it is', two to deal with 'what of it' and three to 'remind'. This is still only dealing with opportunities to see. The definitive work seems to have been conducted in the USA by Lever Brothers via Naples (1979). Naples concluded that the optimal frequency of exposure must be three – one exposure having no real lasting effect, two being the threshold and the third being the point at which the advertisement has the greatest effect. After that the advertisement can be effective but at a decreasing rate so that three becomes the benchmark. This led Naples to the 'S' shape curve. Opponents argue that other factors such as the residual effects of other advertising or brand/company image mean that advertisements have an effect immediately, rise to an optimum, then slow down, producing a convex curve. The one clear message that comes out of this inconclusive area is that frequent exposure brings positive results (Naples, 1979).[2]

Average frequency refers to the number of times a target is exposed to an advertisement over time within a schedule. If

10 per cent of the target is exposed ten times this $= 100$

25 per cent of the target is exposed seven times this $= 175$

65 per cent of the target is exposed one time this $= 65$

Total $= 340$

The average frequency of exposure in this scenario would be 3.4. The use of average frequency figures can be misleading since it is clear from the example above that nearly two-thirds of the target would have been exposed or, worse still, had the opportunity to see the advertisement only once. Added to this is the complex nature of most scenarios where unwanted duplication has to be accounted for.

Weight

Weight is how much the target is exposed in a given period and is the product of reach and frequency. This is usually expressed in rating points. This in reality is not discrete but involves complex viewing, listening and reading habits, and therefore effects on consumption can only be established through the use of qualitative research. Typically a rating will be assigned a monetary value and this has to be added to production and commission costs. Television ratings are a percentage of households tuned in to a specific programme:

$$\text{TVR} = \frac{\text{number in target TV households tuned}}{\text{total number of target TV households}} \times 100\% \qquad [7.4]$$

The TVR for news programme $= 7 \div 9 \times 100 = 78$, i.e. 78 per cent coverage.

One TVR $= 10$ per cent of all television households in an area tuned in to a specific programme, here the news programme, therefore the news programme has a TVR of 780, i.e. $78 \times 10 = 780$.

$$\text{Cost per TVR} = \frac{\text{absolute time cost}}{\text{TVR}} \qquad [7.5]$$

If the cost of the slot is £100 000, then cost per TVR is 100 000 ÷ 780 = £128 (cost per TVR = £128).

Another measure that can be applied is the combination of cost per TVR (CPTVR) and CPT to combine the two measures and form a bridge. The higher the rating, the higher the cost of the slot will be.

If there are a number of targets and one target does not get exposed this means only a percentage is reached. If the average frequency is 3.4 which yields 310 (rounded) GRPs this is the sum of all vehicle ratings in a media schedule. This figure is of course gross and usually takes into account the whole audience and not necessarily the target audience. This coupled with the point made above under 'Reach' regarding objectives might present the planner with a superior choice even though less rating points are provided because frequency is higher. *Cumulation* is a result of the first impact being potentially more powerful than the next where *effective* as opposed to *empty* reach is important.

The *average rating* is said to be 400. A *burst* campaign might be designed to gain 85 per cent coverage with eight exposures/OTS. This rating would then be 680 and considered heavy, but this would not be unusual if the campaign had the prime objective of gaining awareness. The notion of *recency* might be an almost diametrically opposite stance. Messages might be targeted at those who are known to be in the market and are prepared to buy and may be running out of stock/products. In this case reach is of more importance than frequency and the objective would be to reach as many as these as possible in as many weeks as possible. This would lead to a low weekly weight and a long, continuous campaign with frequency spread.

The *complexity* of what appears to be a simple scenario should not be underestimated. Some useful points are:

1   The atmosphere and environment surrounding the vehicle. Editorial tone, experience, credibility of journalists and prestige are all important. Two very similar-looking magazines such as *Cosmopolitan* and *Marie-Claire* are different in some way or other. Different market versions of the same magazine will be different by the same logic, i.e. the environment will be different for *Marie-Claire* UK and *Marie-Claire* France.

2   Repetition. This is beneficial because it helps to limit brand switching and aid believability in the brand. It works through top-of-the-mind awareness and if done properly can be a cue for brand quality. If not, then repetition can be a costly way of damaging the brand.

3   Technical and reprographic characteristics. This involves the usual characteristics of colour, movement and sound but also whether on a front page, back page, particular slots on television and so on.

4   Vehicle fit. Where a complex audience profile exists it may be difficult to match with just one vehicle. Here the marketer might think in terms of segmentation bases so that some of the target is reached through demography, some through psychographics and some through product usage, or a combination of bases.

5   The nature of the product. Clearly some products automatically match particular media and vehicles. Major consumer brands are well suited to peak time viewing of soap operas and situation comedies.[3]

Media scheduling

Scheduling is linked to whether or not objectives are short, medium or long term and achieving these is linked to the frequency of exposures as discussed above. Because of cost there are problems with the frequency of advertisements. Methods of scheduling are illustrated in Figure 7.3.

At least two strategies are available to help in this area. These are *burst* and *drip* as illustrated. A *burst* at the start of a campaign means there is a requirement to achieve high reach, making as many of the target audience as possible aware of the brand but frequency in particular media relatively low. As the campaign progresses less reach but increased frequency may be required, necessitating a much more continuous, regular *drip* or *continuity* campaign.

Certainly this would be the case with more mature products, especially cash cows, where regular maintenance is required. *Rising* or *falling continuity* may be employed when the campaign is linked to an event, such as a cup final or marathon where scheduling builds towards it in a controlled, continuous way or indeed away from it, with the dissemination of information on the product, product modifications and so on. *Flighting* may be chosen when the marketer wants to use resources over a longer period but not all of the time. Flighting may be erratic, regular or used in a burst-like way for the start of a campaign. Schedules will often be constructed around the idea of *pulsing*, which is a combination of continuity and flighting where there is a constant presence coupled with the occasional flight or pulse. Flighting is a flexible way of dealing with seasonality and other such issues and may be regular, irregular or blocked.

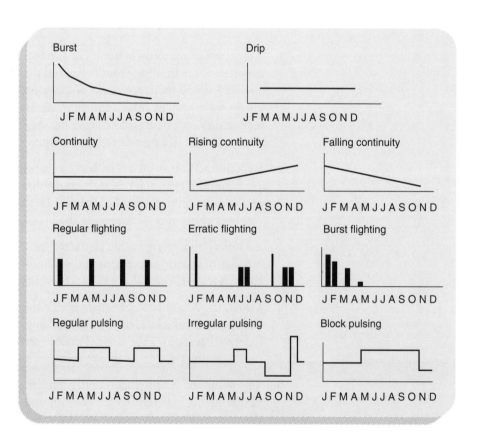

Figure 7.3
Methods of scheduling media.

Costs

Media and media vehicle selection and the choice of other forms of communications in the mix is governed, or at least tempered, in the main by cost. Since many media forms have witnessed fragmentation, this has made it more difficult to generate consistency. Placement and cost of that placement is important regarding relative simplicity. But it is not necessarily a case of simplicity being a virtue. As mentioned earlier, focus groups are now used to help understand targets more fully, rather than simply rely on the aforementioned quantitative measure of reach, frequency and weight leading to GRPs/TVRs and cost per thousand. Absolute costs (of spots, slots, space and so on) and the relative cost per thousand (where CPT = cost of slot/gross reach $\times$ 1000) measure allows the marketer to work out the cost of reaching so many of the target audience. These are of little use on their own. Typically, for example, creative content has an impact on advertising effectiveness and would have to be weighted in some way to be entered into any calculation. This is clearly problematic. Audience duplication is another problem that needs to be addressed. Loss of domination, additional production costs and the importance of concentration, repetition and so on are all considerations (see 'Spend issues' below).

Media strategy

The media strategy document should show how media would be selected to meet objectives. For example: 'Radio spots will be purchased every other week to extend support throughout the period up to and immediately after Christmas'. Media strategy statements include things like rationale for the use of one medium rather than another. For example: 'Television will be used as a primary medium because it offers the optimum combination of mass coverage flexibility in time and place and meets the creative requirements'.

The media plan

This shows how media strategy is to be executed in terms of specific purchases. For example, six one-half pages are recommended in *Good House Keeping* magazine because:

- it provides concentrated coverage of the target market

- it has minimal duplication with other recommended media

- the *Good House Keeping* seal of approval is an asset in this product field.

Another simple example could be the sport of golf whereby a particular magazine would offer a similar rationale around the reader demographics of:

- average age of forty-seven years

- 73 per cent social class ABC1

- average annual income of £25 000 set against the average UK adult salary of £14 000

- 95 per cent male

- Average handicap of 11

- 76 per cent playing golf for ten or more years.

Evaluation of the plan

Two areas for consideration are important as alluded to earlier, i.e. the suitability of the various media types and media vehicles and audience research. This should be an ongoing process, especially in view of new technology and fragmentation. Evaluation as a whole is dealt with in Chapter 18.

Role of audience research

This is an industry in its own right led by Nielsen globally and in the UK by, for example, the BARB (5500 sample drawn from a survey of 52 000 interviews with Peoplemeter[4]). The British Market Research Bureau have a 24 000 sample with TGI and MEAL, and many others attempt to understand audience characteristics and behaviour. Audience research is considered in more detail in Chapter 18.

VIGNETTE

Media selection and planning: how brands like Seiko become world leaders

In Seiko's case it became world leader in watch technology but with the realization that timepieces have an importance and a fascination that extends far beyond their function of measuring and telling time, i.e. they are also fashion goods. This was the view of the President of Hattori-Seiko in 1989 and it says a lot about Seiko's attitude to its business and also its media and advertising strategies. The first quartz watch was introduced in the 1960s with the Ted Bates' slogan 'Some day all watches will be made this way'. Design and fashion therefore played a major role and the need for research of the marketing kind was recognized. This led to the establishing of four distinct target groups with corresponding brands and marketing effort:

1 LASSALE was aimed at successful, professional, urban men and women 30–45 years old. This brand offered an exclusive and limited collection of elegant watches – thinness and sophistication, 'The modern classic', priced at between $300 and $900.

2 SEIKO was aimed at all men and women. This brand was a range billed as the most complete watch collection in the world featuring design and state-of-the-art-technology with a sporty image. 'The world leader in watch technology', prices ranged from $100–$600.

3 PULSAR was aimed at all men and women but particularly women aged 25–35. Fashionable, collectable, priced from $40 to $100.

4 LORUS was aimed at teens/young adults especially 15–30-year-olds. Functional, sporty 'watches for winners' priced at $20–$100.

The advertising was clearly linked with sport. The Seiko Sport-Tech range was advertised in international magazines such as *Time* and *Newsweek*, and also with in-flight magazines using the 'Man invented time, Seiko perfected it' strap line. This caused some problems in Islamic countries such as Malaysia, since for some people it is important that God invents all things. Seiko suggest that with their technology they started a revolution. The company appear to have the combined approach of centrally created advertising in Japan but this is executed nationally. There is a clear and logical link between Seiko and sport and sponsorship for Seiko in sporting areas is not problematic as it is for, say, Marlboro. In terms of media reach, frequency and demographics Seiko used the expertise of Saatchi & Saatchi in order to understand the impact of international campaigns and sponsorship. They used, for example, Skysport to communicate with a pan-European target audience. The net result was that Seiko was viewed as having universal appeal and an enduring reputation and was in the top ten of the 1988 Landor Associates power image study alongside Coca-cola, IBM and McDonald's.

This was in the days before the new electronic media had an even bigger impact. Now these are at the centre of a number of radical transformations in terms of information dissemination, entertainment and other forms of communication. The ways in which customers interact and deal with and buy from organizations have changed. Such organizations have to come to terms with this reality in a number of ways, not least in the area of media decisions and planning in order to protect brands and reputations. In other words, they have to be proactive and see this challenge as a series of opportunities in terms of national and international target audiences. *Bulletin International* is a company based on these transformations. Bulletin is now part of 141 Worldwide under the Cordiant Group but still offers what it started with in 1989 – PR solutions for today's real-time visually led media environment. This includes the usual planning and managing things, of defining the targets and matching the best media to reach them with effective messages, while at the same time understanding journalists' agendas and creating effective editorial content. It also includes a healthy attitude toward evaluation in terms of monitoring coverage, assessing the audience and analysing content and its impact on awareness, attitudes and behaviour. Bulletin started as leaders in video news releases in the UK but can now claim to be truly international. Crucially Bulletin have developed into providing strategic advice and implementing international editorial content management programmes across television, radio and web-based media. They were able to because they were very aware of, and involved with, the communications revolution, from cable to satellite, digital, the Internet and the merging of television and computer screens. Bulletin clearly believe that the new media are so powerful that the old maxim that the medium is the message has to change since these media will not just carry the message but cause it to change. Another maxim is challenged by Bulletin. 'Think global, act local' no longer applies when to think global becomes act local. Brand managers can now create a matrix of relationships through the blurring of editorial, direct marketing and advertising – and fast, in real time. The Bulletin client list is impressive. With the launch of the Edgar Davids-endorsed Nike Air Zoom Total 90 football boot using key websites, the objective was to target these and raise awareness. The Internet is a good match for Nike's targets. Using key sites in the UK, Germany, Italy and the Netherlands raised awareness of the boot ahead of it going on sale, using competitions to achieve this awareness and involvement. For Nike's launch of 'Swift Skin', a bespoke suit for the Winter Olympic Games in Salt Lake City worn by skaters from the USA, the Netherlands and Australia. The question was, would broadcast coverage of key European help position Nike as cutting-edge and innovative in sports apparel design. Tactically, a video was used to maximize exposure during the games and to emphasize the cutting-edge nature of the brand via expressing technology and news. Two hours' worth of this was used on terrestrial and satellite television, aimed for the most part at the target, i.e. the youth market. In all, fifty-four separate reports hit an estimated 20 million audience with the message that Nike in speed skating, and therefore as a whole, is an innovative and cutting-edge brand and corporation.

Sources: Adapted from Rijkens (1993); www.bulletin.com/bulletin-in-depth/about-us/main.asp;www.bulletin.com/bulletin-in-depth/our-services/main.asp; www.bulletin.com/bulletin-in-depth/our-history/main.asp; www.bulletin.com/media-world/commentary/main.asp, all accessed 2003.

STOP POINT

The issues that brands such as Seiko and Nike raise apply to many others. What should brand owners such as these be looking to get out of media planning to help get (and stay) on top? What are the key factors in media decision-making for such brands?

Spend issues

Traditional attitudes toward spend (or funding) are used by most textbook authors and this book is no exception. What is clear is that it is still notoriously difficult to arrive at optimal spend figures. Something that does not help the situation is the lack of certainty as to what the money actually does (recall the Leverhulme quip 'half the money I spend is a waste – the problem is I don't know which half'). Measurement is the key to understanding this but it is clear that senior management, while recognizing the need for communications, have treated it with a certain amount of derision. Arriving at 'spend' is difficult because it is hard to quantify, attitudes toward advertising in particular have been in the 'cost' not 'investment' mould and comparisons between different communications tools have been difficult.

Appropriation

'Appropriation' is the term used to describe the total sum of money available, and there are tried and tested methods of arriving at how this money should be split into various pots to form budgets, i.e. how this money is spent. The conclusion drawn by most, if not all, writers in this area is that no single method prevails or is best at any given time. Things have changed since the 1980s. Advertising expenditure has fallen at the expense of other forms of communication such as direct marketing and sales promotions as accountability held sway during the 1990s and into the new millennium. Even so, advertising expenditure on the part of the likes of Procter and Gamble is still huge. However, it has to be said that the easiest thing for accountants to chop when things are tight is advertising expenditure. It is therefore argued that spending on promotion is an investment and should be viewed as such – and not a cost or expense as some accountants would have it. What is clear is that investment is crucial to brand equity protection.

Budgets

Budgets are to do with timing of spread of financial resources. Budgeting deals with how much money is allocated to the elements of the communications mix.

Appropriation is therefore the total sum allocated, while a budget is specific to the media or a market. These are the two broad tasks the organization faces.

The size in the end depends on objectives that, of course, may have to be revised in the light of the amount of money available. It also depends on the stage the public limited company (plc) has reached and the competitive environment. Costs depend on which media slots are bought and how much is spent on production, administration and research. A reserve of some sort should be considered. Budgets are necessary for planning activities. This means co-ordinating effort across the organization, taking an integrated approach and seizing on the opportunity for mutual support. It also means it is part of the planning approach since the marketer can return to the objectives to check the feasibility and viability of the campaign.

The overall conclusion must therefore be that there is no simple answer to the question 'how much do we spend?' A simple solution for many small businesses is to take the percentage of predicted turnover based upon the sector norm. This is by no means ideal but can be put into practice. The theoretical ideal only serves to complicate matters since it is impossible to put into practice for most organizations and probably not much use in reality for anyone.[5]

The key practical methods employed are:

- strategy-based approaches

- predetermined approaches

- theoretical approaches.

Strategy-based (bottom-up) approaches

Task/objective. This may not be achievable if it is unrealistic in terms of resources. Objectives have, therefore, to be revised in the light of this, as per the analytical nature of the decision sequence model approach. An AIDA-type approach, i.e. cost of achieving varying levels of awareness and the cost of moving through the AIDA sequence, is usually taken. This is the only bottom-up approach and is generally thought to be the most desirable. Often the costs are not all known until the task is complete. There is an appearance of unrealistic budgets needing constant revision, and budget-setting might be seen as farcical. A compromise might be had in a 'sensitivity analysis'[6] approach with adjustments being made incrementally and where it is easier to measure the time scale for recouping expenditure. There is a positive aspect to budgets being evaluated and revised year on year and it is sensible to obtain feedback in order to gain improved performance. However, it is recognized how difficult it can be to estimate all the cost likely to be incurred and to arrive at an accurate, final cost.

Predetermined (top-down) approaches

1 *Inertia* – i.e. to keep at the budget at the same level, which is rare since most organizations, unless in crisis, are at least usually willing to keep in line with inflation.

2 *Affordable* is just that – what is affordable after all costs and required profit. This is hardly analytical and is used by organizations who view

communications as a cost and not an investment. There is usually some form of product orientation where there is a belief that the product or the cause (if a charity) will self-promote. This is often used by smaller organizations such as some charities, micro businesses and SMEs.

3   *Arbitrary*, or the 'chairman's rules' – 'budgeting on the hoof'. This has flexibility but is in no way analytical or customer considerate. Again this is often a feature of smaller organizations.

4   *Percentage of sales* – set either through advertising industry or industry (norm for the) sector sources. This puts a focus on sales rather than profit and is often based on past rather than current sales. Every effort should be made to base figures on realistic projections. However, year on year it is unlikely that *ceteris paribus* will prevail. This can result in a downward spiral, i.e. as sales decline, so to does allocation if based on percentage of sales. This is a cost-orientated approach to communications and, in particular, advertising, rather than an investment approach. If the latter orientation prevailed, clearly if sales declined, consideration of spend as investment to halt decline and rebuild sales would be an option worth exploring.

5   *Historical* – what has been done in the past, what the boss says. The only increase may be where media costs have to be followed, or in line with inflation. This might be allied to the 'all we can afford' approach, which has clear drawbacks, and is based on what is left after costs and profit are subtracted from revenue.

6   *Advertising to sales ratio* – based on the relationship between advertising weight and sales volume. It is therefore possible to compare sector averages and other competitors' ratios and to determine spend figures. The advertising/spend (A/S) ratio, according to Fill (2002), is likely to be higher in sectors where there is:

(a)   surplus capacity
(b)   a high number of new product launches
(c)   high margin
(d)   premium price
(e)   short channels
(f)   low financial risk to the customers
(g)   standardized product
(h)   a large number of customers.

The sector is important as can be seen in the big difference between cosmetics (20 per cent of sales turnover on promotion) and other sectors. Using the A/S ratio helps the marketer to control spend and, if so required, set budgets against the competition or sector average. This leads to the idea of SOV, the voice being the whole of expenditure in a particular context. If this SOV is greater than all the other SOVs then, in theory, this voice has a better chance of being heard. This relies on weight being the important factor and it is this premise that has been challenged by numerous agencies who have produced successful campaigns for clients by cleverly using the media and/or through creative ideas that give the client's brand the edge. Share of voice can be an objective tool, especially if used in conjunction with *competitive parity*. If the data is available the marketer can spend the same as the competition, an action that tends to stabilize the market. But trade/consumer mix has to be taken into consideration so that like with like is compared and, similarly, with the qualitative aspect of the message. If this is equal then SOV may be considered the best option since the weight of advertising spend will be the important factor. This can then be linked to share of market (SOM). When SOV = SOM then equilibrium exists (Figure 7.4). Competitive equilibrium exists when key players make it so in order that the status quo is maintained. This might well be collusion on the part of competitors. At the same time it can be viewed as part of strategy with decisions to attack or defend, assuming reliable data is available. This may lead to more being spent to defend or attack a position than would be the norm. Cash cows are generally high price and low maintenance and therefore have an SOV less than that of SOM. A market leader may well have economies of scale and achieve this position above the equilibrium line. Niche players might also be above this line. Below this line are market followers that may well be stars that need investment if SOV is less than SOM in order to reverse this and move stars toward cash cow status.

Other factors may well influence budget-setting that overrides the SOV/SOM and competitive parity machinations, such as resources or difficulties within product life cycles.

Theoretical approaches

Theoretical approaches include marginal analysis and sales response curves. Overall these are of little use, principally because they are not real and, in any event, the information required is impossible and/or too expensive to acquire. The simple, concave sales response curve follows the law of diminishing returns where sales and expenditure relationship is expressed as in Figure 7.5.

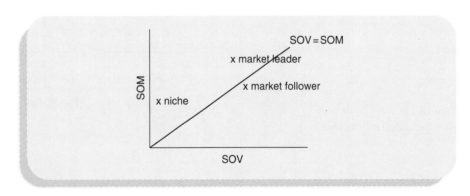

Figure 7.4
The SOM–SOV relationship.

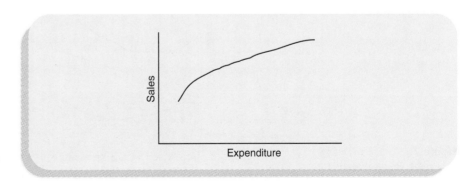

Figure 7.5
The concave sales response curve.

Thus the incremental value of sales decreases as a new unit of expenditure is added. Beyond an optimal point there will be no communications effect and therefore, theoretically at least, a smaller budget can achieve the same results as a larger one, and be just as effective for less expenditure. This also implies that when communications effort is zero, sales will be zero, which may not be the case at all. This gives rise to the S-shaped sales curve. Here the sales produce a concave curve but after an optimal point (A) the curve will plateau and may even decline as a result of irritation or other negative customer perceptions (Figure 7.6).

The marginal approach revolves around the idea that it is possible to predict how many extra sales can be had from an extra unit of spend where the point will be reached where there is equilibrium, i.e. marginal revenue = marginal costs, and P1 is the optimal level of promotional expenditure (Figure 7.7).

However there are too many assumptions not least of which are that promotion is the only cost or influence on sales and that there is no influence from competitive action and reaction. Communications cannot be varied smoothly and continuously as assumed, and not all messages are standardized.

A key question is 'what should the money be used for?' Should the organization spend money on building brand images or selling products, or both? Such objectives are likely to be achieved by particular elements of the communication's mix. This has a bearing on how much is spent on other elements such as sales promotions and PR. Sales promotions costs are easy to measure and

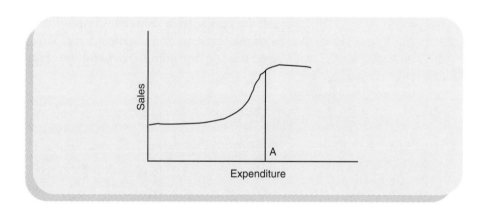

Figure 7.6
The S-shaped sales curve.

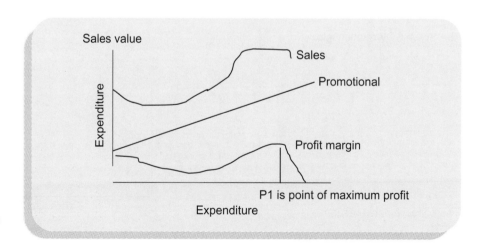

Figure 7.7
The sales value–expenditure relationship.

it is easy to predict the point at which costs will be covered. But this does not rule out anything other than a task approach. Ratio approaches are often more appropriate. Similarly, PR approaches can be costed with a degree of accuracy since mostly it is fixed costs being dealt with such as fees, retainers, expenses and the like, and not buying media space or particular production costs as there are with advertising. Absolute costs can be known, but relative costs of achieving impact and so on have to be based on experience and are therefore subjective.

As suggested in Chapter 4 personal communication is often but not always associated with fixed costs, and the rest of the mix with variable costs. Generally speaking, personal communication dominates in organizational markets and advertising in consumer markets – but this tells us very little indeed. Fixed costs are relatively high and easy to calculate but the relative cost is a more difficult variable to measure.

A combined approach may very well be taken in order to get the best out of all of the above when dealing with appropriation and budgeting. Probably the most used method is percentage of sales. De Pelsmaker, Geuens and Van Den Bergh (2001) maintain that across the consumer market board this is so (50 per cent of all situations). But in terms of business-to-business the arbitrary method is used by 34 per cent of concerns, the affordable method by 26 per cent, percentage of sales method by 28 per cent and the objective/task method (clearly more than one method having been employed) by 40 per cent. This is underlined by the notion of a combined approach. Especially since other factors such as those from the micro and macro environment are constantly present and changing, a crisis may occur or a new situation may arise, for example the opportunity to develop a new product.

VIGNETTE

Spend, spend, spend . . . but on what? How about the magazine medium?

The Internet, multimedia revolution and the information superhighway have been some of the buzzwords and phrases of recent times. Group 7/8 leaders gather in Brussels to discuss the 'information society' and the question has been asked as to what a global communications network will be able to do, who will have access to it – and who will benefit. The information superhighway has been called both a 'yellow brick road' and a 'blind alley'. It uses e-mail, newsgroups/global bulletin boards and the World Wide Web. Cyberspace is used to get information. It is a new way of selling products and services from pizzas that can be designed by the customer and ordered there and then, to business-to-business uses where applications are also for industry and commerce. There is obvious concern for intellectual property rights and data protection, even greater concern over issues such as the dominance of Microsoft and greater still over pornography.

In this world of fragmentation, magazines are perhaps the most fragmented media choice. There are international titles that allow targeting across borders, even though the same title may not be exactly the same in each market it appears. There have been twenty years of rapid growth, with total circulation increasing, yet in terms of media spend, magazines have lost out, despite the likes of Estée Lauder and Gucci building their businesses in them. Despite attempts by the more generalist consumer magazines to use editorial flexibility, some less flexible vehicles have failed. Clearly, marketing has had a role with for example, brand extensions of the likes of Elle with Elle Décor, Elle Cuisine and Elle Girl. Television has been the main medium, often with magazines in a supporting role. However, recently the niche markets have been targeted by SIMs, making magazines more important here than with the major consumer brands. Money spent on the latter has been spent on television. Magazines clearly have high audience involvement, but the characteristics and qualities of magazines vary enormously. Therefore there is evidence that running magazines with television can be cost effective, with Nike, Ford, Coca-Cola and many others endorsing this view. Even Bill Gates is quoted as saying that people buy SIMs as much for the advertisements as for the articles. But it is rather misleading to use the term 'interest' when really lifestyle is involved and it is the successful targeting that comes with such vehicles that has led to the continued fragmentation of this medium. One difficulty experienced because of this is the accurate measurement of audience or readership size, let alone how a magazine might be used or 'consumed'. The usual qualities apply to specialist magazines as with magazines generally, but with some added advantages. They are not casually purchased but are bought and read avidly, being valued for information and lifestyle imagery they provide. They become reference material and have authority, commanding trust in their readership. Because lifestyle is involved in many cases, it is not just specialist products such as golf clubs that can be advertised but also more general products that can be associated with a particular activity. The two key areas here are, first, quantitative data on audience size and, second, qualitative data on consumption. To achieve this in practice there are many and varied research services, systems or models available. Below is a sample of just a few from the (mostly) magazine context.

Research Services Ltd (RSL), responsible for the *National Readership Survey* (NRS), covered ninety specialist magazines in nine sectors ranging from music to specialist sports to classic cars. This research showed, among many other things, that advertising in SIMs is both informative and liked by readers.

The use of magazines for building brand awareness is common, but to act on brand image may require a combination of television and magazines to be able to deal with both the emotional and the rational aspects of brand image. To this end *Axicom* evaluates the effectiveness of individual campaigns. Axicom first selects the criteria that are relevant to advertising objectives, for example brand awareness. Second, it measures effectiveness by comparing segments of the target differentiated by their degree of exposure in each medium used. This uses a representative sample of the target and asks about brand variables and media habits, and then applies this data to media schedules and converts this into a probable OTS for each respondent. Relating this to brand variables measures effectiveness in each medium. All things being equal, if brand awareness is higher among those people most exposed to the campaign then the inference is that this is due to the campaign. If this is repeated a number of times across a number of media then a comparison on advertising effectiveness across media forms can be made as with the *Sesame* design. This then suggests confirmation of marginal effectiveness decrease from the first to subsequent exposures but that performance varies between media. Sesame suggests that a mix of media would be more effective than just one since the first exposure in each medium will have maximum effectiveness. Magazines appear more effective on rational platforms and television on emotional ones but generally, in terms of brand awareness, magazines are well ahead of other media. The *Richness in Occasions to Convince (ROC) index* developed by the *Media Partnership Research* measures the effect of the reading conditions and environment, which is clearly part of the qualitative research support for marketers who would want to increase message efficiency and aid vehicle selection decisions. The ROC index and acceptance scores go beyond mechanistic, substituting OTS with opportunity to convince (OTC). This takes in parameters such as magazine structure or mood of the reader. Beyond impact, ROC is an indicator of receptivity by providing a value measure. The ROC index has three main dimensions. First, the audience must be capable of being attracted to and being moved by the advertising and, second, there must be no irritation or excessive interference. Third, acceptance scores, based on liking, supplements ROC and marketers then have a tool that helps marketers insert advertising into the most favourable context, using readership targeting based on qualitative research rather than demographics and to take account of mood and receptivity.

Sources: Adapted from the BBC (1995); Kilger (2001); Raimondi (1995); Rodger (1996); Smith (1997); Vincent et al. (1997); Walker (2002); www.warc.com/fulltext/bestpractice/77201.htm.

STOP POINT

The magazine medium has a lot of dimensions to it but, despite the changes that have taken place in terms of the Internet, satellite and cable and so on, it still has much going for it. Consider in a general way its characteristics. Think about the added advantages to using SIMs. How can a marketer make sure that particular magazines provide what the publishers say, both in terms of quantitative measures such as size of readership and qualitative measures such as receptivity or mood of the reader?

Assignment

Choose a large company such as Procter and Gamble or Boots. Research one of this company's brands with a view to determining which media are used and why, and how such media might be planned and budgets formulated. In comparison, place the typical smaller enterprise (say with a turnover of £1 million) alongside this. Write a comparative report that teases out the differences at each stage of media selection, planning and spend.

Summary of Key Points

- The characteristics of the various media are fundamental and should be understood by the marketer.

- The media industry has changed and independent media specialists are now the norm.

- The media need to be planned in a way that fits in with IMC philosophy, the roles of the planner and buyer being crucial still to this process.

- There are a number of external and internal sources of data that inform media planning and facilitate media decision-making.

- The key objectives within media planning are reach, frequency and weight resulting in the use of gross rating points and television ratings to help establish which particular spots/slots might be purchased and, therefore, to develop media schedules. Cost is always a key factor.

- Budgets are to do with timings and spend of financial resources. There are top-down and bottom-up practical approaches to setting budgets. There are also theoretical approaches that are available to the marketer but which in practice are of questionable value.

Examination Questions

1 Explain why the various characteristics of the media such as interactivity, dramatic effect or imagination are important considerations during the process of media selection. Use examples to illustrate.

2 Write a job specification for media planners and media buyers, outlining the main tasks facing each.

3 Explain the terms reach, frequency and weight in the media-planning context. Explain what a GRP is and illustrate this in terms of TVRs.

4 Explain why the cost per thousand method is so flawed.

5 Scheduling can use the ideas of continuity, flighting and pulsing among other things. Discuss scheduling in the context of a new brand launch. Use examples to illustrate.

6 Outline the theoretical and practical approaches available to the marketer. Explain the difference between appropriation and budgets. In terms of setting budgets, explain why the objective/task approach appeals to marketers.

7 Theoretical approaches continue to haunt the media planner as an ideal that is unreachable but so desirable. Explain in depth marginal analysis in the media-planning context.

8 Explain why the advertising to sales ratio method is limited to particular contexts and cannot be used by the marketer setting budgets across the board.

9 The valuation of brands has finally arrived with brand equity on the balance sheet. Discuss this in relation to the view that communication is an investment rather than a cost.

10 'Despite the wonders of technology the effects on communications are evolutionary rather than revolutionary.' Explain why this is the case using examples to illustrate.

Notes

1 De Pelsmaker, Geuens and Van Den Bergh (2001) cite Morganstern's B-coefficient analysis suggesting that different media require a different number of exposures to achieve the same levels of memorization where the lower the coefficient then the higher the number of exposures. It is suggested that cinema has a B-coefficient of 70 per cent requiring only two exposures,

whereas radio only has a coefficient score of 5 per cent and requires five to fourteen exposures in order to achieve the same level of memorability.

2 A diversion from this consensus comes from Jones (1995) with his Short Term Ad Strength (STAS) scan data approach. This contends that in the short term, rather than advertising for longer-term brand-building, advertising can be used to get sales. The effect may be small and temporary but enough to warrant the expenditure on advertising rather than a potentially brand-damaging sales promotion tool. Here the first exposure is the greatest part of sales, therefore the most effective frequency is one. After this the impact gets smaller so that it is uneconomic to use heavy bursts because of diminishing returns. The recommendation is to have a low frequency over a longer period. Critical to this is the idea of the STAS differential. This is the difference between market shares achieved with and without the exposure, and this must be large enough to justify the frequency of one.

3 Indeed this is the starting point of the 'advertisers control programming' debate. It is argued by some that television programmes, for example, have to be 'dumbed down' in order to match the ordinary everydayness of consumer products such as toilet rolls. In this way the major players such as Procter and Gamble control television output.

4 Audience research is constantly in the spotlight regarding accuracy that is crucial to the existence and running of a very large industry in its own right, as discussed more fully in Chapter 18.

5 It should be noted that much of this applies to advertising only. Personal selling is mostly kept out of marketing communication and treated separately in this context. Some of the approaches such as objective/task and competitive parity can be used for sales promotion and PR. Often a predetermined ratio based on 'what works' for a sales promotion campaign might be implemented. Here a maximum of a percentage of sales is being used.

6 Another term for this is 'experimental allocation'. There are many ways in which one might experiment with differing levels of allocation. Different areas of the market can be treated differently and this can use a control area approach to keeping some things the same while levels of spend are experimented with. This is rather like a test market and, as such, similar problems occur in reality. For example, there may be different levels and kinds of competitive action and reaction, differing regional media and differing levels of impact of national media in different areas.

References

BBC (1995). *The Money Programme – Superhighway Special.* Television programme on BBC2, 19 February.

Burnett, J. and Moriarty, S. (1998). *An Introduction to Marketing Communications – an Integrated Approach.* Prentice Hall.

De Pelsmaker, P., Geuens, M. and Van Den Bergh, J. (2001). *Marketing Communications.* Financial Times Prentice Hall.

Donnelly, W. J. (1996). *Media Planning, Strategy and Imagination.* Prentice Hall.

Fill, C. (2002). *Marketing Communications: Contexts, Strategies and Applications.* 3rd edition. Financial Times Prentice Hall.

Jones, J.-P. (1995). Advertising's impact on sales and profitability, IPA conference paper, London, March.

Kilger, J. (2001). Media outlook 2001: magazines. *Advertiser*, March.

Krugman, H. E. (1972). Why three exposures may be enough. *Journal of Advertising Research*, **12**, 11–14.

Los Angeles Magazine (1999). Diller instincts. *Los Angeles Magazine*, March. At www.findarticles.com/cf_lamg/m1346/3_44/.

Milmo, D. (2001). Diller the deal maker. *MediaGuardian*, 23 July. At www.guardian.co.uk/broadcast/story/0749356291, 00.htm1.

Naples, M. J. (1979). *Effective Frequency: The Relationship between Frequency and Advertising Effectiveness*. Association of National Advertisers.

Raimondi, D. (1995). New qualitative descriptors of magazines' potentiality to convey efficient advertising messages. *European Society for Opinion Surveys and Market Research (ESOMAR)*. At www.warc.com/fulltext/esomar/10374.htm.

Rijkens, R. (1993). *European Advertising Strategies*. Cassell.

Rodger, N. (1996). Specialist magazine values. *Admap*, May. www.warc.com

Shimp, T. (1997). *Advertising, Promotion and Supplemental Aspects of Integrated Marketing Communications*. 4th edition. Dryden.

Smith, A. (1997). Proof of performance. Magazine advertising sells, but integrated magazine and television advertising is even more powerful. *Esomar*. At www.warc.com/fulltext/esomar/9238.htm.

Vincent, A. and Vincent, M. (1997). Advertising in magazines – why should you? *ESOMAR*, Lisbon. At www.warc.com/fulltext/esomar/9242.htm.

Walker, C. (2002). The challenge for magazines. *Admap*, **433**, November, 47–49.

Advertising management

Chapter overview

Introduction to this chapter

The nature of advertising is understood here to be the traditional 'above the line' media advertising techniques and associated methods and tools such as television, radio, cinema and magazines. This chapter therefore takes the APIC general framework developed in Chapter 4 and facilitates application, via a decision sequence model in the advertising management context.

Aims of this chapter

This chapter provides a case study that can be analysed with the aid of the material presented in Chapter 4 of this book. In particular, the framework presented at the end of that chapter is designed as a facilitation device for this purpose. After completion of this chapter the reader should be able to:

- explain the elements of the APIC system, as applied to advertising, in broad DSM terms

- understand the ideas behind the critique of the adoption of such an approach

- use the framework for the management of the advertising function

- apply the above to the management of advertising for the White Horse brand of Scotch whisky.

A framework for managing advertising employing the APIC decision sequence model

As outlined in Chapter 4 the APIC DSM is a commonly used model that deals with both the 'art' and 'science' aspects of communication. A decision sequence framework is required to help plan advertising in just the same way as any communication might be planned but the difference is in the detail. The reader should refer to the framework provided in Chapter 4 of this book as an aid to analysis of the case studied below.

A case of Scotch whisky: White Horse whisky

Background

Scotch whisky is, as far as the Scotch Malt Whisky Society is concerned, the very essence of Scotland that sums up the land and its people, about 'peat-smoke and bog myrtle, heather flowers and mown hay, white beaches and salt spray: the scents of the land itself'.[1] Whisky, however, is not just about malt whisky, a single product from a particular distillery made in a particular way. The history of whisky is fairly easy to chart up to a point and as might be expected early accounts involve friars, monks and monasteries and 'medicinal purposes'. It was apparently after the Reformation that farming communities began to distil grain liquor – *aqua vitae*, in Gaelic *uisge beatha* and in English 'water of life'. 'Uisge' was then abbreviated to 'usky', which became whisky. The earliest reference to whisky, or at least *aqua vitae*, appears in the Scottish Exchequer Rolls for 1494 where there is an entry that reads 'eight bolls of malt to Friar John Cor wherewith to make aquavitae'.[2] A boll is an old Scottish measure of not more than six bushels, one bushel being about 25.4 kilograms.

Until 1784 it was perfectly legal to make whisky at home from grain grown on one's own land as long as the whisky was not sold. Surplus grain was a catalyst in the development of whisky-making during the eighteenth century. This, coupled with lowland urban population growth due to the Industrial Revolution, saw the advent of what would become the commercial distillery. Businesses may have benefited from the ban on private distilling after this date but legal produce was from the start heavily taxed and, of course, illegal distilling flourished. By the 1820s many of the illegal producers were encouraged to take out licences and go 'legal'.

Scotch can only be called Scotch if it is distilled and matured in Scotland.[3] There is a tradition, then, of distilling and maturing Scotch whisky that uses crafts passed down over the generations. Until 1831 all whisky produced in Scotland was malt whisky. After the advent of the patent still in that year, the production of grain whisky was made possible. *Blends* are usually made from a combination of malt and grain whiskies. A blend could be made from any two single whiskies but usually blending, a 'considerable art acquired only after years of experience',[4] involves a good number of different single whiskies. The job is essentially to blend whiskies of different character that produce a final product that is greater than merely the sum of its parts. There is also the desire to achieve consistency in this combination, which is called *vatting*. When a blend is created, only the youngest constituent part can be used to claim the age of the product. In other words, if a blend is made up of a variety of single whiskies, most of which are over ten years old but one is eight years old, then the product must not try to proclaim itself to be older than eight years. It cannot be called Scotch unless all constituent parts are three years old or more.

Marketing challenge

It is said that Scotch whisky manufacturers are facing the biggest marketing challenge in their history. Bruce-Gardyne (2003) reminds the reader that many brands of Scotch have disappeared over the years or are stronger in overseas markets than in the UK. For example 100 Pipers was the number 4 whisky in Scotland ten years ago but 'its image may have become a little too Scottish for the Scots themselves', yet it sells a million cases in Thailand alone and is big in Asia. The Scottishness country-of-origin effect is important in this context. The 1960s and 1970s were the golden age for the Scotch whisky industry (Jones, 2002). Changing tastes, drink-driving laws and healthier living in the USA and UK alongside the mid-1970s recession have reversed this. The industry itself, according to Jones, was preoccupied with raising output and ignored these trends, reflecting a production rather than a marketing orientation. The structure of the industry has not helped matters, at one stage it looking like an uneasy confederation of fiefdoms (Jones, 2002). Despite starting off in the 1800s having some idea of what customers wanted the ideas of segmentation and branding were slow in coming. Poor marketing research did not help and it took some time before proper qualitative research would provide usable information on what perceptions, beliefs and so on were out there; this with regard to smoothness, price willing to pay and other, relevant parameters. The industry had picked upon the VALS-type typologies with International Distillers and Vintners examining consumer responses to Smirnoff vodka in 1983 that came up with descriptors such as 'London trendsetters', 'young inexperienced' and so on (Jones, 2002).

The takeover of the Bell's brand by Guinness and the merger of Guinness with Grand Metropolitan (as part of Diageo) meant that marketing, including brand-driven strategies that play a major role in maintaining prices and profitability, had finally replaced price competition, and that segmentation became key. In certain markets, the UK included, whisky drinkers are getting older and that makes them literally a dying breed. It is recognized that, for younger consumers of alcohol, whisky still conjures up images of 'briar pipes, cosy slippers and stags' heads over the mantelpiece'.[5] It is known through taste tests that whisky does not appeal to the younger palate. Yet for years whisky was sold on the idea that it should be drunk straight, or with ice or water, a 'real man's drink'. Whisky then was not for mixing, at least in the UK, yet elsewhere in Europe whisky has been mixed freely with the likes of coke to make the spirit more palatable.

The Scotch Whisky Association knows this 'protocol' problem full well. The problem is what is seen as the younger consumer tampering with Scotland's national spirit, debasing it even. The Cutty Sark brand management has abandoned the UK and 'Scottish cues' because they simply do not motivate the younger target. David King, marketing director for Cutty Sark is quoted as saying that the message is 'Its up to you. We're not going to judge you'. In the USA the strategy is unashamedly 'booze, bands and babes'. In Spain it focuses on lifestyle or choice issues such as drugs, sexuality and non-marital partnerships. King argues that the Scotch industry have effectively lost a whole generation of young consumers through being too limiting.[6]

On the other hand, there are those in the industry who see this quite differently. Some advocate targeting mature whisky drinkers with a mature approach. Allied Domecq's Teacher's brand, for example, does just this to the 13.5 million UK scotch drinkers. Chivas Regal is said to favour a classic balanced approach – bring in the new without alienating the old. Gary Cartmell of Cartmell Communications, responsible for youth strategy for Chivas is quoted as saying, 'We'd better not screw around with two hundred years of history. We mustn't lose all those fantastic things that have kept the older end of the market so loyal to the product. I don't want Chivas Regal to suddenly become a fashionable drink among a certain niche'.[7]

The Scotch Whisky Association is confident that people in the UK will get bored with vodka-based pre-mixed drinks and there will be opportunities for whisky. There is a realization that there is a certain amount of cultural baggage and that it will take a substantial marketing effort to attract new drinkers. However, there are opportunities to concentrate on those markets where younger consumers know that Scotch can be mixed. United Distillers and Vintners (UDV), the brand owners of Bell's and White Horse, have sought to recruit a new generation of young drinkers to the whisky market. There is an opportunity to achieve this by repositioning their White Horse brand so that it shakes free of the old-fashioned imagery currently associated with Scotch whisky, but the brand does come with a degree of fame. It is one of the leading brands in Japan for example. This would involve developing a marketing strategy and communications campaign that will change the way younger people perceive White Horse. The blend, however, does contain 40 per cent malts including Talisker, Linkwood[8] and, not surprisingly, Craigellachie, a fourteen-year-old malt bottled by UDV, which would suggest an older palate. While some lighter brands such as J&B might mix well with Coke, White Horse may be perceived as being too heavy to do this. However, people's tastes have changed, as seen with the increasing popularity of single malts and the move towards the more phenolic whiskies (Bruce-Gardyne, 2003).

United Distillers and Vintners, the largest drinks company in the world and one of four operations within Diageo, have already stated their intentions to promote Bell's in a way that continues to appeal to mainstream older, established whisky drinkers by continuing to reflect more traditional values (IPA, 1999). Currently Bell's advertising is led by the Jools Holland[9] campaign 'its in the blend'. The advertisement begins with musician Jools playing individual notes on a piano, which then become chords; the piano is then accompanied by other instruments. The suggestion is that a good whisky is like good music – how things blend together, the whole being more than the sum of the parts. This is therefore intended to attract younger (than the norm) consumers into considering whisky as opposed to the many other options available. This underlines the relevance of certain things for consumers today, as opposed to the more traditional country-of-origin-led signifiers such as tartan or bagpipes.

The UK Scotch whisky market has been in decline for over fifteen years. Drinking patterns generally have moved away from traditional dark spirits (such as rum and whisky) in favour of white spirits (e.g. vodka), wine and lagers. Each generation of new drinkers has been attracted to the marketing and promotion of chilled, long, lighter drinks. Brands that come from other countries such as Russia or parts of Latin America, combining genuine authenticity with exciting contemporary images, have enjoyed persistent growth. The size of the blended whisky market was substantially lower toward the end of the 1990s (8 108 000 × 9 litre cases) than it was in 1990 (10 980 000 × 9 litre cases). Over time the profile of whisky drinkers has gradually become older, within a base that is in itself declining. The number of adults drinking whisky at least once a month has declined by 600 000, and over half the remaining 4.2 million consumers are over fifty years old. The rate of recruitment of people in their twenties and thirties has declined rapidly over recent years (IPA, 1999).

As suggested above, whisky has always been acknowledged as an 'acquired taste' that was unlikely to appeal to novice drinkers, but rather reflected a more mature palate. In the past people made the transition to traditional dark spirits but the evidence seems to suggest that this is no longer the case, or at least not in anything like the numbers they did historically. Consumers no longer seem motivated to rise to the challenge of drinking traditional dark spirits, but are still interested in trying new dark spirits. The growth in malt whisky and bourbon demonstrates this. Table 8.1 illustrates this decline.

The leading brand has consistently remained Bell's (see Table 8.2), but the total share of all the brands is being consistently eroded by less expensive and less famous alternatives. So, in addition to operating in a market that is in overall

Age	Dec 80	Dec 85	Dec 90	Dec 95
18–24	10	11	11	10
25–34	19	14	15	15
35–49	27	27	24	24
50+	44	48	50	51
Total	100	100	100	100

Source: IPA (1999).

Table 8.1
Profile of whisky drinkers (percentage)

Brand share	1993	1994	1995	1996	1997
Bell's	18.9	17.0	17.7	17.0	17.0
Teachers	7.4	7.5	6.9	6.2	6.2
Famous Grouse	13.4	12.8	12.4	12.9	12.8
White Horse	3.1	2.7	2.9	2.3	2.4
Grant's	5.3	5.3	5.1	4.8	4.9
Whyte & Mackay	4.4	4.6	4.7	4.1	4.2
Own Label	18.9	19.0	18.9	19.0	19.1
Cheapest on display	9.1	10.8	12.8	13.3	13.4
Others	19.5	20.3	18.6	20.4	20.0
Total	100	100	100	100	100

Source: IPA (1999).

Table 8.2
Brand share (percentage)

decline, brands are losing their share of that market. The recent recessionary climate has not helped the fortunes of this sector.

The current image of whisky

Recent research (IPA, 1999) used qualitative research among 18–25-year-olds (typically still experimenting) and 25–30-year-olds (usually becoming established in their repertoire) to try to understand what the barriers to drinking whisky are and therefore how a marketer might go about challenging these beliefs through brand presentation.

This research found that there were both product and image barriers to whisky-drinking. It is believed to be a strong and overpowering spirit, with a potent bitter smell and 'rough' or 'fiery' taste that will linger unpleasantly after drinking. It is also universally described as a spirit that is very difficult to mix. Repertoires are usually restricted to 'ordinary' mixers such as ice, water, ginger and lemonade. This makes it more difficult to make whisky accessible in a more dilute form, which is typically how young people learn to acquire a taste for spirits. It is rare to be able to take them neat from the beginning. For some, these product barriers can be seen as an initiation test, with the reward being the acknowledgement of being the aforementioned 'real man'.

There is a fair degree of myth and mystery surrounding Scotch whisky. For example, turning a bottle of Scotch upside down before opening does nothing to it but folklore says one should practise this. It is not injurious to drink whisky with oysters, but legend has it so.[10] Current whisky imagery is seen as outdated and largely irrelevant. It puts out tired, safe old images of tartan, hills, heather and glens, lochs, bagpipers, open fires, old men drinking on their own and so on that are all considered to have once been targeted at young people's parents or grandparents. These images are not felt to reflect the more authentic, real-life images of Scotland and its rich heritage. Films such as *Braveheart* and political moves to give Scotland greater independence are all areas of much greater interest and offer more compelling images of the dignity and depth of Scotland's rich history.

The consumer

The IPA research project also investigated the values of young people generally, not just with respect to whisky. The findings were as follows:

- Today's young people view balance as a necessity to successful life in the twenty-first century.

- They are motivated by success in their desired careers, but the focus for them must also be on enjoyment and escapism in their spare time (hence the popularity of drug and rave culture).

- They are materialistic, but in a less aggressive way than the young people of the Thatcherite 1980s.

- To some extent, an environmental awareness and the need to treat and respect the world we live in has softened this.

During the 1990s it is thought that a shift towards honesty and authenticity – a move away from the contrived lifestyle-orientated 1980s – occurred.

Therefore, being true to oneself is identified as being important. Optimism was also evident, as it is with many young people who have not been hardened by the reality of life. Reflecting the honesty that they view as prevailing in the 1990s, young people appreciate quality, sincerity and unpretentiousness. This reflects a going-back-to-basics mentality. They also consider originality, intelligence and a degree of irreverence (or not taking oneself too seriously) to be particularly important. In sum, 'less is more'.

Humour is seen to be an important vehicle for facing up to the realities of life. Humour that is self-deprecating, subtle and self-referential is particularly liked. British comedians such as Jack Dee are felt to capture this style. The honesty and insight involved with this approach is also appreciated because it credits the viewer with some intelligence.

The values associated with young people today are also tinged with a degree of vulnerability. The prospect of recession has forced many to fear losing their jobs and, therefore, to face the possibility of underachieving in their lives. The thought of contracting HIV or AIDS is also a concern among many young people who are sexually active (IPA, 1999).

Whisky blending and branding

Early blending was not sophisticated and is associated with the ways in which whisky, legal and otherwise, was traded. There was little quality control and not much respect for consistency. Andrew Usher, in 1853, is accredited with the first commercial blend, i.e. the first to be offered for sale to a wider market. Usher was an agent in Edinburgh for Glenlivet and his creation was named 'Old Vatted Glenlivet' and by 1860 it was being advertised in London and sold in India. The same year also saw Gladstone's Spirit Act which allowed blending to occur in bonded warehouses before duty was paid.[11] Peter Mackie, one of the most well-known whisky blenders and distillers of his day, in 1890 created White Horse whisky. He named it after one of Edinburgh's most famous coaching inns, the White Horse Cellar. Indeed the brand logo reflects the pub sign design. In its distinctive 'squat' bottle the brand sells at about £11.99 for 70 cl, which is below that of Bell's (£12.99) and Teachers (£12.69). These would be typical blends on the market. Malts are generally somewhat more expensive, and can be very expensive indeed. A 1998 survey of five of the world's top malt whisky specialists saw the Highland Park and Lagavulin brands come out on top. These brands retail for well over £20. The scoring was based on the quality of the malt, the consistency of that quality over time, the distillery overall and brand expression in the market.[12]

With White Horse, as with most brands, there is a certain amount of legend attached. For example, Yorkshire farmers are said to have always been particularly attached to the brand. They created the very smooth and drinkable 'whisky milk'. This consists of a tumbler made up of 50 per cent cold milk and 50 per cent White Horse whisky. This was seen as a favourite way to wind down at the end of a hard day. Alternatively, the brand may mix very well with ginger ale or orange juice and also coke but, as mentioned above, it may be that White Horse is too heavy to be mixed with the latter.

It is many years since the brand had any advertising support, with most of United Distillers' effort being behind Bell's. However, it is recognized that the successful targeting of a new generation of young consumers is vital to the future of the whisky market. The recent relaxation of the voluntary code whereby whisky brands may now be advertised on television represents a particular opportunity (IPA, 1999).

Assignment

You have been asked to help devise an advertising plan of action that would involve White Horse Scotch whisky. Use the DSM provided in Chapter 4 to complete the following tasks:

- Outline what you feel to be the key background points to the Scotch whisky case from an advertiser's perspective. From this information establish the likely target(s).

- From the information available establish possible objectives and positioning for the promotion of Scotch whisky generally and White Horse in particular. Write an outline advertising strategy proposal for White Horse Scotch whisky and suggest push, pull and profiling ideas as well as creative and media tactics.

- Provide ideas on the implementation of an advertising campaign by using the parameters in the implementation section of the DSM framework and show clearly what you would recommend in terms of allocation, budgets, timings, seasonality and so on.

- Using the final section of the DSM, the control section, suggest what monitoring, evaluation and research methods and techniques you would employ to maximize efficiency and effectiveness of the advertising campaign.

Summary of Key Points

- Most writers would subscribe to the form of decision sequence model when attempting to manage advertising. There are, however, challenges to the APIC type of system without alternatives. A shift has occurred with regard to a move away from communication effects to return on investment in advertising.

- Analysis deals with assessments of customers, products, the organization and its environment. This is the 'Where are we now? question.

- Planning deals with targets, objectives and positioning. This is the 'Where do we want to go?' question. This is followed by consideration of creative and media strategy. This is the 'How do we get there?' question.

- Implementation is a consideration of 'How do we put this into practice?' and involves the allocation of spend to the campaign.

- Control involves evaluation and research and is the 'Did we get there?' question. This is not only a check on whether objectives have been achieved, but also a consideration of the place of research in the entire framework.

Examination Questions

These questions are similar to those outlined in Chapter 4 but should be answered more specifically with regard to advertising and the White Horse brand.

1 Explain why you agree or disagree with the contention that the APIC type model is useful as a framework for advertisers to operate within.

2 Outline what you consider to be the important elements of the analysis stage of an advertising decision sequence model.

3 The planning stage of a DSM involves consideration of 'where do we want to go?' having already established targets. Discuss the importance of establishing targets early on in an advertising campaign.

4 Explain the usefulness (or not) of perceptual mapping in planning advertising.

5 Creative strategy is part of 'How do we get there?' Discuss the different advertising appeals available.

6 Discuss the importance of involvement with particular reference to creative appeals.

7 Media strategy is also part of 'How do we get there?' Discuss the key media characteristics for this case.

8 There are a number of practical issues when considering how to put a campaign into practice. Discuss these in relation to the case.

9 Discuss the logic behind pre-, concurrent and post-testing within advertising.

10 Comment on the idea of advertising as an investment not a cost in relation to building brands.

Notes

1 Scotch Whisky, the essence of Scotland, available at www.smws.com/archives/archives_essence.html, accessed 2000.

2 The history of Scotch whisky, available at www.whiskyweb.com/question/question.asp?ID=91, accessed 2002.

3 At www.whiskyweb.com/history.asp?ID=134, accessed 2002.

4 The art of blending, available at www.whiskyweb.com/question/question.asp?ID=93, accessed 2002.

5 At www.whiskyweb.com/features/features.asp?ID=70, accessed 21 February 2002.

6 Ibid.

7 Ibid.

8 At www.scotchwhisky.net/blended/white_horse.htm.

9 Jools Holland is a well-known British musician famous for his BBC2 music show *Later with*. Having been on the pop music scene in the 1970s with the band Squeeze, he later transformed himself into a presenter, fronting the cult music show *The Tube* with Paula Yates. He performs, records and tours with his Rhythm and Blues Orchestra.

10 At www.whiskyweb.com/question/question.asp?ID=96, accessed 2002.

11 The early blenders, available at www.scotchwhisky.com/english/about/blended/blenearl.htm, accessed 2002.

12 The Millennium Malt Classification, available at www.scotchwhisky.com/latest/malt_classification.htm, accessed 1999.

References

Bruce-Gardyne, T. (2003). Whatever happened to the heroes? *Whisky Magazine*, **32**, 13 June. At www.whiskeymag.com/magazine/index.php?story=249.

Institute of Practitioners in Advertising (IPA) (1999). White Horse Whisky. Advertising and academia seminar. London.

Jones, S. R. H. (2002). Brand building and structural change in the Scotch whisky industry. Dundee Discussion Papers in Economics, Department of Economic Studies, University of Dundee, Scotland, September.

PART THREE

Sales Promotion and Direct Marketing

A promotion is a direct inducement to buy. It adds extra value to a product, something that is above and beyond a product's normal value. Direct marketing is an interactive set of tools that uses more than one media to obtain a response that in many cases is an actual transaction, often using sales promotions techniques to achieve this. As such, sales promotions and direct marketing are established elements of the marketing communications mix in many organizations.

This third part of the book consists of three chapters. Chapter 9 deals with the nature and role of sales promotions and Chapter 10 with direct marketing. Chapter 11, following on from Chapter 4 in Part One of this book, simulates a strategic framework for effective promotions and direct marketing management for a major bank, the ASB Bank in New Zealand.

The nature and role of sales promotions

Chapter overview

Introduction to this chapter

Traditional sales promotions were, until the mid-1990s, growing in status, especially when compared with traditional media advertising. Sales promotions, especially money-off coupons, have been with us for a very long time. Premiums, especially those that are self-liquidating, have been around since the turn of the twentieth century, and many a child has enjoyed the 'free' toy in the cereal box over the decades even if parents have not. As Belch and Belch (2004) point out, it was Ovaltine who first went 'interactive', in 1930, with a decoder ring that required the participant to get information from the *Little Orphan Annie* radio shows. But is not just McDonalds's and Pepsi that use promotions, and this chapter provides coverage beyond the consumer where, admittedly, most ideas have been developed and most money spent. Industrial sales promotions and those within channels of distribution are also addressed as are the problems and benefits of using sales promotions.

Aims of this chapter

This chapter seeks to explore the nature and role of sales promotions in relation to the rest of the communications mix. More specifically it aims to:

- discuss the changing, dynamic role of sales promotion within the integrated communications mix
- highlight the advantages and disadvantages when using sales promotions
- discuss the objectives behind the use of sales promotions
- explain the role of creativity in providing the key notion of added value through promotions
- explain and explore the various types of promotion available to marketers, both consumer and trade
- consider sales promotions beyond the usual tactical level and consider how sales promotions are implemented.

The nature of sales promotions in relation to marketing communications

The nature of sales promotions

It is hard to say in percentage terms what is spent on sales promotions. Sales promotion's role in the communications mix is very much dependent upon the context in which it is used. Consumer packaged goods, the likes of Kellogg, Heinz, Pepsi, Coca-Cola, are big players in consumer and trade sales promotions, and a simple description would be that sales promotions are used to differentiate brands on a shelf in a retail environment. However, other consumer sectors, consumer durables, business-to-business and industrial marketers use sales promotions in one way or another. Estimates vary but a typical promotional budget of an fmcg would be 60–70 per cent on sales promotions with most of the rest on advertising. However, during last decade this has perhaps risen to 75 per cent. Added to this is the fact that advertising often has as a platform a sales promotion message – according to Belch and Belch (2004), 17 per cent of advertisements are of this nature. It can be argued that this sort of communication can be both an incentive and brand image-building if done properly.

In the USA Belch and Belch (2004) reckon direct consumer sales promotion expenditure doubled to \$100 billion between 1991 and 2001 and \$150 billion dollars went to trade promotions. Yeshin (1998) uses Advertising Association figures to suggest that in 1988 sales promotion in the UK was worth £2.5 billion compared with advertising's £6.5 billion. Then, using Mintel figures, Yeshin suggests this spend in 1995 to be £4.9 billion on sales promotion and about £11 billion on advertising in the UK. If such statistics are correct, it is easy to see that sales promotions spend doubled in this period whereas advertising spend did not. Sales promotion can be seen as an acceleration tool to speed up the buying process, to drive up the rate of sale. Ideally, sales promotions should generate sales that cannot be generated by other means and the marketer needs to ensure that they are not selling products through an inducement and at a cost on a product that would have been bought anyway. Also, the marketer needs to make sure that the customer is not merely stocking up on non-perishables without this being part of a planned communication campaign, for example to defend against competitive action.

For some academics and practitioners, sales promotions are a range of tactical marketing techniques designed within a strategic marketing framework to add value, usually monetary, to a product or service in order to achieve specific sales and marketing objectives. In this way of thinking, sales promotions should be short term and used to trigger or induce immediate behaviour, or at best to accelerate the consumer decision-making as with 'buy now, pay later' schemes. However, this book argues for a strategic and integrated marketing communications approach so that this sentiment does not fit. Sales promotions, advertising and the rest should be operating together in an integrated fashion. The view that advertising provides added value that is intangible and other promotions provide added value that is temporary and tangible is rather naive. Sales promotion is certainly a direct inducement that offers added value and often the objective will be one of creating a sale, but the term 'sales promotion' has a broader meaning than this. Sales promotion then can be defined as '*the marketing function that induces the customer to buy through offering something that adds value above and beyond a product or brand's original value'*. In other words, sales promotions add value of one sort or another such as the chance to win a prize or extra product for the same price. But this has to be real value as perceived by the target and not by the company or agency people, and sales promotions can be used in such a way as to help build brand equity and image as discussed later in this chapter.

Buyer behaviour theory and sales promotion

Chapter 2 dealt with communication theory and Chapter 3 with behaviour. More specifically, learning theory is very useful when attempting to understand the role of sales promotion in the customer decision-making process. Much of what the Behaviourists wrote that has been applied to marketing has been applied in the sales promotion area. Classical and operant conditioning, as discussed in Chapter 3, are about predicting behaviour as determined by reward and punishment. It is therefore useful in that sales promotion reinforces the reward that the use of the product produces and should increase the likelihood of repurchase. Pavlov had developed respondent conditioning with the now famous dogs salivating to the sound of a metronome, associating this with the meat powder that Pavlov had rubbed into their mouths, originally to the sound of a metronome. While John Watson, an American psychologist, became the founding father of American Behaviourism and S-R psychology, despite being sacked from his university, it was Edward Thorndyke who created the 'law of effect' that is to do with positive and negative consequences. The 'law' states that the consequences of behaviour will govern the frequency of that behaviour in the future. Using cats, Thorndyke showed that a cat could learn to do the behaviour repetitively in order to achieve the favourable outcome of food by hitting a lever to open the cage, i.e. operant or instrumental conditioning. Fred Skinner distinguished between operant and respondent behaviour, and introduced psychology to the worlds of managing people's lives and managing children, leading to behaviour therapy to deal with phobias and anxiety disorders.

However, from a marketing perspective, it was Watson who came to be most influential. It was he who, post-university, moved into advertising and became responsible for *shaping*, as discussed in Chapter 3. Shaping is the concept of *diminishing reward*. Watson used this in advertising terms to show how, over time, he could manipulate images of cigarette packs and women to gain acceptance of the idea that a woman could smoke. It was no longer taboo for a woman to smoke since the public could be shaped, over time, by moving the cigarette pack closer to the woman, i.e. *reinforcement of successive acts*, whether by advertising or sales promotions. Shaping therefore breaks the desired behaviour into a series of stages and the parts are then learned in sequence. This process is useful for complex decision-making as these behaviours rarely occur through chance. It is also extremely useful when introducing new products because the initial purchase of any new brand involves a complex set of behaviours. Shaping is a process from gaining trial to gaining repeat purchase to regular purchase. Marketers have to distinguish between the inducement and the product. Shaping should move the customer away from the inducement towards purchase of the product at a normal price and quantity. The marketer might begin with free samples to achieve trial, followed by coupons to induce purchase for a small financial outlay and then a larger one until, finally, the consumer purchases without inducement. The use of such techniques are the foundation of sales promotion strategy for new brands but the overuse of them can have a disastrous effect on brand image.

Reasons for the increased growth of sales promotions activities

Sales promotions are no longer just an afterthought in strategic planning terms and, therefore, are no longer short-term tactical tools to 'shift stock'. The sales promotion industry has matured and communications companies have the expertise to fully integrate the communications mix. The shift in power of retailers as discussed in Chapter 1 of this book led Schultz and others to conclude that retailers at one time did very little but now take a more than active part using sophisticated in-store equipment. The aforementioned 70 per cent or more decisions being made in-store from a repertoire of brands have made in-store displays and other promotions all the more important. Retailers know what is working and so do most manufacturers but it is the strength of Wal-Mart and others within a consolidated industry with big companies' own or private labels having such an impact that dominates currently. More specifically:

1   Advertising costs rose dramatically forcing marketers to seek other forms of communication.

2   There has been a decline in brand loyalty and there is now a 'repertoire of brands' approach with greater consumer choice and willingness to experiment and seek variety.

3   Consumers like incentives and rewards and because of time pressures in busy live sales promotion works in store on the spot.

4   The proliferation of brands means that sales promotions can use trial and shape behaviour over time to achieve repeat purchase in conjunction with retailer shelf space.

5   The fragmentation of markets and increased importance of the target has meant a move away from the mass and a move toward one-to-one marketing, often at a local or special interest group level. Sales promotions are often tied to direct marketing activity that uses personalized incentives.

6   Short-termism became a problem with brand managers shifting stock to meet goals and this is part of the reason why P&G moved to category management. Companies with perhaps lots of 'cash cows' in slow or no growth markets might be tempted to use sales promotions as a quick fix solution but deeper problems remain. Creativity that is needed to solve such problems can be hindered.

7   With increasing accountability expected sales promotions are a direct way of knowing what works especially with the technology available.

8   Sales promotions can work fast and there is pressure from the trade end on manufacturers to provide them in the mix.

9   Competition is intense and relationships or co-marketing alliances with particular retailers have developed. Possibly half the sales promotion money is spent in this way.

10   Clutter breakthrough can be achieved through promotional messages but these may work better than non-promotional messages in some media rather than others.

Advantages and disadvantages of sales promotions

The *advantages* associated with sales promotions are that they provide an easy to measure response and are relatively inexpensive, fast and flexible. The *disadvantages* are that they may appear a short-term 'quick fix', cheapen the brand and may not work unless retailers co-operate, and this may have a high cost in terms of allowances. Sales promotions should be about adding value but problems with brand damage and effect on worth of the brand in terms of equity can be real. Yeshin (1998) discusses the overuse of sales promotions by citing a PIMS study from 1991 that surveyed 749 businesses. This study found that those businesses using a lot of sales promotion had an ROI of 18.1 per cent and those with a more balanced sales promotion use had an ROI of 30.5 per cent. While other factors undoubtedly would come into play, this at least is a strong indicator that sales promotions effects are not always what they seem. Advertising may be best for a long-term franchise where a marketer can build image rather than sell volume. Image and position are key but this depends upon whether sales promotions are being used to build brand franchise or simply as a short-term tool. Trade sales promotions can certainly be used to promote the brand to the trade in a 'look what we offer you in terms of partnership/relationship' kind of way, and loyalty schemes such as air miles or redemptions against other things can help build the consumer brand franchise. In addition, offers consistent with brand image, such as a competition to win a holiday, are a consideration. Some sales promotions are short term and damaging and some good trade allowances may not be passed on in the way intended, but this is simply bad practice. Without due care and attention, actions in the sales promotion area can cheapen the brand in eyes of industry.

VIGNETTE

Building or destroying brand equity? The Hoover debacle

Sales promotions traditionally are designed to bring action. As a piece of marketing communication Hoover's 1993 attempt to get consumers more involved rather than behave in way that a short-term sales promotion would induce actually worked. Their 'free flights to America' offer was designed to sell more vacuum cleaners and washing machines but this was an ill thought through scheme costing millions and ultimately lost senior managers their jobs. Hoover were unable to handle the responses – more than double the number expected – and 30 000 complaints were received. The promotion was originally budgeted at £2 million and the company was warned that it could end up at £20 million in terms of fulfilling the promise, but ended up costing at least £50 million with compensation and the company has now been sold for well below its former value. The 'Hoover debacle', as it became known, has the record now of the most expensive failed promotion in UK marketing history and has made a lot of people nervous about sales promotions. This should not be the case, since there were a number of serious omissions from the company's planning. It is easy to offer up sage advice after the fact and hindsight is a wonderful thing, but this is as strong a case to underline the need for research, pre-testing in particular, as the reader might come across. True there are problems associated with this, such as the competition knowing what ideas the company might be developing, but on balance it is worth that risk rather than simply assuming the offer to be similar to a 'two for one' flight offer that had gone before and which had been successful. Hoover was overwhelmed by the response to this promotion.

The promotion centred on an offer of free flights with purchases of over £100 and retailers were reporting a rush on Hoover products, often two vacuum cleaners at a time, just to be able to claim the tickets. The trade was culpable in that by putting up prices on lower priced models this meant any purchase would qualify. Unwanted products were being resold through the classified sections of local newspapers and advertising magazines. The publicity that followed was not good and Hoover had to be saved by its parent company, but not before it sustained corporate image damage.

Sources: Adapted from Woofenden (2000); Practical Marketing Guides (2003); Smith and Taylor (2002); Pickton and Broderick (2001).

STOP POINT

It is interesting to note that Hoover's current offer, at the time of writing, is a free mountain bike but only on selected models. This promotion was designed to run through the summer of 2003, showing that the company has not given up on sales promotion as a marketing communications tool. Borrowing from other sales promotion ideas is frequently practised. It is easy with hindsight to say that Hoover might have put more effort in before making this particular decision. Think about the dilemma of pre-testing ideas when you do not wish to inform the competition. Think also about relations with others such as dealers and retailers and what you might expect of them, and about the minutiae of an offer that allows something like the Hoover sales promotion to get out of hand.

Targeting and objectives

Targeting

The essence of targeting was dealt with in Chapter 4. This is to do with the break-up of mass markets and the creation of target groups, each of which has potentially different needs to be met. Target needs and wants rather than market needs and wants are a requirement that will only be determined by research. Quantitative research is required to establish targets and qualitative research to determine what motivates them, including the kind of sales promotion, if any, they will respond positively or negatively to. This will determine things such as loyalty towards brand and trust in companies and how a particular sales promotion will work and what is required to make it work.

Objectives

Chapter 4 discussed in general terms what marketing communications objectives are and their place in planning communications, so they should be

SMART. The short-term quick fix is often the objective of the sales promotion but is by no means the only one, and there is often more to it than inducing a sale. As mentioned above, sales promotion operates at the action end of the AIDA-type process and, so, usually the purpose of a sales promotion is to make the recipient move in a particular direction and it is therefore behavioural. Usually the recipient is being induced to try a brand, continue using it or to increase use of it and the trade is being encouraged to engage in pushing the brand to the consumers. Objectives can be *offensive*, for example to gain trial or distribution, or *defensive*, for example to defend against competition. Objectives can therefore be short term or longer term. The latter is less likely but it can be a case of keeping in touch with customers and adding to the brand in some way, such as rewarding loyalty. Objectives should be clear and the company should have a clear idea as to what is to be achieved and why, who the targets are and what benefit they will receive and the length of time and money involved.

Some examples of objectives are:

1   Get a *trial* for first time users or for non-users, with an associated reduction of risk. This can be done through, for example, sampling, money-back guarantees or using introductory offer coupons. This can help ensure that a brand is 'right' *in situ* and can encourage *repeat purchase*. The latter is important since the objective of gaining a trial on its own would lead to product failure without repeat purchase at the normal price.

2   Following on from this the objective would be to increase *repeat purchases* or gain *multiple purchases* by the now existing users of a now established brand. New uses may then be found for existing users while incentives can continue for new users and act as a reward for existing users.

3   Sales promotions can be used to introduce an improved product (new improved) or line extension. 'Buy the shampoo and get the new conditioner free' is a common bound-to-pack way of achieving this objective, which of course encourages trial.

4   Defend share against competitive activity by using sales promotions to take users of the product out of the market for a considerable time. By encouraging stocking up through the use of for example coupons they are then unlikely to switch to a competitive brand, even though it is being promoted.

5   Target a specific segment through sales promotions using geodemographic, psychographic or allied techniques such as light users, heavy users or non-users. Competitions, contests and sweepstakes are useful to target special interest groups.

6   Help build brand image and equity through, for example, association with a top prize in a competition.

There are many other, fairly simple, objectives such as easing price increases or introduce a new way of working with the product. Sales promotions can be part of a bundle of offerings to a client, especially on the business-to-business/industrial side of things.

VIGNETTE

Targeting with sales
promotions as gay
marketing comes out

A communication campaign in days gone by usually targeted a message through media advertising. As fragmentation of markets and media has occurred and special interest groups have become the norm rather than the exception, other communication tools have become more relevant in this context. It is now realized that sales promotions programmes can be developed that are an integral part of the target marketing effort, rather than some add-on or afterthought. The phrase 'the pink pound' is used by the *Guardian* to explore and explode what it sees as a myth of double income, no kids (like the old acronym DINKI from 1980s lifestyle marketing) gay couple with loads of money and no commitments. It argues that while this group is known to exist through research, this is based on a database built from credit cards and donations to political causes, and the average income of gay men is lower than average incomes in the UK. Similar information comes out of the USA where early data came from gay publication subscription lists and, as a rule, magazine subscribers are wealthier than the average citizen. Data was also obtained from on-line surveys using self-selecting samples of affluent gays, not random samples.

Fewer family commitments must surely mean more discretionary time for leisure pursuits. However, to generalize gay lifestyles would be a mistake but this is exactly what some marketers have done with advertising. The example of Budweiser's Bud Light campaign 'Be yourself and make it a Bud Light' featured a bottle clad in leather. This stereotype, for the *Guardian*, is in danger of not only patronizing but also alienating, because it mocks sexuality. So at best this strategy would have little effect and at worst appear cynical targeting. Fair point, but the *Guardian* claims that gays are not the attractive monetary target assumed, they are difficult to target and that only a small number of manufacturers will be able to profit from the gay community.

The assumption, however, that the gay community is only one target appears to be a nonsense. As Kinsman (2001) highlights, gay marketing has finally come out, aided and abetted by research agencies like Witeck-Combs who specialize in marketing to gays. The size of the gay market in the USA is not small with some 15–17 million US citizens openly gay with $450 billion buying power. This grouping has a strong self-identity where sexuality comes first, even before ethnicity. This is a neglected group and so a cautious one when suddenly targeted. But targeted it has been and increasingly so, especially in the USA, by major brands. Some marketers use their own staff to begin to facilitate this through advocacy groups and, according to Witeck-Combs, 72 per cent of gay customers prefer brands that pitch directly, suggesting an opportunity to use sales promotions. They may well be prone to brand loyalty, more so than the mainstream groupings, but this will take serious marketing effort and a deep understanding of needs. For this reason, a quick lunge at the gay market with a sales promotion will not suffice, but this does not negate the use of sales promotions. As *Promo* magazine points out, across the USA big name brands are now targeting gays with various forms of communication including sponsorships, advertising and sales promotion. In one sense this is nothing new since Absolut vodka began advertising in gay publications in the 1970s. GuinnesssUDV had a promotional tour, the 'Malibu Loves Fruit Tour', a ten-week West Coast campaign targeted to women aged 21–29. Alongside this was the tongue-in-cheek 'Fruit Loves Malibu' component targeting gay males aged 21–36. Geographically the latter was situated in San Francisco and Los Angeles, while the former went to San Diego, Phoenix and Las Vegas for geodemographic reasons. As long as it is not a case of laughing at and is a case of laughing with, then this can work.

Sources: Adapted from Guardian Unlimited (2001); http://uk.geocities.com/balihar_sanghera/msconsumerculture.html; Kinsman, (2001).

STOP POINT

There is clearly a problem when marketers do not really know their market. How can a marketer communicate effectively unless he or she is aware of needs, sensitivities and so on? Think about targets such as gays in terms of using sales promotions and what research you would further employ to better understand this market and targets within it, such as those targeted with the Malibu promotion who have a particular demographic such as age on the agenda.

Types of sales promotions

Sales promotions can be targeted at consumers or any part of the supply chain. Consumer promotions are typically coupons, premiums, sampling, price-offs or offers and contests, sweepstakes and competitions. Trade promotions include allowances, displays materials and sales contests. There are also different promotional activities recommended for product launches and established product and for consumers and retailers. Then there are other sales promotions that are used in the business-to-business and industrial marketing contexts so that this can be viewed in a number of ways.

Consumer sales promotions

Sampling

If the objective is *trial* then sampling is a key tool in inducing this and to break old loyalties. *Sampling* is associated with products of low unit value and can only be used if the product is divisible and brand features and benefits can be adequately demonstrated. Purchase cycles have to be relatively short otherwise consumers will forget. Sampling therefore is much used by fmcg packaged goods manufacturers. Sampling can be very effective but will not make consumers retry a product that is somehow inferior. Clearly it is difficult if not impossible to sample many products such as forklift trucks or consumer durables like washing machines. Even on the faster side of consumer marketing some products take longer to work or try out, like a brand of moisturizer (the effects of which may take some time and trial to assess), and sampling may not be a possibility.

The means of delivering the sample are many and varied. *Door-to-door* or through the use of newspaper delivery is effective but expensive. *Through the mail* is common but clearly only relatively small, lightweight samples can be delivered. Geodemographic systems such as ACORN or Mosaic (to use two UK examples) can be used as a database for mailings generally but for samples also. *In-store* sampling is common for food and drink, and is used in conjunction with money-off coupons for instant purchase. Related to this is the *in-store demonstration*, mostly food related such as kitchen equipment, knife sharpeners and the like. Both are expensive and need careful planning as well as, in many cases, the co-operation of retailers. Sampling can take place in a similar way at different *events* such as sports matches and samples can be strapped to *packs* of products that would have the same type of buyer. Samples of perfumes have even been placed in magazine advertisements whereby the reader could scratch the paper to release the fragrance. With technology moving forward and the Internet's pace of development, more and more opportunities for creative sampling distribution are being found. Certainly, minus the coupon, sampling avoids the potential brand damage associated with couponing.

Couponing

The coupon is the oldest sales promotion device and now probably the most problematic in terms of cheapening the brand and also of misuse. According to Belch and Belch (2004), in the USA the number of coupons distributed in 1968 was 16 billion, rising to a peak of 310 billion in 1994 and falling to 239 billion in 2001. The average face value has a similar pattern, it being 21 cents in 1981, rising to 83 cents in 2001 (those redeemed 73 cents). Most Americans use them and one-quarter say they always do. Coupons lower the price to encourage trial and they also encourage retrial, but this is the problem. Once price reduction through couponing has started where does it end? This is a problem for both new and existing products where, for the latter, sales promotions can be used to attract non-users or reward existing ones. This, however, does not necessarily make sense in terms of margins. Couple this with the length of time it takes to redeem coupons and the problem is magnified. Belch and Belch (2004) reckon it takes on average 3.2 months to redeem coupons for grocery products, with many being redeemed just before the expiration date. Coupon misredemption is one of the reasons for the demise of the coupon, which has even been forged and passed on as the real thing. One of the more common occurrences is redemption by retailers without the product being sold. Coupon distribution is by similar means to sampling, i.e. through the mail, door and so on, but often through advertising and inserts in newspapers and magazines. But, as Belch and Belch point out, the attractive cost and quality of a free-standing insert has led to clutter. Direct marketing is increasingly being used because of the benefits of this medium (see Chapter 10) and, as said previously, can be use with a sample as well as the coupon but it is expensive. There are other forms of coupons such as the instant coupon, which is redeemed there and then at the till. These can be placed in-store or on packs.

Competitions (or contests) and sweepstakes

Competitions are also quite popular, and can incorporate product-knowledge tests, which can assist in the learning process. Competitions can be fairly low-cost promotions, and often have retailer support, or comprise a competition among staff (see Chapter 16). These promotions can add excitement and, if designed well, tie in with brand management to contribute towards brand image and development. Awareness, attention and interest can be created among a large proportion of the population but this is not necessarily useful in the targeting sense. The difference between a competition and a sweepstake lies in the skill or some other form of ability required for the former. Some sort of judging goes on in competitions but with a sweepstake the winner is determined by chance. Sweepstakes come in many forms, one popular one being a scratch card, and these are used a lot in direct mailing. These promotions have a fixed, known cost and they may allow the marketer to develop the brand by getting consumers so involved that, for example, the essence of a competition may be to engage consumers with naming a brand. This is quite a clever way to suggest that the brand belongs to the consumer. These promotions are now having billions spent on them ($2 billion in the USA in 2001 according to Belch and Belch, 2004) and they continue to be popular in many markets, especially with the popularity of game shows and reality television grows. Alongside this are the growing problems on the legal side, which is why marketers rely on specialist firms and the appropriate regulatory body when designing such promotions. For example in the UK the Code of Advertising Practice (CAP), administered by the ASA, includes a code for sales promotion practice that runs alongside legislation as laid down in Acts of Parliament, typically The Betting, Gaming and Lotteries Act 1963 (Amended 2002).

Money refunds

Refunds, rebates or cash backs involve the consumer purchasing the product in the knowledge that there will be the facility of a refund. Typically this will be 'no fuss money back if not entirely satisfied'. This minimizes risk to the consumer and encourages repeat purchase. Refunds are subject to codes of practice and law also. In the UK the Sale and Supply of Goods Act 1994 is typical of such legislation. Another form of refund or rebate involves saving coupons or till receipts but these can be problematic, especially where more than one proof of purchase is needed. Redemption rates are low, as low as 1–5 per cent, depending on the medium of delivery, print being lower than in-store or in/on pack offers.

Premiums, bonus packs and price-offs

Often the main tool used for promoting *existing products* is a *premium*, which would not be used for new products to induce trial. A premium is an extra item offered at a low price or free. It can be effective at increasing sales but can also be a distraction from the brand properties. Premiums can attract brand switchers and are used with current users to increase repeat purchases. A premium can be free or have some cost to the consumer. A *self-liquidating premium* is one where the consumer covers the cost of the promotion but this will only work if there is an incentive for the consumer. Again Belch and Belch (2004) maintain that in the USA, marketers spend $4 billion on premiums per annum. Many marketers have moved away from gimmicky toys and the like towards real added value with quality premiums, although McDonald's is the epitome of the former and allegedly the biggest toy manufacturer in the world. With the latter Philip Morris's Marlboro is typical, as presented in the vignette in Chapter 1, whereby part of that 'in-the-mail' promotion was merchandise such as a cigarette lighter. Premiums are subject to tight restrictions, not least because of the obvious link with children and television advertising and other promotions. The *bonus pack* is an uncomplicated way of giving extra value and this can be attractive to the consumer who may switch brands. Apart from rewarding existing consumers, giving them extra may very well take them out of the market and away from the competition, but the consumer may very well stockpile since they would probably have bought the brand anyway. A *price-off* price reduction may create the wrong perception of the product. Price-off deals normally involve on-pack price reductions. Bonus packs and price-offs are closely linked. Link-saves are now common in supermarkets because the technology allows for easy stock control and operation. Two for one or 'buy one get one free'[1] is now commonplace.

Loyalty schemes

Many organizations now have a loyalty scheme of one sort or another. Most involve some sort of points system and the ability then to trade points for merchandise such as wine or other less tangible things such as air miles. Clearly the objective is to create and sustain that most illusive of things called loyalty, so that it is about relationship and database marketing, but some might say 'loyalty scheme' is a misnomer and should be called 'frequent purchaser scheme', as with KLM in the vignette below.

Exhibitions

Exhibitions are important forums that are a shop window where actual and potential customers can see, touch and feel products. These are interlinked with trade shows (see below). They provide the opportunity to interact with the consumer, to answer questions and more often than not to sell merchandise. Typical of the large consumer exhibition that is also a tradeshow in the UK is the London Motor Show. Technically this is not a place to actually sell directly but it is a vehicle that is part of many companies' integrated marketing communications and as such is a powerful way of reaching a large number of people. Ordinary people who visit the Motor Show may not do so because they are at the point of purchasing a new car, but clearly they at least have an interest in the products of that particular industry and will gather information to be used in the future. Not all exhibitions are static venues such as London's Earl's Court, the Birmingham NEC or the Palais de Congress in Paris. Road shows are quite common where the product is taken to the buyer and these can be held in hotels, football grounds and arenas such as the Telewest Arenas in the UK and elsewhere. An advantage with road shows is that while a consumer might find it too much hassle to visit a London-based exhibition, they might be willing to visit a local hotel to view the latest ideas from a particular industry.

Packaging

Packaging is a much neglected area of marketing communications that has functional and emotional properties that are important to brand image. Packaging has often been referred to as 'the silent salesman' that sits on retailers' shelves and sells products. But it is so much more than this. Just look at the ingenious way perfume is packaged for an immediate appreciation. Take a look at the malt whisky section of any supermarket and there you will see a number of different images from tartans and bagpipes to shipwrecks and sailors. What you will look at though with most brands is a tube that holds the bottle that holds the whisky. This is little more than an oversized version of the cardboard tube that holds the tissue paper on a toilet or kitchen roll and yet these tubes are designed in such a way as to be extremely attractive items that can scream and shout from the shelves. Packaging, therefore, is much more than the information that must, by law, be provided on it. It has also been referred to as the part of the clothing the product wears in order to become the brand. As such packaging is an essential, visual part of the brand's identity. Indeed, it is part of the brand's personality and therefore contributes towards meaning (in the sense discussed in Chapter 6) and therefore is part of the expression of brand values. Packaging can be used in a number of different ways. Certainly it can be designed to work well on display but that is not to say it will be 'silent'. Pickton and Broderick (2001) summarize Aston Business School's empirical research on the *emotional and psychological benefits* packaging can have. These are:

- a tool to express brand values and images

- aesthetically pleasing

- strong visual impact; stand out, and be eye-catching and differentiated from other brands and gain attention

- a living expression of what the brand stands for

- a value-adder

- a reminder of the brand

- provides cues

- provides an emotional link with the target.

A package has to be attractive, recognizable and different. To achieve this the designer has a number of tools at his or her disposal including colour, form and surface, but also the use of logos, typography, and different materials from tin to plastic and from cardboard to paper. Labels can be stuck or printed on, or indeed engraved, and size does matter, whether this is to encourage product use (larger) or to sample (small).

Packaging is to do with more than appearance. It can have a tactile element to it as well as being visually attractive in appearance. The *functional* aspects of packaging are to protect the product inside, often to hold the product as with liquids for example, and more recently to be in many instances easy to dispose of and in some cases have biodegradable properties. Cost, of course, as always comes into play at some stage.

Trade/retailer sales promotions

A key objective with trade sales promotions is to increase distribution and this means gaining shelf space, especially for new products. Ideas that have developed over the years are discounts, extended credit, point-of-sale (POS) or point-of-purchase (POP) materials, tie-ins, shelf facings and screamers, and displays. These are used in conjunction with advertising, in-store promotions and other promotion allowances and are co-operative marketing ideas, which also help cement good relations. As well as the maintenance or acquisition of distribution and shelf space, other objectives are to acquire better positioning and, obviously, have an effect on consumers in contexts such as supermarkets. However, much of this activity is designed as *'push' strategy*, to get product through the chain. Several types of retail promotions are commonly used.

Incentives

Incentives to sales staff are popular with manufacturers but might not be with the retailer. Such incentives would include prizes, bonuses or simply a cash amount per sale.

Buying allowances

Buying allowances are a price reduction for a period of time where the offer is typically 'buy 100 cases and get a percentage discount'.

Advertising allowances and other co-operative promotion

The commonest form of co-operation is the advertising allowance, that is, money given by the manufacturer to the retailer and which is usually proportionate to orders, typically used in a broader co-operative promotional campaign. For example a manufacturer (say, Heinz) may negotiate with a retailer (say, Safeway) a 50/50 split on costs of the retailer running press advertising with the Heinz products being just some of the lines featured. The manufacturer, within the negotiations, will have use of trademarks, size and so on sorted out with the retailer before the campaign begins.

Slotting allowances

Slotting allowances are buying allowances for new products and are usually fee based and can appear to be blackmail and discriminatory in favour of big and against small business. There may even be a failure fee built into the deal that is a sort of fine on the manufacturer to cover retailers' costs of handling a product that bombs. The problems with trade allowances are real ones with perhaps only one-third being used properly, one-third taken by retailers and another third simply wasted. Forward buying may be practised whereby wholesalers and retailers buy during the promotion but stock up and sell at the regular price afterwards, or they may divert stock to a different area. Companies like P&G take measures to try to stop such practices, such as 'everyday low pricing' which cuts the price of over 60 per cent of its product line while cutting trade allowances, leaving the cost to the trade the same but without the allowance, which can be abused.

POP display material

These are many and varied and, since most final purchase decisions are made in-store, are very important to the retail context. Belch and Belch (2004) report a $15 billion per annum spend on end-of-aisle displays, banners posters, shelf cards and so on in the USA alone. It is hard to say how effective all this merchandising material is. Belch and Belch report a $6–$8 CPM impressions figure for supermarket displays with an average of 2300 to 8000 impressions per week, depending upon the store size and volume (these are Advertising Research Foundation figures). Though effective at reaching consumers, from the manufacturer's point of view, getting the retailer to agree to displays is a potential problem. The power that some retailers have ensures that they dictate the running of things.

Trade shows and exhibitions

Trade shows and exhibitions are important forums that again are a shop window where actual and potential customers can see, touch and feel products. In many contexts these are the only vehicles to display the company's wares and to interact with customers from across the management board. The total number of these vehicles is huge. Belch and Belch (2004) estimate that in the USA and Canada alone 100 million people visit 5000 trade shows with more than 1.3 million exhibiting companies. Blythe (2000), using Advertising Association figures, reckons that during 1995 £750 million was spent at trade, consumer and agricultural shows in the UK. In comparison, half this figure (£378 million) was spent on outdoor and transport advertising, £533 million on consumer magazines, £639 million on business directories and 199 266 million on private events. The amount spent on private events and shows added together was more than advertising spend on UK national newspaper advertising. Trade shows and exhibitions are much more likely to be selling events than those vehicles mentioned above. There is, however, a strong role for public and corporate relations. Managers may view such vehicles as sales vehicles even though, as Blythe (2000) suggests, research shows that visitors do not like such practice. Despite this, managers insist on cramming stands full of sales people. Generally, the reasons why exhibitors partake are to meet new customers, interact with current customers, introduce new products, gather intelligence, meet other channel members and so on, but inevitably they also partake to sell. Planning and managing shows and exhibitions is simple yet detailed, from design and build of the stand to a record-keeping system for visitors, useful leads and contacts.

Free or subsidized training

Manufacturers, as part of the promotional effort but also of relationship-building, can offer free or subsidized training to retail and wholesale staff so that they are well informed and able to communicate the features and benefits of products to end users more effectively and efficiently. This is especially valid when the product is complicated and highly priced. Of course, the manufacturer can provide brochures, manuals and advice for the sales force but training, on the manufacturer's premises, the retailer's or wholesaler's premises or at a hotel venue, is an added extra that promotes sales.

Business-to-business and industrial sales promotions

Some of the above consumer and trade or retail ideas can be transferred over into the industrial marketing context. Certainly much of the trade promotion commentary applies to business-to-business marketers. However, with organizational marketing, much more emphasis is placed on brochure work that is used by sales teams and at shows and exhibitions. The Internet has had an impact in terms of web-based operations, e-mail and so on. Certain ideas can be transferred over from consumer sales promotions but these may have to be adapted. For example, to add value, rather than 'buy one get one free', the marketer of office computer systems might offer free training for staff or free maintenance in the first year. In this way the marketer can offer something above and beyond the normal value of the product or service.

What have Newcastle
Brown Ale and KLM's
frequent flying
Dutchman got in
common? Data, that's
what!

Customers respond differently to different promotional strategies. The likes of Garner (2002) argue that where price-cutting is common, loyalty will not take place with many shoppers displaying promiscuous tendencies. This is probably why most promotional activity involves price (White, 2002). But that is not to say that loyalty does not exist. As with all communication, a promotion has to gain attention and elicit a favourable impression where benefits are clearly understood and the customer clearly understands the incentive offered. The incentive itself should, in accordance with all good sales promotion practice, offer extra value. As Garner and Trivedi (1997) point out, managers too can benefit from careful analysis of their strategy but to do this a strong link to the consumer is necessary.

Getting a sales promotion right in a single market is difficult enough but Scottish and Newcastle (S&N) appear to have achieved this. Scottish and Newcastle is one of Britain's best-performing pub, bar and restaurant operators. Nation-wide it has some 500 restaurants and in 2001 S&N relaunched its customer loyalty scheme. This implements discount at the point of sale that brings together three existing schemes and upgrades them in line with a fourth, 'Leisure Plus', inherited on acquisition of Greenalls in February 2000. Leisure Plus is a sophisticated data-driven system that captures individual consumer transaction data. Loyalty Logic, the company originally responsible for this system, now has the task of supplying S&N with data analysis monthly reports on performance. The scheme is based on magnetic strip cards with stand-alone card readers that send data to a central database. The scheme itself involved members gaining one point for every £1 spent plus vouchers giving 5 per cent retrospective discount. This meant that S&N could operate a loyalty scheme with the performance knowledge, trends, targets and so on clearly understood. The running costs were high but by taking the other three schemes – Old Orleans Club, Diamond Circle over-60s and Premier Club for shareholders – with a total membership of nearly 500 000 into the Leisure Plus scheme after running trials in the North of England, S&N became confident that it could target customers based on the live transaction data and substantially influence buying behaviour. After a final trial in November 2000 (offering Leisure Plus members triple points) designed to assess effects on different targets (active, inactive, new), a single, integrated scheme was put together with the key aim of reducing costs while gaining an effective targeting and data management system. With Loyalty Logic on board as a partner, S&N estimate cost savings to be £350 000 with additional sales at £250 000. Loyalty Logic also run a help desk to support customers and managers alike and a website also supports the operation, allowing customers to find their nearest restaurant, enter competitions, obtain vouchers, check their points balance and take part in research that is rewarded with extra points.

The case of KLM is a different proposition since this Royal Dutch airline operates globally. It is true that the world is becoming the global village, as predicted by McCluhan, but many anomalies exist that hinder trade and characterize law across borders. As Gibb (2003) remarks, change is occurring in the case of promotions law across Europe whereby Germany would no longer be able to prohibit 'buy one get one free' offers. So, for Gibb, this is an opportunity for brands to co-ordinate activity more widely and to gain greater flexibility in planning and targeting but Gibbs warns that sales promotion remains a minefield, especially for inexperienced brand managers. Rather than price promotions, long-term loyalty for the brand is advocated by the use of a number of tools, including frequent users' clubs (Huff and Alden, 1997). Usually, sales promotions are difficult to standardize across borders for the reasons given in Chapter 3. While there are substantial differences in consumer responses to sales promotions as well as many other things, the benefits of frequent users' clubs are clearer and less problematic than coupon and other sales promotion tools. This is especially so when the target is a professional who is likely to clock up points by virtue of his or her job. Typical KLM offers are sent to a database membership via e-mail. The offers and benefits that can be taken up will depend on the grade of membership. Typical offers for ordinary members would be a cruise on the clipper *Stad Amsterdam* for 2100 miles plus 95 euros or the check-in service from office or home via the Internet and earn extra Bonus Miles. For other grades there are free airport lounge facilities and check-in desk facilities. E-tickets are now commonplace and KLM will print a boarding card 40 minutes before departure at one of the self-service check-in centres at the airport. Flying Dutchman members only have to insert their membership card for the boarding pass to be printed out. In all of this operation, data and database management is key to its smooth running and success.

Sources: Adapted from Garner (2002); Garner and Trivedi (1997); Gibb (2003); KLM (2003); Templeman (2002); White (2002).

 STOP POINT

Getting it right is difficult but different kinds of loyalty or frequent use schemes are available for very different products or services. Think about how the right kind of sales promotion can add value and help build and maintain the brand.

Assignment

Assume you are an fmcg marketer engaging with a network of wholesalers and retailers. Choose a product category within which you are intent upon building a brand franchise. You have seen the statistic that suggests that consumers make at least 70 per cent of their final decisions in-store and you firmly believe it. Your task is to in principle design a sales promotion package that includes trade and consumer ideas within a specified timescale and to be realistic with the budget.

Summary of Key Points

- Sales promotion's role has changed and now is a dynamic one within the integrated communications mix.

- There are advantages and disadvantages when using sales promotions. Brand damage and waste should be paid particular attention.

- Added value is key to understanding how sales promotions should work, whether this is in industrial, trade or consumer promotion campaigns. Creativity is part of that added value.

- The objectives behind the use of sales promotions are very different to those associated with advertising or PR. An objective such as trial is key.

- There are various types of promotion available to marketers depending on the context, which might be industrial, consumer or trade. Generally, promotion ideas cannot be transposed very easily from consumer to industrial contexts.

- Beyond the usual tactical level, strategic possibilities for the use of promotions exist and they can be part of an integrated campaign.

- Implementation of a sales promotion campaign should be executed in an efficient manner with timings and deadlines being paid particular attention.

- Evaluation of a campaign is important and constant vigilance is necessary when using techniques such as money-off coupons or competitions.

- Co-operative marketing can be part of the relationship between a manufacturer and middleman such as a dealer or retailer, and sales promotions can be part of this.

- Promotions wars, including price wars are to be avoided and marketers should avoid becoming involved in such situations.

Examination Questions

1 Discuss the changing, dynamic role of sales promotion within the integrated communications mix and qualify this with the use of an example, industrial, trade or consumer, of your choice.

2 Highlight the advantages and disadvantages when using sales promotions, paying particular attention to potential brand damage.

3 Added value is key to understanding how sales promotions should work. Illustrate the role of creativity in providing added value with examples from industrial and consumer promotion campaigns.

4 Discuss the objectives behind the use of sales promotions. Find examples of the objective of trial to illustrate.

5 Explain and explore the various types of promotion available to marketers, both consumer and trade. Choose one such type using at least one example to illustrate.

6 Consider sales promotions beyond the usual tactical level and discuss strategic possibilities. Discuss how this can be part of an integrated campaign.

7 Consider how sales promotions are implemented. Discuss this using a campaign of your choice.

8 Discuss evaluation of campaigns generally, explaining why it is important to be constantly vigilant when using techniques such as money-off coupons or competitions.

9 Outline the rationale behind co-operative marketing in terms of relationships between manufacturers and middlemen such as dealers and retailers. Use at least one example to illustrate.

10 Discuss the notion of price wars in relation to promotions wars. Explain how a marketer can avoid becoming involved in such situations.

Note

1 The 'buy one get one free' phrase now appears to have the acronym 'bogoff' attached to it. 'Bog off' is British slang and an impolite term for 'get lost' or 'go away' and now seems to have crept into ordinary English language.

References

Belch, G. E. and Belch, M. A. (2004). *Advertising and Promotion*. 6th edition. Irwin/McGraw Hill.

Blythe, J. (2000). *Marketing Communications*. Financial Times Prentice Hall.

Garner, E. (2002). Do sales promotions really work? *Admap*, **430**, July, 30–32.

Garner, E. and Trivedi, M. (1997). A communications framework to evaluate sales promotion strategies. *Journal of Advertising Research*, **37** (2), March–April.

Gibb, B. (2003). How to get your promotion right. *Admap*, **437**, March, 40–42. www.warc.com

Guardian Unlimited (2001). The Pulse: exploding the myth of the pink pound. At http://media.guardian.co.uk/marketingandpr/story/0,7494,501323,00.html, accessed 5 June.

Huff, L. C. and Alden, D. L. (1997). An investigation of consumer response to sales promotions in developing markets: a three-country analysis. *Journal of Advertising Research*, March–April.

Kinsman, M. (2001). Promoting to gays is no longer a walk on the wild side. Promotion, 1 December.

KLM (2003). KLM company materials.

Pickton, D. and Broderick, A. (2001). *Integrated Marketing Communications*. Financial Times Prentice Hall.

Practical Marketing Guides (2003). No. 7, *Sales Promotion*.

Smith, P. and Taylor, J. (2002). *Marketing Communications*. 3rd edition. Kogan Page.

Templeman, M. (2002). Data is key to new S&N loyalty schemes. *Admap*, **427**, April. www.warc.com

White, R. (2002). Sales promotion and the brand. *Admap*, **430**, July. www.warc.com

Woofenden, C. (2000). NTL complaints reach record levels. *Network News*, July. www.vnunet.com/news/1106439

Yeshin, T. (1998). *Integrated Marketing Communications*. Butterworth-Heinemann.

Direct marketing

Chapter overview

Introduction to this chapter

This chapter deals with direct marketing as an interactive marketing communications tool that uses one or more communications media to achieve a measurable response. Customer databases are the result of the application of information technology in marketing and as such are very powerful tools. Database and direct marketing have developed significantly in the past few years in terms of a means to deliver a sales message to stimulate demand and supply product information. In order to take advantage of these developments, marketing managers need to understand the characteristics of direct marketing and its role in the marketing and marketing communications mix. They also need to understand creative and media opportunities and limitations. Data protection, particularly electronic data protection, is of topical interest, as is marketing in the digital age generally – the subject of Chapter 19.

Aims of this chapter

The overall aim of this chapter is therefore to explore the nature of direct marketing. More specifically, on completion of this chapter, the reader should be able to:

- explore the nature and role of direct marketing in relation to the marketing communications planning process

- outline the direct marketing process and explain this in relation to other marketing communications elements and media

- become familiar with creative approaches regarding direct marketing techniques including incentives and offers and those that have gained in popularity in the digital age

- appreciate the consumer context but also others such as business to business and not for profit

- explain the emergence of database marketing and appreciate how it has evolved

- understand how database marketing adds value and how it can be used to improve marketing performance

- understand the key elements in the management of data protection and privacy issues.

Direct marketing

Advantages and disadvantages of direct marketing

Direct marketing is in many situations a key component in the marketing communications mix when attempting to develop current customers. Direct marketing has grown with database technology and it is flexible, fast and interactive. It can be tightly targeted so that waste is reduced and it is 'accountable', where responses can be observed and impact seen and, therefore, it can be described as predictable. E-mail and telemarketing in particular are very fast means of getting a result. But this has to be paid for and direct marketing is relatively high in cost, which is why it is critical that correct targeting of the right message via a well-managed database is crucial to being cost-effective. Controlled growth is possible through the application of direct marketing whereby a build-up can be had in an almost test market fashion. In this sense direct marketing can be seen as having low investment costs.

There are many problems associated with direct marketing such as the 'junk mail' image and the fact that a lot of people get annoyed about appearing on databases and their names suddenly appearing on letters. This kind of marketing has always suffered from the lack of the tactile opportunities offered by conventional retail outlets.

The direct marketing process

The process of direct marketing involves the identification and qualification of prospects, the attraction of these prospects to the brand and the conversion and retention of the prospects. This can be understood easily in the relationship–marketing paradigm in terms of the brand development of trust, commitment and loyalty. That is not to say that direct marketing is only used with well-known brands. It is broader than mail order and has been described by the UK Direct Marketing Association as an interactive system of marketing which uses one or more advertising media to affect a measurable response and/or transaction at any location.

Direct marketing is also about targeting and using lists or, more precisely, databases, to be reasonably sure that those contacted are of the appropriate class, as opposed to mass marketing with its associated waste. The concept of direct marketing is simple. It allows effectiveness to be better measured and, therefore, to many it is a more acceptable form of communications, especially with its speed and connectivity. Instead of broadcasting a mass-marketing message through television or print to a wide number of people, a customized message is instead sent to an individual. It is sent direct, to a much smaller number of people who are more predisposed to listening to the message and buying the product or service. There is no 'middleman' but it is interactive, two-way communications where the target receives the offer in some way, whether this is through the mail or through a call centre. National television advertising is very expensive and many organizations are questioning its effectiveness. Where a direct sales force is used, it can cost £100–£200 for a face-to-face sales call and it may take several calls to close a sale. Most would agree that direct marketing is a more cost-effective alternative for generating a sale.

The most common form of direct marketing is 'through the mail' but there are other types, for example direct-response advertising and telemarketing. Direct marketing had its first golden age in the 1950s, in the form of mail order catalogue selling, as the post-war boom drove consumer spending. However, this golden age was came to an end in the 1960s and 1970s as competition from television intensified. In recent years direct marketing has seen a major resurgence. O'Connor and Galvin (2001) maintain this is because of:

1 *The fragmentation of advertising media.* The arrival of commercial television may have heralded the decline of direct marketing in the 1960s, but commercial television itself came under fire in the 1990s from a variety of different cable and satellite channels. Advertisers began to understand what 'the dishwasher powder effect' is, i.e. why advertise dishwasher powder on television if 85 per cent of households do not have a dishwasher and if direct marketing can help you identify the 15 per cent who do?

2 *Increasing retailer power.* Manufacturers are now facing an increasingly tough battle for 'mind space and shelf space'. The increasing power of retailers and the success of own brands have made it more and more difficult for manufacturers to gather information and develop relationships with their customers. An increasingly effective means of bypassing the manufacturer and gaining the mind space of the end customer is via direct marketing.

3 *Declining brand loyalty.* Product proliferation has done nothing for brand loyalty. Direct marketing can help win back that brand loyalty by keeping a particular product or service in the consumer's mind on a regular basis.

4 *Search for long-term customer relationships.* Not all customers are profitable. And those customers who are, often only become so after the company has recouped the costs of recruiting them in the first place. Companies are beginning to understand the desirability of retaining customers and maintaining their loyalty. Regular communication, via direct marketing, can help.

O'Connor and Galvin use the example of Great Universal Stores (GUS) to illustrate this resurgence, which is enabled by the increased productivity and processing power of information technology. Therefore, these authors argue that as the technology is developed and grows in importance, and as long as marketers like GUS can use it, then maximum advantage in targeting key customers will ensue. This results in:

- a target minority, previously underserviced
- a platform for new product introduction
- a cross-selling platform for other products
- the provision of a new channel of distribution, a direct one such as for wine direct
- the identification of prime prospects
- for existing products, consideration of the difference between sales and lead generation and brand response advertising.

How direct marketing works

The way direct marketing works is by using devices such as free phone/toll-free telephone numbers, visiting a showroom/website or joining a club. The response is dependent, at least in part, on the way in which the offer is constructed creatively. The target should not be put on hold, there should be no rudeness or situations arising whereby answers to questions cannot be provided and products should be available. This is customer need fulfilment where product/information is put out in a convenient and timely manner so that the front end and the back end are parts of the same chain. Billing and the like, including the delivery company used (outsourced), become part of the organization's organization.

Responses in terms of interactivity can be real time or delayed and may involve more than one medium. For example, direct response off the page or television may direct the prospect to the telephone or Internet thus lessening the interactivity so that direct response advertising occurs via a medium – mail, television, print, radio and so on.

Duncan (2002) describes a personalization continuum that maps out the degree of personalization whereby this is high when face-to-face personal selling takes place in real time and is company initiated. At the other extreme mass media advertising is low personalization and has a delayed response, usually involving another medium and is company initiated. Sometimes the customer or prospect will initiate the interactivity through e-mail, telephone or fax. In these cases the company should be well placed to take advantage of this, rather than waste a valuable opportunity.

The growth of direct marketing

Growth of direct marketing is happening through increased use of mail, telephone numbers, websites and e-mail. It has grown and is growing in consumer terms, and from this perspective direct marketing is now very visible. Yeltsin's (1998) ten growth factors are:

1 Within consumers there is a desire for experimentation, and people change very little.

2 New shopping outlets.

3 Home focus.

4 Change in society, trends with women working and fragmentation of personal products.

5 Desire for convenience.

6 Services have improved and direct marketing has become a norm of doing business, for example insurance without a broker.

7 The increased cost of reaching fragmented audiences has meant that direct marketing has had to become more sophisticated.

8 Increased segmentation with better marketing research.

9 Cashless society means that people are used to plastic and electronic transactions. Additionally there is data to be had from this.

10 Information technology has created databases.

Marketing, it is argued, needs skilled professionals to maintain this growth.

Incentives

An incentive is usually included in a proposition made to a prospect as to what they will receive and for what in return. They are specific inducements or stimuli but vary enormously in scope from the quick response such as a free gift to more complex situations including loyalty schemes. This is where the direct marketing and sales promotion interface lies and objectives tend to be sales promotion-led objectives such as trial or rewarding loyalty. Whether or not the actual sales promotions work, or are a waste, is a key question as addressed in Chapter 9. In terms of differing targets there is a clear need to make appropriate approaches. With *prospects* there is a need to offer an inducement such as extra free as with, for example, direct wine clubs. For example the offer might be to 'join the club and get 15 bottles for the price of 12 on the first order'. With *competition loyalists* there may be a need to increase the offer in order to seduce them away, but this may not be possible and a waste. *Brand switchers* on the other hand are similar to prospects and, in fact, are prospects. *Company loyalists* have to be retained and extra sales can be had through subtler methods such as newsletters, help lines, loyalty magazines or clubs. These devices provide product involvement, status and association with others, and rewards should be specifically related to loyalty schemes. There is a need to consider upgrading and upselling, cross-selling and even cross-category possibilities such as air miles from, say, petrol purchases.

VIGNETTE

Business to business, not for profit, profit: why direct marketing can fit the bill and why it worked for First Direct

Direct marketing has been practised in the *BtoB* context for many years. There is a smaller sales universe than that of consumer marketing and targets are relatively easy to identify. Direct marketing can be very cost-effective in BtoB. However in terms of targets, the DMU is an important factor when considering communications. There are usually not one but several people to consider in terms of the composite 'MAN', i.e. money, authority and need. A budget-holder may have to be involved but otherwise might have no interest whatsoever in a product or service. Another person may have the need but not the money and may have to seek authorization and so on. It is not unusual for a presentation to be made to the whole of the board of directors where the cost of, say, a new computer system is high. Direct marketing can be cost-effective in this role whereby regular contact can generate leads and brand awareness can be achieved through the creation of specific messages that are tailored to named persons. Sales visits can be more effective given that a preparation has been undertaken to make a prospect aware of the proposition. In *not-for-profit* situations it is the ability to create a database within a niche or a sector and the relatively low costs that attract organizations to direct marketing.

The biggest direct marketing use by far is with the *consumer* and the biggest sector is *financial services*. This is said to have come about because of the sector's professionals, who were confident using the new technology and new ideas. Financial services became an area of early adopters and challengers, which aptly describes *First Direct*. First Direct's strap line 'a challenger brand you can trust' sums this up. No retail outlets, twenty-four hour banking using the telephone and the use of direct response advertising and positive word of mouth to build a customer base is the hallmark of First Direct. The bank doubled its rate of growth in the first two years, after the agency WCRS won the account in 1995, and was well ahead of target in terms of customer recruitment after the relaunch halted the decline in growth that had occurred by 1994 and 1995. The relaunch was done in two stages. The first was to reappraise the situation and to establish the perceptual negatives surrounding traditional banks. 'Tell Me One Good Thing' was developed to use this to separate First Direct from traditional banking. The second stage used comedian Bob Mortimer's 'I hate bank ads' campaign to promote the positives about First Direct. Direct marketing had a major role in this in terms of direct mail and direct response press and television. Millward Brown's tracking study revealed that nearly four out of five people understood First Direct (as opposed to two out of five before the campaign). Further analysis revealed that the bank took one in four of those customers switching banks in the period, so a bank with a 2 per cent share was able to take 25 per cent of the available market. Television investment was paid back handsomely and it was able to magnify the effects of the other media used. Latterly, database marketing has been used for designing mailshots. A closer examination shows how the database marketing system is also used to reduce marketing costs, improve the quality of communication and generally manage the interaction between the company and each individual customer. First Direct's database marketing system builds customer profiles and allows the matching of products to customers' needs. The bank can then predict who is likely to buy a new car and then provide that target with information on loans. According to O'Connor and Galvin (2001), First Direct have cut marketing costs by 40 per cent as a result of lower cost promotions yielding higher returns.

Sources: Adapted from IPA (1998); O'Connor and Galvin (2001); Pickton and Broderick (2001).

STOP POINT

The financial sector uses direct marketing a lot. Why is this so? In what ways can a company use direct response? Is the next logical step to move to Internet banking, or is this too problematic in terms of security?

Types of direct marketing media

Mail

Despite advances in database management the majority of through-the-mail communication is still impersonal, yet worth billions in the USA alone. Financial services and insurance are the leaders in this field, often with personalized offerings but generally, despite software advances, it is too costly to completely personalize every 'mailshot'. The creative element of direct mail advertising is both high and low. The key to success is seen to gain involvement through keeping the brand in front of the recipient using the envelope, a letter, a brochure and reply card. Response rates vary and this medium would certainly lag behind telemarketing or personal selling but can be cheaper, and creativity in the promotion is the key. Videotape, CD and other formats can be included in the direct mailshot. Direct mail is still very important despite the 'junk mail' tag, but critical to this is the quality of the list. Response rates[1] can be enhanced by good database management but lists have to be suitable and internal management committed to the idea of direct marketing so that the right kind of investment goes in. Subtler approaches can eradicate the 'intrusive' factor. Direct mail is a good medium for targeting and it can work if the creative side is right but it also offers an opportunity to provide detailed information, the reason why in the past direct marketing has been a support rather than main medium. With technological and communications changes there are now opportunities to lead with direct marketing, including direct mail.

Television and radio

The infomercial and advertoral as described in Chapter 6 can be programme-length advertisements that might run from 2 to 30 minutes and can be inexpensive to produce because of what they are trying to achieve, which in part will be to educate the viewer. As with print, direct response advertisements are commonplace on television and radio. Costs vary as with advertising generally so that it can be said to be expensive but persuasive. All of the usual advertising pros and cons, such as long lead times, apply.

Print/catalogues

Catalogues are one of the oldest forms of marketing with a lot of history tied to commercial development and doing business at a distance. These days direct marketing is still led by catalogue companies but catalogues are not always simply direct. IKEA, Next and Argos, for example, all have a retail presence but also a catalogue, and of course catalogues have a big place in BtoB marketing. However, the primary target for catalogues is the consumer, usually women. More women than men use them and they can involve the telephone and the retail outlet. Electronically the catalogue is going through an interesting transition from the bulky paper-based book to the CD and now the Internet, making it easy to keep prices, product deletions, stock levels and so on up to date. Print advertising accounts for more than half of direct response and much of this involve cars and financial services. This has both a low response rate and low cost. Magazines can be expensive and have long lead times but are good for targeting. Inserts suffer from the usual problems of falling out of publications and causing irritation. They do get noticed but have a high cost per thousand.

Telemarketing

This might be considered as personal communication (as in Chapter 16) or direct marketing. This book assumes telemarketing to fit within direct marketing rather than within selling where it is considered as just one of the options in terms of personal contact. The distinction has to be made between outward (or outbound) and inward (or inbound) telemarketing. The most common understanding of the term would be the former, with the development of call centres the most prominent idea for both. Calls are taken from responses to other direct marketing such as a direct response press advertisement. It is relatively easy to measure telemaketing's ROI, and the cost per contact, although high, is significantly less than with face-to-face contact and therefore frequent contact is not such a cost issue. Telemarketing should be highly targeted and messages can be tailored. It is fast but can be intrusive and aurally limiting when the message has to be simple, and it needs managing. Outward telemarketing might be seen in the same way as junk mail and viewed with suspicion. Inward calls are positive, immediate and seen as being useful, and can create loyalty.

Internet

The digital age is now also providing companies with a new and richer source of customer information with which they can target selective audiences. Websites gather significant amounts of customer data, and the company or others to whom the information is sold can use this. However, the fact that these increasingly rich sources of customer information are being collated into large customer databases is the source of much concern and debate. The questions discussed later in this chapter are to do with security, limitations that should be put on the use of customer data, special rules that may be required for the Internet and so on. At the moment the Internet is 'king of direct transactions' with low costs of access for customers as the ease of credit card use increases. Low cost of production and web creation and its global nature make the Internet a 'must consider' medium (see Chapter 19).

User groups/membership scheme/loyalty card

These can establish extra benefit and help move the customer towards loyalty as with, for example, air miles. A typical club to join would be the frequent flyer type as with KLM's 'Silver Elite' and other grades of membership where benefits include the cross-selling of wine to members at special rates.

VIGNETTE

Direct marketing, brands and the media: refining the mix for Goldfish

Direct response television (DRTV) commercials are nothing new. According to Lee (2003) they once competed for being the most ugly and intrusive commercials. They were and looked cheap to produce and had no 'big idea' behind them and could only rub off their ugliness on the brand if used, so the tendency was to use a more emotional driver for brands. Direct response commercials, or infomercials as they became known, attempted to work more on behaviour, providing reasons to consider moving in a particular way. There is no luxury of time to create a preference. Since then, direct response has matured and grown more sophisticated and can achieve much more than it used to be able to in terms of being consistent with brand values. Lee (2003) uses the example of Motorola to illustrate effective targeting of eighteen to twenty-four year olds and advocates storytelling and bringing the viewer to an action point for IBM's NetVista A60 system. Other considerations are the length of the television spot, which can be 30 seconds but is more likely to be 60 seconds or more. Lee points out that this is not cast in stone and uses Jaguar's two 15-second back-to-back effort for the S-Type. And when should the telephone number be introduced? This is up for grabs, but Lee reckons toward the end, when the offer is being sold after the story has unfolded as with Motorola, but admits that it could be introduced at the beginning as long as it does no harm. The offer, if one is being used, should be sold, not the product, but otherwise, for Lee, 'you can be successful without one'.

So this is the new direct response television, as opposed to the brasher early days. But DRTV is not the only tool in the box. When considering direct marketing, especially for new products, it can be argued that this is the most important area of use for sales promotion techniques. This is contrary to the established idea that direct marketing is best used with established products. But if a new brand does not get a lot of trial early on it will have problems maintaining a listing in retailers, and once distribution becomes limited the brand may die. Brand failures in the first year are estimated to be around 80 per cent, following the old dictum that most new products fail. When direct marketing is being used behaviour does not follow the usual Leverhulme-type pattern of not quite knowing which or why. It is cause and effect to a large extent. The target is either on board or not and uses the coupon or doesn't. The hostility between advertising and direct marketing was clearly defined for a number of years but now direct marketing has its place in the communications mix. From a brand-owner perspective this is neither here nor there since the brand owner simply wants the best for the brand and the organization, whether this be through advertising, direct marketing or some other means, or through a mix of tools. Douglas and May (1999) use the 1996 work of Pearson in 'Building Brands Directly' on Elida Gibbs to highlight the relationship between branding, advertising and direct marketing. With a direct mail element present, awareness levels were three times higher than they were when advertising ran alone.

The same effects have been seen with the launch of the Goldfish credit card, the winner of the 1998 Institute of Direct Marketing (IDM) Business Performance Award. Direct marketing had been at the heart of a strategy to bring the brand direct to the consumer resulting in a strong brand franchise. Habit, lethargy and inertia had typified the market but Goldfish broke through this clutter with radical positioning away from the mainstream. Humour, intrigue and surprise were used to build warmth toward the brand and its personality had to be built and maintained. Television advertising put across the quirkiness and surprise values of the brand using Scottish comedian and actor Billy Connolly. The direct marketing campaign had to support this and also deliver rational benefits. To achieve this the '75 pound Goldfish' was invented, which referred to the £75 saved on domestic British Gas bills, along with a fully functional credit card. Thus the direct marketing worked on both an emotional and rational level, i.e. it surprised, engaged and excited via wit (clever observation) rather than belly laughs (fishy puns) while being practical, helpful and adding real value. This was communicated clearly without jargon or being too technical. Goldfish achieved 40 per cent awareness through direct marketing and through further research has responded to market dynamics. The view was one of direct marketing leading the integration process, i.e. brand-building in this case was above and below the line but driven by direct marketing.

Sources: Adapted from Douglas and May (1999); Lee (2003).

STOP POINT

The value of direct marketing to Goldfish is clear. What might surprise the reader is the leading role direct marketing had to play in the integration process, or that the campaign had more than one communication element to it. Think about the role that direct marketing has to play for products and services inside and outside the financial sector.

Database marketing

A database is a collection of data, usually collated using a computer, that gives a useful, convenient and interactive access to information on prospective and existing targets. A database can be built up in two ways: through *internal* sources such as previous enquiries or current or lapsed users and through *external* sources such as warranty cards, subscriptions to magazines or through purchase or lease of lists of, for example, 4×4 car purchasers or golf enthusiasts. Database marketing is related to direct marketing, relationship marketing and customer relationship management but is not the same thing as direct marketing and the terms should not be interchanged. Database marketing is much more than 'list building' as it focuses on customers, capturing detailed data on them, not products. Database marketing is an interactive approach to marketing. Clearly it involves list compilation and individually addressable targets who are then approached with marketing materials through mostly conventional media and channels such as the mail or telephone. The task is to manage the database in such a way that contact is made and maintained effectively and efficiently.

The development of database marketing

As suggested above, a database can be built by using both internal and external list information so that lists can be built from actual customers and prospects or they can be purchased or leased from list brokers. These allow marketers to identify their best customers, their value, needs and likely behaviours. Lists can be either response lists (people who have already responded to some aspect of marketing, these being expensive to lease because response rates are known to be higher) or compiled lists (collected from a variety of sources) or both. In other words, you get what you pay for since the quality of the list, rather like a sales lead, really does matter. Frequency of purchase, responsiveness to direct marketing techniques and amount spent directly are all important factors that are likely to be known from response lists (recency, frequency and monetary – Duncan, 2002). Lists can be compiled from a variety of sources such as magazine subscriptions, warranty cards and the like, where the information is bought and sold and the list can be conventional or e-mail addresses. Cost of rental varies and will depend upon whether the client has access or merely provides the information/mailshot to be sent on by a broker or direct marketing company. Outsourcing is common because management of lists or, better still, of a database is best done by experts, although software is available for self-management. Database marketing breeds its own success.

Database marketing used to be about lists, and list management was key since the right people need to be contacted. However, list building and management have moved from a state of lacking sophistication to one of finesse. In the early phase direct mail or telemarketing lists were all that were required, i.e. addresses or telephone numbers. However, the creation of the term 'junk mail' is by no means an accident. Unsolicited material or intrusive telephone calls caused many consumers to either switch off and ignore further mailshots or, worse still, to have a very negative opinion of companies and brands, and the methods themselves. However, the route to more effective direct marketing campaigns came through better customer information to increase the relevance of the offer and better management of the communication between the company and the customer.

Despite the practical difficulties of building a sophisticated database operation, it can be argued that the database is the greatest single application of information technology within marketing. The rapidly declining costs of hardware and software have increased the attractiveness of database marketing, resulting in a massive shift in the last decade towards its importance and use. O'Connor and Galvin (2001) maintain that the cost of storing and accessing a single customer name on a database dropped dramatically over the twenty-year period, 1974–94, from over $7 to less than 1 cent in the USA. Nowadays, companies are becoming much more precise about the type of potential customer they will mail to and the size of mailshots is reducing correspondingly – yet the effectiveness is on the increase.

The advantages of database marketing

A key consideration is how database marketing improves marketing performance. Database techniques, for O'Connor and Galvin (2001), allow marketing managers to improve performance in the following ways:

1 *Increased understanding of customers*, which is difficult. Even where companies have built a customer database, is surprising how few analyse their databases for answers to questions such as how many customers do I have? What products are they buying? Which segments do those customers fit into? Which delivery channels do they prefer? Which customers can I not afford to lose? This presumes an understanding of customers as the first step towards building long-term relationships.

2 *Improved customer service* can come about through the use of database marketing. A wide variety of operational functions can be employed including (a) enquiries that can be supported through marketing databases that allow access to a variety of customer, product, price and transaction information, (b) complaints, where handling is typically supported through the use of databases that categorize, monitor and track customer problems and (c) helpdesks, allowing customers to phone a central telephone number for answers to commonly asked questions and solutions to commonly encountered problems. The Perrier case in Chapter 15 is a good example of this in its telephone form but, of course, there are opportunities for face-to-face applications.

3 *Greater understanding of the market* where integration of marketing research data with other information on the marketing database is key. This facilitates answers to strategic questions such as What direction should we take with new product development? Which new delivery channels should we be experimenting with? Which new markets should we be expanding into?

4 *Better information on competitors* is easily overlooked and very often is not captured in an integrated way in the marketing database. Doing this allows marketing managers to better answer questions in terms of greater speed and accuracy, such as Who are our main competitors by product or market segment? How have their market shares changed in recent weeks/months/years?

What is their pricing structure and what impact have price changes had on market share? How much are our competitors spending on promoting their products and services?

5 *More effective management of sales operations* where four areas of sales activities supported through marketing databases emerge and these are, managing the performance of different sales representatives, managing customer contacts and client portfolios, demonstrating product features and providing quotations, and capturing and fulfilling customer orders.

6 *Improved marketing campaigns* involve a series of steps from initial analysis and planning through to the subsequent monitoring of those campaigns. This considers the different technologies used to support each stage of a campaign.

7 *Better communication with customers* where communication is a two-way process and marketers should use material in order to achieve a meaningful and relevant dialogue with customers. Therefore, databases should be used at appropriate times. Heinz's *At Home* magazine illustrates this in terms of promoting brands through an in-the-mail, database-driven promotion to 4.6 million people – monthly. Where marketing databases are used to support customer service representatives, they should also be capable of reminding such representatives of all previous customer contacts, whether that contact was by mail, telephone or in person.

Measuring results

The number of responses divided by the number of mailed offers has been the traditional way to measure results, as a percentage response rate. Conversion rates are then derived in a similar fashion from orders received divided by responses, so that the latter can be expressed as a higher percentage than the former, or not as the case may be. But the issues discussed in Chapter 18 still remain, i.e. that the marketer may never be sure that it was the direct marketing and not some other factor that worked. Variables working together in an integrated fashion may be the goal but this complicates measurement. Duncan (2002) lists five tests that should be carried out:

1 List testing where sampling techniques can be employed on large lists and therefore risk is reduced.

2 Offer testing where the various elements of an offer, for example length of warranty, can be aired with respondents and the best offer formulated.

3 Creative/copy testing where the ways in which an offer can be explained and presented can be tested, just as with concept testing for advertising.

4 Media mix testing where the best possible media, media vehicles and placement can be arrived at.

5 Frequency testing where the optimum number of offers can be arrived at and waste reduced or effectiveness improved.

VIGNETTE

Norwich Union
Direct: Tots to Teens
Children's Protection
Plan mailshot

With this piece of direct mail, the envelope contained six pieces of information:

1   The letter explaining the product and its benefits. This is a reminder, a follow-on from the original launch, with an extension of the offer for a limited amount of time. This is very rational and sells the benefits of insurance cover in terms of the low relative cost of it. Also included, if the acceptance form is completed by a specified date, is a 'superb family-friendly *touch screen data organizer*' and, if the reply is sent within seven days, exclusive access to the new *Parents Help Line*. Here help is available on all sorts of 'child-related issues'. It carefully talks about the hidden cost of caring, where a hint of fear arousal secures the case to a firm base. It affirms to the reader that they will be reassured, for very little outlay. This is cover anywhere in the world, twenty-four hours a day. There is the added bonus of access to a legal help line where you can talk to professionals all year around. Then there is a reminder that the form must be back by a certain date, another 'special help line' with times of opening. An amazingly deft touch appears towards the end of the letter – 'If you have decided against claiming up to £100 000-worth of cover, please destroy these documents as this offer has been prepared exclusively for you and your child/children and is not transferable' – making it very personal. Then a reminder of the free gift. Then a 'PS' with more fear arousal – 'Return the form so that your child can be protected'.

2   A 'claim your free gift today!' leaflet in yellow with blue writing. This has a picture of the organizer, which is a 'helping hand for every parent!' and will help 'keep track of the whole family' and will be sent 'with our compliments!'

3   An easy to fill in acceptance form with the 'guaranteed acceptance' stamp.

4   Protection plan summary of cover that details the policy.

5   A Tots to Teens Children's Protection Plan leaflet that provides a question and answer approach that explains accidental disability insurance, with a clear telephone number should there be any further information or clarification required. It also reinforces the idea that accidents do happen. Royal Society for the Prevention of Accidents (RoSPA) and Child Accident Prevention Trust data are used to back this up. There is also an endorsement, presumably from a parent.

6   A pre-paid first-class envelope for ease of return and with an 'acceptance form enclosed – please activate immediately!' flash to indicate importance and seriousness.

All in all this mailshot follows the 'rules' of direct marketing well, with a named individual the recipient, already on the Norwich Union database. It is, therefore, a classic piece of cross-selling using database technology and good direct marketing practice.

Sources: Adapted from Norwich Union Direct (2003).

STOP POINT

The value of direct marketing to financial services is clear from this mailshot. The direct marketing process can be seen to be working well in this example. Think about the optimum number of pieces in this type of mailing, the creative approach involved and the employment of the various devices at the right time and place.

Managing privacy issues: digital communications and data protection

Concern about misuse of information

There is concern all round over the ability these days to gather information, especially electronically. The amount of information being gathered on consumers and how this information is used is central to these concerns. For example, the UK's Data Protection Registrar received a large number of complaints from customers of Tesco after the retailer contacted them to ask their permission to target them with a third-party offer using information gathered from Tesco's loyalty card scheme (O'Connor and Galvin, 2001). Digital communications are now also providing companies with new and richer sources of customer information with which they can target selective audiences. The Internet with its many websites will gather significant amounts of customer data and personal information that can subsequently be used by companies (or others to whom the information is sold) for direct marketing. Therefore, the fact that these are increasingly rich sources of customer information that are being made into large customer databases is the source of much concern.

Some questions: are consumers sufficiently well protected from companies that can abuse information? What are the limits to the use of such data? By whom and how should the Internet be policed? Concern is set to grow as the Internet, a huge source of data, grows. For example, small programs known as 'cookies' are downloaded to the hard disks of computers used by Interim users and can be used to trace a surfer's path through the Internet and pass this information back to the website owner. Perhaps as little as 2 per cent of websites that gather customer data (either directly by requesting customers to register in order to use the site or indirectly through the use of cookies) tell their visitors what they gather and how they use it. In 1999 it was revealed that Intel's computer chips and Microsoft's software transmitted unique identification numbers whenever a PC was logged into the Internet. This, potentially at least, would allow consumers' Internet activities and transactions to tracked and monitored (O'Connor and Galvin, 2001).

Options available to deal with data privacy concerns

The Economist (1999) material is a summary of possible options in this area, i.e. more laws, market solutions (self-regulation), infomediaries (brokers), technology (encryption allows consumers to protect information) and transparency (citizens should have access to information). However, *The Economist* concluded that none of these would be adequate, so that, while the debate continues, a combination of legislation and self-regulation will have to suffice.

Legislation and self-regulation guidelines

The 1998 EU Directive on data protection obliges member states to update their data protection legislation. Under such legislation companies can use individual personal data only where the people concerned have given their consent. The exception is where legal or contractual reasons come into play, this being necessary in the area of finance, for example as with loans, but there is still the right to object to being targeted and holding information on individuals. So that this is about controlling the misuse of information and privacy protection.

Because of its pre-eminence within the cyber or on-line world, the USA is further ahead in terms of Internet usage than any other country. By 2001 the USA will be squeezed into adopting more stringent data privacy regulations for the on-line user. Pressure to conform will grow as the trend towards privacy regulation gains momentum beyond the boundaries of the EU. Countries such as Brazil, Chile, Argentina and Canada, as well as several in Eastern Europe, are considering or have already implemented stringent, EU-style data privacy policies. United States companies have been urged to go ahead and make the move to stricter privacy policies in anticipation of changes in US statutes. A 1999 Georgetown University survey examined the privacy practices at top commercial websites. The survey found that, while 93 per cent of websites collect personal information about visitors, only two-thirds give notification of how that information would be used. Worse, less than 10 per cent comply with the privacy protection standards outlined by the Federal Trade Commission. To meet the FTC standards, a site must notify users when data is being collected, give users a chance to opt out of giving information about themselves, give users access to their information so they can correct it, provide adequate security for customer databases and provide access to a live customer contact. It may be that the more progressive organizations are addressing these issues and most might understand the problems surrounding privacy. A key area within database management is the issue of list leasing/re-selling, which some organizations have stopped doing (O'Connor and Galvin, 2001).

VIGNETTE

How technology is influencing and changing direct marketing

The safeguarding of people's personal information has to be one of the most important areas on anyone's agenda. Direct and database marketing and privacy go hand in hand, accentuated by the rapid development of electronic communications. It is all about someone looking into the private life of another, and when that someone is government, the debate widens – Orwellian *1984*-style. The narrower but linked debate regarding marketing can be more clearly understood by looking at particular context, but some generalities can be highlighted. This is about the use and, potentially, the abuse of personal data in a wired society where the fundamental human right to privacy is at stake. The problem is that whereas a few years ago the butcher used to know everything about his 100 customers, these days the butcher is Tesco or Sainsbury and now they want the same with 1 million customers. Hence the use of database marketing through sophisticated technology on a microchip via mail, call centres, direct response and the Internet, with the promise of the ultimate one-to-one, tailor-made transaction. The problems of intrusiveness (and particularly 'spamming' on the Internet) are real. The natural reaction of consumers is to ask Why do you have my name and how did you get it? This is about consent and the choice of opting in or opting out. The EU position is clear, the view being: 'In the interests of the protection of personal data and growth of electronic and mobile commerce there is an overwhelming case in favour of a ban on unsolicited email and other personally addressed messages in the EU.'

However, it is perhaps the perceived lack of privacy that provides the real reason why citizens are reluctant to use new information and communications technology. The EU has stated the need for fair balance between data user and data subject. At the centre of this are the notions of respect and transparency, especially since a person cannot opt out of something they are not aware of. A typical 'trick' would be to offer a free game on a website without the person knowing that personal data would be collected, even down to the type of personal computer they have. European Union regulators already require specific consent for marketing by fax and using auto-calling machines without human intervention. Concern is expressed about especially sensitive issues such as sexual orientation. A US district judge upheld federal regulations to prevent banks/insurance and so on from selling/renting data. There are other examples that are beginning to emerge such as the Swedish Data Commissioner's ruling that all travel agents have to require customers to sign privacy declarations after the American Airlines Sabine Group reservation system was found to be sending data on customers to the USA for processing. For example, dietary requirements that have health and religious connotations were part of the data sent. A Spanish Commissioner fined Microsoft for sending clients' data to the USA without their knowledge.

The Direct Marketing Associations' (DMAs') codes that are negotiated with authorities recognize the need for self-regulation and a set of ground rules. This is complex in any country around the world, therefore the DMAs have taken action. For example, the UK DMA provide a £75 easy-to-use guide to the 1998 Data Protection act (£150 non-members). This guide deals with:

- increased controls over data processing

- the new express provision that gives individuals a right to opt out of receiving a company's own future direct marketing approaches

- the type of information that must be supplied to the data subject

- what opt-outs are necessary and the wording to be used in different circumstances

- the restrictions on the transfer of data to countries outside the European Economic Area

- the increased rights of data subjects and the notification process.

In a sense this is about 'permission marketing' and encouraging the data subject to opt in. The legal obligations of any marketer that holds personal data are clear in that they must comply with the Data Protection Act (1998) Data Protection Principles, namely:

1 The data must be processed fairly and lawfully.

2 The data can only be obtained for specified purposes and processed in a manner compatible with those purposes.

3 The data must be adequate, relevant and not excessive in relation to the purposes for which they are processed.

4 The data must be accurate and where necessary kept up to date.

5 The data must not be kept longer than is necessary.

6 The data shall only be processed in accordance with the rights of data subjects under the 1998 Act.

7 Appropriate technical and organizational measures must be taken against unauthorized or unlawful processing of personal data and against accidental loss, destruction or damage to personal data.

8 Personal data shall not be transferred outside of the European Economic Area unless there is adequate protection for the rights and freedoms of the data subject.

The overall sage advice to marketers from the DMAs is that the penalties for deliberate non-compliance are large enough that no organization could expect to survive prosecution. Mutual benefits are to be had since respect increases trust and trust will result in better targeting and better marketing.

Sources: Adapted from DMA (2003); Experian (2003); O'Neill (2001); Raul and Gomez (1999); Tempest (2001).

STOP POINT

Put yourself in the marketer's shoes. You want information on customers and prospects and you want to use it to its fullest potential, to beat the competition. Think about the consequences of non-compliance with DMA codes and laws of the land on data and data protection. Think about the best way forward for an organization, a data user, to get to grips with what is expected of it when it is dealing with the rights of data subjects.

Assignment

Choose one of the following topics upon which to write a two-page business magazine article. Write the article in the style of a particular magazine, for example *Marketing Week* or *Marketing Business*:

- Targeting and direct marketing generally and more specifically *geodemographics*, making sure to show how the management of databases affects performance.

- *Security*, on the Internet and elsewhere, within direct marketing, highlighting in particular the problems arising through the use of *credit cards*.

- *Sensitivity and regulation* addressing whether a company can be both effective and socially responsible when dealing with databases and direct marketing materials. Include an argument for the extent to which you would *regulate/legislate*.

Summary of Key Points

- Direct marketing is a key component of many a marketing communications mix.

- With direct marketing targeting can be tight and cost-effective if well managed, despite appearing expensive.

- It has at this point almost shed the 'junk mail' image it once had but is still viewed by some as intrusive, annoying and non-tactile. It has re-emerged as a powerful marketing communications tool.

- Direct marketing works best through achieving customer need fulfilment and is growing largely because of societal changes and trends such as lack of time because of work commitments.

- There is a key link between sales promotions and direct marketing. Incentives offered will depend on objectives and targets, for example whether they are company or competition loyalists.

- Direct marketing uses a variety of media and endeavours to be 'personal', where targeting and list creation are key.

- Databases can be made up from internal and external sources but in essence 'you pay for what you get'. Quality is key to success and resources are needed for direct marketing to breed its own success.

- Digital communications are now providing richer data but safeguarding personal data should be high on the agenda of any organization.

- Problems still remain with intrusiveness visible. Organizations should try to persuade data subjects to 'opt in', otherwise this will hamper the marketing effort.

Examination Questions

1 Explain the difference between direct and database marketing using examples to illustrate.

2 Outline the factors have driven the resurgence of direct marketing in recent years and use examples to illustrate.

3 Explain the key role incentives play in direct response advertising and provide examples to illustrate.

4 Explain the workings of loyalty schemes using a specific example to illustrate.

5 Discuss the rationale for setting up a club such as a wine club explaining the advantages to both club owner and consumer.

6 Outline creative approaches to direct response copy and design.

7 Outline the disadvantages and advantages of each medium used with direct marketing techniques.

8 Explain how database marketing can improve marketing performance.

9 Explore what the Georgetown survey on Internet privacy tells you about the way that regulation is likely to develop.

10 Explain the overall ethics of direct marketing practice using examples to illustrate.

Note

1 The use of the average response rate as a measure is dangerous, as response rates will depend upon whether the product and prospect are existing or new and on the sector being dealt with, especially whether this is consumer or industrial.

References

Direct Marketing Association (DMA) (2003). A guide to the Data Protection Act 1998. At www.crm-forum.com/library/dma/dma-006exe.

Douglas, D. and May, D. (1999). It takes two to tango. *Admap*, June. www.warc.com

Duncan, T. (2002). *Integrated Marketing Communications*. McGraw Hill.

Economist, The (1999). The end of privacy: the surveillance society. *The Economist*, **1–7**, May, 105–107.

Experian (2003). How to stay within the law. At www.growmorebusiness.com/DataProtection.html.

Institute of Practitioners in Advertising (IPA) (1998). *IPA Advertising Effectiveness Awards Cases, First Direct*. IPA.

Lee, B. (2003). Direct response television and how it works. *Admap*, **435**, January, 24–27.

Norwich Union Direct (2003). Company materials, July.

O'Connor, J. and Galvin, E. (2001). *Marketing in the Digital Age*. Financial Times Prentice Hall.

O'Neill, G. (2001). *Irish Direct Marketing Association – E-Commerce and Interactive Code of Practice*. IDMA/Federation of European Direct Marketing (FEDMA), 19 September.

Pickton, D. and Broderick, A. (2001). *Integrated Marketing Communications*. Financial Times Prentice Hall.

Raul, A. C. and Gomez, M. A. (1999). U.S. perspectives on consumer protection in the global electronic marketplace (summary of the Federal Trade Commission Public Workshop), 8–9 June. At www.sidleyandaustin.co.uk/cyberlaw/features/ftcjuris.ASP.

Tempest, A. (2001). Electronic communication, privacy and government intervention: issues and actions. International Advertising Association. At www.atalink.co.uk/iaa2001/html/p038.htm.

Yeltsin, T. (1998). *Integrated Marketing Communications*. Oxford: Butterworth-Heinemann.

Chapter overview

Introduction of this chapter

The nature of promotions is understood here to be the traditional sales promotions techniques and their associated methods and tools such as exhibitions and trade shows, packaging and direct marketing. This chapter therefore takes the APIC general framework developed in Chapter 4 and facilitates application, via a decision sequence model in the direct marketing and promotions management context.

Aims of this chapter

This chapter provides a case study that can be analysed with the aid of the material presented in Chapter 4. In particular, the framework presented at the end of that chapter is designed as a facilitation device for this purpose. After completion of this chapter the reader should be able to:

- explain the elements of the APIC system, as applied to promotions, in broad DSM terms

- understand the ideas behind the critique of the adoption of such an approach

- use the framework for the management of the promotion function

- explain the communications mix that helped build the ASB BANK and BankDirect brands

- apply the above to the management of direct marketing and promotions for a direct banking brand, BankDirect as part of ASB Bank, New Zealand.

A framework for managing advertising employing the APIC decision sequence model

As outlined in Chapter 4, the APIC DSM is a commonly used model that deals with both the 'art' and 'science' aspects of communication. A decision sequence framework is required to help plan direct marketing and promotion in just the same way as for any communication, but the difference is in the detail. The reader should refer back to the framework provided in Chapter 4 as an aid to analysis of the case given below.

A case of direct banking: The ASB Bank, New Zealand, and BankDirect

Background

History

The idea of saving money in a bank is quite an old one now. When the Reverend Henry Duncan wanted to encourage his parishioners in Ruthwell, Scotland, to be thrifty, he set up, in 1810, a savings bank.[1] By 1842 the *Auckland Times* was asking why was it not possible to have a savings bank for New Zealand. In 1845, John Logan Campbell, the 'Father of Auckland', drew up rules and regulations and became trustee and Honorary Secretary of a savings bank. Finally, on 7 May 1847 it was announced that Auckland Savings Bank was to be opened and on 5 June 1847 it was opened at 7 p.m.

No gold rush

Business was very slow at first with just £166 4s. deposited in the first year but, as Auckland grew, so did the savings bank and by the 1850s the bank had become involved with mortgage finance. A first loan of £400 was made on a 60-acre farm and the ASB mortgage became known for its easy terms.

Expansion

By 1859 the bank had decided to move into a new building and install a telephone system. From a product perspective, marketing was just beginning. Penny Bank – early targeting aimed at younger customers – was introduced in 1876. There were five new accounts immediately opened. A new head office opened in 1862 and by 1879 the first branch office was open. Prosperity followed as New Zealand grew, and by 1900 there were transactions of more than £1 million.

Ties with the community

ASB was held in high affection and from the early beginnings the bank gave back to its community. In 1906, for example, it gave £10 000 to establish a technical school in Auckland, illustrating how ASB valued its customer base. Another example was the $2500 the bank put into the First World War, War Expense Account, with donations also for the relief of local distress caused by the war. Money was also donated to the Red Cross and $50 000 to the building of the Auckland War Memorial Museum.

The 1920s saw expansion for ASB and community ties continued with local developments, including finance for city projects. The 1930s depression brought problems for many, but ASB kept the community spirit and became an agent of the Reserve Bank helping to deal with finance matters such as deposits, savings transfers to war loans without cash withdrawals and even marketed war bonds to help with the war effort in the Second World War.

Further progress and corporate image

The year 1947 was the bank's centenary year and it had $20 million in deposits. This figure rose to $44 million by 1960 and by the mid-1960s there was a network of ASB branches. In 1965 ASB petitioned the College of Arms and was granted a coat of arms in the following year, with the motto 'tomorrow made secure'. The bank's identity was underlined by this. The depiction of the bank in its natural Auckland setting secured the bank to the community that had given birth to it. A portcullis denotes 'guardian of treasures' and a castle in gold denotes security. A blue marlin and a tui make it distinctively New Zealand.

Moving forward in a technological age

Early use of computer technology allowed ASB to be ahead of the competition. The swift introduction of electronic funds transfer at point of sale (EFTPOS) and Internet banking made ASB unique. ASB is keeping up with the technology, especially now that mobile banking with 'Fastnet Mobile' allows mobile technology to view a mini website bank account.

New name and image

Through amalgamation of various banks ASB became a trust bank and was no longer just a savings bank. The name ASB Bank was underscored by a new logo based on the coat of arms of 1966 but with the use of grey to denote professionalism and security and yellow to denote the future, a progressive organization that was innovative yet friendly. This was used in the usual way with premises and staff uniforms and so on. A tie in with the Commonwealth Bank of Australia (CBA) (75 per cent of ASB Bank bought in 1989) saw a new corporate headquarters by 1991 with state-of-the-art facilities including a professionally managed gymnasium. The rapid changes in banking generally during the 1990s meant much less backroom work and more customer service and, in particular, the introduction of telephone banking. In ASB Bank's case this was 'Fastphone' for bill payments and so on.

The role of the communications mix

Public relations has always featured prominently, with community ties strong from the beginning, so the bank's sponsorship of sport (netball, cricket, rugby), art and culture as well as involvement with a range of projects from flower shows to a children's hospital is not surprising. The year 1997 was the bank's sesquicentenary (one hundred and fiftieth year) and special logo functions for community and business leaders and staff were part of the celebrations. At this point the bank won the Arthur Andersen Service Excellence Award and managing director, Ralph Norris, was named as New Zealand Business Executive of the Year.

Sales promotions have featured to an extent in a sector that is dominated by, effectively, price-cutting in the guise of fixed rates, variable rates and other combinations of offerings such as a nil processing charge, home loan helpline and credit card features such as overseas facilities.

Advertising has consisted of a number of ideas and devices over time. Kashin the elephant became the embodiment of ASB when this character fronted the advertising in 1966. A knot in its trunk was to remind itself (i.e. children and parents) about school banking day. To reflect the impact of technology, in 1996 Robert the Robot, who was a rather amiable, droll character took this fronting role. In January 2000, what became a classic campaign was launched. This utilized the character Ira Goldstein, on a mission from New York, on behalf of a big American bank which was seeking a New Zealand partner. Television advertising depicted Ira at all levels, for example home loans and investments. Ira had to investigate and report back on ASB Bank. Research showed that this lifted awareness still further. The August 2000 sales promotion, using television advertising as the means to get the message across, was of home loans with a difference, portrayed as a fast and efficient service through the '60 minute challenge'. If a home loan application took more than the 60 minutes then a voucher worth $100 would be issued. This was so successful that very few vouchers were issued.

The *Internet* had had a big impact by the mid-1990s and ASB were quick to establish a website, being the first bank in Australasia to offer transactions in a secure Internet environment with 'Fastnet'. With this service, following on from *direct marketing* using the 'Fastphone' service that offered better rates, ASB Bank was able to establish BankDirect.

Media issues

ASB Bank has used television because of its cost-effective reach (for yearly expenditure see Table 11.1). *Corporate brand messages* have been about leadership and have been put across in 60-second slots. *Product messages* have been about things like price, favourable rates and so on, and have been put over in short, 15-second slots. An example is the '60 minute home loan challenge' 60-second slot. Radio and on-line advertising typically accompanied this (Table 11.2).

Table 11.1
Expenditure by year ($)

	1997	1998	1999	2000	2001	2002 (ytd)
ASB Bank	5 243	8 331	3 545	9 556	8 097	3 230
ANZ	6 783	6 173	5 491	7 243	8 030	3 075
BNZ	9 507	8 200	9 531	6 930	6 213	926
National Bank	7 230	8 274	11 645	9 302	7 518	5 315
Westpac Trust	9 612	7 793	17 498	9 968	8 767	1 912

Source: CAANZ (2002).

Table 11.2
Allocation of media by year (%)

Years	Television	Radio	Magazine	Newspaper	Internet	Outdoor	All other	Total
2000	50	5	1	38	5	1	0	100
2001	54	4	4	34	3	1	0	100
2002 (ytd)	57	7	2	33	1	0	0	100

Source: CAANZ (2002).

BankDirect branding

Technological leadership has allowed ASB Bank to develop BankDirect, launched in October 1997. This differentiates ASB from other banks. Other products have been developed since the amalgamation with CBA, including Orbit Home Loans and the Investment Advisory Service that supports on-line trading activities. In 2000 CBA acquired the remaining 25 per cent of ASB.[2]

Targets

In a mature and saturated market different approaches are required. All adults in New Zealand have bank accounts so that getting customers to switch banks or capturing, as customers, children and immigrants are the options. A key target is the personal banking customer who is usually in the age range 25–49 and earns $40 000+. This is the 'quality middle market'. A subset of this, but who would also be interested in home loans, is the owner-occupier.

A second target is the farmer, a third the smaller business and a fourth the on-line shareholder.

Positioning

At the brand level the name of the game is acquiring customers from the competition, and making sure not to lose any customers to the competition. Competition is fierce, especially for home loans. The mission and vision of ASB Bank is to be the best as a brand and as a service provider, and to deliver quality. The bank wishes to be seen as sustainable and stable. Robert the Robot had softened the hard edge of technology and kept the ASB Bank image friendly as well as up to speed. Ira differentiated the brand, keeping it 'one step ahead'. To lead a service the perception barrier has to be dealt with. Both Robert and Ira did this, where the objective was leverage service position to enhance revenue growth.

Marketing challenge

The future of the ASB Bank centres on a number of issues. It is the number 1 bank in New Zealand and wants to remain so. It has investments worth over $1 billion and over 100 000 Fastnet users. It has been successful with its award-winning call centre and has won awards for its Robert the Robot and Ira Goldstein campaigns with whose help the bank has moved to the actuality of being ahead strategically. Despite this success customer perception remains of key concern and there is an ongoing battle against the 'they are all the same' mentality that dogs politics, political campaigning and also banks and banking. Service needs continually to be shored up in order to differentiate from the competition. The problem can be seen as twofold:

- Banks are all the same.

- No bank is really great.

This is clearly not the case. In the last few years there have been numerous examples of developments in promotions in the banking sector. For example:

1 *La Caixa* (Spain) started, in 1998, a *loyalty programme* targeted at younger clients (8–12-year-olds) of Mega Account Book Star (126 136). This involved nil transaction charges, a late night Thursday opening and other activities to gain interest. This resulted in a 68 per cent increase in acquisition of new customers. La Caixa Financial Savings Bank also, in 1998, launched a *loyalty programme* for their usual credit and debit card customers. The programme accumulated points that could be exchanged for gifts. Three thousand three hundred branches helped recruit from a mailing of 300 000 customers with a massive 84 per cent response rate (Direct Marketing Association, 1998f; Federation Europeenne de Marketing Direct, 1998).

2 *Associates National Bank* (USA) in 1998 targeted college students with an unconventional 'breaking all the rules' *direct marketing* campaign that achieved a response rate of 5.5 per cent (previous effort only 3.8 per cent) and cost $44.12 per response. The mailing involved bold graphics, a phone card premium, a sticker design to invoke a response to the card's main benefit, and other bold design features (Direct Marketing Association, 1998a).

3 *SunTrust Bank Card* (UK) in 1997 ran an *alternative media* campaign to promote a generic credit card – but a card that was different in an overcrowded market. This was a push/pull strategy that involved sweepstakes and a nostalgic 1950s music theme using posters, newsletters, stationery stickers and alternative (to conventional) material. The campaign exceeded its goal by 50 per cent on number of applications and approved accounts at a cost that was 50 per cent below industry average for a promotional campaign. All participating branches met or surpassed their individual account goals (Direct Marketing Association, 1998b).

4 *United Missouri Bank* (USA) joined forces with Farmland, a farming co-operative to offer members a Mastercard. A *direct marketing* campaign, through the mail, received a response rate of 5.14 per cent at a cost of $33.94 per response. This positioned the brand as a friend of Midwestern farmers, not a city brand but with the practical benefit of helping with financial management. The entire campaign cost just $69 375 (Direct Marketing Association, 1998c).

5 *The Royal Bank of Canada* used a *direct marketing* campaign that acquired creditworthy customers for Visa. This through the mail campaign communicated the low, 9.5 per cent interest rate in a 'save money now' manner. The mailing dramatically used an oversized envelope with a bold 'save' message. Once opened, benefits were communicated to the 3.64 per cent of the target

who responded, a cost per response of $67.68 (Direct Marketing Association, 1998d).

6   *Banco Real*, a leading Brazilian bank, in 1998 used *direct marketing* to encourage use. Discounts were negotiated across the country with restaurants, clothes stores, petrol stations and so on. Three thousand participant establishments were geodemographically and subject coded so that matching to cardholders could take place and a quality mailing sent out. This 'good for you' mailing yielded a 5.23 per cent response (Direct Marketing Association, 1998e).

7   *Chase Direct* of Chase Manhattan Bank, in 1996, was one of the first banks to offer remote facilities. Two *mail* packages were sent to customer and prospect names, and a 4.08 per cent response rate was achieved at a cost of $62 per response. The first piece of direct marketing was a sign-up kit. This was followed up with the second, a new member kit, for those already signed up (Direct Marketing Association, 1998g).

8   *Okobank* of Finland in 1999 launched a *loyalty programme* aimed at young people, with the objective of establishing a loyal consumer base for the future. A dialogue was opened using the Internet as both medium and service channel. Attention, interest, visibility and image enhancement were all achieved through *direct marketing* on the Internet, television and cinema. Eighteen to twenty-five year olds were approached in a number of ways. The eighteenth birthday programme targeted those having such a birthday. In return for a filled out questionnaire, movie tickets were provided. Graduating students were also approached using direct marketing. The image objectives were exceeded, the television recall figures were excellent and 90 per cent of young people considered the approach to be modern, fun and unbiased. The eighteenth birthday programme, after achieving 95 per cent success in getting the target into the bank and a sales conversion of 100 per cent was made a permanent measure (Federation Europeenne de Marketing Direct, 1999).

Assignment

Differentiation is seen as the only long-term sustainable competitive advantage for ASB Bank, so that 'we deliver on the promise and create advantage' (ASB Bank, 2003).

Assume you have been asked to help devise a sales promotion and direct marketing plan of action that would involve the ASB Bank and build on the bank's advertising and brand driven image. Use the DSM provided in Chapter 4 to complete the following tasks:

• Outline what you feel to be the key background points to the direct banking case from a promotions and direct marketing perspective. From this information establish the likely target(s).

• From the information available, establish possible objectives and positioning for the promotion both generally and in particular. Write an outline direct marketing and promotions strategy proposal for the BankDirect brand, and suggest push, pull and profiling ideas as well as creative and media tactics.

- Provide ideas on the implementation of a promotions and direct marketing campaign for BankDirect by using the parameters in the implementation section of the DSM framework and show clearly what you would recommend in terms of allocation, budgets, timings, seasonality and so on. Pay particular attention to technological leadership and service leadership aspects of ASB Bank as underlined by Robert the Robot and Ira Goldstein.

- Using the final section of the DSM, the control section, suggest what monitoring, evaluation and research methods and techniques you would employ to maximize efficiency and effectiveness of the BankDirect promotions and direct marketing campaign.

Summary of Key Points

- Most writers would subscribe to a form of decision sequence model when attempting to manage advertising. There are, however, challenges to the APIC-type of system without alternatives. A shift has occurred with regard to a move away from communication effects to return on investment in advertising.

- Analysis deals with assessments of customers, products, the organization and its environment. This is the 'Where are we now?' question.

- Planning deals with targets, objectives and positioning. This is the 'Where do we want to go?' question. This is followed by consideration of creative and media strategy. This is the 'How do we get there?' question.

- Implementation is a consideration of 'How do we put this into practice?' and involves the allocation of spend to the campaign.

- Control involves evaluation and research and is the 'Did we get there?' question. This is not only a check on whether objectives have been achieved, but also a consideration of the place of research in the entire framework.

Examination Questions

These questions are similar to those outlined in Chapter 4 but should be answered more specifically with regard to sales promotion and direct marketing and the brand.

1   Explain why you agree or disagree with the contention that the APIC-type model is useful as a framework for direct marketers or sales promoters to operate within.

2   Outline what you consider to be the important elements of the analysis stage of a direct marketing or sales promotions advertising decision sequence model.

3   The planning stage of a DSM involves consideration of 'where do we want to go?' having already established targets. Discuss the importance of establishing targets early on in a direct marketing or sales promotion campaign.

4 Explain the usefulness (or not) of perceptual mapping in planning direct marketing or sales promotions.

5 Creative strategy is part of 'How do we get there?'. Discuss the different creative approaches to direct marketing or sales promotions available.

6 Discuss the importance of involvement with particular reference to creative approaches.

7 Media strategy is also part of 'How do we get there?'. Discuss the key media characteristics for this case.

8 There are a number of practical issues when considering how to put a campaign into practice. Discuss these in relation to the case.

9 Discuss the logic behind pre-, concurrent and post-testing within this case.

10 Comment on the idea of direct marketing or sales promotion as an investment not a cost in relation to building brands.

Notes

1 ASB Bank (2001).

2 It is interesting to note that in 1989 75 per cent of ASB cost CBA $252 million, and in 2000 25 per cent cost $600 million (ASB Bank, 2001).

References

ASB Bank (2001). About ASB Bank history. At www.asbbank.co.uk.nz/about/history.stm.

ASB Bank (2003). At www.asb.c.nz/section114.asp.

CAANZ (2002). ASB Bank – one step ahead. Communications Agencies Association of New Zealand. At www.warc.com/fulltext/CAANZ/76962.htm.

Direct Marketing Association (1998a). Cha-Ching (Associates National Bank, USA).

Direct Marketing Association (1998b). Rock to the top branch campaign (Sun Trust Bank Card, UK).

Direct Marketing Association (1998c). Farmland Affinity credit card (DIMAC, Direct for United Missouri Bank, UMB, USA).

Direct Marketing Association (1998d). Royal Bank of Canada Project Genesis Wave I.

Direct Marketing Association (1998e). Real Visa Ativasao Maxima (Banco Real, Brazil).

Direct Marketing Association (1998f). Star Points (La Caixa).

Direct Marketing Association (1998g). Chase Direct, banking for the 21st century.

Federation Europeenne de Marketing Direct (1998). Mega account book star – La Caixa.

Federation Europeenne de Marketing Direct (1999). Customer loyalty programme for 18–25 year olds – Okobank.

PART FOUR

Public Relations Issues

Public relations (PR) is regarded as one of the classic elements of promotion. Its development into contemporary approaches such as relationship marketing and stakeholder theory threatens the broader aspects of public relations management rather than the core techniques concerning media relations. Stakeholder approaches take on an added significance since they incorporate the ethos of what is regarded as an ethical approach to business. In this part of the book the classical elements of public relations are considered, looking in detail at the contemporary approaches embraced by stakeholder analysis and relationship management. 'Publics' are considered rather than 'audiences' and the chapters deal with information transfer, advice, employees, lobbying, sponsorship and so on. At the heart of Part Four is the idea that PR is a professional discipline (and not some sleight of hand) and should be viewed as being part of the organization's strategic effort.

This fourth part of the book consists of four chapters. Chapter 12 deals with the nature and role of public relations, Chapter 13 with corporate communications and Chapter 14 with sponsorship. Chapter 15, following on from Chapter 4 in Part One of this book, simulates a strategic framework for effective PR management for crisis situations, using Perrier and others as examples.

The nature and role of public relations

Chapter overview

Introduction to this chapter

In this chapter the nature and scope of public relations is explored and explained. Media relations are important but not the be all and end all. Knowing the media is essential but management attitude towards, and use of, PR is an overriding concern. The next chapter deals with corporate communications and hence corporate relations and especially corporate identity, image, personality and reputation. This chapter focuses on the product/market level, where PR might be used, for example, to support brands, assist in the launch of a new brand/product or to help throughout an event. This level has been dubbed marketing public relations (MPR) as opposed to corporate public relations (CPR). The same kinds of techniques might be used on both levels, although ultimately the two levels should be brought together in an integrated, managed fashion (see Chapter 15). This chapter therefore discusses PR's relationship with other communications mix elements and with marketing theory. The chapter also deals with targets or 'publics', PR in practice, PR's ethical dimension and the impact of technology on PR techniques.

Aims of this chapter

The overall aim of this chapter is to consider the nature and role of public relations in the context of what theory has to offer practice. More specifically, on completion of this chapter, the reader should be able to:

- discuss the nature and role of PR in terms of its development and propaganda

- explain PR in relation to other marketing communications

- discuss PR in terms of marketing theory and relationship marketing

- discuss the nature of PR practice

- define PR in relation to the concept of 'publics'

- explain the relationship between internal and external PR

- explain the relationship between PR and ethics, legislation and control in PR practice

- explain the impact of technology and the Internet on PR.

The nature and role of PR

The nature of PR

The term 'public relations' is well understood these days by those in particular walks of life, for example company executives and government officials. Generally speaking, the public at large also understands the basics of PR, although perceptions have changed over time. There is still a view that PR is somehow 'sleight of hand', a con if you will, but this is perhaps less strong than in the past, although some might say that PR is simply organized lying. More positively, others might say PR is about relationships, where maintaining good relationships with various interest groups is seen as a sensible move. Of course, there is a role for PR in achieving this, whether it be maintenance of employee relations or environmental concerns to name but two areas (Dibb, Simkin and Vancini, 1996). There are therefore new challenges afoot for organizations to meet in the future, with PR becoming a strategic necessity as opposed to a tactical tool in order that organizations are able to make the most of opportunities. For Dibb, Simkin and Vancini (1996) such opportunities lie in the areas of:

1   Competition and specialization – for example a high-tech area within the medical or health-care field.

2   Internationalization – where strategic alliances may be important, but it is not clear as to the best means of developing an international capability.

3   Personnel, strategy and evaluation – where investment in people is important but so, too, is the development of PR from tactical tool to strategy formulator. Crucial to this is the measurement of results of the PR effort.

4   Technology – where advances must be mastered and used to advantage.

What is clear is the growth in PR activity in the western world in recent years (Kitchen, 1991). Historically, PR has been used to solve problems such as announcing new products or helping prospects to find information. Latterly, PR has been used more dramatically as a means of 'breaking through the clutter', to capture attention and interest. Public relations can be said to be versatile but its development has been hampered by its lower (than marketing) status in organizations in the past.[1] Duncan (2002) provides the example of the Harry Potter books and films to illustrate how potent PR can be as a tool, where the timely use of embargoes on information created very effective anticipation.

The scope of PR

The scope of PR appears infinite but at its heart there is a need for planned and purposeful communication with whomever is important at any point on a time continuum. Not surprisingly, definitions (which abound in the PR literature, as anywhere else) usually include words such as planned, sustained, mutual and so on. Many see modern PR as an essential part of any organization's marketing mix – an essential form of communication with the organization's market or publics. For the UK Institute of Public Relations (formed in 1948) PR is described as 'the deliberate planned and sustained effort to establish and maintain mutual understanding between an organization and its public'. Others might simply say it is 'goodwill management'. It involves facts and logic but also imagery and imagination designed to win 'hearts and minds' and the ability to sustain this long term. There is a need to achieve credibility where the image matches reality. The organization can polish the image but, as some marketing wags might put it, 'you can't polish a turd',[2] but PR can reach the parts advertising cannot (see Chapter 13 for a discussion on corporate image and reality).

Marketing PR

There is a somewhat pointless debate in some texts as to whether PR is part of marketing or not, a debate that has a definite whiff of 'the Emperor's new clothes'[3] about it. Claiming certain things about issues, articles, objects and so on often will produce problems in terms of what is actually delivered (Baker, 2000). It is true that, historically, PR and marketing came from different routes. The public relations officer (PRO) took over from the press agent. Often a PRO will report directly to the CEO and, in this case, will probably be dealing with corporate PR, but the PR function or department will also deal with MPR issues. In this book the view taken is that MPR is part of the marketing communications mix (and for that matter CPR is viewed as part of the corporate communications mix, and part of an integrated communications whole) and is therefore part of marketing. For some organizations the functions of marketing and PR will still be distinctive departments and the best that one can hope for in this scenario is that marketing and PR are at least allies and not at loggerheads.

The difference between MPR and CPR has been explored at length in the literature (for example, Kitchen and Moss, 1995; Kitchen and Papasolomou, 1997). Whether or not academics argue that MPR is representative of a further attempt by marketers to 'hijack' PR seems rather irrelevant to MPR or PR practice. Marketing PR may not represent a new marketing paradigm or even marketing or PR discipline, as was predicted, but this does not mean that MPR is not an important element of the organization's marketing communications mix. Philip Kotler has declared MPR to be the healthy offspring of two parents, i.e. marketing and PR. It is perhaps safe to assume that MPR has a place in marketing in order to deliver strong share of voice but also to win share of mind and heart (Kitchen and Papasolomou, 1997). On the other hand, MPR and CPR are in a necessary strategic alliance where marketing and PR are allies not rivals. Marketing PR can be effective in building brand awareness and knowledge (in effect 'brand seeding') in a cost-effective manner compared with advertising and, yet, can complement advertising and break through the clutter (Kitchen and Papasolomou, 1997). It can therefore be used to launch new brands and products in a particular position in the market place. Marketing PR can help reposition existing brands, create interest in a product category or help with the defence of a brand in trouble. The positive brand attitude created by MPR can positively influence customers and prospects. Marketing PR used effectively within IMC can be part of a communications mix without the dominance of one form of communication over another (Figure 12.1).

Public relations is about the longer-term rather than the shorter-term commercial considerations of the rest of the communications mix. It should be more than the mere ability to get around legislative restrictions on other communications tools. Public relations should be about, for example, newsworthy events, being objective, advice-giving, being able to reach people in a way other forms of communication cannot or being a good citizen. An underlying feature of PR

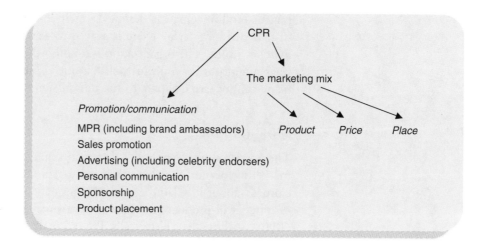

Figure 12.1
Public relations' place
in the marketing
communications mix.

is the lack of control the marketer has when using it, since much of PR is in the hands of media editors and, in some instances, is in the 'lap of the Gods'. Lack of control can be offset against its cost-effectiveness, the ability to create a flexible message, its effective use in a crisis and its perceived objectivity (as opposed to being perceived to be partisan).

In theory PR is about misconceptions and misunderstandings or, rather, the avoidance of these. In practice it is about organizations, chief executive officers, products, policies and so on – in fact anything that interfaces with the various publics any organization inevitably has, i.e. the general public, shareholders, politicians, pressure groups, employees, to name but a few. As society evolves the practice of PR evolves too. Its documented history does not go back beyond this century but its role today is seen as vital by many organizations in the avoidance of crises or having to resort to crisis management. Regardless of the type of organizational situation, specialization is omnipresent in society. So it is not unusual to look at the PR industry and see not a holistic entity but a series of specialists engaging in PR activities. Each organization will have its own discipline, its own way of working. This suggests that while fundamentals might remain, applications and interpretations will differ. After all, if the function of PR is to eradicate misconceptions, incomprehension and therefore avoid misunderstanding, each organization must achieve this within its own context. All would agree, however, that it is about getting it right in the first place. PR can be the catalyst in achieving truly integrated communication.

Some of the ways PR may differ from advertising can be readily seen in terms of audience and purpose. Historically, PR can be seen as a number of associated yet separate entities that are equal partners in the integrated effort. Public relations' own reputation has been at times one of being manipulative or about 'fancy parties' for privileged members of certain groups. However, PR can be seen as being all the communications with all the people with whom an organization has contact. A relationship with others exists whether an organization wants it to or not. Public relations is concerned with the development and communication of competitive strategies. It is a management function that provides visibility for an organization, and this allows it to be properly identified, positioned and understood by all its targets. Public relations at the level of the product/market is still a key tool in the promotional toolbox. Meeting clients, making an appointment, writing a letter or making a telephone call, the office location and décor and the efficiency of the receptionist are all examples of image-forming factors. It is important to note that PR is not the 'free advertising' of some definitions. Certainly successful media relations can lead to free column centimetres, but it is usually as a result of careful planning.

The role of PR

Public relations activities are many and varied but their role is a common one: to contribute to the image of an organization using a 'soft sell' approach. Public relations is not advertising under another name. Many of an organization's clients/customers may view advertising as a 'hard sell' and recognize it as having specific objectives. Public relations activities often have a greater credibility with target groups. For example, an article in the business pages of a newspaper about the impact of new legislation will no doubt be seen in a different light because it is an editorial rather than coming from the organization in a partisan way. The basic premise for PR's role is that a positive image is essential to retain existing customers and clients and to attract new business.

The characteristics of PR

Public relations is characterized by its planned nature and it does not (usually) require the purchase of air time or space in media vehicles such as television or magazines. An editor of one sort or another decides whether or not to transmit messages, not the message sponsor as with advertising, so that it is a question of degree of control. Public relations messages are perceived to come from the media and have a greater credibility than, say, advertising, which is perceived to come from the message sponsor, and while message credibility can be high, management control on the transmission (when and what) can be low. Absolute costs are minimal, and relative costs are very low (cost of reaching target audiences). The main costs are time and opportunity cost associated with preparing literature, press releases and so on. Public relations is not always very good at reaching specific audiences, unlike advertising, therefore wastage can be quite high. In a nutshell, PR represents a very cost-effective means of carrying messages, with a high degree of credibility. However, the degree of control that management is able to exert over the transmission of messages can be limited.

VIGNETTE

From functional material to objects of desire: the case of the European Council of Vinyl Manufacturers (ECVM) leaping the aspirational gap

The case of the ECVM shows the characteristics of MPR in clear relief even though not tackling brand-level problems. Here there is the case of a material like PVC (used to make, for example, water pipes, cable sheathing and blood bags) being made to look aspirational in the minds of consumers. This was an exercise in repositioning products from being perceived as commodity plastics to being the material of choice in the future.

The versatility of PVC that provides a means to enhancing consumer lifestyles was employed by using designers and the design media to get across the concept of 'PVC for life and living'. The PR company's, Countrywide Porter Novelli's, task was to make this concept 'live' and to challenge PVC's traditional image. This was done in several countries, beginning with Italy and

Belgium where interior design and fashion respectively were the unique themes at shows during 2001. Innovative lighting was showcased at the Salon del Mobile (Milan) and a student design competition was created with a leading Belgian fashion institute. By September 2001, involvement with another showcase event in the UK saw a collaboration of English and German designers and the British Plastics Federation, with five marketable PVC products for the home the end result. These quirky products grabbed media attention, as they became commercially viable, desirable objects. What looked like ceramic was in fact PVC, which when dropped, bounced. A video of consumer reaction was made and shown to ECVM internal stakeholders.

This was a campaign with clear and credible objectives that would work in twelve countries. It worked because designers challenged existing perceptions of the product and stimulated discussion about the properties of PVC. A wide range of positive coverage was achieved from national newspapers to the plastics trade press and the 'PVC for life and living' programme repositioned PVC as an aspirational product. Future activities will involve other markets such as Sweden, France, the USA, Japan and Canada, where the ECVM will collaborate still further with relevant PVC trade bodies.

Source: Adapted from www.ipr.org.uk/excellence/case-studies/InternationalPR.htm.

STOP POINT What are the advantages in using an MPR approach to repositioning of a generic product such as PVC? For an organization like the ECVM the collaborative approach appears very appropriate. What alternative communication tools might have been used to achieve similar objectives? What is the likely saving in money terms through the use of MPR instead of advertising?

Public relations as propaganda

Nature and history

Propaganda is often described as being the dissemination of information. In a broad context this involves the whole idea of democracy and issues such as abortion rights, civil liberties and so on. In the court of public opinion, for Center and Jackson (2003), 'PR practitioners are the attorneys' and as such are advocates for companies, causes and issues – in short they are propagandists. Propaganda is best understood when placed in a historic setting. Harrison (2000) uses Hunt and Grunig's (1994) framework for the development of PR in the USA, i.e. that there are five distinct phases in this development:

• the public be fooled

• the public be damned

• public information

• propaganda and persuasion

• public understanding.

Propaganda, then, is preceded by the provision of public information and succeeded by public understanding, and is thus in between the beginnings of honest and truthful stories and what we see today as modern PR practice. The propaganda phase appears to stand alone in a historical continuum but the reality is somewhat different. Harrison gives a clear account of the use of propaganda as part of PR as the 'invisible government, which is the true ruling power of our country' (Bernays quoted in Harrison, 2000: 22).

War aside, the period between the First and Second World Wars saw the beginnings of propaganda being used by governments for more commercial purposes and certainly post-Second World War by commercial organizations, notably Shell and the Royal Mail. Harrison points to the Roman Catholic Church – with its 'Congregation of Propaganda', i.e. a committee of cardinals in charge of foreign missions to seek out unbelievers and makes converts – as a case in point.

Government

L'Etang (1998) maintains that PR today owes much for its development to *local government*, which is where the corps of PR officers was established and who formed those responsible for the setting up of the Institute of Public Relations. They also contributed in an important way to PR ideology and, in particular, to the idea of professionalism in 'the articulation of their own strong public service ethos'. Public relations' initial role was seen as being that of providing information, with 'intelligence' seen as being a complementary service to deliver both internal and external service. The merging of intelligence with information saw local authorities attempting to share understanding with the local populace in terms of legal matters, policy and so on. For L'Etang (1998), public authorities cannot remain the mysterious, impersonal bodies that most were and that many still are.

With local government, the elected members are at the focus of communications. Local authorities usually have a PRO whose job, as a local authority employee (not a political party employee), is to service the people via the elected members. In principle at least this should involve dealing with facts unfettered by distortion. There should be no political axe to grind but it is in this area where accusations of propaganda (as if a dirty word) might arise. Certainly the local authority PRO gets involved with all the useful tools of PR, from press releases to visits and visitors for the purpose of disseminating information.

Central government in peacetime operates differently to that in times of war. Historically, these activities are interwoven with themselves and with changes in technology. The acceptable face of governmental propaganda during periods of war is not necessarily acceptable at other times. This might be the 'Country Needs You' of the First World War or the propaganda battles of the Iraq War of 2003 – where the technological, communications but especially media comparison is stark in terms of what was available during 1914–18. If propaganda is a 'necessary adjunct to diplomacy' (L'Etang, 1998) and as such has a part to play in democracy (rather than simply being a tool of totalitarian regimes), then it can be used by governments for educating and informing its citizens and winning their co-operation.

These days, any government's Chief Information Officer necessarily involves him or herself in advertising, PR and propaganda (or 'spin' if you will) since the duty and function of his or her office is to be primarily a PR and propaganda machine for the government. Here in the UK the Government Information Service (formerly the sinister-sounding Ministry of Information, then the bureaucratic-sounding Central Office of Information) performs a supporting role to the Chief Information Officer and hence the ministerial departments.

National and local government are seen by some as stakeholder groups (Fill, 2002) in the sense that the organization, say a local firm, can use PR to inform the local authority of its strategic intent, in other words, to work with the local authority and seek to satisfy the objectives of both parties. Large organizations and trade associations should seek to influence government and those in power in terms of, for example, the direction and strength of legislation. Select committees and the role of the 'retained' MP have at the time of writing had a number of years of scrutiny, especially the 'cash for questions'[4] issue that gave rise to the debate on what is proper parliamentary practice.

Parliamentary consultants must know the workings of Parliament. Shearer (in Howard, 1985) puts forward two categories of parliamentary lobbying that consultants might be involved in. Defensive action is to do with presenting a case against something you want either abolished or amended. Initiating campaigning is all about stimulating activity in Parliament. To illustrate the former, Shearer uses the example of companies and organizations in the 1970s fighting against Labour legislation and for the latter the animal welfare lobby, especially the Royal Society for the Prevention of Cruelty to Animals (RSPCA) during the period 1979–80.

The relationships government or its ministers/officers have with the media are of course of great interest and importance here. This should not be a question of privileged access to the media by, for example, a minister, but should be a question of the importance and newsworthiness of the statement made. Lobby correspondents perform an important function, the very existence of the lobby greatly influencing communication. The nature of the prevailing party in power, the EU and European Parliament make the entire situation more complex and interesting.

Special interest groups

These would include pressure, voluntary and charity groups. They deal with ideas and attitude change more than the usual tangible products and companies. Barron (in Howard, 1985) points out that 'while education is a charitable activity propaganda is not', especially in the eyes of the Charity Commissioners. This causes real problems for this kind of organization by way of how they present their case. Protesters and crusaders are not a new phenomenon. Nor are 'factionalization' or 'confrontation', which usually lead to a head to head, with a compromise as the outcome. The debates over CFCs, with manufacturers pleading for and getting time to devise and develop roll-ons, pump-action products, wipe-ons and so on are, for Center and Jackson (2003), typical of this process. The same argument could be applied more specifically to, for example, the relationship between Shell and Greenpeace but not, perhaps, to that between Greenpeace and the French government that has a much more sinister dimension to it after the killing of a Greenpeace person by French government agents.[5]

Instruments of propaganda

Many of the instruments that have been developed over the years by PR practitioners could be used for propaganda purposes. For example, television has in the past been used as a prime instrument of propaganda. These days it is perhaps more problematic because much of television is entertainment and therefore not totally suitable – but can be useful to some extent. Certainly television can be viewed at the very least as escapism. There is a modest amount of education and some public service broadcasting including public information films and, in some countries, state television adding to the possibilities. A perhaps more critical, cynical view is that in post-industrial, advanced capitalist, consumer societies the very nature of television as entertainment is an inherent part of the propaganda of those who are in control. Programme sponsorship and product placement are growing and can be viewed as a form of propaganda in the sense that they permeate in an unconscious if not subliminal way into the mind of the audience. House journals are another example, which highlight how propaganda is usually mistrusted, disbelieved or derided. If *Pravda* means 'the truth' in Russian then *Pravda* in state-controlled times was state-controlled truth. This might have a bearing on the effects of house journals (both internal and external) as instruments of marketing communications and which, according to Harrison (2000), are often jokingly referred to by employees as '*Pravda*'.

From Grierson to Goebbels: the role of documentary film in the transition from propaganda to modern PR	The Documentary Film Movement was in a sense born with John Grierson, a Scot influenced in the 1920s by a scholarship in public opinion and social psychology at the University of Chicago where positivist social science and quantitative methods reined. Pessimism of the notion of democracy and fears of the massification of society and the erosion of traditional values led Grierson to use film as a means to inform public opinion by breaking down barriers to an 'informed citizenship'. Grierson was driven not by the love of the medium, like an artist might be, but by a desire for national education with sociological rather than aesthetic aims.

This is about using new and wide-reaching instruments like radio and cinema, public lectures and exhibitions, film libraries and journals. Sir Stephen Tallents, a civil servant who was Secretary of the Empire Marketing Board (EMB), sponsored Grierson. The EMB was established in the 1920s, which advocated imperial preference through market research, supply chain management and publicity. Tallents's associates were publicity and event management people and, notably, Rudyard Kipling. Tallents was credited with binding the Empire together by 'bringing the Empire alive to the minds of its citizens. Later Tallents would write 'The Projection of England', a 'school for national projection' where a recognition and understanding of new technology of the time, the telegraph and wireless, was necessary because such tools would supersede word-of-mouth, interpersonal communication in the battle for understanding. The cinematic word 'projection' was deliberate, Tallents arguing that projection was vital for internal and external trade relations and tourism, the promotion of culture, technology and science being essential for the successful achievement of economic aims.

Thus the links with Grierson's unit. The non-theatrical, early 'hearts and minds' documentary output was directly linked to particular industries. The first such film was *Drifters*, made in 1929 about the herring fishing industry and designed to influence government ministers. Eventually Tallents's EMB Film Unit became the General Post Office (GPO) Film Unit. The GPO's most famous film was probably *Night Mail*, the story of overnight mail between London and Scotland. After the outbreak of war in 1939 the Film Unit was absorbed by the Ministry of Information and renamed the Crown Film Unit.

The key idea of 'cultural propaganda' was now firmly established. The British Council had been established in 1934. Its remit was to 'make the life and thought of the British peoples more widely known abroad', its sub-aims to encourage the use of the English language, to afford opportunities to appreciate British literature and so on. Goodwill would thus be achieved through promotional work and exchange of persons, but against the reality of Britain's decline as a world power and its influence in international affairs.

In peacetime, propaganda is used to inform, educate and persuade, and inside government is seen as a tool to ensure the smooth working of democracy. In reality it helps maintain the status quo. In wartime, propaganda works in a different way. It is about public opinion management with the control and censoring of information that might harm morale. It is also about destabilizing the enemy – to confuse and demoralize – but also to win and maintain political, economic or military alliances. The control of technology of the day has often gone in the British government's favour. Examples can easily be seen from the Boer War to the present day war in Iraq. In print the most celebrated propagandists were Beaverbrook and Northcliffe (credited with securing the Allied victory in 1918). However, film was increasingly being used as a mass propaganda tool. *Britain Prepared* (1915) through to the morale-boosting films used during the Second World War such as the 'careless talk costs lives' film *Next of Kin* (1942) and beyond were part of diverse wartime propaganda activity. How the British Broadcasting Corporation (BBC), the British press and other tools, especially film, handled the British public at home was much admired by Joseph Goebbels. Such activities led to key players such as Colonel Maurice Buckmaster (Colonel Britain), who had worked for Ford before the war and after became Director of Public Relations at Ford, bridging the gap between propaganda and modern PR.

Source: Adapted from L'Etang (1998).

STOP POINT

Explain the links you perceive exist between propaganda and modern PR. What is the difference between wartime and peacetime propaganda? What are the key technologies today that are used in a propagandist way?

Public relations and marketing theory

Marketing theory and the communications interface was broadly discussed in Chapter 1. However, marketing focuses on meeting the needs of the consumer whereas PR has a wider range of stakeholders/constituents or publics to cater for. Public relations can be used throughout a brand's life through what Stone (1995) calls topicality (linking the product to real-time news events), credibility (the endorsement of a third party commentator who generates a degree of trust) and involvement (the creation of interactive opportunities). Some examples of PR's involvement with marketing theory are discussed below.

The product life cycle

Public relations can be applied at any stage of a product life. The first stage of product life cycle (PLC) theory sees the introduction of products or brands but, before this *pre-launch* or *pre-introduction*, PR can have a pivotal role in awareness of the product, informing and educating publics about the *raison d'être* of the product and the problems it will solve upon *introduction*, i.e. in the early days. At the *growth* stage PR can continue to inform publics of the product or brand's progress. At *maturity* and *saturation* stage, PR's role might be one of continuity. In *decline*, PR might be used to help phase out the product and to safeguard against brand or corporate damage.

Boston Consulting Group matrix

The Boston Consulting Group (BCG) model has its origins in the analysis of the performance of strategic business units (SBUs) by the US-based management consultancy. Subsequently it was used in product portfolio analysis. The BCG Matrix is repeated in Figure 12.2.

Since *question marks* lie in the high-growth/low-share quadrant, they are usually at the start of the PLC so that PR's role will almost always be as discussed above, i.e. a key role regarding awareness, information and so on, especially with innovators. *Stars* usually generate significant funds, being in the high-growth/high-share quadrant. They are market leaders and generate significant funds, but the need to recover research and development (R&D) costs and the marketing support that they need (especially with advertising) means that they will not generate a surplus for a while. Traditionally, advertising has been the key communications tool, with PR having a minimal role to play. *Cash cows* have high shares of low-growth markets and are usually successful stars, maintaining market leadership. They produce the cash because R&D costs have been recovered and marketing costs are less than for stars. Again, there is a minimal role for PR to play. With *dogs*, usually at the end of their life cycle, marketing expenditure is reduced and curtailed. However, two ways of spending funds on PR should be considered. First, if any damage is sustained by the decline, PR (at both MPR and CPR levels) can help. Second, a dog might be retained as a gesture of goodwill (as a loss leader) or as part of heritage.

Ansoff's matrix

Ansoff's product/market expansion matrix is a commonly used model in marketing as discussed in Chapter 1. The situation in each of the four cells, as illustrated in Figure 12.3, throws up opportunities to use PR.

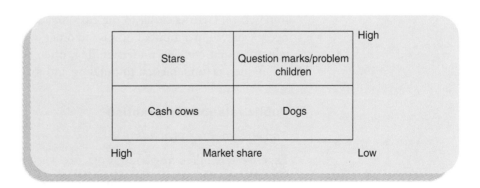

Figure 12.2
The Boston Consulting Group matrix.

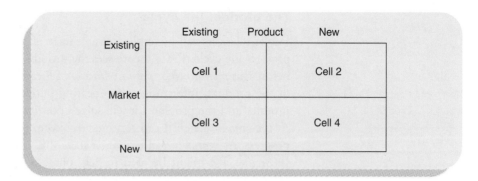

Figure 12.3
Ansoff's product/market
expansion matrix.

Cell 1 – existing product/existing market may highlight the opportunity to use PR to tell existing customers of other product or services available through the company or associate organizations. A mortgage lender may wish to tell of travel insurance or other services. This might include reorganizations where products, brands or markets might be reviewed and regrouped. Various publics such as suppliers and distributors might need to know this. It might also include brand repositioning or even mere refreshment.

Cell 2 – new products/existing markets can see the use of PR to announce innovatory new developments resulting in products and brands within an existing customer base. Core business products such as PC hardware can be supported by new multimedia developments for example.

Cell 3 – existing products/new markets can see the use of PR in the increasing volumes of products sold by gaining new users. This might be done as suggested above within the PLC framework whereby in the new market the product or brand is a different stage of the PLC or brand life cycle (BLC).

Cell 4 – new products/new markets might see the organization using PR in a number of ways to help diversify with new products in new markets. Public relations in this instance would have a substantive educating and informing role within the communications mix.

Relationship marketing and PR

Relationship marketing may have grown up in the business-to-business end of marketing but the efforts on the part of bigger business with consumers as their customers testifies to the importance of relationships across the marketing board. This is competitive advantage through differentiation in a non-price area. How customers are handled or complaints dealt with are of the utmost importance. Getting closer to the customer and moving from prospect to partner is achieved in a number of ways in order to create a relationship. Informing, educating and creating understanding, often achieved through employing PR techniques, is fundamental to building and maintaining relationships.

Public relations in practice

The PR transfer process

Expertise is required for good PR practice. Lack of expertise can lead to mistakes. The PR transfer process, as originally conceived by Jefkins (1995), is a useful device in helping to think about turning what could be negative aspects of PR practice into positive ones. Four possible scenarios can be said to coexist where PR has been demonstrated to have a role to play. This conception is:

Negative>>>>>>>>>>>>>>>>>>>>>>>>>>>>>> → **Positive**

- *Hostility* is based on fear and is irrational. Hostility is often held towards products, companies or brands and can take a number of forms from country of origin (as for example with the boycotting of South African produce around the world until the regime change came) to the use of certain material in products (for example fur products). In many instances the cause of the hostility cannot (and should not) be defended. In others, where hostility has grown out of misunderstanding, PR can be used to set the record straight, where a good case can be presented and the situation adjusted.

- *Prejudice* means that the problems are more deeply rooted, but temporary and often unjustified. The obvious forms of prejudice, the product of environmental conditions, the way people are brought up and so on, are racial and sexual intolerance and bigotry. Public relations can be used to turn hatred into sympathy. In marketing terms, Jefkins uses the example of Thompson Holidays treating journalists to a free holiday to Moscow in the depths of winter. Not only was there a kind of prejudice before the 'Iron Curtain' came down but there was also the cold. Getting travel writers to write copy such as 'The Russians will never be the same again, and nor shall we' and headlines such as 'Better Red Than Med', provided interest and value for readers and allowed successful advertising to follow.

- *Apathy* means that there is a certain inertia on the part of people to products, services and issues. This has been evident in social marketing where advertising alone has not been able to change things. The use of PR has been crucial in moving people on issues such as alcohol and driving, the use of seat belts and crash helmets, and speeding. People can become interested in such issues but in some circumstances it is necessary to use a combination of law, PR and advertising to get the message across.

- *Ignorance* means that the publics are unaware of the company, product or brand and need to be made aware. Clearly, in some cases advertising can achieve this but in many it is sensible to use PR to inform and educate the targets before advertising and other forms of communication can be effective. By providing information and knowledge and stimulating interest that leads to understanding, Jefkins here uses the example of Rentokil in the pest control business, who have used PR to educate consumers and other targets to demolish myths surrounding the causes of vermin and other such problems.

The Mexican statement

A seminal moment in the international PR industry came at the International Conference of PR Societies held in Mexico City in 1978. This, for Jefkins (1995) produced a clear definition of PR practice. Public relations was thus defined in terms of being: both the art and science of analysing trends and predicting their consequences; counselling organization leaders; and implemental of planned programmes of action to service the organization's and the publics' interest.

Public relations practitioners

Public relations can be conducted internally or an outside consultant or company can be used. This often depends on the size of the organization and the resources available. In smaller organizations PR may well be in the hands of an administrator or the managing director's secretary. Opportunities exist to engage a PR consultant on a retainer basis. Larger organizations may have a dedicated PR or customer service function or, indeed, use a specialist company or consultant. In-company people provide expert knowledge of the organization and its strengths and weaknesses, and there should be no confidentially worries. Unless a PR professional or set of professionals is employed there may be a lack of expertise in PR techniques and media. In smaller organizations the people or person responsible for PR may have other duties and responsibilities. In this event, PR activity may not be done well and serious consideration should be given to retaining a PR consultant. This provides a resource but also objectivity and should be a consideration of the larger firm. Of course, employing a consultant or firm of PR specialists may result in a certain lack of expertise. Public relations consultants can be cost-effective but may not be expert in particular industries and technologies, and as such there may be problems with technical aspects and market factors. There might also be problems with confidentiality and conflict of interest.

Public relations costs

As suggested, the retainer nature of PR payment has characterized the PR industry and in the past has stood out in stark contrast to the billing system of the advertising industry. Public relations is labour intensive, the major cost being time. Public relations consultants are paid on a retainer basis and/or by the hour. Other costs would include costs of photography and expenses such as hospitality especially in relation to media relations and events.

VIGNETTE

Creating a relationship at the heart of PR: how charity fundraisers can get closer to donors

Public relations is the natural habitat of the cause-related marketing fundraiser. Money may be the ultimate objective but this relationship is also about storytelling. The fundraiser needs to tell a story to the potential donor. To be successful two things have to be done: first, create effective PR; second, create a long-lasting relationship.

With the first, PR is created by:

1   Creating a simple strategy with aims and objectives.

2   Deciding where, listing names and addresses and cultivating the media.

3   Making a list of interesting people who could talk positively about the charity.

4   Making a list of up-and-coming stories.

5   Having a media contact within the organization.

6   Creating a general media pack.

7   Creating templates such as that for a press release.

8 Being reliable.

9 Being up to date.

10 Being accurate and truthful.

11 Knowing the history of the organization and using it.

12 Offering equal chances to contact so as not to offend.

13 Making the media feel important at events.

Then, with the second, to create relationships:

1 Know who potential, lapsed and actual donors are.

2 Concentrate on a smaller number of important donors.

3 Target donors effectively through knowledge; get financial information as to where the money comes from; know which individuals/groups have a relationship with the charity; know which codes are one-offs and which are regular donations.

4 Develop a system of costing out in time and money the resources needed to obtain a new donor.

5 Carry out simple research to build detailed but effective profiles on what is given, by whom and so on.

6 Organize donors as customers might be organized and know who are the best.

7 Seek feedback and use donor panels to assist in this task.

8 Develop, maintain and monitor a centralized database.

Sources: Adapted from Professional Fundraiser (2003a; 2003b).

STOP POINT

Explain why it is very natural to talk in PR terms within a relationship marketing context. What would you add, if anything, to the thirteen points regarding PR and the eight points regarding relationship marketing listed? Find examples of cause-related marketing and explain any symbiotic relationship you detect.

The concept of a 'public'

Public relations targets or publics

Depending upon objectives, different kinds of approaches may be used at different times with the various *publics* – groups, stakeholders, constituents and so on – the organization might wish to deal with. There may be a desire to simply tell a public about a particular issue through the transmission of information, but on other occasions the organization may engage in a two-way communication that tries to persuade the public through effective dialogue. This may well be part of the integrated effort with other elements of the communications mix. It is important with any form of communication to know to whom the organization wants to talk and what the organization wants to say to them (or what they want to hear from the organization). Publics are therefore carefully selected groups of people with whom the organization communicates or wishes to communicate. Publics need to be defined at the start of the PR planning process in order to:

- identify all groups of people relative to a PR programme

- establish priorities within the scope of a budget or resources

- select media and techniques

- prepare the message in acceptable and effective forms.

Publics can be from the community, potential and existing employees, suppliers, shareholders, the media, the financial community, the profession and professional associations, existing and potential clients, referral sources, and local and central government. Publics can be placed in *external* (*outward orientated*) or *internal* (*inward orientated*) groupings and sub-categorized within *media*, *financial* and *general public affairs*. There is also a consideration as to whether direct or indirect contact is attempted (De Pelsmaker, Geuens and Van Den Bergh, 2001). This is considered in more detail below.

External publics

External relations are important because these are often the channels of communication by which customers see a business. Therefore good external relations should be fostered in order to create a favourable marketing environment and should work in conjunction with internal relations. There are various external publics that the organization needs to consider.

The media and gatekeepers

- The press (national, regional, daily, weekly, newspapers, magazines and so on).

- Broadcast (television, radio, international, national and local).

Financial

- Owners, shareholders.

- Suppliers, distributors.

General public affairs

- Pressure groups, evangelists.

- Educators, information-givers.

- Trade unions.

- The community.

Internal publics

Internal PR should be considered as a very important part of PR generally. Internal relations, and hence internal communications, are all about things like staff morale and sensitivities, which is not just a question of money. The 'grapevine' is pervasive where, for example, industrial disputes can arise from gossip and untruths. Employees can feel left out if they are not included in on 'what is going on'. The internal 'feel' of the organization should reflect and project the external image where internal activities can be made to be effective by effective internal communications. As such, internal considerations are vital to overall communications strategy. In addition, all employees of the organization (including management/directors) are part of wider society. They are therefore influenced not only by what happens in the workplace, but also by being members of the general public, members of professional bodies, members of pressure groups or societies, members of extended families and members of local communities.

Good internal communication is fundamental to good management but the kind of management is important. Management style clearly has an enormous influence on internal communications. Formal (rather than informal) situations dictate relationships and the tools used to communicate with the various publics.

Restoring investor faith – a brand new image for Wall Street

In 2001, Wall Street, it seems, had an image problem brought on by alleged rigged prices and large, hidden fees that had cost shareholders billions of dollars. Investors apparently wanted their money back. Two main accusations were made. That banks doled out to institutional investors wads of underpriced shares that were almost guaranteed to rise once trading started. The institutions then gave the banks a huge commission per share and it was alleged that such payments were not properly disclosed. The second, linked, accusation was that the technique of 'laddering' (artificially inflating prices) caused ordinary retail investors to pay more for shares. When the 'ladderers' pull out, the prices tumble and the retailers lose out.

Wall Street responded with apparent unconcern. Press releases insisted that the firms had followed accepted industry practices but the finance industry more generally apparently had a different view, with predictions of settlements (worth billions of dollars) but also the illumination of additional sordid behaviour. Ethically Wall Street was likened to the tobacco industry in terms of damages.

By 2003 it was claimed that Wall Street had begun to realize that it is hard to win back public confidence after a series of scandals. However, leading American banks have attempted to restore investor faith, but there is some doubt as to whether the effort here is enough. To regain the trust of the investor is one thing. The damage done within and the effect on individuals is another. Pride has been lost as people apparently began to sneer and snigger at the idea of an investment bank worker. So the process of restoring faith began by targeting would-be investors and confidence among employees. The Securities Industry Association (SIA) has the task of approaching the various targets with a variety of means in order to establish an ethical base. In truth American investors might forgive and forget if Wall Street created another bull market. It appears that the banks are not as aggressive as they could be in communicating the changes they have made. There is a clarion call for Wall Street as a whole to articulate a clear programme from top management as to how it is going to do business against the fear that only lip-service is being paid to serious problems.

Sources: Adapted from Miller (2003a; 2003b); Tully (2001).

STOP POINT Clearly, investors and employees have been identified as targets. There appears to be a lack of momentum on the part of Wall Street as an institution, yet its constituent parts – the 600-plus SIA members – are clearly aware of the situation. What more could the SIA do? What kind of PR should the SIA, on behalf of its members, pursue? Who, apart from investors and employees, should PR messages be targeted at?

Tools to reach publics

Information needs to be provided for the relevant, different publics. The PR tool kit to achieve this is quite extensive. Often opinion leadership and word of mouth are used to inform others. There is a big difference between the use of the harder, partisan celebrity endorser, as in advertising, and the softer brand ambassador, a PR device. The latter apart, below are listed the PR tools commonly used to reach publics.

- *Films/video/audio-visual aids* (includes sponsored films/documentaries, tape/slide presentations, photographs, working models etc.)

- *Seminars and conferences* are often sponsored by an organization and connected with a specific subject or event. These may involve a number of speakers, from both within the host organization and other guest speakers/experts.

- *House journals* in the form of a bulletin, newsletter, magazine, etc. Can be for internal or external consumption. Useful for keeping in touch with clients, and helping to generate new enquiries by keeping them up to date on relevant matters of interest. These must be professionally produced and appear regularly for maximum effect.

- *Brochures* contain either general purpose, corporate information or can be designed to communicate information on specific topics. These can be used for clients, employees or the media. Consistency and uniformity in the IMC/Gestalt sense for the personality of organization should be a consideration.

- *Exhibitions/trade shows* can be for the general public or trade or both and can be part of a wider event. Permanent venues exist but mobile exhibitions are common.

- *News/press releases* should have impact and be timely, relevant, topical, accurate, exclusive, and have a special angle or spin, for example human interest. These are short articles containing a newsworthy item that need to appear similar to the editorial of a particular media vehicle.

- *The feature article* is more than just a long press release. It is usually an article commissioned for a particular media with specific timing rather than something destined for a more general release.

- *The media conference's* purpose is to give information and to receive and answer questions. It is usually held at short notice after something newsworthy (a major event) has occurred. Often used by politicians, organizations in crisis and individuals appealing for help (e.g. police). Media kits with detailed information, background on the story, etc. should always be available.

- *The media reception* is more planned and less formal than a media conference that will include a presentation and refreshments. This can be used for new products launches, special announcements and so on.

- *The open day.* A media trip to new premises is an example of an event that usually involves organizing transport, hospitality and so on. The media should perceive this as having something worthwhile and newsworthy involved.

- *The media lunch* is usually organized for the media to meet key personnel in an organization and to informally brief on topics of interest. This should be somewhat intimate as opposed to a large party. There well may be further contacts as a result of this as with, for example, an invitation to write an article.

- *Client entertaining* will have similar objectives to the lunch above, but will involve the entertainment of key clients or potential clients and opinion leaders for the purposes of goodwill and information. Other opportunities may arise but these are not the primary concern.

- *Events* can be product related such as book signings in stores. They can be associated with open days or factory visits and also cause-related marketing activities.

- *Lobbying* is the representation of an organization or industry group within local and national government. Lobbyists provide a flow of information to policy-makers and attempt to represent the views of their client(s) in shaping policy and legislation.

- *Web news page and e-mail.* The use of websites, web pages and e-mail decreases the importance of the traditional gatekeeper, and offers opportunities to profile employees, outline business philosophy and provide information on investments, to name but a few activities.

- *The annual report* offers a vehicle for PR activities such as the Chairman's Statement, fundraising and charitable activities, and so on. The annual report could well be web based.

VIGNETTE

Employee communications: what the documentary video can do that a press release or chairman's letter cannot

The commonest form of PR expression is perhaps the *news* or *media/press release*. With the news release, language is important and must be appropriate. Photography is usually welcome. The story should be clear and succinct. The opening paragraph should tell the whole story in one. This allows the recipient to tell at a glance if the story has some value. Of importance is what the story is about, the organization itself, where the story unfolds, what the advantages are (what is new or special in a factual way), who benefits, how these benefits can be enjoyed and who to contact for more information. News releases can be background, intended to be a briefing or part of a speech. They can also be in report form, a picture caption or an announcement. In effect we can think of this in the serving men of Kipling sense: the what, where, who, why, when and how in every story.

There are many tips from a variety of sources as to how to create the news release:

- Keep the main paragraph short.
- Write stories.

- Match the story to the publication/programme and audience by knowing audiences' interests.

- Write tight copy in a concise journalistic style.

- Keep to short sentences.

- Avoid superlatives.

- Substantiate claims.

- Quote from reliable sources.

- Draft and redraft, edit and polish.

- Get rid of irrelevancies.

- Do not use jargon.

- Be accurate and factual.

- Never exaggerate or create a misleading impression.

In addition, with video news releases:

- Make sure the story has a strong visual impact.

- Make sure of clarity.

- Provide a new perspective on the angle/issue.

- Enable the story to be used as background footage while news copy is read.

- Make the story unique and not available elsewhere.

The *feature article* is similar to the news release but usually an expert or specialist is commissioned by the editor to write it. Alternatively, it might be written by a columnist (such as a wine writer) and actually signed, becoming a *signed feature article*. It is generally bigger than the result of a news release, it possibly being several pages long. The process may involve a proposal to an editor including number of words, illustrations, date for publication, etc. Alternatively a list of general feature articles could be prepared to present in an informative and authoritative way matters of interest to a particular target market. There are many opportunities to take items of topical interest and turn them into articles.

Feature articles should contain:

- an opening paragraph

- the problem or opportunity

- the solution to the problem or benefits of the opportunity

- the results achieved

- a closing paragraph

- sources of information.

However, it must be said that the above two tools are not always the most appropriate. With *employee relations*, fears may have to be allayed and support won. This is not going to happen at a time of speculation, insecurity or criticism that the company's technology is out of date. News releases, articles and letters from the chairman can have the opposite effect to that intended. This can be read as undermanaged communication that lacks objectivity. Allied to the video news release is the technique known as the *documentary video,* which has a professional, independent narrator. The video will typically address problems in an acquired company starting with interviews with a range of employees at differing levels, allowing them to tell of concerns and doubts. This is meant to be frank, open and honest without gloss or platitudes. Executives might be put on the spot or contented employees from previous acquisitions interviewed. The logic is that it is one thing to hear executives say things, quite another to have others such as employees, customers or an external analyst say them. The video will also deal in plans for change with a commitment to keep staff informed about the unknown, as it becomes known. While change can be a difficult thing, far better to be open about it to prevent cynicism and rumour. Other, allied, techniques such as *team briefings* and *brochures* can provide extensive questions and answers and stated, known plans. *Local* and *financial* press and media can be important within this process since employees will seek out information in local media not the financial pages of the broadsheets. The acquirer can use this to advantage by influencing local opinion formers or shapers such as councillors or MPs. Brochures can be sent and meetings arranged. Sincerity is the watchword, as it is with any financial communications. Dealings here can be tricky, and preparation is key. The acquirer should be able to answer questions clearly and honestly, with facts at hand, about the acquisition and the fallout that follows. The media usually wants to know how the deal is being funded, what the strategic logic and a sensible rationale for the announced purchase price are and information on earnings.

Sources: Adapted from CSBS (1998); Duncan (2002).

In what circumstances would news releases be best used? What is the difference between these and the feature article? In terms of acquisitions and the problems this might bring, what is a documentary video and how does this differ from an ordinary documentary? How important to employee relations are local press, media and opinion shapers? How does the acquirer deal with the financial media in such circumstances?

Technology, ethics, regulation, and control in PR practice

A policy to deal with PR projects within a code of professional conduct is essential, especially in terms of today's rather turbulent environment where technology and communications are in a state of constant flux.

Ethics, regulation and control in PR

In terms of human behaviour and social conduct both laws and codes have been developed to regulate and control many things including the PR activities of companies and other organizations. Public opinion and what is acceptable behaviour is important. The phrase 'the court of public opinion' underlines this but in any event actual law may override this, i.e. just what is permissible and what is prohibited by the law of the land. This will vary from country to country as will social mores – what is moral and what is not, often having a religious base. Codes of practice encapsulate the ethical standards set by professions, organizations and the self, based, in theory at least, on conscience, i.e. what is right, fair or just to oneself and to others. This is a general condition, and one that applies within the context of PR.

Entities such as companies, unlike most people, do not have a conscience as such and therefore need a code of conduct – ethics if you will, which inevitably is influenced by the personal values and ethics of key players in the organization. Some form of group consensus as to what is acceptable behaviour may have a powerful influence. The various professional bodies provide a code of ethics that organizations can adopt and they endeavour to educate such organizations through their membership. It is then up to the organization itself to educate its employees on ethical behaviour and practices. Done correctly this would get over the age-old problem of prescription (of ethical standards) for others while not practising such standards themselves. Center and Jackson (2003) illustrate this with the Public Relations Society of America's (PRSA) 1950 (revised in 2000) anti-news manipulation code that has the golden rule of 'If we do unto others as we would have them do unto us, harmonious PR will result'. Thus the code includes, as expected items:

- a statement of professional values that is vital for integrity

- advocacy for informed public debate

- honesty in terms of accuracy and truth

- expertise to be used to advance the profession and help build mutual understanding, credibility and relationships

- independence in the form of objective counsel and accountability

- loyalty and faithfulness

- fairness and respect to all parties and support of the right of free expression.

Codes of ethical practice have emerged across the globe and are maturing, perhaps more slowly than some would like. It has been nearly a century since the four watchwords of 'legal, decent, honest and truthful'[6] were first used in relation to commercial enterprise.

Technology, the Internet and PR

Technology has created its own range of opportunities and problems. Ashcroft and Hoey (2001) maintain that the integration of traditional and on-line communication methods provides the key to successful Internet marketing. Growth in Internet use has been phenomenal in the past decade. The size of the Internet doubles every year in the UK, and worldwide this figure is even more impressive. Chapter 19 deals with these issues in more detail but here the concern is specifically for PR issues. When things really got going with the Internet, *circa* 1995, the main PR tool appeared to be the bulletin board. This was seen as being analogous with the notice board, the electronic equivalent of a communal place where notices could be placed for anyone to read and be informed. In practice this has evolved into a forum for group communication and interaction. There are no real time and place restrictions. Video conferencing is established and mailing lists are available. There are therefore opportunities for enhancing or changing images, how the organization is perceived and how status can be maintained or enhanced. Both internal and external relations have been established by some organizations using web-based tools that are extensions of conventional PR tools such as the news release. News release pages are available on many websites. For example, a new service can be announced in this way, combined with e-mail and the more conventional tools into an integrated whole.

VIGNETTE

Towards a model of integrated Internet communication: the case of biotechnology

According to Hurme (2001), PR practitioners who do not use Internet communications can cause damage to their clients or employers. The move towards dialogue and away from monologue is as visible with PR as it is with advertising – perhaps even more so. Interactive communication generally is gaining ground but the use of the Internet has a number of problems. If this is seen as mere brochure work and not a genuine and intelligent use of the medium, then this is one kind of problem. Since much material that goes onto the Internet no longer passes through traditional gatekeepers such as editors, policing is another kind of problem. Even with the new mobile technology there are problems of underuse. Truly interactive communication is a conversation with at least two discussants. Since Internet users are highly individual, Hurme suggests the following guidelines:

- Consider clients/audiences and adapt media to them.

- Create contacts with web influentials.

- Update content continually even if it costs.

- Use search engines such as Altavista and Yahoo and their persuasion (SEP) techniques.

- Beware of spamming.

- Align yourself with people in similar industries and create links between your web service and theirs.

- Synergy and integration are important.

- Design a media kit or room on your website giving the media immediate access to releases, biographical information, photographs and questions and answers.

Research into the use of PR on the Internet in the biotechnology sector (Ranchhod, Gurau and Lace, 2002) reveals that biotechnology companies attempt to use the Internet as a comprehensive PR medium by explaining complex issues. This is an attempt to turn apathy and ignorance into sympathy and understanding. Diagrammatic information, interactivity through discussion forums and hyperlinks to scientific databases are effective tools for the likes of Monsanto who can forge these into an integrated, on-line communications strategy. However, some companies are not investing as well they might, resulting in mere transference of documents. Hyperlinks and video could be used to great effect for companies involved with a complex, contro-versial and risk-inherent industry such as biotechnology. Key to the effective use of PR on the Internet is targeting the various publics, for example science and technology journalists, purchasers and suppliers and even employees. Dialogue is all important.

Sources: Adapted from Hurme (2001); Ranchhod, Gurau and Lace (2002).

STOP POINT

Consider the three key elements of the above vignette. In terms of interactivity, how can this be achieved by organizations like Monsanto? How important is management attitude to investment in PR? What can be done to convince such organizations that mere transference of documents onto a website is not enough and that the tools available are underused? What would be an ideal integrated communications approach to strategy for a biotech company in your view?

Assignment

You are part of a team of PR consultants for a range of clients in different indus-tries. Illustrate the kinds of work you would typically become involved with by choosing one from the list below. Provide an outline report on topical issues you would expect to be dealing with.

- A regional theatre's new production.
- A children's charity special appeal for nursery equipment.
- A pop music video to be used to launch a new single.
- An industrial hose manufacturer's use of innovative material for firefighting.
- A technical service provider's establishment of a new team of specialists.
- A financial service provider's new range of loan products.
- An international healthcare company's newly established division for 'respiratory therapy care'.
- The introduction of an innovative 'rough terrain materials handler' for use in construction, civil engineering, farming and military contexts.

Summary of Key Points

- Public relations is about relationships with various interest groups.
- Marketing PR (as opposed to corporate PR) has emerged as the commercial brand/product-level function responsible for a set of activities that deal with shorter-term issues.

- The key to any PR is the notion that it fundamentally functions as a creator of a favourable marketing environment.

- Public relations is characterized by lack of control and has very different qualities to those of other communications tools.

- Public relations uses a 'soft sell' approach rather than the 'harder' approaches of other elements of the communications mix.

- Public relations uses objectivity and can be seen as non-partisan.

- Public relations can be viewed as propaganda with many media forms culpable, i.e. house journals and newsletters are propaganda tools.

- With marketing the focus is on meeting the needs of customers. Public relations has a wider range of stakeholders/constituents.

- The used of PR can be explained in conjunction with parts of marketing theory such as the PLC, the BCG matrix and Ansoff's matrix.

- The concept of a 'public' is well established and can be broadly split into internal and external publics who can be reached directly and indirectly.

- There is a raft of tools to reach publics, the most well known of which is the news release.

- Codes of ethics in PR practice have been developed and are available. Such codes have links with other ethical areas such as advertising.

- The key to new PR techniques is interactivity. Good PR practice should strive to create an integrative whole.

Examination Questions

1 Distinguish between marketing PR and corporate PR. Explain, using examples, why the techniques used at both levels might be similar if not the same.

2 Explain what the word propaganda means and why is it such a 'dirty' word. Give your considered view on the opportunities and problems propaganda may provide for PR practitioners, illustrating with examples.

3 Distinguish between advertising and PR in terms of control. Discuss, using examples, the very different qualities PR has to those found in other communications tools.

4 Comment on the notion that the internal feel of an organization will reflect its external reality. Provide practical examples of instances where this is the case.

5 Explain where PR fits in the marketing communications scheme of things. Provide in your answer at least two examples of the interface between PR and other elements of the communications mix.

6 Explain why the relationship between PR and marketing theory is best illustrated by use of marketing theory such as that of the product life cycle or innovation theory.

7 'The PR transfer process as advocated by Jefkins is a simple but effective guideline for use by the PR practitioner when critically assessing PR problems.' Discuss and illustrate.

8 Explain the concept of a 'public'. Choose an internal and external public and illustrate using actual examples how each could be reached directly and indirectly.

9 Discuss codes of ethics in PR practice using examples to illustrate key points. Explain why there are obvious and clear links to other areas of business.

10 Explain how PR tools can be used on the Internet. Illustrate your answer with actual instances you are aware of.

Notes

1 According to White (2002) PR also lacks intellectual firepower and budgets but, with the rise in integrated communication, PR has grown in terms of interest shown.

2 A crude but accurate 'old marketing axiom' meaning that in some circumstances there is no room for spin and nothing can be said. There is no message that can be put out (Armstrong, 1996).

3 This is a reference to the cautionary tale of the emperor who, because of pride and insecurity, was very susceptible to the flattery of his subjects. He was conned into thinking he had new and wonderful clothes where in fact he had none. It took the innocence of a small child to shatter the delusion (Baker, 2000).

4 The 'cash for questions' saga eventually led to the defeat of former Member of Parliament (MP) Neil Hamilton in the 1997 general election by former journalist Martin Bell, famous for wearing white suits, which gave rise to the 'man in a white suit' tag. Hamilton had been accused of taking 'cash for questions', i.e. being paid to table House of Commons questions. He refused to resign his seat in Tatton, Cheshire, and had alleged that the investigation and report by the Commons Standards Committee of MPs was a 'kangaroo court'. The committee had found that Mr Hamilton's conduct had fallen 'seriously and persistently' below standards expected but that there was no concrete evidence that he had taken money from Harrods owner Mohamed al Fayed. The committee added, however, that if Mr Hamilton had still been an MP it would have recommended a lengthy period of suspension. Since then the Hamiltons (Neil and his formidable wife Christine) have carved out quite a career for themselves in the media, for example appearing frequently on British television. The seemingly trivial nature of the Hamilton case belies the very serious problem of business funding many things. For example, the funding of academic research such as that into the impact of wine on heart disease or garlic tablets on hardening of the arteries will be problematic if such research is underwritten by wineries or the manufacturers of garlic tablets.

5 A reference to the 1985 blowing up of the Greenpeace ship *Rainbow Warrior* in Auckland Harbour by French secret service agents. One person was killed.

6 As used by the International Chamber of Commerce (ICC), established in 1919. The ICC code was firmly established by 1937.

References

Armstrong, S. (1996). So much at steak. *Guardian*, 25 March, p. 12.

Ashcroft, L. and Hoey, C. (2001). PR, Marketing and the Internet: implications for information professionals. *Library Management*, **22** (1/2), 68–74.

Baker, P. (2000). Schizophrenia and the emperor's (not so) new clothes. *Magazine for Democratic Psychiatry*, **12** (1). www.critpsynet.freeuk/Bakerhtm.

Center, A. H. and Jackson, P. (2003). *PR Practices*. 6th edition. Prentice Hall.

CSBS (1998). Financial PR and straight talking to employees. *The Antidote*, **13**, 33–34.

De Pelsmaker, P., Geuens, M. and Van Den Bergh, J. (2001). *Marketing Communications*. Financial Times Prentice Hall.

Dibb, S., Simkin, L. and Vancini, A. (1996). Competition, strategy, technology and people: the challenges facing PR. *International Journal of Advertising*, **15** (2), 116–127.

Duncan, T. (2002). *Integrated Marketing Communications – Using Advertising and Promotion to Build Brands*. McGraw-Hill.

Fill, C. (2002). *Marketing Communications: Contexts, Strategies and Applications*. 3rd Edition. Financial Times Prentice Hall.

Harrison, S. (2000). *PR – an Introduction*. 2nd edition. Routledge.

Howard, W. (1985). *The Practice of Public Relations*. 2nd edition. Heinemann.

Hunt, T. and Grunig, J. E. (1994). *Public Relations Techniques*. Holt, Reinhart and Winston.

Hurme, P. (2001). Online PR: emerging organisational practice. *Corporate Communications – An International Journal*, **6** (2), 71–75.

Jefkins, F. (1995). *Modern Marketing Communications*. Blackie.

Kitchen, P. (1991). Developing use of PR in a fragmented demassified market. *Marketing Intelligence and Planning*, **9** (2), 15–21.

Kitchen, P. and Moss, D. (1995). Marketing and PR: an exploratory study. ESOMAR. At www.warc.com/fulltext/esomar/11086.htm.

Kitchen, P. and Papasolomou, I. (1997). Marketing PR: conceptual legitimacy or window dressing. *Marketing Intelliegence and Planning*, **15** (2), 71–84.

L'Etang, J. (1998). State propaganda and bureaucratic intelligence: the creation of pr in twentieth century Britain. *PR Review*, **24** (4), 413.

Miller, S. (2003a). A brand new image. *The Banker*, February, 16–19.

Miller, S. (2003b). Risk management cracks the whip. *The Banker*, February, 18–19.

Professional Fundraiser (2003a). PR and fundraising. At www.professionalfundraiser.org/facts/op20.htm.

Professional Fundraiser (2003b). Relationship marketing. At www.professionalfundraiser.org/facts/op13.htm.

Ranchhod, A., Gurau, C. and Lace, J. (2002). On-line messages: developing an integrated communications model for biotech companies. *Quarterly Marketing Review – An International Journal*, **5** (1), 6–18.

Stone, N. (1995). *The Management and Practice of PR*. Macmillan Business.

Tully, S. (2001). Will Wall Street go up in smoke? *Fortune*, September. www.corante.com/reports/ipo/2.shtml.

White, R. (2002). Public relations in the marketing mix. At www.warc.com/fulltext/Bestpractice/72468.htm.

Corporate communications

Chapter overview

Introduction to this chapter

The nature of corporate communications is explored and relationships developed with the marketing mix and marketing communications mix. Corporate communications are placed within an integrated communications context for the organization as a whole. Organizations can be seen to use three forms of communication: management communication used by senior managers to approach both internal and external targets; marketing communications (as previously discussed) and organizational communications (traditionally corporate public relations and advertising and latterly corporate affairs, with the usual targets groups of the media, shareholders, the community and so on). Broadly, corporate communications, like any other, should be seen as an aid not as a solution per se. Corporate communications can be seen more narrowly as part of corporate strategy but as a process not an object. This chapter is also about relations as well as communications so that things other than corporate advertising have an impact upon performance. Corporate identity needs to be defined in relation to corporate image. This involves a critical analysis of behaviour, symbolism and communication that leads to corporate personality. Consistency and transparency in corporate behaviour and communications is clearly important.

Aims of this chapter

The overall aim of this chapter is to establish how to initiate, develop and maintain an effective corporate communications programme. More specifically, on completion of this chapter the reader should be able to:

• explore the concepts that underpin corporate communications and their functions

• outline the relationship between corporate communications and their functions

• explore the future of corporate communications in terms of integration, social responsibility and accountability, behaviour and symbolism

• outline major corporate communications tools that are at the disposal of the marketer within the framework of an identity and image plan.

Background to corporate communications

Objectives of corporate communications

Corporate communications involve changing attitudes and perceptions that have an impact upon beliefs about an organization and therefore keeping management informed of how the various audiences might react. Ultimately, they are about improving the economic performance of the organization through the creation of awareness, understanding, appreciation, agreement and consensus, and resolving conflicts.

The principles of corporate communications include the analysis of corporate image and corporate identity. This area of study provides techniques to improve the effectiveness of corporate communications programmes via a planning approach. The focus of many campaigns is the immediate relations between corporate strategy, corporate identity and corporate image. There is much more to communications than this and, as discussed in Chapter 1, many things communicate and potentially become part of the vastness and totality of the communications domain, as illustrated in Figure 13.1.

Corporate communications defined

Corporate communications can be defined as 'an all-embracing framework co-ordinating marketing, organizational and management communications that integrates the total business message' or more narrowly seen as achieving organizational goals with a key tool to be used to develop relationships and understanding. The orchestration of this in terms of organizational corporate communications is often in the hands of a communications specialist. However, as van Riel (1995) points out, mistakes can be made as illustrated by a corporate advertisement in the Dutch press claiming that BAT Industries plc were on course for their 1989 forecast. At the same time a report on forthcoming redundancies among BAT employees and the closure of the Amsterdam factory was the subject of an article in the same newspaper on the same day as the corporate advertisement.

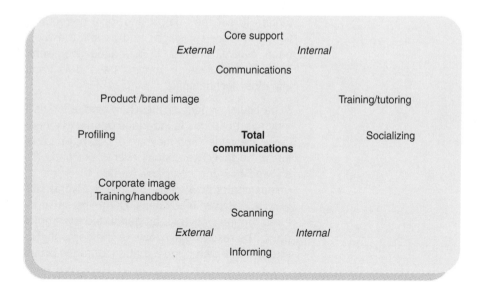

Figure 13.1
The total communications domain.

Audiences for corporate communications

Corporate communication is a significant management discipline. The audiences that receive such communication are variously called stakeholders, publics (UK) or constituents (USA). There are both internal and external audiences and as Dolphin (1999) points out, there is no external communication that does not also communicate internally. The audience list may be the same as or very similar to that of the 'publics' of PR as discussed in the previous chapter, but objectives, messages and so on may differ substantially.

Internal communications and relations, often seen as a Cinderella subject by some, can have a big impact on external communications and relations in terms of the internal feel of the organization. Senior management should nurture enthusiasm, acceptance and respect for the organization itself, and for new ideas, products and so on in order to achieve commitment and loyalty. People project values, they being in effect ambassadors for the organization. Staff morale is crucial in this sense to competitive advantage.

Success with external communications and relations requires an ever-widening knowledge of socioeconomic and cultural concerns. The stakeholders involved will depend upon the size of the organization, whether it is local, international or global in its scope. The list would include the media, opinion leaders and formers, shareholders, politicians and so on with regard to issues such as takeovers and acquisitions, privatization, new directions or positioning for the organization and, of course, perceptions of the organization.

VIGNETTE

Cummins's vision, culture and employees – encouraging innovation and unleashing creativity

The culture of an organization can be changed so that strengths are kept and a shared vision can help re-energize the company. The Cummins example is about facilitation, i.e. the unleashing of creativity of employees to help establish a new dynamic in a rapidly changing business environment. Cummins, a leading manufacturer of high-performance, low-emission diesel engines and power generation systems, are component technology leaders via Holset turbochargers, Newage alternators, Fleetguard filtration and Nelson exhaust products. In the UK, Cummins has been established for almost fifty years. It operates six highly productive manufacturing plants with a strong export focus. The company's aim is to 'improve the lives of people' in helping customers to succeed, improving local communities and generating new solutions to reduce emissions and benefit the wider environment. Cummins has been involved not only in increased geographical diversification, but also in product diversification, moving beyond its traditional diesel engine business into other technologies.

A particular aspect of the Cummins' effort is the VISION programme. The major purpose was to introduce people to a new way of working whereby their ideas are valued and they are encouraged to contribute rather than simply listen or be told. The special events put on by Cummins were very lively and showed how the company wanted to create a culture that encouraged the unleashing of new ideas, so that everyone could make a creative input into what is a dynamic business. Cummins strive for a business culture that nurtures the innovative ideas generated by employees at all levels of the company. The resource available to the company was recognized as the creative energy of its own people that encouraged an atmosphere of thinking 'outside the box'. The VISION programme helped place the emphasis on informality and enjoyment, with high energy, use of music, fun activities, much audience participation and creative-thinking group sessions with feedback being used. Unlike usual training and development activities, events did not generate notes to take away, because the principal purpose behind them was motivational and inspirational. The programme was designed to win the hearts and minds of participants – but with a fun aspect. This was coupled with a serious underlying theme, i.e. that of moving the company forward, so that it becomes 'more flexible, fast-acting, creative, efficient and ultimately more profitable'.

Cummins developed a shared vision where employees were asked to 'act like owners working together'. The culture, or 'the way we do things around here', of the organization refers to shared beliefs, policies and procedures. A starting point in understanding an organization's culture can be observation of employees but by talking to its employees, greater depth can be found. Some organizations appear dynamic where risk-taking and innovation are apparent. Other organizations are more cautious or administratively orientated where risk-taking is less likely to be encouraged or even tolerated. This latter type could well be unable to cope with change, without which the organization might well founder. At Cummins, change was embraced and, in preparing for it, Cummins used focus workshops across the company, which were 'inclusive' of every type of employee worldwide. Thus aspects of working life thought worth retaining, referred to as the organization's 'sacred bundles', such as 'a sense of community' and 'respect for others', were highlighted. This enabled the organization to build on existing values and practice while moving forward.

The focus groups revealed a high degree of pride in the ability of the company, its products and its employees. The strap line 'Making People's Lives Better by Unleashing the Power of Cummins' came from this. The 'Unleashing the Power of Cummins' was achieved by:

- motivating people to act like owners working together, exceeding customer expectations by always being first to market with the best products

- partnering with their customers to make sure they succeed

- demanding that everything Cummins do leads to a cleaner, healthier, safer environment, that creates wealth for all stakeholders.

Cummins has moved to being a globally based organization. This trend is likely to continue and Cummins will need to develop a business culture that is adaptable, flexible and able to respond faster to a dynamic global marketplace. As part of communicating the changing culture at Cummins, four key elements are purpose (to enrich people's lives), values (integrity), performance (helping customers) and personality (driven). For Cummins in the UK, the new vision is cascading throughout the organization with a phased introduction programme to all 5000 employees. As the company puts the mission into practice at all levels, its influence is translated into actions that include the following.

- A shared set of approaches across a diverse UK organization (in terms of locations, products and operating methods); this new way of working enables synergies to be harnessed across all parts of the business. Others can quickly adopt the 'best practice' in one area of the business.

- By encouraging employees to 'act as owners', individuals and teams have identified significant opportunities to reduce overhead costs. Performance cell structures are being developed to devolve responsibility and establish more effective teamworking.

- The company-wide employee 'performance management system' now reflects the commitment to the vision and mission. Managers and teams are assessed not just on how well they meet plans and targets, but also on how well they demonstrate the new values of the company in everything they do. An internal website magazine provides guidance and enables employees to see mission results in action.

- Cummins offers an 'open-door' approach by encouraging customers to visit its plants on a regular basis. Customer councils have also been established to provide feedback on product performance and requirements for the future. A rapid response customer support system has been established which enables users of Cummins powered equipment to register their product on line via the company website. By creating an attractive, energetic corporate culture, Cummins is encouraging new, younger and more diverse people to join the organization and to contribute to its ongoing success.

Sources: Adapted from Cummins (2002a; 2002b).

 STOP POINT

Cummins has successfully re-energized its existing culture by encouraging people to say what they value about the existing culture and by creating a more innovative company that is better placed to deal with a changing and competitive global business environment. The key to success lies in encouraging everybody to become involved and to contribute their own ideas and thinking in a way that models an inclusive and innovative company. Think about:

- organizational culture that is innovative and participatory

- the generation of new ideas within the organization

- the approach to change adopted by Cummins and how this could be adopted by other organizations.

The role of the corporate communications executive and key components

The role of the corporate communications executive is unique and is key in understanding the organization's environment and being able to act upon this in an appropriate manner. The role involves 'looking out for stormy weather' but is one that provides objective and detailed analytical thinking regarding the impact forces from the environment might have on the organization. The executive has to be seen to be making the best of what is available. Key components of corporate communications are:

- *internal communication* – communication between individuals and/or divisions or departments, usually in terms of day-to-day shorter-term activities

- *public relations* – as defined in the usual way, including the establishment and maintenance of mutually beneficial relationships between an organization and its publics

- *corporate or public affairs* – which is a strategic approach involving opportunity for the company or a threat to it, connected with environmental forces that can shape public opinion and decision-making
- *environmental policy communication* – communication regarding environmental strategy with target groups, both internal and external
- *investor relations* – a corporate marketing activity that combines communication and finance to provide an accurate portrayal of a company's performance and prospects, seen as an investment in the value of the organization
- *labour market communication* – planned integrated communication with potential employees and recruitment consultants and agents
- *corporate advertising* – paid-for communication that tries to establish, develop, enhance and/or change corporate image.

This list clearly incorporates those elements of PR that are operational at the corporate level, such as lobbying local or national government, media relations and customer relations, so that, for example, the image of the organization rather than the brand is part of vision or corporate future (van Riel, 1995).

Integration and communication

Chapter 1 discussed integration of communication elements, largely at the product or market level. It is quite obvious that corporate-level communications should also be part of this integrative approach. As well as integration within the marketing communications mix, for a fully integrated approach, application of communication elements should extend to the other functions of the enterprise, where communication must be co-ordinated across enterprise functions and target groups. Contradiction, which could harm the corporate image, should therefore be avoided. In this sense this is not so much a model of IMC but one of integrated corporate and marketing communications (ICMC). A key player in the success of integrated communications activities is the CEO, so the importance of the symbolic role of the CEO cannot be underestimated.

VIGNETTE

The Automobile
Association and
corporate
communications
and stability

History

According to company sources, a group of motoring enthusiasts met at the Trocadero restaurant in London's West End on 29 June 1905 to form the Automobile Association (AA). They initially intended to help motorists avoid police speed traps but as motoring became more popular, so did the AA. One hundred members in 1905 grew to 83 000 members by 1914 and as the AA membership expanded, so did its activities. In 1906 the country's first effective danger and warning signs were seen. The AA has been involved with promoting road safety ever since. It was responsible for all signposting until the early 1930s when it became a local authority responsibility, and AA Signs' distinctive yellow and black signs for special events remain a common sight. To cater for the increased popularity of touring by car, the AA appointed agents and repairers throughout the UK, listing them all in the *Members' Special Handbook*, which first appeared in 1908. In 1909 the AA introduced its free legal system for drivers summoned to appear in magistrates courts. The AA still supports members involved in legal test cases. From 1912 the AA also started to inspect hotels, and those receiving the AA's famous star classification were included in subsequent editions of the handbook. In the early 1920s, pre-purchase and post-accident repair checks were introduced (now AA Vehicle Inspections). The first AA routes were introduced around 1910 with handwritten details and, by 1929, the AA was issuing 239 000 routes a year. The AA has always produced routes and travel guides, a business activity that has grown rapidly in the past two decades. AA Publishing is now the UK's largest travel publisher; it produced more than 10 million books last year. By 1939, 2 million cars were on UK roads and 725 000 motorists had joined the AA.

After the Second World War, the AA led the protest against petrol rationing, which was finally lifted in 1950. It was a campaign that reflected the AA's traditional role of championing motorists' rights. Since that time the AA has led a number of major campaigns, including the compulsory wearing of seatbelts, which became law in 1983, and the introduction of lead-free petrol. In recent years, the AA has lobbied successive governments over unfair motoring taxes and the lack of investment in transport. The AA has always been innovative in harnessing new technology. The introduction of two-way radio after the Second World War saw the 1949 launch of a night-time breakdown service in the London area, which was gradually extended to cover most of Britain. Paper-based operations began to be replaced by an AA computer system, Command and Control, from 1986. The system's award-winning successor, AAHELP, together with automatic vehicle location technology, using global positioning satellites, has been key to achieving the AA's current speed of response at the roadside. Although the AA began selling motor insurance in 1907, twenty-three years before UK motorists were obliged to have such insurance, it did not establish its current AA Insurance underwriting service until 1967. After a number of cut-price companies had crashed in the 1960s, motorists wanted absolutely secure motor insurance cover from an organization that they could trust and they turned to the AA in their thousands. AA Roadwatch, Europe's biggest traffic broadcaster, came into being in 1973 with the advent of commercial radio in the UK. Fast and accurate collation of road and traffic information is universally recognized as key to the future of motoring and, in 1997, the AA won the first telematics contract in the UK to provide in-car breakdown, route-guidance, and accident and traffic information. Motorcycle combinations for AA patrols, introduced from 1920, together with roadside telephones, had been replaced by four-wheeled vehicles by 1968, but solo motorcycles were reintroduced in 1972 to combat urban congestion. Then, in October 1973, AA Relay was introduced, guaranteeing to transport any seriously broken-down vehicle, together with driver, passengers, luggage and trailer or caravan to any destination in Britain. That same year also saw the AA move its headquarters from London's Leicester Square (it had moved to the area in 1908 and occupied premises in New Coventry Street from 1929) to Fanum House in Basingstoke, Hampshire. The AA moved to its current Basingstoke headquarters, Norfolk House, in 1994. In 1992, the AA Driving School was launched. It is the only national body to employ fully qualified instructors and today employs more than 1000 franchises. In November 1994 AA membership reached a record 8 million. Today it stands at 9.5 million, of whom 4.4 million are personal members.

A year-long review of the AA's activities began in 1997. At the end of the year, the AA committed to three main strategic planks, i.e. to be pre-eminent at the roadside, to manage its portfolio of other businesses to achieve excellent financial returns, and to re-establish the AA as, unmistakably, the motorists' organization. In 1998, the AA reduced its call-to-arrival time at breakdowns to 35 minutes, 84 per cent of members' vehicles were fixed at the roadside and these were fixed in under an hour. This was nearly 10 minutes faster than in 1997. In addition, AA call handlers responded to 93 per cent of emergency calls within 15 seconds and 81 per cent of non-emergency calls within 20 seconds. In August 1998, the AA announced that it was pulling out of its retail network of 142 shops, insurance underwriting and 'home assistance' services. In January 1999, the AA announced the centralization of its deployment operations at three supercentres in Halesowen, Thatcham and Cheadle. In June the AA received further, independent confirmation of its vastly improved service levels when it set a new standard for the breakdown and recovery industry, and came first in the annual J D Power survey of 25 000 drivers. In July, Centrica, the leading supplier of energy and services to the home in Great Britain, announced its intention to buy the AA for £1.1 billion. The sale was completed in September, after members voted overwhelmingly in favour. In July 2001, the AA acquired the car-servicing arm of Halfords, acquiring Halford Garages for £5.75 million, which has been rebranded as AA Service Centres. Centrica owns British Gas, Goldfish, One.Tel as well as the AA and other brands. By February 2002 the AA had its twelve-millionth member and in May 2002 it launched the £22 million 'Just AAsk' brand repositioning campaign for all of its services. In June 2002 the AA, with its 3600 highly trained patrols, won the UK top roadside assistance spot for the third time in four years. AA Insurance, which also sells home cover, is the UK's largest motor insurance intermediary. Personal loans and instalment payment facilities are available to members and customers through AA Financial Services.

Values

The company values are expressed as passionate, pioneering, confident, responsive, approachable and providing value for money. While today the AA is a commercially driven business, it retains elements of its heritage as a 'membership' organization. AA Breakdown customers are still referred to as members and the AA remains an active lobbying force on behalf of motorists through its policy unit.

Range of Products

The AA operates in different markets due to its widening product range. The consumer range splits loosely into three core areas:

1 *Motoring services* – The AA has developed a large range of products within this area, which represents its core competence in consumer eyes. AA Breakdown is the dominant product for customer acquisition and driving revenues. Of the other products, the new AA Service Centres represent the most significant opportunity going forwards. The AA is the market leader in Roadside Assistance. Of all 30 million motorists in the UK, 30 per cent are AA members, 19 per cent are with the RAC and 13 per cent are with either Green Flag or Direct Line. Thirty-one per cent are not members of any motoring organization. Membership of any motoring organization can be 'voluntary' (taken out by a private consumer) or 'involuntary' (given as part of the manufacturer or dealer package as part of a car purchase). Quality of service is the AA's core strength in the breakdown market. The AA has over twice as many trained and liveried patrols as the RAC (3700 vs 1300) and gets to breakdowns more quickly. The AA has won the J D Powers survey (best roadside provider) in three out of the last four years.

2 *Financial services* – primary products are motor and home insurance (buildings and/or contents). The AA is the UK's largest intermediary with a panel of some twenty insurers and around 1.6 million customers. It currently has around 4 per cent market share. A few big players dominate the market, led by Direct Line, Norwich Union, Churchill and the AA. The market, especially motor, is heavily price driven, with premiums seemingly ever on the increase. The AA has a unique proposition in terms of saving the consumer time and, potentially, money through its intermediary status. However, there is also a common consumer view that the AA is very expensive for insurance – possibly a legacy of when it had a smaller panel of underwriters or due to 'received wisdom' about the premium the AA brand carries. Loans are a development area for the AA, with a range of products on offer. The most well known of these is AA Car Loans, which is simply an unsecured loan with a free AA Car Buyers Inspection – a unique proposition which has proved successful at growing AA's market share. AA Loans compete with the high street banks and building societies, as well as supermarkets and direct players such as Lombard Direct and Direct Line. The AA currently has around 1 per cent of this market. The AA has also had a credit card offering for many years. A new AA Visa card was launched earlier this year, offering a series of specific AA benefits and a mid-rate annual percentage rate (APR) of interest. In this competitive, mature market, the AA strategy is to use a highly targeted approach, focusing on gaining incremental value from existing AA customers. So far, the product has remained low key, sold through internal customer channels and on the website, theAA.com.

3 *Travel services* – this area primarily encompasses information services (e.g. AA Roadwatch) and publishing. The AA uses its extensive traffic information network to provide data through a number of channels – radio, mobile phones and theAA.com, as well as routing and navigation services. Last year AA Roadwatch received over 7 million calls. The AA is the UK's largest travel publisher with over 650 titles and is in the top five worldwide. It has sold 36 million overseas travel guides since 1990 and is the UK market leader in road atlases. In total, AA Publishing sold 30 million books last year – key products for cross-selling purposes.

Corporate brand development and the Just AAsk campaign

The AA claims to have one of the most trusted brands in the UK, having built its brand on the breakdown product ('The 4th Emergency Service', 'A very nice man'). But the very success of this brand-building means that breakdown has eclipsed the other products within the portfolio that are now critical to the AA's future. The rebranding campaign, with the new logo and strap line 'Just AAsk' was launched in May 2002 to help overcome the dominance of AA Breakdown. The campaign aims to focus consumer attention on the wider range of AA products available. The key to its effectiveness will be how successfully it demonstrates that the AA's brand values (reassurance, expertise, quality and consumer championship) are equally applied to the other products it offers. The simple consumer insight at the heart of the AA rebranding is that 'The AA rescues you from uncertainty' whatever the product or service. The aim of the rebranding campaign is to get the AA out of the customer's mental glove-box (filed firmly under 'Breakdown') and into more frequent consideration across a range of products. In the advertising, consumer needs in different scenarios are framed as questions, with the AA supplying the answer through the product and the strap line 'Just AAsk'. The rebranding has been introduced across all consumer-focused communications from brand advertising on television to direct sales force posters to provide complete consistency. The campaign is starting to generate awareness of a wider range of products and is raising the credibility of the AA in new areas.

Other opportunities for customer communication

TheAA.com was relaunched in 2001 and is positioned as the AA's 'shop window' where users can seek information and purchase products and services. There are over 30 000 pages of content on all aspects of owning and buying a car. TheAA.com served 112.4 million page impressions last year to 7.5 million unique visitors. The number of people using the site since January 2001 has grown 6 per cent faster than general Internet growth and it is currently one of the top twenty corporate sites (i.e. excluding Internet service providers and portals). TheAA.com 'share of audience' is second only to Autotrader in the motoring arena – and is twice as high as competitors such as RAC and Direct Line. As well as attracting high volumes of site traffic through functionality like route planning (6 million routes generated per year), traffic alerts, car-buying information and accommodation guides, the AA website also drives revenue. Currently, around 25 per cent of AA Insurance quotes are done on line, up to 30 per cent of loans business is done on line and 7 per cent of roadside membership is bought on line. Sales of AA books on line have increased fourfold. *The AA Magazine* was started in 1992 and is currently the second widest circulation magazine in the UK (around 4.5 million). It is published twice a year and has been traditionally only sent to AA Breakdown members as part of the benefits of membership. Recently, however, insurance and financial services customers have been included both to help promote roadside cross-sales, and also to involve and recognize non-breakdown customers as part of the AA brand. A contract publishing company publishes the magazine. It currently raises revenue directly through the sales of advertising space (both to external companies and internally to AA products and services). It is also a key response medium for the AA and generates response and sales for products through the advertising they place, and through editorial and promotional offers. It is possible currently to use elements external to the magazine itself – the personalized letter, carrier, inserts, outserts, supplements, etc. – to tailor the magazine to different audiences. There are three *AA call centres* that are structured around product/service requirements at Cheadle, Newcastle and Cardiff. Both inbound and outbound calling can be managed and the handlers are well trained. There is capacity in off-peak times to accommodate marketing initiatives, including cross-selling of other products.

Sources: Adapted from IDM (2002); www.centrica.com/textsite/learningzone/h_theaa.htm; www.theaa.com/aboutus.html; www.theaa.com/aboutaa/history.html; www.theaa.com/aboutus/news/newnewso55.html.

STOP POINT

Consider the key components of the AA's marketing and corporate communications. While the AA is clearly committed to marketing communications, it is also acutely aware of and committed to corporate communications also. What role if any has history to play in this? To what extent is the AA's communication integrated? Is there potential for conflict or contradiction within what the AA does?

Corporate identity, personality and image

Corporate identity

There is a clear distinction between corporate image and corporate identity. The latter is the way in which the organization presents itself to target groups (as opposed to image, which is a perception of the organization by the target groups). Corporate identity has to be created, through the use of some forms of signs and symbols to capture the essence of the organization, and then experienced through everything the organization says, does or makes and has to be managed. The corporate identity is revealed through communications policies. The corporate identity mix consists of symbols, communications and behaviour. Corporate personality can be defined as the manifestation of the organization's self-perception including intent, i.e. the cultural glue for often disparate parts of the organization that binds.

Corporate identity should be strategically planned and measured. It should also be based on company philosophy, long-term company goals and a particular desired image. In effect it is the sum of all methods of portrayal, visual and non-visual, that the company uses to present itself to relevant targets. It is a reflection of the distinctive capabilities and the recognizable individual characteristics of the company. It can also be said to be the tangible manifestation of the company and a reflection and projection of the real personality of the company meant to be experienced, and is therefore an aesthetic, formal expression and behaviour. Corporate identity should, if it is worth anything, be an enhancer of performance and efficiency and a co-ordinator of values and information – in short an integrator (van Riel, 1995).

Dolphin (1999) distinguishes between corporate identity and image by placing identity within the mission statement, the first formal act of the organization's identity that defines the corporation and its goals and principles. Identity is also embodied in a sense of self in terms of history, beliefs and philosophy. Corporate identity change is therefore not a 'face-lift'. There should be a concrete, not cosmetic, link between identity, communications and image. For Baskin (1998) it is also about leadership and vision since 'identity can focus managers' attention specifically on what they need to do to keep their organization competitive. As with IBM, managing a corporate vision/culture is a leadership responsibility. Thus, change can be a deliberate management act, for example in positioning and repositioning situations such as a move from being seen as a national to a global corporation, as is classically the case with British Airways. With the strap line 'the world's favourite airline', BA also attempted a new identity that was global, caring, more modern, open and cosmopolitan – and proudly British.

Identity is made up of signs and symbols such as name, logo, colours, icons, heraldry, flags, marks, uniforms and even the corporate headquarters. Other communication whether verbal or non-verbal is important too, as is action or behaviour, for example signs and symbols bring with them associations. On its own a new logo will not work beyond the cognitive. With other forms of communication and the ways in which an organization behaves something quite different can be produced. There may be a new house style but couple this with a collegiate feeling, a sense of belonging and of recognition and the impression of high esteem, quality and performance, and you have something more than a cognitive impulse.

Grayson (2002) offers a seven-step model aimed at helping managers marry corporate identity with responsibility. This suggests that corporate identity is indeed much more than signs and symbols, and is summarized below:

Corporate identity and responsibility: a seven-step marriage model

Nicola Hill (2002) considers David Grayson's (2002) management handbook, *Everybody's Business: Managing Risks and Opportunities in Today's Global Society*. His book suggests a seven-step model aimed at helping managers marry corporate identity with responsibility. There are seven 'win-win' steps:

Step 1 is a trigger for action: It suggests thirteen common triggers. This may be an externally generated event, for example, a media exposé of conditions in the company's third world factories or the threat of a campaign against the business. The trick, however, is to get ahead of the wave – and generate your own trigger for action.

Step 2 then involves articulating a compelling business case for action appropriate to the specific business.

Step 3 suggests that a business needs to scope the critical emerging management issues it faces. Tools include stakeholder dialogue, benchmarking, assessing business impacts and using scenarios.

Step 4 is about committing to action, which may involve changes to a company's vision and mission; new governance arrangements, and perhaps making a public commitment through signing up for something like the global compact or joining a business coalition promoting socially responsible business.

Step 5 suggests that a business needs to integrate strategies, by stretching existing policies and processes or, for example, where there is a strong risk management culture or a commitment to total quality management, these can be extended to incorporate the emerging management issues. Almost certainly, however, there will also need to be some new strategies developed.

Step 6 is about implementation, engaging with stakeholders, for example incorporating these issues into job specifications, appraisals, management training and rewards systems, and addressing community needs.

Step 7 suggests measuring and reporting on impacts that the business has, and using these as a trigger to start the process again.

Measurement of corporate identity

An accepted categorization of types of corporate identity (Id) to explain the possibilities of different depictions of the organization in terms of style, policy and strategy is:

1   Monolithic Id where the whole organization uses one visual style (Shell, Philips, BMW).

2   Endorse Id where subsidiaries have their own style but where the parent is recognizable (GM, L'Oreal).

3   Branded Id where subsidiaries have their own style but the parent is not recognizable (Diageo, P&G).

It should be noted that a combination of these could be used and that other language might be used to describe the same thing, such as umbrella and endorsed. The visibility of the parent is pivotal and this, of course, has to do with degree of control and of 'content guiding' whereby the parent might have high/low visibility and strict/no content guiding, or some degree of each.

Methods of analysis of corporate identity

There have been a number of methods developed to analyse corporate identity. Two are worthy of consideration:

1 *Bernstein's cobweb method.* This is useful for putting managers' ideas into a more explicit form. It facilitates a means, for example, to arrive at areas of conflict within the management team and to expose them. This brings out in the open the terms in which the managers are thinking so that they can arrive at an unambiguous statement of the corporate identity desired by the management. This method measures, in the first instance, the view that they may have of their company, which is not necessarily the same as the view of the company held by other observers. This is the weakness of the method since it does not actually measure existing identity of the company and should perhaps mainly be considered a method for initiating discussion of the goals of the organization. The eight attributes of quality, integrity, value for money, imagination, reliability, service, social responsibility and technical innovation are then mapped on a scaled graph and the collective view of participants and their estimation of the public view can then be compared.

2 *Lux's star method* is similar to Bernstein's cobweb. The value of this also is limited to the stimulation of discussion among senior management along the lines that corporate identity should be following. This is still a useful and practical tool. With the Lux method the distinguishing attributes of the company are predetermined, i.e. that there are seven dimensions that always underlie personality of a company – needs, interests, attitudes, temperament, competencies, origin and constitution (this after Guilford's 1954 study that established such characterizing dimensions).

Corporate identity and personality

Corporate personality is, as one might expect, 'who the organization is' (Olins, 1989). Symbols, other communication and behaviour add up to corporate identity. This is a story that can be told. Communication can, for example, say 'we are innovative'. The behaviour of the organization can back this up. A logo can be an instantly recognizable sign. The culmination of these leads to corporate personality. Corporate personality emerges from the concrete triangle of symbolism, communication and behaviour and therefore corporate image consists of all forms of expression by which the organization reveals its personality and therefore the uniqueness and organization (Figure 13.2).

The relevance of corporate identity can be summed up in four ways:

1 Rising moderation among employees; this is an internal effect of corporate identity, allowing employees to identify with the organization. This is an

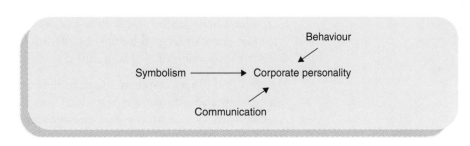

Figure 13.2
Factors affecting
corporate personality.

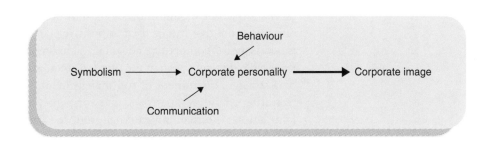

Figure 13.3
Factors affecting corporate
image.

internal feel that increases commitment to the organization and that has an external projection. This is better use of human capital (van Riel, 1995).

2 Inspiring confidence among external target groups since consistent signals help such targets to develop a clear picture that reduces the risk of inconsistency.

3 Acknowledging the vital role of customers to help build customer confidence and relationships for the longer term.

4 Acknowledging the vital role of financial target groups, which inspires confidence in the company especially since they are dealing with financial risk.

Of course, the notion of the desired identity leading to desired image is different from the notion of the actual identity leading to actual image. At least in part, self-preservation of the company lies in the corporate identity, in the manifestation of a bundle of characteristics (or distinguishing features), that form around the organization, displaying its personality. Corporate identity can be seen as existing in cues offered about itself by the organization in its self-presentation via behaviour, communication and symbolism, which are forms of expression. The persona therefore reflects the reality of the organization and on this basis the observer can judge an organization and its people.

Corporate image and reputation

The corporate identity should mirror or match corporate image. If corporate identity combines symbolism, communications and behaviour to form corporate personality, corporate image is determined not by the organization, but by the perceptions of the target group, and can be good, bad, indifferent, bland or confusing. This is illustrated in Figure 13.3.

Corporate image can be described as a set of meanings by which a corporation is known that can be used by the observer to describe, remember and relate to it via the interaction of beliefs, feelings, perceptions and impressions.

Dolphin (1999) sees corporate image in the same way as a photographic image can be seen and asks the key question 'how does an organization see itself?' A receiver will decode an encoded message and, even if nothing has been deliberately encoded and the receiver apparently does nothing consciously, there will still be an image. The organization must therefore realize that it has to manage the expectations of its potential publics, especially with regard to corporate reputation. A stable and consistent reputation can only be viewed as the overall estimation of the organization by its stakeholders. A favourable corporate reputation is a tool that can be used to positive effect. It is created by other tools and is necessary for competitive advantage. The importance of a favourable image, a favourable representation in the mind, is unquestionable. Corporate image should be a strategic instrument of top management, an incentive for sales, an aid to recruiting employees, partners, investors, analysts and customers, a generator of faith among internal and external groups, a provider of authority, a creator of emotional added value, a provider of a means to competitive advantage, a changer of attitudes and potentially behaviour, a decider for consumers when the situation is too complex, when information is sparse or too wide-ranging, or when obstructions such as time constraints affect buyer behaviour (van Riel, 1995).

Herbig and Milewicz (1995) highlight the relationship between reputation and credibility as key for competitive advantage where 'credibility transactions' (negative or positive) can have an impact upon an organization and its competitors. This study supported the idea that an organization's 'reputation and subsequent credibility are a result of the continuous process of credibility transactions'. They argue that it takes many transactions to get back to a position after some fall from grace has taken place or where an organization has not lived up to its claims.

Symbolism as an agent in binding corporate identity and image

Symbolism as a binding agent is not new. Names, symbols, traditions, rites of passage and so on all need to be invented or reinvented: for example, a sense of grandeur though palatial corporate headquarters or a house style that promotes unity and recognition. This is the establishment and maintenance of corporate identity. Done successfully and, for example, company pride among employees can produce a readiness to co-operate. There are basically two forms: indicative (pragmatic, that which is recognizable, the symbol), and thematic (dogmatic, an expression of the strategic principles of the organization that transmits values). Thus name choice can be allied to flags, ceremonies, rituals, as with BA, leading to the rebirth of British Airways as 'the world's favourite airline'. Visual devices such as logos have to be designed to work on a number of levels. They have to be recognizable, distinctive, easily remembered, reducible and flexible in order to work in different media contexts such as magazines and television. The Internet in particular has had a big influence on the simplification of visual devices that will work in that medium. Mostly, however, they have to symbolize something and therefore metaphors, metonyms, allegories and the like are used to achieve this. For example, the organization can humanize itself to communicate that it is about people, as with the Peugeot lion to suggest strength.

Identity, image and reality

Image, identity, personality, character, impression, representation and presentation are words that to Bernstein (1984) are fundamental. Musing on the large company's state of being, Bernstein suggests that the company should question whether it has an image problem or that identity might be out of line with product performance, whether a consistent personality is expressed, whether all communications convey the character of the corporation and whether what is said conveys the desired impression. What Bernstein is concerned about is actuality and perception, where any mismatch is the perception itself in the mind of the transmitter. This makes a lot of sense in the real world of everyday experience. The experience may be the observation that a relatively small travel company calls itself something like 'Target Travel'. It calls itself that because it gets people to the destination like a dart or an arrow. They then choose a target, as in archery, because a target looks like an attractive logo. The problem is there is no real link, just a perceived link in the mind of the transmitter.

The notion of 'detachable entities' – what a company does and how it is perceived – is a useful construct, i.e. there is a potential mismatch between what it would like to be and what actually appears to be reality, the danger being distorted perception on the part of the transmitter. Companies therefore seek to have image(s) for the company itself and/or its brands and these are usually strong rather than weak, open rather than devious, warm rather than cold and flexible rather than rigid (Bernstein, 1984).

For the receiver the perception of the reality is the everyday reality where the reaction is not to an abstract reality but to the perception of this reality. It is this perception that is reality. In other words consumers are highly likely to accept a degree of illusion and choose a particular brand to join a club. In this sense, products (or for that matter politicians) are not packaged as is normally assumed but are given more than this – they are given a personality. For this Bernstein's analogy of the baby's clothes equating to packaging of the brand/politician in terms of growing and developing personalities is useful. With corporate advertising the image is adjusted. With product advertising the image is built into a product offering, usually a brand that becomes the embodiment of the person – the company, VW or Guinness. The difficulty lies in the problem of reality shifting and, therefore, is one of control. The corporate communications manager (if not the CEO) is the guardian of the corporate image and the product/brand manager is the product/brand image-maker. Image is therefore 'a fabrication' and an impression that appeals to the audience rather than reproduces reality. This implies a 'degree of falseness' whereby the reality 'rarely matches up to the image' of a 'product or a politician' (Bernstein, 1984).

The company should therefore be concerned about being perceived at all and, if so, how signals are being received and how the company is perceived in relation to its self-image. This is a continual struggle, not something that the company can sort out once and for all. We find most change uncomfortable and is unfortunate because modern management is about change. We cling to a set of values and conditions that we recognize and that are undemanding of our own commitment and effort. John Harvey-Jones (1988) in his book *Making it Happen* underlines the importance of the ability to create and manage the future in the way that we wish. This is what differentiates the good manager from the bad and appears in its starkest form in this century of industrial change.

Corporate image levels

In terms of transmitting the identity, the broader communication sender-message/signal-receiver model applies here also (Figure 13.4).

Any form of communication can therefore be placed within the model and the failure to project an effective image can be explained in these terms. Obviously, without distortion a clearer image or picture will appear. Bernstein (1984) sees image as one would a photographic image that develops in the mind of the viewer. The true image is therefore the viewer's perception and not that of management. If management want to look into a mirror and see something target groups do not, then they do so at their peril. As van Riel (1995) has it, an image is therefore a strategic instrument and has been defined in a number of ways. Image is subjective knowledge and a representation or imprint of reality, the sum of 'functional qualities and psychological attributes in the consumer's mind', the result of 'the way the object is assessed in terms of tangibility, relevance and degree of correspondence with self-image' or the 'sum of impressions and expectations'. Image is also a 'combination of product aspects such as brand names and other advertising symbols' and a 'hierarchical meaning structure consisting of means–ends value chains'. Image can also be viewed as 'a holistic and vivid impression held as a result of information processing (some of which will have been transmitted by the organization itself as marketing and corporate communications) by particular groups regarding the organization'. Van Riel recognizes three areas of opinion on how image works: social critics, analytic writers and utility writers. The first group are interested in *learning* as the way of viewing organizations. The second are interested in *cognition and elaboration*. The third, *utility*, consists of both academics and practitioners, and is by far the commonest approach taken by the industry in terms of image creation. This approach, which is key to corporate communications, is illustrated in Figure 13.5.

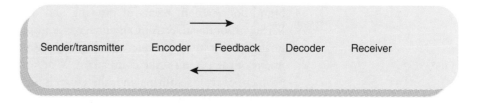

Figure 13.4
Sender–message/
signal–receiver model.

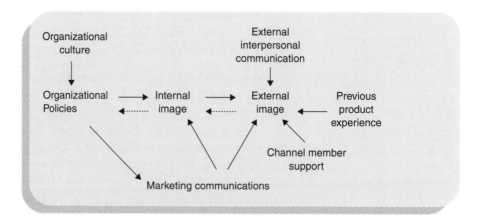

Figure 13.5
The utility approach to
image creation.

Impression management and measurement of corporate image

As with any managed programme, clear objectives, strategy and tactics have to be stated. One organization may wish to move to a radically new position because of some major upheaval in its environment. Another may have a more incremental, subtle approach to impression management. However, first the image has to be created, then protected. Having created something favourable, it then makes sense to maintain this. Assertive impression management is proactive. Defensive impression management aims to protect the image. Coupled with this, impression management can be both tactical (short term addressing specifics) and strategic (longer term and not tied to one particular issue but achieving organizational goals), and as such corporate communications should be core to the overall strategic plan to ensure performance. Strategically, corporate communications should be influential on every business decision as fashioned by the CEO and communications executive team relating to corporate values, culture and mission/vision. The nature of the organization should therefore be relayed to the key constituencies and this should support management functions. Through such synergy should come management of the organization's reputation and building of public consent.

Tactically, an effective dialogue with constituents is required but there is a need to know their perceptions and behavioural inclinations in order to be in a position to mutually benefit both them and the organization. Dolphin (1999) sees the role of 'boundary scanners' – the eyes and ears of the organization – as vital here. Formal scanning consists of things such as surveys, focus groups and media content analysis. Informal scanning consists of things such as media contacts and monitoring complaints of one sort or another. This is exchange of knowledge in order to learn more about significant constituents in the pursuit of competitive advantage. The corporate communication tools of, for example, lobbying and advocacy, can then be used more effectively.

In terms of both corporate identity and impression management, models have been developed to aid practitioners. These are very much akin to the general decision sequence model found in the marketing communications literature. Van Riel's (1995) Corporate Image Policy Programme (CIPP) follows the APIC system espoused in Chapter 4 of this book with steps from problem analysis through to evaluation.

Crisis management and avoidance

In a similar vein to the above APIC model, crises have to be managed (or preferably avoided). This was discussed fully in the previous chapter in general public relations terms but this becomes part of corporate relations and affairs when the crisis is at corporate level and corporate communication is a requisite part of problem-solving. Dolphin (1999) highlights a 'crisis index' based on the notion that 'one person's crisis is another person's incident'. This then ranges from 'being the focus of a political controversy' to financial problems to organizational restructuring. The solutions to the highlighted problems can be followed through using a decision sequence framework. The nature of the problem will simply be at the corporate rather than product level.

Like Dolphin and many other writers, Davies et al. (2003) advocate not only defending a reputation and crisis management but also pre-emption of crises. Once in place corporate reputations are constantly in danger of being eroded or damaged – even destroyed. Foreseeing a disaster is a great skill at any level. The argument and discussion surrounding this area at the product level was dealt with in the previous chapter and the particular example used was Perrier. This crisis has a number of interpretations. The one presented in the previous chapter was the company's view. However, at the corporate level, Davies et al. maintain that 'Perrier's credibility fell between the cracks' whereby the headquarters response was inadequate because of the international dimension. Perrier, of course, maintain otherwise (see Chapter 15).

Understanding of the customer/consumer corporate brand relationship

Chapter 5 discusses how the customer/consumer knows to trust a brand. At the corporate level this comes about through confidence, integrity, consistency, competency, honesty, responsibility, helpfulness, benevolence – perceived or otherwise. This is a build-up, over time, of communications, performance and functional and representational values. There has to be a mechanism whereby trust can be aroused and sustained. The role of communications is to take the aspect(s) of the corporate brand that matter and seal it, remembering that fundamentals like product defects will kill the effort even when the communication, say, the strap line, does the job. Communications are there to reinforce the idea that, say, 'Tesco will look after me' and 'if they say so it must be true'. For Morgan and Hunt (1994) relationships characterized by trust are highly valued and within these benefits, termination costs and shared values directly influence the trust–commitment–loyalty process, but communications and opportunistic behaviour also have a role. Within this framework, marketers have to ask questions like 'why do some brands appeal and others repulse?' 'Is there something symbolic about the brand configuration that does this?' Or 'Is it the brand's associated communications that does this?'

Traditional/conventional research or semiotic research

In Chapter 6 of this book it was argued that the postmodernism of Brown (1995) contends that individuals do not have unmediated access to external reality and questions the existence of the free-thinking 'subject'. The human condition is not constitutive but constituted where knowledge people imagine they possess is 'unreliable, dispersed, fragmented, pre-existing and an epiphenomenon of language'. A semiotic analysis approach to the consumer/brand relationship is an attractive proposition. This is at least equally so at the corporate level. There is interest in relationship quality that stems from trust and the high degree of certainty of predictable and obligatory behaviour that leads to sales, giving the seller integrity and the process a high degree of certainty (Crosby, Evans and Cowles, 1990). The components of brand or corporate image are seen by many as being both rational and emotional, as reported in Chapter 6, which is fundamental to the notion of what a brand or organization really is in any given situation. Bhat and Reddy (1998) use the terms 'functional' and 'symbolic' in respect of brand or corporate positioning where a brand can be both, or one or the other. The symbolic offers either (or both) prestige and self-expression. The functional meets immediate practical needs. The Research Business have developed, for example, their Brand Works brand facet model which when applied to a particular brand would yield a mix of facets. Taking Toshiba as an example of corporate branding, this corporate brand apparently has saliency (emotional closeness/distance of consumer to brand) and a corporate brand personality (personification of the organization that demonstrates how the corporate brand's core emotional character has been projected to the consumer).

Conventional research looks at what, say, advertising, brand or corporate images mean to respondents willing to participate in the research study. It also looks at signs and symbols through the use of conventional procedures, e.g. free response, multi-choice, etc., and may go as far as employing a third party usage with rating scales (Foster, 1995).

Semiotic research looks at meaning on a different level. The basic premise is that social attitudes and values are embodied in signs and symbols. These can be found everywhere but in particular in logos, advertising, retail design, media exposure, etc., which build up brand and corporate images in the minds of consumers. Just how signifiers set off chains of ideas in the minds of consumers so that the image feels like the true and natural representation of the company/brand and how it thinks and feels is of prime importance here. Hetzel and Marion (1995a) then go on to discuss five models of influence of messages – transmission, construction, impression, stimulation, and insemination – and are concerned with two types of contributions of semiotics to consumer behaviour (research), i.e. co-interpretation and enunciation. Thus the semiotic approach provides researchers with the means to both find new hypotheses and to analyse collected data.

Semiotics can be used in conjunction with qualitative research techniques (Lawes, 2002). With the above commentary regarding postmodern marketing research in mind, it is thought worthwhile to explore the usefulness or not of *projective techniques*. Born out of psychoanalysis, the nature of these vary enormously in form but are generally attempts to use the chain of ideas mechanism, to project the corporate/brand image into something else, for example what a third person might say, think and feel about an idea, object, brand or company. The researcher might ask the respondent to think about, say, Tesco (the multiple) as an object or an animal in order to get at the inner-most self and cultural meaning – which is not accessible to the conscious mind. The argument is that if you are a food company then your image can only be interpreted within the parameters of cultural meaning and, in this case, within the context of the rituals of eating, socializing, etc. Advertising in many cases is in the business of manipulating people's emotions and can either be dreamt up by practitioners or can be devised after some form of research be it a conventional focus group or a projective technique. Those who take part in studies may/may not be representative of a particular target group.

Applying projective techniques and semiotic analysis

Projective techniques have gained some credibility through their use by large companies like Guinness. The idea is to fit the product or the organization to the message and the message to the product or organization. It is interesting to note that Tesco have recently run a graduate recruitment campaign which uses the line 'If Tesco is just a shop, here's a village in the south of England' accompanied by a photograph of London Bridge, Big Ben, etc., i.e. London. If semiotic analysis is applied in such situations, the hope is that structured recall of advertisements designed on this basis leads to the creation of pleasurable/positive emotions that will be triggered when the brand/company is viewed. Jhally (1987) uses Williamson's (1978) work to illustrate the importance of transference of meaning from one sign to another where the transference is accomplished by the juxtaposition within the formal internal structure of the advertisement but requires the active participation of the viewer.

Advertising campaigns and corporate brand images can therefore be coded in the language of signs that can be understood by a shared consciousness principally using the symbolic workings of colour and form. For example, red is urgent, forward, leaping, and the symbolic use of this would be things like red for danger or leaping flames. In contrast blue is cool, distant and the colour of an apparent recession into the distance as seen in a cool pool, an infinite sky or a faraway horizon. Consider the examples of application in the vignette below.

Measuring corporate image and identity: examples of application from the conventional to the semiotic

General Motors

The General Motors (GM) case of the mid-1980s involved traditional research regarding policy decisions in the area of corporate communications of a worldwide marketing company, in relation to its UK operations. The research therefore falls into the category of conventional, survey-type research that looks into what certain attributes mean to respondents rather than the category of how meaning is created (Fountain et al., 1986). In essence, survey work was carried out to determine the value of the GM connection to local (and here this means UK) operations. Here it is claimed that the results show that GM had a very low profile in the UK but, with proper handling, a higher profile and a more strongly perceived relationship between the UK companies and their American parentage would be beneficial to their operations. These results were put to the GM senior management and made a significant contribution towards the development of GM corporate strategy in the UK.

Guinness

The credibility of getting participants to cut up pieces of magazine images in order to research the personalities of brands such as All Gold and Dairy Box, how they express themselves, and also, how role play is a means to exploring ways of segmenting markets and developing brand personalities, how clay modelling is an exploratory tool and how psychodrawings have been used to explore the innermost and outermost properties of the ideal Guinness drinker were all the subject of the QED team (QED, 1995). Guinness used such techniques in order to create advertisements that would embody the inner and outer properties of the Guinness drinker. Projective techniques, tarnished somewhat by the lingering associations with motivational research, have gained some credibility through their use by large companies like Guinness. The Guinness 'dolphin' campaign that ran for several years is an example of the outcome of this kind of research. More recently Guinness have developed the Guinness Advertising Decoding Kit to aid the unlocking of the 'power of culture and communications in shaping consumers' perceptions and behaviour today' (Harvey and Evans, 2001). The claim is that semiotics offers cost-saving research for advertising at product or corporate level.

Heinz/M&S/British Home Stores (BHS)

Applying semiotic analysis to various companies, Valentine (1988) describes Heinz appearing to be a giant rocket-powered container driven by Mary Poppins. At the semiotic level, the container, shaped like a baked bean can is a symbol that gives Heinz power in the world. Heinz is all around the consumer and has the power of presence in supermarkets, weight in its advertising, the huge scale of promotions. Thus Heinz is an enormous enterprise 'piloted by a fairy story figure' who 'feeds children with a basic moral goodness, sweetened with a spoonful of sugar. A bit like Mum, really'. With M&S, the way the sign becomes the symbol of the mythologies guides our deepest and most emotional decisions. The semiotic structure is intact where there is a deep-seated belief about the M&S corporate mind. There is no problem with M&S shifting the paradigm of the image of a company. M&S were good at knickers and knitwear (K&K, a second order signifier regarding fashion in clothes). They were also good at putting fashion in food, i.e. it is not the products themselves but what can be done by M&S. The BHS logo was the focus of the semiotic work. The basic outcome was very bold and blue to emphasize and maintain a corporate distance commensurate with such an institutional identity, i.e. a definite emphasis on British with a 'dancing h' taking a much less prominent role, it being a kaledioscope of colour – red, blue and green: 'The red ascender, red tip, the blue-green base all a-shimmer and a-sparkle matching its excited tones with an informal, witty, lower-case typographical style'. The old BHS thus became BhS where the B and S are semiotically flanking the h for home, presenting and supporting a home which is exciting, bright, adventurous and a place to be. Using one of Pascal Fleury's (director of the Paris-based agency 'Trilogy') ten semiological rules for understanding corporate imagery, this work attempted to keep a distance, provide a coldness, a seriousness, integrity by using the B and S, and tempered this by creating warmth around symbols. The 'new' BhS was therefore endowed with a corporate seriousness coupled with a home-centredness with the h as the embodiment of the domestic sphere. The main problem in all of this is that the research is never really discussed, just the outcome, so it is impossible to know what was done to arrive at such conclusions and decisions. Later BhS became bhs, caligraphically written in lower case 'real writing' and all in one blue colour.

Levi (jeans)

Using Kapferer's (1991) and Semprini's (1992) work on brand identity elements, Hetzel and Marion (1995b) see the real challenge for companies as understanding the relative importance of each element of brand identity and the nature of relations between the various elements. Semprini's hierarchy of mutual relationships, based on semiotic theory, is based on the notion of the brand offering a discourse and meaning being produced by generation and narration, coming about through gradual enrichment around an elementary core in which only the constitutive values of society exist. Such values only acquire reality by 'rising back upward towards the discursive surface' where they are 'implemented by narrative structures' and are subsequently 'enriched by the figures and objects of the world as we know them around us'. So a journey by meaning is travelled through these levels, i.e. the sign is transformed into signification through a generative journey in three stages: axiological, narrative and discursive. Hetzel and Marion are concerned with two types of contributions of semiotics to consumer behaviour (research), i.e. co-interpretation and enunciation.

Another example, therefore, of deconstruction is Levi jeans. Hetzel and Marion (1995b) use Semprini's model to illustrate the various levels Levi might operate on, the advertisements for which usually feature young people with sensual and attractive bodies that seduce and attract attention to the Levis they are wearing. The characters love life and enjoy it to the full. This is the surface (simplest) level. At the most complex or deepest level of the brand's identity, the axiomatic, the values are anti-conformity, freedom and adult virility. These allow the brand to continue over time, a permanent, lasting entity in the minds and memory of those concerned. At the second level, the narrative, a tellable character is assigned which allows the axiological values to be told, i.e. from what is implicit in the brand to that which is explicit. This requires two things: first, the organization of the values that are defined at the axiological level among themselves; second, affording these values a dynamic force using relations of opposition, search, de-possession, complicity and confrontation. So for Levi it is the hero (different each time) that underlies the values of anti-conformity and individual freedom. So realistic narration, a polemical structure, confrontation and exclusion form the basis of this level for Levi. This enables the advertisements to vary since the hero has several ways of showing anti-conformity, free will, etc. Thus the brand has a narrative role through which it displays itself. At the third, surface level of discourse(s) the narrative is enriched by figures such as objects, people (actors), etc. At this level the hero is no longer abstract, he is real and so is his motorcycle. This is the context in which the brand is presented so that the audience can identify and differentiate the brand through him, the hero. The variants at this level are numerous. In Levi's European advertising you will see that the actor (discourse level) who plays the hero (narrative level) who embodies the values (axiomatic level) does not have to be the same. The discursive elements, while at the sociocultural sensitivities end of the ways of life and attitudes of consumers, do not represent the essential aspect of the identity of the brand. The discursive elements may play an important part in brand recognition but do not necessarily represent its value system. They are surface, i.e. it is no longer a question of simple analysis of themes and codes (same actor, colour and so on) but more a question of structuring the levels of the generation of meaning in order to work out what constitutes stability and permanence of identity and what is superficial. That which is axiological gets to the core of radiation of meaning from which everything else is generated. It is easier, according to Hetzel and Marion (1995b), for a manager to change the elements at the top than rather than at the bottom.

Sources: Adapted from Barthes (1973); Fountain et al. (1986); Harvey and Evans (2001); Hetzel and Marion (1995a; 1995b); IPA (1995); QED (1995); Valentine (1988).

STOP POINT

Think about the different approaches taken to measuring image or identity in the above cases. The more conventional approach may provide acceptable data to management but does it really say very much about the workings of images, logos and so on? The use of projective techniques and semiotics may facilitate more in-depth analysis but will the outcomes be acceptable to management? Is there a compromise position that would be an acceptable one?

Assignment

Select a corporate identity and explain its composition in terms of shape, colour, form and so on, and comment on what it symbolizes. Explore other forms of communication and behaviours currently engaged in by the same organization and explain its corporate personality. Comment on the likely corporate image and reputation this organization will have with its various constituents.

Summary of Key Points

- Corporate communications are ultimately about improving performance and gaining competitive advantage.

- Corporate communications' role is that of the integration of functions to project the total business message.

- Corporate communications management should know that that there is no external communication that does not impact internally and this can affect staff morale, adding or subtracting to competitive advantage.

- There is a clear distinction between corporate identity and image involving corporate personality and reputation. Identity is the way in which an organization presents itself; image is the way it is perceived by various constituents.

- A combination of signs and symbols make up the corporate identity. This symbolism along with other communication and behaviour of the organization add up to corporate personality. This projection becomes the corporate image as perceived by target groups and over time. Corporate reputation then ensues, it being a collective representation of an organization's past action and results.

- The link between branding, brand strategy and corporate identity and image is crucial. Other factors such as behaviour help take the new logo beyond mere cognitive impulse.

- There is an intimate relationship between corporate identity, personality, image and reputation. Presentation, perception, representation and reality are important considerations in impression management.

- Impression management involves strategic and tactical activity that is part of the strategic corporate plan.

- To get to the true meaning of corporate identity and imagery, more than traditional/conventional research is required. It is easy and tempting to survey and gather information on recall/recognition. It is much more difficult to get to true meaning, but qualitative techniques are emerging as an aid to this end.

Examination Questions

1 Explain why organizations need to develop a culture that is innovative and participatory. Include in your answer consideration of the generation of new ideas within the organization.

2 In terms of the employees of an organization, discuss why it is important to make people feel that their ideas and opinions count, and why passion

about the job and the organization and the opportunity to work as a member of a team matter.

3 'The IMC concept is misleading when consideration of the corporate level is made. The acronym ICMC is more appropriate in today's competitive world.' Discuss this statement in relation to the idea of 'total corporate communications'.

4 With reference to a particular example, explain how an organization might seek to communicate its corporate brand identity.

5 Explain why an organization might use the colours red, blue or green in its identity. Using examples to illustrate, bring into your discussion consideration of shape and form and any other devices that are used for identity development.

6 Discuss how the creation of a new brand identity might help an organization to steer its way through difficult as well as easy times. Explain the relationship between identity, communications and behaviour.

7 Examine the relationship between corporate personality and corporate image. Explain where the notion of reality comes into the picture.

8 Corporate reputation is said to be the result of past and present actions and results. Discuss corporate reputation in the context of an organization of your choice.

9 'Traditional research into corporate identity can deal with meaning, but only in a superficial way. The only way to get beneath the surface and get to true meaning is through the use of semiotic research techniques'. Explain why you agree or disagree with this statement using examples of your choice.

10 Projective techniques are some of the tools at the disposal of the psychologist or semiotician. Discuss the credibility of the use of such techniques, bearing in mind their somewhat chequered history, in corporate brand, identity and image development.

References

Barthes, R. (1973). *Mythologies*. Paladin.

Baskin, K. (1998). *Corporate DNA – Learning from Life*. Butterworth-Heinemann.

Bernstein, D. (1984). *Company Image and Reality*. Cassell.

Bhat, S. and Reddy, S. K. (1998). Symbolic and functional positioning of brands. *Journal of Consumer Marketing*, **15** (1), 32–43.

Brown, S. (1995). *Postmodern Marketing*. Routledge.

Crosby, L., Evans, K. and Cowles, D. (1990). Relationship quality in services selling: an interpersonal influence perspective. *Journal of Marketing*, **54**, 68–80.

Cummins (2002a). Cummins – powering forward with a new vision. At www.thetimes100.co.uk.

Cummins (2002b). Unleashing the power of Cummins. At www.cummins.com/eu/pages/en/index.cfm.

Davies, G. with Chun, R., Vinhas da Silva, R. and Roper, S. (2003). *Corporate Reputation and Competitiveness*. Routledge.

Dolphin, R. (1999). *The Fundamentals of Corporate Relations*. Butterworth-Heinemann.

Foster, J. (1995). It's very nice, dear, but what does it mean? *Research*, May, 20–21.

Fountain, E. et al. (1986). The contribution of research to GM's corporate communications strategy in the UK. *Journal of the MRS*, **28** (1), January, 37–47.

Grayson, D. (2002). *Everybody's Business: Managing Risks and Opportunities in Today's Global Society*. Dorling Kindersley (in partnership with Business in the Community and The Prince of Wales Business Leaders Forum).

Harvey, M. and Evans, M. (2001). Decoding competitive propositions: a semiotic alternative to traditional advertising research. *International Journal of Marketing Research*, **43** (2), 171–187.

Harvey-Jones, J. (1988). *Making it Happen: Reflections on Leadership*. Collins.

Herbig, P. and Milewicz, J. (1995). To be or not to be . . . credible that is: a model of reputation and credibility among competing firms. *Market Intelligence and Planning*, **13** (6), 24–33.

Hetzel, P. and Marion, G. (1995a). Contributions of French semiotics to marketing research knowledge. *Marketing and Research Today*, February, 35–40.

Hetzel, P. and Marion, G. (1995b). Contributions of French semiotics to marketing research knowledge. *Marketing and Research Today*, May, 75–85.

Hill, N. (2002). Corporate identity: a seven step model. At http://society.guardian.co.uk/conferences/story/0,9744,672417,00.hml.

IDM (2002). *The IDM Competition Case Study (AA and EHS Brann)*. IDM.

Institute of Practitioners in Advertising (IPA) (1995). *The Advertising Effectiveness Awards*. Notes and video. IPA.

Jhally, S. (1987). *The Codes of Advertising*. Routledge.

Lawes, R. (2002). Demystifying semiotics: some key questions answered. *International Journal of Market Research*, **44** (3), 251–264.

Morgan, R. and Hunt, S. (1994). The commitment-trust theory of relationship marketing. *Journal of Marketing*, **58**, July, 20–38.

Olins, W. (1989). *Corporate Identity: Making Business Strategy Visible through Design*. Thames and Hudson.

QED (1995). *It's Not Easy Being a Dolphin*. Channel 4 television series.

Valentine, V. (1988). Signs and symbols. *Survey*. Winter, 24–25.

Van Riel, C. B. M. (1995). *Principles of Corporate Communications*. Prentice Hall.

Williamson, J. (1978). *Decoding Advertisements*. Marion Boyars.

Sponsorship

Chapter overview

Introduction to this chapter

The nature of sponsorship is explored and relationships developed with the marketing communications mix. Sponsorship is placed within an integrated and strategic context. Sponsorship involves an exchange whereby one party permits another an opportunity to exploit an association with an activity, for commercial advantage, in return for funds, services or resources. This is often seen in relation to sports (particularly when televised) due to high coverage on television. This is part of event-related marketing and the sponsorship of events of all sorts from sport to the arts. Venues can also be used as a focus for corporate entertaining, as with football boxes or racecourse marquees. Cause-related marketing includes the sponsorship of causes, most often charities. Sponsorship of television programmes is now commonplace. Ambush marketing and product placement are included as an allied but somewhat different marketing communications optional tool. This chapter explores these areas and makes a case for sponsorship's elevation to strategic status.

Aims of this chapter

The overall aim of this chapter is to consider the nature and role of sponsorship in the context of what theory has to offer sponsorship practice. More specifically, on completion of this chapter, the reader should be able to:

- discuss the nature and role of sponsorship

- explain sponsorship in relation to other marketing communications tools

- discuss sponsorship in terms of marketing theory and relationship marketing

- discuss the various types of sponsorship in the three broad areas of causes, sports and arts events and television programming

- discuss the nature of sponsorship practice in relation to strategy

- explain the notions of ambush marketing and product placement in relation to sponsorship.

The nature and role of sponsorship

The nature of sponsorship

Coca-Cola advertising chief Segio Zyman, according to Admap (2002), in his book *The End of Advertising as We Know It*, says the term 'sponsorship' should be dropped (because it is patronizing) and that it should be replaced with 'marketing property utilization'. Sponsorship is about someone paying to be part of something else – a project or an activity – or it is about someone entering into an agreement on behalf of another. Or it may be about someone who makes him or herself responsible for certain things (Sleight, 1989). However, this view, for Sleight, may be rather erroneous, Sleight choosing to define sponsorship in terms of relationships. The provider of funds, resources or services to an individual and event or organization is offered, in return, some rights of association, usually to be used for commercial advantage. The sponsor is the provider of the funds and some other resource, and the sponsee the receiver of the funds or resource and the giver of the rights of association.

It is no longer simply the chairman's wife who gets to choose a charity to support. Sponsorship often occurs at the marketing operational level and, increasingly, certain partnerships are to do with the marketing of brands. Sponsorship is not at all new and can be traced back to, for example, Roman times where the sponsorship of the arts was common. A famous example would be the De Medici family sponsoring Michelangelo (De Pelsmaker, Geuens and Van Den Bergh, 2001). Sponsorship has been, and still is, about altruism, making people aware, or creating a positive feel for the company, among other things, but with less control than is to be had with many other forms of communication.

Reference to sponsorship in the marketing communications literature is often found under either cause-related marketing or event-related marketing (Shimp, 1997). With the former in particular there has been an increase of in-kind sponsorship at the expense of cash. There is also a worthwhile distinction that can be made between corporate philanthropy and commercial sponsorship where, respectively, one is pure giving the other giving but seeking reward (Bennett, 1998). The latter appears to be the stronger trend with in-kind sponsorship having a number of additional benefits, including community involvement and staff training and development. Event-related sponsorship would now include the name of Marlboro, which has been associated with Formula One racing, but this has been the case for many years. Likewise Benson and Hedges is synonymous with both cricket and golf. Sponsorship, therefore, has a long history of involvement with athletes/sportsmen and women and causes/philanthropy. The term 'soap opera' has become part of the English language and is used now in a wider context than its origins – the sponsorship of drama by soap companies. Apart from the now obvious and some might say despicable sponsoring of (usually sporting) events by tobacco companies in order to avoid advertising restrictions, in recent times there have been two identifiable occurrences. First, the highly publicized 'marriage' between brand names and non-profit-making organizations, such as charities like Save the Children being associated with Cadbury's, is established practice. Second, television programmes have been sponsored by brands, again such as Cadbury but this time sponsoring *Coronation Street*, the UK's premier soap opera. Other examples of such sponsorship are Pepsi and the Pepsi Chart Show, HSBC and

ITV Drama, M&S and Age Concern and Mencap, and Unilever's Flora margarine brand and the London Marathon.

There are different types of brand sponsorship. Brand sponsorship is a tool now thought to be an essential part of the programme of communications due to the decline in advertising effectiveness (Kitchen, 1998; Stewart and Short, 1997). Consumers are more sophisticated and perhaps respond less to traditional forms of advertising thus making it less cost-effective. Allowing the brand name to be associated with charities, events, sports people (rather than athletes, which allows the inclusion of golfers or darts players) or television programmes is thought to make the communication more direct and, as such, more effective. Brands are said to work by 'facilitating and making more effective the consumer's choice process' (Doyle, 1989). This implies that, if brands are positively associated with events, favourable causes, sports people or television programmes then this will help to limit the need for choice. Whatever the type of sponsorship, it can be said that the parties involved gain some degree of mutual satisfaction. Research by the author (Copley, 1999) maintains that beyond the marriage analogy there is a suggestion of an emergence of symbiotic alliances between sponsors and causes and between the causes themselves. The charity, event, sports person or television programme/station gains valuable financial help and the organization or brand benefits by public association where such publicity will enhance image, enlist consumer loyalty and, even, increase sales (Savage, 1996). Brand image encompasses the total set of brand-related activities engaged in by the brand/manufacturer (Doyle, 1989). Obviously such sponsorship will form part of that total set of activities and thus affect the consumer's understanding of the brand.

Targets

The targets for sponsorship will depend upon the context in which the sponsorship takes place. Targets might be at a corporate or marketing level. The participants, media and a section of the general public might all be the target of the sponsorship effort. Clearly, the target might be younger people (rock event) or older and more specific, say, golf, or the arts. Usually there are a number of targets, for example employees as well as the general public, in the minds of the people at companies that sponsor.

Objectives of sponsorship

Corporate and marketing objectives can be seen as primary, for example awareness, or secondary, for example to support the channel members or staff morale-building. However, this depends on management outlook. This becomes more important as management attitudes change and sponsorship becomes a more strategic tool. The degree of involvement is also important. Does the sponsor simply donate money or become involved in reshaping an organization, perhaps sending out a specialist member of staff, rather like a footballer, 'on loan' to a sponsee such as a charity. The distinction between the objective of achieving the status of the corporate good citizen and that of achieving brand or market led media coverage through sponsorship is clearly an important one. The organization has to decide if it wants to reinforce brand values or use sponsorship in a secondary role, for example as a source of information.

Much of the activity in the sponsorship area is to do with awareness and image[1] at both the corporate and brand levels. However, effects of sponsorship might be long term, so that benefits might be missed if the immediate effect appears to be very limited. The outlook may differ between those who sponsor and those who are non-sponsors. Advocates of sponsorship should not normally be looking for direct sales but rather should be wishing to link the brand to, say, an event. For example, Guinness have sponsored the arts in order to build image and corporate goodwill, while Sony's Play Station 2 has a different intent with its (European football) Champion's League sponsorship. The former is therefore more like old-style PR. Perhaps the biggest objective is to get media coverage. That is why Formula One sponsorship is such an important issue. In situations like this, no media coverage means the sponsorship deal collapses and there is no point in companies such as Scottish and Newcastle (brewers) sponsoring Newcastle United (English Premiership football) if they can no longer have the Newcastle Brown Ale motif on players' chests.

A typical list of objectives is:

- awareness

- image

- alter perception

- good citizen

- trade relations

- motivate employees

- recruitment

- create good arena for sales to operate within

- media attention and coverage

- stockholder reassurance

- big player image.

The role of sponsorship

Why organizations sponsor

There are many reasons why an organization might wish to sponsor. Some of these reasons are:

- government policies on products such as tobacco and alcohol

- the high costs of media advertising

- the ITC-type restrictions on the nature and form of sponsorship have been relaxed so that programme sponsorship is more flexible

- sponsorship can be a standardized method of communications on an international or even global scale, and is often used for market entry

- the desirable relationship with marketing connections

- positive senior management attitude change

- soft brand association achieved through sponsorship.

A lot of money is now dedicated to sponsorship activities around the world. De Pelsmaker, Geuens and Van Den Bergh (2001) maintain that in 1984 $2 billion were spent in the USA. By 1996 this figure had risen to $16.6 billion, and according to Sponsorship Research International (as quoted by Duncan Grehan Partners, 2003) by 1997 it was $18.1 billion. In the UK £4 million was spent on sponsorship in 1970, rising in 1996 to £491 million. Another statistic to ponder is that advertising expenditure rose by 6 per cent in the period 1983–97, whereas sponsorship year on year rose at a rate of 15–20 per cent in the UK. Unilever alone spent $4 billion in 2002 on communicating to customers and they intend to increase dramatically the amount spent on sponsorship, but such sponsorships 'have to be great' (Unilever, 2002).

If the name of the game is getting through the clutter, then sponsorship provides a means to obtaining media exposure (channel of communication) and also getting names – brand or corporate – positively associated with people or events (message). There are two basic outcomes for the sponsoring organization: increased visibility of brand or organization; and image-building or enhancement in terms of being seen as socially responsible (Bennett, 1998, after Logan, 1993) or excellent or a winner. This philosophy can maximize benefits for all concerned in a win-win symbiotic alliance kind of way (Copley, 1999). Bennett (1998) uses Dabon's 1991 work on twenty large European companies to illustrate consumer demands for greater social accountability. Bennett also uses Casson's 1991 work to illustrate why companies suggest that giving comes as a direct result of more cash being available because of takeovers, increased profitability, increased sophistication in the manner consumers perceive things and behave, and government pressure on companies to help with community needs. There is evidence in the literature that suggests sponsorship is now an essential part of the marketing mix and even the organization's mission and that it should be managed in a professional way as any other investment. Companies may not expect short-term sales but in the longer term there is an expectation of ROI through positive image-building and maintenance. In this light, research that suggests managers expect little from sponsorship appears somewhat out of synchronization. Lee's 1996 study of 400 companies (as reported in Bennett, 1998) suggests that 67 per cent of informants expected no links with products in order to form valuable relationships, that 40 per cent expected only enhanced public awareness of their companies and that 60 per cent had no expectation of joint promotions to increase sales. If managers are saying this in academic research, then this is in conflict with observed practice but results would very much depend on the size of the organization. Large companies are much more likely to want sponsorship by results whereas smaller companies are more likely to be philanthropists (Copley, 1999).

Motives of the sponsor almost certainly vary between the various forms of sponsorship. Research has shown that those organizations that become involved with charities wanted to enhance reputation (87 per cent) and increase sales (21 per cent), as reported by Savage (1996). Savage (1996) also reports a 1990 MORI poll that showed 71 per cent of consumers in the UK stated that they were more likely to buy from a company that supported the community (78 per cent in 1996 in the USA, according to Bennett, 1998). It is reasonable to assume, however, that for those organizations sponsoring through television the motive would be increased brand awareness and sales. These organizations seek to communicate with the consumer through the programmes or films that they like to watch. By using these immediately pre and post programme and commercial break slots the advertiser has a greater opportunity to catch the consumer's attention before they switch channel to see what else is being shown. Also sponsorship-type deals are more cost-effective (Mazur, 1998). Pepsi have taken sponsorship one step further by actually producing the Pepsi Chart Show. This allows Pepsi total control over the image and therefore enables them to remain consistent with all other forms of advertising taking place (Mazur, 1998). As for event-related sponsorship, this is almost certainly to do with excellence and with winning, as well as extra media exposure. Quester and Farrelly (1998), with a four-year longitudinal study of the Australian Formula One Grand Prix, show this to be the case whereby uppermost in the sponsors' mind is (the strength of) the association between the event and the sponsors' brands. Positive image associations are achievable because sponsorship has been seen as being less commercially biased (than advertising) and has helped sports to develop, the sports people to develop and, of course, causes. Internationally the non-verbal components of the company/brand's sponsorship helps build brands like Nike (Quester and Farrelly, 1998).

How sponsorship works

Problems with awareness, attitudes and behaviour

Clearly marketers are interested in exposure effects where one-off sponsorship exposure differs considerably from continuous exposure. A key question is, 'does a one-off exposure manage to get into the target's evoked set?' Part of the answer to this is that if sponsorship is congruent with expectations then it will work better. Additionally, longer exposure may increase involvement. If people like the event, they are more likely to like the sponsoring brand. The expectation or assumption that if there is a positive mood or atmosphere then this will pass on to the brand is a prevalent, cognitively driven one. On the other hand, behaviourists argue that operant conditioning is at play where reinforcement and vicarious learning are important in terms of how a product can be used. For example, the credibility of the athlete (positive in many cases but negative in other cases where credibility is lost) will either positively reinforce brand image or, conversely, damage it.

It can be safely said therefore that sponsorship is not a panacea for the communication ailments of the would-be sponsoring firm. Apart from the obvious (athletes taking illegal drugs, sex scandals, embezzlement of the cause's funds and so on) and the inevitable (spiralling costs, 'ambush marketing'), there is clearly a need to understand the sponsorship–brand association and memory decay effects (Crimmins and Horn, 1996). Much has been written in the area of awareness, usually through some form of recall testing. Quester and Farrelly (1998) have focused on awareness and recall but admit that emotion is missing from the equation thus far. Asking for recall of events and then the brand associated with it, however well this is done, tells us nothing more than association. Consumers may know that it is the 'Nationwide' League but this says nothing about how they really feel about the Nationwide as an organization or the league itself. For Gwinner (1997), repeated exposure is key while for Quester and Farrelly (1998), long-term impact is important whereby spontaneous awareness may be initially low but over the long term the message might sink in. This is fair enough but still says nothing about how the consumer feels about the sponsor or the sponsored. Using sales measures to indicate success is, of course, inane and goes back to the age-old 'controllable variables' argument (Copley, 1999). Also, it is quite easy to see how the value of the exposure sponsorship brings can be measured in a sort of 'opportunities to see' or 'cost per thousand' kind of way, but the merit of this is questionable. When this is done the results are rarely published, being private/syndicated and any information on worthwhile aspects such as constraints on sponsorship message (Hansen and Scotwin, 1995) are unobtainable. Claims in the literature of real image change or sales increases are often accompanied by lack of evidence (Copley, 1999).

Bennett (1999) looks at recall in terms of Zajonc's (1968) 'mere exposure' hypothesis and the 'false consensus' theorem of Ross (1977) in terms of football match spectators and posters around the perimeter of the pitch. The key to this research appears to be more in the area of 'false consensus' where it is believed that fellow devotees purchase the brands sponsored at the event and so, too, does the general public. This is, therefore, a measure of the impact of the exposure and is a way to evaluate sponsorship effects. This effect is found in occasional attendees suggesting the importance of sponsorship in strengthening brand image. Even if the brand is not the main sponsor, the greater the frequency of exposure, the higher the level of recall, i.e. it is more likely that informants will name perimeter advertising of specific brands as examples of product categories. Bennett suggests also that studies show that percentage recall increases as aiding or prompting is increased but that this is still relatively low. When dealing with an official team sponsor, however, recall is dramatically increased. Bennett highlights a number of other issues such as length of association and social cohesion of attendees that have an influence, particularly on message decay. Bennett makes reference to literature which suggests that, after twenty to thirty minutes, recall can be down by as much as one-quarter and after twenty-four hours by as much as one-half. Even after prompting using product categories as a stimulus, recall can fall back substantially so that the 'emotional environment' affects recall in terms of involvement. This might be especially so where a team sponsor's message might be more than 'mere exposure' but might have a positive effect in terms of attributes that are attractive in some way to the recipient of the message.

From the cognitive to the affective domain

There is an argument that suggests that sponsorship can have an effect within each of the established stages of the hierarchy of effects model but that such a model should be used with caution (Hansen and Scotwin, 1995). Association between sponsor and sponsored can be important but emotional involvement (attitude strength, actual purchase and positive word of mouth) is crucial in terms of recall because of the way attitudes towards the brand are shaped within an environment (Hansen and Scotwin, 1995). A strong emotional response and positive moods increase the value attached to the brand (Quester and Farrelly, 1998). Here the source of the message in terms of the usual parameters such as trust or perceived expertise might be important. There is evidence to suggest, for example, that the sponsee can be seen as being more neutral than the sponsor (Quester and Farrelly, 1998). This again is plausible but not new. For years PR has been seen in this light and it is not unusual to see writers place sponsorship in a PR box. So, to suggest that sponsorship can be used as a sales proposition or platform for other marketing activity is merely restating an old definition of PR. Involvement appears to be the key. With sports sponsorship the affinity between viewer and sport appears to get stronger with, for example, the opportunity for displays of great skills (say football), to see danger (say motor racing) and so on. If there is excessive involvement in an event this can be detrimental to recall, i.e. there is a threshold of involvement whereby more sponsorship beyond that point would be a waste (Quester and Farrelly, 1998). Involvement with the event is not, of course, the same as involvement with the brand unless the event and brand are inextricably linked. There is often the assumption that the sheer volume of the exposure will result in penetration with desirable results. This argument has, of course, been used before in terms of advertising and other communication tools.

Nicholls, Roslow and Dublish (1999), who were interested in the demographics of brand recall but also preference, used the Ryder Cup Golf and Lipton Tennis events to look into spectator awareness (via recall) and image (via brand preference). This research found that previous exposure to the brand was important to recall but that the length of the association and local familiarity with the sponsor was important to both recall and preference. However, these researchers concede that where the sponsorship is a vehicle to obtain mass coverage (or at least wider coverage, especially via television), the importance of the local parameter is lessened. The key finding seems to be that high recall is associated with high expressed preference and low recall with low expressed preference.

Ultimately the question within the hierarchy is 'does increased exposure and familiarity lead to increased preference and positive behaviour toward a brand?' (Copley, 1999). In this chapter there is an attempt to deal with the cognitive (perceptions, awareness, associations) but at the same time the affective (the nature of attitudes – whether attitudes are positive or negative and the strength of those attitudes). This is important in terms of attitude-related effects since brand and/or sponsorship awareness alone tells us very little. Actual behaviour is more problematic in terms of the paucity of research in this area.

Marketing communications, branding and sponsorship

Consumers are more discerning than ever before and their higher level of understanding demands that amusement and innovation are a necessary part of communications. New approaches to accessing the consumer's mind are thus being sought. Innovation in communication media as well as communication message has been at the forefront of (necessary) change. This change encompasses the further development of brand sponsorship. As the stakes rise, with the ever-growing 'own labels', so manufacturers seek new ways to differentiate and build their brands. Sponsorship can be seen as a clever way of reminding the consumer of the brand and in some cases associating the brand favourably with other, familiar, names (Copley and Hudson, 2000).

Brands are now recognized as valuable assets that appear on a firm's balance sheet. Brand equity may be difficult to measure but this must somehow be done for the sake of the development of effective brand strategies (De Chernatony,

1998). As Farr (1998) argues, brands that create strong attitudinal bonds with the consumer through investing in rational, emotional and saliency based advantages are likely to be worth more to their owners in the future than brands that are bought on availability or pricing. Copley and Hudson (2000) use the argument that long-term brand-building requires that manufacturers invest a great deal of time and money developing communications between the brand and the desired customer. As television and other forms of media become increasingly cluttered, the manufacturer and the advertiser have sought more sophisticated methods of communicating with, and capturing, their customer. This is linked to the idea that, historically, advertising was thought to be sufficient, then in the late 1980s and early 1990s quality and service were deemed the best way of creating brands (Doyle, 1989). Sponsorship offers new ways of reaching targets or extending brands because of its unique properties.

The scope of sponsorship

Sponsorship's potential

With the clutter now associated with modern media communications, sponsorship seems a good way for the brand to fight through and regain the customer and the consumer's attention. Apart from the more aloof question as to whether sponsorship should be more corporate philanthropy than commercial and the irrefutable argument that sponsorship should be managed professionally (for the benefit of all concerned), there are numerous other directions for thought. Bennett (1998) asks: should we be worried about being viewed as exploitative with negative connotations? Which level should sponsorship be used at – brand, SBU, organizational/corporate? Should the sponsorship be singular and therefore substantial or spread (perhaps too thinly)? There are, therefore, many ways to proceed in this rich area.

There is an opportunity to clarify the motives of both the sponsor and the sponsored engaging in a sponsorship deal where there may or may not be some sort of symbiosis occurring. Research by the author (Copley, 1999) explored the notion that the situation has arisen in the past whereby the consumer has liked the advertising but could not remember the brand and asked, 'Could this happen with sponsorship messages?' Propositions, which can be derived from the various stages of the hierarchy of communications effects model, i.e. from the cognitive, affective and behavioural stages, were derived as being:

- to do with memory, recall and so on, and therefore issues such as awareness, for example consumers do not remember the brand that sponsors their favourite television programme

- to do with attitudes and feelings and therefore issues such as liking, desire and so on, for example consumers dislike such forms of television sponsorship

- to do with actions and therefore things such as purchase, for example consumers do not buy brands that sponsor television programmes.

It is contended that brands can create strong attitudinal bonds and they are worth the cost of investment and that sponsorship has unique properties that can be used to great effect. Brand sponsorship works by enhancing the consumer choice process through positive association with events, causes and so on. There is, therefore, a symbiotic relationship between sponsor, sponsee and consumer.

The consumer gains through a better understanding of the attributes of the sponsoring brand. For the sponsor and sponsee, the key question is 'how does this work in terms of both awareness (recall) and involvement/emotion (expressed preference in terms of enhanced brand image)?' – directly because of the sponsorship.

It is, however, recognized that this does not exist in a vacuum. It has to be looked at within differing settings to reflect different situations, for example product categories or consumption contexts. The movement is, therefore, from awareness to attitudes (including strength of attitudes) to actual purchase. This reflects Hansen and Scotwin's (1995) contention that 'attitudes are shaped toward the brand within an environment' or Quester and Farrelly's (1998) equation of 'strong emotional response + positive mood = increased value attached'. Consideration of involvement should also be included, especially Quester and Farrelly's (1998) 'threshold of involvement', where waste can occur beyond a specific point. Also, the 'increased frequency of exposure will lead to enhanced expressed preference' (Nicholls, Roslow and Dublish, 1999), whereby the sponsoring brand has 'mentally desirable characteristics' is of interest here.

It is possible to deduce that sponsorship has a positive effect on attitudes towards brands but the strength of attitude will depend upon a number of variables such as length of time in front of the message, and the intensity and strength of involvement with brands and activities. The greater the involvement with the activity the less chance the sponsorship message has of getting across. If this is the case then sponsorship can be used to change attitudes. If not then perhaps sponsorship should be viewed rather more simply, it being more to do with things like awareness, i.e. the cognitive aspects of the hierarchy of effects model and should be used in conjunction with other techniques. Research by the author (Copley and Hudson, 2000) explored this area in two ways. First, respondents were asked a series of questions to ascertain their opinions about brands and branding but the questions were designed so as to be able to derive opinion about sponsorship without respondents knowing this. Second, rating scales were devised using a series of statements such as 'the brands on offer are of excellent quality' and respondents were asked to rate each statement according to how strongly they agreed or disagreed with each for their favoured brand. Respondents were asked to do this in a number of given settings such as 'Eating out for a snack'. There is some evidence in this research to suggest that sponsorships have a positive effect on attitudes towards brands. The study did not provide any support for the notion that strength of attitude will depend upon variables such as length of time in front of the message but did suggest, however, a relationship between intensity and strength of involvement with brands and activities. The study also found there was an apparent link between recalled brand and preferences, suggesting that when recall is high, brand preference will be high and where recall is low, preference will be low. The evidence also supported the notion that brands can have positive mental characteristics and, where this is the case, strong attitudes are developed towards chosen brands. The study supported the idea that the greater the involvement with the activity the greater the chance the sponsorship message would work.

Since there is a paucity of research in the area of behaviour, it may well be the case that sponsorship should be viewed by practitioners rather more simply, it being more to do with things like awareness and liking brands rather than being able to predict actions. This is an important consideration when managers are dealing with objectives in a campaign.

VIGNETTE

Vodafone, Manchester
United and Ferrari:
shared visions, global
appeal and sponsorship

The appeal of sponsorship as a tool to be used in achieving corporate and marketing goals is now well recognized. Carol-Ann Heavey, corporate sponsorship manager of Ford Europe is quoted as saying 'for the first time ever we have a central medium through which we can drive all Ford's UEFA Champions League activity. This launch is a crucial part of Ford's overall strategy, allowing us to interact individually with both our current and future customers' (Customercomms.com, 2002). The central medium of a fully integrated media campaign was the website, www.destinationfootball.com (a new site is currently under construction). The campaign included advertising but also featured none other than sponsorship as a key tool.

Ford is not alone in their attitude to sponsorship. The Vodafone UK/Manchester United co-operation was set up in order to help achieve corporate- and brand-level goals. With these two companies, both of which have global appeal and are leaders in their field, it is easy to see why corporate and marketing communications are important. The brand vision for Vodafone is making life easier for customers but for Manchester United it is the relentless pursuit of excellence. Vodafone sell to everyone – private individuals, small businesses and large organizations. Manchester United have 50 million fans globally and an estimated 6 million in the UK. It is one of the most watched football club sides globally, with 139 countries televising games.

Vodafone is a leading global brand and in some markets is the sole brand. Brand strategy includes local branding, appearing to follow the mantra 'think global act local'. Vodafone has grown through geographic expansion, the acquisition of new customers, retention of customers and through increasing usage via technological innovations, including wireless application protocol (WAP). It is estimated that by 2005 there will be 1 billion global users and two-thirds will be WAP enabled which will go beyond the current photo-messaging and allow all sorts of activities including video conferencing. The global strategy employed classically provides cost savings from standardization in many areas of operation. Vodafone's aim is to be market leader and this is product led, the brand often being ahead of customer thinking. Part of this is achieved by listening to the customer and feeding back into the strategy.

Many markets for mobile phones are now mature so that it is a necessity to add value. Part of this is in the area of how the brand is communicated and part of this is the sponsorship deal with Manchester United. This was finalized in February 2000. It is effectively a commercial alliance that has Vodafone as principal sponsor as well as being telecommunications and equipment service partner to the club. The four-year deal began in June 2000 and took Vodafone into markets hitherto unknown. Clearly the deal exhibits symbiosis but Vodafone in particular are paying for:

1 *Enhancement of brand awareness and image* – Vodafone logo on playing kit, the right to use the Manchester United logo on promotions, advertising, perimeter signage at home games (not Champions League) and involvement in other material such as the match programme. Clearly, association with Manchester United brings excitement, passion and so on to the Vodafone brand, which helps retain customers and win new ones.

2 *Extension of range of products and services* – the Manchester United connection has been a way of directly increasing sales and adds a range of Manchester United products to the repertoire, creating brand awareness globally.

3 *Adding value to services* – the official mobile service for the club is 'manUmobile', which allows fans extra, direct access to news and so on, and they can use www.manumobile.com from a personal computer. Text messages are used to keep fans informed about a host of issues. Vodafone have been able to use this UK base to enhance its own brand globally.

The deal has cost Vodafone £30 million over four years and, of course, the company needs to make sure that objectives are achieved, something, according to The Times 100, that looks to be the case.

Vodafone's sponsorship deal with Ferrari is about similar issues. It is about awareness of the brand but also about positive corporate PR. It is about positioning but also about internal feel and obtaining hospitality facilities. Again Vodafone have used their technological expertise to good effect but it is the high-profile exposure that features with particular sponsorship. Vodafone have 360 million television viewers per race and 100 million customers worldwide in twenty-eight countries. The deal was announced at the Monaco Grand Prix (25 May 2001) and by 6 February 2002 the Vodafone car was launched at Ferrari headquarters in Italy and the following March was team raced in the Australian Grand Prix. Vodafone expect Ferrari to be an ambassador for the Vodafone brand. The qualities of being dependable, empathetic, innovative, a 'can do' brand and having vitality and life are the essence of the brand. In a similar vein to the manUmobile example above, Ferrari fans can subscribe to Multimedia Messaging Services – news, chat, games and so on. There is also the Vodafone Race Track racing simulator. These are value-adding connections that are 'the batteries that make the toys work'. Ferrari and Formula One provide Vodafone's customers with updates texted to Vodafone mobiles for each 2003 race with a range of race information. With Vodafone Live!, images are available and there are the voices of Schumacher, Barrichello and others talking about races, testing and other relevant issues.

More broadly the entire integrated communications campaign includes advertising around 'Vodafone Live!' and mobile Internet. Public relations is linked to the sponsorship deals with positive press coverage one of the goals.

Sources: Adapted from Customer Communications (2002); The Times 100 (2003).

STOP POINT

Think about why Vodafone sponsored Manchester United and why Manchester United wanted the association. Think about whether or not the partnership has resulted in objectives being met. A key question might be, 'Are Manchester United and Ferrari compatible sponsorship deals for Vodafone?' Consider the possibility of problems surfacing for Vodafone after a period of time given that not everyone supports, follows or even likes Manchester United or Ferrari. Do you agree that intelligent sponsorship involves much more than putting the sponsor's name on a football shirt or racing car?

Sponsorship in practice

Measurement considerations

The world of sponsorship is increasingly complex and 'big business' and so, with large budgets involved, inevitably sponsorship has come into play in terms of opportunity to see and the sponsorship's effectiveness. The former is relatively easy to measure in terms of reach and frequency with some agencies claiming that both quantitative and qualitative audience research can be used but that the quality of audience delivery is important as is the impact on brand perceptions (Thompson and Vickers, 2002). The sponsorship insight tool combines detailed audience profiling with comprehensive understanding of the relevance of the partnership. Olivier and Kraak (1997), interested in the consumer response to sponsorship exposure, conclude among other things that sponsorship exposure can be as effective as television advertising in terms of brand name recall but challenge the industry sponsorship exposure value norm that uses a down weighting factor to measure effectiveness. Olivier and Kraak also advocate Research International's Sponsorship Publitest tool as a pre- or post-test effectiveness measurement tool.

Choice considerations

The type of event, cause or programming is always a consideration as is the quality, reach, length, media impact and geographic scope. Strategic fit, protection against ambush, the amount of support, the ability to integrate into the mix, the interest of employees, cost, whether cash or in-kind and implications for employees, are all important choice considerations. As mentioned earlier, the money spent varies enormously, especially if money for supporting communications is included. Appropriation runs from millions (for example Coca-Cola and the Olympics) to very little (for example a smaller firm engaging with minority sports).

The ability to measure the effect of sponsorship is important. Numbers can be physically counted at an event and television audiences measured, therefore reach and frequency can be ascertained. The communication effects can be measured (as with Quester and Farrelly above), usually in the area of awareness and interest rather than behaviour, as discussed. Focus has been placed on sponsor confusion or whether there is a clear link between brand and event. A number of authors use 'PIE', the persuasive impact equation, i.e.:

$$\text{Persuasive impact} = \text{strength of link} \times \text{duration}$$
$$\times \text{ gratitude felt due to link}$$
$$+ \text{ perceptual change due to link} \qquad (14.1)$$

This suggests that the more the target is aware of the link and the longer it is in front of them and the more positive the perceptual change is about image, then the more impact the sponsorship will have. More simply, sales or market share could be a measure of the effectiveness of the sponsorship deal. As with advertising and other communications tools, feedback is an option via research and evaluation.

Types of sponsorship

The type of sponsorship chosen will depend to a large extent on top-level management involvement and whether the investment required is put in at the corporate or marketing level or both. De Pelsmaker, Geuens and Van Den Bergh (2001) offer evidence that sport sponsorship is more akin to advertising at the marketing level but cause-related sponsorship is more akin to corporate PR. This has led to change regarding sponsorship and the goals behind investing in it.

Global projects like yacht races are more relational than the many more tactical events that could be chosen. Many forms of sponsorship exist. Motor racing might involve TagHeuer timekeeping, as might water polo (Dunhill) and golf (Dunhill) or the London Marathon (Flora). Most are long-term associations and so ride the storm of recession and budget-cutting so that sponsorship becomes a means of defending a market and providing triggers for recall and recognition.

Most of the money spent is spent on sport, followed these days by television programming, with arts now a close third. Most sponsorship deals can be put into these boxes. But other sponsorships exist across a wide variety of projects, a most infamous example being the ill-fated London Millennium Dome. Sponsorship is not, therefore, strictly cause-related, arts or sport. It may be the environment with which the sponsor has a vested interest, such as a car manufacturer sponsoring motoring or aspects of the community that are not causes as such but which release money to be spent on other things. As an example of this Fill (2002) cites Volkswagen (VW) sponsoring the attire of 'lollypop people', normally funded by local authorities that can then put the resource into something else. This is an interesting twist in social marketing campaigns whereby a sponsor provides for a slot with a social message, for example a car company could sponsor an anti-speed campaign.

Cause-related sponsorship

Cause-related sponsorship may have a positive effect with people willing to pay more or to brand switch but as much evidence exists to the contrary as it does to support this proposition. Sponsorship of causes needs to be understood in terms of both sponsor and sponsee practitioner perspectives. It is also important to understand the effects of sponsorship on the sponsor's customers and consumers generally. Donor motivations and other processes lead to corporate donations and possibly partnerships or strategic alliances and 'lateral partnerships' (between causes which may or may not be in competition), where 'strategic fit' is seen as pre-eminent. Research by the author (Copley, 1999) enabled the construction of a 'strategic and lateral partnership/alliance' conceptual model. This attempts to explain how symbiosis is increasingly becoming important to the success of such activities and how changes from within the causes themselves are driving them towards alliances in a more positive way.

As sponsee practitioners become increasingly more professional with very different expectations to their predecessors, this is not only inevitable but good news for better, more efficient use of resources. It appears that this is due to the ways in which the donations process works and the consequent approaches that are perceived to be required of the various charitable organizations. While there appears to be a tendency towards positive messages in the 'consumer' field, it also appears that people can be made sensitive to both emotional and rational appeals and both negative and positive messages (Belhout and Copley, 1997). With corporate giving, enhancing the corporate image appears to be the overriding concern (Savage, 1996) but with movement towards more tangible goals being in evidence (Sargeant and Stephenson, 1997). Things like the *Guardian*'s 'Investment Challenge', a scheme to help investors put money into Barnardo's (Guardian, 1998), underline the move toward legitimacy of supporting causes. Moreover, it appears that to help causes in what they promote the marketer should perhaps first consider a fundamental approach to segmentation and targeting (Sargeant, 1996; Denney, 1997; Sargeant and Stephenson, 1997) but should also consider much more than advertising message strategy in terms of integrated communication. More generally, causes appear to be becoming more marketing orientated but the incidence of this is still comparatively low (i.e. when compared with commercial organizations), this being linked to, for example, size of the organization, ideological or attitudinal barriers posed by management and also an identified time lag which has affected performance (Balabanis, Stables and Phillips, 1997). Issues such as strategic fit and matching and becoming more like a business (although not necessarily more business-like) where the begging bowl is replaced by a systematic approach (Bird, 1997), are surely important within this more general context and perhaps there is a the need for both cause and donors to focus directly on an integrated marketing communications approach which, for Stewart and Short (1997), can be brought about through sponsorship.

Cause-related marketing communications

The pressures upon practitioners involved with the marketing of causes generally may not allow them to take full advantage of approaches that might well help them better understand the variety of processes that surround them. An initial analysis of communication theory provides the important elements a communicator should consider in order to enhance the effectiveness of communication with various audiences. The role of marketing communications in cause-related organizations is not, as some may assume, only to solicit donations. Of course, an important function of, say, advertising might well be to create public awareness of the problems the cause is confronting as well as seeking to motivate the public to donate financially. The need for advertising has become all the more important because of restrictions on the amount allocated through government funding and the competitive market situation. The ability to advertise on television increases advertising's crucial role in building awareness and for securing future support in terms of covenants, legacies, trusts and so on, but most advertising has been, and is expected to continue to be, conducted through local and national press, because of lower costs than those associated with television (Campaign, 1993; Key Note, 1993). This, of course, is by no means seen as a hard and fast rule. There are a growing number of examples to the contrary, as in the case of a major children's charity running a television campaign as part of an integrated effort. Added to this are the dynamics across marketing such as the activities in retailing and distribution of, say, Oxfam, or the recognition that there has been an overemphasis on tactical approaches, say, selling to raise funds, perhaps at the expense of more strategic approaches. Buttle (1996) adds that expectations have also been greatly raised with respect to response (to appeals) rates (from perhaps 2 per cent a few years ago to perhaps 25 per cent) and that 'Charities and other voluntary bodies have also to understand that they must compete for donations, grants or other contributions and that they need to satisfy their customers' requirements more effectively, whoever their customers might be'. In short there is a need for not-for-profit organizations to move to a more strategic perspective.

Cause-related marketing sponsorship

A key question is 'Why sponsorship?' For Stewart and Short (1997) there are five good reasons companies should consider sponsorship: the decline of the effectiveness of advertising; the decrease in government funding of non-profit organizations; the requirement to (be seen to) achieve objectives and therefore become strategy-orientated; sponsorship makes news; and sponsorship offers new ways of getting through the clutter.

Often little is really known of the activities of companies in this area beyond the contents of the company report, talk of deserving charities and social responsibilities with over £10 million worth of 'community involvement'. However this is 'cash and kind' with £9.8 million worth of cash and staff secondments, the latter being, typically, a management secondee like the one to Marie Curie Cancer Care to develop a merchandising strategy for the cause's retailing operation. It also mentions the £400 000 raised by employees, taking the total to £10.2 million. These kinds of activities, the report argues, are the reasons why M&S won the Business in the Community Award for Corporate Commitment. Thus the well-known and established PR value of the company report remains intact in this example. More can be derived from the example of the Norwich Union/St John's Ambulance tie-up, as described by Mawdsley (1998), which appears to be sponsor driven, where the sponsee is almost incidental apart from the Saatchi and Saatchi research that preceded the decision and allowed for strategic fit. Here the benefits for both parties are derived from symbiosis but appear to be greater for the sponsor than the sponsee, making the activity much less of a partnership. Also from this the role of agency (Saatchi and Saatchi) as 'marriage' broker is clear. The whole thing is driven from the sponsor's end with the sponsor's advertising agency doing the driving. As Farquarson (1998) points out, 'dating agencies' may be resented by fundraisers but until now such agencies have been seen as being crucial to success and, presumably, are the reason why Saatchi and Saatchi have over 120 causes signed up to its particular unit. Successful matching, then, is central to success of the particular activity and beyond.

Strategic partnerships/alliances through symbiosis

There are, therefore, mutual benefits to be had through the creation of strategic partnerships/alliances. Survey evidence (Research International for Business in the Community) as reported by Savage (1996) seems to indicate that it is the enhancement of corporate image rather than to increase sales that is the goal behind cause-related marketing sponsorship. Other survey evidence by MORI (again as reported by Savage, 1996) suggests that nearly three-quarters of UK consumers are more likely to buy from companies who support charities. Business in the Community report that 86 per cent of consumers claim they would change brand or retailer to buy products linked to a good cause and that 70 per cent of company chairmen see cause-related marketing as a high growth area (Farquarson, 1998). Denney (1997) distinguishes between those whom the cause benefits and those who donate – both business/corporate sponsors and the public – and recognizes the need to understand target segments, lifestyles and so on, advocating the need to understand why recipients of messages might not behave in a pro-social manner and the need to attack the barriers which inhibit communication. While Denney shows this to work for Barnardo's, it is clear from a survey of the charity sector by Sargeant (1995) that, with the exception of a few of the large organizations involved, market segmentation is not part of the thinking – or at least the practice – of most other charity organizations.

Sargeant and Stephenson (1997) identify two distinct types of corporate givers: opportunists, who see staff morale-building, corporate image enhancement and general awareness-building as what they get in exchange for corporate giving; and philanthropists, who appear to be only interested in the cause and therefore do not look for exchange for their corporate giving – which tends to be considerably less on average for philanthropists than for opportunists. Buttle (1996) also identifies the 'in-kind' philanthropist where the donation is not money but the offer of support in other ways, say, a service or management expertise. There is also the mutual benefit derived from two or more charities sharing resources – or costs/expenses – which Buttle calls 'lateral partnerships' and which can exist even if partners compete for the same donor support. Clearly, there is scope for consideration of some form of relationship marketing model here, along with the recognition that such relationships are not necessarily panaceas (see, especially, Blois, 1997). The changing relationship between charities and corporate donors is at an important phase of its development. If causes are more business-like then corporate donors can be said to be more strategy-minded when it comes to donating to or sponsoring causes. For Bird (1997), if it is more desirable to create social businesses than to create beggars, and if it is more desirable to be self-sustaining than appealing to businesses and the public for alms, then this requires a fundamental shift away from dependency. This means learning the art of self-sustainment in order for this social transformation (whether in the UK or Ethiopia) to take place. Bird therefore advocates paying taxes and bragging about it – to remove the stigma of 'Mr Blair's giving age' and to try to create a social engine within business, 'social capitalism' to create jobs and so on – a move towards a more realistic symbiotic relationship between cause and corporate donor.

Matching and strategic fit is now firmly on the agenda of both sponsors and sponsees. The strategic partnership idea is not a new phenomenon but it could be said to be changing and evolving. Partnerships are emerging between very different causes, say, between a children's charity and an animal cause where the partnership is really about connections between the cycle of domestic violence and animal abuse, and where the partnership offers a number of advantages to each partner which they would not have if left in isolation. This is on the one hand a lateral partnership between two causes as full members of a 'humane society'. Savage (1996) comments from the sponsor viewpoint citing Lever, who is said to believe in the search for 'a partner suitable for your own needs', i.e. that charities should systematically search out the right partner. An example of the afore mentioned is that of Cadbury and Save the Children where a strong relationship has developed. There is a lack of systematic research in this area but it appears to be a very attractive proposition for the likes of Cadbury who apparently believe that cause-related marketing 'will become a natural part of all successful businesses'. There is an opportunity (some might say a strong case) for marketing research to establish its own role. In other words, if organizations like Cadbury, Lever and so on are to consider becoming involved with cause-related marketing (as opposed to, say, event-related marketing), they should be considering not only matching and strategic fit but also where research (and presumably evaluation) fit into the whole process. This would then allow for, in terms of corporate or brand image, three things: consistency in style; consistency in tone of voice; and consistency in personality projected (Sargeant, 1998). There is a clear indication that causes are becoming more aware of their own brand potential, and the potential for great success but also for disaster. As Farquarson (1998) underlines, cause-related marketing demands a quantifiable payback whereby the cause's good name, values and image must help sell products. At the same time causes should beware of prostituting themselves while in the process of exploiting opportunities. Farquarson quotes one cause practitioner as saying 'any charity which allows its good name to be raped is incompetent', a sentiment which to many is an understatement. Alternatively, from the sponsor viewpoint, it should be clear that it is no longer the case of throwing money at a good cause because it 'looks good'. As Pope (1998) suggests, sponsorship can work and sponsorship awareness can affect consumption values but this needs to be clarified. Pope therefore suggests that sponsors need to fully examine what aspects of particular values they wish to affect prior to signing up to a sponsorship programme.

Donor–cause relationships within corporate and marketing strategy

This leads to consideration of just what a sponsorship programme is and how it can be planned and managed. A rather conventional, linear view is expressed by Stewart and Short (1997) regarding the 'sponsorship step process' that has eight hierarchical steps to be followed in a linear fashion and which follows the decision sequence model approach that provides a framework for the management of sponsorship activities. Challenging this conventional linear view of the planning process, Moss and Warnaby (1996) attempt to build a conceptual model that places PR at the heart of strategic management but with a model that is much more relational with the environment that surrounds the organization. This provides a schema to describe the role of public relations in the strategic management of organizations that can be usefully considered here, especially from the viewpoint of donor organizations, i.e. a more specific focus on a tool – sponsorship in the form of corporate donation – which is viewed by most as belonging in the corporate or marketing PR box.

VIGNETTE

Cause-related sponsorship, matching and strategic fit

The idea of matching and strategic fit within the sponsor/sponsee partnership/ alliance along with lateral activities between causes is a logical one for practitioners to pursue. Research suggests that only slight differences exist between corporate donor and cause practitioners in terms of their views in this area, depending upon the size of the organizations concerned. Alliances may be the way forward where cause and donor are equals and where there is recognition of the fundamental difference between the terms 'partnership' and 'alliance'. This might appear to be playing semantics but alliance motives are important from both sides. The interrelationships between the sponsor and sponsee clearly matter and, in particular, there appears to be a strong advocation of planning campaigns so that nothing clashes, and in this there is a strong resonance with Crane's (1998) 'green alliance' situation. Interrelationships between causes are important also in that it is felt that causes can coexist, not compete head on. Therefore the lateral partnerships (Buttle, 1996) are recognized but there is a need to clarify just what terms like 'partnership', 'alliance', 'co-operation' and 'collaboration' really mean. What really matters are the issues of importance as seen by the parties concerned. This includes the recognition that causes are often branded and that such brands have value.

Good (or bad) matching of sponsor/sponsee with issues such as cultural differences is seen as having the potential to make or break a match. The elements of the usual micro and macro environments also begin to show (and again there appears to be a good deal of resonance with green issues).

Research into practitioners' views reveals:

1   That such people are concerned with 'donor fatigue' and that this might be present and that in times of crises the hard-hitting negative appeal is necessary to get a result. Also the idea of different appeals for different people being necessary in the light of segmented or fragmented markets is held. Certainly both negative and positive appeals were seen as having a place in the bigger picture, the latter for underlying stability and longer-term planning.

2   Corporate giving as corporate image enhancement or philanthropy is not as simple as the literature might have us believe. Certainly a correlation is perceived between size of company and reasons for donating. Smaller companies are perceived as being likely to donate for personal/emotional reasons, whereas with larger companies there is a tendency to donate for non-emotional/objective/professional reasons which are performance related. The possibilities of 'putting something back in' features strongly but with care given to the nature of the cause the organization donates to and benefits of the brand as owned by the cause (as opposed to the donor) in terms of brand damage.

3   Causes generally market themselves in terms of segmentation and marketing communications (or, more accurately, advertising and the move away from mere advertising towards more of an integrated marketing communications situation). More specifically, there is concern for tangible outcomes in marketing terms, the perception being that in some cases (smaller) causes do no formal marketing at all. Larger organizations are perceived to market themselves much more like commercial organizations – something that is in direct opposition to some views in the literature. A time element was introduced in terms of short-, medium- and long-term activity – a reference to planning (or lack of it) generally but to marketing planning in particular. Waste of resources surfaced as a key issue where charities might be perceived to simply send material out on a mass basis with the resultant waste and loss of message, because 'what they do is poor'.

4   Resistance to causes is more business-like because of the people involved and their values expressed but that causes must be seen to be business-like and not wasteful. Causes have needs; businesses have resources. The question is, 'can businesses afford to miss some of the opportunities in this area?', to which the answer is probably 'yes'. To the question 'should they not consider such opportunities?', the answer is probably no. Causes should hang on to their values but at the same time causes should be setting goals, targets and so on as a fundamental activity.

5   Competitive market situations and the role of government in terms of resources and controls are dependent on the size of the cause and of the constituency in which it operates. Specific concern for the ability to do things like 'advertise on television' and 'limited resources' is prevalent. Some causes simply cannot compete with others or deal with unwanted and unmanageable growth without extra resources. There is clear concern for the 'size of the pie' in consumer donation terms. There is concern too

about 'overlap' and 'waste'. Causes appear to prefer alliances rather than partnerships.

6 The assumption that mutual benefits are to be gained from partnership formation and just what is in it for the donor and for the recipient appears to be goodwill (and hence corporate image-building and enhancement) on the part of the donor where direct sales increases are not expected at all. Causes appear not to be looking necessarily for money injections exclusively, but appear to be quite interested in receiving in-kind donations (equipment, etc.). Measurement of outcomes of any donation is seen as essential (if difficult) for both parties. The key benefit for causes' informants is seen as being awareness, and for the donor also, but awareness in a sort of omnipresent way – being seen as an organization that does 'good works' and provides real benefit on a long-standing basis.

7 The nature of the relationship, expectations of outcomes including which business functions would be of importance, and the role of matching/ marriage broking if any are important. The reason appears to lie in the synergy that is available to both parties within a symbiotic relationship where the two can meet. Notions of 'stake-holding' and 'alliance' are welcome; both causes and donors are more cautious on the definition of matching and strategic fit. This reflects the relationship marketing literature view on the problem with the marriage analogy. The relationship is not so much a marriage as an affair – a different kind of relationship with different needs and so on. Therefore, a role for a partnership or alliance professional is identified (as opposed to a marriage broker) who might come from the Confederation of British Industry (CBI), the government, the Charity Commissioners, trade associations – some organization or body that can act as a facilitator that has objectivity and other requisite qualities. A key concern from both sides is of becoming involved with something that was (or might become) inappropriate. Concern is expressed from both the cause and donor informants (most of the latter being involved in SMEs) that a sensible choice of broker be made from organizations beyond PR or advertising agencies. The size of the company is important in terms of the ability of a small firm to make a large enough contribution to be considered as a real sponsor.

Sources: Adapted from Buttle (1996); Copley (1998; 1999); Crane (1998).

STOP POINT

Think about this alliance (as opposed to relationship) model. Think also about why donors should consider actually segmenting/categorizing the potential causes, why market causes too should segment/categorize in some way the donor market, and why causes should also segment/categorize the causes market in order to achieve 'lateral alliances'. This would pave the way for a much clearer symbiosis and there may well be a role for some sort of 'alliance broker' in both these cases. The resultant corporate and marketing (including, of course, corporate and marketing communications) activities might well be a naturally integrated approach that would reflect an effective and efficient set of alliances. The setting up of such alliances should involve practitioners from either side being aware of their environments thus allowing them to be able to use research effectively as part of that process – aided, of course, by an appropriate broker.

Event-related sponsorship

This includes any kind of event but is usually either sport related or arts related, this latter category including rock/pop music events. Events can be sponsored in cash or in kind. Most of the money in sponsorship is spent on sport, followed by the arts, but in some countries television programming has caught up with or exceeded cause-related sponsorship. Compared with advertising, event sponsorship is very cost-effective in terms of reaching a target. From opera to sports, event targets can be reached in order to meet several kinds of objectives. However, spending lots of money on deals that cannot be justified; alienation of some customers and potential customers by having a particular sponsor rather than a rival; mistakes if, say, a sponsored footballer or athlete gets into trouble; culturally unacceptable sports in some markets so that other national sports or stars have to be used, are all problem areas. More generally, some research indicates that spectators are less likely to pay attention to the sponsor than to the sport itself, which compounds difficulties in measuring effectiveness.

Sports sponsorship

Sports sponsorship was worth £400 million in the UK in 2001 (Admap, 2002), or £450 million according to Thompson and Vickers (2002). This is not far off the figure spent on radio advertising (£600 million). However, sports sponsorship is growing faster, with some sports being accused of being greedy and making great demands on sponsors. The problem for sponsors is that sports sponsorship is attractive, usually because of high media coverage and large audiences, it facilitates targeting with large targets of shared characteristics, and events are visible and there are a lot to choose from, especially for big corporations like Coca-Cola. Usually, sponsorship of an event precedes that of a team and then a league. Then an individual might follow but this is not always the case and certainly not in, for example, David Beckham's (the England footballer and captain, and Real Madrid player) case. Golf has been used to promote things like whisky (Johnny Walker at the Wentworth World Matchplay Championship), Toyota then got local golf involvement to build dealerships, and Guinness was promoted at the Rugby World Cup. During the 1999 Rugby World Cup the £4 million spent on sponsorship saw sales rising by 15 per cent during the cup with Guinness spending £16 million on communications to ensure the brand would benefit (Fill, 2002). Coca-Cola has exploited sponsorship of football (soccer) by the choice of sport but also the use of all forms of media PR, sales promotions and internal communication. For example, together with the retailer Sainsbury's, 3000 fans around the country at four venues were able to hold the trophy, even though England was not the host country (Earl, 2002). The Sydney 2000 Olympic year alone saw total sponsorships worth more than $1.4 billion (Quester and Thompson, 2001).

Ambush marketing

Ambush marketing is the association of an organization with an event without being an official sponsor so that through the use of the media they appear to be a big sponsor, or by sponsoring one team or one player or by overstating involvement the organization achieves a similar effect. This verges on the illegal. For example Sony sponsored ITV coverage of the Rugby World Cup and managed to get first mention on the programming even though Sony was not a sponsor of the event itself. Corporations like Coca-Cola will try to stop Pepsi ambushing them in this way and vice versa (De Pelsmaker, Geuens and Van Den Bergh, 2001).

Arts sponsorship

Business is now a key funder of the arts. Ten to fifteen per cent of all sponsorship is in this area and worth more than $650 million in the USA alone (Quester and Thompson, 2001). There was an upsurge of arts sponsorship during the 1980s. This has now slowed and, whereas it began as philanthropy, it mutated into activities such as corporate hospitality and making appeals to particular targets, for example women. Arts sponsorship is less expensive than sports sponsorship, generally speaking, and it involves many things from art galleries to music festivals to ballet and so on. Much sponsorship of the arts is to do with image-building by association. Mobile phones and a younger target saw the sponsorship by Orange of Glastonbury, but less obvious might be the example of Becks as sponsor of Gilbert and George and Damien Hirst to get at a younger audience. In-kind sponsorship – supporting local artists with materials, photocopying services and so on – is less common than it used to be. Given the risks involved in sponsoring sports or sports people, such as positive drugs testing or corruption, arts sponsorship can be an attractive proposition.

Brand sponsorship at dance music events is now worth tens of millions of pounds (Bagnall, 2002). If an organization wants to target youth, and Rizla, Durex, Carling and Smirnoff do, then sponsorship of such events is not only logical but allows the brand owner to communicate its proposition, develop style and tone, to sample and even sell, with opportunities to promote the brand to a wider audience outside the event. Bagnall (2002) cites Miller beer as an obvious example of this kind of sponsorship: Miller's Yacht Party in Ibiza offers clubbers a ticket to a one-off exclusive party on a privately chartered schooner. Research into more conventional arts sponsorship by Quester and Thompson (2001) reveals that, unlike advertising that is viewed as self-serving, arts sponsorship is perceived as facilitating the staging of performances that can be viewed and enjoyed for what they are. Before and after tests revealed a significant attitude shift, although Quester and Thompson concede that their research is general and 'many questions remain unanswered' such as whether particular demographic groups are more sensitive than others to sponsorship.

VIGNETTE

Thank goodness its Guinness: Guinness does it for the arts and sport

Sports sponsors normally seek audience reach and product/brand awareness through media exposure, whereas arts sponsors look towards image via community relations and hospitality. NTL's sponsorship of the British Lions tour to Australia in 2001 is a classically good example of sport sponsorship. The benefits sought by NTL were presence, awareness and integration. NTL had good awareness but not in terms of understanding what it did, especially since broadband for most people had no meaning. NTL consisted of a number of businesses and needed something to portray the organization as a cohesive one. If these were the primary benefits, then secondary benefits were synergy between the brands – passion, inspiration, the pinnacle – strategic fit, internal motivation and film production that would be usefully played elsewhere within the mix. Thus sponsorship was used effectively to bring brand awareness to the ABC1 target but also to motivate employees. The contract included shirt-branding and other signage, player appearances and a full squad appearance, website rights and behind-the-scenes rights.

The NTL mix included the 'Close up and personal' advertising campaign that used appropriate print and television vehicles to hit the target. In particular, a comprehensive guide to the British Lions tour was the subject of a *Sunday Times* supplement. The website, NTL.com/lions, allowed straight access to information and a giant advertisement was erected outside the Millennium Stadium, Cardiff, to coincide with the Six Nations' matches. Radio input was designed to bring fans 'Up close and personal' by having access to referees' comments and there were other web-based activities and more use of footage on the Lions' television channel. National and regional PR was undertaken using the players, resulting in over £2 million worth of media coverage (over £1 million press and nearly £1 million television). The results overall were more than satisfactory for NTL with good awareness scores and web click-through rates. During the tour there were nearly 1 million hits per week on the website and 100 000 games players. According to Karen Earl (2002) this well-conceived sponsorship was a success because of 'the way in which it was used by all the business divisions within the company'.

The sponsorship by Guinness of the Rugby World Cup is a different affair to the NTL/Lions tour. The 1999 deal was clearly seen as a success and the 2003 (under way at the time of writing) deal is likely to be also. In the UK the ITV network agreed a £4 million deal with Guinness for the sponsorship of television coverage of the 1999 World Cup and similar details of the 2003 deal will ultimately emerge. But this is not the only sport, or indeed sponsorship of events, Guinness is involved with, despite the merger with Grand Metropolitan and the formation of Diageo. Hurling may have been around since the thirteenth century BC and as an organized sport since 1884, but it was in 1995 when Guinness began its sponsorship of the All Ireland Hurling Championship, and brought together two uniquely Irish icons. The final is played in September each year. However, despite being the fastest field sport in the world, hurling, by the 1990s, was out of favour. Fans had turned to Gaelic football not least because of sponsorship. Hurling's ruling body, the GAA, realized they had to find sponsorship but not just any old sponsorship. They had to find the right one and Guinness was seen as ideal, not least because the Guinness brand was enjoying much success with a high-image profile. With over 1000 clubs and almost one-third of the population as members, hurling offered Guinness something quite substantial in return. The Guinness injection sponsors the sport on two levels. First, it has provided funds to the GAA to use to develop the game at all levels. Second, it has invested funds and marketing expertise in the promotion of hurling. Therefore, the Guinness sponsorship has been instrumental in raising the image and perception of the sport. The four key area tackled originally by this sponsorship were:

- changing the name of the championship (to include Guinness in the national and regional championships)

- linking in with a poster and television advertising campaign that was extended to tickets, programmes and so on. The consistent imagery throughout attempted to capture the spirit of the game and the public's imagination

- PR effort played towards the needs of journalists in terms of phones and other facilities, and a media guide was produced for all journalists, keeping them up to date and informed with contact points and so on. Match programmes provided a strong link between Guinness and each game

- an ongoing promotional programme including a launch at the beginning of the season and university scholarships are a fundamental part of the sponsorship.

Attendance figures for 1994 were 289 281 but by 1999 they were 543 335, with an increase of 50 per cent in participation (67 000 new players) and an increase in live televised matches (The Irish Times, 2000). The initial investment by Guinness for the first five years was a IR£7 million and this was increased to IR£10 million for the next five-year period.

Guinness is good at sponsoring sport. But they do sponsor other things, in fact a wide range of events including jazz (Guinness Cork Jazz Festival) and horse racing. In Cork while Guinness sponsors jazz, rival brand Murphy's sponsors the film festival. The jazz event is internationally renowned, has 40 000 visitors and is worth £40 million each year. Guinness spent £1 million in 2001 (Flood, 2001). Guinness's Michael Whelan reckons the Cork jazz event to be the top event in Europe and in the top five or six in the world. The Guinness money makes the event 90 per cent free to jazz lovers yet attracts top acts and it is claimed that the festival remains unchanged, with the whole of Cork behind it. Big names who have played the festival are, for example, Ella Fitzgerald and Dizzie Gillespie.

Meanwhile, in Wexford, Guinness have for the last thirty years been involved with the Wexford (opera) Festival as sponsors. Guinness has been joined by Unilever and Merril Lynch and despite a cut in its Arts Council grant, Wexford has continued to produce outstanding events and maintain its spirit of adventure in exploring lesser known operas. This is only possible on a non-commercial basis and is why the sponsorship is so important. Three main operas for 2003 were *Die Drei Pintos* (Mahler and von Weber), *Maria Del Carmen* (Granados) and *Svanda Dudak* (Weinberger). There were more than forty other events including highlight scenes from *L'Elisir d'Amore* (Donizetti), *Hansel and Gretel* (Humperdinck) and *Tales of Hoffman* (Offenbach). Others involved the Prague Chamber Choir, lunchtime recitals and concerts by the Belarus Philharmonic (O'Riordan, 2003). Apart from awareness, image enhancement is an important objective for Guinness and this form of sponsorship is an important tool in achieving that end.

Sources: Adapted from Earl (2002); Flood (2001); O'Riordan (2003); Quester and Thompson (2001); The Irish Times (2000); UK Business Park (2003).

STOP POINT

Explain the difference between the two forms of sponsorship – sports and arts – as outlined above. Distinguish between the NTL and Guinness approaches to these sporting events. Think about achieving awareness as well as image building and enhancement through sponsorship of the arts such as opera, jazz and other art forms, institutions and people.

Programme-related sponsorship and product placement

In a sense programme sponsorship is new, yet at the same time it is an old concept, especially in the USA where the 'soap opera' was born and well established by the 1980s. However, 'soap opera' is relatively recent to Europe but is growing. It might well be the case that public-owned television allows sponsorship of programming if not commercial advertising (as in Belgium, according to De Pelsmaker, Geuens and Van Den Bergh, 2001). There may be links between the sponsorship and celebrity endorsement if a principal actor becomes involved, but largely so far this has not been the case, and this should not be confused with the notable example of Ray-Ban/Tom Cruise/*Top Gun* but which is product placement. De Pelsmaker, Geuens and Van Den Bergh suggest that only long-term relationships produce positive effects (Belgian research). Certainly programme sponsorship is now valued at hundreds of millions in the UK (Fill, 2002, maintains the figure was £180 million in 2000) as compared with 1992 when sponsorship was worth just £11 or £12 million (Bryant, 1992). A fundamental point to make is the critical relationship between programming and the very nature of television. Links between programmes and brands at times may be difficult to make. Others are more than obvious. The fizzy drink brand, Tango, for a while sponsored the youth-orientated programme, *The Word*, with clear synergy for the particular target concerned. Others are not so easy to understand, such as the Prudential Assurance Company's sponsorship of Film on Four on British television's Channel 4, compared with the much clearer feel for Stella Artois's sponsorship of the same, the Belgian beer brand having sponsored this programme for several years now. One ethical argument has it that sponsorship is now so influential that, like its communications cousin, advertising, it can affect the nature of television programming so that programmes have to fit in with the needs of the sponsor and 'be like the brand'.

Programme sponsorship can only really work through association, and not try to be another way of advertising. For example, a client may want association with a sport where some of the glamour rubs off on the brand (Bryant, 1992). The sponsor's brand, if targeting is done well, is clearly identifiable with the programme's audience and can be more focused than advertising, since the sponsor's message is there right at the start and restart of the programme, as well as the end. Clearly, the audience profile has to match as closely as possible the brand target characteristics. Tracking research developed by the agency TSMS looks at, for example, brand and sponsorship awareness, television advertising awareness and the image of the sponsor of programming. The creation, maintenance and awareness of the brand and brand's presence on television is an accepted outcome of sponsorship but it is the appropriateness links and image transference that makes sponsorship more than spot advertising (Millman, 2000).

Product placement

Television and film have been used for a very long time for placing products in a particular context. The IKEA couch in a television programme or James Bond using a Philishave or BMW are examples of product (or brand) placement. The consumer is not necessarily aware that this is a deliberate act. Indeed, this is one of the technique's strengths, where it can be more potent than advertising but with more people noticing the product or brand without knowing it. This has been called 'subliminal product placement'. Research indicates that brand recall is stronger with product placement than with advertising but that a combination of both almost potentially doubles the effect. This will, of course, depend upon product categories. A brand can be incorporated into any script. In a film a protagonist may smoke a cigarette but not just any cigarette or drink a whisky but not just any old whisky, depending upon any sponsorship deal that has been cut. In a similar vein, in magazines a piece of fashion photography might be accompanied by a particular car marque or models wear particular clothes. This is a form of merchandising where the product or, more accurately, the brand is placed within a set.

Most product placement is thought of in terms of feature films and television programmes. The objective behind product placement is usually to build national recognition but it may be used to enhance brand image, bring excitement to the brand, especially where there is implied celebrity endorsement, in an (often) uncluttered environment. For this privilege companies have to pay and pay handsomely. Ray-Ban aviator glasses and Tom Cruise in *Top Gun* is a classic example, as is BMW in the Bond movies. The Bond cars are a particularly good example of the history of the development of product placement as a marketing tool. At first the makers of the films were told by manufacturers that they would have to pay for the cars they needed as part of the film script. It took a little while for this particular tail to stop wagging the dog, but eventually it did and the value of placing a product or a brand was realized. Belch and Belch (2004) list the *advantages* of product placement or tie-ins as exposure (can be billions of OTS), frequency or repeated exposure, good as a support medium, uses source association well, cost can be low but recall can be high, can be used to bypass regulations and product placements seem to be acceptable to people generally. *Disadvantages* are listed as high absolute cost (even if CPM is low), lack of guarantee of exposure time, limited appeal that is indirect, lack of control, lack of acceptance (some people do not accept the idea), there is competition for key placements and, finally, negative placements can occur, for example when a product is placed in a very negative setting within a film.

VIGNETTE

Why Cadbury and Corrie went hand in hand

The ITV network, like all television networks, does not want to lose viewers. There is evidence to suggest that BARB's (the official ratings researcher's) research might have underestimated audience size in the past. Research commissioned by Carat, a media agency and one of the top five media buyers in Britain, suggested that around 3.3 million viewers of *Coronation Street* are 'lost' meaning that, yearly, 40 million viewers of 'Corrie' are not accounted for. Carat claims that this could be costing ITV as much as £150 000 in advertising revenue for every 4-minute break because the lower viewing figures are putting off potential advertisers. On the one hand, the new BARB system, introduced in January 2002, has had its problems, with ratings considered so unreliable that a two-week blackout was imposed. The changing of the 5000-strong panel appeared to lead to up to 25 per cent of viewers suddenly being lost (Cozens, 2002). On the other hand, Cadbury are one of Carat's clients.

In 1996 Cadbury signed a £10 million deal with Granada, makers and broadcasters of the UK's premier soap opera *Coronation Street*. The existing deal is said to be worth £50 million over the period 2001–05. This is real relationship marketing in the sense of linkages between Cadbury's targets and Corrie audiences. Those aware of this regard the parties in higher esteem and the two partners appear equal. Many see Cadbury as being up to date and a community supporter[2] while others view Cadbury's efforts in the sponsorship of Corrie as tedious and downmarket such as the caricature of a man telling his po-faced wife that they're having egg and chips for tea 'in unfunny, tortured French' (Flett, 2003). Flett asks, 'C'mon Cadbury's – what's it all about?', thereby missing the point entirely (Millward Brown research suggests this to be 'the most favourable sponsorship relationship researched to date'). Corrie's average of 15 million viewers love the Cadbury 'characters', as the company prefers to call the Aardman Animation (Oscar winners for Wallace and Gromit) creations. These characters bring *Coronation Street* to life and are seen at the beginning, middle and end of each episode. These characters include a milkman, postman, the Corrie cat and a 'Jack Duckworth' pigeon, Jack being one of Corrie's key characters within the soap.

This is the biggest sponsorship deal on British television. Carat and Granada Media Sales struck a deal after extensive research had suggested a perfect balance between 'the integrity of the programme and the commercial expectations' of Cadbury. This has both a large audience and frequent exposure, achieving impact without 'wear out'. Tracking research by the agency TSMS revealed that the earliest days of the sponsorship provided improvements to an already fine image for Cadbury (Millman, 2000).

Advertising, sales promotions and PR activities play a part so that the sponsorship does not stand alone. The Cadbury 'master brand' and its brands such as Cadbury Cream Egg feature, and even seasonality factors that influence particular brands can be catered for, not least because this is a fifty-two weeks a year deal. There is even the possibility of product placement, with the Cadbury brands featuring as part of the props in the corner shop, an integral part of the soap's *mise-en-scène*.

Sources: Adapted from Cadbury company information (2003); Cozens (2002); Doherty (2000); Flett (2003); Millman (2000); Munster Express (2001).

STOP POINT

Everything points to the Cadbury-Corrie consumer sponsorship deal being just about the perfect match. Think about this matching process and the nature of target markets and television audiences. What would you suggest could improve this deal for either or both parties? What role, if any, would you advocate for product placement as part of the deal?

Assignment

Choose a car company that you feel would benefit from a sports sponsorship deal. Map out the communications objectives behind the sponsorship programme and the reasons why sponsorship would be a better choice in achieving these than advertising. Describe the targets for the sponsorship and the nature of activities that potentially would be undertaken. Highlight key advantages and disadvantages to such a deal and how its effectiveness might be monitored.

Summary of Key Points

- Marketing and corporate sponsorships are about relationships with various interest groups.

- Marketing sponsorship (as opposed to corporate sponsorship) has emerged as the commercial brand/product level function responsible for a set of activities that form the basis of a relationship between a sponsor and a sponsee.

- Sponsorship follows communication theory and can fit in with the integrated communications mix.

- Sponsorship is constantly changing and evolving. One constant is the need to evaluate its effectiveness.

- Objectives may vary with different forms of sponsorship. There are basically two broad objectives: on the one hand, to raise awareness and, on the other, to enhance image. A number of sub-objectives coexist with these.

- There are fundamental differences behind the use of different forms of sponsorship within the three broad categories of event, cause and programming.

- Sponsorship has a relationship with both product placement and ambush marketing.

Examination Questions

1 Distinguish between marketing sponsorship and corporate sponsorship. Explain, using examples, why the techniques used at both levels might be similar if not the same.

2 Explain what the word 'sponsorship' means. Distinguish between this and other forms of communication such as advertising or PR.

3 Discuss how sponsorship works in theory, using examples to illustrate.

4 Comment on the notion that sponsorship is changing and evolving using examples of instances where this is the case to illustrate.

5 Explain where sponsorship fits in the marketing communications scheme of things. Provide in your answer at least two examples of the interface between sponsorship and other elements of the communications mix.

6 Sponsorship comes in a number of forms. Explain the objectives behind sponsoring a sporting structure such as a football league.

7 Cause-related sponsorship can be used to achieve objectives very different from those of event sponsorship. Discuss this notion and illustrate with examples.

8 Explain the concept of television programming sponsorship. Choose an example of such sponsorship to illustrate why an organization might engage with this form of communications.

9 Discuss sponsorship practice in terms of the dangers of ambush marketing.

10 Explain how the effectiveness of sponsorship can be evaluated. Illustrate your answer with actual instances you are aware of.

Notes

1 Witcher et al. (1991), on organizational sponsorship, note from their research that while functional objectives for sponsorship generally differ, 'the primacy of the corporate image objective is manifest'. The indicators are, however, that since this research the situation could well have become different, depending upon the context the sponsorship is applied in. With organizational marketing this observation could well remain a truism.

2 It is quite well known that John Cadbury in 1824 founded Cadbury in Birmingham, England, this becoming a small family business that developed into a very large international company. Cadbury was a Quaker and his and his family's personal values became the hallmark of Cadbury Limited, although this is now part of Cadbury Schweppes plc.

References

Admap (2002). Sponsorship. *Admap*, **432**, October. www.warc.com

Bagnall, M. (2002). Event sponsorship: is the worst yet to come? *Admap*, **427**, April. www.warc.com

Balabanis, G., Stables, R. E. and Phillips, H. C. (1997). Market orientation in the top 200 British charity organisations and its impact on their performance. *European Journal of Marketing*, **31** (8), 583–603.

Belch, G. E. and Belch, M. A. (2004). *Advertising and Promotion*. 6th edition. Irwin/McGraw Hill.

Belhant, L. and Copley, P. (1997). Message strategies for promoting humanitarian causes in the UK. *Proceedings of the Academy of Marketing Conference*, Manchester University, pp. 1245–1249.

Bennett, R. (1998). Corporate philanthropy in France, Germany and the UK. *International Marketing Review*, **15** (6), 458–475.

Bennett, R. (1999). Sports sponsorship, spectator recall and false consensus. *European Journal of Marketing*, **33** (3/4), 291–313.

Bird, J. (1997). Let's do business with the underclass. *The Guardian*, 29 November, p. 21.

Bliois, K. (1997). Are business-to-business relationships inherently unstable? *Journal of Marketing Management*, **13**, 367–382.

Bryant, N. (1992). Breaking down the barriers. *Admap*, July. www.warc.com

Buttle, F. (1996). *Relationship Marketing*. Paul Chapman Publishing.

Cadbury company information (2003). At www.cadbury.co.uk.

Campaign (1993). Charity fatigue. *Campaign*, 14 May, 29–30.

Copley, P. (1998). Does 'strategic fit' have a key role to play in the marketing communications practice of UK charities? – preliminary results of a qualitative study. *Proceedings of the Academy of Marketing Conference*, Derby, Derby University.

Copley, P. (1999). Street walking with the Saatchis? Symbiosis through sponsorship in strategic alliances – a conceptual model from the humanitarian cause-related marketing field. In McAuley and Sparks (eds), *Proceedings of the Academy of Marketing Conference*, Stirling, University of Stirling.

Copley, P. and Hudson, J. (2000). Consumer perception of the brand/sponsorship relationship. In Mayer et al. (eds), *Proceedings of the Academy of Marketing Conference*, Derby University, Derby.

Cozens, C. (2002). TV ratings under fire after Corrie 'loses' 3m viewers. *Guardian Unlimited*, 30 January. www.guardian.co.uk/Archive/0,4271,00.html.

Crane, A. (1998). Exploring green alliances. *Journal of Marketing Management*, **14**, 559–579.

Crimmins, J. and Horn, M. (1996). Sponsorship: from management ego trip to marketing success. *Journal of Advertising Research*, **36** (4), 11–21.

Customer Communications (2002). Ford and the UEFA Champions League. At www.customercomms.com, accessed 1 March.

De Chernatony, L. (1998). Dynamic brands need dynamic methods of measurement. *Researchplus*, January, 4.

De Pelsmaker, P. Geuens, M. and Van Den Bergh, J. (2001). *Marketing Communications*. Financial Times Prentice Hall.

Denney, F. C. (1997). Advertising in the charities sector: a case of a large promotional campaign. *Proceedings of the 1st Academy of Marketing Conference*, Manchester Metropolitan University, Manchester, pp. 301–311.

Doherty, C. (2000). Tension builds as RTE and TV3 vie for rights to Corrie. *The Post.ie*, 6 August. www.archives.tcm.ie/businesspost/2000/08/06/story291616.asp

Doyle, P. (1989). 'Building successful brands: the strategic options', *Journal of Marketing Management*, **5** (1), 114–132.

Duncan Grehan Partners (2003). Sponsorship law. At www.duncangrehan.com/pages/english/advert1.html, accessed 28 October.

Earl, K. (2002). How sponsorship can always win. *Admap*, **432**, October, pp. 16–18.

Farquarson, A. (1998). Two causes, a single choice. Which one gets your cash? *Guardian*, 25 November, pp. 9–10.

Farr, A. (1998). How brand values sort the strong from the vulnerable. *Researchplus*, January, 12–13.

Fill, C. (2002). *Marketing Communications: Contexts, Strategies and Applications*. 3rd edition. Financial Times Prentice Hall.

Flett, G. (2003). The way I see it (chasing customers away). C-Outside. At www.coltas.co.uk/c_outside.

Flood, L. (2001). Corporate cash brings city to life. The Post.ie, 10 June. www.archives.tcm.ie/businesspost/2001/06/10/story300706.asp

Guardian (1998). Guardian investment challenge. *Guardian*, 31 October, pp. 14–15.

Gwinner, K. (1997). A model of image creation and image transfer in event sponsorship. *International Marketing Review*, **14** (3), 145–158.

Hansen, F. and Scotwin, L. (1995). An experimental inquiry into sponsoring: what effects can be measured? *Marketing and Research Today*, August, 173–181.

Key Note (1993). *Charities*. Key Note Publications.

Kitchen, P. and Erdogan, B. (1998). Managerial mindsets and the symbiotic relationship between sponsorship and advertising. *Market Intelligence and Planning*, **16** (6), 369–374.

Mawdsley, C. (1998). Measuring the effects of integrated campaigns. *Proceedings of the Advertising and Academia Seminar*, IPA, London, September.

Mazur, L. (1998). Getting the most bang for your media buck these days calls for a much smarter, more lateral approach – something too many marketers have yet to master. *Marketing Business*, July–August, 24.

Millman, I. (2000). Broadcast sponsorship works. *Admap*, April. www.warc.com

Moss, D. and Warnaby, G. (1996). Towards a strategic perspective on public relations. *Proceedings of the 1st International Conference on Marketing and Corporate Communications*, Glasgow, University of Strathclyde, pp. 63–74.

Munster Express (2001). Entertainment, TV review, soap money. At www.munster-express.ie/010119/fun3.htm, accessed 19 January.

Nicholls, J. A. F., Roslow, S. and Dublish, S. (1999). Brand recall and brand preference at sponsored golf and tennis tournaments. *European Journal of Marketing*, **33** (3/4), 365–387.

Olivier, A. and Kraak, M. (1997). Sponsorship effectiveness. What is driving consumer response? ESOMAR.

O'Riordan, D. (2003). Classic notes. The Post.ie, 5 October. www.archives.tcm.ie/businesspost/2003/05/10/story333774.asp

Pope, N. (1998). Consumption values, sponsorship awareness, brand and product use. *Journal of Product and Brand Management*, **7** (2), 124–136.

Quester, P. and Farrelly, F. (1998). Brand association and memory decay effects of sponsorship: the case of the Australian Formula One Grand Prix. *Journal of Product and Brand Management*, **7** (6), 539–556.

Quester, P. and Thompson, B. (2001). Advertising and promotion leverage on arts sponsorship effectiveness. *Journal of Advertising Research*, **41** (1), 33–47.

Sargeant, A. (1995). Market segmentation in the charity market sector – an examination of common practice. *Proceedings of the Marketing Education Group Conference*, Bradford, University of Bradford, pp. 693–702.

Sargeant, A. (1998). Charity giving: an exploratory model of donor behaviour. *Proceedings of the Marketing Education Group Conference*, Sheffield, Sheffield Halam University.

Sargeant, A. and Stephenson, H. (1997). Banishing the battleship ladies – the emergence of a new paradigm of corporate giving. *Proceedings of the 1st Academy of Marketing Conference*, Manchester, Manchester Metropolitan University, pp. 903–916.

Savage, M. (1996). Rich and needy in perfect partnership. *Research*, August, 20.

Shimp, T. E. (1997). *Advertising, Promotion and Supplemental Aspects of Integrated Marketing Communications*. Dryden.

Sleight, S. (1989). *Sponsorship*. McGraw Hill.

Stewart, D. and Short, S. (1997). Sponsorship: a facilitator of commercial communication. *Proceedings of the Academy of Marketing Conference*, Manchester Metropolitan University, pp. 1501–1504.

The Irish Times (2000). Sponsorship: a successful partnership between GAA and Guinness. *The Irish Times*, Business 2000 Millennium Edition.

The Times 100 (2003). Vodafone – Superbrand sponsorship. At www.tt100.biz, edition 8.

Thompson, I. and Vickers, S. (2002). Sponsorship: the real deal. *Admap*, **432**, October, 19–22.

UK Business Park (2003). Guinness company search. At www.ukbusinesspark.co.uk/guinness.htm.

Unilever (2002). Unilever to boost sponsorship spend? Press Office Unilever, 12 March.

Witcher, B., Gordan Craigen, J., Culligan, D. and Harvey, A. (1991). The links between objectives and function in organisational sponsorship. *International Journal of Advertising*, **10** (1). www.warc.com

CHAPTER

15

Planning and managing public relations

Chapter overview

Introduction to this chapter

The nature of PR is understood here to be at both the marketing and corporate levels. The techniques and their associated methods and tools such as press releases and receptions, exhibitions and trade shows (from the PR as opposed to sales promotion perspective) were dealt with in previous chapters. This chapter takes the general framework developed in Chapter 4 and facilitates application, via a decision sequence model in the PR management context.

Aims of this chapter

This chapter provides a case study that can be analysed with the aid of the material presented in Chapter 4. In particular, the framework presented at the end of that chapter is designed as a facilitation device for this purpose. After completion of this chapter the reader should be able to:

- explain the elements of the APIC system, as applied to PR, in broad DSM terms

- provide some critique of the adoption of such an approach

- provide a framework for the management of the PR function

- explain the communications mix that helped salvage Perrier and other brands from crises that enveloped them

- apply the above to the management of PR for such brands in pre and actual crisis situations.

A framework for managing advertising employing the APIC DSM model

As outlined in Chapter 4 the APIC DSM is a commonly used model that deals with both the 'art' and 'science' aspects of communication. A decision sequence framework is required to help plan PR in just the same way as any communication might be planned, but the difference is in the detail. The reader should refer back to the framework provided in Chapter 4 as an aid to analysis of the case given below.

A case of Perrier and other crises

Background

Perrier Vittel is the world leader in mineral water. This includes the brands Perrier, Vittel, Buxton, Pure Life, Aquarel and Calistoga. During the 1970s in the UK it was only 'cranks and foreigners' (*Financial Times* survey, as reported by Wilson, 1986) who bought mineral water in a bottle, but by the mid-1980s the mineral water market in the UK was worth £50 million with 88 million bottles sold. In one decade the market saw a 30 per cent growth. This was achieved, it is said, through the marketing efforts of Perrier where, for example, the shape of the bottle and other aspects of packaging were important factors (Wilson, 1986). However, it is conceded by those involved that the market was underdeveloped and there was a twofold need. First, a distribution base was required and would have to be built. Second, the need was to gain the classic awareness and trial among consumers so that there was a clear role for advertising from the beginning.

From the start the brand was, through advertising, characterized as chic, having quality and exclusivity. Leo Burnett had focused from the late 1970s on the playful word 'eau', French for water and a very useful copy tool. The result for a number of years was 'Eau la la', 'H2Eau', 'Bistreau' and so on. The original targets had been Francophiles, then the upmarket young until a broader market was created where the brand had a strong national presence and the message that other than Perrier, 'anything else is pseudeau'. The media had been posters but then the brand moved on to television with posters and quality magazines as support. Targeting with the latter was typically a clever tag line such as 'yoicks tally heau' for *Country Life* magazine or 'VDSQ? AC? Chateau' for *Decanter* magazine. The key to all this was Perrier's personality development that would help erode the massive resistance to bottled mineral water, with Perrier as champion to this cause.

Origins of the Perrier brand

Perrier is a great post-Second World War success according to its promoters, but it is the aforementioned period from the 1970s (half a million bottles sold in 1974) to the end of the 1980s (157 million sold in 1989) that is impressive. Clearly, the brand was very successful during the 1980s. In the UK alone during this period sales grew from 12 million bottles to 200 million bottles (Setford and Crispin, 1990). The brand's origins, however, go back to the turn of that century. In 1903 the urbane Englishman, St John Harmsworth, while holidaying in Provence, was introduced to the water from the village of Vergeze's spring by one Dr Perrier. Harmsworth called it the 'champagne of table waters', bought the spring, modelled the shape of the bottle on Indian clubs used for exercising and named the brand after the doctor. By 1933, when Harmsworth died, 19 million bottles had been sold, half of these exported. From then until 1990 Perrier was French family owned and all water originated from the source.

More on Perrier communications

Qualitative research had revealed the value of the French pedigree and the importance of the 'sparkling personality', 'unique elegance' and the chic, exclusive image. *Media* choice had started with posters (first 4-sheet then 48) with an initial budget of £400 000 for the UK. *Creatively*, Perrier became, through the use of the '*eaus*', 'what the French drink when they are not drinking', where there is 'no substitute for Perrier' but where the execution provided the right feel and simplicity to allow for personal interpretation. After a short relapse, 1984 saw the return of the 'eaus', this time on television. The suggestion was that in following Perrier the consumer was not part of the herd. A previous deviation into childlike animation was replaced with an adult theme around a distinctive, elegant brand with a soft and enticing French name. The actual product (water) was natural, clear and pure, and the 'eau' made it fun. The key, having built the brand franchise with Francophiles and yuppies was to make the brand accessible but not lose the magic. The 'eau' continued to be used with the likes of 'who put the eau in bottles' and 'eau come all ye faithful' 1985 efforts. The result was:

- Perrier became the generic term for bottled water
- Perrier became more than bottled water, it being mysterious, flowing and natural; other aspects of its personality also define the brand
- Perrier was classy, above all others and classy enough to put on the dinner table
- Perrier was unique, 'like diving into a lake'
- Perrier users were rewarded by being part of an exclusive club.

Reputation

By 1990 the inevitable crisis had arrived at Perrier's door. In America a known carcinogen, benzene, was found in the product. Ironically, it was discovered by accident because of Perrier's reputation for purity. The product was being used as a standard in a North Carolina laboratory where it was discovered to have 6 parts per billion of the contaminant. Not a lot in reality but in marketing and PR terms 'six parts too many', and the product was withdrawn from the American market place.

Perrier were primarily concerned with reputation. Swift and responsible behaviour including the provision of a ten-line telephone information service ensured a swift return to the 60 per cent market share it enjoyed. Perrier were also spurred on by the very good response by callers who both expressed sympathy and the assurance that, at least in 85 per cent of cases, they would return to the brand. This was achieved by the implementation of a £4 million UK advertising campaign that featured the bottle (as an icon) before returning to the long-running 'eau' campaign. This was described by the company as its 'welcome back campaign'. The role of PR was very much in the classical mould, i.e. that of creating a favourable marketing environment for advertising to work more effectively in. Perrier claimed to believe that:

- it is not possible to create a good public face for a company that is behaving badly

- a PR stunt is bad PR

- a company should have a director of communications, i.e. bring it into the boardroom

- the use of outside agencies/consultants is highly desirable for objectivity

- objectives must be realistic and attainable

- campaigns should be monitored and results measured (BBC, 1991).

Public relations and planning

Negative publicity might be inevitable but there are ways to minimize impact. Any *situation* should deal with how the organization has been perceived and how it would like to be perceived among certain target audiences. Any attitudes that need to be changed should be identified. *Publics* (or targets) should be defined. *Objectives* are essential and no kind of PR activity should be planned without objectives. Objectives direct the PR activity to the right publics, using the most appropriate media and techniques, and also allow for evaluation to take place. Some examples of objectives are to build awareness and interest in the organization and its services, to differentiate the service offered and organization from those of competitors and to build and maintain the organization's image and reputation. The selection of *media and techniques* then follows so that media will be available that will reach the various publics. A clear understanding of what the organization can offer the media and what is likely to attract its audience in return for exposure is required. Planning the *budget* is crucial, of course, and this may be set, for example, on the basis of what the organization can afford. Alternatively, having decided the objectives, the appropriate resources are allocated to enable these to be achieved. What is important is that the PR function is recognized as a legitimate business expense and that appropriate resources are allocated for the objectives to be realistically achieved. *Assessment of results* will depend to a large extent on the objectives. Quantitative measures may be used, for example changes in enquiries, numbers of new clients or increase in turnover. There may also be a qualitative assessment, for example whether the organization's image or reputation has changed. *Evaluation* is a logical conclusion of any PR activity if the organization is to see the effectiveness of the programme. Answers can be had on a number of issues such as whether the organization is getting increased business, positive feedback from customers, staff motivation and so on.

Crisis planning and management

An important part of PR is crisis management or, as some would have it, crisis avoidance or prevention. Crises arise from a range of sources in the business environment. Certainly there is the likelihood of pressure groups being involved and acting as a catalyst of change. As suggested earlier with Perrier, incidents can become global – very quickly. Information can be disseminated around the world minutes after an event has occurred.

As is usual within marketing some things can be controlled and others not. Fill (2002) explains this by providing an organizational crisis matrix that involves *wide impact, controllable* elements such as product defects or customer accidents, and *non-controllable* elements such as product sabotage. Narrower, *local impact* involves thing such as employee accidents (*controllable*) and terrorism (*non-controllable*). This suggests that crisis management is about averting controllable crises, and managing the impact of uncontrollable ones through, for example, the flow of information from the organization to interested parties, especially the media. However, others argue that PR can play a major part in crisis avoidance as well as management, where non-controllable elements are involved. This requires that management have the vision to engage with particular activities. Dye (1997) suggests that, when things take a turn for the worst with perhaps the media digging deep into corporate affairs and with the public taking notice, it is vital that a PR team is in place to play a vital role preventing a crisis getting out of hand. This requires senior management involvement, especially on a global stage. Armstrong (1996) advocates *contingency planning* to act swiftly and effectively. This suggests a plan should be in place to deal with a crisis, whatever that crisis may be.

Perrier and other crises

Armstrong (1996) suggests the mid-1990s British government could have learnt a thing or two about PR. The absence of contingency plans for an issue that was bubbling under the surface for years is remarkable. At a very late stage and after *CJD* evidence emerged, Ogilvy and Mather were given £250 000 to stop the rot – probably a clear case of too little too late. Armstrong maintains that a strengths, weaknesses, opportunities and threats (SWOT) analysis would have revealed a lot about the problems of the government itself, and advocates:

1 Destroy cattle now to save lives (or at least show potential to).

2 Destroy cattle now because a strong solution is required to solve a strong crisis.

This is perhaps best exemplified by some managers who cleverly plan for crisis avoidance rather than relying on the managing of (or way out of) a crisis. Armstrong (1996) lists the PR company Hill and Knowlton's eight-point PR plan to alleviate the *government*'s problems with the *BSE* crisis:

1 Gather hard data.

2 Use legislation.

3 Have an education and enforcement department.

4 Consider the entire food chain.

5 Decide whom to protect.

6 Take action against poor advice.

7   Get rid of the Chief Medical Officer's position.

8   Find out what the public wants and therefore be able to reassure and so on.

On the basis that 'you can't polish a turd' the sage advice with BSE, with hindsight, was to destroy cattle and get all solid facts out through senior people and to 'do a Ribena'. *Ribena*, the then SmithKlineBeecham (SKB) brand of blackcurrant cordial drink, had run into trouble with the alleged levels of sugar in the product and its potential to damage teeth (especially children's). This saw SKB directors drinking the product on news programmes for months until the company was believed.[1] After the 'benzene in the water' crisis, *Perrier* can be credited with not making too much of a drama of it. They had, with their UK PR agency, Infoplan, prepared well for a crisis. They did not hesitate to put a damage limitation exercise in place that involved a telephone facility with trained people to deal with a crisis. Perrier claim to have been honest, telling people what had happened, not hiding things (BBC, 1991). This, along with the advertising work of Leo Burnett, put the brand firmly back on the market. Perrier's view of international PR is that it is the how the organization delivers the message that differs, not necessarily the message itself. The proliferation of the media is important, as are the various segments that might exist in different markets. On the other hand, according to Davies et al. (2003), things internationally were not as smooth as they appeared to be in the UK and the USA. The Perrier Paris headquarters's attempt at a single conference on the subject was not the success they had hoped for. In the UK there were problems with the recycling of the glass bottles and local authorities did not like the idea of the water being poured down drains. The claim of a blocked filter causing the contamination exposed the idea that carbon dioxide might be added to a product that was supposed to be natural, and UK retailers demanded changes in labelling. Seventy-two million bottles were withdrawn in the UK and 160 million worldwide. Market share dropped from 32 per cent to 17 per cent in the UK in one month. In the USA the figures were 24 per cent to 5.7 per cent, but this situation was salvaged somewhat by the other brands in the stable. The lessons for Perrier, according to Davies et al. (2003), are the inevitability of crises, the need to co-ordinate centrally, that media are global and that some markets will respond differently than others. There is a need to:

- dispose of the product even if it is just suspect

- apologize

- explain with authority

- co-operate

- recover.

Many other crises have arisen over the years from the *Exxon Valdez* to Johnson and Johnson's (J&J's) *Tylenol*. Tylenol was totally pulled from stores and J&J introduced tamper-proofing and had a high-profile campaign to reintroduce the brand. This attitude agrees with Henley Centre research that suggests loyalty can rise to its former levels rather than the average of a drop to 60 per cent of sales after a crisis. Tylenol, an analgesic brand in the USA, had cyanide supposedly injected into it. Johnson and Johnson's response was to pull all products completely, repackage it and relaunch it. The result was not only retention of customer loyalty but also an expression of increased customer confidence. *Walkers Crisps* had the problem of glass fragments in only five or six packets of crisps but withdrew 9 million packets from the UK market and had press work and a helpline under way in twenty-four hours using a number of agencies. This scenario had been rehearsed, despite not knowing exactly what it would be, twice a year, and was executed with mechanical precision. In Australia, Sanitarium's soymilk brand *So Good* had to be recalled and pre-recall figures were met despite competitive activity while the brand was absent. A rapid response using advertising and PR to a contamination crisis saw the deployment of a plan that was already in place to execute an immediate response. The potential damage to the brand and to other brands in Sanitariums's stable and to market slowdown and to the product category was huge. The recall was made within six hours with 300 000 units taken off the shelves across Australia and sent for testing and destruction. The CEO became a figurehead for public contact while the campaign was co-ordinated by the marketing manager. Sanitarium advocated:

- open communications for trust from the public

- communication across all stages of recall and in real time

- share must be won back, even though the last portion of this is difficult to achieve

- all possible communications should be used in conjunction with PR measures

- the need to create confidence and win back loyalty

- effectiveness and swiftness to protect other products/brands

- the CEO should speak directly to the public

- reactions and change should be monitored.

The net result of this campaign was that 95 per cent thought that new stock of So Good was safe, and damage was limited on Sanitarium's other products and others in the category. Sanitarium was able to turn a contamination nightmare into success. Advertising spend had to be increased but the adoption of an open and integrated communications strategy meant that maintenance of So Good in the marketplace was assured (Advertising Federation of Australia, 1999).

Marketing challenge

Most companies have crises. Many organizations plan for this as best they can by using scenario training – 'what ifs' if you prefer. An organization might, for example, run scenarios where the brand has been poisoned. The training might involve getting the news out quickly and getting information across, having the product used publicly and using credible third parties to endorse it, planning ways to remove it from shelves and destroying it. Certainly the emphasis should be on solving the problem and bringing it back.

There may not be a crisis per se but it may be that PR can be used to take the sting out of potentially devastating news (Durban, 2002). Or it may be 'image nurturing' or some other form of protection from scandal. It may be a reactive or proactive art in practice but in any event, the challenge is to:

- be believed
- come across in the right way, efficiently and effectively
- be prepared, and preparation is essential
- get the whole story first and not to rely on only one source of facts
- facilitate through the use of dedicated help lines, office facilities and so on
- be honest, but this does not necessarily mean full disclosure
- not be economical with the truth
- be prepared for the worst
- define the real problems
- co-ordinate centrally response activities
- have a dedicated crisis team
- be prepared to sacrifice product or market
- resist a combative instinct
- contact all relevant publics across the spectrum
- assume the worst
- identify allies within the industry
- broaden to put incidents into perspective (adapted from Durban, 2002; Fallows, 1998; Phillips, 2001).

 Assignment

Planning for a crisis or even negative publicity is seen as the province of PR, which is then often used in conjunction with other forms of communication.

Assume you have been asked to help devise a crisis avoidance and management plan of action that would involve a major consumer brand such as Perrier, Tylenol or So Good that would fit in with that brand's advertising and image. Use the DSM provided in Chapter 4 to complete the following tasks:

- Outline what you feel to be the key background points to the brand. From this information establish the likely target(s) or publics.

- Establish possible objectives for the brand facing a potential crisis. Write an outline crisis management strategy proposal for the brand, suggesting ideas on creative and media tactics.

- Provide ideas on the implementation of a crisis management campaign for the brand by using the parameters in the implementation section of the DSM framework and show clearly what you would recommend in terms of allocation, budgets, timings and so on. Pay particular attention to any leadership aspects that the brand might have.

- Using the final section of the DSM, the control section, suggest what monitoring, evaluation and research methods and techniques you would employ to maximize efficiency and effectiveness of the brand's campaign.

Summary of Key Points

- Most writers would subscribe to a form of decision sequence model when attempting to manage PR. There are, however, challenges to the APIC-type of system without alternatives. A shift has occurred with regard to a move away from communication effects to return on investment in communications.

- Analysis deals with assessments of customers, products, the organization and its environment. This is the 'where are we now? question that involves various publics as targets.

- Planning deals with targets, objectives and positioning. This is the 'where do we want to go?' question. This is followed by consideration of creative and media strategy. This is the 'how do we get there?' question.

- Implementation is a consideration of 'how do we put this into practice?' and involves the allocation of spend to the campaign.

- Control involves evaluation and research and is the 'did we get there?' question. This is not only a check on whether objectives have been achieved, but also a consideration of the place of research in the entire framework.

Examination Questions

These questions are similar to those outlined in Chapter 4 but should be answered more specifically with regard to PR and crisis management and the brand.

1 Explain why you agree or disagree with the contention that the APIC-type model is useful as a framework for PR generally and crisis management in particular.

2 Outline what you consider to be the important elements of the analysis stage of a crisis management DSM.

3 The planning stage of a DSM involves consideration of 'where do we want to go?' having already established targets. Discuss the importance of establishing targets early on in a crisis management campaign.

4 Explain the usefulness (or not) of perceptual mapping in planning a response to a crisis.

5 Creative strategy is part of 'how do we get there?' Discuss the different creative approaches to crisis management and avoidance.

6 Discuss the importance of honesty with particular reference to creative approaches.

7 Media strategy is also part of 'how do we get there?' Discuss the key media characteristics for this sort of context.

8 There are a number of practical issues when considering how to put a crisis management campaign into practice. Discuss these in relation to the context.

9 Discuss the logic behind pre-, concurrent and post-testing within the context of crisis management.

10 Comment on the idea of scenario planning and crisis avoidance as an investment not a cost in relation to brand maintenance.

Note

1 The government that had to handle a full blown BSE outbreak a few years later appeared to have learnt little from this experience.

References

Admap (2002). Best practice – public relations in the marketing mix. *Admap*, **426**, March. www.warc.com

Advertising Federation of Australia (1999). *So Good Soymilk Product Recall: A Remarkable Recovery*. Advertising Federation of Australia.

Armstrong, S. (1996). So much at steak. *Guardian*, Media Guardian, 25 March, p.12.

BBC (1991). *Executive Business Club – Public Relations*. BBC video.

Davies, G. with Chun, R., Vinhas da Silva, R. and Roper, S. (2003). *Corporate Reputation and Competitiveness*. Routledge.

Durban, M. (2002). *Are You in Control of an Effective PR Strategy?* Microsoft Central for Small Business.

Dye, P. (1997). Emergency services: crisis management, *Marketing Week*, 17 April, pp. 73–74.

Fallows, R. (1998). *Marketing Theory: How Do I Handle a Crisis?* Marketing Council/Business Link Hampshire.

Fill, C. (2002). *Marketing Communications: Contexts, Strategies and Applications*. 3rd edition. Financial Times Prentice Hall.

Phillips, D. (2001). The public relations evangelists. *Corporate Communications: An International Journal*, **6** (4), 225–238.

Setford, A. and Crispin, R. (1990). Perrier: Eau and success over the long term. In IPA, *Advertising Effectiveness Awards*, notes and video.

Wilson, R. (1986). The story of eau – the key to Perrier's success. In IPA, *Advertising Effectiveness Awards*, notes and video.

PART FIVE

Personal Communications

'Personal communications' is a broader term than the often used 'personal selling', another of the classic elements of promotion. Its development into contemporary, and perhaps more subtle, approaches in terms of internal stakeholders and customer relations has become part of personal communications management, rather than the sales and selling techniques developed over a very long period of time. In this part of the book the classical elements of personal selling are considered, looking in detail at traditional and contemporary behavioural approaches to this key function that may find itself threatened by new ways of delivering messages on a one-to-one basis. There is also consideration of the management of other personal communication tools that are at the disposal of most organizations.

This fifth part of the book consists of two chapters. Chapter 16 deals with the nature and role of personal selling, and Chapter 17, following on from Chapter 4 in Part One of this book, simulates a strategic framework for effective personal communications management, using the case of Audi.

16

The nature and role of personal selling

Chapter overview

Introduction to this chapter

This chapter deals with personal selling's role in marketing and the marketing communications mix. This book takes a marketing concept-type view of selling but recognizes the more aggressive variants of selling that exist. The approach taken in this book is therefore to treat personal communication as part of the marketing communications mix. Personal communication and selling are put into the context of the selling/buying process. The nature and role of personal communication and selling are obviously changing over time to reflect changes in the communications mix as well as in society. Technological advances that threatened to mean fewer jobs in terms of what were conventional sales forces may now play a role more supportive of the sales person/representative, who can concentrate more on interpersonal skills. Selling is portrayed here in terms of ideas around motivation, objectives and the role of sales training rather than other related topics such as sales force management that are left to more general marketing management texts.

Aims of this chapter

The overall aim of this chapter is to explore the nature of personal selling and its role within the marketing and communications mix. More specifically, on completion of this chapter, the reader should be able to:

- explore the nature and role of personal communication and selling within integrated marketing communications

- outline the advantages and disadvantages of personal communication and selling

- explain the place that personal selling in particular has within the integrated marketing communications mix

- consider different types of selling in differing contexts

- investigate personal communication as a process that informs personal selling

- assess approaches to sales training and development

- understand and appreciate selling performance and effectiveness.

The nature of personal selling

The nature of personal communication

In terms of other forms of communication, personal communication is relatively expensive. Fill (2002) suggests the cost per contact will exceed £100, while Duncan (2002) expresses this as at least $300 upwards but these are, of course, very general figures. Personal communication is often called dyadic communication because it involves more than one person, but this is somewhat of a misnomer since it suggests a dyad, i.e. two. Personal communication, and especially personal selling, very often involves more than two people. It is, inevitably, constantly in competition with other forms of communication, especially with electronic forms. However, advances in technology should make life easier and more effective for those involved with personal communication, although advances in interactivity (see Chapter 19) appear to threaten the one-to-one hold that personal communication has had over other elements of the communications mix.

Like any other form of communication the basic model of the communication process is a useful starting point in understanding the nature of the beast one is dealing with. The sender–receiver model outlined in Chapter 2 of this book again applies but here, of course, the person doing the selling becomes the source of the message, usually for and on behalf of the organization. The receiver may be a channel member customer, a direct customer or the consumer depending upon the selling context. As discussed later in this chapter, the selling process is basically different from other forms of communication in terms of message, noise and feedback, but the general model still applies.

Advantages and disadvantages of personal communication

The *advantages* of using personal communication are that it is at least a two-way interaction and instant feedback can be received. There is much less noise in the system compared with other communication tools. In terms of personal selling, participation in the decision process is greater on the part of the seller. Messages can be tailored, particularly in response to feedback that should be actively sought by the seller, which becomes part of the organization's marketing information system. The net result is that the selling process, if handled and managed well, has a huge potential to solve consumer problems. Targeting, negotiation and flexibility help make personal selling efficient and this function can genuinely break through the clutter and engender behaviour change. The *disadvantages* are the aforementioned high cost per contact, low reach, frequency and control over the message in terms of being told by the organization what to say and not say. There are some situations therefore that arise whereby the reason for using the personal approach in the first place is defeated. Some of these problems, such as motivation, can be solved through training and development as discussed later in this chapter.

The nature of personal selling

Personal selling is a form of personal communication, or forms, since personal selling varies a lot in its style. It is sometimes described as the 'hard sell' that is epitomized by the 'foot in the door' sales type, characterized by unscrupulous timeshare operators or the archetypical second-hand car salesman. Clearly this is not the case for the most part. Selling activities take many forms in the buying/ selling process, depending upon the context in which selling takes place. Sometimes the sales people are information providers and representatives of the organization, sometimes order-takers and at other times order-makers. The main difference between personal selling and the other types of marketing communication is that this form of communication is two-way, enabling immediate feedback and evaluation of transmitted messages. Personal selling messages can be tailored to the consumer's individual needs. A key part of personal selling is that objections can be overcome by providing explanation and, if needs be, information, quickly. As will be discussed later, another important part that personal selling has to play is the encouragement of the placing of orders and closing the sale. This is not something that can be done with much of the rest of the communications mix, but it is set against a backdrop of recently introduced consumer protection by way of cooling-off periods and so on. As the environment has changed so, too, have selling styles. The old, ethical, position that once dominated and that followed the marketing concept of meeting customer need and so on, was superseded by a much more aggressive approach during the 1980s and beyond. The links have now been made with the *relationship marketing* (and indeed the *customer relationship management*, CRM) paradigms. Here long-term cost-effectiveness is linked with mutual benefit as opposed to what can be termed *transactional marketing*.

Personal selling *activities* have changed, although the nature of personal selling in essence has not, as indicated above. What have changed are the methods of contact with the advent of e-mail, video conferencing, voice mail and the virtual office but also team meetings, PowerPoint-type presentations, the ubiquitous mobile phone and the laptop. Sales people are involved still with, as expected, actual selling, working with channel members, route planning and guiding (servicing products and accounts), surveying (collecting and feeding back information), training and recruitment, entertaining, travelling, conferences and seminars. *Key account management* is not new but has gained a certain prominence in recent times whereby a kind of 80/20 rule-of-thumb Pareto-type principle applies to the selling situation, i.e. that 80 per cent of the organization's effort goes into 20 per cent of its client base that comprise key accounts. Some see a danger in this in that too much of the company resources might go to too small a number of clients. Others see the benefits and have set up key account divisions or teams.

The future of selling

Personal communications generally, and selling in particular, are changing radically. The integrating of direct marketing (especially telemarketing) in field sales operations has already occurred for cost reasons if nothing else. Screening leads and credit ratings are all possible thanks to technology and better, faster communications. The net results are cost reduction and higher rates of closure. This will become even more potent should organizations improve their relations with audiences through public relations activities and improve their aftercare. Worries over technology wiping out the selling function appear at this point to be unfounded.[1] However, in terms of dealing with various other players, including customers and suppliers, sales people will have to acquire new skills. They will have to become more opportunistic but also better market analysts and researchers, and much more team orientated, contributing more towards things like new product development.

Types of selling

Sales people can be many things. For example, they can be providers of information, persuaders, prospectors, problem-solvers and even procreators (Duncan, 2002). Some commentators see selling as simply order-related. For Fill (2002) there are order-takers at some form of reception or till, order-getters, typically those who demonstrate and persuade, order-collectors in terms of new and existing customers (often now telesales) and order-supporters, who provide secondary information, advice and so on. There is, however, a broader view. Personal selling, as hinted at above, should be viewed as part of personal communication and as such as a discipline that is multifunctional, including relationship building and maintenance and servicing accounts.

There is a need to clarify the context in which selling is to be applied since the nature and role of the function varies enormously depending upon the context. Basically, the divide is between consumer and business to business. Selling activities can therefore be classified according to customer type. Fill (2002) uses the following categories:

- Consumer, where the type of selling requires contact with the retail trade (channel BtoB, including other channel members) and/or the consumer direct.

- Professional BtoB, where the type of selling requires 'specifications' and the offering is often tailored and sold on to clients of the professional.

- Industrial or organizational BtoB where, for example, components will be sold to manufacturers to be incorporated into a finished product.

Selling activity can also be classified according to *customer buying behaviour* and, consequently, the type of approach needed. *Creative selling* occurs in 'first buy' situations where analysis and assessment, preparation and presentation are required for a successful sale. *Order-taking*, as mentioned above, is routine and either a straight or modified re-buy. *Missionary selling* does not involve persuasion or taking orders but is more of a supportive function, where influence is key to a successful sale. *Retail selling* should involve sound product knowledge in many situations since customers need advice and assistance in order to make buying decisions (but sadly this is not always the case in reality).

Back to the future: re-routing selling towards relationships	The shift toward longer-lasting relationships between an organization and its customers is not a startling revelation. Relationship marketing has been called the 'new marketing' by some and a 'new paradigm' by others. Still further, other writers maintain good marketers have always built good relationships. Since the sales force traditionally has been the vital link between the organization and its customers, it is not surprising to find that there is an intimacy between the two entities. Sales people in many contexts have the task of managing and maintaining relationships, and this is the reasoning behind the study by Kyziridis et al. (1996). This study, among other things, explored the nature of long-tem relationships and what was going on regarding sales and sales management. It also examined sales management practices such as recruitment, training and so on and the impact on relationships. Relationship marketing is all about moving away from competition and conflict, and towards co-operation and mutual benefit. The

resource that forms the sales function must surely have a role since under-standing customer characteristics and needs can (or should) be enhanced by the surveying opportunities provided by a sales team. Relationship marketing has its roots perhaps not so much in the marketing concept but, rather, in the societal marketing concept (where all players win, including society generally – see Kotler, 2000). Certainly many writers of the relationship marketing persuasion propagate the 'new reality of marketing'. There was a move from the marketing concept philosophy of the 1960s and 1970s to a more aggressive incarnation during the 1980s. Traditional marketing in a sense was rescued from this by the relationship 'paradigm'. The sales function in particular, especially with services, appears to have played a vital role in this. Relational selling in service markets has been a significant force, especially where services are difficult for customers to evaluate and where the service may be complex and the environment very fluid and dynamic. Relationship marketing and hence relational selling appears to offer the best way of achieving competitive advantage.

For some, the relationship marketing paradigm is an illusion, just as the marketing mix is. However, the history of marketing thought demonstrates the 'mix' idea came out of empiricism and observation. Culliton's 1948 study, which had antecedents going back to 1929, on the management of marketing costs was acknowledged by Robert Bartels, who first coined the phrase 'marketing mix', as being the first to discuss marketing in terms of ingredients. By the 1950s the marketing mix was born and by the 1960s was established as one of the cornerstones of marketing thought. Observable phenomena had essentially become shorthand and were put into convenient boxes, only to be extrapolated, interpreted and expressed as broader marketing activities within particular contexts. Exploratory empirical research in the UK by Copley and Robson (2001) concluded that marketing occurs regardless, and techniques are adopted as a result of a socially constructed reality within a particular context. Since the context chosen to study – arts tourism marketing – was a highly sensitive area of cultural development and expression, the suitability of certain techniques within the 'mix' was of crucial importance. The tension between the arts and commercialism, and especially selling things, could have been cut with a knife.

In a similar vein, relationship marketing evolved from traditional marketing as 'the new marketing', and not for the first time a new marketing was born. Greek exploratory, empirical research conducted by Kyziridis et al. (1996) led the authors to conclude that there is indeed a new 'type' of relationship-orientated sales person with a differing role to the conventional 'type'. This, argue these researchers, can be seen in the metaphor of the 'Ambassador' where the sales person promotes by means of the establishment and maintenance of long-lasting and close relationships where there is network rather than hierarchical knowledge. Goldsmith's (1999) conjecture that certain consumers are not happy with the standardized offerings in the marketplace is new marketing. However, if there is a resurgence of interest in bespoke products, then this is not necessarily new but a kind of retro marketing – not in the sense of the retro VW Beetle, Chrysler PT Cruiser or BMW Mini Cooper S, but a move back to the ways in which products are supplied, albeit with the selling aid that is the World Wide Web. This suggests that marketing remains but the means of bringing the product to market to sell has changed.

Sources: Adapted from Ballantyne, Christopher and Payne, (2003); Copley and Robson (2001); Culliton (1948); Goldsmith (1999); Jones (2000); Kotler (2000); Kyziridis et al. (1996).

Consider the different types of selling in different contexts with which you are familiar. Think about when it may be appropriate to assume the role of mere order-taker. When is it appropriate to try to persuade? When does the missionary or ambassadorial role have a part to play? A key question to ponder might be, are we going back, or back to the future in terms of sales and marketing?

Personal selling as part of the communications mix

Personal selling, as alluded to above, is the most expensive part of the communications mix when analysed on a cost per contact basis. Personal selling is generally most effective at the latter stages of the hierarchy of effects and is more closely associated with action and decision-making than building awareness. This is important when considering the integrated marketing communications mix. Each tool should be used when it is most appropriate within the marketing communications plan.

When to use selling in the marketing and communications mix

The marketing mix

When the *product* or service is a complex one or the purchase decision is a major one the features of the product will have to be shown, and this may require demonstration and/or trial. This would be typical of any BtoB situation. Where *channel* members are involved, product/service training might be needed. *Price*, especially final price, may be subject to negotiation and, as with the larger manufacturers, large margins are usually available to support the selling operation.

The communications mix

There are clearly key areas for consideration within the selling/other forms of communications interface. Fill (2002) lists four. First is *complexity*, associated with the product itself or the environment in which the negotiations are taking place. The degree of complexity and the need for customization is clearly important. When there is a high level of complexity, advertising and PR cannot convey the benefits in the same way personal selling can. Personal selling allows for demonstration/explanation and for points that are of concern to a particular buyer to be discussed. Second, *buyer significance*, or involvement in a product decision involves considering whether, if risk is high for the consumer, more complex or problem-solving decision-making will occur. This type of decision-making is information intensive making the two-way, interactive communication message a preference. Third is *communication effectiveness*, where the communication tools most effective at delivering a message will depend to a great extent on the communications objectives. For example, advertising will be more effective at communicating brand awareness but selling will be very effective at closing the sale or doing a deal. Business-to-business marketing, being characterized by a small number of customers and suppliers, means that often the products or services are tailored and price, delivery and so on will be subject to negotiation, making personal contact essential. Finally, there are *network factors*, which are where network or channel of distribution factors such as the amount of information needed by members of the network and the extent to which a collaborative relationship are required. There is also the question of whether push or pull strategy (or both) is being employed and the nature of relationships.

More specifically the interfaces have the following qualities:

1　*Personal selling and advertising.* Advertising may not be an appropriate tool when information needed by the buyer is too complex or detailed to convey. The message may be too specific for the more general media and the targets dispersed, meaning that advertising does not reach the target market effectively. Therefore, both media and effectiveness of message issues arise. The relative importance of the mix functions was discussed earlier in this book in relation to, for example, stages of the product life cycle where advertising may be relatively important in the early stages to create awareness but selling is more important when explanation is needed. The size of the target is important, as is information need, value of the purchase, resources available, product complexity and post-purchase requirements in terms of assurance and support. Much of this could be resolved by injecting money but this could prove wasteful. Advertising could be used before the sales person makes contact. In industrial selling, certainly, advertising can be used to provide information, especially facts, before contact is made, making the communication process more efficient by saving on personal contact time. Personal selling improves reach and can increase profit, or have the opposite effect if done badly, i.e. increase costs and harm profit. Advertising can be an aid to selling when it:
    (a)　saves time
    (b)　provides useful information before contact
    (c)　can be used as a visual aid in follow-up
    (d)　is an ego booster
    (e)　is a refresher
    (f)　helps build brands
    (g)　gets the customer involved.

2　*Personal selling and PR.* Similar logic can be applied to PR where the situation is much the same as with advertising but with an emphasis on the 'feel-good factors' associated with PR. It has long been argued that the *raison d'être* for PR is to provide a better marketing environment in which to sell. Sales people are bound to feel better if they are operating against a backdrop of good publicity, a strong corporate and/or brand image and so on. Of course the opposite will be the case if negative PR ensues.

3　*Personal selling and direct marketing.* This includes the obvious link to database marketing and telemarketing as discussed in Chapter 10. Direct marketing support leads to, for example, better closing, more time selling and more information disseminated.

4　*Personal selling and sales promotions.* This link has always existed in terms of incentives and other promotions and the selling function. The usual rationale for sales promotions was discussed in Chapter 9. At the selling/sales promotions interface free merchandise, offers and other sales promotion techniques can add excitement to the selling situation, giving it that extra buzz and a real lift, if handled with care.

VIGNETTE

Polo – 'the mint with the hole': what role for selling within the product life cycle?

The Polo mint *is* a British institution but even British institutions (and established brands) need an injection to breathe new life into them as circumstances change. With brands such as Polo the market is constantly changing and good marketing practice is to constantly monitor the PLC, or BLC, and invest in the brand. Injecting new life can mean any number of things such as changing the product to better meet changing needs and wants, changing the price relative to the competition or changing ways of distribution. This, of course, alludes to managing the marketing mix and, not surprisingly, this includes promotion – or communication, as it is better known. Within the communications mix, of course, there are choices such as developing a new advertising campaign in order to raise awareness with existing consumers of alterations to the product (product improvement) that provide new or improved benefits to the consumer or customer.

Polo was the market leader in the UK for decades with its 'Polo – the mint with the hole' distinctiveness invented by family owners, Rowntree, that became part of the Nestlé group by the 1990s. Sales of Polo declined from 1980 as an index (base) year (100) to 77 by 1993. The decline was slow at first during the 1980s and had risen above the base in 1988 to 102, but this appears to have been an aberration as the decline continued and Polo appeared to have lost its value as a brand in the eyes of the consumer. The brand, facing new competition in the marketplace, was staid and it had not carried people with it. Innovation was coming from elsewhere, particularly Trebor Extra Strong Mints, and Trebor Spearmints and Softmints. There was now a repertoire to choose from and Polo's advertising in particular was to become the key tool to revitalize the brand by making it distinctive once again, but also more interesting. The objectives therefore were to revitalize the brand and sales, but also to broaden Polo within the repertoire. This meant moving away from the one product, 'Polo – the mint with the hole', towards what research had shown to be the right direction, namely, spearmint, strong mint flavour and sugar free, reflecting a more diverse marketplace and more distinctive targets. This is a good example of a previously undifferentiated market becoming differentiated. The original mint appealed to all adults. The strong mint had a male bias, the sugar free mint a younger adult female bias and the spearmint an all young adults bias. Such targets, of course, drove the marketing and hence communications mix for the Polo brand as a whole. The media and the message obviously had to be different. For Polo Original, television advertising put across 'the original and best taste'. Polo Spearmint used television and posters to suggest 'a younger, trendier mint'. Likewise Polo Strong used television and posters to get across 'a smooth, strong taste', while Polo Sugar Free used women's magazines to get across 'the sugar free mint with a hole'. The core strengths of Polo (unique physical form and friendliness, built up over the years through the use of humour) and the character of its variants were therefore communicated by advertising in various media. The advertising campaign, according to Polo's owners, Nestlé, was a success in terms of growing the market and regaining supremacy. The index figure for 1994 rose to 94 from the 77 figure of 1993. The total mint market grew by £6 million to £207 million and the increase continued into 1995. By April 1995 Polo Spearmint had captured 4.3 per cent of all mint sales, Polo Strong 1.7 per cent and Sugar Free 1.5 per cent.

While it is not surprising that Polo's communication was led by advertising, the marketing mix clearly included distribution. The trade needed to be convinced that by stocking Polo retailers could increase mint sales rather than simply substituting one brand for another. Trade interest was created by the selling activity that explained the rationale behind differentiating the market and the reasoning behind media and creative strategy. Thus a supportive role from the selling function and an innovative set of ideas meant that retailers would want to be part of a campaign that would create a lot of interest and demand, and therefore would want to stock the product.

Source: Adapted from The Times 100 (2003).

STOP POINT

Consider the revitalization of any brand with the PLC/BLC concept. There is clearly a potential role for many things including personal selling. In the context of an fmcg brand like Polo, the selling function is clearly going to be restricted to dealing with trade issues. Consider how vital this role is in informing and educating the trade about other elements of the marketing and communications mix in action.

The selling process

Before a salesperson can begin to sell to customers she/he must research and plan. The selling process therefore contains:

Sales person → Research → Plan → Sell → Customer

This fits within the overall framework of the sales process that begins with a search for (potential) customers and moves through a sequence of events to closing the sale and aftercare. In terms of the AIDA model, as discussed in Chapter 2, selling involves:

Attention Interest Desire Action
(Attract) (Rouse) (Develop) (Close)

The hierarchy of effects is therefore revisited in terms of personal communication. The message is not a monologue but part of a dialogue, the aforementioned dyadic communication, and as such the sender/messenger is in a much better position to explain, discuss, meet objections and so on.

Other schema can be used to explain the selling process, including the S-R behaviourist model that includes mediated feedback and a problem-solving (cognitive) model that suggests a problem–solution–purchase sequence that has the brand as the solution that leads to satisfaction. Fill (2002) uses Pitt et al.'s work of the same year to argue that high levels of communication apprehension will result in higher levels than the norm of sales performance. This appears akin to the notion that an actor needs to feel some apprehension to avoid a blasé performance.

The selling process advocated here is:

- *Preparing* – prospecting, qualifying targets, developing relationships.
- *Presenting* – presenting sales materials, meeting objections, closing.
- *After-sales support* – further developing relationships, maintaining trust and commitment.

Table 16.1
The selling process

PREPARATION	Pre-call planning	Approach	Needs
Analysis to build profiles and lists, qualified into types	Knowledge of products, the company and objectives and of channels, DMUs, history	Developing rapport Using telephone, e-mail for advance appointments Avoid mistakes and assumptions	What are needs, wants, desires, features, benefits sought?
PRESENTATION	*Objections*	*Closing*	*Follow-up*
Of features and benefits Tailored or 'canned'/ pre-done presentation?	Make clear what the objection is Agree and counter Compensate objection with benefit Boomerang the objection Probe/feel if objection is emotional Deny/contradict	Look for buying signals – gestures, nodding, comments, questions Assumed close (assume deal is done) Either/or close (give reasons) Social validation close (what others do) Impending event close (tie in to event) No closing close (leave to trust)	Check on satisfaction Check even when nothing bought Trust may be highest with no close

More practically, on the one hand, there is *preparation* and, on the other, *presentation*. The selling process thus becomes as shown in Table 16.1.

Things that make a sales person an effective communicator

Several things help do this. The level of *flexibility* exercised by the sales person should be as high as possible since the freedom to adapt messages is a positive thing if the sales person can be trusted to use this facility well. If training is of high quality there should be no need to exercise control since 'quality control' will be in place (Fill, 2002). One of the advantages and strengths of personal communication, and hence personal selling, as discussed earlier in this chapter, is the ability to create a dialogue and dyadic communication.

Build customer relationships, remembering that, depending upon the selling context, relationships can be very simple or very complex. They may or may not have a pivotal role to play in the success of a deal. The fmcg, Polo, example above is a good illustration of a relatively simple relationship with channel members compared with, say, a £2 million deal on dump and fork-lift trucks with training, maintenance and other issues as part of a long-term contract. With the latter, personal selling, representation, customer care and support, after-sales support and relationship development become much more relevant than other elements of the communications mix such as PR or advertising. The latter, as discussed above, would be the key element with Polo, Mars Bar and so on. Personal selling has long been seen as the marketing function that increases in importance over other forms of communication as one moves along the spectrum of companies from fmcg towards heavy industry. Alongside this is the relationship with behaviour models, with the emphasis on search and risk as discussed in more depth in Chapter 3. Other factors such as timelines become more important in organizational/industrial markets. Of course, it is recognized that consumer behaviour will start to look something like organizational buyer behaviour as one moves from Polo mints to consumer durables, but the same logic applies since consumers will behave in many instances in a much more rational (as opposed to emotional or impulsive) way.

Traits of effective sales people have been identified as healthy and strong self-esteem (ego strength), urgency sense (getting things done), ego drive (competitiveness), assertiveness, risk-taker, sociable, concept understanding, sceptic and creative empathy (Duncan, 2002). Thus the old argument that sales people should have knowledge, empathy with the prospect, be punctual, organized, energetic, enthusiastic, honest and so on still holds when dealing with personalities and what is required to do the job well. The opposite of the effective sales person is, of course, one who is unprepared, a problem-avoider, not dependable, presumptuous, late for appointments and so on.

Source considerations were deemed important generally in the discussion in Chapter 2 on source characteristics. Since personal selling is based to a large extent on the relationship between seller and buyer, source characteristics become personal characteristics, and these are clearly very important to achieving effective communication. Likeability and credibility are crucial if the communication is to be effective. First impressions are important and can have an impact on whether a customer likes or dislikes the sales person. Dress code and personal hygiene therefore matter. Relationships are important and familiarity is useful in terms of liking, but it can breed contempt. Rewarding the customer engenders likeability where reward may be material and/or psychological, and empathy is a positive thing. Similarity of the sales person to the customer can engender likeability. Credibility will make the sales person more persuasive, therefore being trustworthy, honest and expert in the field are useful.

Message considerations include appeals to interests and/or immediate concerns and needs, have empathy with the customer's predisposition and allow the customer to participate. Benefits not features should be transmitted and the USP considered. A unique or unusual sales presentation can work but may also backfire, and simple messages might work best of all. There is a case for both one-sided and two-sided messages, depending upon the education platform of the prospect. The interest shown by the prospect is important in terms of where the key benefit is used. If interest is low, then key benefits should be expressed quickly. If interest is high, then a build-up should be considered, with key benefits being used near the end of the sales interview. Relative advantage(s) of new products over old should be expressed in terms of benefits.

Noise considerations include the atmosphere in which the sales meeting takes place, the attitude of other players such as secretaries, receptionist and other gatekeepers, and the knowledge levels of the sales person. Many things can constitute noise, or barriers to communication.

Feedback considerations can be formal or informal perceptions of the sales person and the extent to which the sales person is receptive to signals and other cues. The extent to which sales people are willing to disclose information along with feedback determines the size of the information base that is public.

VIGNETTE

To close or not to close, that is the question

To some this might be a strange proposition. Surely a sales person must close the sale and get the order directly? However, over time, effective closing techniques have been developed that do not follow this logic. The importance of such techniques cannot be underestimated. Recognizing different types of closures for different situations, but also cues like buying signals, are important. The seller is looking for commitment of one sort or another, and this may be a sale or merely an agreement to receive literature or visit a seminar or exhibition stand. In this sense this is akin to 'permission marketing'. In many instances the prospect will want to buy but will not commit because they are uncertain and indecisive or they do not know how to make a purchase. It may be the case that there is no real rush to buy or that they simply need reassurance, more information to overcome inertia or objections.

As the sales interview proceeds there may be many instances of buying signals or other cues. Questions are common buying signals, as these may be about delivery, availability, quality, price and many other things. The key difficulty for the seller, however, is not so much recognizing such cues but how and when to act upon them. When deciding to close it is important that the right language is used and therefore the sales person needs to be aware of the kinds of closing statements and questions that are useful. The choice of which ones to use will, of course, depend upon the situation. If no real interest has been shown without any real objection, this suggests apathy on the part of the prospect. In this case the sales person can ask if there is anything further that can be provided and if there are any further questions. In other situations a trial close may be in order so that the question might be related to availability such as, 'I know we have these in stock, would you like to order?' It may be that the situation is so positive that an assumptive close is appropriate, as in 'we can deliver on Friday' or it may even be that things are agreed and the direct close can be made. Most closures are indirect, however, such as the trial close, alternative close ('would you prefer to pay by direct debit?'), summary close ('we are not the cheapest but . . .'), the quotation close (quotation sent) or the concession close ('of course if you buy now there will be a discount of . . .'). The point is therefore reached when persuasion and information-giving come to an end and the sale is closed, abandoned or saved for another time.

The kind of selling situation does have an effect on closing. On-line is very different to the conventional face-to-face situation and telesales are something else altogether. Time is a factor, as is the ability to read cues through body language and so on. However, the biggest problem remains being able to close the sale and secure commitment. One last thought. Despite all that has been written on closing the sale there is a lot of credence in the suggestion raised by Fill (2002), that greater trust and commitment might be had by not attempting to close at all.

Sources: Adapted from Fill (2002); Hersey (1988); McDonald (1988); Sticky-marketing.net (2001); Venn (1999).

STOP POINT The remark on not closing, above, underlines what in some instances may be a dilemma. Think about closing the sale and the number of alternative ways to do this. Is it possible to have a situation where not trying to close gives added credence to the seller? What kinds of situation exist where you feel this would not work and the choice would be one of the many other ways to close a sale?

Making personal communication work for selling

Planning and managing the selling process

There is a need to plan and manage personal communication, especially the sales effort (not sales management per se, which is not the matter for discussion here, i.e. things like territory design are obviously important but are part of the broader sales management issues as opposed to the management of a form of communication). The concern here is with prospecting and identifying potential need, and sufficient resources for acquiring products/services requires pre-call planning, finding sales leads and qualifying prospects, preparing for initial contact through training and establishing which style may be appropriate to follow. The impact of the technological and communications revolution on personal communication and the selling function are the future.

Prospecting and making appointments

Prospecting includes identifying someone who has a potential need and sufficient resources for acquiring products/services. The process begins with pre-call planning – finding sales leads, qualifying prospects and preparing for initial contact. Prospecting also includes the activities in the establishing and the analysis part of the persuading styles discussed earlier. Prospecting therefore deals with:

- identifying market geographically
- researching and identifying market potential
- instigating the approach, checking on buying days
- confirming appointments
- gaining understanding of consumer tastes, needs, other brands and competitors
- preparation of testimonial material, advertising copy, coupon information, samples, market surveys and so on
- recognition of buyer authority and location in organization, and ways of getting to the decision-maker.

Barriers to communication

Some of the barriers to communication are lack of knowledge, ways of greeting, indifference, personal appearance, distractions, emotion and competitive offering. Some of the ways in which these and other barriers can be overcome are through good sales training and preparation. Good sales practice includes consideration of sales training and presentation (techniques of closure, meeting objections and so on) and helping develop selling styles for particular situations using interpersonal awareness. As mentioned above, the sales person needs to research in order to obtain knowledge, integrity and trustworthiness. Sellers must have these attributes to match buyer/customer desire, for them to have knowledge of problems and their needs and the ability to show they are trustworthy. The seller should therefore remember that:

- the customer is important regarding needs
- identification and analysis of needs to explain behaviour is required
- benefits, not features, should be sold
- demonstration as to how needs can be satisfied should be shown.

There are four basic areas of knowledge that a sales person should be concerned with:

- themselves
- the company
- the product(s)
- the customer(s).

There are four basic ways to drive away customers:

- slow greeting
- indifference
- poor personal appearance
- lack of knowledge.

The main barriers to communication are distractions, reception, emotion and competitive offerings. Overcoming these and other barriers can be achieved by the following:

- enthusiasm – act on it
- self-organization
- silence; listen and observe, and show interest and seek agreement
- use questions to find out wants
- be sincere, show confidence and attention
- knowledge and know the key issue(s)
- honesty and praise where due
- remember names and faces
- do not forget a customer
- close the sale in a final action.

Sales training

There are many sales training packages available. Most follow the basic idea that there is a need to train to prepare and a need to train to present, including closing. There is greater recognition now that sales people need to be aware of relationships and the importance of after-sales care and support and the further development and maintenance of the relationship. This, of course, assumes that relationships are indeed important, which they may not be in some contexts. The following is a typical example of scenario training.

Preparing for the sales interview

Research the customer (find out who it really is).

Research the product (be trained in it and carry literature).

Research relationships (between the organization and the customer).

Objectives (number of calls required).

Objectives (regarding other products for the same customer).

Objectives (regarding other customers for the same product).

Ask questions (to gain information about client needs).

Ask questions (to obtain leads).

Ask questions (to keep control of the interview).

The sales presentation

Explain benefits, not features, and talk in terms of customer need.

Meet objections and probe to make any objection specific. Put any objection into perspective.

Close the sale by looking for buying signals and then keeping quiet.

Questions to ask about *preparing for the interview*:

WHAT should a sales person do to determine prospects?

WHAT information should be kept on customers or potential customers?

HOW can a sales appointment be arranged?

SHOULD all calls be by appointment?

WHAT system should a sales person develop to know on whom to call – and when?

HOW should sales literature be used at a meeting?

HOW should any products/samples be used?

WHAT techniques can be used to keep control of a sales interview?

WHAT should a sales person know?

HOW would you find leads for cold calls?

Questions to ask about *the presentation*:

WHAT techniques can sales people use to close the sale?

HOW can a price objection be handled? How can objection be overcome?

WHAT are the differences between features and benefits?

HOW should a sales person conclude an interview that has not resulted in a sale?

WHAT should sales people avoid doing in handling objections?

WHEN offering alternatives to close the sale, how should this alternative package be structured?

HOW should a salesperson use customer needs – identified by questions – to help close?

Motivation

How best to motivate is a key area in terms of positive versus negative treatment, where a reward and punishment approach may not work on its own. A more 'cultivate rather than threaten' approach to sales people's needs can motivate, and keep motivated, people in what can be a very difficult job where they can feel autonomous and good about themselves. Positive reinforcement can enhance job satisfaction rather than merely telling people within a sales force what to do. Role models are very appropriate, whereby leading by example can be the appropriate behaviour to build trust and have a positive effect on overall performance. This can be facilitated by:

- regular meetings

- clear definitions of roles providing freedom from emotional exhaustion

- remuneration, guidance and incentives that all help to avoid emotional burnout in what can be a lonely job and can bolster commitment and loyalty.[2]

Selling styles

Training courses today address issues surrounding the use of new technology such as the Internet, laptops, electronic record-keeping and so on, but the core of many sales training programmes remains prospecting, presenting, closing, 'keeping the doors open' and so on. In the 'situational selling' approach there is an emphasis on adapting styles to meet the needs of customers. Changing styles requires the ability to use a variety of different behaviours, depending on the situation. Selling style is the sales person's pattern of behaviour as perceived by customers, and it is the way the sales person comes across to customers that influences them. The customer's interpretation can be quite different from what the seller intended.

Hersey (1988) offers four selling styles, the first being *establishing competency* that deals with the product, company and sales person. This is necessary when the prospect is uninformed and uncommitted, providing information about the sales person, product and company, stating the purpose of the call and asking a transaction question, carefully designed to have a positive consequence – specific and related to the purpose or to build rapport. The second, *persuading competency* deals with persuading, and is appropriate when the prospect is uninformed but interested, and involves questioning to gain insights into the prospect's needs and problems, encouraging and guiding – showing the prospect that the seller is interested, probing to find important information and advocating by matching features of the product to the prospect's expressed needs. Features that fulfil needs become benefits, and acceptance of benefits a critical bridge. The third is *committing competency* whereby prospects are knowledgeable but encouragement and problem-solving is required since interest brings apprehension, enhancing needs, and should be addressed by summarizing acknowledged needs, strengthening to evolve buying signals, asking for the order, following buying signals (trial close of sale) and responding to objections. These may reflect scepticism misunderstanding, drawbacks, postponing and should be responded to, i.e. customer commitment. The fourth, *fulfilling competency*, comprises continued follow-up to ensure a long-term relationship based on customer satisfaction by maintaining and monitoring the account, expanding business inside (new products) and outside (referrals) the client's organizations and responding to complaints, i.e. listening, understanding and reflecting back to the client, where acknowledging problems helps to maintain rapport. A sales person could have a wide range of flexibility and be able to use all four (or a combination of all four) selling styles.

Style adaptability

Diagnostic skills are the key to adaptability since these provide indications of what style(s) to use and when to use it/them. Selling personality differs from selling style in that it combines the sales person's self-perception with the perceptions of others. A useful framework for describing selling personality and helping increase interpersonal awareness is the Johari window (Joe Luft and Harry Ingham) in Figure 16.1. This is used to depict the relationship between a sales person's self-perception of selling behaviour and the perception by others (i.e. customers).

- The *public* area is known to both the sales person and the customer.

- The *blind* area is unknown to the salesperson but known to the customer, either because of lack of feedback (customer says nothing) or because the sales person has been inattentive to verbal and non-verbal customer communication.

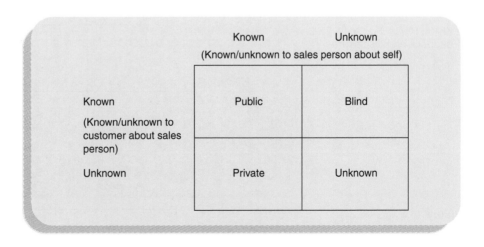

Figure 16.1
The relationship between self-perception and perception by others.

- The *private* area is known to the sales person but unknown to the customer and is private because the sales person has not disclosed information to customers (or customers have not received and understood any communication).

- The *unknown* area is often referred to as the subconscious. The aim is to reduce this as far as possible.

The size and shape of the areas are important. *Feedback* and *disclosure* (Figure 16.2) can affect these. *Feedback* is the extent to which customers are willing to share their perceptions with the sales person and the extent to which the sales person is receptive to customer communication. *Disclosure* is the extent to which sales people are willing to share information with customers and the extent to which customers are interested in and receptive to other sales person communication. Feedback and disclosure determine the size of the public area since information can evolve which was previously unknown to both parties.

Successful sales people constantly monitor their relationships with the customers they contact. If things are going well then the seller must try to determine the reasons why. If they are not going well the seller must try to determine what to do for success next time. There are various ways of getting the information they need on the customer in order to build up customer profiles but these are often built up over a long period of time. Figure 16.3 shows an example of selling styles or types.

S_1 – formal, controlled, disciplined, head orientated, organized (appears reserved, withholds feelings, task orientated, cool, distant).

S_2 – aggressive, pushy, communicates readily, appears confident, authoritative, takes charge, assertive, overbearing, direct, active.

S_3 – passive, gentle hesitant, quiet, difficult, submissive, accepting, shy, thoughtful, subtle.

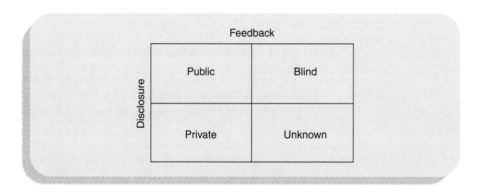

Figure 16.2
Feedback and disclosure.

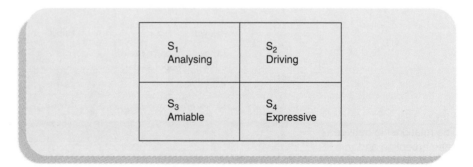

Figure 16.3
Selling styles or types.

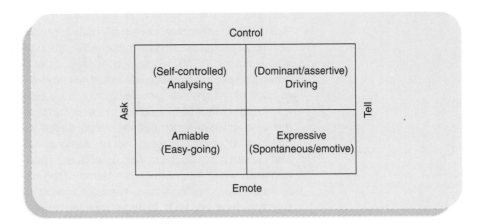

Figure 16.4
Customer profile of each
selling style.

S_4 – informal, responsive, spontaneous, gut orientated, appears disorganized, impulsive, expresses feelings, warm, close, relationship orientated.

With different types of customers the sales person needs to adjust his or her behaviour accordingly (change style). If the sales person's customers are all of one type – let us say, for example, they always want facts and figures and have little time for chit-chat – then an analysing style (Figure 16.4) would match the customer profile and the sales person would need to control the interview in this fashion.

Figure 16.4 also describes the kinds of customer profile each of the other three selling styles would match. Amiable takes time to be agreeable, wants relationships, needs guarantees and assurances, and has an acquiescent style when tense. Expressive needs to be estimated, needs to share effort needed to support their dreams and institutions, and has an attacking style when tense. Driving measures personal progress by results, wants to save time, takes time to be efficient, and has an autocratic style when tense.

Performance evaluation

Any organization that takes selling seriously will invest in sales training, and will also wish to know how well the function is working. Performance evaluation relies on both quantitative and qualitative measures. *Quantitative* measures are things such as call reports, number of calls, which customers or prospects, what was disclosed, the outcomes of sales meetings in terms of volume and value. *Qualitative* measures are much more subjective and deal with things like attitude and commitment, product knowledge and appearance. In short, the latter are more to do with behaviour and how to control sales people rather than having more concrete, tangible outcomes.

VIGNETTE

Only fools and genuine, solid silver-ish: why it is understandable that the Del Boy stereotype exists

There are many articles and other writings on stereotyping in different contexts. Many are to do with gender role portrayal and gender stereotyping. In marketing terms it is in the advertising arena that much is published on this subject whether this is body-isms, face-isms or the number of times more than men that women are portrayed in swimwear in beer commercials. The concern is often for the dehumanizing influences such images have, particularly when used in association with alcohol use and violence in sporting events. Women are often portrayed as 'bodies' rather than 'some bodies' (Hall and

Crum, 1994) or women are significantly more likely to be portrayed promoting particular products such as those within the bodily health category (Furnham and Thomson, 1999). Gender stereotyping, of course, can be looked at from other perspectives. Particular industries and sectors have been studied and notions of masculinity and femininity, masculine and feminine subjectivities and gender identities explored. In the occupational context this is important to the ways in which sales people are portrayed in many walks of life, and which have an effect on the actual job of selling and how selling itself is perceived, and indeed how the sales man or woman is perceived. This can be positive or negative. Much has changed in terms of the role. Selling, itself, has become more serious, perhaps as a reaction against the negative stereotyping and damage done not least by the characterization of the seller as an archetypal 'wide boy' or barrow boy such as that of Del Boy. Del Boy is the central character from the BBC's longrunning situation comedy *Only Fools and Horses*. As well as other things Del Boy sells decidedly 'iffy' stuff. The media, it seems, are quick to portray selling and sales people as 'sharp practice' and a 'con', as in 'confidence trick'. Yet sales training has never been in a better state and, for the past decade or so, it is no longer a question of straightforward talking about how to sell. Workshops, simulations, case study analysis and, in particular, role-play have become the staple ingredient of sales training that will help the seller better meet client need through the cultivation of interpersonal and intra-personal skills.

Sources: Adapted from Blythe (1999); Furnham and Thomson (1999); Gatton, Dubois, and Faley (1999); Hall and Crum (1994); Hodge (1990); Lane and Crane (2002); McDowell and Court (1994).

STOP POINT

The problem is that while the media and other forces continue to portray the sales person in a negative stereotypical manner and certain industries such as financial services have problems and have to be regulated, selling as a profession will suffer. Think about the role of the seller in various contexts and how the sales people themselves can help change perceptions. What role is there for sales training within this?

Assignment

Use Figure 16.5 to considering the following:

Think about yourself in relation to others and other people in relation to others, how they perceive themselves and how others perceive them in order to help develop selling styles. Someone who knows you well and likes you has been asked to give a brief description of your general behaviour or character style. How do you imagine their description reads? How would someone who does not like you alter this description?

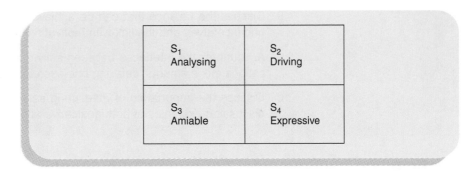

Figure 16.5
Grid for the assignment.

Summary of Key Points

- Personal selling is a form of personal communication that lies within the integrated marketing communications mix.

- Communicating personally has advantages and disadvantages, and this is the case also for personal selling.

- There are different types of selling that operate in differing contexts. The sales person may be out to get a sale or to represent the organization in a missionary or ambassadorial way.

- Personal communication is a process that informs the personal selling process. This is usually denoted as a sequential set of events or stages.

- Approaches to sales training and development have become more sophisticated in the past decade or so. Stereotyping still exists, and can be problematic and a hindrance to successful selling.

- Selling performance and effectiveness should be and can be measured.

- The emergence of the Internet and other technology has had an impact upon the selling function. As technology evolves, this impact will be even greater.

Examination Questions

1 Discuss the difference in meaning between the terms 'personal communications' and 'personal selling'.

2 Examine how personal selling can best be incorporated into the IMC mix.

3 Discuss changes that have taken place in the personal selling function and the impact of relational ideas on these.

4 Outline the personal selling process, highlighting, with examples, the fundamental importance of interactivity.

5 Discuss the importance of closing the sale, illustrating with at least one closing method.

6 Write a brief account of emerging roles within the selling function, taking account of the impact of new technology.

7 Examine the relationship between frequency and cost per contact in selling terms.

8   Discuss the balance that can be achieved between fixed salary, bonuses and incentives and the link with motivation of sales people.

9   Account for the interfaces between selling and other marketing communications mix elements, detailing one such interface with examples.

10 Discuss the importance of measuring sales performance. Include in your discussion examples of both qualitative and quantitative measures.

Notes

1   At the time of writing there is anecdotal evidence of high-street retailing and hence retail-selling jobs becoming under threat from the success of the Internet and e-commerce.

2   The remuneration debate over what is the best balance between commission only, fixed salary or a combination of both is recognized but not developed here as it is more of a sales management issue. The pros and cons to this can be found in most standard marketing management texts.

References

Ballantyne, D., Christopher, M. and Payne, A. (2003). Relationship marketing: looking back, looking forward. *Marketing Theory*, **3** (1), 159–166.

Blythe, J. (1999). Exhibitor commitment and the evaluation of exhibition activities. *International Journal of Advertising*, **18** (1), 1–14.

Copley, P. and Robson, I. (2001). Practitioner perspectives on arts tourism marketing. *Journal of Travel and Tourism Marketing*, **10** (2–3), 23–46.

Culliton, J. W. (1948). *The Management of Marketing Costs*. HBS.

Duncan, T. (2002). *Integrated Marketing Communications*. McGraw Hill.

Fill, C. (2002). *Marketing Communications: Contexts, Strategies and Applications*. 3rd edition. Financial Times Prentice Hall.

Furnham, A. and Thomson, L. (1999). Gender role stereotyping on two British radio stations. *Sex Roles: A Journal of Research*, **40** (1), 153–162.

Gatton, D. S., Dubois, C. L. Z. and Faley, R. H. (1999). The effects of organisational context on occupational gender-stereotyping. *Sex Roles: A Journal of Research*, **40** (7–8), 567–577.

Goldsmith, R. (1999). The personalised marketplace: beyond the 4Ps. *Marketing Intelligence and Planning*, **17** (4), 178–185.

Hall, C. and Crum, J. (1994). Women and 'body-isms' in television beer commercials. *Sex Roles: A Journal of Research*, **31** (516), 329–337.

Hersey, P. (1988). *Selling – A Behavioural Science Approach*. Prentice Hall.

Hodge, A. (1990). Fun, games and training in ad sales. *Admap*, July. www.warc.com

Jones, B. (2000). Historical research in marketing. In *Marketing Theory* (M. J. Baker, ed.), Thomson Learning.

Kotler, P. (2000). *Marketing Management*. 10th edition. Prentice Hall.

Kyziridis, P., Saren, M. and Tzokas, N. (1996). Sales management: re-engineering the sales force for relationship marketing. ESOMAR. EMAC Symposium. www.warc.com

Lane, N. and Crane, A. (2002). Revisiting gender role stereotyping in the sales profession. *Journal of Business Ethics*, **40** (2), 121–132.

McDonald, M. (1988). *Effective Industrial Selling*. Heinemann.

McDowell, L. and Court, G. (1994). Missing subjects: gender, power and sexuality in merchant banking. *Economic Geography*, **70**, 229–251.

Sticky-marketing.net (2001). Closing the sale. At www.sticky-marketing.net/glossary/closing_the_sale.htm.

The Times 100 (2003). Nestle – injecting new life into the PLC. The Times 100, September.

Venn, P. (1999). Closing the sale. At www.users.globalnet.co.uk/~adrest/Dpages/Closingskill.html.

Planning and managing personal communications

Chapter overview

Introduction to this chapter

The nature of personal communications is understood here in its broadest sense and not simply the traditional personal selling function with its techniques and associated methods, and tools such as those outlined in Chapter 16. This includes the obvious interfaces with events such as exhibitions and trade shows, seminars and conferences, but also the ways in which all employees interface with customers and potential customers. This chapter therefore takes the APIC general framework developed in Chapter 4 and facilitates application, via a decision sequence model in the management of personal communications in a particular context.

Aims of this chapter

This chapter provides a case study that can be analysed with the aid of the material presented in Chapter 4. In particular, the framework presented at the end of the chapter is designed as a facilitation device for this purpose. After completion of this chapter the reader should be able to:

- explain the elements of the APIC system, as applied to personal communications, in broad DSM terms

- provide some critique of the adoption of such an approach

- provide a framework for the management of the personal communications function

- apply the above to the management of personal communications for a major car brand, Audi

- facilitate the application of the above to the management of personal communications in a broader context.

A framework for managing advertising employing the APIC decision sequence model

As outlined in Chapter 4 the APIC DSM is a commonly used model that deals with both the 'art' and 'science' aspects of communication. A decision sequence framework is required to help plan personal communications in just the same way as any communication might be but the difference is in the detail. The reader should refer back to the framework provided in Chapter 4 of this book as an aid to analysis of the case given below.

The case of Audi

Background

As the role of personal communications has changed, focus is no longer purely on the selling function. Of course, this remains of prime importance as does the role of sales representative and other associated roles in terms of selling but also in maintaining relationships. However, it is now recognized that people within the organization, through their skills and expertise, are (or should be) very valuable assets as the organization's human resources are at its heart (The Times 100, 2003).

History

The history of Audi is a colourful one in car and motorcycle manufacture. From the start technological innovation has been the key driver, endorsed in 1971 by the 'Vorsprung durch Technik' campaign. The first car was completed in 1901 in Cologne and there was a move to Saxony in 1902. The first design incorporated the idea of a coachman and was a right-hand drive machine, but left-hand drive had been established by the 1920s. By the 1960s, with NSU as part of the organization, the Wankel Spider was born and, in 1972, the Audi 80 was launched, of which 1 million were sold in the first six years. By 1980 the four wheel drive Audi Quattro was the sensation of the Geneva Motor Show.

Heritage

Heritage is, of course, important. Audi drivers like to be associated with an old-established and successful brand. Audi originated in Germany in 1909, founded by August Horch. The thirteen-year-old son of one of the original directors suggested that Horch should translate his name into Latin. Horch in German means 'listen' and the nearest to listen in Latin is 'audi' meaning audio. Audi first appeared on a car in 1910 and from the start the company had a reputation for innovation. One such innovation as early as 1912 was headlights that turned sideways to reduce drag.

During the 1930s the four leading German manufacturers were Audi, Horch, Wanderer and DKW, and from 1932 until 1969 the company was known as Audi Union, with the now famous four rings that form its logo. The company briefly became Audi NSU (1969–77) and then Audi AG. Connections with Ferdinand Porsche were strong, Porsche having worked on Wanderer designs in the early 1930s. By the late 1980s Audi had assembled cars for Porsche. Audi have also had some success with Grand Prix racing.

Structure

In 1964 Audi joined the VW group which included Bentley, Lamborghini and Buggati. But Audi was clearly in a position of technological expertise with, for example, the first catalytic converters in the 1980s and the four-wheel drive Quattro in the 1990s. By 1994 Audi had separate dealerships and centres from VW and were clearly positioned differently in the marketplace. There was further investment in showrooms and buildings but, more importantly, in 'people and processes' that would dominate customer experience and help create positive word of mouth.

Mission and brand values

Many companies aspire to the lofty mission to be recognized as a world leader in the field or fields they operate in. In Audi's case this is engineering, manufacture, and marketing of attachments and related services. In addition, Audi believe that following fundamental values will assure both the company's success and the personal fulfilment and well-being of employees.

Commitment

Audi are committed in several ways:

1 *To customer service and satisfaction.* Audi believe in building loyal, trusting partnerships of employees, dealers, and customers by striving to exceed customer expectations and consistently providing high value for their investment, and being responsive to their needs.

2 *To leadership.* Audi believe that innovation in the development of products, processes and services is necessary to achieve and sustain leadership, and that this is accomplished by encouraging creative risk-taking and using leading technology.

3 *To co-operation and communication.* Audi believe that co-operation among employees, shareholders, dealers, customers and suppliers is essential for continued success and that open communication and co-operative teamwork produces a work environment for constructive decision-making.

Overall, Audi believe in supporting the environments, communities and partnerships that contribute to success.

Audi the brand

Branding influences perceptions of products. Customers have confidence in reputable brands. Brands are more often than not emotional things. With Audi, competitive advantage is gained through recruitment – training and developing skilled, intelligent people. By investing in its people, Audi are investing in the brand.

Audi's position

Audi have positioned themselves as design leader – a blend of technological innovation and design excellence. Romulus Rost, head of design at Audi is quoted as saying 'you sell image, you sell design, you sell the brand through the design of the car, its as simple as that' (Youson, 2002). Design for Audi provides a USP but active and astute management is needed to translate brand intent into 'customer experience'. This process thus involves:

- creating brand intent

- aligning the organization

- delivering the customer experience

- refining this process.

In short, it involves making and fulfilling promises to stay on top (Barron, 2003).

Audi's advertising

Audi effectively joined the Prestige Car Club in 1995 alongside BMW, Mercedes and Jaguar, and above Volvo and Saab but below the super prestige status of Porsche and Ferrari. Audi has done this on its strong technical credentials and brand desirability. Audi lie at the high end of the market where less than 10 per cent of new car sales in the UK occur. They have, in fact, joined a kind of aristocratic club where the usual emotional and rational factors are at play but in addition there is a 'Factor X' to do with prestige and which is a kind of co-efficient on demand. A Toyota and a Porsche may have some similarities, for example the 6.1 seconds it takes to go from 0 to 60 miles per hour, or they may have similar top speeds, but the Porsche image commands a much higher price. Thus the prestige brand dynamic affects the manufacturer (volume growth, higher margins), the dealer (volume growth, selling price and margin on cars, parts and service) and the customer (the second-hand market, higher re-selling prices and less depreciation on financial outlay).

Audi in the 1980s produced bland Eurocars similar to Ford Sierras. Perceptions had to be changed and this was achieved through the Audi Quattro. By the 1990s Audi was still on the prestige waiting list behind Mercedes, BMW and Jaguar, and needed to achieve at least parity with these via an image change.

Audi's image

In 1995 Audi entered the Prestige Car Club. From research Audi had decided that they needed to be three things:

- modern, with strong design

- innovative, following their history and heritage rich in technological ideas

- individual, with independence and understatement.

This meant positioning away from Jaguar (establishment, successful, British, conservative, old school tie), Mercedes (established, rich, successful and inflexible) and BMW (ambitious, competitive, ostentatious, confident and successful) to being successful, intelligent and different, a position away from the others in the club, but on their own terms.

To achieve this Audi avoided the use of print advertising to underline imagery. Rather print was used to underline Audi's technological credentials, a crucial hygiene factor for the Prestige Car Club membership. Product innovations were explained using witty, wry tone of voice to portray Audi as modern, innovative and individual.

Audi used television to get across these three fundamental brand values of being modern, innovative and individual but using emotional appeals, suggesting that some buyers of cars, i.e. Audi customers, are one step ahead of the rest.

Audi had cemented its membership of the Prestige Car Club by 1997 but realized that understanding the customer was key to success.

People and culture

Audi is a classic case of an organization needing to change culture. This is not as simple as it may seem. It requires patience because cultural change cannot happen 'just like that'. It takes management attitude and ability to create and sustain a momentum, and it needs senior management with the power and status to lead change. This also requires effective communication within the organization. People are at the heart of Audi's culture. The development of Audi's people, technicians in particular, has meant the creation, development and provision of service excellence, and key to this is the understanding of individual customer need so that solutions to repair and service problems exceed customer expectation. Customers have come to expect that they will always come first, so that this expectation must be delivered for continued success.

Audi therefore believe that providing employees with challenges for growth and recognition demonstrates a long-term commitment and provides a promising future for them. Respect for every individual builds a team of empowered, self-motivated and creative employees, committed to excellence. Audi believe that continual improvement of products, processes, services and skills provides long-term success for employees, dealers and customers.

The Audi career path plays an important role. Apprentices graduate to celebrate successful completion of their studies. They may be vehicle technicians, parts personnel or body repairers or finishers, but each striving for technical excellence, and understanding leading-edge technology and, not least, customer expectations. Direct contact with the customer means being able to build relationships is of paramount importance.

Recruitment

Recruitment in Audi is based on the identification of people most likely to fit in with Audi's ideals. This means having the same values as the Audi brand values. Individuals therefore must want to be part of a team, want to self-develop, contribute to the success of Audi and, above all, seek to improve customer service.

Training

Training people in order to meet company objectives is a given for many organizations, and Audi is no exception. The acquisition of skills that enables employees to then deliver brand values is a key goal in itself and is essential in the car environment where technological changes and issues are of paramount importance. Dealers and customers benefit from high-quality, enterprising and confident employees. Training in Audi is therefore about personal improvement to meet customer requirements.

Development

Development is encouraged in order that employees meet their own needs so, for example, education is central. However, this is personal development that goes hand in hand with organizational goals. For this reason Audi leave their own Centre for Technical Excellence with an appraisal system to identify training and development needs and appropriate courses to attend. Individuals are actively encouraged to become involved in this process via training needs analysis with the use of multimedia hardware and software. This activity:

- enhances the Audi brand

- means that dealerships have high-quality, enterprising and highly motivated employees who produce high-quality service

- means that the consumer comes first, and the consumer knows this

- ensures that employees benefit via a careers progression ladder for motivation

- provides continuous development of the brand via the Audi Academy.

Customer satisfaction and the 'Know Your Customer' programme

Employees need to be motivated and need to want to provide high standards of customer service. There is a link between customer satisfaction and employee satisfaction. But to know how customers really feel, qualitative research of some sort needs to be enacted. Audi decided to use a workshop approach that brought customers and employees together, not to test concepts as Audi could with focus groups, but to focus on the business context. The workshops were run in the dealerships, on premises familiar to employees and customers. This gave local managers ownership of the process, which could be viewed by all employees via video link. Kemp and Atkins (1999) call this 'Customer Theatre' and that it is 'a mechanism which highlights the power of the voice and presence of the customer to a captive audience'. This means that employees hear at first hand what customers think about service and in this sense it is also a team-building tool. Employees hopefully gain understanding of how all roles feed in to the customer experience.

This tool used rational assessment, not exploration, to understand the employee/customer interface. It was purposefully designed to perform this task and, as such, went against a number of the conventions of qualitative research such as dress code and style of questioning. Kemp and Atkins (1999) list the main benefits of this approach. It:

- brings the voice of the customer alive

- offers all employees the chance to hear customers' opinions

- filters information and findings throughout the whole organization

- shapes and changes culture by placing the customer at the heart of the company

- acts as a catalyst for change

- complements and builds on existing research

- gives up-to-the-minute feedback on how a business is performing

- identifies emerging issues and reveals strengths and weaknesses

- brings all parties of the service profit chain together

- highlights best practice customer-handling skills and processes

- provides public relations opportunity – local and for the brand

- demonstrates commitment to customer care

- uses video clips from the workshops for training and information purposes to brief all departments within the organization.

The Audi 'Know Your Customer' programme was referred to as this from the start and in all communications. The worry was that, despite successes by 1997, customer loyalty was not strong and there was no understanding of why valued customers were defecting. This programme was designed to give the customer a voice and would drive Audi at a micro (Audi Centres) and macro (Audi UK) level with the result being 'From Inverness to Ingolstadt the voice of the Audi customer regularly influences business' (Kemp and Atkins, 1999). A video library of commentary has been developed that contains 'workshop criticism, not fan club sycophancy', which is the preferred experience for Audi, and a customer-driven organization has emerged.

The marketing challenge

Audi's marketing challenge was to enter the Prestige Car Club. This has been achieved. The challenge now is to make sure that customers keep coming back. Audi have achieved this so far by the successful development and implementation of skilled delivery of service. It is clear from research that the better the reputation for service, the higher the turnover will be, the converse also being the case, i.e. the poorer the reputation for service, the lower the turnover. This is the case on every measure. For example, there is a much higher profit per employee where service reputation is high. However, the service encounter can be highly complex and Audi adhered to three things:

1   Alignment of service offers in each dealership. This initiative was spurred on by the fact that Audi had come last in a luxury car marques' survey in terms of satisfaction and loyalty. The key challenge was consistency, which Audi met with a 20 per cent hike in after-sales revenue in little over one year.

2   Investment in people through a focused and sustained effort via technicians trained in customer service skills, who understood customer need and were able to engender customer confidence.

3   The use of metrics for high performance using Gallup measures so that low performance could be avoided and higher profits achieved.

The key challenge to Audi has been to understand what satisfies customers but also deliver real improvements in customer care in order that retention can be achieved. The key to this was to facilitate the link between customers, management and those at the customer interface. In Audi's case these was the army of technicians who were able, after training and development, to liaise with customers and meet customer need. This was only possible through the creation of a corporate culture that placed employees and customers at the heart of the organization. This meant technicians had to be trained to understand customer expectations and the importance of the customer service promise, including such employees getting to know what the customer thinks of them and the service the organization provide through them.

Assignment

Assume you have been asked to help devise a personal communication programme that would help an organization achieve what Audi have managed. This would build on the company's already established brand or corporate image. Use the DSM provided in Chapter 4 to complete the following tasks.

- Outline what you feel to be the key background points to the Audi case from a personal communication perspective. From this information establish the likely target(s).

- From the information available, establish Audi's objectives and positioning, and the role for personal communication within this. Write an outline strategy for the Audi situation.

- Provide ideas on the implementation of the personal communication campaign by using the parameters in the implementation section of the DSM framework and show clearly what you would recommend in terms of allocation, budgets, timings and so on.

- Using the final section of the DSM, the control section, suggest what monitoring, evaluation and research methods and techniques you would employ to maximize efficiency and effectiveness of the campaign.

Summary of Key Points

- Most writers would subscribe to a form of decision sequence model when attempting to manage advertising. There are, however, challenges to the APIC-type of system without alternatives. A shift has occurred with regard to a move away from communication effects to return on investment in advertising.

- Analysis deals with assessments of customers, products, the organization and its environment. This is the 'where are we now?' question.

- Planning deals with targets objectives and positioning. This is the 'where do we want to go?' question. This is followed by consideration of creative and media strategy. This is the 'how do we get there?' question.

- Implementation is a consideration of 'how do we put this into practice?' and involves the allocation of spend to the campaign.

- Control involves evaluation and research and is the 'did we get there?' question. This is not only a check on whether objectives have been achieved, but also a consideration of the place of research in the entire framework.

- Audi's attitude toward and commitment to this form of personal communication allows for enhanced customer satisfaction.

Examination Questions

These questions are similar to those outlined in Chapter 4 but should be answered more specifically with regard to sales promotion and direct marketing and the brand.

1 Explain why you agree or disagree with the contention that the APIC-type model is useful as a framework for personal communication to operate within.

2 Outline what you consider to be the important elements of the analysis stage of a personal communication decision sequence model.

3 The planning stage of a DSM involves consideration of 'where do we want to go?', having already established targets. Discuss the importance of establishing targets early on in a personal communication campaign.

4 Explain the usefulness (or not) of perceptual mapping in planning a programme such as that described in the Audi case.

5 Creative strategy is part of 'how do we get there?' Discuss the very different personal communication and customer satisfaction programme that Audi put into practice.

6 Discuss the importance of recruitment, training and development within a company like Audi.

7 Outline the major reasons why dealership involvement was important to Audi's programme.

8 There are a number of practical issues when considering how to put a programme such as the one described into practice. Discuss these in relation to the Audi case.

9 Discuss the logic behind pre-, concurrent and post-testing within personal communication and customer care.

10 Comment on the idea of Audi's customer satisfaction programme as an investment not a cost in relation to building the Audi brand.

References

Barron, J. (2003). How strong brands get 'on intent' – and stay there. *Journal of Business Strategy*, **24** (2), 36–41.

Kemp, A. and Atkins, R. (1999). Customer theatre – bringing the voice of the customer alive. ESOMAR.

The Times 100 (2003). Audi – investing in people and in brands. At www.tt100.biz.

Youson, M. (2002). Four-ring circus – look after your brand and your brand will look after you. *Engineering*, **243** (7), ss7 (2).

PART SIX

End Piece

The last part of this book is an attempt to pull together some of the strands of thought that have been alluded to throughout the previous seventeen chapters. Research interactivity and international aspects of marketing communications are felt to be worthy of consideration in their own right, since issues within these areas are at the very edge of change in marketing (and corporate) communications.

This sixth part of the book consists of three chapters. Chapter 18 deals with research in and evaluation of marketing communications, Chapter 19 with interactivity in marketing communications and Chapter 20 with key international marketing communications issues.

Research in and evaluation of marketing communications

Chapter overview

Introduction to this chapter

This chapter deals with research and evaluation in marketing communications. The notion that each element of the communications mix needs to be part of a carefully planned strategy in order to maximize effectiveness to obtain a 'unified message' was put forward in Chapter 1. A decision sequence model/ framework was described as a framework for the development of this integrated strategy, the key stages being some form of situation analysis followed by decisions on targeting, objectives and positioning, then strategies, budgets, implementation and, finally, evaluation and control. In other words, the final stage of the model attempts to answer the question 'did we get there?' or, put another way, 'how can this be evaluated and controlled?' This chapter uses the DSM and maps out where research has a part to play in what is essentially a risk-reduction set of exercises designed to enhance and facilitate decision-making. As such this is the marketing research–marketing communications interface. The nature of research at the pre-, during and post-stages of campaigns is considered in terms of message creation and achievement of objectives.[1]

Aims of this chapter

The overall aim of this chapter is to explore the nature of research and evaluation in terms of marketing communication as part of the overall marketing effort. More specifically, during the course of this chapter, the reader should be able to:

- understand the nature and role of research and evaluation in relation to marketing communications and, in so doing, define the role of integration in this

- outline research issues at the varying stages of a marketing communications plan

- explain the types of research and data collection methods that are appropriate and available at each stage, and how a research and evaluation attitude adds value and how it can be used to improve marketing performance

- become familiar with research techniques, particularly those that have gained in popularity in recent times

- become familiar with tracking studies used in marketing communications

- explain the elements of monitoring and evaluation of marketing communications campaigns.

The nature of research and evaluation

Why the organization should research and evaluate

Creatives in agencies or communications companies may very well be prone to disregarding research findings but many in the industry or in companies are in favour of using some form of research process to aid decision-making, improve spending effectiveness, reduce risk and generally improve knowledge and understanding. Not everyone is in favour, however, and it may be that this is politically motivated or simply that spend on research is viewed as a waste, and that resources should be spent on actual communication. On the one hand, research helps avoid costly mistakes, and provides alternative ideas and objectivity. On the other hand, it is costly, it is not easy to measure the specific effect of any piece of communication in isolation, it can cause friction within the organization and it takes time.

Return on customer investment

As outlined earlier, in Chapter 4 of this book return on customer investment is mandatory for Schultz and Kitchen (2000), who see much of what is done under the name of evaluation as being 'too soft'.

Schultz and Kitchen therefore advocate:

- Tackling the more difficult measurement of ROI rather than supply communication effect.

- Highlighting the importance of time frames in communications planning.

- The use and completion of a communications planning matrix.

- Separation of short- from long-term returns.

- An 'outside-in' rather than 'inside-out' approach to budgeting, i.e. the amount spent is driven by the amount spent by customers which will drive down spend and push profits up.

- A closed-loop system for identifying the value of customers and prospects which requires incremental returns in order to calculate ROCI.

- That the older rates (minimum percentage returns) for investments shall be set.

- Short- and long-term brand aspect measurement in terms of brand equity.

In the end Schultz and Kitchen can be said to advocate communications as an investment and not a cost, as these authors are still interested in attitude and behavioural measurement via Activity-based costing (ABC) and economic value assessment (EVA).

Research and evaluation explained

Evaluation of the marketing communications effort can involve the obvious as with sales increases for example. This kind of evaluation is very tempting, especially in today's climate of pressurized performance. But cause and effect, especially with advertising, is not as concrete as it is with, for example, sales promotion coupon redemption.

The research process involves the creation of a data bank that is the combination of regularly collected marketing information and data collected from marketing

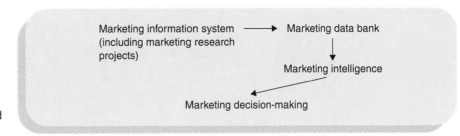

Figure 18.1
Research process and
decision-making.

research projects. This then provides a platform of marketing intelligence that allows for informed decision-making, as shown in Figure 18.1.

Marketing research itself is the process of systematically collecting, recording and analysing data pertaining to specific markets or segments of a market for which the company caters. The problem is one of control of variables, which is a hard and sometimes impossible task. There are often residual and cumulative effects, especially in the case of pre-existing brands and also decay effects, which will vary from context to context. Other considerations might be the lifecycle stage of the product, market or brand, where objectives in each stage will also vary.

The difference between good and bad research depends on input, including effective control over the entire marketing research process comprising:

1   *Defining and locating problems.* There is a need to agree on research objectives, i.e. matching the best research to the task of obtaining information which will help solve the problem. There is a need for a clear definition of the problem, i.e. not vague or broad, but focused. Three types of research might help: *exploratory* (to help better define the problem or to suggest hypotheses), *descriptive* (to enable the marketer to describe customer profiles, segmentation and so on), and *causal* (to test hypotheses about cause and effect relationships).

2   *Determining relevant information.* This involves, for example, demographic and/or psychographic characteristics such as consumer usage, uses, when used, penetration of product, retailer reaction and support needed.

3   *Designing and doing research.* There are basically two types of data collection: *secondary* and *primary*.

Two documents are important in this area. First, the *research brief*, i.e. a verbal or written instruction outlining the problems as perceived by the marketer. The *research proposal* is a remedy to fulfil the brief, but it also has to sell the agency or research/communications company who will wish to 'pitch' for the work based not just on the proposal content but with a CV, i.e. relevant experience, reputation and so on.

Research has a number of components, which are usually represented as in Figure 18.2.

Secondary research, the examination of which is often termed 'desk', needs to be relevant (current, up to date), accurate and impartial. Obvious examples of external secondary data are government statistics or data in periodicals or trade magazines. Bought-in secondary data comes from the likes of Mintel. Internal data are things like sales records. Often, secondary data provides a good starting point for further, (primary) research.

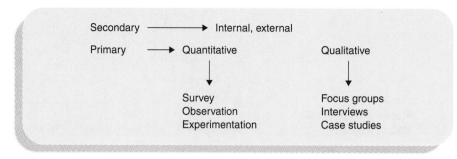

Figure 18.2
Research components.

Primary research is by definition original, exclusive and tailor-made for a specific problem. It has been likened to a commission (rather like a painting or a photograph) for the first time. Primary means first-hand *quantitative* or *qualitative research*. There are basically three types of *quantitative research*:

1   *Observation* attempts to record the actions of people in situations. This is often explanatory research and includes observing traffic in supermarkets, use of eye cameras in advertising or packaging research, use of hidden cameras and one-way mirrors. These techniques are limited and often used in conjunction with other techniques and methods.

2   *Surveys* usually gather descriptive information on beliefs/knowledge/preference/ levels of satisfaction. The work can be very structured (using dichotomous questions), semi-structured or unstructured (using open-ended questions).

3   *Experiment* seeks causal information, often using matched groups of subjects giving them different treatments. Controlling certain parameters, it seeks differences in responses from the various groups. This kind of work often involves control groups against which comparisons can be made.

There is also a need to gain an appreciation of the advantages and disadvantages of the various quantitative *contact methods*. For example, *postal surveys* are inexpensive but likely to be unrepresentative if only a proportion of the sample bothers to reply. Rewards or incentives are used in order to improve response rates. *Telephone surveys* gained popularity because of speed and relatively low cost, and they are cheaper to administer. The usual associated problems include length of time on the telephone, which can irritate and be an intrusion, especially if held at a bad time. These surveys are perhaps more successful in business/organizational/industrial research. *Electronic contact* is becoming increasingly important not just for questionnaire analysis, but for design and actual contact as with, for example, Random Digital Dialling, bar coding and electronic point of sale (EPOS)-type systems.

Qualitative research includes:

1   *Depth interviews*. These are expensive and time-consuming. The commonest form is the semi-structured interview that yields very rich information. This can be expensive but, when used within a structured schedule, can be cost-effective and the only way of getting answers to questions that have depth to them, as opposed to the superficial, highly structured questionnaire approach. Other techniques may be employed beyond the interview schedule (see *semiotics* later).

2 *Focus groups* can result in useful discussions leading to new and spontaneous ideas and revelations that are not possible by other methods. The small numbers involved are often cited as the main problem with such a method but if representation is not the goal and idea generation is, then this criticism is negated.

3 *Case studies* and *histories* are easy to understand and use in the general sense but are rather more problematic from a research standpoint. For Bell et al. (1987) case study research is a 'study of an instance in action', where the instance is a representative entity of a class of things, such as a particular religious group being an instance of religious groupings. This is a bounded system, i.e. the 'case' chosen transcends the principle of selection of a sample that is representative of a class. Case study research can be current or historical and interpretative, offering 'a surrogate experience' inviting the reader 'to underwrite the account' by appealing to tacit knowledge of the context.

There are also other sources that are external to the company but can be bought in. *Continuous research* is usually bought by subscription where data are based on audits, panels but also on surveys. Sometimes this is *syndicated* with a base of subscribers as with TGI which surveys products. *Omnibus Surveys* are regular and ongoing and the marketer can buy into these with some questions or perhaps just one question.

VIGNETTE

What's in the non-ad hoc research shop? Geodemographics, psychographics, TGI, ACORN, Mosaic, data audits, EPOS . . . to name but a few

The layperson in marketing can be forgiven for raising a smile when confronted with the myriad, jargonized terms that abound in this area of marketing activity. Clever acronyms and other uses of language to describe what are essentially the tools of the market researcher's trade have evolved over the past forty or so years. Certainly the *TGI*, an international tool but offered in the UK by the British Market Research Bureau (BMRB), has a 24 000-strong sample of adult informants who are willing, for a small incentive, to self-complete a very large questionnaire. This seeks to gather data on a wide range of products and product usage, on brands and extent of use, that is cross-tabulated with a range of things from demographics, psychographics and media consumption. Thus buying into TGI provides the marketer with not only an aid to targeting but also to message construction and media selection. *Audits* more generally are an aid to monitoring and these days can often be had in an on-line format. Electronic point of sale and other electronic auditing such as *loyalty/bonus cards* have added to both quantity and speed of data, to the point where a high percentage of grocery products can be accounted for.

Geodemographic systems have developed since the 1970s and *ACORN* and *Mosaic*, to name but two commercially branded services, offer links between geography and demography, allowing for targeted campaigns and research; similarly with *psychographic* systems such as those that have evolved from the original *VALS* as developed in the USA by Maslow and Rockeach in 1975 and which modelled American society in terms of attitudes, interests and opinions *AIO*. VALS II followed in 1989 and by then commercially driven systems were in place and have been developed since, such as Young and Rubicam's *4Cs* (a cross-cultural consumer classification) or Pegram Walters International's *Global Village* systems. Such systems allow the marketing communicator to fire messages at a much better known target, domestically and internationally.

Syndicated research is relatively inexpensive to buy into. The best examples of this in the UK are Mintel and Keynote, and these are also much used by students. Much less heard about outside particular industries or sectors are the many examples of syndicated research of use to marketers and marketing communicators that may even be bought in alongside competitors.

The *Omnibus Survey* is a form of continuous research that covers particular industries, sectors or special interest groups. Pickton and Broderick (2001) use the example of Martin-Hamblin's monthly telephone panel of *500 general practitioners*, maintaining that a defining feature of the Omnibus Survey is the choosing of a fresh sample every time it runs. Another feature is the control the subscriber has in terms of spend; the marketer may choose to have only one question in the survey, but this method can be very cost-effective. This allows for at least some data where none at all might be had if a marketing research project were to be considered cost-prohibitive. Speed of obtaining data is another factor. *National Opinion Poll* claim, because of the ability of a food manufacturing client to very quickly put questions on NOP's weekend *Telebus*, a nationally representative sample of 1000 respondents, the company was able to receive actionable research data within three working days after a health-scare story broke. This allowed the client to take appropriate market action and protect brand image as well as sales. *Media* research can also be bought in in a non-ad hoc manner, so that the marketing communicator can buy in to *NRS* or *BARB*'s Nielsen-generated 'peoplemeter' facilitating the electronic audience measurement service, among others.

Marketers can also test marketing communications before 'going commercial' by using *test marketing*, classically trying out certain ideas or materials in one area (a test market) of the country first, using regional media and so on. This can let the marketer know to a certain extent whether things are working at all or even too well for current production capacity and so on. A variation on test marketing is the *mini-test market* whereby certain outlets only are used and on a very finite scale. Here for example devices within point-of-sale or in-store promotions can be tested.

Sources: Adapted from Dealer Magazine (2000); Pickton and Broderick (2001); www.mrnews.com 12t3ny/ news/tns0699.html, accessed 13 September 1999; www.nop.co.uk/ omnibus /hp_omnibus. shtml, accessed 2003, www.tgisurveys.com/about/aboutmenu.htm; www.tutor2u.net/ business/ marketing/research_types.asp, accessed 2003.

STOP POINT

Consider what non-ad hoc marketing research is, or alternatively, what it is not. Consider also the cost advantages of buying into continuous, syndicated or other forms of non-ad hoc marketing and audience research. Think about how such research can be useful to the marketing communicator in particular.

Research and evaluation within a decision sequence framework

The question of when to apply research and evaluation can be answered simply by considering the decision sequence framework or model as advocated in

Chapter 4. Research and evaluation can be appropriate in one form or another at each stage but in broader terms takes place before, during and after a campaign in terms of pre-, concurrent and post-testing. Pre-testing is carried out before a campaign is launched. After implementation, monitoring and evaluation comes in the guise of concurrent and post-testing, after the target has been exposed to the communication. For example, attitudes may be tracked via tracking studies over a long period, with regular testing at intervals to measure the effects of a particular communication so that the communication itself, a brand and purchase intentions may be involved.

Evaluation of the marketing communications effort can involve the obvious, sales increases for example. It is desirable to be 100 per cent sure, but this is not possible. This kind of evaluation is very tempting, especially in today's climate of pressurized performance, but cause and effect, especially with advertising, is not as concrete as it is with, for example, sales promotion coupon redemptions. According to Rothschild (1987), research has become one of the cornerstones of modern advertising management; it is a 'vital force in giving direction to the ultimate strategy of the campaign, and it is regularly used to assess the creative product that finally emerges'. It is common for the diagnostic testing of messages to be carried out for the development of effective advertising, as well as assessment of how well objectives have been achieved in terms of sales or market share indicators, or attitude changes. Rossiter and Percy (1997) divide the research and evaluation process into the categories of advertising strategy research, concept development research and advert testing, and campaign tracking and evaluation. As mentioned in Chapter 4, the research and evaluation process can be linked into the marketing communications DSM:

Situation analysis and targeting – consumer research, competitive research and product research.

Targets, objectives and positioning – internal and feasibility research.

Strategy development – developmental pre-test of concepts.

Budget – final pre-test and execution of production.

Implementation – test marketing and internal feasibility research.

Evaluation – post-test against objectives.

New situation analysis research – cycle begins again.

Research can be conducted either *in situ*, i.e. in the field, or artificially in the 'laboratory'. With the latter, respondents are exposed to a variety of devices such as concept boards or animatics/photomatics (see below) and asked to discuss various aspects or answer questions regarding certain issues. This is controlled by the researcher but lacks the realism of actual situations where marketing communications has to operate. A discussion around a coffee table about certain concepts, however, is not meant to be a substitute for a piece of communication that is absorbed with distractions or noise of one sort or another. Research conducted 'in the field' sees communication being examined under more natural settings but leads to different kinds of issues being tested, such as competitive activity or media content. Marketing research reaches out to people to find out who they are, what they prefer, what attitudes they have, what appeals to them most, what they respond to, how they react and ultimately who buys. In other words,[2] whom does the target audience consist of, what do they want, when do they need it, where does it sell best, how does it reach them and why do they buy it?

Advertising effectiveness testing can be divided into the two components of communication and behaviour. This can then be combined with a consideration of the three stages of pre-, concurrent and post-campaign research testing (Figure 18.3).

Clearly this incorporates the hierarchy of effects models where communications move consumers through a series of stages from source to the purchase (the usual unawareness, awareness, knowledge, liking, preference, conviction and purchase), as discussed in Chapter 2, and considers the type of testing appropriate at each stage. As can be seen, pre-, concurrent and post-testing are considered under *communication factors* where *source* variables factors include attitude change, trust or credibility, likeability and, on the negative side, the possibility that the source might dominate the message at the expense of the brand/ product/service. The *message* and the means by which it is communicated (delivery, usually a *medium* of one sort or another) are bases for evaluation. The message is usually tested to see if the intended meaning has been communicated to the receiver, and this might include the effectiveness of individual message elements, for example copy, strap lines, headlines and so on. *Media* decisions need to be made based on research so that the marketer is better able to decide on media class (broadcast or print) and sub-class (newspapers or magazines), or specific vehicles (one magazine rather than another). Placement within vehicles can also be the subject of research, as can number of insertions, length of a television commercial and best means of scheduling, possibly using bought-in audience research such as the aforementioned NRS, BARB, and so on, data (see also Chapter 7).

Behavioural factors include intent to buy, trial and purchase, and brand loyalty. The actual practice of consumers can be very different from the theoretical stance of the hierarchy of effects, and therefore *action measures*, which allude to an intent to purchase rather than actual behaviour and include brand choice,

	COMMUNICATION Source, message, media		BEHAVIOUR Pseudo-purchase, purchase
PRE-TESTS	Focus groups Checklists Split-run Readability	Physiological Direct mail Theatre On-the-air	Test marketing Single-source
CONCURRENT	Recall Attitude Tracking Coincidental		Single-source Diaries Storecupboard checks
POST-TESTS	Readership Recall Awareness	Attitude Association Audience assessment	Single-source Split-cable Enquiry Sales counts

Figure 18.3
The three stages of pre-, concurrent and post-campaign research testing.

calls or written contact and store visits. Such measures are important in the early stages of the PLC where one objective will almost certainly be awareness. Clearly the objectives of the communication need to be stated at the outset and measured accordingly. Burnett and Moriarty (1998) maintain that there is firm evidence that shows a strong correlation between intent to buy and actual purchase when involvement is high, as with, for example, cars or expensive fashion goods.

Before the marketing communications effort (pre-testing)

Unfinished communication

This largely relates to communications materials, marketing or corporate, that is to say, visuals, copy, mock-ups, roughs, animatics/photomatics and the like. Pre-testing the ideas contained within this decreases risk but costs money. This might be viewed as a waste or it might be done as a matter of course, in conjunction with testing the broader marketing mix as with new product development. Whether or not these devices represent the real thing is questionable, but both qualitative and quantitative testing can be conducted. The most common methods and tests are highlighted below.

Concept testing is used to weed through creative ideas, positioning and so on. Roughs are used, i.e. early artwork or storyboards or some other form of expression are used to get across the gist of the concept to informants who are usually part of a *focus group*. This is the commonest form of qualitative research, where a small number of people will freely discuss meanings or other aspects of mock advertisements, roughs and so on. The direction of the discussion will depend upon the brief and the objectives of the research. For example, the group may discuss alternative ideas, be expected to suggest other directions or choose between competing concepts. Participants might be observed through the use of videotaping or digital cameras or 'live' through one-way mirrors. Informants' reactions to images, advertisements/roughs etc. can therefore be observed. The *consumer jury* is a more formal (quantitative) evaluation tool where juries are made up of representatives of a target group. The jury is asked to rank concepts on rating scales and this again can be facilitated by the employment of tools like roughs.

Finished communication

Finished communication can be tested by *dummy vehicles* (allied to the *folder* or *portfolio* tests, designed to expose a group of informants to advertisements), being mainly used with press advertising, mostly magazines, but also employed with packaging research. An advertisement being tested is inserted into a dummy magazine and given to informants, who are asked to consume the magazine in the normal way. Later on they are asked questions about the entire magazine – editorial and advertisements. This type of testing is more realistic than the methods above that tend to take place in 'laboratory' conditions (Fill, 2002). *Readability tests* developed by Flesch in the 1970s employ a formula to assess the ease with which print copy can be read. This involves working out the average number of syllables per 100 words, the average length of sentence and the percentage of personal words and sentences. If the educational level of the target is known and a comparison can be made with established norms, then comprehension is best when sentences are short, words are concrete and familiar, and personal references used frequently (Fill, 2002). *Theatre tests* are mainly used to test finished broadcast advertising. An advertisement can be placed among others and shown to informants who then evaluate what is shown. However, this can be very simple or rather more complex, with the introduction of some form of time-lapsed recall test being used to measure the effect in terms of what Fill (2002) calls 'persuasion shift', having already gathered demographic and attitudinal details. This means that, overall, the test is both qualitative and quantitative but, as Fill notes, this is both artificial and unrealistic, and therefore the wisdom of using resources on such techniques is very questionable. It is rather ironic that the pressure or even requirement to be 'accountable' drives the use of this type of quantitative technique. *Physiological measures* involve involuntary physical responses. Examples are:

1   The pupilometer, where pupil dilation is measured in reaction to a stimulus. A constricted pupil is equated with low levels of interest and the opposite suggesting arousal. This test is used for packaging design and determining interest in particular advertisements but has a high cost and is used infrequently.

2   The eye camera, whereby cameras track the movement of the eye as it scans an advertisement or packs on a mocked-up shelf. Strap lines, headlines, pictures, illustrations and other such devices can be tested in this way, but the interpretation of results is a critical factor.

3   The psychogalvanometer, which tests galvanic skin response and measures amount of sweat produced by looking at advertisements and other images. This is the same principle as a lie detector and the pupilomenter in that, if an informant is aroused or interested, they are more likely to sweat. One problem with the psychogalvanometer is that while no doubt some form of emotional arousal is detected, the research does not reveal whether this is positive or negative.

4   The tachistoscope, which measures the ability of an advertisement or packaging to attract attention. The time of exposure is varied from very short exposure to light in a blacked out field to relatively much longer. The range may be something like 1/1000th of a second to 2 seconds. This is useful to identify those elements that are perceived first, often in a subliminal manner, so that shape is perceived before colour of a logo on a piece of packaging.

5   The electroencephalograph, which measures brain activity. Its use in marketing is very questionable, although claims are made that it essentially performs the same function as some of the above, i.e. the measurement of arousal and interest.

6   Voice recognition or, more accurately, pitch analysis, which determines when a voice is raised. If this occurs and positive comments are recorded then this is seen as a positive reaction to the stimulus.

Unfortunately the use of strange equipment and the fact that informants are aware that testing is occurring makes the use of these tools problematic for marketers. They are also costly and can really only achieve small-scale studies, but used intelligently can be invaluable and yield insightful data.

During and after marketing communications effort – concurrent and post-testing

This is a large and important area of marketing research, and certainly the largest area of communications research in terms of spend. Research for management decisions in communications therefore tends to be concentrated in this area. Much of the research in advertising deals with the ability to get through the clutter to consumers, using devices such as pictorial value or empathy. 'Are we getting there?' and 'did we get there?' or 'are we getting it right/did we get it right in the field?' are, of course important but different questions relating to research and evaluation. The option to leave things with pre-testing is there but this might only save a small sum and leave the organization with little or no information and knowledge on how things have worked in practice. The advantage of doing research during and/or after the campaign over mere pre-testing is that the communication is being tested *in situ*, in the real world. Most concurrent and post-tests concentrate on awareness of the communication, sales data and market share data.

Inquiry tests are quantitative approaches such as coupon counting and are real to life, i.e. they measure the numbers of enquiries or direct responses stimulated by communication, as with telephone numbers used in the commercial. They can be used on a single piece of communication or on an entire campaign. Similarly with *on-air tests* the same can be done. Both can use a *split run*, where different versions of the same communication are run in the same issue (Pickton and Broderick, 2001). Clearly this is quantitative information, but data gathered are merely inquiries, not sales, and the reasons why consumers did not respond may never be known.

Concurrent and post-testing involves *recall* (aided and unaided) and *recognition* tests. Here the concern is to draw the threads of research together and show how different research techniques can be applied to the totality of marketing communications. *Recall tests* are designed to assess the impression the communication has on the memory of the target market. Typically, informants are asked what programmes they remember watching on television and what advertisements they recall seeing. Unaided recall signifies no prompt used to aid recall but if a prompt is used then this is aided recall, and both are usually day-after recall (DAR). The reliability of such tests is high since these can be repeated without great difficulty. Though used a lot, validity is low since there is no known relationship between recall and sales, and they are expensive, making their use more difficult to justify. Fill (2002) suggests also that rational messages may be easier to recall than emotional ones but that programming will be an influencing factor in recall. Also, the mere fact that informants are involved in a process of agreeing to view programmes and be asked about it the next day must effectively drive up recall levels.

Recognition tests require informants to look at a media vehicle and then the informants are asked to look at particular features, articles, advertisements and so on. They are then asked about particular aspects of what they are seeing and what they thought about particular aspects. Fill (2002) suggests four types of scores that are reported:

1 Noted, i.e. the percentage of informants who remember seeing the advertisement.

2   Seen-associated, the percentage who recall seeing any part of the advertisement identifying the offering.

3   Read most, the percentage who report reading at least 50 per cent of the advertisement.

4   Signature, the percentage who remember seeing the brand or logo.

Here, like recall tests, reliability is high but, unlike recall, validity is high also, but this does not get over the problem of informants falsifying things. Costs are lower and it is easy to put into place the required simple questioning procedure. The *Starch Readership Service* is a non-random, '30000 advertisements in 1000 publications' survey (Pickton and Broderick, 2001) that tries to establish which ones work. It is very subjective. The service uses interviewers who find people who have seen a publication and takes informants through what particular advertisements they read and what components they have seen. This allows the communicator to assess several dimensions such as colour, size and copy but there is the danger of an assumption that readership tests translate into sales or the penetration of an idea. In many cases informants may be confused as to where they saw the advertising (Burnett and Moriarty, 1998).

Other tests

Market-based tests can be difficult to use. They are historical and expensive and it is difficult to identify the direct link between one form of communication and sales because so many other variables may also be factors. The use of the test market, the mini-test market and single source data using controlled exposure to advertising correlated to sales are all options, but expensive ones. *Tracking studies* are ongoing pieces of perceptual research and, as such, are designed to monitor the effect of communications and also competitor activity. There are many types of tracking study, for example retail-based tracking studies or monitoring of stock levels. Continuous tracking studies may be more appropriate for new products, and periodic tracking studies more appropriate to existing products (Fill, 2002). *Financial analysis* and in particular *variance analysis* are used to provide a picture of spend and especially the biggest item of communications expenditure, media spend. The drive for accountability and spiralling media costs has brought about a greater emphasis on, for example, effectiveness of media buying that can be analysed with reference to product type and overall expenditure norms. *Likeability* is, for Fill (2002) to do with being:

1   Personally meaningful, relevant, informative, true to life, believable and convincing.

2   Relevant, credible, and having clear product advantages, product usefulness, and importance to 'me'.

3   Stimulatory of interest or curiosity about the brand and of warm feelings through enjoyment of the advertisement.

This means then that likeability has to be measured at the deepest level of meaning (see semiotics later and in Chapter 6) so that it can be shown that a piece of communication has significant value that will ensure it will be effective.

Application of research and evaluation to the communications mix

Advertising

Many of the above tests have been developed in the advertising area. Evaluation has to be conducted on the basis of what is trying to be achieved. If the objective is awareness, then this is what should be tested for and not something else. For this reason guidelines or checklists have been developed to help marketers choose appropriate tests. In following the DSM approach it is then possible to identify communications objectives, use AIDA-type model approaches and so on in a systematic way. One such system developed within advertising is PACT, a set of guidelines developed primarily to assist in the research for television advertising, but can be applied to advertising in other media also. PACT stands for Positioning Advertising Copy Testing, and was developed in 1982 by twenty-one of the largest US advertising agencies to improve research used in testing advertising, and thereby provide a better, creative product for clients and control costs of, especially, television advertising. The nine principles of PACT are listed below:

1 Provide measurements that are relevant to the objectives of the advertising.

2 Require agreement about how the results will be used in advance of each specific test.

3 Provide multiple measurements because single measurements are not adequate to assess advertising performance.

4 Be based on a model of human response to communications – the reception of a stimulus, the comprehension of the stimulus and the response to the stimulus.

5 Allow for consideration of whether the advertising stimulus should be exposed more than once.

6 Require that the more finished a piece of copy is, the more soundly it can be evaluated, and require, as a minimum, that alternative executions be tested in the same degree of finish.

7 Provide controls to avoid the biasing effects of the exposure context.

8 Take into account basic considerations of sample definition.

9 Demonstrate reliability and validity.

Most communication and research companies would agree with this, and commercial products are born because of such rationale. For example, in the UK, the Millward Brown Group, in terms of multiple media use to extend reach and use of budgets more effectively, have developed their *TotalLink*, which is a version of its core advertising copy testing solution *Link*, clearly to measure the effectiveness of multimedia campaigns. Thus TotalLink works by evaluating brand visibility, persuasion and communication for each medium but also identifies synergies created between the various media being used (Millward Brown Group, 2002).

Every part of the communications process, as explained in Chapter 2, can potentially be tested and evaluated, and this is particularly true for advertising. For example, the *source* of the message, say, a celebrity, can be evaluated in terms of audience response to any trust, liking, respect that is generated. It may be that the goal is to have an effective spokesperson for the organization. A corporate or brand image can also be part of the source and be tested in some way. The *signal*, *message* or *channel* can be tested in terms of effective delivery and whether the message is working, using the research tools outlined above. In short the communication should be achieving the objectives set and, hopefully, be decoded by the recipient in the way the sender intended.

Other promotional tools

The rest of the communications mix can, to a lesser extent, be subjected to testing. Point-of-sale material, packaging, sales promotions, for example coupons or competitions and special offers, can all be tested at each of the pre-, concurrent and post-testing stages. Most communications research has been in the area of advertising, probably because of advertising's pre-eminence in the communications mix, with much of the allocation assigned to it. The changes that have occurred in the media, life styles, technology and the environment generally, have meant that sales promotion, public relations, direct marketing, selling and, more recently, sponsorship, product placement and the like have become significant enough to warrant testing and evaluation. After all, the goal should be to communicate effectively with the target market in an integrated manner. Each of the broad elements of the communications mix is briefly assessed below.

Sales promotion

For Burnett and Moriarty (1998), measuring the effectiveness of sales promotion can be just as complicated as measuring the effectiveness of advertising. While advertising tends to be longer term and deals with awareness and so on, sales promotion devices are shorter term and attempt to change behaviour and research, and evaluation has for this reason tended to be more quantitative than qualitative. Usually the objective is to increase sales in some way, and therefore sales-based measurement techniques, often customized, are used. There is some diversity of sales promotion objectives that might involve, for example, enhancing product value and brand equity or reacting to the competition. Sales promotions evaluations have the appearance of speed, ease and precision but there is still an element of uncontrollable variables in the equation, even though compared with advertising this is much smaller. Technology plays a major role in effective promotions and can help marketers target spend at certain periods when consumers are known to be most responsive.

Pre-testing should involve the perceived value (Burnett and Moriarty, 1998) of the offer whether this is immediate as with a price-off offer or promised value as with a continuity offer. In terms of the communication involved, informants can be balloted with a questionnaire or a portfolio test or a jury could be used. Focus groups and panels are also used. Behaviourally the test market or mini-test market is a much used pre-test of sales promotion *in situ*. During and post-campaign scanning and tracking devices can be used as well as actual figures generated, observation, and survey methods. As might be expected, piloting is a choice to help identify problems and simple measures such as the counting of redeemed coupons offer reliable sales measurement. As Fill (2002) points out, mathematical regression models are used to determine the contribution of various sales promotions tactics to sales, but it is well known that much of sales promotion activity focuses on the behavioural, especially on the consumer side. Fill conveniently breaks this up into:

1 *Manufacturers to resellers.* Here the main objectives are to get trial for new products and to increase shelf space for the promoted brand. Retail audits such as that of Nielson are a useful form of feedback as these measure stocking levels. Before/after testing can be carried out and agencies with appropriate experience used. Resellers should always be consulted.

2 *Resellers to consumers.* Retailers also can monitor stock movement especially against a non-promotion period. The reseller may also have an instinctive opinion as to trading levels of particular brands and the kind of informal feedback that sales representative visits may obtain. Store traffic can be monitored and reseller image tracked.

3 *Manufacturers to consumers.* The objective is usually trial, or increased usage. Targets can be set for the redemption of coupons and for other promotions such as self-liquidating premiums, and this can be assessed against actual returns. Retail audits, for example Nielsen's 'Homescan', can track sales patterns but not distinguish between new and existing customers. The volume of special packs sold and the volume of premiums used can be tracked.

4 *Manufacturers to sales force.* Usually, the objectives behind activities are to build performance, morale and allegiance to the manufacturer and their products/brands. The effectiveness of these promotions can be monitored by sales performance and is hard to assess, but attitudinal studies are not uncommon and benchmarking can be used.

Public relations

Public relations is probably the most difficult element of the communications mix to evaluate because it is used in conjunction with other things. Much of PR activity deals with opinions and therefore is not easily observable. Corporate PR, dealt with in Chapter 13, is concerned with the likes of corporate identity and image, and crisis management. Many image studies are ongoing tracking studies that measure interest, attitudes, goodwill and so on. Work can be done with stakeholders to determine important attributes that can then be measured against standards and the competition. Employees should be seen as a stakeholder group and surveyed regularly in some way. Crisis management, as discussed in Chapter 13, should have research and evaluation built into any DSM used, with an in-built pre, concurrent and post attitude towards image and so on.

Feedback is often received through a 'cuttings' or 'clipping' service. These at least identify any media coverage, i.e. the types of media, journalists and audience. Here the quantitative measure of column inches is used and often the erroneous comparison made with the same coverage using advertising, with the huge savings that go with this. Content analysis should be applied to such coverage to establish quality, but the mere opportunity to see the argument is equally as valid here as it is with advertising. Press releases can be pre-coded, with the technology in place to measure effects on sales and sales leads and to enable improved analysis. Survey methods can be used to monitor change.

Personal selling

Personal selling requires an approach to evaluation different from the rest of the communications mix. Burnett and Moriarty (1998) maintain that factors assessed include the number of planned and unplanned sales calls, the number of presentations, the frequency with which the showroom has been used, the mix of accounts visited and so on. These can be measured against organizational standards and are quantitative measures. Qualitative measures are things such as skills and knowledge of the *sales person*, so that both types of research have their influence. Quantitatively, Fill (2002) uses ratios to look at volume analysis. This includes the standard cost per call ratio, which reveals the cost of a territory and which can be compared with others. Similarly, the sales to expense and orders per call ratios provide quantitative data that in combination can be a powerful tool and provide benchmarks to work with. However, of more current interest is the notion of contribution towards profits, and this has a different set of inputs and expectations. At the *sales force* level this kind of work can be applied in an aggregate fashion but changes are occurring that have to be managed, so that managing customer relationships has led to a move away from short-term orientation regarding selling. Added to this is the multi-channel reality of selling these days, which has a profit rather than a cost perspective.

Fill (2002) uses Oliver's (1990) work on personal selling evaluation. Here analysis of inputs and outputs (performance) is a factor of the effort and costs (inputs) that an organization contributes.

Other marketing communications tools

Sponsorship these days needs to be separated out from the rest of the mix and then evaluated. One problem is the temptation to use audience size as a measure, but it is the event or other sponsorship activities that the audience wants to see, so this, not the sponsor, is the reason they watch motor racing or football. It may be an opportunity to see. Fill (2002) advocates customer surveys rather than audience data. Bought-in data can be had from the likes of Taylor Nelson, who provide panel data in this area. *Direct marketing* can be monitored by actually recording telemarketing and managing and controlling databases. *On-line research* is growing but suitable measuring standards have to be achieved. Simple quantitative measures such as how many pages have been requested, time spent and type of computer used are accurate but yield superficial data (Fill, 2002). Simple behavioural measures such as click-through rates are no substitute for reach, frequency, weight or attitude measurement. Nielsen offers a panel of 9000 informants special software that records their web page visits (Fill, 2002). Distinguishing between qualitative and quantitative on-line research, Fill finds, for example, that both are less expensive than conventional research, quantitative more so than qualitative. On the downside there are sampling and technical problems. Evaluation is made more difficult because of the varied reasons why websites are created and the reasons why people surf and search the web. The strengths and weaknesses of on-line research are allied to those generally for the Internet as discussed in the next chapter of this book. *Product placement* research and evaluation is only just beginning to emerge as an important issue, principally because of its success as a marketing tool.

VIGNETTE

Taking the biscuit: how United Biscuits launched the United chocolate bar but lost out to Jacob's Club who then lost out to life style

In 2000 United Biscuits was sold for £1.26 billion and is now owned by a consortium of venture capitalists. French owner, Danone, have now put up Jacob's Club Biscuit for sale. This is typical of a sector that has undergone a massive transformation and becomes ripe for consolidation. In the early 1980s United Biscuits decided to launch an orange-flavoured chocolate biscuit to complement the original product, the United chocolate biscuit. This period of time has turned out to be the chocolate biscuit bar's heyday. In a sense the Club bar had won the early battles and probably the war. The Club bar is still with us, and many will remember the jingle and the concept of 'joining the club'. Other promotional devices used are still in place for Club, and some have been very successful, like the 1996 'Music for Schools' initiative under which schools could collect wrappers from Jacob's Club biscuits and redeem them for musical instruments. Over 16 000 schools registered, with 30 334 975 wrappers being sent in, and the promotion achieved the production of specially commissioned teaching packs, Play Centres, set up with families. Tens of thousands of young people tried out instruments nationally, and schools received 36 600 instruments worth over £900 000.

'United' never did make the grade it seems. One inevitable problem was the message in the television advertising and how best to get this across to the target audience. United Biscuits were asking the right kinds of questions before the launch of their orange bar. They were clearly seeking, via pretesting, an answer to the question as to how a particular brand image might be communicated, whether the selection of television with women's magazines as support would be sensible for a product like 'United' and how tight the deadlines were in the various media. United Biscuits had the foresight to pre-test advertising using animatics (as opposed to storyboards). The concept that they evolved and wished to test used King Charles and Nell Gwyn to symbolize the 'orangeness' of the brand. This relied on the audience's knowledge of the relationship between the monarch and the street-seller of oranges, and all that this entailed. Potential confusion with this concept and the United football theme may have caused problems, with ideas clashing. In the mean time Jacob's Club was set to have an illustrious career as the biscuit with a lot of chocolate on, which anyone could get by joining the club, i.e. buying Club biscuits, and this was to be the case for over twenty years.

United in the end did not have the longevity and staying power of Jacob's Club. Now however, the market has changed. Poor sales in Britain and Ireland are thought to be the reason for Danone's decision to dispose of the business. Jacob's has a 7 per cent share of the £1.5 billion UK biscuit market and in Ireland a 50 per cent share. Jacob's is still worth £130 million but chocolate biscuits it seems are being replaced by healthier alternatives.

Source: Adapted from Jacob's Orange Club (2002); Macalister (2000); Promoting the industry, expanding its market, at www.mia.org.uk/mia/about/promo2.htm; RTE Interactive News (2000); United Biscuits (2003).

STOP POINT

What kind of research might United Biscuits have used in order to arrive at advertising concepts before pretesting? What would you suggest companies like United Biscuits do now in terms of the healthier alternatives? Think about lifestyle research and the kinds of concepts that might be relevant now, and how these might be tested, tracked and evaluated.

Assignment

Your company has the leading brand of domestic bleach in most European markets and other markets worldwide. Through research you have discovered that consumers, mainly female, aged 25 plus, want a product that can be used on a daily basis to freshen the toilet, while still using bleach on a regular (say weekly) basis to thoroughly clean the toilet. Draw up a list of items for the agenda of a meeting that will decide on what goes onto the brief to research companies in order that they can in turn draw up proposals that would in the end aid your company's marketing communications campaign.

Summary of Key Points

- There are clear benefits to evaluating campaigns.

- There are clear difficulties in measurement because of lagged and cumulative effects of different stimuli and individual differences.

- Briefing and proposal writing are an integral part of developing research.

- Pre-, concurrent and post-testing is commonplace in marketing practice.

- Both quantitative and qualitative research has a role to play in communications research.

- During a campaign it is common to use DAR, unaided or aided tests. Recognition testing can be used to establish elements of a piece of communication.

- Post-campaign is dominated by quantitative sales effect-type research.

- Most of the research and evaluation methods and tools have been developed in advertising and packaging research, but other communication elements are being evaluated as their use increases.

Examination Questions

1 Explain what is meant by the term 'research and evaluation' in marketing communications' terms.

2 Write a typical research brief for an fmcg brand and explain what a research company would have to put in a proposal to have a chance of getting the account.

3 Explain the difference between primary and secondary research in marketing communications, using examples to illustrate.

4 Explain the difference between quantitative and qualitative research in marketing communications, using examples to illustrate.

5 Discuss the kinds of 'off the peg' research a marketer can buy into that are useful in marketing communications terms.

6   Outline media research issues that are relevant for today's marketing communicator.

7   Outline the kinds of research typical to sales promotion campaigns.

8   Discuss PR in relation to research, and in particular image studies, using examples to illustrate.

9   Distinguish between qualitative and quantitative research that might be used in sales person or force research.

10 Discuss other elements of the communications mix, such as sponsorship, in relation to the kinds of research that might be advocated in order to assess effectiveness, using examples to illustrate.

Notes

1   Following on from the work on semiotics in Chapters 6 and 13, consideration of the role of semiotic research within corporate and marketing communications research was given. Therefore, nature and role of semiotics as a research system in corporate and marketing communications is left within these chapters and more conventional marketing communications research discussed here.

2   Kipling's 'Serving Men' as discussed in Chapter 1.

References

Bell, J., Goulding, S., Bush, T. and Fox, A. (1987). *Conducting Small-Scale Investigations in Educational Management*. Harper and Row.

Burnett, J. and Moriarty, S. (1998). *An Introduction to Marketing Communications – an Integrated Approach*. Prentice Hall.

Dealer Magazine (2000). Plunge into the knowledge pool – the benefits of marketing research. *Dealer Magazine*, February. At www.business-advantage.co.uk/ba/articler.htm.

Fill, C. (2002). *Marketing Communications: Contexts, Strategies and Applications*. 3rd edition. Financial Times Prentice Hall.

Jacob's Orange Club (2002). At www.nicecupofteandasitdown.com/biscuits/previous.php3?it, accessed 12 December.

Macalister, T. (2000). US group takes biscuit empire. At www.guardian.co.uk/print/0,3858,408 3965,00.html, accessed 31 October.

Millward Brown Group (2002). Testing multimedia campaigns. *Perspectives*, **20**, September, 1.

Pickton, D. and Broderick, A. (2001). *Integrated Marketing Communication*. Financial Times Prentice Hall.

Rossiter, J. R. and Percy, L. (1997). *Advertising, Communication and Promotions Management*. 2nd edition. McGraw Hill.

Rothschild, M. (1987). *Marketing Communications*. Heath.

RTE Interactive News (2000). Danone plans to sell Jacob's biscuits. At www.rte.ie/news/2000/1018/business.html, accessed 18 October.

Schultz, D. E. and Kitchen, P. J. (2000). *Communicating Globally*. Macmillan.

United Biscuits (2003). An enterprising approach to a marketing re-launch. At www.tt100.biz.

Interactivity in marketing communications

Chapter overview

Introduction to this chapter

The main concern in this chapter is the fall of the monologue and the rise of the dialogue in communications. Perhaps more than this, the fragmentation of markets and that of the media that has followed targeting and the interactivity as predicted by Schultz (as discussed in Chapter 1) has led to what might be called the 'electronic frontier'. In practice marketing communications is a mix of old and new elements, including website design, and is based upon the mix of interactive media, e-commerce and relationships, and so on. This chapter therefore explores the meaning of interactivity and discusses the emergence of the electronic media and, in particular, the Internet. The integrated marketing communications mix elements are considered, particularly in relation to the Internet, as is e-commerce and not least website design and management, including qualitative and quantitative measurement.

Aims of this chapter

The overall aim of this chapter is to explore the importance of interactivity and, in particular, that of the Internet. More specifically, on completion of this chapter, the reader should be able to:

- discuss the nature and importance of interactivity

- define interactivity in terms of the 'electronic frontier'

- explain how new electronic media forms have become part of IMC

- discuss the Internet as a major development and key driver in twenty-first century IMC

- explain e-commerce and the impact of the new media on trade generally and sales support in particular

- understand the relationship between company and customer and how web-based marketing can enhance brand loyalty

- understand the principles of advertising and other forms of marketing and corporate communications activities on line

- explain issues surrounding website design, characteristics and management

- explain visitor website 'hits' and the need for effective monitoring of Internet activity.

Technology and communication

Background

If the Industrial Revolution took workers from farm to factory, the Information Age is a time of migration of workers from manufacturing to service industries. Because of microchip capacity, news about companies and brands can be spun around the globe in a day via Internet chatrooms and other such inventions. The use of direct response television is indicative of the changes that have taken place in terms of the ability to process information and the improvements in database creation and maintenance. The recent introduction of broadband in the UK is an example of this in terms of the amount of digital information that can be sent backwards and forwards despite the increasing complexity of messages and the space required to handle them.

The growth of teletext, the Internet and other important areas such as mobile phone technology, in particular text and photo messaging, is evident in everyday life. Somewhat ironically, this has led to a decline in television advertising yet, at the same time, radio has been revived and survived and now flourishes around the world. Newspapers and magazines are now able, through technology, to be cost-effective enough to be profitable with much smaller (often special interest group) audiences. On-line newspapers, magazines and radio may very well threaten traditional forms, offering the same kinds of content from gossip to serious news to the weather report. It is possible that other forms of business communication, such as the ubiquitous fax machine will soon be obsolete. Outdoor displays are not immune from technological advance with the marketer's ability to throw images almost Batman-like into the skies, or at least onto buildings such as the Houses of Parliament for dramatic effect. Electronic displays, database technology that allows for loyalty programmes, EPOS systems and so on are all evidence of the effects of technology.

The digital not analogue age

A number of activities are now possible because of the way technology and, in particular, digital technology have transformed the marketer's arena. The broadcast media are still available in analogue form but also in digital form. The interactive media, though, are driven by digital technology. The delivery of television and radio is now via satellite, cable and terrestrial means. Digital television offers much improved picture quality but it is the future impact of interactivity in terms of home shopping, home banking and many other activities in life that makes the prospects of this mouth watering to marketers.[1] Videotext is now two-way. The failed Prestel system was never a match for the impressive French government-sponsored 'Minitel', still used as part (20 per cent) of the French company La Redoute's mail-order business (O'Connor and Galvin, 2000). Digital teletext will ensure greater interactivity with improvements in viewer control, especially regarding navigation, graphics and animation. The CD-ROM has not been passed over totally yet. Video conferencing, whether with PC or room-based, still has potential but has equipment and time zone problems. Perhaps the most exciting area is that of mobile technology, where the wonders of WAP technology are leading to mobile e-mail, text and photo messaging, among other things. As ever, however, the commercial viability aspects of applying such advances have a bearing. Digital radio is with us but has not developed like its broadcasting counterpart, television, because the commercial benefits are not the same. Price is thus a barrier with the only possibility for commercialization being some sort of relationship with in-car entertainment. The telephone systems that are fully automated in call centres can be viewed either as an asset that helps build relationships or as a hindrance to this process. Successful automated answering systems are still required to meet customer needs and not least the interactive voice response (IVR) has to be supported by good design and a system with response capabilities and menu options. The system must be able to capture customer response and be monitored and updated continuously.

The nature of interactivity

The technological advancements alluded to above have ensured that communications have become operationally interactive. The advent of the Internet is important but so, too, are other developments. Digital television in particular and broadcasting more generally sees interactive services arriving at a rapid pace. The Internet, discussed in more detail later in this chapter, has stimulated commerce in many ways, including locally with, for example, on-line shopping from supermarkets such as Tesco in the UK. In this instance, and somewhat ironically, the shopping may be conducted on line but delivery still has to be conducted in a conventional way. In this sense making a list on line at Tesco and having it delivered is not that different to drawing up a list for the local department store or supermarket and placing it with the store on a regular basis, a practice that harks back to decades earlier.

Interactivity defined

The desirability of one-to-one targeting in marketing and the dream of two-way transactions are approaching a reality as the passive audience becomes active in real time, where targets are not only accessible and recognizable but are also responsive. Interactivity in essence is adding two-way communication to one-way communication and facilitating it to achieve connectivity with the target whereby messages can not only be retained but also engaged with. One-way communication is about awareness but two-way is about relationships that are personalized, social and responsive.

Marketing on the Internet and e-commerce

The Internet is about interactivity and about real-time, targeted, personalized brand messages. By the mid-1990s the Internet had moved from being a leisure pursuit of 'anoraks' and, before this, the tool of academics and, before that, a military tool. The Internet soon became a commercial necessity, many companies, without understanding its true nature, rushing to be on 'the Web' or 'the Net' if only to be able to say 'visit or website'. Having a website became a 'must have', even if the site was little more than a simple leaflet on a screen. There was kudos to be had from being 'on the Web', thus following the Marshal McCluhanism 'the medium is the message' whereby merely being on the Internet said something about the organization, i.e. 'progressive, up to date, go-ahead and so on. The converse would be that not being on the Internet suggests a slow, non-progressive and behind-the-times organization.

These days the Internet is an important part of IMC. What started with website addresses being communicated via conventional advertising has evolved into something completely different. The Internet has a social dimension with a style reminiscent of television but somehow more synchronized. The most important aspect is, of course, the way the customer or consumer has control of content and contact. The Internet thus far has been characterized by banner advertising, boxes that are the commonest way of alerting the user to a facility that provides a click-through to a relevant page on a website. These are often animated and, when in a pop-up form, irritating and the cause of overload on the user's system. This can lead to 'freezing' of screens and the need to reboot the system. Despite industry predictions of big business, the Internet was worth \$4.2 billion in 2000 and was expected to be worth \$7.8 billion in 2002 (O'Connor and Galvin, 2000). Duncan (2002) reports the figures to be more like \$300 million in 1996, \$5.3 billion in 2000 and a predicted \$16 billion in 2005. De Pelsmaker, Geuens and Van Den Bergh (2001) use similar figures but usefully break this down by product category or industry. For example, in the USA in 1998 over \$1 billion was spent on travel, another \$1 billion on PC hardware and software and \$0.5 billion on entertainment, whereas the whole of Europe in the same year spent \$298 million in total on line. However, the optimism is still in place with the march of technology and the recent introduction of broadband, and these sums are expected to be much higher. This is dependent upon the challenge from digital television.

The Internet is a worldwide system of linked computers that has provided a commerce base since the mid-1990s. It was made commercial by the advent of a web browser that provided user-friendly graphics and other facilitating features.[2] The characteristics of the Internet are like those of many other media with news stories, letters and other formats that are familiar to the reader of a newspaper or magazine or a viewer of television or, indeed, a listener to radio. The predicted power shift to the consumer from the manufacturer, channel and even the media (Schultz, 1996) does, however, mean that the Internet is similar to other media, the difference only being that it is on line. Rather, this is an indication of the nature of interactive communications in the future. This interactivity, however, is dependent in the first place on the accessibility of the Internet, the increase in and range of information available and the fact that the Internet is 'fast and vast'. Business-to-business commerce on the Internet has led the way but as consumer access has risen so, too, have the number of websites and e-mail usage and, by 2004, the ratio of Internet activity should be 90:10 (consumer:BtoB). Overall the cost of selling and buying has been decreased by the advent of the Internet, as have prices (Clow and Baack, 2001).

The Internet is made up of websites and e-mail, bulletin boards, forums and chatrooms to variously send e-mails and attachments, post notices or engage in real-time interaction with others. The part of these activities that is actually involved with selling is usually referred to as *e-commerce*, and accounts for nearly half the activity on the Internet. Many people use the Internet to look for information, use e-mail or visit chatrooms. Some companies are strictly on line only, such as eBay or Amazon. Bricks and mortar organizations such as Comet or Tesco, of course, engage with both traditional and on-line commerce. The key to successful e-commerce has been developments in navigation and the design of home pages, and the use of search engines such as Google or Ask Jeeves. Such engines find websites based on key words. A portal is a search engine for a selected number of sites so that, for example, Yahoo is both this and an on-line shopping centre. Such organizations have helped to develop navigation across the World Wide Web, which has become a graphical communication medium which uses hypertext mark-up language (HTML) that allows text images, icons and sounds to be shared in a user-friendly way.

It is worth noting that it took centuries for print as a medium to reach millions and decades for radio to do the same. For television this figure was probably only ten years once properly launched, but the Internet has achieved this in five years.

Communications networks

Web-based technology has had a high impact on networking and networks in terms of customers, employees, business partners and any other significant stakeholders. The key, of course, is interactivity. *Intranets and extranets* are related to the Internet. *Intranets* preceded the Internet but were expensive, although relatively secure. These internal, password-protected systems were used for document management, project management, knowledge management, training and other support. The material shared consisted of, for example, calendars, newsletters, discussion documents or even a cafeteria menu. An *extranet* takes this outside to other stakeholders. Again this network would be password protected. Both could be Internet-enabled and allow access from home. The *benefits* of networks lie in the areas of speed, cost-reduction and a more integrated approach to issues and concerns. Improved records, information, knowledge, flexibility and barrier-reduction are other benefits that can be had and the Internet can be said to have contributed greatly to globalization, not least for smaller businesses. *Wireless communication* is a new infrastructure, which for some developing nations, means that they can skip the old (for the developed nations) infrastructure and put investment into the newest generation, unhampered by the 'baggage' (cables and wires) of the past. *Mobile technology* in particular is at the forefront of this, whereby wireless messages can be used to redirect customers to websites. It remains to be seen if consumers will revolt against commercial text and photo messaging, especially in the light of a number of scams that have been exposed whereby the phone user has had to pick up the bill for accepting messages that turn out to be either meaningless or for commercial gain of some sort. In Chapter 10 the use of direct mail was discussed and a similar argument can be transferred into the *e-mail* domain. Unsolicited e-mail can cause similar problems to those generated in the more conventional field and 'permission marketing' is a possible part of the solutions to such problems. With the electronic form, spam (or spamming) is a tempting prospect but is a practice that does not fit in well with the IMC approach advocated in this book and many other places. If the situation is an 'op-in' one whereby the recipient is happy to receive e-mail and attachments, then advertising messages can be sent via rich media such as video, newsletters, press releases and so on. Specialist companies can handle this work and there is a relative low cost associated with it if compared with conventional media. Potentially, there will be a better response from e-mail than from banner advertising, provided permission is granted.

According to many writers and sources, including Ernst (2001), there is an unprecedented revolution taking place that will reshape human civilization. This is a profound change that is difficult to imagine. It is, of course, the digital revolution in communication that is changing the face of the media and more. Television and radio are obvious candidates but other media such as newspapers and magazines are being affected. This is all about responding to listeners, viewers and readers in a new context, often referred to as the information and/or digital age. The Internet has been the catalyst for change and the introduction of interactivity, which is set to develop in many forms, including the Internet itself. This change is now being driven by digital technology and converging platforms.

The infrastructure was, of course, needed to provide delivery systems, leading to the ability at least for people to interact, not just via the Internet but via television in their own homes. The consumer no longer has to pick up a telephone and respond to an on-screen number. The advent of broadband allows many of the digital devices that have been developed to come into play and television will be at the centre of this convergence. This will be important in the home, but also elsewhere, i.e. in the car or some other location. The television is almost universally acceptable with a near 100 per cent penetration of homes and is a natural choice for most who are used to using the television to view video and DVDs for films, games and even karaoke. First mooted in the early 1990s, films on demand are becoming a reality as interactivity kicks in. Not everything will be interactive, but the proportion of real-time broadcasting is predicted to reduce, leading to a new form of communication that will synthesize the 'traditional advertising's brand strength with the power of customized communication' (Ernst, 2001) and that will incorporate media consumption, interactions and purchases.

In many ways there is still a waiting game being played, as there has been for a number of years, regarding the scale of this revolution and the impact it will have on marketers. The opportunities from fragmentation are there to be had by those who can capitalize on personalized interaction. It is quite clear that in this area the adoption and diffusion of innovations theoretical curve of Rodgers can be applied in practice and it is clear that the adoption time is getting shorter for each major innovation to be adopted, and therefore the curve is becoming sharper. The implications of the interactive revolution are far reaching. For marketers, looking at two of the things that have come into play already, the form and content of messages have to change because of the nature of interactivity but there is also a realization that there is a need for at least a rethink of the marketing communications model and how communications works at each stage of the journey.

The journey to this point, at least for the past decade, has been a frustrating one. The plethora of articles in the earlier 1990s is testament to the 'promising but not delivering' situation that emerged. For example, King (1994) quotes a senior US advertising figure saying that interactive television 'is here now' and that infomercials would be the only choice, presumably because consumers would want them since the consumer would take control and want to search. What happened between then and now is called the Internet and the advertising industry's fascination with it and the possibilities of e-commerce. Many marketing and advertising people believe that the breakthrough ideas that enable more user-friendly applications will not come from the 'technologists' but from building relationships with customers, consumers and prospects. Others argue that the slowness of take-up of new technologies has been in the 'wait-and-see' approach companies have had towards technology (Grupe, 2000).This argument aside, the Internet has for the past decade been the medium where developments have taken place. In the past, large companies could quite easily live with small companies developing ideas in niche markets before being 'swallowed up' by a bigger predator. The Internet did change this situation to an extent since the resources needed to enable communication internationally were dramatically reduced. For BtoB SMEs in particular, the Internet was good news.

However, Grupe argues that 'the sleeping giants' have woken up and have started to evolve leading edge e-commerce strategies – or, if they have not done so, then they should. This, of course, means investment in communications technologies is required in order to develop and maintain cutting-edge brands. This applies not only to the Internet but all sorts of technologies from mobile to voice and as Emmerson et al. (2000) conclude, there is a need to understand the 'meta-products' that are tied to communications and that will be required to meet information-related needs, i.e. meeting consumer needs and not being information or communications-centric for the sake of it.

The Internet has come from its Cold War beginnings through to what is now a new era of interactivity with the re-emergence of the 'web television' idea that was mooted in the early 1990s. Some argue that the large corporations have been lax in their commitment to the Internet and have allowed others to develop the various media at a somewhat slow pace than might have been. The sex and pornography industries are said to have played a large part in Internet developments in order to sell their wares. Perhaps instead of using the phrases 'digital age' or 'information age' a better way to express what is happening is in terms of waves and tides and the realization that some organizations will get washed over by waves and miss the tide while others most certainly will not.

Sources: Adapted from Di Iorio (1999); Emmerson et al. (2000); Ernst (2001); Grupe (2000); King (1994); Merz and Roberts (1998).

STOP POINT

What do you think the digital revolution will bring in the coming year? Are we on a perpetual shoreline of a digital sea whereby some of the promised waves do not quite reach us? We are said to be on the verge of seeing home entertainment systems with digital television at the centre. How long before this happens will depend upon the commitment of companies to such an ideal but also upon ourselves as consumers and whether we really want what is on offer or soon to be on offer.

The intercommunications process: IMC and the Internet

Websites and e-commerce as a complement to other activities are now quite common. The Internet may be weak on awareness in the first instance and may require more traditional media to create initial awareness. In a similar way, measuring effectiveness is difficult; but it is increasingly possible to go beyond site 'hits' and measure in a more qualitative fashion. The Internet is clearly a medium that is good on product and company information. It is also a cost-effective way of doing business. For example, current advertising on British commercial television can create awareness of the brand and its potential benefits and take the prospects on a website where they can buy on line. This is the case with Esure, an on-line insurance company who typically offer a 10 per cent discount if the prospect buys on line rather than off line (the option is there to use the telephone if needs be). Thus this integrated communications campaign draws attention to the offering of the company with conventional television advertising, but by way of a special on-line promotion a prospect can be turned into a customer. This allows for greater use of the creative platform to be used to work cognitively and affectively until an action is taken since once on the site the prospect is involved with something that is interactive, flexible and targeted.

Advertising, branding and brand loyalty

Branding and brand loyalty are part of this process on line just as much as off line. Branding brings with it a greater use of emotional elements, although this is less significant on the Internet where the tendency is to be more informational. Once on a site, delivery can be a simple click-through, i.e. the same method used to get on the site in the first place in many instances. Delivery is therefore consistent, and getting a sale and then improving retention to achieve some degree of brand loyalty are the objectives. Once a company has an *e-mail* address an advertisement or promotion of some sort can be sent, although this would be inherently dangerous if unsolicited. *Banner advertisements* are a more likely option and can be static or more interactive as the medium moves towards a more television-like presentation.[3] Clearly position, animation and other ways of drawing in the prospect are important, and research suggests that animation is marginally more effective than asking questions (as reported by De Pelsmaker, Geuens and Van Den Bergh, 2001) but this is by no means clear-cut. Chatroom banner advertising can be bought but, as De Pelsmaker, Geuens and Van Den Bergh point out, this may be ineffective since the 'chatters' are there to chat, not click-through on banners, although the targeting in this sense would be efficient. *Buttons* are smaller versions of banners that take the prospect straight to a site. *Classified advertising* is popular but dependent upon search engines such as Google (see below regarding design). To support the brand, *interstitials*, which are transitional on-line advertisements, and *pop-ups*, are available but should be used with care. There is a balance to be achieved between irritation and attention. Once on a site, some form of novelty factor can grab attention but again this should be used with caution. *Cookies* are text files that are embedded on the hard drive of a site visitor and which allow companies to repeat offers to that visitor once the cookie is established. Allied to this is the idea of *pushed advertising* where information is downloaded onto the prospect's hard drive, which then allows an advertisement to be played. The same logic over the danger of irritation applies.

Sales support comes in the form of managing and analysing data. There is no selling per se unless some form of video conferencing is arranged. Communication is impersonal and therefore unmediated. Customer service helps build relationships and part of this service is the solution to problems on a full-time basis. For 365 days of the year, fifty-two weeks of the year, seven days a week and twenty-four hours a day there is the potential for solving problems on the Internet. Easy-to-use information on site with an index or search facility helps this process. A custom-built service would underline interactivity and there may be possibilities for human interaction, even if only by e-mail.

Other marketing and corporate communications on the Internet

Promotions

Interest and involvement will encourage a return to a site where a prospect may have registered on line and be part of a database. E-mailing is then possible so that, for example, Amazon or eBay typically e-mail offers and attachments. The ideas behind on-line promotions are the same as for off-line – competitions, prizes and so on. The outcomes of using promotions on line will be the same as if used off line, as discussed in Chapter 9. Promotions on line may get visits and clear stock and so on but, as with traditional promotions, this is not usually part of a brand-building exercise.

Direct marketing

Direct marketing on line using e-mail uses the same logic as direct marketing off line as discussed in Chapter 10. As mentioned above, direct e-mail can be used to contact prospects with promotions and attachments or with offers. The idea of *viral marketing*, akin to word of mouth and opinion leadership (see Chapter 3) or even a chain letter, is where a message is sent to a small number of people who then send it on to others. This might be a humorous message or one with special interest. Such special interest groups may, or may not, be interested in commercial offers so that this is a kind of permission marketing where affinity groups and even affinity sites exist to share information, ideas and so on.

Public relations

The Internet provides the ideal context for information to be posted about the organization, the company and its brands. Both marketing/product and corporate levels benefit from Internet PR activities such as investor and corporate relations through published accounts and press releases, past press releases, history, newsletters, photography, downloadable files such as screen savers and so on.

Sponsorship

Sponsorship deals and materials can be announced but there is also the prospect of sponsorship opportunities on line such as the sponsorship of a good cause's website. The usual goals such as targeting particular groups with the brand and achieving goodwill are the same as discussed in Chapter 14. The means are different since on-line communities, special interest groups and chatrooms for real-time interaction can be used.

VIGNETTE

Developing an IMC model that includes the Internet as an integrating corporate and marketing tool

The Internet has played a key role in the development of IMC. It has changed the way information is presented and displayed, and indeed the way organizations communicate both internally and externally. Traditional communications strategies have been radically challenged by this 'new kid on the block' that has both threatened and opened up new opportunities for companies and other organizations in terms of their corporate and marketing activities. The Internet as a communications tool performs many functions. The fragmentation of mass audiences means that it has become increasingly difficult for companies to deal with issues around reputation, awareness and perception. The cure for this difficulty appears to be the Internet – at least for a while. The Internet has become a medium upon which trade takes place. E-commerce has gradually moved from BtoB trading to business-to-consumer trade. But the Internet offers much more than this in an age of instant global communication. Ranchhod et al. (2002) use Drobis's 1999 work of four basic pillars for effective communication to underscore the challenge ahead. If an organization wishes to move ahead it needs *dialogue* with its targets for understanding and better communication. It needs *borderless communication* that can cope with time zones and be consistent in marketing and communication elements such as advertising and PR. Communications should be *inclusive* for all audiences, internal and external, to avoid conflicts and confrontation. Finally, communications need to be *continuous*, especially where PR is concerned, and not simply turned off.

The Internet offers scope for all of this via connectivity and interaction, rather than detachment and monologues. Communication is no longer some form of conduit or pipeline and not even simply bidirectional, but rather multidirectional. Members of the organization are connected to each other and targets. Target members are connected to the organization and to each other. The task is to take control of the interconnectivity and this can be done to an extent in chatrooms and communities. The target today is much more informed than in the past and more shrewd, with very quick access to other information. This makes pushed information less readily accepted than in the past.

Incorporating the Internet into an organization's marketing armoury is not necessarily as easy a task as it first might appear. It is not that the Internet would not fit in. Research by Rodgers and Chen (2002) indicates that one stumbling block might be the inability of advertising executives to warm to the new medium or at least they appear to be less confident handling it. The Internet has, it seems, levelled the competitive landscapes across agency types. Public relations and new media companies apparently are more comfortable with the Internet. These researchers conclude that no one type of agency is ideal to handle the Internet and that co-operation may be the way forward. Indeed,the way forward may very well be incorporated in the way in which communications companies have been formed from the various types of agency.

Research into technology and communications underscores the importance of the role of technological advance as a catalyst for integration in communications. However, this will depend on the orientation of the organization concerned and as Molenaar et al. (1996) found in their research, internal orientation corresponds with relatively low responsiveness because of limited knowledge of the external environment leading to limited integration of marketing in the organization. A way to change this is through developing and changing this orientation, and building relationships that lead to integration of activities that, in turn, lead to customer participation and interaction. The Internet has been developed and now has a vital role to play in this.

Sources: adapted from Cham (1996); Chen (2003); Meyer (1999); Molenaar et al. (1996); Ranchhod et al. (2002); Rodgers and Chen (2002); Wegert (2003).

STOP POINT

Think about the meaning of integration in the context of the Internet. Think about the words dialogue, borderless, inclusive and continuous. The stumbling blocks to integration might well be human ones and not technological ones. Agency or communication company personnel may need to become more Internet friendly and managers in companies more customer orientated before IMC can be achieved.

Internet design and management issues

A server is required to link a user's computer to the web. This involves software that an Internet service provider (ISP) can have with the capacity to provide this service. Apache.org (2003) claim to have had the most popular server since 1996 and the company cite the October 2003 Netcraft Web Server Survey which states that 64 per cent of websites on the Internet are using the Apache server. Many of the disadvantages of 'being on the Internet' are technical and technological. Many Internet difficulties are quickly resolved, but just as this is done other difficulties pop up. Such is the ever-changing nature of this particular beast. There should be clear links to marketing strategy when considering the use of the Internet and not just a 'number of visitors on our web site' mentality. Indeed, as advocated in this book a DSM approach to managing Internet activity should be taken. In the past an on-line brochure may have been the requirement, but much more is desired now and this demand is set to continue to increase.

Web design

The key to successful Internet use is interactivity and the key to interactivity is ease of use. The characteristics of web design are crucial to the length of stay, activities undertaken and potential for a return visit. This applies whether dealing with corporate or marketing/product/brand issues. Key to this is customer search. The prospect is searching and, apart from cross-cultural issues and variances such as language, speed is of the essence as is accessibility and the incidence of personal computers. Wireless connectivity for business is a key issue at the time of writing, as is the availability at airports, railway stations and so on of wireless connections to the Internet, provided by companies such as BT.

Visitors to websites can be categorized by type. Experienced users need directed information but there are those who require this less. Experienced buyers may need no information. Other visitors might be bargain hunters or entertainment seekers. These types could be classified as active or passive and as far as hits on the website goes, the argument is still around the quality of the hit, which is rather like the argument about the quality of visitors to an exhibition stand. The designer therefore has to take account of the relevancy of the material in meeting need and not simply using design as an end in itself. However, the site has to excite and might engender curiosity, if this is appropriate. In a similar manner to advertising, the website must be interesting, likeable and so on. The site should be user-friendly and the interface interactive. Messages should not be concealed by overuse of gimmicks, graphics and so on. Navigation will become difficult if the site is too complex or has too many levels. Menu options should be clear and complete with easy return and exit buttons. As ever, irritation should be considered carefully.

Banners

Banners can be placed at the top, side or bottom of the screen and click-through takes the prospect elsewhere. During this process sound and animation added for effect is activated, such as for a car the 'vroom' sound associated with starting off. The costs of banners are relatively low but so, too, are response rates, although involvement is a factor. Animation and other novelties can lift the rate of click-through on low-involvement situations but have little effect on high-involvement ones for obvious reasons.

Front pages

Front pages have been designed with some of the above considerations on sound, animation, and search through to 'classifieds' via key words.[4] Decisions to use the interstitial or pop-up have to be balanced against the irritation factor, which can do damage and drive prospects away. A similar consideration has to be made with the use of multi-screens.

Managing websites

A webmaster is normally hired to manage a site. This includes analysis and monitoring of site activity and checks on navigation and connectivity. *Privacy* in terms of personal data sold to others and third party involvement is clearly an important management issue as it has been with traditional database management for decades. Similarly, *security* remains one of the biggest barriers to e-commerce and the use of the Internet generally. Despite industry claims, perceptions, especially of credit card fraud, remain, and this is not surprising when this kind of fraud regularly crops up in more traditional telephone and over-the-counter contexts as well as, these days, in on-line transactions. The Internet at this point is therefore not seen as a medium that is adequate against theft and there is still no great confidence regarding credit card fraud. Customer expectation seems still to be that a transaction should be comprehensible, flexible, adaptable, predictable, easy to understand and transparent. These expectations may very well militate against secure transactions.

Measurement

In terms of measurement of website activities De Pelsmaker, Geuens and Van Den Bergh (2001) use the InSites model that measures five core constructs to explain performance in terms of content productivity (is content sufficient, relevant and up to date), browse efficiency (ease of navigation, home page performance), design efficiency (layout, style), exchange level (the site's interactive capabilities) and emotional appeal (the site's attractiveness, likeability and so on). Four peripheral indicators are overall satisfaction, intention to revisit, influence on the brand and company image, and visit intensity or duration of the visit. This is a good move away from mere counting the hits on a website, yet hits are the equivalent of OTS and are still the basis for CPM charging for advertising. There is therefore room for growth and development in terms of tracking and measurement. Possibly less than half the companies with websites actively seek feedback, as recommended within any DSM of management such as the APIC model used in this book. De Pelsmaker, Geuens and Van Den Bergh (2001) use a study in Belgium to illustrate this, where only 41 per cent of companies used feedback and two-thirds of these only measured hits on the website and only half tracked individual users. Only 6 per cent of these companies sought some form of site appreciation by users.

Feedback can be asked for at the website but this is inherently biased. Organizations are advised to use the specialist web research companies that are emerging who can handle both on- and off-line web surveys and both qualitative and quantitative research. This would involve, therefore, not simply number of hits but a range of techniques including depth interviews, focus groups and panels to investigate design issues such as positioning of banners, effectiveness of click-through or quality of classified advertising lists in relation to key words.

VIGNETTE

Search engine optimization: the improved way to marketing on the Internet

The motivations of web users are an important area of study. Understanding why people use the Internet will surely help understand attitudes and ultimately behaviour. However, according to Rodgers and Sheldon (2002), web motivation research is in its infancy. Motivations may differ between different types of people, different genders, different computing skills, different use rates and so on. Since the Internet serves different needs for different people this further complicates the situation. Rodgers and Sheldon's research supports the notion that people are most motivated when situational opportunities meet personal needs but these researchers concede that it is not yet known why such motives change across time.

Making it easier and quicker to find what you are looking for can be an important aspect of Internet use and of e-commerce. Search engines are central to this and central to search engine activity is *Google*, the main player in this area with massive distribution across a network of partnerships including *AOL* and *Ask Jeeves*. *Yahoo!search* now has a stable of first-class players and *MSN* now has its own crawler-based search service. Grehan (2003a; 2003b) uses Andrei Broder's work on informational, navigational and transactional characteristics of search to explain changes that are occurring. Informational is the classic information retrieval on, say, a medical condition. Navigational is all about reaching a particular website and many people searching will go directly to the site. Transactional means shopping, the searcher wishing to enquire about or actually buy something, rather like using *Yellow Pages*. It is this latter area that makes the friendliness of the search engine – or crawler – attractive. The nature of digital technology turns search words into numbers. The speed of return on a search is phenomenal as is the breadth and depth of information. The resultant classified pages are crucial to the search process. If the company's entry is in the first or maybe the second, then it has a chance of success. Beyond this the surfer will get bored and re-search or move on to something else. Crucial to this is the way in which linkage is set up and, as with many situations, companies get what they pay for. Better placement in the listings will cost the company more. Pay per click is growing as an alternative to traditional techniques but this has its difficulties such as 'click fraud'.

This apart, the concern is for search optimization, or more precisely search engine optimization (SEO). This offers companies the opportunity to take advantage of *key term* research. Key terms are the foundation of search engine positioning programmes but clearly these have to be relevant to the content on the website. This means understanding which terms are most and least searched, those that are competitive and those that are secondary or, even, tertiary. Understanding this means understanding how people search the Internet. Other important issues are *meta tags* (descriptive terms within the HTML code of a web page), *title tags* (given great consideration by search engines and important because of hyperlinks) and *body text* which includes words, phrases and descriptive paragraphs that tell the story of the company and its product or brands.

Sources: adapted from Grehan (2003a; 2003b); Oneupweb (2003); Rodgers and Sheldon (2002).

STOP POINT

The ascent of search engine optimization has been, as one might expect from the Internet medium, extremely rapid. Have banners and buttons fallen by the wayside during this ascent? Can more 'traditional' Internet devices survive in the face of SEO pre-eminence? Think about the important of getting other things right such as payment systems and website design, remembering that it may be more beneficial to pay someone with the expertise to get design/layout changes, new text for title tags, meta-tags and so on 'right'.

Assignment

You are required to write a consultative report for an organization of your choice. Assume this organization's managers have no knowledge of interactivity and especially Internet websites, search engines and web design issues. The report should cover all aspects of interactivity and highlight the options available to the client, given the context in which the client operates. The report should included commentary on two websites of your choice. One of these sites must be what you consider best practice and another what you consider to be not good practice.

Summary of Key Points

- Technological change has led to an increasingly complex situation with the Internet but also with intranets and extranets, WAP technology and wireless communications.

- Interactive media have evolved into digital technology and an 'electronic frontier'.

- The new electronic media are not in conflict with more traditional media and at present IMC is perfectly feasible using all form of media.

- The Internet and especially website design have been key drivers in IMC.

- E-commerce has begun to pick up momentum and as long as the Internet can deliver customer service this will threaten more traditional commerce.

- The Internet and e-commerce can enhance brand loyalty because of positive relationship-building.

- The electronic frontier is an exciting and daunting prospect at one and the same time. 'Traditional' Internet advertising is changing at pace, with search engine optimization threatening to overtake website design as the key driver.

- Effective evaluation will still be required, regardless of which form of technology dominates.

Examination Questions

1   Define interactivity in communications terms, using examples to illustrate.

2   Examine the Internet and its relationship with intranets and extranets. Use examples of each to illustrate this relationship.

3   Highlight the benefits of the Internet in terms of branding and relationships, illustrating with pertinent examples.

4   Briefly explain IMC in relation to the Internet. Use examples to illustrate the role of mail and phone within this.

5   Discuss the importance of the 'electronic frontier' in terms of technological change.

6   Assess the impact of the transient nature of advertising on the Internet using relevant examples.

7   Explain, in broad terms, the strategic options available to marketers regarding advertising on the Internet. Discuss in particular the difference between banner advertising and pop-ups and how these work in relation to click-through and web pages using examples to illustrate.

8   Discuss website creation in terms of design and the practical implications for navigation using examples to illustrate.

9   Explain why you agree or disagree that digital television will ultimately be more important to commerce than the Internet.

10 Examine the quantitative measure of number of hits against more qualitative measures of search engine and website use, using examples to illustrate.

Notes

1   Some argue that it is digital television not the Internet that will lead commerce. Others suggest that business and marketing will be integrated activities anyway so that it is the integration not the medium that is important.

2   It is said that much of the advance in connectivity and user-friendliness is driven by the needs of the pornography and sex industries.

3   There is much speculation as to what the future on line will bring. Virtual reality is set to happen, especially now that broadband is established and able to carry much more information. Virtual technologies have been in place for some time but the means of delivering these has just been established. Virtual towns, stores and other venues or contexts are an interesting marketing prospect.

4   Search engine marketing is currently, according to Grehan (2003a; 2003b), the next big thing. Grehan uses the terms 'informational', 'navigational' and 'transactional' to describe the process from search to actual purchase, search engines having a much more important role now and in the future than the actual website itself. De Pelsmaker, Geuens and Van Den Bergh (2001), however, make the valid point that the informational to transactional model is the luxury of the multinationals, whereas small companies opt for a transactional approach due to lack of resources. This may then develop into informational, i.e. from a transactional to informational model.

References

Apache.org (2003). Apache HTTP Server Project. At httpd.apache.org.

Cham, E. (1996). How to market and do business on the Internet? At www.cntek.com/paper_1.html.

Chen, B. (2003). Rural women in China. At www.arwacc.org/media/p4.html.

Clow, K. and Baack, D. (2001). *Integrated Advertising, Promotion & Marketing Communications*. Prentice Hall.

De Pelsmaker, P., Geuens, M. and Van Den Bergh, J. (2001). *Marketing Communications*. Financial Times Prentice Hall.

Di Iorio, N. (1999). Technology: need-to-know interaction. *Agency Magazine, Spring*. www.warc.com

Duncan, T. (2002). *IMC – Using Advertising and Promotion to Build Brands*. McGraw Hill.

Emmerson, R., Parsons, S. and Rutkowski, J. (2000). Voice over Internet Protocol (VoIP) – impacts on communicatios carriers and consumers. ESOMAR, October.

Ernst, D. (2001). Assessing the value of interactive communications. Advertising Research Foundation, October.

Grehan, M. (2003a). Search engine marketing. Lecture give to the Newcastle Business School Postgraduate MA Marketing students, 19 November.

Grehan, M. (2003b). Search engine marketing. At www.search-engine-book.co.uk.

Grupe, R. (2000). Riding the new digital waves. *Admap*, July. www.warc.com

King, H. (1994). Interactive future. *Agency Magazine*, Spring. www.warc.com

Merz, T. and Roberts, B. (1998). Analogue and digital television in Europe: measuring change – a challenge for research. ESOMAR.

Meyer, E. (1999). 'Netting the brand: ad agencies can – and should – play a crucial role. *Agency Magazine*, Fall. www.warc.com

Molenaar, C., Plat, F., Hoekstra, J. and Leeplang, P. (1996). Information technology: its role in the era of 'new marketing'. ESOMAR. www.warc.com

O'Connor, J. and Galvin, E. (2000). *Marketing in the Digital Age*. Financial Times Prentice Hall.

Oneupweb (2003). The consumer's guide to search engine optimization services. At www.oneupweb.com.

Ranchhod, A., Gurau, C. and Lace, J. (2002). On-line messages: developing an integrated communications model for biotechnology companies. *Qualitative Market Research: An International Journal*, **5** (1), 6–18.

Rodgers, S. and Chen, Q. (2002). Post-adoption attitudes to advertising on the Internet. *Journal of Advertising Research*, **42** (5). www.warc.com

Rodgers, S. and Sheldon, K. (2002). An improved way to characterise Internet users. *Journal of Advertising Research*, **42** (5). www.warc.com

Schultz, D. (1996). New trends in communication and advertising. Lecture to the University of Strathclyde Business School, 16 October.

Wegert, T. (2003). Contextual advertising: the consumer's point of view. At www.clickz.com/media/media_buy/article.php/2195211.

Key international marketing communications issues

Chapter overview

Introduction to this chapter

This chapter raises some of the key communications issues that affect the existing international marketer or the marketer who has decided that it is time to 'go international'. It may very well be the case that for all but the very local micro business, going international is no longer an option but is an inevitable consequence of being. The last few decades have seen tremendous growth in world trade and this growth has been accompanied by a very large growth in communications, not least, of course, the Internet and e-commerce. Having a global or international presence throws up even more barriers to communication for organizations that struggle in the first place to communicate effectively in the domestic market. Different cultural elements, a different media landscape and different legal requirements impact in different ways in different markets. The continuous struggle is not just to do with what is different but is also to do with what is (or can be) the same, with an inevitable drive towards marketing and other economies of scale. There are other drivers in this, such as using up excess capacity or downtime or the benefits of diversification and not having one's eggs in a particular market basket. However, the difficulties and consequences of trading in different markets should never be underestimated. The literature is littered with examples of blunders perpetrated by the most unlikely of large corporations, not least of all in the communications arena.

Aims of this chapter

The overall aim of this chapter is to provide a final platform upon which the reader can contemplate further study in a number of international directions. More specifically, on completion of this chapter, the reader should be able to:

- explore international communications and underscore the parameters that make them different from the communications outlined in Chapter 1

- examine the communications process in the international context and highlight any differences to the process outlined in Chapter 1

- examine the idea of achieving uniformity of marketing and marketing communications effort in terms of the adaptation/standardization debate

- outline environmental patterns around the world and explore some of the consequences of going or being international

- outline the APIC managerial framework espoused in Chapter 4 in the context of managing international communications campaigns.

The nature of international communications

A brief historical note on international communication

The term 'advertising' happens to be French, probably fifteenth century and was defined in 1694 as being 'a crime committed with many witnesses' (De Mooij, 1994). Since that time it has evolved as information and this can be observed by looking at early copies of *The Times*. This demonstrates that advertising was a continual repetition of information. Artwork costs were more expensive due to letterpress print technology. Advertisers learnt to promote products effectively, sometimes through glamour, sex, humour and so on in order to make them more effective, grabbing attention more readily. The development of communication worldwide (which follows that of marketing and business generally) is in itself fascinating. Advertising grew quickly between 1850 and 1900 and developed with the change to lithographic printing techniques. The emergence of television in 1950s, and radio between the First and Second World Wars also influenced its development. In socialist states such as the USSR and China, advertising emerged as an instrument of propaganda, whereas in free market economies such as the USA, advertising of processed foods, tobacco and drugs was the order of the day. After Stalin's death socialist countries recognized that advertising encouraged sales and therefore was a necessary evil. In China, however, during the time of Mao (after 1949) commercial advertising was denounced. Not all countries therefore believed advertising to be a good thing. However, since the 1960s advertising has become established in many countries including those in the Third World. International advertising has grown in particular, with companies having offices in many countries. The advertising industry has many agencies today that are international, the USA, UK, France and Japan being important base countries. Important agencies include the WPP Group plc (J Walter Thompson and arch-rival O&M being part of this group), and Lowe Howard, Spink and Bell plc. Most are privately owned and would now consider themselves to be communications agencies (IPA, 1999), reflecting not only the growth of sales promotions, public relations and direct marketing techniques, but also the move towards IMC as addressed in Chapter 1. Recently, the impact of the Internet and rapid growth of e-commerce as discussed in the previous chapter has forced the industry and clients to move with the times, or at least to try to. Factors influencing growth include the growing world markets for consumer goods; local agencies needing modern techniques to promote products; and reduced tax costs in some countries on foreign advertising. Consumerism emerged in the 1960s and endeavoured to redress the balance of power in an imperfect market and protect individual consumers in the process. Consumerists exist either as organizations or loose groups of individuals with similar minds. They are stronger in developed countries. In the Third World they have little power, but this is perhaps about to change.

International communication defined

Communication involves the skilful use of all the capacities of language organized into a system of tools, techniques and transmission devices. For example, if the idea of advertising is to create in the customer's mind utility and value, this means that the marketer has to position the product in a way that makes it desirable to the customer, enabling transference of a basic need into a want.[1] International integrated communication involves the formulation of vision that results in a strategy and implementation of an integrated communications plan in more than one country in various parts of the world, as opposed to the entire world, which would then make it global.

The international communications process

The communications process generally was dealt with earlier, in Chapter 2. Both the international marketing and marketing communications literature deal with this by adding some international elements to the basic process. The task that the sender has is to use sociocultural cues and symbols familiar to the receiver and to select media that are socioculturally and legally appropriate (if available). The increased difficulties are underscored by the idea of both the sender's and the receiver's 'realm of understanding' and 'field of experience'. Clearly factors affecting communication in the international context are such things as language (for example brand names) perception (for example colour), values and beliefs (for example veneration of the elderly) or local advertising regulations (for example comparative advertising). This is depicted in Figure 20.1.

The complexity of the situation is clear to see. The difficulties of getting the message across the sender–receiver divide were explained in Chapter 2. These difficulties are exacerbated in the international setting and key factors are discussed in more depth in the rest of this chapter. The Cinzano vignette below provides an illustration of some of the difficulties international companies encounter.

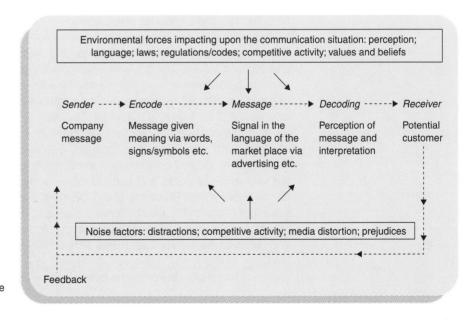

Figure 20.1
The international marketing communications process.

Sources: Adapted from a variety of very similar models, for example De Pelsmaker, Geuens and Van Den Bergh (2001), Toyne and Walters (1993).

On 19 December 2000, after months of speculation, a joint bid from Diageo (formed in 1997 by the merger of Grand Met and Guinness) and Pernod was successful in the auction of Seagram's drinks business. The $8.15 billion ($5 billion paid by Diageo) price tag was seen as being worth it by Lex/FT and this is another step in the rationalization process whereby 1999 saw the operator selling brands, including the world's number two vermouth, Cinzano. It had announced that it wished to concentrate on the development of other global brands such as Johnny Walker, Guinness, Gordon's and Smirnoff. By early 2000 Diageo was announcing increased first half profits principally on Burger King, Haagen-Dazs and spirits rather than beer. The Seagram's spirits brands include market favourites such as Chivas Regal Scotch and Absolut vodka. At the time of writing the split up of Seagram has to be decided, but it is likely that Diageo will take Captain Morgan rum and Crown Royal and others, while Pernod Ricard will acquire Martell Cognac, Chivas Regal, Glenlivet and Glen Grant. Diageo had announced the sale of Cinzano a year previously, on 29 September 1999, to privately owned Italian rival, Campari. Cinzano is the number two global vermouth brand after Martini (made now by Bacardi, one of Diageo's rival bidders for Seagram's). Campari International is a minority owner of Skyy, the San Francisco based spirits operator, and the two have a distribution alliance whereby Skyy markets Campari, Cutty Sark, Glenrothes and now the Cinzano line – Extra Dry, Rosso, Bianco vermouths and also Asti Spumante sparkling wine.

Brands of vermouth like Cinzano and particularly Martini have long been associated with the high life and much of the communication has been highly aspirational. This might be reflected in the advertising, the high-profile sponsorships or the range of branded clothing. Much of this has to do with winning and winners, being ahead, being at the top of the pile. So it was rather curious to find that during the 1980s Cinzano had attempted to market the brand using advertising as a key element of strategy. They used a humorous campaign that starred Leonard Rossiter (a British comedy actor of some repute, especially for his performances in television sitcoms) and Joan Collins, the international film star. This suffered in translation not least of all because humour is a notoriously bad traveller.

Many people thought the advertisements successful but the reality of sales figures was somewhat different. In response to the campaign's failure a British film director was hired and a small town in Italy was chosen and taken over for the location of the film shoot that was to be the basis of the new campaign. The shoot was controlled from London but overseen from the client's headquarters in Geneva. The problems were many and varied. The creativity was handled by another agency whose brief involved bringing back a youthful feel to the brand. The danger lay in dealing simultaneously with young people from diverse cultures, with one message. The attempt was made, therefore, to tap a nerve of the (international) younger consumer of the time by using a series of 'slice of life' situations. Problems in the legislative area lay in different attitudes toward alcohol consumption in different countries. In the UK, for example, age of participants and aspirational images are of prime importance but not so everywhere. Problems in the client–agency relationship were not necessarily to do with the international dimension, although as in many business situations there may be communication problems. The client here was particularly keen to be involved and was persistently on the set, having input into the 'look' of the film. On the one hand, this is understandable given that the client was trying to revitalize the brand after a period of failure. On the other, what is the point of hiring creative people at great expense only to interfere with what you are paying them to do?

The outcome was a 30- and 60-second version of a piece of communication that attempted to get around the usual problems of crossing national boundaries. This was an attempt to make a Coca-Cola type commercial that would help rebuild the brand using music, atmosphere and a sense of occasion to position the brand – one piece of film that could be adapted very, very slightly in terms of the kinds of parameters in Figure 20.1. The 30-second commercial was used on Channel 4 in the UK in a small way, but both versions were never used fully. The client dropped the international strategy.

Sources: Adapted from Frayling (1987); Rijkens (1993), Diageo selling more brands, at www.cnnfn.com/1999/04/27/europe/diageo/; Cinzano sold to Campari, at www.cnnfn.com/1999/09/29/europe/diageo/; Skyy picks up Cinzano's US rights, at www.adweek.com//daily/december/bw/bw121999-5.asp; Diageo, Pernod to buy Seagram brands; Diageo profit inches ahead, at www.adweek.com//daily/december/bw/bw122000-11.asp and www.cnnfn.com/2000/02/24/europe/diageo/; Diageo buys Seagram portfolio, at www.guardianunlimited.co.uk/Archive, accessed 20 December 2000.

STOP POINT

What are the key components of the communication process that are different in the international context? Briefly describe the role of each element. What role do you think the source will have in the communication of the brands like Cinzano? Is there any scope for using its inherent Italianicity? Is it possible to create one piece of film that will work anywhere for a brand like Cinzano? Could Cinzano learn anything from Coca-Cola?

Uniformity or not: the standardization/ adaptation debate

The theme of standardization/adaptation runs across the subject of international business, marketing and communications. It is associated with economies of scale generally but more specifically here with creative production and number of personnel involved. At the level of the organization there are three 'models' available to the international marketer. The first is central control where marketing and communication effort is directed from the centre (for example, Unilever Europe). Second, the head office acts as a resource centre where the locals are free to develop within central directives on agencies and media buying (for example, Nestlé). Third, there is complete autonomy where minimal justification of actions is required (for example, Heinz). Generally speaking the notion of products being culture-bound is well used in the literature. Alternative strategy in terms of just what can be kept the same and just what might have to be adjusted, even if only slightly, in different part of the world has to be a consideration. This applies in the communications arena probably more so than in any other type of parameter.

Standardized brand/product and standardized communication are possible but there are other choices, such as:

- standardized brand/product and locally adapted communications
- locally adapted product/brand and standardized communications
- locally adapted brand/product and locally adapted communications.

The organization may or may not have to adapt or customize or modify promotional strategy because of local differences brought about socioculturally, economically, legally or by the availability – or not – of particular media and media vehicles. With this in mind communications strategy has to be developed and implemented. The usual kind of DSM as propagated in Chapter 4 is also appropriate here and this is dealt with in the last section of this chapter. The central debate remains that of degree of uniformity. The pros and cons are obvious, i.e. economies of scale, consistent message across markets, centralized control, different market characteristics, media availability and costs and government regulations. The stronger argument appears to be that different strategy appears to work in different situations, rather than a totally standardized campaign. Once these geographical issues are decided upon then the scope of the campaign, objectives and elements of strategy can be worked on.

If the organization develops a message for one market and then transposes this intact into others or if it develops a message with a number of markets in mind from the start, it may be centrally conceived in both cases. This is popular because of co-ordination and control providing the benefit of speed of roll out. With easier production and fewer staff involved the cost benefits are easy to see. The danger is that voiceovers/dubbing and so on may not be adequate or may even be disastrous. However, the search for universal symbols and meaning transference in many markets with the same message is an attractive proposition. There are three ways to choose – *adoption* (the whole thing is exported, language and all, and can work for, say, French perfume), *prototype* (where concepts and central ideas remain intact but where local input is made use of and the control of this remains in the hands of the company but depends on the quality of the local input), and *concept co-operation or guideline* (that keeps a certain amount of the brand and company facets intact, for example company colours, strap lines, and raises the dangers of lack of control but also imposition of facets that are wrong for particular markets). Four creative impediments to centralization might exist: locals wishing to take control and prove themselves; cost reduction through adapting campaigns that pays less to the agencies than creating a new campaign; local managers who do not wish to see their authority decline; and the 'not invented here' syndrome (De Mooij, 1994).

Standardization is possible where audiences are similar (for example, lifestyles), where image can be used, where the target has similar characteristics (for example, social status), where the product is high tech (for example, involving innovation/innovators and a common technical language) and where products have a nationalistic flavour (for example, country of origin can be important). *Adaptation* is necessary where concentration on the differences is seen as important/necessary to tackle problems encountered by a standardized approach across the marketing environment (from political to social/cultural to media infrastructure) and where internal differences such as stage in the product/brand life cycle can be catered for (Mueller, 1996). Examples of companies such as Parker (pens) and Colgate who have realized to their cost what it can mean to fail with a standardized approach are common in the literature. There is also recognition that the adaptation approach does not necessarily mean changing fundamentals such as core values of the brand. In communication terms the actors in a commercial may be changed (as with Coca-Cola using different national sports and therefore players) at a surface level. An illustration of the possibilities for marketers to acquire and develop strong signifiers that can have worldwide meaning is provided in the vignette below.

VIGNETTE

'Scottishness' and single malt whisky: the Bunnahabhain and other single malts

Going international with a brand of whisky raises many issues. Perhaps the beginning of the relationship between the spirit and 'Scottishness' was Compton Mackenzie's *Whisky Galore* in which the Hebrideans conspired to defeat the excise man. Recent Hollywood interpretations of Scottishness through the likes of movies such as *Highlander*, *Braveheart* and *Rob Roy* may have done no harm to the Scottish (or Scotch) whisky campaign. In recent years a number of acquisitions by the big international players in the spirits market have taken place. The rationale for this is that global distribution over the past couple of decades has been achieved. What is missing is a full range of good to premium brand offerings – hence the acquisitions. Seagram were central to this and have a history now of global distribution of many things including Chivas Regal. This brand is now in the Pernod Ricard stable having been part of the aforementioned Diageo/Pernod Ricard deal.

The Bunnahabhain Distillery was founded in 1827 on the Isle of Islay, northwest Scotland. The distillery produces a single malt whisky, marketed under the Bunnahabhain brand name. Single malt whiskies are produced by over 100 distilleries in Scotland, and the Bunnahabhain is a medium, smooth, soft, mellow, light, gold-coloured drink with a hint of peat. Traditionally, malt whiskies are classified according to how old they are – generally the older, the better and more expensive. Price plays an important part in brand choice, but this does depend on the product and the occasion. Generally, blended whiskies are cheaper, for example a bottle of Bells would cost around £12; a supermarket branded single malt will retail at around £14.99; an established brand could retail at anything from £16 but most are around £25 unless on special promotion as, for example, around Christmas and New Year. If the product is to be 'mixed', for example with ginger or Coca-Cola, a cheaper brand may be adequate, but consumers are willing to pay a lot for a quality malt, especially when it is bought as a present or for a special occasion. In the whisky market, packaging is at least as important as advertising – some would say is as important as the product itself! Image is a highly relevant factor in customers' decision-making. The Scottishness of the product is crucial. Traditionally, Scotland and good whisky go hand in hand; consumers see the origin of a whisky as a quality indicator when making a purchase decision. Jack Daniel's has very successfully exploited their 'Southern' US roots when marketing their product to the UK. Similarly, the story of the Stone of Scone, mentioned earlier in Chapter 6, is part of Scottish folklore. For many years whisky has had an old image to go with its ageing customers. In recent years whisky marketers have woken up to the fact that if they do not introduce their products to younger drinkers then they are facing a declining market. Whisky, particularly when mixed, has more appeal to younger drinkers, and many of the younger age groups have been targeted recently, for example, Bell's with their 'good crack' campaign and Teachers with pub-based promotional campaigns. However, all the distillers have a common marketing problem – how to make their product appealing to the new younger markets without alienating the current older customer. Before the aforementioned sale, earlier in 2000, Seagram had attempted to target younger drinkers with a 'trendy makeover'. With both Chivas Regal 18 and its sister brand, Chivas Regal 12, revamped, an attempt was made to attract the younger drinker without alienating the traditional drinker – the age-old problem, especially in alcoholic drinks product categories. This involved adding to the brand's aura of quality and heritage. The objective was to reinforce Chivas Regal as the perfect gift for the sophisticated whisky drinker. It is argued that the single malt can survive drowning in cola but it is the pipe and slippers image that is damaging a key industry (billions of pounds in export earnings, tens of thousands of jobs, communities' survival in danger and so on).

It was probably by accident rather than design that a positive association between television's *Inspector Morse/The Sweeney*/John Thaw and whisky evolved. Burns may have known that 'freedom and whisky gang the gither' – but today's twentysomethings are more likely to associate whisky with middle age. However, all is apparently not lost. In Spain Scotch is seen as part of the aspirational nightlife culture but to be taken long with cola rather than sipped and savoured. In Greece whisky has overtaken ouzo as the favoured drink with 'disco machismo' favouring the Dimple blend (suggestive shape of the bottle and the name) and France is now the biggest market for Scotch.

The finest whiskies have always had snob appeal but Scotch is seen as one of the most highly prized products in the spirits industry and one of the few bright spots of the alcoholic drinks business. Brands such as Laphroaig are said to have literary appeal in a sort of 'Islay chic' kind of way (as used by, for example, Dick Francis, Will Self and Edwin Black). Visitor centres, brand ambassadors and bartender evangelists are some of the ways to get the 'Scotch is the new fine wine' message across, creating Scotch buffs along the way – or at least this is the hope of Jack Keenan, boss of United Distillers and Vintners, Diageo's spirits subsidiary. Apparently Mr Keenan's dream is to have dinner party guests chat about the qualities of one malt against another in the same way as they might with fine wines – in terms of taste and discernment. Brian Ivory of Highland Distillers points out that the strong tastes of single malts can find favour with drinkers in their late teens/early twenties and uses the example of the distinctive Islay malt that is 'strong enough to assert itself even through a half-pint of cola'. Alistair Robertson, manager of the Glenkinchie distillery, admits to wanting to preserve the mystique of (malt) whisky – a miraculous product of Highland air and water, and a unique part of Scottish heritage that can never be completely understood, where the taste is only part of the appeal. This is reflected in advertising for Glenmorangie – 'come to the glen (morangie) of tranquillity'.

Sources: Adapted from company materials (2000); Barr (1998); Bell (n.d.); Buckingham (1999); Cozens (n.d.); Jackson (n.d.a; n.d.b); McKie (n.d); Mueller (1996).

STOP POINT What are the key considerations regarding standardization/adaptation for brands such as the Bunnahabhain regarding the communication process? What is likely to differ in the international rather than simply the domestic context? How important do you consider the source of the message to be in the communication of brands like the Bunnahabhain? What is the viability of the proposed position using 'Scottishness' for such brands just as Levi, Harley-Davidson or Marlboro have used 'Americaness'?

Key factors affecting international marketing communications

There are myriad factors that potentially affect the international marketing communications process. Key factors have been placed into the three broad groups of (1) constraints/restraints, (2) culture, creativity and branding and (3) media and production.

Constraints and restraints on communication around the world

Standardization/adaptation has to be seen in terms of the context of communicating with members of the 'Global Village'.[2] In other words, there is a need to deal with the communication process as a whole and to include all the environmental factors as an integral part of the communications model. The world appears to be rapidly converging in terms of activities, interests, preferences and demographic characteristics, leading to readily accessible, homogeneous market groupings. This will have a fundamental effect in terms of the communication (and, of course, the marketing) process. The marketer, in short, has had to question the idea of stereotyping across cultures, which might be possible but not desirable or even necessary. The marketer needs to be aware of differences in many things, including regulation, laws and unwritten customs and practice. STEP/PEST-type factors (social, technological, economic, political) that are used to look at situations from a strategic marketing viewpoint are, of course, relevant to international communication. It is these that underpin activities across markets around the globe. Of course it may be the case that because of the differences that exist in environmental factors in different countries, certain elements of the communications mix, say, advertising, may not be possible in some markets. Or it may be that for some situations (say, machine tools), advertising will take a lesser role. The major communication tool might be personal communication of some sort but this will be very different in application in one market than in another. The scope of communication will depend on the type of society. For example, in Saudi society much of what goes on is a function of religion and, hence, the law; in the UK communication (and, in particular, advertising) excesses are restrained by a different code and a different ethic. Here four broad areas for consideration are proposed as being key: what is legal or allowed; cultural differences and similarities; the importance of branding internationally; and the media and production across borders.

International rules, regulations and codes

The notion that marketing (advertising in particular) is intrinsically good/bad is important here with respect to different countries' and governments' attitude towards it. If the statistics on advertising expenditure and GDP are scrutinized the inference is often drawn that there is a positive correlation between advertising expenditure and stage of economic development. The types of media availability vary enormously around the globe and this is not just a function of economic status. It could be easy to draw wildly inaccurate conclusions in this area, however, there is a good correlation for example between economic status and the number of television sets per capita (Toyne and Walters, 1993). It is argued here that ethical and regulatory questions have to be addressed since the social benefits of advertising – or the reverse – are particularly sharpened in the international context. The issues include economic value, competitive practices and consumer protection.

Economic groupings such as the EU offer an interesting insight into the legalistic wrangles. There are a number of issues that are important, such as subsidiarity, product issues (the usual tobacco, pharmaceuticals, alcohol, financial services), allowance of comparative advertising, and sensitive issues such as contraception. Most people believe it is wrong to misrepresent a product. For example, by 1893 the English had a Sale of Goods Act, and under a fairly mature legal system advertisers are not allowed to misrepresent facts or breach confidence. In America the Federal Trade Commission Act of 1938 set restrictions on the advertising of food, drugs and cosmetics. As long ago as 1925 the International Chamber of Commerce was shaping things to come and in 1937 established a Code of Standards in Advertising Practice (Mueller, 1996). Some *international regulation* takes place through the auspices of a small number of international bodies. The regulations regarding advertising and sales promotions are many and varied. The host countries are important and usually are the principal regulators because international law allows for national state sovereignty over their people and resources when at home. The United Nations (UN), however, acts as an international regulator and has a restricted role through the General Assembly's adopted 1985 guidelines on consumer protection, especially in the Third World.[3] Some organizations exist to check on specific matters, for example the World Health Organization (WHO). Marketers should, therefore, be interested in regulations, taxes, restrictions and the monitoring of any changes. Many in the industry believe they should support regulation but at the same time are pro self-regulation (see below). Advertising (and sales promotion) regulations are developed to a reasonable extent in only twenty or so countries with a further fifty or more that at least have some regulation. This is less so for other forms of communication.[4] Restraint is still very much domestic driven. In the UK the Advertising Standards Authority is a typical domestic body, but, for example, EC Directives are becoming increasingly important in all member states. A fundamental proposition is that either the business community is capable of self-regulation or, left to their own devices, some firms would break the rules. After all, business exists to make money not moral or ethical judgements. Alternatively, intervention is justified for consumer protection. In 1989 within the EC the Consumer Consultative Council (consisting of thirty-nine consumer bodies) existed to express consumer protection opinion (Mueller, 1996).

Regulations made by a country depend on the cultural and otherwise make-up of that country as to whether advertising is negative or positive. There are different types of regulatory controls. These include *national governments* able to control the operations of multinational enterprises through their own law. They can decide which companies can promote which products and how. This means a multinational company needs to seek advice about what it may do in each country. This will vary because of the different origins of laws in different countries, e.g. civil law, common law, socialist law, Islamic law, Confucian law and traditional law. In market economies regulation is used only to enable fair competition and to protect the consumer. In the Third World the needs of the economy to develop are important. There may be rules to prevent the promotion of many Western goods that may be viewed as too tempting. Some countries will only allow advertising of their home-produced goods in order to encourage local demand. Religious principles may prevent certain products from being advertised. General laws tend to exist to ensure that advertising content is not false, misleading or unfair. These may be adopted and become mandatory. They tend to involve restrictions on the media. For example, especially after the Nestlé infant formula disaster, in Third World countries restrictions on the usual marketing communications tools may be fierce (Terpstra and Sarathy, 1991).

Commercial advertising is not allowed in some countries for certain products. Time restrictions exist in many countries. Some countries have laws as to whether foreign language can be used in the advertising. *Self-regulation* has three objectives. The first is to protect consumers against false or misleading adverts, against adverts that intrude on privacy, or adverts that are of an offensive nature. The second is to protect legitimate advertisers against false or misleading advertising by the competition. The third is to promote the public acceptance of advertising so that it can remain effective. The industry established its own codes of practice to prevent the interference of governments in its affairs. The aforementioned ICC (set up in 1919) established Codes of Standards of Advertising Practice in 1937 whose objectives are referred to above. Others have followed, for example the Caracas pact in Latin America and the European Advertising Standards Alliance, formed in 1992, from more than twenty bodies (the UK ASA for example) from more than twenty countries. Mueller (1996) gives more detail on the hard (i.e. deception, fraud) and soft (i.e. tasteless, indecent, sexy, sexist, suggestive, objectification of women, violence against women) perceptions. Attitudes of bodies around the world vary. For example the National Advertising Review Board in the USA tends to concentrate on the hard issues of accuracy etc., presumably because these can be cut and dried, rather than the soft issues, which are not (Shimp, 2000).

The importance of *product categories* in this area cannot be underestimated. Specific laws and regulations exist with those products associated with health and safety. The main areas for concern in terms of products appear to be the most obvious. Some examples are tobacco, alcohol, pharmaceuticals, financial services, children's products (especially toys), baby food and cosmetics. For instance, with tobacco, much is debated but basically there are two viewpoints. First, a ban on advertising will cut cigarette consumption. Second, advertising only affects brand differentiation, not the number of smokers. The UK has gone for a ban while Germany, the Netherlands, Denmark and Greece still oppose a total ban. With France, references to social and financial success are not permitted, adding to an already severely restrictive situation for alcohol marketers that have a requirement to include health warnings.

Country groupings are an important consideration for the international marketer. The International Advertising Association lists fourteen countries as being particularly restrictive – Germany, the UK, the USA, France, Canada, Australia, Sweden, Austria, Belgium, Argentina, Mexico, Italy, Finland and Denmark. As indicated above, restraint is still very much domestic driven, for example in the UK through the ASA. Article 3 of the EC Consumer Consultative Council's Misleading Advertising Directive deals with the characteristics of goods (geographical origin, purpose, uses and so on), pricing and supply, and the advertiser's nature and identity. Article 2 deals with deception, causing injury to competition etc. and Article 7 appears to be in contradiction of this by giving individual states autonomy by not precluding them from keeping or adopting provisions that furnish more extensive protection in that state. Harmonization seems distant in this light. Another example is the Gulf Co-operative Council (Saudi, Qatar, Kuwait, Oman, United Arab Emirates and Bahrain) that operates on the principle that the basis for all laws is the Qur'an and Hadith where shariah is Islamic law.

Creative content is of particular concern for marketers, especially those who use advertising, sales promotions and direct marketing tools. In Germany comparative advertising has been banned since 1909 but the EC appears to like comparative advertising since it apparently assists consumers. Further afield than the EU and EC Directives etc. the world picture is rather diffuse. In the Arab world Islam plays a huge part, it being a fusion of culture/religion and law. Of not least importance here is the role and representation of women. Here the directive is that children should not be used in advertising. As in many countries, there is concern for dishonesty in advertising. Of interest in particular are products such as alcohol and activities such as gambling. Real rather than perceived benefits are valued, otherwise fraud is seen as being committed. In Saudi Arabia a government ministry (Commerce) sees that commercials are legal in shariah terms and another (Information) controls television. There is concern for the prevention of sins and ordering of good deeds.

The area of *social responsibility and ethics* encompasses many things. International marketers should be concerned that the consumer movement is generally in favour of legislation to provide consumers with information (data, especially comparative), education (knowledge, how to deal with companies and so on), and protection (health and safety, against deception). Basically self-regulation is not trusted. Advertising in particular is seen by supporters as being a positive force serving to educate, inform, provide lower prices and improve quality, stimulate the local economy and provide jobs, and can generally be used for the social good as with AIDS/condom campaigns etc. Alternatively, detractors see it as a negative force that engenders cultural imperialism, raises expectations and causes agitation, and militates against consumer protection. It hits local competition hard, especially where status is attached to having the big brands, and it is responsible for exaggerated claims and even deceit (deception is considered a crime in most countries) and so on. Or maybe, for some, it is just advertising. There is, for example, the aforementioned distinction between hard and soft advertising issues of sex, decency, tastelessness, sexist, racist, demeaning through stereotyping, violence against and objectification of women (where there is no relevance) and obscenity. In most cases, however, it is down to interpretation.

If it is legal then shout about it? Some examples of constraint and restraint globally

Many countries are in a state of flux and there may be no self-regulating bodies. Businessmen who oppose bans on the advertising of alcohol and tobacco, feel that merchandised items produced legally should have the right to be advertised. Roger Neill, the then President of the International Advertising Association, has said at the 1990 Hamburg congress, 'Any product that is legally allowed to be produced, legally allowed to be sold, should be legally allowed to be advertised' (De Mooij, 1994). In Malaysia Seiko ran into trouble with their worldwide 'Man invented time, Seiko perfected it' campaign because, for a lot of people, God not man invented time. So the strap line became 'Man invented time-keeping . . .' and changes had to be made to television, outdoor and press advertising. China is in a state of flux. If the textbooks are to be believed, claims such as a herbal tea can prevent and even reverse ageing and make the drinker more virile and a spray that stops one contracting AIDS and is a 'love solution' are commonplace in advertising in China. This is because of lack of control and consumer protection. Puffery might be acceptable in the USA – the legitimate expression of biased opinion – but the strap line 'The strongest driveshaft in Canada' would be deemed misleading in Canada unless absolute proof were available. South Africa's ASA may change its attitude towards comparative advertising but at present no comparisons are made nor are rival brands shown. In Taiwan adverts have now to live up to their claims. In the past there was much puffery and, even, lies. In many instances it is not the products themselves but blatantly offensive advertising that causes the problem – whether this be real or imagined. For example, in 1995 a poster campaign in the UK caused division in the advertising industry itself. The adverts for Club 18–30 had headlines such as 'Beaver Espana' and 'the summer of 69' The ASA, after receiving 314 complaints, asked for them to be withdrawn. One could comment on similar examples in the Arab context, particularly regarding Islam, the place of women in Islamic society, attitudes towards the giving to charity and, generally, what can and cannot be said. Of course, Saudi Arabia is very different from Dubai but many of the concerns are common and the aforementioned Gulf Co-operative Council does exist and has an impact upon the management side of advertising in particular.

Sources: Adapted from Alderson and Olins (1995); De Mooij (1994; 1998); Mueller (1996).

STOP POINT

In what ways do the constraints and restraints in different contexts shape marketing practice? If it is legal to produce cigarettes then what is the problem with their promotion? Find further examples of restrictions on communications, especially ones that interface with other environmental elements such as religion.

Culture, creativity and branding

Culturally plausible international communication

A popular position seems to be the idea of 'plan global, act local' as a strategy. There is a great temptation to engage in stereotyping. The manager who talks about the various nationalities involved with the organization (whether this be in a 'selling in' or a 'country of origin' context) in very general terms plays with fire. Examples of this are where the Germans are seen as being rational, descriptive and informative, the British as subtle, understated, ironic and humorous, the French as innovative, modern and attention-getting, and the Americans as emotional, lifestyle obsessed and glamorous. This is not at all helpful unless based on a firm foundation of sound research. The relationship between culture and behaviour is important. Culture has many definitions. Hofstede (1990) defines culture as 'the collective mental programming of the people in an environment' where culture is not a characteristic of individuals but rather it 'encompasses a number of people who were conditioned by the same education and life experience'. Culture is important in marketing because it differs between societies. What may be very acceptable in one country will not be in another. This is because culture is learnt. Culture may also be defined as 'the sum total of learned beliefs, values and customs that serve to direct the consumer behaviour of members of a particular society' (De Mooij, 1994).

Levels of culture

The idea of levels of culture is a useful one. There are a number of different aspects of culture that are important to a company. They include things like national culture (if this exists there is a danger of stereotyping, but this is often used in a humorous way), corporate culture, age and so on. The usual aspects of culture are not necessarily appropriate to all three. Consider eating habits, dress habits at work, Sunday dress habits, gender roles, and social class. Mueller's (1996) adaptation of a maximum/minimum continuum of compared cultures is a useful construct for the manager wishing to understand cultural differences and similarities. One example at the maximum end of the sociocultural continuum is the apparent difference between what is Western and what is Asian. The argument is that if we look deeper into this divide we might find that in some respects a farmer in China has more in common with a farmer in the USA than the latter does with a Wall Street executive.

Expressions of culture are described by De Mooij (1998), by using Hofstede's 'onion model', i.e. symbolic, heroes, rituals, values and beliefs, and customs and practices, with the resultant *expressions of culture*. This is usually presented rather like an onion with layers from core to skin. *Symbols* carry meaning that is interpreted differently according to culture. These symbols include objects, pictures, gestures and words. Words, of course, are obvious; the language is not just the words and their individual meanings in different countries but the jargon specific to that part of a region of a country. Gestures are important. The Japanese, for example, smile a lot when they do not understand. Some people nod their head up and down when they mean no. Pictures of dresses and hairstyles are important. For Eskimos there are many words for snow. The Hopi deals in facts not present/past. The word 'coke' has lots of meanings in the West and this is increasing elsewhere. There are lots of faux pas around because of poor translation, from the Nova (a 'won't go' car) to the lack of understanding of the symbolic importance to meaning of colour (white can mean mourning, yellow death). A *hero* is a person who has characteristics that are valued by society. The person may be living, dead or imagined. Therefore Superman, Donald Duck, King Arthur and James Dean are all useful in establishing cultural values and links in communicating attributes of a product. The links with product merchandising are obvious, as can be seen from any one of the Marlboro cowboy images that were used for such a long time. *Rituals* are considered essential within society until they are eroded. Nationalism and pride can be tied up with rituals. For example, consider the Olympic Games. It is often not possible for an observer to understand the reasoning behind the ritual, but get it wrong in an advert and your product will be doomed. Certain values are held by some cultures to be more important than others. A recent car advert for the VW Golf in the UK deals with a divorce. This would not be seen as an appropriate storyline in a country where the divorce rate is very low. *Beliefs* are feelings we have about things, often expressed through non-verbal communication or verbal statements. *Values* are more important than beliefs because many in a society see them as a guide to what is appropriate. These mental images affect how a person will respond to an advert and whether the effect will be desirable. People tend to have values to do with what is good/evil, rational/irrational, natural/ unnatural, beautiful/ugly, dirty/clean, normal/abnormal, logical/paradoxical and, because of increasing world business and communication, it is believed by some that certain global cultures exist. There exists some global advertising, for example Pepsi and Marlboro. However, the images will die unless supported by advertising. The corporate cultures of multinational companies tend to reflect the cultures of the companies involved. Undeniably, advertising in particular can have an influence on people in countries as diverse as the USA and Estonia. Global companies such as Benetton and McDonald's influence most people throughout the world. Pressure from the World Bank creates an impossible framework to resist these companies. However, the success of the company will still depend on the customer's willingness to buy. How much change occurs from advertising and how much from the product itself is debatable. However, product consumption can lead to a change in behaviour as can be seen with the National Lottery in the UK. Similarly, certain behaviour is seen as correct in certain societies and situations. Get this wrong in an advert and the product can easily fail. For example, in making tea putting in milk at a certain stage may not be appropriate. Using a mug in this scenario might send the wrong message, as might showing a product in a group situation or in a pair. These are examples of *customs and practices*. One reason why global communication is so difficult to achieve is because our individual understanding of it is different owing to our differences in values and beliefs and hence customs and practices (De Mooij, 1994; 1998).

The context of culture

Mueller (1996) after the work of Hall (1977) distinguishes between high- and low-context culture, citing Japan as collectivist and the USA as individualist, and illustrating the importance to marketers of the difference when they are dealing with Japanese or American culture. We have to consider how useful the concept of context is when looking at different cultures from an international marketing and communications management viewpoint, and the kinds of differences there might be between Japanese and American culture, and what similarities there might be. This may mean the differences in high-low-medium product involvement in the marketing process are more important in some contexts than in others. Appeals and associations might therefore work differently in different cultures. De Mooij (1998), using the example of individualism, looks deeper into the American and Japanese context and concludes that individualism exists in both cultures but these are very different. From a management perspective this means that individualism can be used creatively in both but obviously with different treatments. Since 90 per cent of content is silent or unspoken (De Pelsmaker, Geuens and Van Den Bergh, 2001) there is plenty of scope to take advantage of similarities and differences, especially in the knowledge that a 'picture says a thousand words'.

Culture, consumer behaviour and creative strategy

Things such as visual imagery were looked at in Chapter 6 but clearly in the international setting there are certain additional constraints on the creation and execution of communication. Hofstede's[5] (1989; 1990; 1991) five dimensions of culture, i.e. power distance, individual versus collective, masculine versus feminine, uncertainty avoidance and Confucian dynamism (or long-term orientation) might be acceptable to some as might Mueller's context work. To others, however, generalizations of culture can often be more harmful than useful. Two fallacies appear to exist. First, that segmentation studies are useless unless the 'segment must be substantial and accessible' dictum applies. Second, that self-actualization is an individualistic concept therefore self-actualizers will only exist in low-context cultures. A cornerstone of the systems that have been developed to look at cross-cultural classification is the original VALS system devised by Maslow and Rockeach in 1975. VALS 2 came along in 1989, as discussed in Chapters 3 and 4. Others have followed. Here we are concerned not only with how advertising may work creatively but also with the international setting. Do we simply like the advertising – and hopefully the brand – or does it also provide a real proposition? This is an area where literature abounds. Prescriptions from admen, theories from academics, social commentary from journalists – it seems that most people are fascinated by advertising and how it works and this has been the staple diet of many a Sunday newspaper supplement. The approach taken to international advertising will very much depend on the company and its understanding of international marketing. International communication may be seen as being designed to help market the same product in different countries and cultures. However, this implies that the communication can be standardized; many authors agree that this is not the case, with even companies such as Benetton who may appear to be creating standardized images perhaps not quite getting things right. Mueller uses Frazer's 1985 definition of creative strategy, i.e. 'a policy or guiding principle that specifies the general nature and character of messages to be designed. Strategy states the means selected to achieve the desired audience effect over the term of the campaign' – in other words 'what is said'. This includes consideration of both verbal and non-verbal approaches to message content.

Creative themes and concepts

This can be viewed as 'how it is said' rather than what is said and involves copy and dialogue (verbal) and visual and illustrative (non-verbal) communications. The two broad kinds of appeal are, on the one hand, rational and, on the other, emotional – often referred to as hard sell and soft sell respectively. The reality of situations is more complex than this rather simple distinction. Mueller uses her own and others' work on the differences between Japan and the USA (referring back to high- and low-context cultures) but it should be remembered that most would agree that these are very large generalizations. The French are said to like humour and sex appeal, while the British display a great fondness for class division, eccentric behaviour and puns. Mueller's comparison between the USA and Japan is a very useful one.[6] With verbal communication (copy and dialogue) things like brand names come to the fore but it is much more than this. Mueller gives both linguistic and managerial guidelines. For example, with non-verbal communication (visuals and illustrations), the usual claim is that less confusion will be the outcome because of the lack of translation difficulties. Mueller recognizes settings, backdrops, etc. as having different meaning to different people of different cultures. These hinder standardized campaigns. In the same vein, it is dangerous to ignore symbolism. The assumption that there are universals available is also made. De Mooij (1994) makes the distinction between the appeal and the execution whereby the strategy may be universal but the execution may well be localized. The family appeal of McDonald's is universal but, within Spain, the execution is, for example, Catalan and presumably different again in other parts of Spain. Ideas generated centrally might remain while surface level treatments differ.

De Mooij[7] (1994) lists *universal* themes and concepts as case histories (difficult but worthwhile, usually offering solutions to problems and a mixture of landscapes and environments), improved quality or productivity (especially useful B-to-B wise), basic everyday themes (for example motherhood or jealousy) new products (novel features or new concerns such as environmentalism), service (particularly in industrial marketing), special expertise (particularly technology or engineering), the 'made in' concept (country of origin effect, appealing to national pride or particular expertise), demonstration, universal images (such as the Red Cross), media-driven concepts (such as the youthfulness of MTV), lifestyle concepts (but where adaptation of execution may be necessary) and heroes (possible but with adaptation of execution). *Culture-bound* themes and concepts are personal ideas and opinions (for example, the notion of slimness being attractive is not universally held), customs and moral values (for example, nudity in France is not such a big deal as it seems to be in the UK), humour (does not travel well apart from the use of incongruity, i.e. contrast highlighted by that which is expected and unexpected; other writers might add slapstick comedy of the Chaplin kind to be a universal), motivation (can be seen in examples of household products that are convenient, i.e. there is an incentive so that time can be freed up), individuality and the role of women (involving clothing and sexual overtones) and comparative advertising (the differences between markets, for example Japan and the USA, where losing face is looked on very differently in these two cultures).

VIGNETTE

National stereotypes

The French are arrogant, the Germans cold and disciplined, the Italians . . . well they're Italian! Enough said? Not for the Harris Research Centre, who have developed a system to help them better understand more reliably and robustly cultural differences in Europe. Semiometrie is a system based on a 12 000-strong survey of people aged fifteen and over in five countries – Germany, the UK, France, Italy and Spain. The system uses stimulus material to facilitate the scoring of 210 words that enable researchers to discover values and emotions. The word list is a result of extensive qualitative and quantitative research and is representative of European values and culture. According to Morrisson (1998), the Sofres group has validated Semiometrie through more than 500 surveys in Europe. There are myriad values and opinions on myriad topics across the sociocultural divisions that exist in all the countries of Europe. Factor analysis brings out divisions. In Europe these have been found to be:

1 Duty versus pleasure. Characteristic words respectively are homeland, morals, discipline and voluptuous, adventurer, humour.

2 Community versus singularity – friendship, family, charitable and rebellion, detachment, attack.

3 Materialism versus culture – jewel, wealth, desire and book, poetry, art.

4 Idealism versus pragmatism – infinite, sacred, hero and build, accuracy, logic.

Country differences are shown by Semiometrie to be stronger than standard demographic ones, so national identity can be stronger than age, sex, etc. and, therefore, mentalities are different. Examples from the use of Semiometrie are that the English accept conflict and have a lack of inclination to form bonds. This is singularity for life with a respect for rules, institutions and conventions. Here is strong national pride and identity. There is a difficulty in expression of feelings and a requirement to display control and reject pragmatism. The French search for quality of life in terms of status-valorization rather than materialism and for pleasure, well-being and pleasant sensations. They have little time for rules and authority, and rely on the rules of social life to guide them. The Italians it seems value community and they subscribe to a sensitive kind of pleasure rather than a more concrete kind. There is a curiosity, open-mindedness and sensitivity to art, aspiration for imagination rather than reality. The Italians have a profoundly rooted religious side to their idealism. The Spanish are similarly rooted but have a much more feminine side. The Spanish aspire towards learning and knowledge, and are most attracted to sharing and harmony, i.e. the values of human interaction, and they do not like violence or repression. The Germans are strong pragmatically. They have a tangible reality and therefore adhere to concrete pleasure and a strong desire to be free from restraint.

This kind of analysis tallies with the realities of communicating across the different states of Europe. Pepp and Becattelli's (1998) observation of German advertising leads them to conclude that there is much reference to ecology yet reference also to hedonistic consumption and technology. With the French it is personal style and patriotism. In the UK in particular, the metaphor is used frequently as with BMW. A six-pronged lightning bolt on a new six-gear box is used to symbolize power and speed. However, in Germany the metonym – a device laden with lifestyle clues – is used rather than the metaphor. The central character is used to represent the wider audience as in the aspirational Ferrero Rocher 'Ambassador's Reception'. Therefore the metaphor can only be used in certain situations, whereas the metonym can be used across the pan-European board and frequently shows consumers and consumption. Its use, however, is vicarious and is not good at communicating intangible brand attributes. This is not looking for a common denominator or research for common ground. Rather it is a search for a theme that motivates across markets and then an examination of how best to express it. Prevailing advertising codes should be understood in order to achieve pan-Europeanism via common values. Pepp and Becattelli advocate this and a single underlying creative idea that is capable of local variations to maximize its appeal in each market. In other words, alongside understanding each market there should be a research programme to support advertising development. First would be brand evaluation and choice of theme while considering the brand's position in each market and how advertising can support it with, for example, humour. Second would be creative development of the theme using research to identify how the theme can be expressed in different cultures. This is fine-tuning the chosen core message to maximize appeal using technical changes or varying symbols or references to tie brand communication to local need. Third, creative evaluation and assessment helps create advertising that offers best brand fit in all markets.

Sources: Adapted from Morrisson (1998); Pepp and Becattelli (1998).

STOP POINT

How useful is the Semiometrie system to managers of marketing or corporate communications? Will it help solve the problem of the tendency to stereotype across cultures? Does it present a better way of addressing cultural differences? Are Pepp and Becattelli right to advocate a local tailoring approach?

Branding in the international context

Chapter 5 dealt with branding and advertising. The relationship between brands and communication (particularly advertising) at the international level is crucial. International communication of one form or another is therefore placed within the management of the organization and is a link between the philosophy of the organization, say, Coca-Cola, and its advertising, say, a global message of one-world harmony. The standardization/adaptation debate is inescapable. The importance of *corporate mission and vision* that deal with 'what you are doing' and 'where and what you want to be doing' at some time in the future, cannot be overlooked. Mission should be viewed as a strategic discipline, part of the intellect of the organization, the cultural glue that binds the organization's often disparate elements – in essence the soul of the organization and the reason for being.

Branding as *competitive strategy and comparative advantage* can be achieved through the product trade cycle (product life cycle, trade and investment) where notions of 'trickle down' as opposed to 'waterfall' effects should be considered. The latter represents the rapid diffusion of brands internationally. The configuration and co-ordination of the business and marketing effort and the ease or difficulty of implementing a standardized strategy are determined by culture, infrastructure, and economic and technological effects but are driven by such things as economies of scale and global corporate/brand image. Branding and advertising have their place in emerging homogeneous, single markets where successful brand names and personalities are themselves determined by linguistics, distinctiveness, adaptability, international applicability, logos and graphics, national characteristics of brand attributes and culturally plausible advertising platforms.

International and global branding and communication therefore involves the encouragement of competition, economies of scale, product development, stimulation of economic growth, improved products due to competition among brands, lower prices and greater variety. These are seen to be the case irrespective of whether the economy is centrally planned or market orientated. Conventional wisdom seems to say that no amount of advertising, however good, will enable a poor product to succeed. It is clear, however, that communication plays a vital role in getting across the benefits and availability of a product and also can explain how a product may be used to best advantage. Consider Levi in the vignette below in this light.

VIGNETTE

Levi: quality never goes out of style with Flat Eric and Angel

The history of Levi is well documented both in writing and on film. The brand has celebrity status not least because of its advertising, which to a large extent is localized, i.e. selling and overall strategies are local responsibilities while the central marketing function concentrates on identifying consumer trends and developing marketing strategies. The main product in the last fifteen or so years has been 501 jeans and jeans have put Levi up there with Coca-Cola and Marlboro. As Rijkens (1993) puts it 'it is not surprising that the basic positioning of Levi's advertising is virtually the same all over the world'. The Levi mission, while not denying the goal of commercial success, claims to be one of wishing Levi to be a 'responsible citizen' with credentials to prove it. This, of course, can be seen as part of the Levi global PR effort. The position of Levi is such that its products are seen by men and women aged between fifteen and twenty-five as being straightforward, honest, independent, adventurous and rebellious. These consumers, say Levi, care for what is genuine, enjoy one another's company, feel attracted to the opposite sex and express their sense of freedom and enjoyment – in an acceptable manner irrespective of age. In theory it should be possible to use the same advertising everywhere. Levi advertising sees moving pictures and music combining to produce the desired image so that television and cinemas are the ideal media vehicles. The actual commercials are familiar to most across Europe – no worries about language or complicated (and often disastrous) dubbing or the need for any icons other than those with universal appeal to the target audience – especially in the age of satellite television, as long as non-verbal communication works. An example in the UK would be a spot around an appropriate programme to reach the target group with a commercial on the ITV network. Hoardings, trade magazines and merchandising are also used but the all-important form of communication is the film, which is expensive but clearly effective so far. Responsibility lies locally in close consultation with Brussels. Time must be held over for international commercials or cinema films.

Flat Eric changed Levi Strauss's fortunes in Europe in the year 1999, it is claimed. Also claimed by the same source (the agency responsible, BBH) is that this was a campaign that generated thousands of column inches in the press across Europe, has been endlessly deconstructed in the media but most importantly was a great international campaign that 'impacted brilliantly on a brand's fortunes'. In early 1999 denim was looking like it was in the early 1980s – on the slide and not in fashion. Research was showing the brand to be 'less-top-of-mind', purchase intention scores declining and the reality was a worldwide drop in sales and redundancies. *The Times* proclaimed jeans to be the 'badge of middle age' rather than the 'uniform of youth'. Levi asked BBH for an earthquake. BBH research revealed three things. First, Levi had become a mono-product brand, i.e. Levi = 501. Second, 501s were ageing, best summed up by the *Daily Mail*'s 'Clarkson effect' (a reference to a 'past his prime' jeans-wearing television presenter, Jeremy Clarkson). Third, the world of Levi's as seen by consumers was formulaic – the same story for the past fifteen years. A 'new' product in the form of Levi Sta-Prest (this had been around in non-denim form before) denim that a new generation could call its own was given a new world. The brand in this new world could express itself with behaviour (less glitzy, more everyday), attitude (upbeat and positive not ironic or cynical or about lone heroes) and styling (simple and uncluttered and relevant to street culture with lots of unspoken codes and personalization).

The Sta-Prest proposition was not the 60-second film with narrative structure but, instead, a pair of sharp-thinking and sharp-acting characters who were also sharply dressed friends (a partnership not unlike that of Clint Eastwood and Clyde the orang-utan in the film *Every Which Way But Loose*). Three 30-second commercials were produced and the first, 'Dancing', was deliberately launched on the Internet to match the medium to the production treatment (compressed into quicktime movie format). This was mailed to opinion leaders to get a snowball effect. In addition, the agency designed a new form of moving banner advertising for the Internet called overts. Here, as the consumer downloaded, a moving banner would appear in the background and Flat Eric would skateboard in from the side of the screen or parachute in from the top. Click on Flat Eric and they are taken to Levi.com. Supporting television peak weekend spots (around sport, music and the soaps) were booked to ensure the word of mouth was secured during the week. Across Europe this campaign scored a hit in all departments from sales increases to awareness, likeability and enjoyment, hits on the Levi.com site, the music (Flatbeat) becoming a number one in six markets (in the UK, Italy, Norway, Belgium, Austria and Germany). BBH claim the PR value runs into millions of pounds.

Sources: Adapted from Armstrong (1995); BBC (1987; 1997); Levi-Strauss company information (2000); McCormick (1995); Moyle (1992); Rijkens (1993); Smith (1999).

STOP POINT

BBH work with Levi in thirty-seven countries. Across Europe they work for the likes of Electrolux, Polaroid and Lynx. They always go for the 'big idea' rather than the lowest common denominator to take brands across borders. The key for BBH is the creative team being given free rein to act in a think tank-like way – but only after appropriate consumer research. Do you think that branding will be enhanced in all cases if the 'highest common denominator' is sought rather than the lowest when crossing borders with an international campaign? What do you think of the BBH 'big idea' philosophy?

Media and production

The media and production across borders

Chapter 7 dealt with media and media planning generally, and made some allusion towards the international context. Put in this context the various media can be severely limiting. For example, there is no alcohol allowed in French cinemas and a poster ban except in the region of production. Another example is that of television and radio advertising that has only recently been allowed in Saudi Arabia (1992), Denmark (1987) and Sweden (1992). With advertising materials there is a vast array of restrictions. For example, foreign words are often banned and there are restrictions on the use of foreigners in certain countries. Footage and music may have to be prepared locally, as in Malaysia where actors and voice-overs have to be native. The UK and Australia have similar regulations on local crews attending shoots, whereas the USA has a union agreement that is slightly less stringent. Peru bans foreign-inspired models and materials in order to protect national identity. Certain countries, for example Australia, have a nominal tax on media billings (0.01 per cent) that funds the Advertising Standards Council. While advertising agencies may grumble, this is supported by advertisers such as Kellogg's and McDonald's (Mueller, 1996).

Government attitudes towards public ownership, especially of the broadcast media, are important here. In the UK the BBC may not survive very much longer in its current form. There is constant debate on the poor/healthy state it is in. Per capita advertising spend varies enormously, even within the EU, and peak spots available vary widely. Italy has highly fragmented television. Fifty per cent of adspend in France goes on TF1. Satellite (and now cable) has caused change. BskyB has created a number of target audiences. Sixty per cent of viewing in the UK is still with the four terrestrial channels. The UK has national tabloids and broadsheets. Some circulation figures are high, for example the *Sun* (5 million). Compare this to the 0.5 million of *Le Figaro*, one of eleven Paris-based newspapers. Germany has local regional dailies some of which have more than 0.5 million, for example *Die Welt* (Hamburg). There are international titles, mostly American, but the *Financial Times* and *The Economist* (both UK) are international titles that are doing well. *Reader's Digest* has more than 6 million subscribers but these are thirty-five plus years of age and it is particularly strong in the UK, Germany, France and Scandinavia (De Mooij, 1994). The list of such titbits of facts is endless.

The technological and communications revolution

As discussed in the previous chapter, we are said to be on the verge of a cataclysmic transformation of the information world thanks to the techno miracles of the multimedia. On the one hand, there is the ubiquitous CD-ROM that is apparently turning out to be too small and too slow. The computing power required to overcome problems is too expensive and temperamental. Sony was pushing double-speed and double-density discs while Time Warner was talking double-sided discs. The mini disk and the mobile phone are making the news. On the other hand the network – the global information infrastructure – has still to be established. As one media analyst has put it, 'these problems and obstacles will eventually be overcome but, until they are, talking about multimedia in terms of revolution may be like talking about the *Titanic* in terms of the future of maritime transport' (Davis, 1994). This is still the case and perhaps always will be where technological advance is concerned. Standards in terms of format/compatibility, neglect of the end-user, the potential myth of video on demand and so on are a product of over-promising/under-delivering. We are still waiting. Satellite and cable have led to a fragmentation of viewing and this has had a knock-on effect on audience research. Advertisers should be worried about the ways in which consumers might take command of their television consumption and concerned about the explosion of new services potentially available. Some argue that the notion of the 'medium is the message' is dead and that the message is the message, or at least a bit of the message is created for the medium, deliberately. There is great concern from some quarters on the question of ethics and the creation of a multimedia underclass. Many people will not be able to afford to take part in the revolution and therefore cannot participate in society. There is a question mark over whether or not aspirational programming and, hence, advertising can be a positive force as well as a negative one. The alternative is the creation of a Jeffersonian[8] community rather than a centralized state/authority – putting power in the hands of the people.

The media landscape and audience research

There are a number of trends that have occurred in the past and are still relevant today. For example, electronic media expenditures have grown at the expense of print. Magazine producers have reacted to the new electronic media by replacing some general interest magazines by special interest ones. Outdoor media are a growing phenomenon. The growth of satellite delivery has supported both television and cable networks, which have been particularly important in the distribution of programming and advertising internationally. The international media are the Internet, newspapers, magazines, professional and technical magazines, television, interactive communication, radio, outdoor/ transport, place-based, folders, POS material, direct mail, trade fairs/exhibitions and sponsorship. Mueller (1996) provides some examples of international media vehicle promotion: magazines such as *Playboy*, *Vogue*, *Elle* and so on and newspapers such as *International Herald Tribune* and the *New York Times*. There are also television vehicles such as MTV and CNN. De Mooij (1994) points out that still much advertising space worldwide is bought and sold on circulation. The kinds of research undertaken are more mature in some countries than in others and there is a fight for harmonization of research techniques to achieve meaningful comparison – equivalence being the international marketer's goal. Perry (1995) deems Peoplemeters inappropriate for the kinds of research future 'TV buyers are likely to demand from satellite channels, such as detailed targeting descriptions, involvement with the channel, and compatibility with the agency's requirements'.[9] Gill (2000), on the other hand, argues that, although not perfect, 'Peoplemeter' panels have now become the almost universal standard method for measuring television audiences, being used in seventy countries around the world'.

International media planning

The role of the GRP/TVRs[10] was discussed generally in Chapter 7 but is obviously important internationally. De Mooij (1994) suggests both horizontal planning (global brands aimed at cross-cultural groups) and vertical planning (culture-bound products in multilocal settings) as ways forward in media planning. The simplistic measurements such as reach, frequency, opportunities to see, the tools used in order to seem to be getting the message across in terms of budgets available, optimization by matching schedules to the profile, are of little use in two ways. First, the quantitative side of this particular coin is not in dispute but there is debate about this kind of measure and what it actually offers. Merely having an opportunity to see or be exposed to a piece of communication needs, for many (see, for example, Galpin and Gullen, 2000), a qualitative understanding. Second is where the notion of primetime viewing cannot be equally applied in each market of an international and, hence, global campaign. Pan-European, let alone global scheduling cannot easily occur unless it is done so in a multilocal way. Media planning should also be put into the context of the client–agency relationship and how media spots are bought. This takes into account the role of advertising agencies and the ownership of the media. Media planning internationally is therefore a different function from the domestic situation. The company needs to decide which approach to media planning it will take. The choice is either to use an international advertising strategy and international media supplemented by national media, or a standardized campaign based on national plans using national media and supported by international media. These are referred to as horizontal planning and vertical planning respectively. It is appropriate to choose horizontal planning where you are launching a new product and where you intend the brand to be global. This is because at the start the brand will be culture free. Where a brand is established and culture bound, vertical planning on a multilocal base is appropriate. The difficulties that are likely to be encountered with this are the budget and splitting of it, comparing the costs for coverage and media spill over. The media briefing should give those involved a clear idea of media objectives, targets, balance and placement.

VIGNETTE

Media around the world

The industrialized countries

The *USA* is the most important area for advertising, given the value of the business conducted. Most multinational agencies are based in the USA. The USA leads the world in creativity, technique, organization, management and research, and important media: print, radio and television. Advertising is more regulated than in other free-market countries, being subject to federal, state and local regulations. People are also likely to sue for injury. *Europe* sees the UK, Germany, France, Italy and Spain dominate advertising, and media opportunities and trends vary though in different member countries. *Other developed Commonwealth countries and South Africa*, i.e. Australia, Canada, New Zealand and Africa have a lot of involvement with foreign agencies. All are dominated by print, with television being important to a lesser extent. Radio is more important in Australia, New Zealand and Canada than Africa where it represents around 4 per cent of total expenditure. Regulations are largely similar to those of the USA and the UK.

Japan has advertising that is different in many ways from that in Western societies. The culture prevailing includes much tradition rooted in ancient eastern philosophies. This combined with attitude and religious heritage influences both the economy and advertising. Tariffs, quotas and invisible trade barriers discourage foreign business. Distribution channels make it difficult for foreigners to compete. Advertising has to appeal to the customers' ideologies. Print, radio and television are important. Issues of group and frugality influence it. *Eastern Europe* has in excess of 300 million customers and budgets were small but growing due to former socialist philosophy recognizing the need for advertising. *Perestroika* and *glasnost* translated into reforms that enabled foreign goods to be advertised. In some cases joint ventures between foreign advertising agencies and state commercial organizations had occurred. Hungary, for example, already had similar advertising to the West, so that many states were in a good position to develop commercial communications. *China*, because of its size, could be the largest market in the world. However consumer products have been scarce, hence limited advertising. The situation is changing rapidly and will do so even more in the future.

The newly industrialized countries and the Third World

This includes 120 countries in the Middle East, Latin America, Asia and Africa. Many countries are unstable and weak. The Third World is an untapped market for advertisers where they can offer low-priced, suitable goods. The newly industrialized countries (NICs) such as India are a mixture of Third and First Worlds. Clearly, it is the latter market that is of interest to advertisers and includes the *Arab Middle East*, a challenging market not least due to the influence of Islam. Countries are fundamentally democratic, concepts combining both capitalist and socialist ideologies. Advertising has only existed since the 1950s. Print media is most important but radio is limited. *Latin America and the Caribbean* is an area that includes twelve republics of continental South America, eight central American republics, and the West Indies (thirteen Caribbean Island republics). Many aspects of this market are European in character. Population is European, Mestizos and Indian. Spanish is the official language, except for the Caribbean where it is French or English. Although advertising is allowed, trade is difficult because of political and economic problems. *Asia* sees many different languages, attitudes and policies exist. Asia is made up of low-income, middle-income and high-income groups. Advertising is most important in the high-income areas because customers are able to spend on goods. Print and television are particularly important. In *(South of Sahara) Africa* advertising expenditure is low because of little economic development and much illiteracy. Luxury items are severely limited, perhaps to village elders. The élite, largely foreigners, are into heavily branded goods. Quality goods are sold on the black market, advertising not being necessary.

Sources: De Mooij (1994), De Pelsmaker, Geuens and Van Den Bergh (2001).

STOP POINT

The media around the world picture is complex to say the least. What are the differences between the opportunities for advertising and other forms of communication in industrialized countries and the rest of the world? What choices have to be made because of media availability? How will these affect message considerations? How will it affect overall media planning considerations?

Managing international communications campaigns

The APIC system of management, as advocated and explained in Chapter 4, is applicable to the international setting (as are the more detailed aspects of the system that follow in the chapters after Chapter 4).

Analysis

Included at the analysis stage, for example, is consideration of (international) marketing research. Here, the difficulties of comparative marketing research in different markets are important. For example, in terms of secondary/desk research certain products might not be categorized in the same way in all markets, so size of the market becomes problematic. Government statistics might be unreliable or even deliberately misleading. Conducting (especially) primary research is far from easy in many markets because of gender role differences, differences in infrastructure and so on.[11]

Planning

After consideration of the usual things but at the international level, the manager is then able to plan, i.e. set objectives, seek direction and position the brand in the various marketplaces. Inevitably, when constructing a communications mix, adaptation/standardization may or may not be dictated by the communications tool being used. Advertising is more likely to be standardized than anything else other than sponsorship, which is often approached in a standardized package kind of way. Certainly, personal communications and sales promotions are likely to be adapted for local contexts. The key word here is again integration. That is to say, the notion that one can study advertising (whether international or not) in isolation from other elements of the communications mix, while not impossible, is improbable or undesirable.

Advertising internationally is much less culture bound than the rest of the communications mix. With BtoB marketing this is not so. Direct marketing has been used for some time internationally, as have trade fairs. Sponsorship, especially of international and global sporting events like the Olympic Games and the (soccer) World Cup, has long provided a means to strengthening brand awareness and image, and providing a 'single tone of voice' worldwide. It has become clear that in the past twenty years media advertising has seen less spend in favour of (especially) sales promotion. In 1976 the media/non-media spend ratio was 60:40. Recently this has become more like 30:70. There is also a trend towards using a wider range of methods both nationally and internationally.

Sales promotion (SP) is about added value. Devices like coupons or competitions should add to a brand above and beyond its normal value. In consumer terms there are both tactical, short-term promotions and longer-term strategic promotions. Short-term (classical) promotions are usually applied in a very localized fashion, often varying within a particular country or region. Exceptions to this rule are things like samples in magazines, e.g. perfume in a sachet, which can be used in the international media. Value promotions are more to do with image. They are thematic, integrated with media advertisements/direct marketing/PR/sponsorship. The changing relationship between manufacturer and retailer is important here. The trend appears to be toward the more strategic use of SPs, integrating with thematic advertising campaigns, sponsorship and so on, while at the same time short-term tactical SPs are being used locally. For De Mooij (1994) the challenge for integrated marketing communications is to link these two – the global, strategic approach with the local tactical approach in order to maximize communication effects. The thematic approach embodied the 'round-the-clock protection' idea for a deodorant and used a pan-European television campaign. Strict product positioning was maintained and, while promotional

material was developed on a local level, the artwork etc. was contrc
trally. Watches and clocks were controlled centrally and used as free gifts ιυ
in with the theme. Point-of-sale material was adapted for local conditions. The
object was twofold: to achieve trial and to strengthen brand image. The three
major elements were a special trial offer, a special smell test and the chance to
win a holiday at Club Med's 'Club Natrel' in Turkey. The latter was in keeping
with the healthy image of the brand. Overall the campaign's main strength was
its creative consistency. Internationally, SPs are prone to problems. Price promotions are not acceptable in some countries. Links with gambling and lot-
teries are problematic. Links with good causes are generally prone to success.

Trade fairs, exhibitions and congresses can be either the broad, general, annual
event like the Hanover Fair or rather more specialized events like the
International Materials Handling Exhibition. Such events can be very important international media vehicles if the company is at the export stage where
market possibilities can be explored before committing, and products can be
seen, tried, tested and demonstrated. The trade element is obvious as is the integrated nature of communications around such events. Measurement of effectiveness remains a challenge.

Public relations can be viewed as corporate or product/market. Basically the former deals with corporate image and has become more and more important
internationally as borders blur. Publication relations is particularly important to
organizations like Exxon, Shell etc. in relation to the environment, and in this
context is becoming more similar throughout the world. The media (including
the Internet and especially news groups/bulletin boards) may play a crucial role.
At the product/market level PR was originally supposed to be different from
other communication. Theoretically its aim is to create goodwill and understanding – a favourable marketing environment in which the rest of the mix can
operate more effectively. Good PR can therefore save the organization money,
thereby easily paying for itself. There are many potential publics both internal
and external to the organization but, in particular, the media are important in
terms of presentation. Credibility is often much higher with a PR message
rather than advertising, which is partisan in nature. News, whether real or made
up, is crucial to PR. Publicity is never free (just like the lunch) but some see it
as a cheap, quick way of getting known and even selling directly. But just as
with politicians, spin doctoring alone is not enough. You really do in the end
need good policies/products.

Sponsorship includes relationships with events, clubs, persons, institutions and
so on, and is not new. Mostly sponsorship internationally is to do with enhancing corporate image. Sometimes it is to do with circumventing advertising regulations (especially alcohol and tobacco). There are many advantages to the use
of sponsorship which advertising cannot offer. It is much more personal.
Corporate hospitality can enhance reputations and images of companies,
brands and individuals. The difficulties of measuring the effects of sponsorship
are well known, not least because it seems that if a brand is well recognized then
the effect appears to be less than it would be for a less well recognized brand.
There is also the relationship with advertising to consider.

Direct marketing (DM) includes television, print/off-the-page, radio, mail,
phone and the Internet. Internationally the drawbacks are things like underdeveloped infrastructure/communications/media, e.g. poor mail service, but also

levels of literacy and other such environmental considerations. Of course, BtoB marketing uses DM a lot for the obvious target groups that have been relatively easy to access for years, particularly with the sales effort. Direct mail has been well used over the years to aid personal communication, which is made a lot easier if the ground has been prepared. This is particularly the case with export selling. Direct marketing can be used effectively as an integral part of an integrated communications campaign. There are obvious links between trade fairs, DM and personal selling at the international level as well as domestically. A typical run-up to a trade fair or exhibition would be the use of direct marketing to announce the organization's intention to exhibit while personal selling (or at least multilingual representation) would be an obvious feature, once the event had started. There are problems however. Direct marketing, and in particular direct mail, can only be used in a standardized way if, for example, decision-making units in each country's market are similar, or attitudes towards what is often seen as an intrusion differ and so on. The English language is seen as *the* international language yet can only be used in certain situations. Poor standards that have led to junk mail, junk phone calls and perhaps junk Internet use threaten the positive aspects of DM.

Personal communication (including selling and representation) includes some of the above points, which are also relevant here. Clearly, at the international level trade fairs, direct mail and certain kinds of international advertising and publicity are particularly important. At the motivational level, incentives, often grouped with sales promotion, are critical, as are sales conferences that exist to aid the 'sharp end'. Sales people need encouragement but also information – on how the rest of the mix is working, on databases, on new promotional material and how to use it, and on product knowledge and back-up, i.e. sales support. This is not simply a question of translation but goes much deeper with the development of marketing information systems that cater for many things at the international level. Care should also be taken with performance measurement incentives, especially as the international grapevine can be as pervasive as the national one.

Implementation

In just the same ways that budgets are worked out thoroughly in terms of media use and coverage and geographical coverage, all over particular time periods, so it is in each market. Putting things into practice in a multi-market scenario is fraught with the kinds of standardization/adaptation issues discussed above. Parameters such as religious festivals can have a profound effect on timing. Execution of a campaign can be severely affected by local requirements on content, use of local actors and so on. Indeed, when considering standardization it is often these elements that are the hardest to achieve.

Control

Finally, some sort of pre-, concurrent and post-testing is recommended. The aforementioned complexity regarding international marketing research and testing therefore applies when attempting to measure and control across the chosen communications mix. The absence of equivalence (Toyne and Walters, 1993) among very different markets makes this task difficult and sometimes impossible. Life is made a little easier if some sort of targeting system has been used, where relatively homogeneous lifestyle groups have been identified and attacked. In this event, research can be designed relatively easily to monitor and control a campaign. This also enhances the effective use of tracking studies in a multi-market campaign. Mueller (1996) also points towards three kinds of control of international campaigns, the approach adopted being influenced by the overall manner in which the organization is structured and its size. Thus, *centralized control* is headquarters based and has the usual advantages such as a highly developed research base and the regularity of research. The downside to this is, for example, lack of local knowledge. With *decentralized control* it is the knowledge locally that is a positive factor, and often the reason for doing it this way. *Co-ordinated control* attempts to get the best of both worlds and strives for comparability – or equivalence of research between markets.

Agency selection at the international level

The management of international campaigns must also include some reference to international communications agencies, including international marketing communications research. The selection of an agency to deal with marketing communications – particularly advertising – will depend on the type of company, i.e. its level of international involvement and its organization. Where standardization is prevalent the company will increasingly choose an international agency rather than use a domestic or local one. There are many reasons for this, for example economic, i.e. where agencies do not exist in say Third World countries. On the other hand, where experience of culture and the rest is necessary, local agencies may be a better choice. The usual criteria operate – market coverage, quality of coverage and supporting activities (whether or not full service). Multinational agencies provide centrality, have experience of the culture (or can buy in the services of a local agency) and usually have research experience in many locations. Selection considerations include issues of control, campaign planning, administration, operations and media. There is also some uncertainty regarding boundary-spanning roles whereby clients are the initiators of change (Beard, 1999).

Assignment

You are required to write a consultative report for an organization of your choice. This could be your current employer (or a previous employer/placement host). The report should include an outline communications plan that follows the steps of the APIC decision sequence model advocated in Chapter 4 and at the international level as in the last section of this chapter. In effect you are designing a case, rather like the cases in Chapters 8, 11, 15 and 17. Your case should deal with all aspects of international communications for the chosen organization. The case should have specific, international communications 'problems' as its focus. The quality and relevance of the communications problems posed are important. If you do not have an organization in mind, you might prefer to choose a situation that involves an existing company or brand or even something hypothetical such as the launch of an international brand or brand extension. The focus might be the launch of a new product into a marketplace where the company is unknown or already known, the addition of a new brand to an existing range and so on applied to a country or countries of your choice.

Summary of Key Points

- There is a history to international integrated marketing and corporate communications. International communications is well defined and understood in the literature.

- Problems within the communications process are exacerbated in the international context.

- The standardization/adaptation debate is very important in international communications. There are strategic choices to be made but many would agree that it is best to 'think global, act local' or go 'glocal'.

- The four broad areas that have the biggest impact on international marketing communications are legalities, branding, culture and media and production.

- There is an international dimension to the elements of the environment in which communication has to work.

- The APIC decision sequence model is equally apt in the international marketing communications context.

Examination Questions

1 Define international communications. Examine how a historical perspective can give an insight into present-day change for marketers using marketing and corporate communications.

2 Highlight what is likely to be different about the communications process in the international context as opposed to the domestic situation.

3 Briefly explain the standardization/adaptation debate as applied to marketing and corporate communications. Explain, in broad terms, the strategic options available to marketers.

4 Distinguish between laws and codes that affect company communications. Use examples to illustrate social responsibility in the international context.

5 Explain the relationship between branding and communication at the international level using examples to illustrate.

6 Explain why you agree or disagree that national stereotyping is a dangerous thing to do in international communications campaigns.

7 Discuss the importance for managers of having some form of target market classification system rather than relying on an aspects of culture approach within particular markets.

8 Given the advent of the Internet and other media forms and the fragmentation that has taken place in recent years, examine the current trends in media worldwide using examples of your choice to illustrate.

9 Outline the key sources of information for effective international media selection.

10 Explain the use of the APIC decision sequence model as an aid to international integrated marketing communications.

Notes

1 Abraham Maslow is famous for a number of things but not least for the 'hierarchy of needs' used extensively throughout marketing in the last four decades.

2 The term 'global village', as coined by Marshall McCluhan in the 1960s, refers now not just to the media and advertising in particular, but to the entire business world and beyond. 'New world order' is a term used to describe the economic power shifts occurring continually and has its origins in the study of the development of the world economy.

3 Mueller (1996) provides a useful discourse on the role and nature of *transnational agencies*. This deals with the usual pros and cons of advertising and agencies in especially the Third World – from raising expectations and agitation to cultural imperialism and changing the nature of the media to providing money to develop local advertising and media industries.

4 There are so many situations worldwide and the whole issue is compounded by the nature of integrated campaigns, i.e. the marketer is not usually dealing with advertising in isolation but with PR, sponsorship and so on.

5 From his large study of IBM employees around the globe, Hofstede had originally constructed four dimensions of culture. The fifth, at first called Confusion Dynamism then Long Term Orientation, was added because of the bias toward Western societies. Michael Bond and a number of Chinese social scientists who developed a Chinese Value Survey created this. See De Mooij (1998) for excellent application of Hofstede's work to marketing and advertising.

6 See also De Mooij (1994) for comparisons between Japan and the USA, France, Taiwan and the USA, the USA and the EC, Germany and the UK.

7 De Mooij provides useful guidelines on organization, creative development and production for the execution of campaigns as well as some useful examples.

8 This is a reference to the egalitarian notion of power to the people that can be manifestly seen in some community programmes. Currently, those who are not able to gain access to personal computers and the Internet are helped to do so in a kind of class struggle against the poverty of the underclass.

9 Mueller (1996) and others use McCann-Erikson-type figures in order to discuss things like household penetration of broadcast media. The textbooks, however, by their very nature are much less up to date than industry sources in this area.

10 Gross rating points and television rating points have become a universal measure of the 'total exposures produced by an advertising schedule' (Donnelly, 1996).

11 There are myriad differences to consider. This topic is covered particularly well from the international marketing point of view by Toyne and Walters (1993).

References

Armstrong, S. (1995). The bottom lne. *Observer*, 8 December, p. 26.

Barr, A. (1998). Single minded. *Observer*, 10 October, p. 16.

BBC (1987). Design classics – Levi 501 jeans.

BBC (1997). Branded – Levi, October.

Beard, F. K. (1999). Client role ambiguity and satisfaction in the client-agency relationship. *Journal of Advertising Research*, March/April, pp. 69–78.

Bell, A. (n.d.). Islay faces farcical whisky waste law. At www.guardianunlimited.co.uk/Archive, accessed 20 December 2000.

Buckingham, L. (1999). Drop a dram afore ye trance. At www.guardianunlimited.co.uk/Archive, accessed 20 December 2000.

Cozens, C. (n.d.). Chivas Regal targets young drinkers with trendy makeover. At www.guardianunlimited.co.uk/Archive, accessed 20 December 2000.

Davis, J. (1994). The perils and pitfalls of the multimedia revolution. *Admap*, November. www.warc.com

De Mooij, M. (1994). *Advertising Worldwide*. Prentice Hall.

De Mooij, M. (1998). *Global Marketing and Advertising: Understanding Cultural Paradoxes*. Sage.

De Pelsmaker, P., Geuens, M. and Van Den Bergh, J. (2001). *Marketing Communications*. Financial Times Prentice Hall.

Donnelly, W. J. (1996). *Media Planning, Strategy and Imagination*. Prentice Hall.

Frayling, C. (1987). *The Art of Persuasion*. Channel 4.

Galpin, J. and Gullen, P. (2000). Beyond the OTS: measuring the quality of media exposure. *International Journal of Marketing Research*, **42** (4), 473–493.

Gill, J. (2000). Managing the capture of individuals viewing within a peoplemeter service. *International Journal of Marketing Research*, **42** (4), 431–438.

Hofstede, G. (1989). Organising for cultural diversity. *European Management Journal*, **7** (4), 390–396.

Hofstede, G. (1990). *Marketing and Culture*. University of Limburg, Maastricht.

Hofstede, G. (1991). *Cultures and Organisations: Software of the Mind*. London: McGraw-Hill.

Institute of Practitioners in Advertising (IPA) (1999). In *Global Advertising. Proceedings of the 4th Annual Marketing Educators' Advertising and Academia Forum*, London. IPA.

Jackson, M. (n.d.a). Why the Islands are beating the Highlands. At www.guardianunlimited.co.uk/Archive, accessed 20 December 2000.

Jackson, M. (n.d.b). Bourbon creams. At www.guardianunlimited.co.uk/Archive, accessed 20 December 2000.

McCormick, N. (1995). Darling, they're playing our advert. *Daily Telegraph*, 8 December, p. 25.

McKie, R. (n.d.). Blend of the affair. At www.guardianunlimited.co.uk/Archive, accessed 20 December 2000.

Morrisson, V. (1998). The real values behind national stereotypes. *ResearchPlus*, Autumn, 6–7.

Moyle, F. (1992). Laying the Russians bare for Western brands. *Marketing Week*, 27 March, p. 25.

Mueller, B. (1996). *International Advertising – Communicating across Borders*. Wadsworth/Thompson.

Pepp, M. and Becattelli, I. (1998). Researching the way into adland Europe. *ResearchPlus*, Autumn, 18–19.

Perry, J. (1995). Measuring change – how TV audience measurement might develop in a fragmentary and interactive future. *Admap*, February. www.warc.com

Rijkens, R. (1993). *European Advertising Strategies*. Cassell.

Shimp, T (2000). *Advertising, Promotion and Supplemental Aspects of Integrated Marketing Communications Management*. Dryden.

Smith, M. (1999). Planning an international campaign. In *Global Advertising. Proceedings of the 4th Annual Marketing Educators' Advertising and Academia Forum*, London. IPA.

Terpstra, V. and Sarathy, R. (1991). *International Marketing*. 5th edition. Dryden.

Toyne, B. and Walters, P. G. P. (1993). *Global Marketing Management*. 2nd edition. Allyn and Bacon.

Index

Page numbers in *italics* refer to vignettes; those in **bold** type indicate figures. A letter n following a page number refers to a numbered note on that page

Marketing Communications
Management